Enlightenment in Dispute

Enlightenment in Dispute

*The Reinvention of Chan Buddhism
in Seventeenth-Century China*

JIANG WU

2008

OXFORD
UNIVERSITY PRESS

Oxford University Press, Inc., publishes works that further
Oxford University's objective of excellence
in research, scholarship, and education.

Oxford   New York
Auckland   Cape Town   Dar es Salaam   Hong Kong   Karachi
Kuala Lumpur   Madrid   Melbourne   Mexico City   Nairobi
New Delhi   Shanghai   Taipei   Toronto

With offices in
Argentina   Austria   Brazil   Chile   Czech Republic   France   Greece
Guatemala   Hungary   Italy   Japan   Poland   Portugal   Singapore
South Korea   Switzerland   Thailand   Turkey   Ukraine   Vietnam

Published by Oxford University Press, Inc.
198 Madison Avenue, New York, New York 10016

www.oup.com

Oxford is a registered trademark of Oxford University Press.

Library of Congress Cataloging-in-Publication Data
Wu, Jiang, 1969–
Enlightenment in dispute : the reinvention of Chan Buddhism
in seventeenth-century China / Jiang Wu.
     p. cm.
Includes bibliographical references and index.
ISBN 978-0-19-533357-2
1. Zen Buddhism—China—History—17th century.   I. Title.
BQ9262.9.C5W8 2007
294.3'927095109032—dc22   2007029033

9 8 7 6 5 4 3 2 1

Printed in the United States of America
on acid-free paper

This book is dedicated to my father Wu Shaoyao (1939–1985) and my father-in-law Liu Shisong (1940–2002).

Preface

Many excellent works on the history of Chan (Zen) Buddhism in China and Japan have been written in recent years. Conspicuously absent from these studies is a thorough investigation of Chan Buddhism in the seventeenth century, when China was undergoing a series of religious transformations. This topic has been neglected largely because the golden age of Chan was long past, and most scholars assume that Chan communities were in decline during the Ming and Qing dynasties.

In fact, as this book will show, Chan Buddhists were extremely active in this period, and various Chan communities had been rebuilt according to the Chan ideals of antiquity. For example, one of these communities, based in Huangbo monastery in Fujian, was particularly prominent in China and also became so in Japan. The third Huangbo master, Yinyuan Longqi (1592–1673), migrated to Japan in 1654 and laid the foundation for the third largest Zen denomination in Japan, the Ōbaku school. His story demonstrates the vitality of Chan Buddhism in seventeenth-century China.

This book, unearthing this forgotten segment of Buddhist history in China, should be of interest to various readers. Students of Chinese religions will find that it fills a significant gap in the history of Chan Buddhism. Historians will be interested in learning the temporary ascendancy of the Chan monks in the Manchu court and the Yongzheng emperor's fierce responses to some Chan works. Specialists in early Chan history will be surprised to learn that in the seventeenth century the identity of a Tang Chan master became the focus of a controversy and that beating and shouting were resurrected as primary methods of training Chan students. Historians of Japanese Buddhism should be interested in the chain of events that led to the founding of the Ōbaku school in Japan. The primary focus of this book, however, is the transformation of the Chan tradition in the seventeenth century.

Readers might find this book not easy because so many people's names, book titles, and place names are mentioned and discussed. Reading this book requires great patience to focus on seemingly trivial but extremely important pieces of evidence, which were often disguised in the intricacy of easily confused names and complex relationships. It is my intention to reproduce in this book the complexity of the controversies by focusing on some "small" details. The benefit of doing so is that this book can be used by researchers and students as a handbook of seventeenth-century Chan Buddhism. Such a meticulously documented book is needed because when reading Buddhist sources from this period, scholars will inevitably come across many references to the major events and figures I study in this book. If readers use my comprehensive index properly, together with the reference books listed in the bibliography, it will be relatively easier to locate more information about the subjects for which they are looking. For a long time, the main obstacles that lay ahead of scholars and students of Buddhism in late imperial China were exactly these names and relationships. To figure out the connections among these monks, I actually have built a relational database, which I hope to release in the future.

I wish to thank those who helped and encouraged me to struggle through various stages of research and writing: my mentors Robert Gimello and Tu Weiming and Professors Peter Bol, Michael Puett, Eugene Yuejin Wang, Beata Grant, Helen Baroni, Robert and Elizabeth Sharf, Albert Welter, Miriam Levering, Anne Blackburn, Timothy Brook, Jonathan Spence, Lynn Struve, and Joshua Fogel. In particular, I want to thank professors Chün-fang Yü, Chia-lin Pao-Tao, and Lewis Lancaster for their support of my career and research. Two anonymous reviewers read the manuscript carefully and helped to finalize this book. John McRae and Charles Jones read an early version of the manuscript and offered their professional insights to improve my writing and the organization of materials. Charles Jones also generously shared with me several rare Chan sources written or compiled by the late Ming literary figure Yuan Hongdao.

Several recent trips back to China, especially the one to Eastern Zhejiang, where active Chan communities grew in the seventeenth century, allowed me to add new perspectives to this study during the final stage of revision. I thank

Gene Reeves for inviting me to join a conference on the *Lotus Sūtra* and later a tour to Ningbo and Tiantai in June 2006. This trip was generously financed by Risshō Kōseikai. I appreciate having had this opportunity to talk with abbots and monastic officials in famous monasteries in the area. I also thank Lewis Lancaster for inviting me to travel with him to Nanjing, Shanghai, and Beijing in August and November 2006 for a database project of contemporary Chinese monasteries. These two trips were funded by the Electronic Cultural Atlas Initiatives at University of California, Berkeley. During my trips, Professors Li Fuhua and He Mei (Institute of World Religions, Chinese Academy of Social Sciences), Wei Dedong (Institute of Buddhist Studies, Renmin University), and An Husheng (*Buddhism Online* at www.fjnet.com) provided useful information about contemporary Chinese Buddhism from a different angle. I want to thank all of them.

Among my teachers and friends in China, I am grateful to Professor Chen Zhichao, grandson of the famous historian Chen Yuan (1880–1971), who first taught me at Harvard and later provided guidance for my research when I stayed at his home in Beijing. Professors Pang Pu and Chen Lai, during their stay at Harvard, also taught me how to read early Confucian texts and newly discovered texts by Wang Yangming and his follower Yan Jun. Professor Fang Keli of the Chinese Academy of Social Sciences, formerly from Nankai University where I graduated, has been encouraging me and providing his support for many years. Credits also go to my friends Wei Dedong and Huang Jiqian, who coordinated my trip to Huangbo monastery in Fuqing in 2001. The abbot Beisheng of Huangbo monastery and his disciple Mingkong welcomed me warmly during my visit to the rebuilt Huangbo monastery in the summer of 2001. I thank all of them. In addition, I am grateful to the staff at Harvard-Yenching Library for their generous help and to Professor Liu Yuebing, then at the Institute of Japanese Culture at Zhejiang University, who helped me to photocopy rare sources from Komazawa University Library and shared with me his research on Meiji Confucianism. Professor Qin Zhaoxiong of Kobe Foreign Language University provided valuable assistance by helping me to acquire rare sources from the Manpukuji archive, where Tanaka Chisei kindly assisted him.

I presented the contents of appendix 3 at the Center for Buddhist Studies at UCLA in February 2003 and at the Conference on the Study of Chinese Buddhism held in Hsi Lai monastery, Los Angeles, in June 2005. I am grateful for the feedback from the audiences. Kamada Hitoshi at the University of Arizona Library checked all of the Japanese transliterations. Cynthia Read, Paul Hobson, Merryl Sloane, and other editors at Oxford University Press have taken care of the production of this book. I deeply appreciate their work.

I want to extend special thanks to the Chinese Buddhism Electronic Text Association (CBETA), which has made many Chan genealogies compiled in late imperial China available online during my revision of this book. Their efforts allowed me to locate references efficiently and to check the validity of various pieces of evidence relating to the controversies examined in this book. Any remaining errors are my own. My colleagues at the University of Arizona provided continuous support by making all of their resources available to me. I also received generous funding from the Office of the Vice Provost for Faculty Affairs at the University of Arizona for indexing this book. Finally, I want to thank my wife, Jing Liu, for her care and support and my daughter, Shalan, for the good luck she brought to me. I dedicate this book to my father, Wu Shaoyao, and my father-in-law, Liu Shisong.

September 30, 2007
Tucson, Arizona

Contents

Conventions and Explanatory Notes, xv

Chronology, xvii

Introduction, 3

The Revival of Chan Buddhism in the Seventeenth Century, 4
Controversies and Chan Buddhism, 7
The Transformation of Chan Buddhism, 8
The Reinvention of the Chan Tradition, 11
Chapters and Sources, 14

PART I THE CONTEXT OF SEVENTEENTH-CENTURY
   CHINA

1 Reenvisioning Buddhism in the Late Ming, 21

From Margin to Center, 22
Ambiguous Chan Communities, 31
Conclusion, 44

2 The Literati and Chan Buddhism, 47

Wang Yangming and Chan Buddhism, 48
The Literati's Textual Spirituality, 53
The Literati's Influence on Chan Monks, 64
The Advent of Chan Buddhism in Eastern Zhejiang, 73
Conclusion, 81

3 The Rise of Chan Buddhism, 83

   The Rise of the Linji School, 85
   The Rise of the Caodong School, 93
   The Further Spread of Chan Buddhism, 96
   Chan Buddhism within Seventeenth-Century Chinese Society, 105
   Conclusion, 109

PART II   THE PRINCIPLE OF CHAN

4 Clashes among Enlightened Minds, 113

   Hanyue Fazang's Distinction between Tathāgata Chan and
      Patriarch Chan, 114
   Hanyue Fazang's Encounter with Miyun Yuanwu, 118
   Exchange of Polemical Essays, 121
   The Antagonism between Miyun's and Hanyue's Lineages, 129
   Conclusion, 133

5 The Divergence of Interpretation, 135

   Objectifying the Subjective Experience of Enlightenment, 136
   The Mystery of the Perfect Circle: Hanyue Fazang's Esotericism, 144
   The Encounter Dialogue in Question, 151
   Conclusion, 161

6 The Yongzheng Emperor and Imperial Intervention, 163

   Yongzheng's Journey to Chan Enlightenment, 163
   The Chan Society at the Imperial Court, 168
   Yongzheng's Works on Buddhism, 173
   The Emperor's Polemical Writing, 176
   Conclusion, 182

PART III   LINEAGE MATTERS

7 The Debate about Tianhuang Daowu and Tianwang Daowu in the
   Late Ming, 187

   The Myth of the Two Daowus, 188
   Summary of Major Evidence, 190
   The Use of Evidence in the Debate, 194
   The Role of the Confucian Literati, 196
   The Literati's Initial Discovery of the Two Daowus, 197
   The Dispute about Muchen Daomin's Chandeng shipu, *200*
   Conclusion, 205

8 The Lawsuit about Feiyin Tongrong's *Wudeng yantong* in the
   Early Qing, 207

   The Publication of the Wudeng yantong, *208*
   Accusations and Responses, 214
   The Intervention of Local Authorities, 218
   Conclusion, 223

9 The Aftermath, 225

   The Rebuilding of the Dubious Tianwang Monastery, 225
   Caodong Monks' Continuing Efforts to Falsify the Two-Daowu Theory, 227
   The Debate over the Wudeng quanshu, *229*
   The Literati's Involvement, 235
   The Debate about the Two Daowus in Japan, 238
   Conclusion, 241

PART IV   CRITICAL ANALYSIS

10 Explaining the Rise and Fall of Chan Buddhism, 245

   Textual Ideals and Monastic Reality, 246
   The Formation of Chan Textual Communities: Monks and the Literati, 249
   Drawing the Boundary: Monks and Emperors, 256
   Institutional Implications of Dharma Transmission, 258
   Conclusion, 262

11 The Pattern of Buddhist Revival in the Past, 265

   Legacies of Seventeenth-Century Chan Buddhism, 265
   The Place of Chan in the History of Chinese Buddhism, 273
   The Meaning of Buddhist Revival Revisited, 276
   In Search of a Pattern, 280
   Conclusion, 283

   Concluding Remarks, 287

   Appendix 1. Translation of Official Documents, 291

   A. *Huang Duanbo: "Public Notice Issued by Judge Huang Yuangong [Duanbo]*
       at Xuedou Monastery", 291
   B. *Surveillance Commissioner Lü (Li Rifang): "Investigative Remarks*
       on Banning the Spurious Book Wudeng yantong", *294*
   C. *"Public Notice by the Bureau of Police Chief", 295*

   Appendix 2. Major Controversies in the Seventeenth Century, 297

   A. *The Debate over the "Five Superfluous Generations" in the Song Caodong*
       Lineage, 297

B. *The Debate over the Two Linji Monks Named Haizhou Ci in the Early Ming,*
    301
C. *Other Controversies Related to the Linji Monks, 306*

Appendix 3. Survey of Evidence Concerning the Issue of Two Daowus, 311

A. *Evidence Supporting the Two-Daowu Theory, 311*
B. *Evidence against the Two-Daowu Theory, 324*
C. *Modern Scholarship on the Two-Daowu Theory, 330*

Glossary, 333

Abbreviations of Dictionaries and Collections, 353

Notes, 355

Bibliography, 403

Index, 441

Conventions and Explanatory Notes

1. This book uses the style name (*zi*) or literary name (*hao*) plus the dharma name throughout to identify a monk. For example, for the name Miyun Yuanwu, "Miyun" is the style name and "Yuanwu" the dharma name. In monks' dharma names, the first character is usually the so-called generation character (*beizi*) that is taken from a verse composed for the purpose of dharma transmission. In some sources, this character is omitted. If the generation character cannot be identified, a monk's name will appear in three characters. If the style name cannot be found, the dharma name is used. Certain famous monks, such as Miyun Yuanwu, Feiyin Tongrong, Hanyue Fazang, etc., are sometimes identified by their style names after their first appearance.

2. This book uses the names of mountains on which famous monasteries are located in place of their official names. For example, Mount Huangbo or Huangbo monastery refers to Wanfu monastery, formerly Jingde monastery, in Fuqing.

3. All Chinese titles and names are transliterated using the pinyin system. Titles of primary sources mentioned in the main text are translated in English at their first appearance in the main text.

4. Full citations of primary sources from collections such as the Taishō canon (T), *Shinsan dai Nihon Zokuzōkyō* (Z), and *Mingban Jiaxing dazang jing* (JXZ) are given in the following fashion at their first appearance: title, fascicle number (where relevant and abbreviated as "fasc."), serial number, volume number, page number, and

register (a, b, or c), if necessary, e.g., *Wuzong yuan*, Z no. 1279, 65: 102–11. Some sources are tracked through the "CBETA Chinese Electronic Tripitaka Collection" (CD-ROM) released by the Chinese Buddhist Electronic Text Association (CBETA) in February 2006. Citations from the *Zhonghua dazang jing di er ji* (ZH) are not provided with serial numbers because, due to poor editing, the serial numbers of titles listed in the catalog do not match the actual numbers in the main volumes.

5. The lunar calendar is used for months and days while the approximate year is given using the Western calendar. The Western months and dates of some important events are given in parentheses.

6. Because all emperors in the Ming and Qing dynasties used one reign name consistently throughout their rule, their reign names are used to designate the emperor. For example, Yongzheng, the reign name of the Shizong emperor Yinzhen, refers to the emperor himself.

7. For the dates of Buddhist monks, I largely rely on the *Zhongguo Fojiao renming dacidian* (ZFR; 1999), which contains 16,973 entries and is so far the most comprehensive biographical collection of Chinese monks. As a general rule, dates for all historical figures, if known, will be given at their first appearance and in the glossary in the book.

8. I use the term "literati" throughout this book to refer to a social group of cultural elite in Chinese society. I chose this term instead of "gentry" or "elite" in order to emphasize their professional training in literary composition and connections with the civil service exam rather than their social and economic status. I mark some important literati figures with their terminal degrees in the civil service exam: *shengyuan* (licentiates at the county level), *juren* (recommended scholars at the provincial level), *jinshi* (presented scholars who passed the metropolitan exam).

9. Readers may find that the use of "Chan" in Chinese sources is quite fluid. Sometimes it refers to meditation only and sometimes to the specific teachings of the Chan school attributed to Bodhidharma and Huineng. I use "meditation masters" to refer to those teachers who engaged in meditation without affiliations or claims to Chan lineages and "Chan masters" to refer to those who consciously associated themselves with Chan dharma transmissions and the Chan rhetoric. I use "Chan monasteries" to refer to the institutions whose abbots had clear dharma transmissions and identified themselves as "Chan institutions." As many have pointed out, this doesn't mean that these institutions necessarily followed "pure" Chan practices, excluding influences from other traditions.

Chronology

1526　Official ordination platforms in Beijing and Nanjing were closed.

1529　Wang Yangming died.

1585　Wang's follower Li Zhi shaved his head and retreated to a small cloister in Hubei as leader of a group of monks.

1586　The Wanli emperor bestowed fifteen sets of the Buddhist canon to famous monasteries.

1589　Zibo Zhenke initiated a private edition of the Buddhist canon, which was later referred to as the Jiaxing Buddhist canon.

1602　Qu Ruji compiled the *Zhiyue lu* in which the issue of two Daowus was raised for the first time in the late Ming; Li Zhi committed suicide in Beijing; Wuji Zhenghui revived the transmission of the Northern school at Mount Yuquan in Hubei.

1603　Zibo Zhenke died.

1607　Miyun Yuanwu met Zhou Rudeng and Tao Wangling in Shaoxing, Eastern Zhejiang.

1609　Guxin Ruxin offered the Triple Platform Ordination Ceremony in Linggu monastery at Nanjing and Hanyue Fazang received full ordination.

1615　Yunqi Zhuhong died.

1623   Hanshan Deqing died; Miyun was invited to Mount Jinsu, and
         Hanyue became the head monk; Miyun offered dharma
         transmission to Hanyue soon after.

1625   Hanyue wrote the *Wuzong yuan*.

1630   Miyun was invited to Mount Huangbo in Fujian.

1631   Miyun was invited by Huang Duanbo and Qi Biaojia to
         Ayuwang monastery and later to Tiantong monastery.

1632   Miyun and Muchen Daomin published the *Chandeng shipu*,
         adopting the two-Daowu theory.

1633–1634   Miyun wrote a series of letters and essays to criticize Hanyue's
         Wuzong yuan.

1635   Hanyue died; the rebuilding of Tiantong monastery was begun
         by Miyun; Miyun wrote three treatises to refute Christianity.

1636   Feiyin wrote four treatises to criticize Matteo Ricci; with his
         disciple, he also compiled an anti-Christian anthology in
         Fujian.

1637   Hanyue's disciple Tanji Hongren wrote the *Wuzong jiu* to defend
         his teacher; Huang Duanbo publicly denounced Miyun for
         altering transmission lines based on the two-Daowu theory.

1638   Miyun ordered the compilation of the *Pi wangjiu lueshuo* to
         refute Tanji Hongren.

1639   The anti-Christian anthology *Shengchao poxie ji* was compiled by
         Miyun's and Feiyin's disciple Xu Changzhi.

1642   Miyun died; Feiyin Tongrong and Muchen Daomin argued over
         the names of Miyun's official dharma heirs appearing in his
         epitaph.

1645   Nanjing fell to the Manchu army; Huang Duanbo was executed
         as a Ming loyalist; Qi Biaojia committed suicide in his home
         at Shaoxing.

1654   Feiyin's *Wudeng yantong* was published; a lawsuit was filed
         against him and his book was banned; documents about the
         lawsuit were collected in the *Hufa zhengdeng lu*; Feiyin's
         disciple Yinyuan Longqi arrived in Nagasaki, Japan.

1657   Feiyin's *Wudeng yantong* was reprinted in Fumonji, Japan, by
         Yinyuan Longqi.

1659   Yulin Tongxiu and Muchen Daomin were summoned to Beijing
         by the Shunzhi emperor; a dispute over Miyun's and
         Hanyue's epitaphs, written by Qian Qianyi and Huang
         Zongxi respectively, started; the Japanese *bakufu* government

granted land at Uji, Kyoto, to Yinyuan Longqi to build Manpukuji.

1662   Zheng Chenggong died after conquering Taiwan in 1661; the last regime of the Southern Ming, the Yongli court, collapsed in Yunnan; a dispute over rebuilding Tianwang monastery started.

1672   Weizhong Jingfu wrote the *Zudeng datong* and *Zudeng bian'e* to question the "five superfluous generations" in the Caodong transmission during the Song.

1683   The Qing government reclaimed Taiwan.

1693   The *Wudeng quanshu* was published and stirred a controversy.

1695   Weizhi Zhikai wrote the *Zhengming lu* to dispute the *Wudeng quanshu*; Shilian Dashan traveled to Vietnam.

1733   The Yongzheng emperor wrote the *Jianmo bianyi lu* to condemn Hanyue and his disciple Tanji Hongren.

1754   The Qianlong emperor officially abolished the government-controlled ordination system.

Enlightenment in Dispute

Introduction

The issue of transformation is crucial to the understanding of Buddhism in China because, as an imported tradition, Buddhism introduced a set of new beliefs and practices that involved creative tension between a foreign religion and Chinese cultural norms. Early scholarship on Chinese Buddhism is fascinated with the question of the sinification of Buddhism and favors a paradigm that dates the completion of this process to the seventh and eighth centuries when the mature Chinese philosophical schools, such as Tiantai and Huayan, took shape. This normative paradigm, privileging philosophy over religion, tends to perpetuate a sinicized form of Buddhism as static and ultimate. Accordingly, scholars regard the following centuries as a period of steady decline characterized by the impoverishment of sophisticated philosophical thinking.[1]

The paradigm of transformation should not be confined to religious thought. The transformation of Buddhism in China was multidimensional and was synchronized with transitions of Chinese culture and society. For example, Chan Buddhism survived the destructive persecution of Buddhism in A.D. 845 and continued to grow in the Song and Yuan dynasties. After a long dormancy during the fifteenth and sixteenth centuries, Chan Buddhism once again became prominent and influential in the seventeenth century, when China was undergoing a political transition from the Ming dynasty (1368–1644) to Manchu rule. During this turbulent period, Chan Buddhism was revived in an institutionalized form. The ideal of sudden enlightenment was valued; the spread of dharma transmission, an institutional mechanism for the formation of Chan fellowship, created dharma masters at an accelerating rate; the recorded sayings of Chan masters and Chan genealogies of dharma transmission were published more often than they had been in earlier times; and a large number of Chan monasteries emerged, claiming to be typical Chan institutions and professing to follow the Chan Pure Regulations (qinggui). In this sense, Chan Buddhism was reinvented based on the ideals created in Tang (618–907) and Song times (960–1279). Although many aspects of this reinvented tradition resemble its counterparts in the Tang and Song, it can not be solely measured by the same yardstick we use in earlier periods. Rather, we have to examine closely this reinvention—in its own right—as the compound result of a historical process.

The Revival of Chan Buddhism in the Seventeenth Century

In Chinese history, the seventeenth century is a time of social transitions resulting from the Manchu conquest. The process of conquest was prolonged and its implications for culture and historical memory were far reaching. In addition to China, other East Asian countries were also deeply troubled by political unrest. Some scholars thus consider the seventeenth century in East Asia to be a period of crisis.[2] Not only did political and economic changes trigger social upheavals, but crisis also manifested itself in the collective human consciousness, which spelled out through writing and remembrance the nostalgic memory of the past and the loss of ideals, values, and identities.

Although Buddhism was deeply involved at all levels of social change and provided spiritual counsel and healing to wounded souls and dislocated communities, scholars have not yet fully explored the spiritual transformation in this period. Seventeenth-century Chinese Buddhism, as demonstrated in the controversies I discuss in this book, was a formidable religious and social force that configured and reconfigured itself in response to the spiritual, social, and political crises of that time.

The appellation "seventeenth-century Chinese Buddhism" reflects a view of Buddhism as part of the intellectual and social transformations of Chinese history. This view describes the Buddhist world as continuous and uninterrupted by the Manchu conquest in 1644, which did not disturb the growth of religion and even created an urgent spiritual need for religious salvation. My use of the term "seventeenth-century Chinese Buddhism" also calls attention to the period following the deaths of three eminent Ming monks, Zibo Zhenke (1543–1603), Yunqi Zhuhong (1535–1615), and Hanshan Deqing (1546–1623), who had in large part shaped the course of the Buddhist revival in the late Ming (1550–1644). Previous scholarship regards "the late Ming Buddhist revival" as taking place during the Wanli reign (1573–1620), with the developments in the early Qing dynasty as simply the aftermath of this revival.[3] I intend to show, however, that this view is not quite accurate. After the three eminent masters died, the Buddhist revival entered a new phase, in which Chan masters, such as Miyun Yuanwu (1566–1642), Hanyue Fazang (1573–1635), Feiyin Tongrong (1593–1662), and Muchen Daomin (1596–1674) rose to prominence and dominated the Buddhist world.

The rise of Chan Buddhism in the seventeenth century was first of all characterized by a remarkable textual revival of Chan literature. Two types of Chan literature, recorded sayings and Chan genealogies of dharma transmission, were predominant in the publications of Buddhist sources. Recorded sayings are collections of Chan masters' remarks about Chan enlightenment under various circumstances. They are lively representations of encounter dialogues between Chan masters and their students. This genre is a combination of textuality, orality, and performativity because it has textualized oral discourses and the bodily actions associated with them. The compilations of Chan recorded sayings reached their height in the Southern Song and the Yuan but gradually ceased to appear after the early Ming, corresponding to the decline of Chan institutions. The reemergence of Chan recorded sayings as a genre only occurred in the late Ming, during which early Chan texts, such as the *Platform Sūtra* and the recorded sayings of the Song master Dahui Zonggao and the Yuan master Gaofeng Yuanmiao, were extremely popular. In addition, some early Chan texts were rediscovered and reproduced. For example, the recorded sayings of five early Chan masters, Guishan Lingyou (771–853), Yangshan Huiji (808–883), Caoshan Benji (840–901), Dongshan Liangjia (807–869), and Fayan Wenyi (885–958), were reprinted in 1630 and widely distributed.[4]

The second Chan literary genre, Chan genealogies of dharma transmission, usually called the "Histories of Lamp Transmissions" (*dengshi*), was a generational organizing scheme of the hagiographies of Chan masters. Although these texts also incorporated the quintessential spiritual experience of Chan masters, emphasis was given to the relationship between masters and disciples and to the notion of an unbroken dharma transmission that could be traced back to the Śākyamuni Buddha. The most influential among these are the *Jingde chuandeng lu* (Records of lamp transmissions during the Jingde reign) and *Wudeng huiyuan* (Compendium of five genealogies) compiled in the Song. The format and arrangement of Chan generations by the authors of these two books were considered standardized conventions that were officially sanctioned.

In the seventeenth century, not only were previous Chan genealogies re-printed, but a large number of new histories of dharma transmission were also produced. According to Hasebe Yūkei, the Ming and Qing dynasties saw the production of eighty new editions of histories of lamp transmission. Ming authors were responsible for seventeen titles. In the Qing dynasty (1644–1911), twelve new histories were written during the Shunzhi reign (1644–1661) alone, and in the first half of the Kangxi reign (1662–1692), forty additional titles were published. Based on Hasebe's data, we can see that most writings about dharma transmission from 1400 to 1900 were produced in the seventeenth century. Hasebe's statistics show that from 1597 to 1703, sixty-five new books about Chan histories of dharma transmission and biographies of eminent monks were published.[5] These records not only provide sources for the study of Chan history but also reflect the thriving growth of Chan in seventeenth-century Chinese Buddhism. Judging from the number of textual productions of Chan literature, it becomes evident that in addition to the early stages of Chan history in the Tang and Song, the seventeenth century was indeed the third "golden age" of Chan Buddhism.

The Chan textual revival shows that there were active Chan communities that emphasized the practice of encounter dialogue and organized the monastic hierarchy based on the relationship of dharma transmission, which was supposed to be a spiritual process of transferring the ineffable Buddhist truth and patriarchal authority from an enlightened teacher to a disciple who is believed to have reached the same level of spiritual attainment. In the seventeenth century, both the Linji and Caodong lineages, traditional rivals since the Song dynasty, developed from certain Chan figures who claimed to have orthodox dharma transmissions. The Linji lineages of Miyun Yuanwu, Tianyin Yuanxiu (1575–1635), and Xuejiao Yuanxin (1570–1647) originated from Huanyou Zhengchuan (1549–1614). The Caodong master Zhanran Yuancheng (1561–1626) received transmission from Cizhou Fangnian (?–1594), a master upholding the Caodong transmission from Shaolin monastery. The Caodong masters Wuyi Yuanlai (1575–1630), Huitai Yuanjing (1577–1630), and Yongjue Yuanxian (1578–1657) were dharma heirs of Wuming Huijing (1548–1618), who also received recognition from the Caodong lineage derived from Shaolin monastery. Through dharma transmission, these masters' dharma heirs multiplied their followers exponentially. Among these subdivided lineages, the transmission of Miyun Yuanwu's Chan lineage was the most aggressive. Miyun alone had twelve dharma heirs in the first generation. Through these heirs' independent transmissions, within twenty years, his second-generation dharma heirs numbered 495, and the third-generation heirs reached 1,168, surpassing all other transmissions in Chan history.[6]

Controversies and Chan Buddhism

While Chan Buddhism was on the rise, controversies among Chan monks ensued. In this book, I intend to explore two major controversies in order to investigate the transformations of Chan Buddhism in the seventeenth century.[7]

The first controversy is the debate between Miyun Yuanwu and his dharma heir Hanyue Fazang. When Miyun Yuanwu revived the Chan performance of beating and shouting in the 1620s, Hanyue Fazang challenged his master's interpretation of Linji Chan teaching and his orthodox position within the lineage, insisting that the enlightenment experience should be subject to authentication by the "principle" (zongzhi) of Linji Yixuan's teaching rather than by the excessive use of beating and shouting. A hundred years later, in 1733, the Yongzheng emperor (1678–1735) finally settled the dispute in Miyun's favor, writing an eight-fascicle book Jianmo bianyi lu (Records of selecting demons and discerning heresies).[8]

The second controversy involves Miyun Yuanwu's dharma heir Feiyin Tongrong's ill-fated book, Wudeng yantong (The strict transmission of the five Chan schools), which agitated a notorious lawsuit in 1654. Advocating a strict criterion of dharma transmission, Feiyin Tongrong intended to clarify the confused lines of dharma transmission. In his view, self-proclaimed Chan monks without proper dharma transmission personally conferred by their masters should be relegated to the category of "lineage unknown" (sifa weixiang). Not only did he marginalize some eminent monks, such as Yunqi Zhuhong, Hanshan Deqing, and Zibo Zhenke, he also ignored or underrepresented the Caodong monks derived from Wuming Huijing and Zhanran Yuancheng. The major charge against him, however, was that he had deliberately altered the lines of dharma transmission in the officially approved Chan history of lamp transmission, Jingde chuandeng lu.

Disputes about dharma transmission characterized Chan Buddhism from its beginnings. Various "transmission" theories were produced in early times to legitimize a particular group of Chan monks. After fierce competition among rival groups, the Song imperial court approved a surviving version of transmission and codified it in the Jingde chuandeng lu.[9] However, making this version official did not mean settling the disputes about dharma transmission. In the following centuries, this orthodox version was constantly challenged, and Feiyin Tongrong was among the most audacious contenders. Based on the "discovery" of a new inscription of Tianwang Daowu (737–818 or 727–808) in the Tang, he argued that this monk had been confused with Tianhuang Daowu

(748–807) in the official *Jingde chuandeng lu*. According to this new inscription, Longtan Chongxin, from whom the Yunmen and Fayan schools were derived, was actually Tianwang Daowu's heir rather than Tianhuang Daowu's. The real significance of this confusion was that Tianwang Daowu belonged to Mazu Daoyi's (709–788) transmission and Tianhuang Daowu belonged to Shitou Xiqian's (700–790). Based on these new pieces of evidence, Feiyin Tongrong boldly altered the official dharma transmission lines, adding the dubious figure Tianwang Daowu to his version of the genealogy and consequently switching the Yunmen and Guiyang schools to Mazu Daoyi's and Nanyue Huairang's (677–744) line. Because this alteration hinged on the shaky evidence of Tianwang Daowu's identity, Caodong monks sued Feiyin in Zhejiang and the provincial governor ordered the book to be burned.

The Transformation of Chan Buddhism

This book investigates the transformation of Chan Buddhism by reconstructing history through the lens of controversy. In the history of religions, controversies have led to major schisms, to the formation of new denominations, and even to religious wars. Controversies have defined the religious landscape in China as well. For historians of Chinese Buddhism, controversies are extremely informative because they disclose keenly felt spiritual issues. Controversies also have a social and political dimension from which social changes and the function of the existing power structure within and outside the Buddhist world can be examined. For Buddhists themselves, engaging in controversies has been a way to reconstruct identities as new denominations emerge and the boundaries among religious traditions are renegotiated.

For scholars of Chinese religion, controversies are an index to the rise of new religious groups and to the transformations they embodied. By using such controversies to reconstruct Buddhist history, scholars can avoid the pitfalls and oversights often created by Buddhist historiographers who have been consciously or unconsciously influenced by open or hidden ideological agendas. For instance, certain historical works by Buddhist scholars have reformulated or even suppressed formerly influential dissident voices and texts. Early Chan history provides a perfect example of how Buddhist historiographers manufactured an orthodox version of history that gave voice only to certain Chan lineages.

The two controversies upon which I focus can be equally used to understand the transformation of Chan Buddhism. The first controversy shows that Chan monks paid much attention to the fundamental spiritual issue of Chan teaching, which they called the meaning of "principle." The issue in dispute is the practice of beating and shouting as a way of Chan training and enlightenment, indicating the popularity of this practice. It reveals that at the spiritual core of the revived Chan Buddhism was an idealized version of Chan teaching and practice that fully displayed the antinomian spirit of Chan rhetoric. Various Chan works of this period, such as recorded sayings and histories of lamp transmission, create the impression that certain eminent masters have attained enlightenment through the use of enigmatic language and performance in their daily encounters with their teachers and other masters. During the process of interaction, the spirit of spontaneity is supposed to have been fully displayed through puzzling conversations and symbolic actions, such as beating and shouting. These episodes can be loosely referred to as "encounter dialogues," a translation of the Chinese term *jiyuan wenda* (Japanese: *kien mondō*) coined by Yanagida Seizan.[10]

For Chan monks in the seventeenth century, who commonly believed that enlightenment was attainable through sudden awareness, encounter dialogue was a real performance involving master and disciple, intended by Chan masters to induce enlightenment in their students. My study of the two controversies shows that Chan Buddhists regarded beating and shouting during encounter dialogues as the hallmark of the authenticity of their tradition. Here, readers must bear in mind that encounter dialogues can be performed in different contexts. There is no doubt that they can be carried out as a private training tool without much publicity. However, in the seventeenth century, encounter dialogues were performed publicly, usually in the ceremony of ascending the hall, and later were publicized through printing the master's recorded sayings. More important, these public performances, which were even ritualized or rehearsed in advance, had to demonstrate the spirit of spontaneity by imitating the dialogues and actions found in Chan records without any sign of falseness. In other words, situational spontaneity, or imitated responsiveness based on existing Chan kōans, became the implicit principle underlying the use of encounter techniques such as beating and shouting.

For example, the distinctive characteristic of a monastery controlled by Chan monks was its abbot's ability to "open the hall and preach the dharma" (*kaitang shuofa*), or "hold the ceremony of ascending the hall" (*shangtang*), during which beating and shouting took place. In the late Ming, Miyun Yuanwu was acknowledged as the embodiment of the "true Chan spirit" especially because of his frequent use of beating and shouting when this ceremony was under way. In a religious culture dominated by the joint practice of Chan and Pure Land Buddhism, this style of Chan teaching was novel and refreshing. Thus Miyun Yuanwu won the title "the second coming of Linji Yixuan," after the founder of the Linji school, who had been skillful in beating and shouting during the Tang dynasty.

In the second controversy, dharma transmission is obviously the crucial subject under discussion. Within Chan communities, dharma transmission literally means the process of transmission of the ineffable Buddhist teaching from teacher to student. In practice, it bonds a group of monks with a special kind of spiritual relationship comparable to that of father and son in a secular Chinese lineage organization. In the course of the debate, we learn that the focus of the debate was not the spiritual content of the transmission. Rather, all parties were concerned about the evidence or credential of dharma transmission and about how to apply a strict standard of dharma transmission to eliminate false claims and imposters. This controversy shows that the transformed Chan Buddhism in the seventeenth century was distinguished by its emphasis on a strict definition of dharma transmission: The authenticity of dharma transmission had to be verified through examining the evidence of transmission.

In practice, Chan Buddhists, especially Miyun Yuanwu and his followers, considered certain aspects of dharma transmission to be corrupt. Because specific lineages were often discontinued for various reasons and dharma masters often could not find suitable candidates, two widespread practices of dharma transmission, *daifu* (transmission by proxy, in which a master transmitted the dharma to a monk on behalf of his deceased master) and *yaosi* (transmission by remote succession, in which a monk declared himself the master's legitimate dharma heir without meeting the master in person), were extremely popular. Because such practices would inevitably confuse the lines of transmission, Chan monks advocated a strict method of authenticating dharma transmission and used it as an organizing principle to extend their monastic network.

To better understand the significance of these debates, we must be aware of the recent institutional changes in some newly revived monasteries. According to Hasebe Yūkei, in the seventeenth century, a new type of Chan institution, the "dharma transmission monastery" (*chuanfa conglin*), emerged as the dominant Chan institution. He defines the dharma transmission monastery in this period as a hereditary institution "attached to a certain dharma lineage being deprived of publicity," which selected candidates for abbot only from among its own dharma heirs.[11] In my own study of this type of monastery, I find that a dharma transmission monastery took form after a monastery was revived by local patrons and a renowned Chan master with dharma transmission was invited as abbot. This Chan master would reorganize the monastic bureaucracy by appointing his dharma heirs as officers and successors. After several generations, the abbot succession system was established according to the principle of dharma transmission. Because the abbots of many monasteries in a region maintained a close relationship of dharma transmission, these monasteries formed a loose institutional network. Periodically, there was a great need to update Chan genealogies, such as records of lamp transmission, in order to incorporate the newly certified dharma heirs and to perpetuate their group control over certain monasteries. Therefore, the accuracy of dharma transmission was not a small matter, and a false claim was a potential threat to the established abbot succession system. The controversies about dharma transmission simply reflect this institutional change in reality.[12]

The Reinvention of the Chan Tradition

If Chan Buddhism underwent a series of transformations in the seventeenth century, how can these changes be characterized? On the surface, Chan Buddhism in the seventeenth century merely revived some archaic forms of practice, showing no innovations. Chan monks attempted to follow the Chan ideals faithfully and to create an impression of continuity with the traditions in the Tang and Song. However, I contend that Chan Buddhism in the seventeenth century was a systematic reinvention of Chan ideals characterized by the performance of beating and shouting and a hierarchy of dharma transmission.

By "reinvention," I mean the historical process by which a largely defunct religious ideal was intentionally revitalized and transformed into something real and practical for a religious community. This reinvented Chan tradition, appearing and claiming to be a historical continuation of the Chan school in antiquity, in fact originated in the seventeenth century.[13] Its proponents claimed that their own Chan teaching and practice were deeply rooted in the past and that the Chan tradition was a coherent unity without disruptions. However, "traditions" that claim to be descended from antiquity are often reinvented by applying old forms in response to new situations. Eric Hobsbawn defines this type of "invented tradition" as follows:

> "Invented tradition" is taken to mean a set of practices, normally governed by overtly or tacitly accepted rules and of a ritual or symbolic nature, which seek to inculcate certain values and norms of behaviour by repetition, which automatically implies continuity with the past. In fact, where possible, they normally attempt to establish continuity with a suitable historic past.[14]

In other words, invented traditions dressed up novelties as antiquities by repeating a set of behavioral norms and claiming an ancient origin for them. Although certain symbols or practices appeared to be the same as their precedents, these symbols and practices were newly created out of cultural and social circumstances completely different from those of earlier times when these symbols and practices were first used.

The phrase "invented tradition" is an apt description of the transformation of Chan Buddhism that sought to restore ancient practices and ideals. For instance, some archaic practices, which can be read about only in Chan literature such as kōan stories, were literally enacted in seventeenth-century Chan communities: Beating and shouting—violent expressions of enlightenment—were performed live in front of the assembly; the legitimacy of dharma transmission was emphasized in its strictest sense; and monastic rituals recorded in the Chan Pure Regulations (qinggui) were followed sincerely. These reinventions created a sense of authenticity and authority among Chan monks, best expressed by the phrase "the orthodoxy of the Linji school" (Linji zheng-zong),[15] a forceful claim intended to reestablish continuity with the lost Chan traditions of antiquity.

Certainly, this movement of reinvention was not unique, and the Chan tradition in China has constantly been invented and reinvented. For example, the emergence of Chan in the Tang dynasty was predicated on the claim of an unbroken mind-to-mind transmission that traced the origin of Chan to the Śākyamuni Buddha. Without historical basis, this theory functioned as a legitimizing tool for the birth of a new tradition. Later, the rhetoric of sudden enlightenment was manufactured to denounce gradual cultivation even though the actual Chan practice was rooted in various ritual forms, such as meditation and the cult of patriarchs. During the Song and Yuan dynasties, the Chan tradition was invented again, and the Chan monastic system, a recent creation of the Song, was imagined as modeled on the fully functioning institution in the Tang dynasty. Although Chan Buddhism was considerably weakened in the early (1368–1450) and mid-Ming (1450–1550), in the seventeenth century, Chan masters reinvented the antinomian Chan ideal characterized by the methods of beating and shouting and the strict definition of dharma transmission.

To claim that the Chan tradition in the seventeenth century is a reinvention implies a historical thesis that the development of Chan was disrupted before Chan Buddhism was systematically revived. As I will demonstrate in part I of this book, Buddhism in general, especially Chan Buddhism, suffered serious spiritual and institutional decline during the hundred years between the mid-fifteenth and mid-sixteenth centuries, when many Chan institutions famous in the Song and Yuan (1271–1368) became obsolescent and regular Chan practice ceased in most Chan monasteries. In this sense, the Chan tradition was unquestionably disrupted.

The rise of Chan Buddhism in the seventeenth century therefore has to be explained by looking at influences from outside the monastic world. Prior to the rise of Chan in the monastic world, there was a cultural and intellectual craze for the Chan spirit among the Confucian literati. Here, in my chronological analysis of the revival of Chan Buddhism, I have noticed a conspicuous delay of the emergence of the Chan masters such as Miyun Yuanwu: They became prominent only after Chan was promoted in the elite literati culture. The literati's craze about Chan, stimulated by some of Wang Yangming's (1472–1529) disciples, was already visible during the middle and late sixteenth century while Chan communities remained obscure: There were few eminent Chan masters and few recorded sayings of contemporary teachers were compiled, published, and circulated. At that time, the Chan craze was only part of the literati culture and Wang Yangming's intellectual discourse rather than a natural outcome of a monastic movement of Buddhist revival. As I will show in chapter 1, the first type of Buddhism that was revived was not Chan but Buddhist scholasticism characterized by frequent lectures on scriptures, and the learning of Tiantai, Huayan, and Yogācāra flourished. There were indeed monks practicing the iconoclastic "Chan" in obscure communities, but their influence was still limited. However, the majority of monks understood Chan as a diligent or even ascetic style of meditation rather than as the antinomian performance of beating and shouting that dominated Chan communities later. For some of the eminent Buddhist teachers, the use of beating and shouting was a despicable act that demonstrated the shallowness of a faked imitation. The shared opinion about Chan among clergy, represented by Zibo Zhenke, Yunqi Zhuhong, and Hanshan Deqing, was that a serious Chan practitioner must combine the practice of meditation with other forms of Buddhist vocations, such as Pure Land and doctrinal studies. As I will show in chapter 2, the fact that Chan Buddhism arose after the emergence of the intellectual discourse of Chan thought in elite culture means that the literati played an essential role in fostering a Chan culture not only in the secular society but also in the monastic world.

If the intellectual transformation in the late Ming explains the rise of Chan Buddhism, it also accounts for its demise in the eighteenth century, in which Wang Yangming's teaching and the entire movement inspired by him was under scrutiny, and some even blamed it for the loss of the Ming dynasty.[16] As Timothy Brook points out, a conservative movement resurged among Confucian intellectuals who "sought to isolate Buddhism's influence within the elite."[17] Here, the motive was not even anti-Buddhist. Rather, the Confucian literati wanted to delink their overt associations with Buddhism, especially with Chan Buddhism. In other words, Confucian intellectuals in the eighteenth century no longer regarded Confucianism and Buddhism as one unified ideology as their predecessors in the late Ming did. Rather, they believed that they were separated on their own rights.

Although, as I will show, Chan Buddhism dominated the Buddhist world in the seventeenth century, neither modern historians nor even Buddhists themselves mention these Chan masters prominently. Holmes Welch has interviewed modern Buddhists extensively, but none was aware of the role of Miyun Yuanwu and the legacies of his lineage although most of them could trace their transmissions to him.[18] This shows that another disruption occurred after the seventeenth century and contributed to the neglect of these Chan monks. The Chan teaching and practice revitalized in the seventeenth century ceased to inspire monks in later times, and modern Chinese Buddhism has taken other trajectories, such as the pursuit of Yogācāra study.[19] It is true that in some local traditions, Miyun Yuanwu and his followers are still remembered as reformers of local monasteries, such as Tiantong. However, in today's Buddhist world, Miyun Yuanwu and his Chan style are seldom mentioned.[20]

Chapters and Sources

I divide this book into four parts followed by short concluding remarks and appendixes. The first part provides the background for seventeenth-century Chan Buddhism. In chapter 1, I trace the development of various Buddhist communities that revitalized Buddhist scholasticism and ordination in the late Ming. As I will demonstrate, in the early stage of Buddhist revival, Buddhist communities followed a "syncretic path," which emphasized the joint practice of meditation on critical phrases (huatou), Pure Land incantation, and doctrinal study. The radical practices of beating and shouting and dharma transmission were disparaged. However, the situation changed dramatically in the early seventeenth century: Both the Caodong and Linji lineages were revived; the role of dharma transmission was reemphasized; and Chan monks were eager to seek their unique sectarian identity. Chapter 2 focuses on the literati's influence on Chan Buddhism because the rise of Chan had been greatly promoted by the literati. In chapter 3, I introduce major Chan masters in the Linji and Caodong lineages and the spread of Chan lineages in the seventeenth century.

Part II focuses on the dispute between Miyun Yuanwu and Hanyue Fazang. Chapter 4 examines the polemical texts from both sides in chronological order. In chapter 5, I single out three points of contention to clarify the grounds for disagreement. Chapter 6 details the Yongzheng emperor's involvement in this controversy, showing how he became involved in the dispute and why he suppressed Hanyue Fazang's lineage.

The controversy about dharma transmission is investigated in part III, which is divided into three chapters. Chapter 7 focuses on the key issue of the controversy: the identities of Tianhuang Daowu and Tianwang Daowu and how evidential research played a role in the debate during the late Ming. Chapter 8 shifts the focus to the process of the debate in the early Qing and to the following lawsuit by examining various sources. In chapter 9, I examine the aftermath of the debates over the lawsuit, especially the one about the most comprehensive Chan history compiled in this period, *Wudeng quanshu* (The complete genealogy of the five lamps). In addition, I will briefly account for the impact of the debate about the *Wudeng yantong* in Japan because Feiyin Tongrong's heir Yinyuan Longqi reprinted his teacher's book in Japan in 1657.

I added part IV during the final revision of this manuscript to tighten up loose ends and to offer some of my observations about Chan Buddhism and Chinese religion in general. Readers who are not familiar with the historical background of this period and feel obstructed by the detailed information discussed in the main text might want to read this part first to get into this research through thematic discussions of some key issues. In chapter 10, I introduce the concept of "textual communities" developed by the European historian Brian Stock to explain the rise and fall of Chan Buddhism in the seventeenth century and highlight the institutional implications of the debates over dharma transmission. In chapter 11, situating the Buddhist revival in a larger historical context, I seek to identify the legacies of the Chan revival and the pattern of the Buddhist revival in the past.

After short concluding remarks, in appendix 1, I translate several important polemical essays and official documents from the *Hufa zhengdeng lu*, which was discovered during a field trip to China. In appendix 2, I list other major controversies in the seventeenth century in addition to the ones I have studied. I believe that these debates are crucial for us to understand the seventeenth century. In these debates, one can sense that the entire Buddhist world in that period was connected by the exchange of polemical essays, and controversies provided the fabric for monks' social networking. In appendix 3, I list all of the evidence pertaining to the Tianhuang and Tianwang debate as mentioned in the seventeenth-century sources, hoping that my efforts here can aid scholars of early Chan history to solve the puzzle.

To reconstruct the history of these controversies, I have consulted various Buddhist and historical sources, even the Jesuit missionary records. The Jiaxing Buddhist canon and its supplementary volumes, which cover Buddhist works produced in the seventeenth century, are my major sources. Because of the existence of a large number of Chan texts in this collection, Buddhist scholar Lan Jifu claims that this canon is the "Dunhuang discovery" in the study of Ming-Qing Chan Buddhism.[21]

To recover Buddhist history between the early Ming and the late Ming, I have also relied on monastic gazetteers, which have not yet been fully exploited by Buddhist scholars.[22] In my study, I have found that these gazetteers not only contain detailed information about monastic institutions in the seventeenth century but also include precious materials pertaining to early Chan in the Tang and the Song. In particular, because many monasteries were rebuilt in the proximity of the original sites of Tang and Song temples, during the reconstruction some important relics were discovered and documented in the gazetteers. Many gazetteers were compiled by accomplished literati, and sources relevant to the monastery but scattered in other historical and literary sources were assembled together as well.

Some of the sources with which I am dealing are highly normative discourses, such as recorded sayings and history of lamp histories, which we must treat with caution and sophisticated methods. These ideological and normative discourses are unique Chan literary genres that represent the textual ideals of Chan Buddhism. However, even in highly normative sources, such as recorded sayings and chronological biographies, descriptive statements have proved to be useful for reconstructing historical events.[23] In order to mine the maximum amount of historical information from these normative sources, we should be more sophisticated about them. For example, although lamp histories cannot be used as accurate sources for studying early Chan history, these compilations can still be useful for reconstructing Chan Buddhism around the time when these works were compiled. This is because although the records about early Chan masters might contain romantic imaginings and rhetorical hyperbole, the records of those recent masters close to the time when these records were created have the highest rate of accuracy since these works are genealogical and public in nature. They were often subject to further investigation and examination by all concerned Chan masters and their disciples who cared about their status in the entire Chan hierarchy. Besides, for the study of Chan Buddhism in this period, we are lucky to have a plethora of surviving texts that provide multiple records of the same events from different angles.

In addition to these collections, a number of rare sources have shed new light on the subject matter of this book. The first set of rare sources comes from the Manpukuji archive in Japan: 117 letters from Yinyuan Longqi's master, Feiyin Tongrong, disciples, and lay followers in mainland China were discovered by Professor Chen Zhichao in 1995, and their reprints are available now to the public.[24] These correspondences provide valuable information about Buddhism during the Ming-Qing transition. Second, two collections of polemical essays I retrieved from Japan have also been extremely helpful for reconstructing the controversies: The *Miyun Yuanwu chanshi Tiantong zhishuo* (Straightforward remarks of Chan master Miyun Yuanwu at Mount Tiantong, nine fascicles, often referred to as *Tiantong zhishuo*) collects the polemical essays that Miyun Yuanwu wrote in response to Hanyue Fazang.[25] *Feiyin chanshi bieji* (Separate collection of Chan master Feiyin Tongrong) in eighteen fascicles includes Feiyin Tongrong's polemical essays about his work *Wudeng yantong* (Strict transmission of the five Chan schools).[26]

Finally, three collections I came across in the Shanghai Library are also crucial for understanding the issues surrounding dharma transmission. First, Weizhi Zhikai's *Zhengming lu* (Records of the rectification of names, fourteen fascicles) is a systematic review of all disputes about dharma transmission in the seventeenth century.[27] Second, the anonymous *Hufa zhengdeng lu* (Records of protecting the dharma and rectifying lamp transmissions, one fascicle) contains documents relating to the lawsuit against Feiyin Tongrong in 1654. Finally, when I visited the Shanghai Library the second time in June 2006, I found a rare source entitled *Dongming yilu* (Remaining records in Dongming monastery), which includes biographies of three abbots in Dongming monastery in the early Ming. These documents were compiled by the Chan monk Shanci Tongji and published in 1635. I believe that this is the forgery commonly referred to as the *Dongming zudeng lu* (Records of patriarch lineage in Dongming monastery), which pertains to the controversy of the Linji patriarch Haizhou Ci in the early Ming.[28]

In many ways, all of these sources reveal that the rise of Chan Buddhism left its marks on seventeenth-century China. But somehow, these traces were intentionally or unintentionally neglected by later Buddhist historiographers. The purpose of this book is to recount and reconstruct this reinvented tradition, which was full of tension, negotiation, and contradiction.

PART I

The Context of Seventeenth-Century China

I

Reenvisioning Buddhism in the Late Ming

The reinvented Chan Buddhism grew out of the nationwide revival of Buddhism that started in the late Ming and reached its height in the early Qing dynasty. In a short period, Chan Buddhism was restored to an unprecedented level of prominence marked by the appearance of thousands of ostensibly enlightened Chan masters and the increased production and reproduction of Chan literature. This was in sharp contrast to the situation in the mid-Ming, when neither famous Chan masters nor active Chan communities were recognized in Chan historiographies. Publications about Chan, such as recorded sayings and histories of lamp transmissions, were scarce as well. This contrast requires a fresh look at late Ming Buddhism.

My study suggests that the first signs of Buddhist revival appeared in Buddhist scholastic traditions such as Huayan, Yogā-cāra, and Tiantai. The Vinaya school was also revived in response to the great demand for proper ordination. Meanwhile, Confucian philosopher Wang Yangming's followers created a pro-Buddhist intellectual movement that promoted a close association between the Confucian literati and Buddhist monks. Against this background in the late sixteenth century, Chan Buddhism started to be revitalized as one of many traditions. However, Chan teachers and communities still lacked their own identities because most practitioners of Chan followed a syncretic method, such as the joint practice of meditation and Pure Land.

From Margin to Center

In a study of early Ming policies toward Buddhism, Timothy Brook has aptly characterized the social status of Buddhism in the Ming as being "at the margin of public authority" because the Ming rulers adopted pragmatic policies of restriction and control. In general, the development of Ming Buddhism can be roughly divided into three stages. First, in the early Ming, the first emperor, Zhu Yuanzhang (1328–1398), initiated a series of institutional reforms to reorganize Buddhist establishments, successfully disrupting the institutional structures handed down from the Song and Yuan. In the second stage, his successors continued this policy while lavishly patronizing Tibetan Buddhism. The turning point occurred in the Jiajing reign (1522–1566), during which the emperor favored Taoism over Buddhism and attempted to suppress Buddhist institutions. Although the anti-Buddhist fervor ended a short time later, some policies, such as the prohibition against Buddhist ordination, had a serious impact on late Ming Buddhism. In the third stage, which was near the end of the Ming dynasty, the Wanli emperor and his mother, the Dowager Empress Cisheng (1546–1614), promoted Buddhism as a means to perpetuate their personal welfare. During Wanli's reign and through his influence, Buddhist monasteries were gradually revived and doctrinal studies flourished.

The Restriction of Buddhism in the Early and Mid-Ming

The reform of Buddhist institutions in the early Ming is well documented by such scholars as Tatsuike Kiyoshi, Chün-fang Yü, Hasebe Yūkei, Guo Peng, and, more recently, Timothy Brook and Zhou Qi.[1] Their studies indicate that the Ming founder, Zhu Yuanzhang, who had been a monk in his youth, was very conscious of the role of Buddhism in the formation of a unified state ideology.[2] More important, his institutional reforms disrupted the continuity with the previous system and established a new monastic hierarchy in the capital, Nanjing. Modeled on a bureaucratic hierarchy, three "super-monasteries" were created to administer affairs in three different divisions of Buddhism: Chan, doctrinal instruction (jiang), and esoteric ritual performance (jiao). Different from the Song monastic system, which designated the name jiao to "monasteries of doctrinal instruction," Zhu Yuanzhang redesigned the tripartite monastic classification and used the title jiao to refer to the monasteries specializing in esoteric ritual performance (yuqie jiao).[3] Government regulations required that Chan monks should aspire to "see their true nature without establishing words"; teaching (scholastic) monks should "illuminate the meaning of all scriptures"; and the *jiao* monks should "eliminate all karma created by human beings" through performing Buddhist rituals.[4]

The most significant impact of this policy was Zhu Yuanzhang's attempt to separate Buddhism from society. His "Biqu tiaoli" (Regulations preventing [monks'] currying [for favor]), issued in 1394, stipulated that monks could not travel freely nor associate with government officials and ordinary people.[5] To a large extent, these new measures amounted to religious suppression, as Brook notes.[6] Clearly, the emperor intended to set a strict boundary between Buddhism and secular society while acknowledging the utilitarian value of Buddhism for state ideology.

Later emperors continued to carry out the early Ming policies, though with some revisions. The regulations set by Zhu Yuanzhang were reiterated in 1412 by the Yongle emperor (r. 1403–1424), in 1432 by the Xuande emperor (r. 1426–1435), and in 1441 by the Zhengtong emperor (r. 1436–1449).[7] While these emperors showed various levels of personal interest in Buddhism, the Ming government viewed Buddhist establishments as ordinary institutions for tax and covée purposes. Because monasteries were subject to taxation to cope with fiscal emergencies, they resorted to selling ordination certificates to increase revenue.[8] Perhaps for similar financial reasons, the emperors prohibited the building of new temples unless their sponsors acquired a plaque granting permission. A new temple erected without such a plaque would be destroyed by government officials.[9] Even during the Wanli reign, when the building of private monasteries was widespread, officials invoked this prohibition to punish the emperor's favorite monk, Hanshan Deqing, who built Haiyin monastery at Mount Lao in Shangdong province.[10] Thus, Ming policies toward Buddhism could hardly be considered favorable given the strict limitations imposed on Buddhist institutions.

From the mid-fifteenth to the mid-sixteenth century, there is a lacuna in historical records about Buddhist activities. Few Buddhist histories had been written and official records seldom mentioned Buddhist institutions. In most monastic gazetteers compiled in the seventeenth century, a palpable silence about Buddhist activities envelops this period: Little royal patronage is evident, fewer donations to repair dilapidated buildings appear, and records of presiding abbots are missing. The monastic gazetteer of the famous Ayuwang monastery in Ningbo reveals that the succession of abbots stopped abruptly in 1444 and was renewed only in 1576, when a new Tiantai teacher was invited.[11] Historical studies show similar results. For example, the social historian Wolfram Eberhard observes a low level of temple building during this period. His statistics on Buddhist monasteries, based on local gazetteers, indicate that

Buddhist monasteries did not receive significant patronage until the years between 1550 and 1700.[12]

Communications between Buddhist communities and the social elite, as an indicator of frequent Buddhist activities, also dwindled significantly. Brook has surveyed eighty-six datable poems about monasteries preserved in the *Jinling fancha zhi* (Gazetteer of Nanjing monasteries) and found that after a few poems in the early Ming, almost nothing was written until the end of the fifteenth century. At the beginning of the sixteenth century, the number of poems increased sharply.[13]

Government policies contributed to the further decline of Buddhist communities in this period. From 1514 to 1546, a strong anti-Buddhist campaign was initiated to curb the lavish patronage of Tibetan monks.[14] The enthronement of the Jiajing emperor, a practitioner of the Taoist technique of attaining immortality, brought further decline to Buddhist communities: He ordered that Buddhist temples and cloisters be destroyed or sold and Tibetan lamas be expelled. In 1544, the Ministry of Rites carried out the emperor's decree to disrobe all Buddhist monks and nuns.

The plight of Buddhist institutions was worsened by the Japanese pirate invasion of coastal regions where many monasteries were located, with both pirates and local defenders exploiting monastic property for their own purposes. For example, during a pirate raid in 1554, government troops burned Zhaoqing monastery, a famous Vinaya institution in Hangzhou. In 1556, the government once again ordered its destruction for fear that pirates might use the rebuilt monastery as a strategic base.[15]

The Revival of Buddhism in the Wanli Reign

During the late Ming, the Wanli emperor and his mother, the Dowager Empress Cisheng, also known as Madame Li, stimulated the recovery of Buddhist communities throughout the nation. Madame Li was a devout Buddhist. As a pious and powerful woman, she was responsible for many renovations of Buddhist institutions and supported such famous monks as Hanshan Deqing and Zibo Zhenke. In 1584, she summoned Hanshan Deqing to Beijing and allowed him to enter the inner quarters of the palace. She also convened a grand ceremony in Mount Wutai to pray for the begetting of a new heir for the emperor. In addition, she befriended Bianrong Zhenyuan (1506–1594) and erected a seven-story memorial pagoda for him after his death.[16] Under her patronage, monasteries were rebuilt with imperial donations.

Among these pious activities, the bestowal of the imperial Buddhist canon is particularly noteworthy. Throughout the Ming, the imperial court had organized the official compilation and printing of the Buddhist canon. When the Yongle emperor established the two-capital system in 1420, the Buddhist canon was also divided into the Northern edition, an updated version for royal patronage, and the Southern edition, stored in Bao'en monastery in Nanjing for commercial printing.[17] In 1586, the Wanli emperor bestowed fifteen sets of the newly compiled canon on famous monasteries throughout the empire. In 1614, he bestowed six more sets.

Besides these official editions, Ming Buddhists sponsored a private edition of the Buddhist canon which had gained increasing popularity because it adopted the usual Chinese style of stitched volumes rather than the Indian style of accordion-pleated binding. This new binding style facilitated the production and distribution of the canon. This private canon, initiated by Zibo Zhenke in Mount Wutai and later moved to Lengyan monastery at Mount Jingshan in Jiaxing county, was thus named the Jiaxing or Jingshan canon.[18] Its main body contains the reprinted official edition of the Buddhist Tripiṭaka of the Ming, but its supplementary sections preserve many contemporary Buddhist writings.

The Rise of Buddhist Scholasticism

The Buddhist revival was heralded by the rise of Buddhist scholasticism, represented by doctrinal traditions such as Huayan, Yogācāra, and Tiantai. Throughout the Ming, the government patronized public lectures given by learned monks and preserved the exegetic tradition of Buddhist texts in official monasteries. Monks attended these public lectures on popular Buddhist texts, such as the *Avataṃsaka*, the *Laṅkāvatāra Sūtra*, the *Heart Sūtra*, and the *Śūraṃgama Sūtra*.

The survival of these exegetical traditions indicates that doctrinal studies are much more enduring than other sectarian establishments. For example, the study of the *Śūraṃgama Sūtra* (*Shoulengyan jing*) has been a long-lasting scholastic tradition in Buddhist monasteries since the Song dynasty. Despite its dubious nature as a Chinese apocryphon, the *Śūraṃgama Sūtra* generated tremendous interest among scholar-monks and literati followers.[19] While exegeses of this text had been popular during the Song, commentaries by monks and literati followers were even more prolific in the sixteenth and seventeenth centuries. According to my calculation, forty-six such commentaries from the Ming and the Qing have been preserved in various Buddhist canons, surpassing the

number of titles relating to other popular scriptures and indicating a special interest in this text.[20]

A complete picture of the function and operation of these doctrinal traditions awaits further study. But in the mid-sixteenth century, Beijing was the
undisputed center of Buddhist doctrinal studies.[21] According to Susan Naquin, many scholar-monks visited Beijing from the 1570s to the 1620s and
made themselves famous by offering lectures in large monasteries, attracting
eunuchs and Confucian intellectuals interested in Buddhist scriptures.[22] Kongyin Zhencheng (1547–1617), a scholar-monk who had studied Huayan teaching in Beijing, recollected three dharma masters, Yijiang Zhenfeng (1501–
1572), Xifeng Shen, and Shou'an Zhong, who were promoting doctrinal studies
in Beijing in the 1550s.[23] Other sources traced the rise of Buddhist scholasticism to the monk Lu'an (or Lushan) Putai (fl. 1511) of Da Xinglong monastery
in Beijing. Focusing on Huayan teaching, he also studied Yogācāra doctrine
with Cao'an Weng'ao.[24]

Lu'an Putai's disciple Wuji Mingxin (1512–1574) came from the south to
study in Beijing and later returned to Bao'en monastery in Nanjing, where two
promising young monks, Hanshan Deqing and Xuelang Hong'en (1545–1608),
became his best students. Later, while Hanshan Deqing determined to pursue
the life of an itinerant meditation monk, Xuelang Hong'en became the most
famous dharma master in the Jiangnan area, specializing in Huayan. He was
also particularly instrumental in the promotion of Yogācāra study. According
to his biography written by his good friend Hanshan Deqing, he was attracted
to doctrinal studies at twelve and thus entered the Buddhist order. At Bao'en
monastery in Nanjing, he studied with Wuji Mingxin, who had traveled to
Beijing and transmitted the knowledge of Huayan learning and Yogācāra
teaching to the south. Since the Yogācāra school no longer existed, Xuelang
Hong'en assembled eight essential Yogācāra texts and compiled a collection
entitled *Xiangzong bayao* (Eight essential Yogācāra texts) that laid out the foundation of the revival of Yogācāra study.[25] Revered as the patriarch who revived
the Huayan school, his influence was extended through his disciples, among
them Yiyu Tongrun (1565–1624), Cangxue Duche (1588–1656),[26] Tairu Minghe (1588–1640), and Gaoyuan Mingyu (fl. 1612). The Huayan tradition continued in the Qing dynasty when Baiting Xufa (1641–1728) and Datian Tongli
(1701–1782) became the most prominent Huayan teachers.[27]

In addition to monks' effort to revive Huayan teaching, the literati also
paid attention to the Huayan commentaries. However, instead of honoring the
authority of the Huayan patriarch Fazang (643–712) in the Tang, the late Ming
literati favored the Tang hermit Li Tongxuan's (647–740) *Huayan helun* (Expla-

nation of Huayan collated with the scripture), which provided a straightforward Chan understanding of Huayan teaching free from formulaic commentarial conventions. Because of his simplification, Li's commentary appealed to the Chan-minded literati in particular.[28]

The Tiantai school was also revived by the efforts of Miaofeng Zhenjue (1537–1589), who claimed to have attained supreme understanding of Tiantai doctrine and thus considered himself to be a true heir of the Tiantai school. He first lived in Jingshan and studied with Yueting Mingde (1531–1588), who was well versed in various doctrines but without any specialties.[29] According to his biography, Miaofeng Zhenjue did not benefit from studying with his master. Instead, he comprehended the Tiantai teaching of "nature inclusion" (*xingju*) through reading Siming Zhili's (960–1028) works preserved in the Buddhist canon.[30] Thus, without any personal connection to Siming Zhili, he declared himself a "distant dharma heir" of Siming Zhili.[31] He started to lecture as a Tiantai master in 1554, and his influence was further extended by his disciples Wujin Chuandeng (1554–1628) and Wulou Chuanping (1565–1614).[32] The former revived one of the ancestral monasteries of the Tiantai school, the Gaoming monastery, also known as "Youxi," at Mount Tiantai in Zhejiang, and the latter revived Ayuwang monastery. In the early Qing, Chuandeng's disciple Tianxi Shoudeng (1607–1675) was one of the most influential Tiantai teachers and exegetes.[33]

The vitality of doctrinal studies can be seen in the debate over Sengzhao's (384–414) treatise, *Things Do Not Shift* (*Wubu qian*), in which almost all the famous monks, including Zibo Zhenke, Yunqi Zhuhong, Hanshan Deqing, and Huanyou Zhengchuan, participated. Kongyin Zhencheng, a follower of the Huayan tradition at Mount Wutai, wrote the *Wubuqian zhengliang lun* (The correct reasoning on *Things Do Not Shift*) in 1588 to refute Sengzhao's arguments. In this work, he used Buddhist logic to point out the inherent errors in Sengzhao's reasoning. Employing Buddhist syllogisms consisting of thesis, reason, and example, he commented that Sengzhao's argument is incorrect: Sengzhao argues that things are immutable because their nature is permanently abiding, indicating that the nature of things is an enduring substance. However, according to Zhencheng, the standard Madhyamaka theory should assert that things do not shift because their inherent nature does not exist. Therefore, Sengzhao's conclusion is similar to Madhyamaka thought, but his reasoning is entirely wrong. Chinese scholar Jiang Canteng has shown that Kongyin Zhencheng's "heretical" views immediately met with opposition. The majority of scholar-monks challenged Zhencheng and defended Sengzhao's position.[34] The content of this scholarly debate is not relevant to my study in this book. However, the scope and depth of this discussion show the popularity of doctrinal studies.

The Revival of the Vinaya School and the Invention of the Triple Platform Ordination Ceremony

The Vinaya school was also revived in response to the ban on Buddhist ordination during the Jiajing reign. Throughout the Ming dynasty, the government established strict rules to control the monastic population through examinations and a national registration system. In the early Ming, a monk acquired his status through a test of his proficiency in Buddhist scriptures by rote memorization. (Such tests were still administered in the late Ming, but according to some accounts, the students composed essays on the scriptures, rather like the Buddhist version of a civil service exam.)[35] Since 1391, ordination ceremonies had been regulated and were only offered once every three years. In this way, the monastic population could be kept at a desirably low level: forty per prefecture, thirty per county, and twenty per town. In addition, the Central Buddhist Registration (Seng lu si) prepared a nationwide register of monks in 1392.[36]

Little is known about the activities of Vinaya masters in the early Ming. The late Ming literatus Qu Ruji (1548–1610) noticed this unfortunate neglect of the Vinaya tradition in the Ming as he remarked:

> In Tang times, Vinaya masters were the most respected among all and thus no Buddhism in other times surpassed that in the Tang. Down to the Song, it was more often the case that Vinaya institutions were converted to Chan monasteries and thus Buddhism declined gradually. Till now, Vinaya masters are seldom heard and in the Buddhist world, only statues and scriptures remain.[37]

The genealogies of Vinaya masters compiled in the Qing dynasty such as the Nanshan zongtong (Genealogy of the southern mountain) and the Lüzong dengpu (Genealogy of the lamp of the Vinaya school) are also sketchy about the Vinaya tradition in the early and mid-Ming. However, both records mentioned the prominent Vinaya master Zhihuan Daofu, commonly known as "Goose Head Patriarch" (E'tou zushi), who was active during the Zhengtong reign (1436–1449) in Beijing. According to his biography, he presided over Ordination Platform Monastery in Western Mountain (Xishan Jietai si) in Beijing, which was the designated imperial platform.[38] Many Vinaya practitioners in the late Ming claimed that they received his transmission. Although their claims lack evidence, it is clear that in the early Ming, the government centralized the practice of ordination in Beijing and promoted certain Vinaya masters as approved ordination providers.

However, in the fifth month of 1526, the Jiajing emperor ordered the Western Mountain ordination platform in Beijing and the one at Tianning monastery together to be closed because men and women were found intermingling during the ordination ceremony. The emperor took similar actions against these monasteries in 1546, arresting Master Tong and the abbot of Tianning temple, who had built ordination platforms there. Daniel Overmyer translated this record as follows:

> In recent years large groups of monks and laity have been gathering
> together in the T'ien-ning monastery, outside the Hsüan-wu gate [of
> Peking], frequently holding worship services to take vows of absti-
> nence and preach the dharma. [The people] are jammed together,
> excited and stimulated, while from everywhere Buddhist clergy
> gather, [forming crowds of] up to 10,000. They reverently worship
> and obediently listen, gathering by day and dispersing at night, with
> men and women mixing together. There are very many escaped
> criminals in their midst. [These monks] initiate disciples by burning
> marks on their scalps and giving them tonsure, but they carry out
> criminal acts [on the grounds of] hidden karmic affinity. Therefore,
> from the fourth month [of this year] robbers and bandits have
> secretly flourished within and without the capital. Surely such
> activities should not be going on so close to the emperor![39]

Official records show that in 1566 the emperor once again prohibited ordination platforms in Beijing.[40] This event is confirmed by the accounts of Buddhist monks affected by this policy. As Chan master Zhanran Yuancheng recalled, the close-down occurred around 1566 during the Jiajing reign, and ordination platforms were officially closed throughout the late Ming.[41] Hanyue Fazang, who was both a Chan and a Vinaya master, hinted that this occurred because the Jiajing emperor considered the extravagant Buddhist rituals too costly.[42] According to him, the close-down occurred because some eunuchs introduced prostitutes onto the platform to provide sexual services to monk-soldiers recruited for the anti-pirate campaign.[43]

The actual reason for the closing is not known. We do know, however, that even after the Jiajing emperor's death, ordination platforms remained closed. The Jiajing emperor's ban on mass ordination was reiterated in 1572 by his successor, and monks who offered ordination in Wanshou and Guangshan monasteries were arrested.[44] In 1579, when the Wanli emperor's mother attempted to restore the ordination platforms, Zhang Juzheng (1525–1582), the powerful prime minister, aborted the idea, once again based on the former emperor Jiajing's prohibition of Buddhist ordination.[45]

The prohibition of ordination during the Jiajing reign delayed a great number of novices who should have been properly ordained, and the resulting bottleneck promoted the consciousness of autonomy among monks. Even after the Wanli emperor allowed three official ordination platforms to be built, such a small number could hardly satisfy the demand for ordination throughout the country, and many monks still had no chance to be ordained properly. Hanyue Fazang, for instance, approached Yunqi Zhuhong for proper ordination in 1601 because, despite joining the Buddhist order as a boy, he still had not received full ordination at twenty-nine years. However, Zhuhong declined his eager request on the excuse that the ordination platform was not officially granted. Zhuhong could offer the novice precept only.[46] In 1604, Hanyue requested full ordination for the second time, and Zhuhong again rejected him. He did not receive full ordination until 1609 when Guxin Ruxin (1541–1615) began to offer full ordination ceremonies in Linggu monastery under the royal decree. Although the revival of the Vinaya school in the seventeenth century was commonly attributed to the Vinaya tradition in Baohua monastery, especially to the Vinaya patriarch Jianyue Duti (1601–1679), several Vinaya genealogies such as *Nanshan zongtong, Lüzong dengpu*, and a more recent source, *Lümen zuting huizhi* (Collected records of the patriarch hall of the Vinaya school), compiled in 1904, indicate that the Baohua tradition was actually derived from Guxin Ruxin in Nanjing.[47]

In the late Ming, Guxin Ruxin was widely acknowledged as the reviver of the Vinaya tradition. According to his biography, Guxin Ruxin entered the Buddhist order at an early age. He first became a novice under Su'an Zhenjie (1519–1593).[48] During a pilgrim tour at Mount Wutai, he had an encounter with the bodhisattva Mañjusrī and claimed to have received ordination from him. When he returned to the south, he became a reformer of the ordination ceremony and declared that he had the true transmission of the orthodox lineage of Southern Mountain (*Nanshan zhengzong*). In 1584, he lived in a small chapel called Gulin at Nanjing, which he transformed into a monastery.[49] In 1613, when Guxin's fame reached Beijing, he was awarded the purple robe and placed in charge of the Wanshou ordination platform. In the same year, at the Wanli emperor's request, he offered "Triple Platform Ordination in an expedient way" (*santan fangbian shoushou*).[50]

The so-called Triple Platform Ordination was an innovation in Chinese Buddhism that is still popular in today's China. In the Mahāyāna tradition in China, a monk must participate in three different initiation ceremonies. The first is the novice initiation, which requires the taking of the three refuges and

the ten precepts; the second is the full ordination, which demands the observance of all 250 precepts stipulated for adult male members of the monastic
community. In addition to these two kinds of ordination, which are universal
to all Buddhist monks and nuns, the apocryphal *Fanwang jing* (The scripture
of Indra's net) stipulates that Mahāyāna Buddhists in East Asia confer bodhisattva ordination on both Buddhist clergy and laity. Instead of administering
these three rites separately, the Triple Platform Ordination held novice initiation, full ordination, and bodhisattva ordination all together in one place and
within a short time.[51]

References to Guxin Ruxin as a reviver of ordination ceremonies show
that he invented the Triple Platform Ordination Ceremony although he did not
leave any works explaining the procedure of the ritual. However, he left twelve
dharma heirs, including two capable Vinaya leaders, Sanmei Jiguang (1580–
1645) and Hanyue Fazang. Sanmei Jiguang created the Baohua Vinaya tradition, which was further promoted by his disciple Jianyue Duti. Hanyue Fazang, the protagonist of the first controversy discussed in this book, received
dharma transmission from Miyun Yuanwu and became a Chan master. However, he continued to promote the Triple Platform Ordination in Chan communities by composing the *Hongjie fayi* (The rite and procedure for spreading
ordination), which detailed the procedures for ordination.[52] It should be noted
here that through Hanyue Fazang and other Chan masters' efforts, the Triple
Platform Ordination Ceremony was also frequently performed in Chan communities and administered by Chan monks. It was a new phenomenon that,
beginning in the seventeenth century, ordination ceremonies were no longer
monopolized by the state and the Vinaya masters.

Ambiguous Chan Communities

The general environment of Buddhist revival in the late Ming fostered the
growth of Chan Buddhism. As young monks, the would-be Chan masters fre-
quented public lectures on Buddhist scriptures and sought for proper ordination while wandering around the country. However, Chan Buddhism was not
initially prominent compared with other traditions. During the early stage of
Buddhist revival, Chan communities were still not clearly defined. Huang
Zongxi's (1610–1695) retrospective observation of the rise of Chan Buddhism
illustrates this point well. In an epitaph he wrote for Hanyue Fazang, Miyun
Yuanwu's major disciple and opponent, Huang Zongxi pointed to an important fact about the revival of Chan Buddhism: No noticeable Chan communities existed before the Wanli reign:

> Before the Wanli era, the Chan style of teaching had almost disap-
> peared. The Yunmen, Fayan, and Guiyang [lineages] were all extinct.
> The learning of Caodong was only transmitted secretly. Linji seemed
> also on the verge of extinction. Tens or hundreds of them gathered
> together transmitted [the dharma] from master to disciple. Among
> them vagabonds were not a few. Zibo and Hanshan thus advocated
> Buddhist teaching distinct from them and showed contempt to those
> Chan monks. This is why these two masters were expelled as
> "lineage unknown."[53]

Huang Zongxi's observation is accurate for several reasons. First, during the mid-Ming, the compilation of Chan genealogies of dharma transmissions and recorded sayings had been discontinued, indicating the dwindling of Chan communities. Second, when the signs of Buddhist revival appeared in the late Ming, the remaining Chan communities, intending to bridge the gap created by lost records of dharma transmission, became eager to claim continuity with previous generations, even if their claims lacked historical basis. This chaotic situation revealed the need to reorganize Chan communities and to regulate dharma transmission. Third, the mainstream Buddhism represented by the three eminent monks disparaged such nominal claims of dharma transmission and the iconoclastic Chan style, which they regarded as based on shallow understanding and awkward imitation.

Dormancy of Chan Buddhism in the Mid-Ming

In the early Ming, a few works on dharma transmission were compiled. At the end of Zhu Yuanzhang's reign (1368–1398), the monk Juding (?–1404) compiled the *Xu chuandeng lu* (Continued records of lamp transmissions) to continue the *Jingde chuandeng lu* initiated by Daoyuan in the Song. In 1417, the monk Wenxiu (1345–1418) once again updated this work in his *Zengji xu chuandeng lu* (Supplements to continued records of lamp transmission). In 1489, Rujin compiled the *Chanzong zhengmai* (True transmission of Chan lineage). These works show that Chan communities were still active in the early Ming. However, there is a major lacuna between the mid-fifteenth century and the end of the sixteenth century, during which no major records of Chan genealogy can be found. Late Ming Buddhists certainly noticed this gap. The late Ming literatus Qu Ruji, for example, while reading stacks of Chan recorded sayings from the Tang and Song, felt sorrow about the absence of eminent Chan masters in his own time.[54] Zibo Zhenke also lamented this situation and vowed to compile a new genealogy.[55]

Chan literature for this period, especially the recorded sayings that were supposed to document Chan masters' spontaneous interactions with students, is also scarce. Certainly, some names of Chan monks are known to us through fragmented accounts. For example, Yunqi Zhuhong, in his *Huang Ming gaoseng jilue* (Biographies of eminent Ming monks) recorded only four Chan masters for the entire 150 years from the late fourteenth century to the early sixteenth century: Konggu Jinglong (1387–1466), Chushan Shaoqi (1403–1473), Dufeng Jishan (1443?–1523), and Xiaoyan Debao (1512–1581). However, these monks left no recorded sayings, probably because, as Chün-fang Yü points out, they all favored certain joint practices with Pure Land and asceticism rather than "authentic" Chan teaching.[56] Although the number of records of dharma transmission and Chan masters' dialogues cannot be the sole indicator of the condition of Chan communities, they at least show that in the Buddhist world of this time the Chan spirit was not valued as it had been in the Song and the Yuan.

During this period of decline, monasteries, including formerly renowned Chan establishments, adopted a strange institutional system. This system can be only glimpsed from scant reports that rarely surface in historical sources. According to my reading, under this system, a large monastery was divided into several separate houses (*fang*) that operated independently. Monks affiliated with the houses were referred to as "house monks" (*fangseng*) and the monk in charge of the house as "house head" (*fangtou*).[57] For example, Timothy Brook notices in his study of Tiantong monastery that around 1460, the corporate structure of the monastery collapsed, and five separate houses controlled monastic affairs.[58] In the gazetteer of Zhaoqing monastery, a record was preserved about such a system. After Zhaoqing monastery was designated as an official ordination platform and renamed Wanshan, the community was divided into thirty-three houses, which traced their transmissions to an early Ming monk called Daqian Putong. The abbot of the monastery was selected only from members of these houses.[59]

According to sparse sources, each house had its head monk, who recruited monastic officials by himself. Apparently, when such houses took shape, they divided monastic property, including the buildings and especially arable lands, among themselves and collected rents from tenants. After some years, however, sojourners reported that land was encroached by powerful local families and even rents were difficult to collect from tenants because of weak supervision of the houses. The heads of these houses were more willing to trade monastic properties for their personal gain. More important, monastic discipline ebbed to the lowest level: Monks dressed in various kinds of clothes, and eating meat and drinking wine were not unusual in monastic compounds. Some of them even lived in the villages as farmers, perhaps with their families, and raised livestock for slaughtering. This was exactly what Hanshan Deqing witnessed when he visited Caoxi monastery in 1596. Although it was not clear if this famous Chan institution, where Huineng had lived, adopted the house system, the degradation urged such monks as Hanshan to reform the monastic system.[60]

Confusions Regarding Chan Dharma Transmission

Because of the revived interest in Chan Buddhism in the sixteenth and seventeenth centuries, the so-called Chan monks started to trace their lineages backward in order to resume their spiritual connections with the tradition. Some records preserved in monastic gazetteers indicate that Chan monks in the seventeenth century had tremendous difficulties in restoring the broken lines of dharma transmission. As a result, claims of dharma transmission became nominal, if not deliberately fabricated, and gaps in dharma transmission were rife in many rejuvenated Chan communities. Although later Chan historiographies appear to have repaired these broken lines, some alarming signs of discontinuity can be detected from the two most popular ways of assuming continuities with the past: remote succession (*yaosi*) and transmission by proxy (*daifu*).

Chan lineage is perhaps the largest and longest lasting lineage organization in China. Unlike lineages in the secular realm, the Chan lineage is maintained by an imagined form of reproduction. By means of dharma transmission, dharma heirs gain legitimacy to succeed to the patriarchal position in an imagined family. Therefore, the continuity of dharma transmission is central to the survival of Chan lineages. In reality, however, a specific lineage was often discontinued for various reasons and would-be dharma heirs could not find a living dharma master to transmit the dharma personally. In such cases, a proxy could be introduced to transmit the dharma on behalf of a deceased master. A precedent for this practice can be found in the case of Touzi Yiqing's (1032–1083) dharma transmission. When the Caodong master Dayang Jingxuan (943–1027) died, he had found no desirable candidate for his dharma transmission, so he left his portrait, dharma robe, and shoes to Fayuan and asked him to find a suitable heir. Later, when Fayuan met Touzi Yiqing, he conferred these credentials of Dayang's transmission to Touzi by proxy.[61]

The practice of claiming a remote succession was also rooted in the Chan tradition of mind-to-mind transmission, which allows anyone who feels a resonance with an early master's teaching to claim a transmission from that master. A seventeenth-century example that appeared in the Linji school is Miyun

Yuanwu's dharma brother Xuejiao Yuanxin. Being ordained by Huanyou Zhengchuan, he should have claimed to be an official dharma heir of the Linji school. However, when his name was listed in the Linji lineage in the new Chan genealogy *Chandeng shipu* (Generational genealogy of Chan lamps), Xuejiao Yuanxin asked to have it removed because he personally admired the founder of the Yunmen school, Yunmen Wenyan, and considered himself a dharma heir of the Yunmen school even though the Yunmen school had been defunct since the Song. Given that there were no living dharma heirs in the seventeenth century, Xuejiao Yuanxin's claim was a clear case of remote succession.[62]

Traces of such doubtful attribution of dharma transmission can be also identified in the gazetteers of some famous monasteries. The most daring and dubious claim was made by a certain monk called Wuji Zhenghui (?–1628), who offered the dharma transmission of the Tang master Shenxiu's Northern school. Certainly, he had evidence of the "Fifty-six Characters of the Northern School" (*Beizong wushiliu zi*), a transmission verse containing generation characters for all descendants of the Northern school, inscribed in a stele erected at Dumen monastery in Mount Yuquan.[63]

A late Ming member of the literati, Wang Weizhang's inscription of Wuji Zhenghui delineated a clear lineage of the Northern school from Hongren (600?–674?), to Shenxiu (606?–706), to Puji (651–739), to Yixing (685–727). According to this record, a certain master called Fadeng Murong during the Song and another master called Zhongshan Guangzhu (1248–1341) in the Yuan were the most prominent teachers of the Northern school. During the Chenghua reign of the Ming (1465–1487), Ruiyan Guanglei (1369–1481) and his dharma grandson Yu'an Changzhen (?–1581) restored the Northern school. Yu'an Changzhen had five disciples who formed five lineages. According to his epitaph, Wuji Zhenghui hailed from Dangyang and entered the Buddhist order when he was ten. He studied Confucian classics and esoteric ritual performance. Later, he visited Tianzhu Manxiu (?–1568) at Puyang monastery. Wuji studied with him for three years and received a verse of fifty-six characters recited by him, who noted that this verse was also carved in Shenxiu's stele in Dumen monastery at Mount Yuquan, where Shenxiu had lived in late seventh century. Later, Wuji Zhenghui found this stele at Mount Yuquan. Claiming to be an heir of the Northern school, he revived Dumen monastery in 1602.[64]

In other obscure places, efforts to revive Chan practice and dharma transmission can also be observed. For instance, in an undated text preserved in the Buddhist canon, entitled *Zhengzong xinyin houxu lianfang* (Linked flowers continued after the true lineage of mind-seal), lively encounter dialogues between masters and disciples were recorded.[65] Not only were their dialogues

full of the spirit of spontaneity, the consciousness of continuity was also manifested in the master's emphasis on "continuing the linked flowers" (*xu lian
fang*), a euphemism for dharma transmission.[66]

In famous monasteries such as Shaolin, an "unbroken" dharma transmission has apparently been maintained since the Yuan. It is well known that
Shaolin monastery was revived by Xueting Fuyu (1203–1275) during the early
Yuan dynasty. Not only did he revitalize Shaolin as the ancestral monastery of
Chan Buddhism, he also established the Caodong transmission there.[67] In the
late Ming, dharma transmissions derived from him were still alive. To prove
the authenticity and continuity of their dharma transmission, Chan practitioners often referred to the *Shaolin lianfang bei* (Inscription of linked flowers in
Shaolin) as evidence.[68] The revived Caodong lineage in south China, which I
will describe in chapter 3, was indeed derived, at least nominally, from the
Shaolin transmission.

However, the genealogical sources about the Caodong school in the seventeenth century were often inconsistent about listing the generations of the
Caodong masters. For example, in some sources, the famous Caodong
teacher Zhanran Yuancheng was recorded as belonging to the twenty-sixth
generation and in others as belonging to the thirty-first generation of the
Caodong lineage. This inconsistency resulted from a seventeenth-century
debate about the elimination of five generations of Caodong transmission in
the Song, which I explain in appendix 2.A. Here, I summarize the two con-
flicting versions of the Caodong transmission during the Song in chart 1.1 to
illustrate how significant the change had been. On the right side, the conventional Caodong transmission continued after the Caodong patriarch Furong Daokai (1043–1118) through five generations down to a monk called
Lumen Zijue (?–1117), from whom later Caodong masters received transmission. Meanwhile, there was a monk called Jingyin Zijue listed as Furong
Daokai's dharma heir, but his transmission became an obscure collateral
lineage in traditional Chan historiography. However, a new discovery in the
seventeenth century showed that these two monks were actually the same
person. Then, a revised transmission line should follow the one on the left
side of chart 1.1, eliminating the five generations on the right (between Furong Daokai and Lumen Zijue) completely and thus lifting all later Caodong
masters five generations ahead.

The Linji transmissions seemed to be more widespread. Xiaoyan Debao,
for example, was a respected Chan master with the Linji transmission, which
can be traced to Yuanwu Keqin's heir Huqiu Shaolong (1077–1136). The revived
Linji school was derived from Xiaoyan Debao's dharma heir Huanyou Zhengchuan. In addition to Huqiu Shaolong's transmission line, Dahui Zonggao's

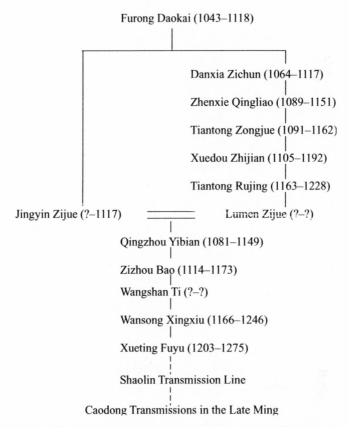

Furong Daokai (1043–1118)

Danxia Zichun (1064–1117)

Zhenxie Qingliao (1089–1151)

Tiantong Zongjue (1091–1162)

Xuedou Zhijian (1105–1192)

Tiantong Rujing (1163–1228)

Jingyin Zijue (?–1117) ====== Lumen Zijue (?–?)

Qingzhou Yibian (1081–1149)

Zizhou Bao (1114–1173)

Wangshan Ti (?–?)

Wansong Xingxiu (1166–1246)

Xueting Fuyu (1203–1275)

Shaolin Transmission Line

Caodong Transmissions in the Late Ming

CHART 1.1. The Five Superfluous Generations in the Caodong School during the Song

(1089–1163) lineage was also supposedly continued but not without controversy. For example, the Chan monk Chuiwan Guangzhen (1582–1639) claimed that he was the fourteenth-generation heir after Dahui Zonggao, but he incurred some objections.[69]

However, some problems occur in this lineage with the identity of Haizhou Puci (1393–1461) and Haizhou Yongci (1394–1466) in the early Ming.[70] Because both names were abbreviated as Haizhou Ci in Chan literature, confusion developed regarding which man was the real Linji patriarch from whom later generations derived. Chan polemicists used inscriptional records to argue that they were two individuals with different dharma transmissions and that the official version of this lineage had confused these two people.[71] As shown in chart 1.2, there were at least three different versions of the Linji transmission in the early Ming: (1) Some found that Haizhou Ci was actually listed as Wanfeng Shiwei's dharma heir. Thus, the two generations between

FIGURE I.I. First page of *Dongming yilu*, 1635. Photocopy from the Shanghai Library.

them should be eliminated; (2) A collection called *Dongming yilu*, whose first page is shown in figure I.I, identified that Haizhou Ci was actually Haizhou Puci, who first studied with Wanfeng Shiwei. He later received Dongming Huichan's transmission and his dharma heir Baofeng Xuan was ascertained to be Baofeng Mingxuan; (3) A new inscription discovered in 1657 showed that the so-called *Dongming yilu* was a complete forgery because this new source specified Haizhou Ci as Haizhou Yongci, who had a dharma heir called Yufeng Zhixuan. Some Linji monks quickly switched positions, claiming that Haizhou Ci should be Haizhou Yongci and Baofeng Mingxuan should be Yufeng Zhixuan. In addition, the transmissions of some individuals in the line were also questioned.

Such nominal or ambiguous claims of dharma transmission caused certain confusion not only because of their shaky accuracy but also because dharma transmission, Chan teaching, and sectarian identity no longer corresponded to each other. That means that a certain monk could have received a Linji transmission but engaged in doctrinal studies while claiming to be an heir of the Yunmen lineage. A good example is the self-proclaimed Northern Chan master Tianzhu Manxiu (?–1568), who transmitted the verse of fifty-six characters of the Northern school to his disciple Wuji Zhenghui as mentioned earlier. According to his biography, Tianzhu Manxiu was first ordained in the Northern school and belonged to the twenty-eighth generation after Shenxiu. Later, he practiced meditation in Mount Funiu

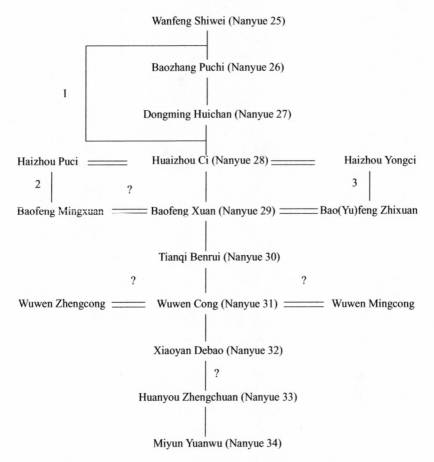

CHART I.2. Disputed Linji Transmission Lines in the Early Ming

and achieved awakening. For this reason, his teacher Huanyou Zhengchuan conferred the Linji dharma transmission on him. Thus, he was famous
as an heir of the Northern school who advocated the "Southern doctrine"
(*Beizong ren Nanzong fa*) because his dharma transmission was from the
Linji school. It seems that he felt free to transmit the dharma of either
school: He transmitted the dharma of the Northern school to Wuji Zhenghui and that of the Linji school to another disciple, Zhenghai.[72] In this case,
dharma transmission, Chan teaching, and sectarian identity could be configured at will.

Even among those Chan masters with dharma transmissions from the
Southern school, such as Linji and Caodong, it was not necessary to uphold
the antinomian spirit that corresponded to their sectarian identities. On the

contrary, because of the popularity of Buddhist scholasticism, famous Chan masters in both the Linji and Caodong schools were largely engaged in doctrinal studies characterized by frequent lectures on Buddhist scriptures and doctrines. For instance, Wuji Mingxin, the monk who was viewed as a reviver of Buddhist scholasticism in south China, was actually a claimant of the twenty-sixth generation in the Linji school.[73] Miyun Yuanwu's masters Xiaoyan Debao and Huanyou Zhengchuan had both lived in Beijing as scholar-monks and specialized in doctrinal studies.[74] Obviously, such a situation called for a great movement to regulate various kinds of unwarranted claims and, as we will see in later chapters, Feiyin Tongrong's *Wudeng yantong* was a direct response to the chaos.

Varieties of Chan Understandings

At the end of the sixteenth century, Chan practice was widely understood as meditation, especially the meditation on critical phrases (*huatou*) advocated by Dahui Zonggao. As Hanshan Deqing recollected, the first Chan master who propagated Chan meditation training was Yungu Fahui (1500–1579). He offered a seven-day meditation retreat in Tianjie monastery in 1549, which Hanshan Deqing attended. He taught students to use the critical phrases of kōan as a meditation technique. He advocated the use of the critical phrase "reciting the name of the Buddha." By urging students to raise the question "Who is reciting the name of the Buddha?" Yungu Fahui emphasized the role of doubt, in a way similar to Dahui Zonggao's method.[75] Inspired by him, Hanshan Deqing was determined to become a Chan monk with the understanding that "Chan" meant arduous efforts in meditation. He thus embarked on a journey of ascetic and meditative practice in Mount Wutai. Hanshan Deqing's experience was typical of many so-called Chan monks at that time. They lived in secluded areas, engaging deeply in meditation, together with devotional and ascetic practices. Other forms of meditative practice, such as solitary confinement (*biguan*), were popular, and small meditation cells (*chanku*) were widespread in such places as Mount Wutai.[76]

Because meditation was understood as the basic characteristic of Chan Buddhism, practitioners such as the three eminent monks sought to integrate methods like meditation on critical phrases in kōan (*huatou*) with other practices. Hanshan Deqing, who devoted himself to Chan meditation in his youth, emphasized the role of doctrinal studies in the path toward enlightenment. Yunqi Zhuhong, as Chün-fang Yü has shown, became an exemplar in synthesizing Chan meditation and Pure Land practice.[77] According to them, enlightenment was a gradual process involving strenuous training. For them, sudden enlightenment without the accumulation of effort was out of the question. Inspired by the Song master Dahui Zonggao, Hanshan Deqing's views on meditation on critical phrases illustrated this spiritual orientation:

> This method is not meant for you to think about the meaning of a
> *kung-an* as if the *kung-an* were a question for intellectual solution.
> Speaking of the *hua-t'ou* method, Ta-hui taught his disciples to kill
> the "sneaky mind" with a cold-blooded hand. According to him, the
> first principle of Ch'an practice is to empty one's mind. One must
> first paste the two words "life-death" on the forehead, and regard
> them as seriously as if one owed a debt of a million taels. In day or
> night, while drinking or eating, traveling or staying at home, sitting
> or lying, entertaining friends, in a quiet moment or at a noisy hour,
> you must hold on to the *hua-t'ou*.[78]

Here, according to Deqing, the meaning of a kōan was not a question for a Chan practitioner to fathom. Rather, all efforts should be directed to mental discipline.

A marked difference between these eminent monks and later Chan masters in the seventeenth century was their view on the role of Chan teachers. For Yunqi Zhuhong and Hanshan Deqing, training through self-cultivation was encouraged, and nominal and formulaic instructions from pretentious masters were despised. Eminent monks, who practiced meditation and asceticism but without proper dharma transmission, were acclaimed as acquiring "wisdom without teachers" (*wushizhi*), a laudable title for them but a misfortune in the eyes of the more orthodox Chan masters in later generations, for whom dharma transmission defined their identity as Chan monks in a certain lineage.

The negative attitude toward the role of teacher can be seen from Hanshan Deqing's perspective. Though never receiving dharma transmission, he was often asked to write prefaces to the records of transmission in some obscure lineages. His writings testify that although the practice of dharma transmission was revived, Hanshan Deqing questioned its value seriously. For him, the enlightenment of the mind was more important than the nominal claim of dharma transmission.[79] Because true enlightenment experience was valued, a few self-proclaimed Chan masters in the late Ming gained reputations as eminent monks without acquiring dharma transmission.

Despite these unfavorable comments about the Chan rhetoric of sudden enlightenment and dharma transmission, a visible change in the understanding of Chan practice emerged in various Chan communities. Chan novices,

without serious studies of Buddhist doctrines and without committed meditation practice, favored "bizarre" behavior that looked like the reenactment of kōan
stories. As Huang Zongxi correctly pointed out in the observation that I quoted
earlier, all of the three masters, especially Zhuhong and Hanshan Deqing, observed this new trend with disdain and contempt, considering Chan Buddhism
as such to be "shallow." Zibo Zhenke, for example, visited Shaolin monastery in
1575 and found the Chan practice there rather "phony": The Caodong master
Huangxiu (Daqian) Changrun (?–1585), following his teacher Xiaoshan Zongshu
(1500–1567), simply lectured on kōans (*jiangxi pingchang*) without emphasizing
true understanding.[80] Zhuhong, disdaining the pedantic discussion of Chan
kōan literature, considered monks who "recreated" kōans in performance to be
"charlatans sporting counterfeit testimonial[s]" without genuine enlightenment.
As Chün-fang Yü points out, Yunqi Zhuhong protested bitterly against this bur-
geoning phenomenon:

> Nowadays, there are people who do not have any enlightenment in
> their hearts, but because they are quick-witted and clever with words,
> they sneak a look at various recorded dialogues and imitate some of
> the phrases. They only value the absurdity and strangeness of the
> phrasing. As long as the phrases can delight and startle the ordinary
> people, they [are] satisfied. . . . They open their mouths to say all
> kinds of nonsense. People who do not know better praise them with
> one voice and frequently imitate them. To talk about wisdom fool-
> ishly and vainly is indeed a great sin.[81]

Hanshan Deqing was equally critical of Chan practitioners who paid lip service to enlightenment:

> Today's youth announce the news of enlightenment before they have
> sat firmly on their meditation mat. They show off the so-called
> enlightenment by using their little mouths and minds in the
> exchange of quick wit and in the composition of praises to ancient
> masters. The praises are really produced from illusory thought; they
> are without any point. How can they have even dreamt of the
> existence of ancient masters? If enlightenment is so easy to attain,
> then the ancient masters were the most stupid persons in the
> world.[82]

Hanshan Deqing was particularly critical of the newly revived Linji lineage. As he wrote in Zibo Zhenke's epitaph around 1615, he noticed that the
spread of Linji transmissions was a fairly new phenomenon in the beginning

of the seventeenth century because he recollected that when he was young the Linji transmission had been lost for at least a half century. He said:

> Only has Linji's lineage spread all over the world. Its Way was revived by Dahui (Zonggao) during the Song. Down to the beginning of our dynasty, there were eminent monks such as Chushi (Fanqi, 1296–1370) and Wunian (Shengxue, 1326–1406). Later, at the end of Hong-zhi and Zhengde reigns (ca. 1500–1521), there was a master called Ji (Fazhou Daoji, 1487–1560), one of whose disciples was my formal teacher Yungu [Fahui]. Although all the rules and scriptures re-mained intact, in the past fifty years, transmissions from [Linji] masters have ceased to exist. Recently, [some monks], not yet having sat on the meditation mat firmly and illuminated their true eyes, even dare to falsely claim themselves as "the how many tens and how many generations of the Linji lineage." Alas! How could we not lament these demons and their false teaching![83]

Here, as a senior monk in his seventies, Hanshan felt uncomfortable with the rising claims of Linji transmissions because in his memory, in the past fifty years (ca. 1565–1615), he had heard that no one was offered the Linji trans-mission. He implied that all of the transmissions therefore became nominal and insignificant. Even if eminent masters such as Zibo Zhenke could have claimed to be disciples of Linji Yixuan and Dahui Zonggao, because of the extinction of dharma transmission, he would not even think about a false claim.

Both Chen Yuan and Chün-fang Yü notice that in these monks's critical remarks on Chan Buddhism, neither Zhuhong nor Hanshan Deqing men-tioned Miyun Yuanwu and his disciples, who represented this shallow Chan style in its extreme.[84] For these monks, those Chan fellows were not trustwor-thy. This is understandable because during the later years of these masters, Miyun Yuanwu and his followers were still young monks, wandering around the country seeking like-minded fellows. The three eminent monks were no doubt right about the proper method of Buddhist training. Unfortunately, after their deaths, the Chan communities they had criticized grew rapidly through-out China. In this regard, Huang Zongxi was correct once again: Because of their critical stance toward a rising Chan movement, in several major Chan genealogies compiled in the seventeenth century, these three masters, none of whom sought dharma transmission from established Chan masters, were la-beled as eminent monks with "lineage unknown." It was telling that the lin-eages of the three eminent masters did not last because they did not want to extend their influence by seeking and offering dharma transmission.

Conclusion

The movement to revive Chan Buddhism was intertwined with various social, cultural, and political circumstances of the seventeenth century. In this chapter, I have outlined the revival of Buddhism in some areas of Buddhist learning and practice starting from the Wanli period. The Buddhist revival, according to my reading, preceded the rise of Chan Buddhism in the seventeenth century because during the late sixteenth century Chan communities had not acquired their distinctive identity, and certain values, such as the antinomian spirit and strict dharma transmission, had not gained overwhelming acceptance in the Buddhist world.

If we list chronologically all of the important events concerning the Buddhist revival in the late Ming, an important discovery is that Chan Buddhism was revived at the final stage after many other Buddhist traditions were reestablished. This time delay has been easily overlooked by historians. However, the belated arrival of Chan Buddhism as a monastic movement might be the key to explaining a perplexing paradox that Chan scholars have faced. That is, while the Chan rhetoric of antinomianism is highly exclusionary and sectarian, the actual monastic practices in the so-called Chan institutions are extremely syncretic. In part IV, I will discuss in detail this seeming contradiction between ideal and reality. Here, I want to point out the fact that the already revived Buddhist traditions, such as doctrinal studies and the ordination ceremony, contributed to the formation of a syncretic Chan monastic practice. This is because Chan communities, which were revived on the basis of an existing monastic routine, had the opportunity and advantage to assimilate all available resources to create a syncretic monastic practice. Many Chan masters who established themselves later, in the first stage of Buddhist revival in the late sixteenth century, were young monks visiting different types of Buddhist communities and gaining knowledge about all aspects of Buddhist religion. It was natural for them to synthesize various kinds of Buddhist practice while choosing to position themselves as authentic Chan monks.

My description of this stage of Buddhist revival also shows that the Buddhist world needed a powerful and appealing ideology that would attract attention from the elite and allow Buddhism to be part of the most prevalent cultural and intellectual movement at that time. In addition, a rationalized organizing principle was needed to connect the various Buddhist communities scattered in the country into a more integrated whole. In the last twenty years of the Ming dynasty, the social and intellectual conditions for such reorganization were ripe, and an ideal ideology and organizing principle indeed emerged. The performance of beating and shouting, which embodies the anti-nomian Chan spirit, was appreciated by some Confucian intellectuals who favored the Chan rhetoric and anticipated its strong presence in Buddhist communities. Meanwhile, Chan Buddhists demanded a strict definition of dharma transmission to fend off imposters and pretenders.

However, not all of these could happen without the literati's promotion of Chan Buddhism. Some followers of Wang Yangming's intellectual movement, in particular, actively promoted Chan Buddhism because they saw a similar antinomian spirit in both. Such an intellectual climate nourished a Chan culture in which Chan masters emerged.

2

The Literati and Chan Buddhism

In the late Ming, we see a clear pattern of the literati's influence on Chan Buddhism: First, an intellectual movement initiated by Wang Yangming around 1500 opened the door for the literati's legitimate immersion in Buddhist scriptures. Some of Wang's followers consciously incorporated Buddhist thoughts into the Confucian discourse about learning. During this time, Buddhist scholasticism was greatly promoted. Then, in the subsequent decades, Wang's followers, especially the Taizhou scholars, focused more on Chan thoughts as one of the sources of their intellectual and spiritual inspiration. During this time, however, there had been no visible Chan communities and eminent Chan masters, indicating that the prevalent Chan craze in the literati culture was not a direct result of the rise of Chan Buddhism, which should have become the major impetus for such a Chan craze. On the contrary, as we will see in this chapter, these Chan-spirited literati not only disparaged the literarily inferior monks but also played the role of Chan masters to instill the spirit of spontaneity in the monks who associated with them. Only around the turn of the seventeenth century, certain forms of organized Chan communities started to take shape under the sponsorship of local literati and officials in Eastern Zhejiang. After that, the literati were more involved in appointing Chan masters they favored to be abbots of monasteries.

This observation corroborates Timothy Brook's calculation of abbots' appointments by gentry patrons in the late Ming. According to him, the majority of these appointments occurred between 1612 and 1648, not in the early periods.[1] This shows that the rise of Chan Buddhism as an institutional establishment was a gradual process of building up momentum under the intellectual, cultural, and economical influence of the literati. In addition to materially depending on the literati's patronage as Timothy Brook suggests, Buddhism, especially Chan Buddhism, relied on the literati for intellectual or even spiritual guidance because, as experts in handling China's rich textual tradition, which includes Chan literature, the literati had the necessary authority over the interpretation of Chan's textualized past.

Along this line of reasoning, I regard the way in which the literati read Chan texts to be the most important factor that affected their views about Chan Buddhism. This is because, as educated elite, the literati were much more capable than Buddhist clergy of delving into Chan's past through thoroughly examining various kinds of Chan texts. In other words, in comparison to monks, they had superior textual skills to handle Chan literature and thus had ultimate authority over textual matters of Chan literature. Thus, in the late Ming, we see some interesting phenomena: Some literati, simply approaching Chan thought through reading recorded sayings without any monastic experience, believed that they had obtained enlightenment by themselves and started to look for Chan monks in order to challenge them. More strikingly, some Confucian intellectuals who were highly proficient in reading Buddhist scriptures and Chan literature began to act like Chan masters, training monks in order to induce their enlightenment experiences. Such a somehow reversed relationship attests to the extent of the influence of the literati on the formation of Chan communities.

In this chapter, I will describe in detail the influence of the literati and their intellectual and spiritual orientation toward Chan Buddhism. Unlike other scholars who focus on the intellectual similarities between Chan Buddhism and Confucianism, I tend to emphasize that the intellectual approximation of the two arose from a similar interpretation of the common textual tradition shared by both the literati and the monks. However, because of the literati's authority in textual practice, their view on Chan greatly influenced Buddhist clergy.

Wang Yangming and Chan Buddhism

The revival of Buddhism was stimulated by a pro-Buddhist intellectual movement, which justified the gentry's desire to lavish their wealth on Buddhist institutions. A continuing trend of economic development in the sixteenth and seventeenth centuries allowed local gentry to reallocate wealth to public projects, such as building monasteries. Despite some observations about the decline of Buddhist institutions at that time,[2] statistics show that temple building increased at an unprecedented rate between 1550 and 1700.[3] Timothy Brook reveals that Buddhist monasteries during the late Ming were rebuilt under the sponsorship of local gentry, whose patronage of Buddhism reflected a wave of local activism that further separated the state and society. As Brook points out, gentry patronage in the late Ming took many different forms: The gentry could provide financial support to a monastery directly by donating land or supervising monastic affairs or indirectly through "literary patronage," such as writing a poem or essay for the monks' fundraising efforts.[4] Brook has documented the revival of four monasteries in particular, including Tiantong and Ayuwang, where Miyun Yuanwu and his dharma heirs reformed Chan institutions.[5] It is evident that reviving Buddhist monasteries became a national movement.

Wang Yangming's "Learning of the Mind"

Behind the lavish patronage toward Buddhist institutions was an intellectual transformation initiated by Wang Yangming (1472–1529), which aroused great interest in Buddhism among the Confucian literati. Wang Yangming, rising at the end of the fifteenth century as an insightful philosopher and successful statesman, provided an attractive alternative to the orthodox neo-Confucianism represented by Zhu Xi (1130–1200). Considering the mind as the original substance of the universe and of human beings, Wang Yangming initiated a "subjective turn" from Zhu Xi's emphasis on the objective principle (li), which is accessible only through a rigid and gradual program of learning. Wang argued forcefully that human beings could achieve sagehood through sudden comprehension of the ultimate moral truth, transcending the duality of good and evil. The pivotal concept of his "learning of the mind" (xinxue), "the innate knowledge of goodness" (liangzhi), calls for introspective reflection to search for the ultimate moral ground in a way that strikingly resembles the Chan rhetoric of nonduality and sudden enlightenment.[6]

The influence of Wang Yangming extended beyond the realm of ideas. His thought heralded a new era of intellectual and social movement that mobilized a group of Confucian elite and commoners to search for the meaning of being an individual by freeing themselves from socially imposed Confucian codes of behavior. His followers pursued a new kind of learning through organizing "lecture meetings" (jianghui) and establishing Confucian academies. After Wang's death, they were divided by different interpretations of his teaching. Many of them showed considerable interest in Buddhist teachings, especially in the teaching of the mind, an obvious connection with Wang's learning of the mind. For instance, scriptural studies on texts such as the *Śūraṃgama Sūtra* were popular among the literati. In the *Śūraṃgama*, the sophisticated description of the phenomena of mental states and vigorous programs for the training of the mind through meditation and asceticism attracted Confucian intellectuals like Guan Zhidao (1536–1608) and Zhao Zhenji (*hao*. Dazhou, 1508–1576, *jinshi* 1535), who encouraged the use of Buddhist scriptures to enrich Confucian self-cultivation.[7] Some of Wang Yangming's followers such as Mu Konghui (*jinshi* 1505) deliberately used the Tang Tiantai master Zhiyi's (538–597) commentary on the *Lotus Sūtra* to interpret the *Great Learning*, one of the four books grouped by Zhu Xi.[8]

In the late Ming, many Confucian intellectuals who favored Wang Yangming's thought came close to Chan Buddhism and promoted certain Chan masters whose teachings reflected their values and intellectual orientation. The majority of Wang's followers found Buddhist teachings, especially Chan teachings such as sudden enlightenment, congenial to their understanding of Wang's Confucianism. For this reason, Wang's teaching was often referred to as "Yangming Chan" by late Ming intellectuals. As a result, an intellectual atmosphere of integration of all three teachings (*sanjiao heyi*), including Confucianism, Buddhism, and Taoism, took form and led to a more accommodating attitude toward Buddhism, especially Chan Buddhism.[9]

The Taizhou School and "Mad Chan"

The promotion of Chan Buddhism had much to do with a group of Wang Yangming's followers, often called the Taizhou school. These Chan-minded intellectuals included active figures like Wang Gen (1483–1540), Li Zhi (1527–1602), Yan Jun (1504–1596), He Xinyin (1517–1579), Luo Rufang (1515–1588), and Jiao Hong (1540–1620), who tended to display what William Theodore de Bary calls "individualism" through challenging traditional Confucian values.[10] Among them, Li Zhi was a central figure.

In the late sixteenth century, a literati community influenced by Chan thinking took shape surrounding the iconoclastic Confucian intellectual Li Zhi, who lived in a Buddhist cloister in Hubei. Li was born into a Muslim family in Quanzhou, Fujian province.[11] After obtaining his *juren* degree (recommended scholar in provincial exams) at twenty-six, he started his official career by serving as a low-rank official and clerk. Although he was a talented man, his career was significantly curbed by the fact that he never acquired the prestigious *jinshi* degree. His last post was an appointment in the remote Yunnan province as a prefect when he was already fifty-one years old. He soon retired from this position in 1581 and sojourned in northern Hubei. He finally decided not to return to his hometown in Fujian but devoted himself completely to reading and writing in a local Buddhist monastery there. Because he dismissed his wife and children back to home and shaved his head, he was often referred to as a monk despite the fact that he never took Buddhist vows seriously.[12]

Although he lived in a remote monastery, his social and intellectual connections with the outside world were national in scope. He had access to all kinds of books, and his writings were sought after by publishers because his iconoclastic personality and sarcastic writing style guaranteed his books to become bestsellers. He kept correspondences with friends and other intellectuals to discuss various kinds of intellectual, social, and political issues, often initiating serious debates among the Confucian literati. Surrounding him, an intellectual community developed. Members of such a community, including prominent figures such as Jiao Hong, Yuan Hongdao and his two brothers, and Tao Wangling (1562–1609), kept close contacts through correspondences and traveling. In the late Ming, their writings and thoughts had direct impact on the literati culture. However, Li Zhi did not survive a political campaign against him: He was thrown in jail in Beijing in 1602 and soon after committed suicide. After his death, the center of this community shifted to the Eastern Zhejiang area where the Taizhou figures Zhou Rudeng (1547–1629) and Tao Wangling became leaders. These leading intellectuals patronized Chan Buddhist monks, and eventually both Linji and Caodong lineages were revived in Eastern Zhejiang.

Represented by Li Zhi and his close associates, the so-called Taizhou school had certain intellectual orientations that allowed its followers to embrace Chan Buddhism. First, their belief in a human being's innate capacity for moral perfection privileged intuitive knowledge of morality transcending such dualistic distinctions as good and evil. This idea resembles Chan teaching, which favors immediate enlightenment, a direct "seeing" of the truth unmediated by cognitive knowledge or dualistic thinking.

The second Chan-like characteristic of the Taizhou school was its iconoclastic teaching of morality demonstrated through unconventional behavior. Wang Yangming's leading disciple Wang Gen, who hailed from Taizhou and thus the Taizhou school was named after him, was the son of a salt merchant but aspired to pursue Confucian learning. Believing that he had acquired the truth about Confucian sagehood, he imitated the appearance of an ancient sage by dressing in antiquated costumes. In 1523, mimicking ancient sages, he toured Beijing in a chariot he designed and caused a great sensation.[13] Li Zhi, who placed the "childlike mind" (tongxin) at the center of his value system, shaved his head and lived in a Buddhist cloister without any intention of full

ordination as a monk should have done. He Xinyin subverted the Five Relationships of Confucianism by emphasizing the virtue of friendship and led
the life of a wandering dissident.[14] More strikingly, social barriers between
Confucian elite and commoners began to break down within the group. Yan
Jun, a commoner inspired by Wang Yangming's teaching of the innate knowledge of goodness, traveled in the country as a lecturer to propagate Wang's
teaching and gained a following of Confucian students, among whom Luo
Rufang and He Xinyin became leading Taizhou scholars.[15]

The Taizhou scholars also displayed a certain inclination toward spontaneous expressions of their enlightenment experiences. For example, the Confucian scholar Geng Dingxiang (1524–1596) records that, in the middle of a session of discussion, Yan Jun "suddenly fell on the ground and rolled over in the
middle of a public lecture, saying, 'Look at my innate knowledge.'"[16] Readers
who are familiar with records of Chan masters' iconoclastic encounter dialogues
can easily identify the commonality between Yan's spontaneous reaction and
the typical antinomian behavior of Chan masters. In this case, Yan Jun must
have been greatly inspired by Wang's teaching and therefore demonstrated his
ineffable experience through spontaneous actions. It shows that, at least in appearance, some of Wang's followers, either consciously or unconsciously, found
Chan-like spontaneity to be the best way of expressing their ultimate understanding of moral truth. Once again, the Taizhou scholars' iconoclastic views
and behavior paralleled the spontaneous spirit often found in Chan literature.
For most of them, Chan and Confucianism were the same, without distinction.
In other words, their practice was better referred to as "Confucian Chan Buddhism" as Li Zhi's follower Yuan Hongdao (1568–1610) put it.[17]

However, their public displays of such antinomianism caused a great stir
in society, and their opponents characterized them as embodying a kind of
"mad Chan" (kuangchan). Huang Zongxi's unfavorable comments on the Taizhou school, especially on Yan Jun and He Xinyin, reveal its connection with
Chan Buddhism:

> The teaching of Master Yang-ming became popular everywhere under
> Heaven on account of Wang Ken (Wang Gen) and Wang Chi (Wang
> Ji). But it gradually lost its transmission in part due to Wang Ken and
> Wang Chi. . . . Thus they pressed Yang-ming into the ranks of Ch'an
> Buddhism. . . . In Wang Ken's case, many of his disciples could fight
> the dragon and the snake with their bare hands. By the time his
> teaching passed down to men like Yen Chün (Yan Jun) and Ho Hsin-
> yin (He Xinyin), it was no longer within the boundaries of Confucian
> moral philosophy. . . . However, in my opinion, what attracted others to

them was not their so-called cleverness but rather their teachings. What we call Patriarch Ch'an is the teaching that regards the transformation of consciousness as direct perception of nature. These men turned Heaven and Earth upside down. There has been no one like them among the ancients and the moderns. The Buddhists practiced beating and yelling, acting wildly according to the situation; however, once the stick was laid down, they were like fools. But these men bore everything with their bare bodies, never letting down their stick, for which reason they have caused so much harm.[18]

In this unsympathetic account of the Taizhou school, Huang suggested that Wang Gen and his followers, such as Yan Jun and He Xinyin, had led Wang's teaching away from Confucianism toward Chan Buddhism, especially to Patriarch Chan (*Zushi Chan*).[19] Like the Chan monks' beating and shouting, their behavior was antinomian from the Confucian perspective. However, Huang insinuated that they caused great harm because they did not understand that sticks were simply tools and should be put down when the goal was achieved. Huang's report accurately depicted how Wang's teaching evolved and merged into the revival of Chan Buddhism.

The Literati's Textual Spirituality

Although not all of the literati agreed with Wang Yangming and his followers, Buddhism had a visible presence in the general literati culture. Timothy Brook has thoroughly examined the pro-Buddhist elite culture in the late Ming. According to him, during that time, it was common and acceptable for the literati to befriend monks and to visit monasteries, which were largely open spaces for literati gatherings and retreats. They even joined lay associations and participated in Buddhist rituals, such as releasing animals. Writing a poem or essay and making a donation after a visit to a monastery did not tarnish the fame of a good Confucian. Buddhism and its institutions fit so well into the literati's cultural life that it became completely unnecessary to repudiate Buddhism as a foreign religion.

In particular, the literati were deeply immersed in reading and writing Buddhist texts. In their religious reading and writing, the literati displayed a unique spiritual orientation that shaped their understanding of Buddhism. For most of them, reading and writing Buddhist, especially Chan Buddhist, literature was one of the many cultural pastimes in which they dabbled during their leisure time. Because their entry into Buddhism did not begin with faith in the Buddhist belief system, they tended to emphasize the supreme and most sophisticated expressions of philosophical wisdom rather than precepts and devotional activities. Many of them simply dismissed the Buddhist teaching of retribution and reincarnation because for them this coarse reasoning of punishment and reward was obviously designed for the unsophisticated minds. Even in their meditation practice, the literati preferred to use Dahui Zonggao's method of meditating on the key phrases (huatou), a spiritual exercise transformed from the attentive contemplation on doubts that have been aroused from intensive kōan study. This practice has a clear trace in their habit of religious reading because of its origins in textual study. Because their spiritual experience was largely generated and fostered during the process of reading, writing, and discussing, without leaving a carefully constructed textual realm, I tend to call such a religious experience "textual spirituality" to distinguish it from a more devotion-based religious experience. Exploring the characteristics of textual spirituality is important in this study because, through reading and writing, a shared mentality took form in some literati's communities, in which Chan monks were members and were deeply influenced by such a text-based spiritual orientation.

The Role of Reading in the Literati's Understanding of Chan Buddhism

Although not all members of the literati class had the economic means or high political status to free themselves completely from work, most literati maintained their lives without engaging in labor and thus had more leisure time for cultural and literary production and consumption.[20]

In this sense, Chinese literati can be described as a typical type of "leisure class" as American economist Thorstein Veblen (1857–1929) defines it. According to Veblen, as a kind of "non-productive consumption of time," enjoying leisure was the hallmark of one's wealth and social standing, which enabled that person to afford the life of idleness and to consider industrial labor as unworthy. For the leisure class, complete abstention from productive work was honorific, meritorious, and decent. Moreover, "conspicuous leisure" led to ostentatious "exhibition of some tangible, lasting results of the leisure so spent," such as luxuries, fashionable clothes, and exquisite furniture. But more important results were immaterial achievements, such as "quasi-scholarly or quasi-artistic accomplishments" and knowledge in impractical things. Because members of this leisure class were largely exempt from industrial labor work, they thus had leisure time to devote to various kinds of "conspicuous consumption" with distinctive tastes.[21] The canon of tastes they developed and cultivated was in turn emulated by the rest of society as elite fashions.

As Craig Clunas shows, the Ming literati were especially notorious for indulging in "superfluous things," such as stylishly decorated scholars' studios, strange-looking rocks, ancient vessels and utensils, etc., which exuded a cultivated elegance and exquisite taste. After withdrawing from official careers, the literati led a life of "pure enjoyment of cultured idleness,"[22] which was devoted to cultivated literary and artistic pastimes. In addition to the high standard of living, elite social etiquette and protocols, and the consumption of luxuries, the Chinese literati distinguished themselves from the leisure classes in other cultures by their penchant for reading and writing books. The Chinese literati loved or even worshiped things written: Not only did they read all kinds of literature voraciously, they also became the curators of books. Venerating ancient books, they roamed in book markets in search of rare editions. After collecting them, they stored them carefully in their private libraries as family treasures. During the late Ming, the Song prints of various kinds of books, including Chan texts of Song and Yuan origins, became coveted commodities and valued collectibles. Under the influence of such a book-centered elite culture, a large number of educated people became "book readers" (*dushuren*) or even bookworms regardless of their social background.[23]

Among these books were also texts related to religions. Some literati were extremely interested in reading religious texts and even engaged in a kind of religious reading that generated a particular viewpoint about religion. Because of their leading role in shaping the taste of elite culture, their view on religion influenced all educated people, including monks with literary backgrounds. For most literati, indulging in Chan literature was a cultural pastime that fit in their leisurely lifestyle very well. If a literatus was satisfied with the terminal degree he received in civil service exams, with enough economic means, he could easily retreat to his scholar's studio without the disturbance of public affairs. Without the pressure of examinations, the literati, as active readers, could be influenced by any texts to which they had access. China's rich religious traditions offered the Ming literati a wealth of ideas upon which to ruminate. To a large extent, those who were interested in religion led a contemplative reading life, meaning that they tended to grasp the sense of transcendence solely from reading religious texts. With little help from spiritually accomplished priests, the literati could claim that an experience of enlightenment or a feeling of thorough penetration of the meaning of life was achieved.

The literati's reading of Chan texts can be regarded as a kind of religious reading. As Paul Griffiths defines it, based on his case studies of reading practices in Buddhist India and Roman Africa, "religious reading requires and fosters a particular set of attitudes to what is read, as well as reading practices that comport well with those attitudes; and it implies an epistemology, a set of views about what knowledge is and about the relations between reading and the acquisition and retention of knowledge."[24] The Chinese literati's reading of Chan texts certainly fits into Griffiths' definition of religious reading: While reading Chan texts, they developed their own perspective and often jotted down their thoughts in miscellaneous notebooks.

Because of the extensive scope of their reading, it can be expected that the literati's view of religion would be eclectic and accommodative, showing the spirit of unity and harmony without ostensibly discriminating one tradition against another. The Northern Song scholar-official Chao Jiong (951–1034), for example, was one such figure who led a contemplative reading life and left extensive notes about his reading, in which he expressed an eclectic attitude toward all three teachings.[25]

Chao's reading notes on Buddhist scriptures and Confucian and Taoist classics indicate that the purpose of Chao's reading was for his personal cultivation, and therefore he tended to focus on those teachings that would contribute to his spiritual well-being. He described his reading method as follows:

> When I read the books of the three traditions I find something
> to be gleaned from each and to cherish. Reading Confucian books
> I have learnt the arts of "great refinement" and I cherish the
> absence of depravity that comes with the rectitude of conduct they
> expound. Reading Taoist books I have learnt the technique of
> "expansive vision" and I cherish the catharsis that comes with the
> transcendence of wisdom that they preach. Reading Ch'an books
> I have learnt the method of "ultimate awakening" and I cherish the
> condition of non-obstruction that comes of the perfect interfusion of
> nature they reach. None of these three methods is dispensable. How
> then could one possibly set up invidious distinctions between
> "theirs" and "ours" by wrangling over their respective merits and
> deficiencies?[26]

In the above confession translated by Robert Gimello, Chao Jiong tended to harmonize and synthesize the three traditions. This approach might have emerged from his reading habit of including books from all traditions without discrimination because there was no evidence showing that Chao Jiong was influenced by any renowned clergy who guided his reading. As he declared, "When first I read the books of Lao and Chuang I subscribed to their governing principle of 'expansive vision' . . . . . . Later, when I read the Indian books of the Buddhists, I gained the method of the great vehicle. . . ."[27] Clearly, reading was his major source of religious knowledge. In this sense, Chao Jiong had led a spiritual and contemplative reading life.

The Literati Reading Chan Literature

The Ming literati enjoyed reading Chan literature such as collections of kōans, recorded sayings of Chan masters, and Chan genealogical records. These collections, containing witty and lively conversations between master and disciple, had a prominent place in the literati's reading life, which was leisurely, carefree, and serene. It is somehow ironic to see that the literati, who were eager to draw a line between elegance and vulgarity, actually enjoyed reading Chan materials because those texts often contained iconoclastic encounters and remarks expressed in unsophisticated vernacular languages. However, as we have seen in the process of the production of Chan texts, some literati in the Northern Song had consciously participated and edited the texts to the extent that they became acceptable for literati readers. As Albert Welter documents, these Song literati helped to define the image of Chan as "a tradition separated from scriptures."[28] More important, when the actual encounter dialogues were recreated in a textual form, these seemingly vulgar activities were transformed into a reading experience, which created an idealized portrait of Chan in an imagined world. Under this circumstance, for the literati, reading Chan texts became the most important source for seeking the feeling of transcendence.

However, the sense of transcendence generated from reading Chan texts can be described as a kind of textual spirituality, which largely depends on textual manipulations rather than on devotion and ritual performance. Such a reading life, though spiritual, can hardly be regarded as devotional by pious Buddhist believers. At best, the literati's piety can be termed as a kind of "worldly devotion," an oxymoron Mark Halperin uses to characterize the Song literati's engagement in Buddhism.[29] To a large extent, the literati who led a contemplative reading life were at best spiritual rather than religious because in their reading the literati tended to focus on conceptual understanding and doctrinal profundity rather than on religious cultivation. This dilemma was perfectly demonstrated in the popular *Śūraṃgama Sūtra*, in which the most learned Ānanda, who could be interpreted as representing Confucian literati, was accused of lacking sufficient cultivation.[30]

Most Confucian literati only dallied with Chan texts during their leisure reading time to taste the "joy of Chan" (*chanyue*) in the same way as they enjoyed poetry, drama, antiques, tea, wine, or other "toys." The late Ming literatus Tu Long's (1542–1605) delightful poem describes the life of a Chan dilettante:

> A spotless desk and a clear window;
>> Good incense and bitter tea;
>>> Discussing Chan from time to time with an eminent monk.[31]

What was conspicuously missing in such a leisurely pursuit of Chan was faith and devotion, which most literati were loath to discuss because they apparently had transcended such a standard intended for the unsophisticated masses. Juelang Daosheng, a Caodong monk who had frequent interactions with the literati, acrimoniously pointed out how superficial such a Chan life was. He vividly described that, according to these literati, the ideal way of being a Chan person was to simply lead a comfortable reading life focusing on the supreme teaching without the hardship of Buddhist cultivation and meditation: They came to monks only for the most profound teaching; they were not accustomed to ascetic practices and meditation, not to mention managing monastic affairs for the monastery; they believed that they had the superior understanding; and they desired an ideal reading environment for their enjoyment. I translate this caricature as follows:

> I must be given a small room that should be well-lit and clean, with supplies of books, paper, brushes, and several dishes of fruits and desserts. [I can] either read some recorded sayings, or practice the cursive-style calligraphy, or compose some short poems, stanzas, songs, and eulogies. If I feel tired, I just take a nap for a while. Together with several friends of the Way who study Chan Buddhism, we can often read several "turning phrases" and discuss some kōans. We drink tea, talk something, criticize somebody, or discuss current affairs. Sometimes we laugh and clap our hands; sometimes we lift our eyebrows and sigh deeply. This [way of life] would not ruin our reputation as people transcending the mundane world.[32]

The literati's understanding was therefore largely a textual imagination distanced from monastic reality. Certainly, such a textual experience can later turn into a more serious religious life of faith and devotion at the juncture of a life crisis or social upheaval. Some literati-turned-monks, after a number of years of Buddhist training, became in fact critical of their understanding of Buddhism before their ordination. For example, in the following, Yunqi Zhuhong, in his short essay "Discussing Chan" ("Tanzong"), described the dramatic change of his understanding of Chan and Buddhism before and after his ordination:

> When I didn't leave family, I once came across the recorded sayings of the Chan school. Understanding superficially with my own deluded consciousness, I wrote to a Buddhist monk with ambitious and splendid remarks. The monk was surprised [by my understanding]. After I had been a monk for several years, I met this monk again in a

hospice. During the conversation, he noticed that I had set my mind on Pure Land and had no words related to Chan teaching. Being surprised, he asked: "Your understanding was so brilliant before, why now are you so shallow?" I replied with laughter: "A proverb says 'a new-born cub is not afraid of tigers; only those who know tigers are frightened.' Do you know this?" That monk was silent.[33]

Like all literati, Yunqi Zhuhong was fascinated by Chan literature before his ordination. Through reading, he seemed to have obtained a sense of enlightenment that urged him to write eloquently and ambitiously about Chan teaching. However, only after he became a monk did he start to realize how superficial his understanding was if he was only relying on reading texts. From Zhuhong's perspective, genuine Chan enlightenment must be achieved through arduous cultivation in a gradual way. Attaining sudden enlightenment solely through the mystagoguery of Chan kōan is simply the illusion of an audacious beginner who has not yet arrived at the entrance into Buddhism.

The Literati's Chan Writings

As part of their reading life, the literati also composed various kinds of Chan literature to spread their understanding. As Paul Griffiths points out, as byproducts of religious reading, people often compose anthologies and commentaries on the scriptures they read to express and reinforce the particular kinds of attitudes cultivated during religious reading. Indeed, during the late Ming, the literati were enthusiastic in commenting on Chan-related scriptures and compiling Chan anthologies. In addition to these two genres of religious writings, some Chan-minded literati even compiled their own recorded sayings that documented their encounter stories in a way similar to Chan masters' recorded sayings.

The first type of literati's Chan writing was commentaries on Chan-related Buddhist scriptures. Among all scriptures, the most popular one on which the literati chose to comment was the *Śūraṃgama Sūtra*, which had close intellectual ties with Chan Buddhism. The sūtra centers on a plot that evolves around Buddha's chief attendant Ānanda's seduction in sexual desire. Because of Ānanda's weakness in cultivation, the Buddha provides detailed analysis of his fall. In this scripture, many important themes of Mahayana philosophy, such as *tathāgatagarbha* thought, the relationship between gradual cultivation and sudden enlightenment, and Buddhist cosmology and meditation, are discussed. The literati were particularly attracted by this scripture because it spelled out their intellectual concerns over issues of self-cultivation, such as how to keep balance between the accumulation of fragmented knowledge and the quest of the meaning of life and death. For the literati who excelled in learning, it was easy to identify themselves with the main character Ānanda because he was the most knowledgeable person among Buddha's disciples but had problems with his moral cultivation. It appears that the scripture addressed the issue of learning, the most crucial concept in Confucian teaching because the Buddha explicitly identified Ānanda's problem as "excessive knowledge (duowen)." He admonishes that even Ānanda has excellent memory and learning, he is weak in genuine practice and cultivation. In this sense, the popularity of this scripture in the late Ming lay in the fact that it discusses the relationship between knowledge and action, a pivotal issue for the Confucian literati, especially for the great Ming Confucian philosopher Wang Yangming and his followers.[34]

The second type of the literati's Chan writing was Chan anthologies and genealogies. During the late Ming, the literati customarily gleaned inspiring encounter dialogues and biographies from their extensive reading of Chan texts and accordingly compiled their versions of Chan anthologies and genealogies. For instance, as early as 1589, when the late-Ming poet Yuan Hongdao was only twenty-two years old, he assembled a collection of encounter dialogues from Chan recorded sayings and titled it *Jinxie bian* (Collections of gold scraps). In this collection, not only did he select about seventy passages from Chan encounter dialogues he also wrote his own comments after each selection.[35]

Among all such works authored by the literati, Qu Ruji's (1548–1610) *Zhiyue lu* (Records of a Finger Pointing to the Moon—a famous allusion from the *Śūraṃgama Sūtra*) is the most popular one and was organized in genealogical order. Qu hailed from a prestigious family in Changshu of Jiangsu whose descendents owned one of the four famous private libraries in the eighteenth century, "The Storehouse of the Iron Harp and the Copper Sword" (Tieqin tongjian lou).[36] His teacher was Guan Zhidao, a Confucian intellectual who believed in the unity of the three teachings.

According to Qu's 1602 preface to the *Zhiyue lu*, his collection initially resulted from his extensive reading of Chan recorded sayings without the intention to publish it. As he confessed, being simply fond of reading Chan literature in his youth, he began to jot down notes about his reading in 1575 when he studied under his teacher, Guang Zhidao. Even after his teacher distanced himself from Chan Buddhism later, Qu claimed that he continued to spend time in reading Chan literature, believing that a true Confucian scholar had to understand the ultimate meaning of Confucian learning through reading Buddhist texts, especially Chan literature, which was the quintessence of Buddhist teaching, in his opinion. His notes were accumulated up to thirty fascicles in 1595. Urged by his friends, he finally decided to publish the collection in 1601.[37]

Because Yuan Hongdao's *Jinxie bian*, compiled in 1589, was only printed around 1617, Qu's work appeared to be the first Chan anthology published by the literati in the late Ming. It immediately emerged as a new classic of Chan literature and quickly became one of the bestsellers in the book market. According to Araki Kengo's study, although Qu and his friends intended the work to be a correction to the iconoclastic teaching of sudden enlightenment and to promote a gradual approach of cultivation, this anthology incited even more enthusiasm among the public for an idealized version of Chan understanding.[38] (Qu's *Zhiyue lu* was particularly important in this study because, as I will describe in chapter 7, Qu rediscovered the issue of Tianhuang and Tianwang Daowu and thus triggered a great controversy.)

In addition to Chan anthologies, the literati also compiled collection of excerpts from lengthy Buddhist texts according to their preferences. For example, Yongming Yanshou's *Zongjing lu* (*Records of the Source-Mirror*), a significant Chan work that synthesizes various kinds of Buddhist doctrines, was popular in the late Ming.[39] However, it was composed of 100 fascicles and required considerable effort to fully absorb all the doctrinal implications. Therefore, some literati, after reading the entire work, compiled excerpted versions of the *Zongjing lu* based on their reading to help others to grasp the essential meaning of this work. In 1603, Yuan Hongdao selected some essential passages from the *Zongjing lu* and compiled them into an anthology entitled *Zongjing shelu* (Summarized records of the *Zongjing lu*). Equally intrigued by the *Zongjing lu*, his friend Tao Wangling compiled a similar work called *Zongjing guangshu* (extensive collections of essentials of the *Zongjing lu*).[40]

However, the literati's writing strategy was highly selective, and some literati authors even deliberately alter the original texts to fit them into their own understanding. For example, many Chan texts contain vernacular expressions, dubious historical facts, and offensive languages. Among them, the *Platform Sūtra* was perhaps one of the most popular but unpolished Chan texts. Some of its coarse and unrefined language styles and expressions bothered the literati, such as Yuan Hongdao. To satisfy his taste for literary elegancy, Yuan deliberately abridged the text by cutting off those offensive expressions and usages. In his *Tanjing jielu* or *Liuzu tanjing jielu* (Excerpts from the *Platform Sūtra*), whose preface is shown in figure 2.1, Yuan made significant changes according to his likings: Completely changing the conventional structure, he condensed the whole texts into five sections: encounter stories, sermons, students' requests, dharma transmission, and inscriptions. As he declared in the preface of this work, he also deleted all references which he considered as forgeries, colloquial expressions, and repetitions.[41]

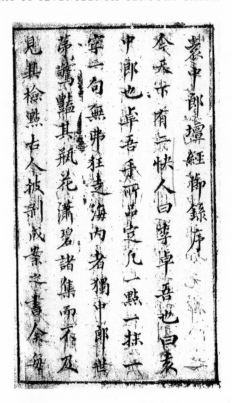

FIGURE 2.1. First page of Yan Diaoyu's preface to Yuan Hongdao's *Tanjing jielu*, 1617 edition. From the *Naikaku bunko*, Japan.

In addition to writing commentaries and anthologies, the third genre of the literati's Chan writing was the collection of recorded sayings, which was common in both the Confucian and Chan traditions. Since the Song, Neo-Confucians tended to document their teachings in the form of oral discourses. In the late Ming, Wang Yangming heralded a new era of compiling Confucian recorded sayings by allowing his students to record his conversations about issues in self-cultivation. After him, recorded sayings became a popular form of writing among his followers because this writing style could document the literati's discussion about issues of moral self-cultivation. However, when Buddhist teaching became a topic in these gatherings and some literati consciously or unconsciously behaved like Chan masters, these recorded sayings resembled Chan recorded sayings in many ways.

In the late Ming, a collection of miscellaneous notes of conversations by Yuan Hongdao and his brother, Yuan Zhongdao (1570–1624), entitled *Shanhu lin* (Coral grove), can be considered a product of a literatus's religious reading in Confucian classics, Buddhist scriptures, and Taoist texts. Yuan was a leading literary figure in the late Ming. With his two brothers, he advocated a fresh style of writing that fully expressed human emotions and individuality. One of his sources of inspiration was Buddhism. He befriended Li Zhi and was sympathetic to Li's iconoclastic teaching. He also became one of Zhuhong's followers and wrote the famous *Xifang helun* (Combined treatise about Western Paradise). Although he was often perceived as a devotee to the Pure Land practice because of this work, Yuan continued to pursue Chan teaching, regarding the Pure Land practice a remedy and correction to an unbalanced approach to Chan.[42]

In the fifth month of 1604, Yuan Hongdao and several friends, including both clergy and lay people, gathered in a place called Shanhu lin in Gong'an county of Hubei. Later, touring Mount Deshan in the nearby Taoyuan county to spend summer, they continued to discuss fundamental issues in self-cultivation. Their conversations, centering on Yuan Hongdao's remarks, became the source of a book entitled *Shanhu lin*, which was later published.[43]

As shown in the *Shanhu lin*, Yuan read extensively in all three traditions. As a Confucian scholar influenced by Wang Yangming's thought, he was deeply concerned about the meaning of the *Great Learning*, which caused great controversies in the late Ming. In addition to reading Confucian classics, he had the works of Wang Yangming's followers, such as Wang Ji and Li Zhi, on his reading list. Although Laozi and Zhuangzi's Taoist philosophy was also one of the topics in his discussion, the majority of the notes were about Buddhism, showing his broad knowledge of Buddhist thought, especially Chan Buddhism. As evidenced in this text, Yuan was particularly knowledgeable in Buddhist scriptures and writings such as the *Huayan Sūtra* (*Avataṃsaka*), the *Lotus Sūtra*, the *Śūraṃgama Sūtra*, the *Sūtra of Perfect Enlightenment* (*Yuanjue jing*), the *Laṅkāvatāra Sūtra*, the *Vimalakīrti Sūtra*, Sengzhao's treatise on *Things do not shift* (*Wubuqian*), Yongming Yanshou's *Zongjing lu*, Li Tongxuan's commentaries on the *Huayan Sūtra*, Dahui Zonggao's recorded sayings, and so forth. In terms of his intellectual orientation, he had no specific preference for any of the three teachings. Rather, it is common in his conversations to interpret the meaning of Confucian classics by referring to Buddhist thought because for him, at the ultimate level, all three traditions revealed the same truth. Nevertheless, Chan Buddhism has a special place in his understanding of the three teachings.

This collection also indicated that a literatus such as Yuan Hongdao not only read religious texts as intellectual enrichment but also practiced meditation as part of self-cultivation. A significant portion of Yuan's discussion centered on the issue of meditation on key phrases (*huatou*) as Dahui Zonggao advocated, indicating that Yuan practiced meditation regularly and had insightful observation regarding how to deal with various problems in the practice. However, for Yuan Hongdao, such a practice focused on the supreme understanding of the ineffable Chan meaning instead of on devotion and piety. In his *Shanhu lin*, in the presence of the clergy, he publicly denounced popular devotional practices such as blood-writing, seven-day meditation sessions (*daqi*), and vegetarian feasts because in these practices the practitioners allowed themselves to attach to phenomenal existence rather than to penetrate the supreme truth as iconoclastic Chan followers presumably had.[44] Although he authored a highly influential Pure Land work several years before to praise the practice of chanting Buddha's name, Yuan pointed out paradoxically in his conversation that "chanting Buddha's name is also a sort of illusion" because the practitioners' "understanding has not yet become solid," just like his previous immersion in the Pure Land beliefs.[45] It is clear that although Yuan tended to assimilate all religious thoughts together, he was still largely inclined to a more idealized Chan understanding that distinguishes itself as a unique practice superior to all other conventional ones.

In sum, the *Shanhu lin* shows that, in the late Ming, the literati's reading and writing religious texts had both intellectual and spiritual dimensions. Intellectually, they adopted an accommodating attitude toward other traditions; Spiritually, reading these texts, together with engaging in meditative practice (rather than devotional activities), generated a special kind of spirituality.

The Literati's Influence on Chan Monks

To understand the extent to which the literati influenced Chan monks, it is important to pay attention to the literati's reading experience because intensive reading motivated by a specific hermeneutic purpose engenders new understandings of Chan's texutalized past. These interpretations are largely imagined literary representations that reflected the readers' current intellectual and spiritual concerns. In the late Ming, the literati read Chan texts and discussed Chan issues with friends in various occasions of gathering to which monks were often invited. However, in regards with the scope of reading and the level of literary skills, most monks were not on a par with the literati who received professional training in literary composition and Confucian classics. Thus some literati who were confident about their own enlightenment experiences through reading Chan texts challenged monks on their Chan understandings. Some even assumed the position of Chan teachers and tried to guide monks to achieve enlightenment. Under the influence of these literati, some monks, quickly adopting a similar hermeneutic stance, began to emulate the literati's literary style and to echo their Chan understandings.

The Literati Challenging Monks

The literati certainly had all kinds of reasons to despise the devotional life of Buddhist believers because they possessed the literary power to manipulate texts, including Buddhist literature. In terms of reading, it was natural for them to develop an arrogant attitude toward monks, whose literacy and literary skills were inferior to professionally trained literati. In this sense, the literati had authority over textual matters. In fact, the quality of Buddhist monks, especially their literacy rate, had fallen to a deplorable level at the end of the sixteenth century. Even in the most prestigious Bao'en monastery in Nanjing, monks were often ridiculed by the literati for their ignorance and illiteracy. As Hanshan Deqing recalled, when he entered Bao'en monastery as a youth, monks engaged themselves in regular ritual practice "without the ability to respond to even one word from the literati."[46]

Monks were indeed disparaged because of their inability to articulate their own understandings of the Buddhist faith. Juelang Daosheng complained that, in his day, the literati who acquired their own understanding of Buddhism often challenged Buddhist masters, even insulting monastic communities: "If only one word does not agree with their thought, they left immediately with a hateful heart and a resentful mouth. Endlessly slandering the master and cursing the monastery, they harbor the hatred for their life time without entering the door of that monastery even when passing by."[47]

Hanshan Deqing mentioned a certain literatus named Zhong Yuchang, who was such an arrogant man that he challenged monks by imitating encounter dialogues in front of them, expecting monks to respond to his puzzling words and actions in a similar way. He had such a reputation that he was never defeated by monks. One day, when he passed Tianjie monastery in Nanjing, he asked for a real Chan person to come out to meet him. Being so afraid of him, the monks in Tianjie asked the sojourning master Huiguang Benzhi (1555–1605) to greet him. During their encounter, Zhong asked, "Is Tianjie monastery located within the mind or without the mind?" Huiguang Benzhi replied: "Don't even mention Tianjie monastery! Even the three thousand Buddhas are just located at the tip of my whisk." Zhong was impressed and thus left.[48]

Some literati even challenged Yunqi Zhuhong, a widely respected eminent monk, for his effort to synthesize Chan and Pure Land. Despite their esteem to Zhuhong, not a few literati felt that his emphasis on the single-minded chanting of Buddha's name was inferior to Chan's direct comprehension of the ineffable truth. The late Ming literatus Cao Yinru was among these daring literati. Deeply influenced by the Taizhou figures Geng Dingxiang and Luo Rufang, he believed that Chan teaching was compatible with Wang Yang-ming's interpretation of Confucianism. He was also well versed in Huayan teaching, especially in Li Tongxuan's commentary on the *Huayan Sūtra*, which brought Huayan closer to Chan teaching. In a series of letters addressed to Zhuhong, Cao challenged Zhuhong's reliance on the *Amitābha Sūtra* and the practice of chanting Amitabha's name. For him, the *Huayan Sūtra* represented the highest teaching and the *Amitābha Sūtra* ranked much lower in terms of its level of sophistication. What Cao felt unsatisfied was Zhuhong's exclusive emphasis on the Pure Land belief and on the chanting practice for all people of different capacities. He suggested that Zhuhong should differentiate people such as the literati who possessed superior abilities of understanding and the masses who could only be enticed by the promise of rebirth in the Pure Land. According to him, for the literati, Chan practice was the appropriate method because if one truly followed the principle of "Pure Land within the mind" (*weixin jingtu*), Chan teaching actually subsumed the Pure Land practice and the Pure Land was only one of the illusions manifested from the mind.

In his reply, Zhuhong could not hide his contempt for this kind of Chan rhetoric because for him, within this unfortunate era of the degenerating dharma, there were few—if any—who had the superior ability to understand the profound Chan teaching. In Zhuhong's opinion, most literati who claimed to have understood Chan were only playing with the words of Chan. In princi-ple, he agreed to understand the existence of the Pure Land within the frame-work of the mind. This is because for him having faith in Amitābha's other-power and relying on one's self-power generated from an enlightened mind were mutually inclusive. However, in practice, he insisted that chanting Amitābha's name was the sole effective method for all, regardless of their so-cial status and spiritual attainment.[49] For Zhuhong, "he who clings to Ch'an but denigrates the Pure Land belief is denigrating his own original mind; he is denigrating the Buddha. He is denigrating his own Ch'an doctrine. How thoughtless!"[50]

Even the commonly held Buddhist precept against slaughtering animals was disputed by the literati who believed in the amorphous mind precept. In the ninth month of 1604, Zhou Rudeng, one of the leading Taizhou figures, whom we will revisit later, organized a lecture meeting in Yan county of Sha-oxing prefecture. The Caodong monk Zhanran Yuancheng was also invited. During the meeting, when Zhanran saw cooked fish and meat being served, he urged the literati participants to observe the Vinaya rule of non-killing. Zhou Rudeng immediately seized the opportunity to argue with Zhanran, defending his obvious breach of Buddhist precepts. He considered that although Buddhism and Confucianism are different in practice, their common goal is to eliminate the mind of desire. Therefore, as long as the mind of killing is gone, one should follow the natural course of one's life, including eating meat and drinking wine. As a result, "the precepts," Zhou argued, "are the precepts of the mind. Not to seek [the precepts] in the mind but to believe in the retribution of sins and blessings is the view of the small vehicle. This is too far away from the ultimate Way."[51]

After a while, they began to discuss a doctrinal issue about the relationship between the perception of the external world and the dream experience. Zhanran Yuancheng argued that "dream is not the perception of the external world. It is different from the experience in the daytime." Zhou Rudeng refuted him again: "Zhanran is renowned as a Chan master but he separates the dream and the world into two. No need to discuss further." Then the meeting was dismissed. The second day, when the discussion touched upon this issue again, Zhou again ridiculed the Yogācāra teaching that Zhanran used to support himself, citing the sixth patriarch Huineng's teaching of no-thought.[52]

Zhanran Yuancheng, who will be discussed in more detail in chapter 3, was an established Caodong monk who advocated the joint practice of Chan and doctrinal studies. His distinction of the dream experience from the normal perception in daytime derived from the Yogācāra discussion of dreams. According to the Yogācāra understanding of dreams, in the dream experience "a complete and unreal world is created with objects felt to have spatio-temporal localization in spite of the fact that they do not exist apart from the mind which is cognizing them."[53] Zhanran's understanding of dreams was exactly based on the Yogācāra theory. However, Zhou Rudeng appeared to be more Chan-like than a real Chan master. He rudely accused Zhanran of dualistic thinking, which a "pure" Chan master would have shunned.

For Zhou Rudeng, his understanding of Chan seems to have been superior to that of a Chan master who, according to him, not only obstructed himself with precepts but also used dualistic thinking to perceive things. Zhou's authority, as he referred to it, relied on his reading of Chan texts such as the *Platform Sūtra*. His reading prompted him to imagine an absolute and ultimate reality that renders morality and cognitive thinking as relative and even harmful for the attainment of enlightenment. In this sense, the textual authority generated from a kind of textual spirituality would invest the literati and the literati-turned-monks with a particularly advantageous position in the Buddhist world, especially in Chan Buddhism, which is largely textually constructed.

The Literati Becoming Chan Teachers

The literati who were well versed in Chan thought not only challenged monks but also dared to judge the monks' spiritual attainment. Some of them even became Chan teachers. Wang Yangming, for example, rather than being influenced by Chan monks, had helped a monk to achieve enlightenment by preaching his learning of the mind to him.

Although it has been assumed by many that Wang Yangming must have been deeply influenced by Chan Buddhism, there is little evidence to suggest that Wang had fruitful interactions with Chan monks. Wang did visit many Buddhist temples and widely engaged with Buddhist monks, as the Japanese scholar Kusumoto Bunyū has demonstrated in detail.[54] However, Wing-tsit Chan seriously questions the assumption that Chan Buddhism at this time actually influenced Wang Yangming's thought. Wing-tsit Chan observes that Wang had no Chan masters as close friends from whom he benefited intellectually. Wang quoted only a limited number of Buddhist scriptures and even criticized Buddhism more severely than the Song neo-Confucians did.[55] Tu Weiming also has the same concern about Wang's Buddhist connection: In the two most important spiritual moments in Wang's life, his enlightenment in Longchang in 1509 and his elaboration of the extension of the innate knowledge of the good in 1520, there was no direct influence from Chan teachers.[56]

Wang Yangming indeed had a close relationship with one Chan monk, Yu-zhi Faju (1492–1563).[57] However, this monk had no place in Wang's intellectual world. On the contrary, evidence shows that he was actually greatly inspired by Wang Yangming. According to his biography, before he met Wang Yangming, he was only an ordinary monk without any sign of distinction in his Buddhist practice. However, around the year 1524, he was introduced to Wang Yangming by a literati friend who had been converted to Wang's teaching. After their meeting, Wang judged him as not yet being enlightened.[58] Although it is not certain if Yuzhi Faju obtained the enlightenment experience from Wang Yangming, Araki Kengo believes that he later became a Chan monk who consciously introduced Wang's teaching of innate goodness into Chan Buddhism.[59] In this case, Wang Yangming's interaction with Yuzhi Faju suggests a reversed relationship: The literati, without relying on monks' knowledge of Chan, could actually judge the level of spiritual attainment of these monks; and monks had to resort to these literati to gain insights into their own religion.

The most interesting case of such a reversed relationship is the Chan monk Wunian Shenyou's (1544–1627) enlightenment experience under the iconoclastic intellectual Li Zhi, who chose to live in a monastery and had monks as his disciples. Strictly speaking, Li was not qualified to be a Chan master because although he shaved his hair and lived in a monastery, he never took Buddhist vows and precepts seriously. Based in the monastery where he lived, there was a small community that was devoted to the discussion of spiritual issues. This community was composed of both literati and clergy. Wunian Shenyou, as one among them, was deeply influenced by Li Zhi, whose understanding of Chan was regarded as superior. Although a monk, his enlightenment was actually induced by Li Zhi rather than by a Buddhist master.

Wunian Shenyou hailed from Macheng county in Hubei province. Becoming a monk at sixteen, he traveled around China to seek instruction from eminent monks. In 1579, he was invited to Zhifo cloister in Longhu in his hometown. At almost the same time, Li Zhi came to visit him and the two became friends. In 1585, Li Zhi decided to send his family back to Fujian and lived in Zhifo cloister as a hermit permanently. In 1588, he moved to Zhifo cloister to live with Wunian Shenyou and his disciples. In 1593, their relation did not go well, and Wunian Shenyou decided to leave for Fayan monastery in Huangbo mountain, which is located in Shangcheng county of Runing prefecture in Henan (not be confused with Mount Huangbo in Fuqing, Fujian). Wunian Shenyou must have been a very influential Chan master in his time because his literary collection contains many letters from renowned literati, such as Li Zhi, Yuan Hongdao, Yuan Zhongdao, Jiao Hong, and Zou Yuanbiao (1551–1624).[60]

Before Wunian Shenyou met Li Zhi in 1579, he had been seeking eminent Chan masters for years but still had not reached enlightenment. As a result, he often felt depressed. Li Zhi seems to have understood the reason for his depression. Li, therefore, invited some literati friends to help Wunian Shenyou to reach his spiritual goal. Wunian's biography contains the following account of this gathering:

> When he saw [Wunian], Layman [Li Zhi] asked: "How is your cultivation?" Master [Wunian] replied: "I have a doubt." Li Zhi asked again: "What do you doubt about?" The master said: "If I have insight I will know." Li Zhi became serious and remarked: "This is not your insight." The master was confused again. [Later], Li Zhi invited his friends to meet [Wunian] at Sima mountain. There was also a scholar-monk who came and joined the meeting. Sitting at night, Li Zhi asked: "How can the pure and original [mind] suddenly produce mountains, rivers, and the earth?" This is a famous phrase from fascicle 3 of the *Śūraṃgama Sūtra*. After the scholar-monk explained, Li Zhi said: "Wunian, would you explain it?" When Wunian Shenyou was just about to open his mouth, Li Zhi gave him a push on his knee and said: "Good (*ni*)!" Wunian was suddenly

awakened. When he returned to Longhu, he practiced quiet sitting for several days and all he had learned in his lifetime disappeared completely. Since then, all doubts and anxieties were gone forever.[61]

In many ways, this scene resembles Chan encounter dialogues as recorded in Chan literature, except for the role reversal between the monk and the layman. In the case above, Li Zhi obviously assumed the role of a Chan master and completely reversed the relationship between laymen and Buddhist clergy: Here, Chan masters must reach enlightenment under the guidance of their literati patrons.

In this episode of spiritual encounter, Li Zhi acted as a Chan teacher by imitating a famous enlightenment story from Chan kōan collections. His use of the word *ni* was based on the encounter story between the literati follower Feng Ji (?–1153) and Yuanwu Keqin's disciple Foyan Qingyuan in the Song. The record says that one day Feng Ji and Foyan Qingyuan passed the dharma hall and heard a novice reciting the phrase "among all phenomena only he shows his body." Hearing this, Foyan stroked Feng Ji's back and said: "Good (*ni*)." Feng Ji was thus enlightened.[62] However, Master Foyan could not possibly have imagined that, after about 500 years, his word *ni* would be used in a totally different context: A layman assumed his position and the disciple turned out to be a Buddhist monk.

Although Wunian Shenyou considered himself enlightened, he still did not receive Li Zhi's approval. Li wrote an essay entitled "San chun ji" (Record of three stupid people), in which he considered three monks who served him as stupid. Li Zhi evaluated Wunian as follows:

Although [Wunian] Shenyou has the intention of pursuing the Way, he is not that kind of person who is determined to reach the ultimate. He often focuses exclusively on "dead sentences." He is fettered by routine works and takes wealth, fame, and pleasure as the most pleasant and carefree dharma gate. As a result, he cannot avoid harming himself and others.[63]

Obviously, Li Zhi held negative opinions about this Chan master's spiritual attainment. When they appeared together in literati gatherings, Li Zhi was often revered as a true Chan master and Wunian was only introduced as an attendant and messenger.

For example, She Chanji and Wu Dechang, two literati from She county in Huizhou visited Nanjing in the summer of 1598 and recorded their meeting with Li Zhi and Wunian Shenyou there. Both men came to study with Yang Qi-yuan, a student of Taizhou scholar Luo Rufang and an admirer of Chan Buddhism.[64] Learning from Yang that Li Zhi came to Nanjing, as well, and stayed in Yongqing monastery, they planned to pay a visit to this famed figure. One day, they went to Yongqing monastery with two other friends. It happened that some other people also came to visit Li Zhi. For She Changji and Wu Dechang, the meeting was a little bit strange because there was no greeting and introduction to each other in the beginning. When all people were just seated, a senior named Li Zhushan first spoke. He praised Li Zhi: "How empty and shallow your stomach is!" Li Zhi replied loudly: "I just had two bowls of gruel. How empty and shallow can it be?"[65] Here, Li Zhi largely behaved as a Chan master and had lively exchanges of conversation with visitors. The two men from Huizhou were deeply impressed by this kind of spontaneous and witty repartee. Obviously, in many occasions, Li had been respected by the literati as a quasi-Chan teacher and as the Taizhou scholar Jiao Hong aptly pointed out in his preface to the records of this meeting collected by the two men, Li's conversations and behaviors were just like the kōan stories in Chan literature.[66] However, according to these records, in the literati gathering in Yongqing monastery, Wunian was only mentioned once in passing, indicating his minor role in such a gathering.

The Literati Promoting Dharma Transmission

Although Li Zhi shaved his head, lived in a monastery, and even acted like a Chan master, he was basically a Confucian intellectual, a rebel growing within the literati culture. He read Buddhist texts extensively and was able to provide guidance to other literati, but in terms of spiritual authority, he lacked the essential qualification of dharma transmission that would have delegated patriarchal power upon him. The Chan-minded literati could certainly feel this deficiency and actively promoted authentic dharma transmission if it was available. In the late Ming, because social mobility increased the exchange of information, the dharma transmission of famous monasteries such as Shaolin began to be known and sought after. The literati promoted these transmissions and even helped to arrange dharma transmissions to the monks they favored. The famous Caodong master Zhanran Yuancheng's transmission, for example, was negotiated through Tao Wangling.

The relationship between Zhanran Yuancheng and Tao Wangling will be discussed later, and Zhanran Yuancheng's biography will be detailed in chapter 3. Here, my focus is the process of dharma transmission, in which a Confucian intellectual served as a middleman. While Zhanran Yuancheng became famous in the literati circle, he had not yet received any legitimate dharma transmission. Tao Wangling thus negotiated an arrangement with the Caodong master Cizhou Fangnian (?–1594) from whom Zhanran Yuancheng received dharma transmission under Tao's urging. The episode occurred in 1591, and I translate this record as follows:

> The Caodong master Cizhou Fangnian visited Eastern Zhejiang after returning from his trip to Mount Putou and Mount Tiantai. When Tao Wangling met him, Tao recommended Zhanran Yuancheng to him: "In the Jiangnan area, Master Zhanran is the only Chan person." Cizhou Fangnian was silent after hearing this. So Tao put his request more straightforwardly: "You are the only person who has the ortho- dox transmission of Caodong. Zhanran should inherit your transmis- sion." Master Cizhou Fangnian remained silent. For seven days like this, both Cizhou Fangnian and Zhanran Yuancheng did not agree on dharma transmission. When Cizhou Fangnian was about to leave, Tao asked him to preach the dharma in the night. After ascending the hall, every one was as quiet as if they were eating meals. After a while, Cizhou Fangnian looked around, saying: "It is late tonight. Let's talk tomorrow if you have something to say." Then he left his seat. At this moment, Zhanran Yuancheng moved forward and bowed to him. Thus, Cizhou bestowed and entrusted dharma transmission to him.[67]

According to this record, this dharma transmission appears to be a bit forced and superficial, lacking intimate relationships and intellectual engagement.[68] However, Tao Wangling would like to see a monk he favored be empowered by a prestigious dharma transmission. As shown in this record, he initiated the pro- cess and urged both sides to compromise. Eventually, an agreement was reached, and Zhanran received the Shaolin transmission. This move proved to be crucial in Zhanran's career because he became one of the few Chan monks who could offer the authentic Caodong transmission in the south.

In my reading of late Ming sources, it is evident that Confucian literati had great influence over monastic affairs. These literati directed cultural, social, and economic resources to the institutions they patronized. Through their direct or indirect influence, they could choose abbots they favored and secure a large amount of donations. For a sustainable Buddhist revival, no clergy could afford to overlook these people's opinions about the Buddhist faith. Although during this period, there were no active Chan communities or eminent Chan masters in the monastic world, the Chan-minded literati were consciously or uncon- sciously anticipating the emergence of certain kinds of Chan Buddhism that would meet their expectations. Even though there were no such establishments in the existing monastic world, they would use their influence and control to cre- ate an ideal Chan community. Such a move indeed occurred in Eastern Zheji- ang, where a group of literati, largely Wang Yangming's followers, invited their favorite Chan monks to their communities. These Chan monks, backed by the powerful elite, immediately attracted a following and formed the nuclei of early Chan communities, from which most Linji and Caodong lineages derived.

The Advent of Chan Buddhism in Eastern Zhejiang

If we delineate a chronology of the late Ming literati's pursuit of Buddhism, especially Chan Buddhism, their interest in Buddhist texts only started around the beginning of the sixteenth century. During the Longqing reign (1567–1572) and the Wanli reign (1573–1620), their fervor over Chan became manifest: In various kinds of public lectures organized by the literati, the topics about Chan Buddhism dominated the intellectual discourse about Buddhism.[69] However, as I have shown in chapter 1, around that time, there were few well-established Chan institutions or capable Chan teachers to respond to the literati's increasing demand for Buddhist knowledge. Buddhism started to show signs of vitality in the mid-sixteenth century, but the establishment of Chan Buddhism came to the scene even later. The full-fledged Chan lineages that flourished in the seventeenth century did not emerge from the well-established Buddhist communities such as Zhuhong's Yunqi monastery. Rather, they developed under the literati's tutelage. Several powerful Eastern Zhejiang literati and their families patronized Chan Buddhism in particular.

Zhou Rudeng and Tao Wangling

The Taizhou scholars in Eastern Zhejiang played an important role in promoting Chan teachers such as Miyun Yuanwu and Zhanran Yuancheng.[70] The rise of Chan Buddhism in the seventeenth century can be actually traced to this area, where the most famous Chan centers such as Tiantong, Ayuwang, and Yunmen monasteries were located. During the sixteenth and seventeenth centuries, intellectual life in Eastern Zhejiang once again became extremely active, and Confucianism and Buddhism grew side by side. Inspired by their teacher, the followers of Wang Yangming built Confucian academies and frequently organized lecture meetings to pursue Wang's learning of the mind. Confucian literati Zhou Rudeng, Tao Wangling and his brother Tao Shiling (?–1640), and Qi Biaojia (1602–1645) and his brother Qi Junjia were some of the local leaders of this movement.[71] They organized various kinds of lecture meetings, to which Buddhist monks were often invited.[72] Using their local influence, they patronized Chan masters whom they favored by inviting and appointing them as abbots of rebuilt monasteries.

Among these scholars, Zhou Rudeng and Tao Wangling were the leading figures in the so-called Taizhou school, and their intellectual preference for Chan Buddhism had a direct impact on reviving Chan communities. Zhou Rudeng, often referred to by his courtesy name Haimen, was a *jinshi*-degree holder of 1577. During his official career, he had served as a supervisor in the Ministry of Works in Nanjing and as an assistant in the Ministry of Military Affairs and in the Ministry of Personnel. The highest office to which he climbed was chief director of the Seals Office. In Huang Zongxi's historiography of Ming Confucians, Zhou was classified as an adamant follower of the Taizhou school. Intellectually, Zhou was deeply influenced by Wang Yangming's leading disciple, Wang Ji, who came to Ningbo in 1570, when he met Zhou for the first time. After reading carefully Wang Yangming's works, Zhou was completely convinced and decided to follow his teaching. Later, Zhou also studied with another distinguished Taizhou figure, Luo Rufang, whose teacher was the commoner Yan Jun. Through him, Zhou inherited some radical views about Confucianism: He believed that Confucianism and Buddhism were the same and that the Confucian program of self-cultivation had to include the study of Buddhist teaching.

Inspired by this idea, he compiled the *Fofa zhenglun* (The true wheel of Buddhist teaching) in two fascicles, which is also referred to as *Zhixin bian* (Collections of the straightforward mind). In the first fascicle, he collected eighteen Buddhist sayings from sources such as the *Platform Sūtra*, the *Linji lu*, and Dahui Zonggao's recorded sayings. After each excerpt, he added his own comments. The second fascicle collected eighteen passages from Confucian sayings and seven passages of Taoist sayings. All of these selected sayings show a clear feeling of sympathy toward Buddhism and favor an eclectic approach to the three teachings. Zhou's argument, as he stated in the preface, is that "if one realizes the ultimate truth, even Confucianism and Buddhism exist separately, no distinction can be made; even Confucianism is Chan and Chan is Confucianism, no merger can be seen."[73] This attitude shows clearly that for him there is no need to distinguish Confucianism and Buddhism at all.

Zhou was also an active participant and organizer of lecture meetings in which both Confucians and Buddhist clergy were invited and philosophical questions were discussed, as was shown by his debate with Zhanran Yuancheng quoted in a previous section. In one of the famous meetings in Nanjing, he had a debate with Liu Zongzhou's (1578–1645) teacher Xu Fuyuan (1535–1604), who opposed a radical interpretation of Wang Yangming's teaching that gave Confucianism a Buddhist flavor. Represented by Zhou's teacher Wang Ji, this view bent Wang Yangming's teaching toward Chan Buddhism: The ultimate moral ground, *liangzhi*, according to this view, transcends the

distinction of good and evil. Xu worried that such a radical stance of nondual-
ity would eventually eliminate moral standards in social life. Zhou, as Wang
Ji's faithful student, defended his teacher. As he stated, he understood Wang
Yangming's teaching as follows:

> [For the purpose of] maintaining the world and regulating the
> ordinary people, to do good and to eliminate evil are precautionary
> measures. However, to realize human nature and to understand
> Heaven, one must consider no good and no evil as the ultimate. No
> good and no evil is exactly to do good and to eliminate evil without
> efforts. It is truthful to do good and to eliminate evil only when [one]
> understands no good and no evil. The true teachings are mutually
> penetrating without contradictions; their words are supplementary
> rather than conflicting.[74]

In this passage, Zhou argued that his position of nonduality does not im-
ply the elimination of moral judgments. On the contrary, a mind without the
distinction of good and evil would allow the natural flow of goodness out of
the ultimately good human nature and thus prevent evil doings. Here, Zhou
appealed to the idea of spontaneity shared by iconoclastic Chan Buddhists. According to him, this state of mind is free from the intention or will of doing
good as well. Rather, true goodness is without intentional effort to produce the
good because the will of doing so is by nature selfish and hypercritical.

Tao Wangling, an intellectual companion of Zhou Rudeng, acquired his
jinshi degree during the Wanli reign and served as a compiler in Hanlin Academy and the National Confucian School. He retired from office in 1603 after
being implicated in court politics. As an accomplished poet, he was affiliated
with a group of literary figures such as Yuan Hongdao and his brothers, who are
often referred to as the Gong'an school. Intellectually, because he studied with
Zhou Rudeng, he was deeply influenced by Zhou's thought. As Zhou's close associate, he often worked together with Zhou to compile new anthologies such as
the *Fofa zhenglun*, and they shared views about Confucianism and Buddhism.
He was also a lay disciple of Zhuhong, from whom he received bodhisattva precepts. Following Zhuhong's example, he actively promoted and organized lay
associations for releasing animals.[75] Together with his brother Tao Shiling, he
also befriended Chan masters and helped figures such as Miyun Yuanwu and
Zhanran Yuancheng to achieve prominence among the local literati.

As Huang Zongxi recorded with an accusing tone, because of Zhou's and
Tao's open embrace of Chan Buddhism and close relationship with clergy,
they were responsible for introducing Chan masters such as Miyun Yuanwu
and Zhanran Yuancheng to Eastern Zhejiang:

During the Wanli era, Confucians were giving public lectures all over China, and so Buddhists like Zibo Zhenke and Hanshan Deqing came to prominence in the same way. Monks like Miyun and Zhanran followed in the wake of Zhou Rudeng and Tao Wangling. Confucianism and Buddhism became like meats on a skewer, each taking on the flavor of the next.[76]

Huang Zongxi's observation was validated by the records in Miyun Yuanwu's and Zhanran's chronological biographies. Miyun Yuanwu's record indicates that his encounter with Zhou Rudeng in 1607 was indeed remarkable, displaying Miyun's "true color" (bense). I translate their encounter as follows:

Master [Miyun] traveled to Mount Tiantai and visited the layman Zhou Rudeng. When they were seated, Zhou asked: "Where are you?" The master replied: "I traveled from Nanjing to Tiantai and paid a special visit to you." Zhou then asked: "Your reverent name?" The master uttered a shout and then left [the room]. Zhou followed him to the outside and asked: "Where are you staying?" The master said: "Yesterday I rested in the chapel next to your academy." Zhou continued: "I have some fruits. Come and steal some to eat, won't you?" The master gave him a slap and said: "You old thief!" And he thus left.[77]

This was indeed an extraordinary encounter. It was not a kind of conventional exchange of greetings between two people for their first meeting. The shouting and slapping made the encounter dramatic but very confusing. Their conversation did not refer to Buddhist teaching directly, and no doctrinal concepts were discussed. Zhou was greatly surprised and deeply admired Miyun.

Zhanran Yuancheng's meeting with Tao Wangling was equally dramatic. As Zhanran Yuancheng's biography shows, the encounter between him and the literati was accidental and dramatic. One day in the year 1588, when Tao Wangling and some other literati visited Baolin monastery, they heard snoring from Zhanran, who was sleeping outside the hall at that time. Awakening him, they asked, "Who are you?" Zhanran replied, "A monk who has nothing to do." Again they asked, "Where are you staying?" Zhanran replied: "I beg when I am hungry and sleep here when I am tired." After a short conversation, the literati believed that Zhanran was a true Chan master. Through their introduction, more literati followers were willing to meet him and to invite him to various literati gatherings.[78]

In both cases, Zhou and Tao favored a particular kind of Chan Buddhism that fully displayed the antinomian spirit. Among self-proclaimed Chan teachers, Miyun and Zhanran appeared to these literati as the right representatives of this kind of Chan spirit and thus were welcomed in Eastern Zhejiang. After Zhou Rudeng and Tao Wangling died, local officials and influential literati families in Eastern Zhejiang continued to patronize Chan Buddhism, especially the revived Linji and Caodong lineages, from which most Chan transmissions derived.

Huang Duanbo

In Chan Buddhism's further development in Eastern Zhejiang, Chan masters relied on the support of local officials who leaned toward Chan teaching intellectually and spiritually. Miyun Yuanwu's ascendancy in Eastern Zhejiang, for example, was largely attributed to the Ming loyalist Huang Duanbo (zi. Yuangong, hao. Hai'an Daoren, 1579–1645), who served as the judge of the Mingzhou prefecture (Ningbo) at the end of the Ming; both Tiantong and Ayuwang monasteries were under his jurisdiction.[79] In 1636, he was transferred to Hangzhou, and in 1642 he started to serve in Nanjing. In 1645, Nanjing fell to the Manchu army. Refusing to surrender, Huang was executed.

Huang received his *jinshi* degree in 1628. In 1629, he was appointed as the judge of the Mingzhou prefecture. Because of his interest in Chan Buddhism, during his tenure, he provided substantial support for Chan institutions in the region by exercising his power as a local official. He kept good relationships with both Caodong and Linji masters and was deeply involved in the controversies among them, as I will describe in later chapters. Because of his patronage, he was even praised as the reincarnation of the famous Song lay Buddhist Zhang Shangying (1043–1121).

His interest in Chan Buddhism was aroused when he read Chan recorded sayings in his youth. Meeting with the Caodong master Wuming Huijing in 1617, he began to study Chan Buddhism with him and his disciples Wuyi Yuanlai, Yongjue Yuanxian, and Huitai Yuanjing. Under the Caodong masters' guidance, it was said that he achieved enlightenment. In 1630, he came across Miyun Yuanwu's recorded sayings and was deeply impressed by Miyun's style of Linji Chan, which was characterized by the use of beating and shouting. Thus, in the same year, only shortly after his appointment in Ningbo, Huang Duanbo and Qi Biaojia formally invited Miyun to preside over Ayuwang monastery. But Miyun soon left Ningbo for Huangbo monastery in Fuqing, Fujian. In 1631, Huang Duanbo extended his invitation again to Miyun and asked him to head the prestigious Tiantong monastery. This was an offer that Miyun could not refuse.

The many prefaces that Huang authored for Miyun Yuanwu's works demonstrate his unusual relationship with Miyun Yuanwu. For example, in his preface to Miyun's recorded sayings, Huang praised Miyun as the "second coming" of Linji Yixuan. He admired Miyun so much that he was even willing to be listed as a formal disciple of Miyun Yuanwu. However, their friendly relationship ended abruptly in 1637, when he realized Miyun's deliberate alteration of the conventional transmission lines.[80]

The Qi Family

The Caodong master Zhanran Yuancheng's success relied on the long-term support of the Qi family, especially Qi Chenghan (often mispronounced as Qi Chengye, 1565–1628), and his sons Qi Biaojia and Qi Junjia (*zi*. Jichao, dharma name: Jingchao).[81] Qi Chenghan was not a high-ranking official. Passing the *jinshi* exam in 1604, he had been appointed as the local magistrate in several prefectures. However, he is renowned in Chinese history as a bibliophile and garden designer.[82] He befriended Zhanran Yuancheng and helped him to revive Yunmen monastery. After he died, among his five sons, Qi Biaojia and Qi Junjia were most active in promoting Chan Buddhism.[83]

Qi Biaojia was a famous child prodigy of this time. When he was just seventeen years old, he passed the provincial exam and at twenty-one he received the *jinshi* degree. He was appointed as censor and governor of the Suzhou circuit and the Songjiang prefecture. He was a student of another Ming loyalist, Liu Zongzhou (1578–1645), and committed himself to Wang Yangming's learning of the mind. He and his brother Qi Junjia, who was a devout Buddhist, practiced meditation and discussed philosophical issues in Yunmen monastery, which was headed by Zhanran Yuancheng and his disciples.[84] When Beijing fell to Li Zhicheng and later to the Manchus in 1644, he joined the Southern Ming government in Nanjing.

Qi Biaojia also kept a good relationship with Miyun. According to Miyun's chronological biography, Qi Biaojia had been involved in inviting Miyun to Ayuwang monastery.[85] Later, both Qi Biaojia and Qi Junjia joined other literati to invite Miyun Yuanwu to Tiantong. Qi Biaojia's name was also listed among Miyun's many lay followers. The relation between Miyun Yuanwu and the Qi family must have been very close because in the winter of 1641 Miyun Yuanwu stayed in the private garden of the Qi family to recover from an illness.[86]

However, the Qi family was more closely associated with the Caodong lineage headed by Zhanran Yuancheng. After helping Zhanran to revive Yunmen monastery, the Qi family continued to support Zhanran's dharma heirs. For example, Qi Biaojia invited two of Zhanran's students, Shiyu Mingfang (1593–1648) and Er'mi Mingfu (1591–1642), to head Yunmen monastery.[87]

Qi Biaojia's other brothers also actively supported the Caodong masters. Qi Junjia, a *jinshi* degree holder as well, became a lay dharma heir of the Caodong master Sanyi Mingyu in 1638 and was given a dharma name: Jingchao. Evidence shows that the two other Qi brothers Qi Xiongjia and Qi Zhijia were also deeply involved in Caodong monks' monastic affairs. For example, during a controversy about dharma transmission in 1654, Qi Xiongjia wrote a preface for Sanyi Mingyu's rebuttal essay, and Qi Zhijia listed his name as one of the petitioners to ban Feiyin's work *Wudeng yantong*.[88]

Chan-minded Literati Becoming Martyrs

In 1645, the Manchu army marched to the south after capturing Beijing. Quickly, Nanjing was surrounded, and the first Southern Ming regime fell apart. The Eastern Zhejiang region was immediately threatened. Some local literati began to organize resistance movements. But many Ming officials, such as the famed literary man Qian Qianyi, chose to surrender and welcome the new ruler. Among a few exceptions, both Huang Duanbo and Qi Biaojiao, two of the most important patrons of Chan Buddhism in Eastern Zhejiang, died heroically for the Ming cause in 1645.

It is difficult to explain their deed by resorting to their close relationship with Chan Buddhism. However, as Huang Zongxi observed, some literati such as Huang Duanbo, Cai Maode (1586–1644), Ma Shiqi (1584–1644), Jin Sheng, and Qian Sule (1606–1648), who were close to Chan Buddhism, became the most adamant loyalists and were willing to sacrifice themselves to the lost Ming dynasty.[89] In addition to Huang Duanbo and Qi Biaojia, Huang Yuqi, often referred to as Miyun Yuanwu's only literati dharma heir, was also captured and killed after a covert plot of resistance was discovered.[90] Another Buddhist layman, Jin Sheng (1598–1645), joined the resistance movement after the fall of Nanjing. He was captured and later executed in Nanjing.[91] Qian Sule, grand secretary of Regent Lu of the Southern Ming regime, also befriended Chan monks, and after he died, he was buried at Mount Huangbo by Yinyuan Longqi.[92]

To explain this phenomenon, Huang Duanbo's Chan thought might offer some clues for his conscious choice of death. Although he was a minor figure in late Ming intellectual history, Huang Duanbo's radical Chan thought was close to that of Zhou Rudeng. For him, Chan meant nonduality in all aspects of life:

> It is all right to talk about filial piety; it is all right to talk about brotherly fraternity; it is also all right to be fond of bravery, sex, and profit. Then one will believe that brothels and wine shops are all the fields for pursuing the Way. [Only those who are] not obstructed by Buddhist precepts and cognitive knowledge are the ultimately enlightened.[93]

It is clear that Huang was deeply attracted by the Chan rhetoric of antinomi-anism. In this passage, Buddhist precepts and doctrines are described as obsta-cles for enlightenment while brothels and wine shops become the right places for self-cultivation and salvation as idealized in the *Vimalakīrti Sūtra*. Certainly, this does not mean that monks or literati actually deviated from monastic norms in their daily life. Rather, as Huang understood, all of these actions, no matter whether they are moral or immoral, depend on situations: For a fully enlight-ened person like Huang, he could visit brothels and wine shops if necessary; he could also face death courageously if sacrifice was called for. Huang proved his words at the fall of the Ming: In the face of the Manchu invasion, while most Southern Ming officials became turncoats, Huang chose to die as a martyr.[94]

In 1645, Huang served in the Ministry of Rites in the Southern Ming gov-ernment led by the prince of Fu. After the fall of Nanjing, the Manchu general Dodo (Duoduo, 1614–1649) offered amnesty to all former Ming officials who were willing to collaborate with the new regime and asked them to register in Prince Yu's (Dodo) tent. Not only was Huang among the few who declined the offer, he even put on a poster outside his house, declaring himself as a Ming loyalist. In the following, Frederic Wakeman describes Huang's heroism in the most vivid fashion:

> Huang Duanbo, on the other hand, chose a more defiant martyr's death. A protégé of Jiang Yueguang serving in the Ministry of Rites, Huang had sternly rejected one friend's advice to dress up as an old monk and escape to the hills, and had ostentatiously refused to attend Prince Yu's audience. The Manchu prince sent soldiers to bring Huang to him by force, but even then Huang refused to wear a hat or be politely obeisant in Dodo's presence. Dodo, who was said to have been impressed by Huang Duanbo's haughtiness, offered him a position. When Huang refused to accept it, Dodo asked him what kind of a ruler the Prince of Fu had been. "A sage ruler," responded Huang. On what basis had Huang decided this? "A son does not speak of a father's faults," Huang answered. Huang Duanbo even defended Ma Shiying to Dodo on the grounds that Ma, at least, had not surrendered to him: "'Not to surrender is what it means to be worthy [*xian*]." In the end Huang was executed, but the tale of his stubborn independence was carefully preserved by historians eager to find some evidence for scholarly integrity when Nanjing fell.[95]

As Wakeman suggests, after Huang died, he was soon enshrined as a paragon of loyalists among the literati. Soon after, Hangzhou was threatened. In despair, Qi Biaojia returned to his hometown of Shaoxing and drowned himself in his own family garden, following his Confucian teacher, Liu Zong-zhou. In his recent book on the late Ming figure Zhang Dai, who was Qi Biao-jia's good friend, Jonathan Spence describes Qi Biaojia's death as follows:

> Qi talked things over with his wife, put his affairs in order as well as
> he could, arranged for a large plot of family land to be given to the
> Buddhist monastery nearby and wrote the last entries in the diary he
> had kept meticulously for the previous fourteen years. On July 25, he
> had his son warm several cups of wine, and he invited a number of
> relatives and friends to visit. Then, as they departed, he summoned
> an old friend called Zhu Shanren to talk with him . . . . . . [After their
> talk,] Qi himself, however, walked to the Baqiu Pavilion and wrote a
> farewell letter in the great hall of his ancestors there. He then wrote
> a short will, which read: "My loyalty as a subject demands my death.
> For fifteen years, I have served the Ming ruling family with great
> loyalty. Those who have attained higher intelligence than I might not
> wish to end their lives in this lowly fashion but I, a dull scholar, can
> find no alternative." He wrote these words in red ink and then threw
> himself into a nearby river. [96]

As Spence depicts in his skillful narratives, at the last moment of this life, as a Confucian scholar deeply influenced by Chan Buddhism, Qi didn't forget to leave a fortune for the Buddhist monastery nearby, which must be Yunmen monastery patronized by his father, himself, and his brothers. He drowned himself in the shallow water in his beloved garden and close to his treasured library, which he would rather give up for a higher moral purpose. Maybe for him, as well as for Huang Duanbo, the Buddhist sense of emptiness did help him to make the final decision to step into the eternal realm of nonduality, and only in appearance his suicide made perfect moral sense in the Confucian world. After Qi Biaojia died, the Qi family declined. But some of his sons remained defiant to the Qing conquerors. They continued to patronize Chan Buddhism, and it was rumored that even the Qi family's book collection had been given away to Buddhist monks in Yunmen monastery.[97]

Conclusion

There is little doubt that through the Confucian literati's promotion, Chan Buddhism gained momentum in the seventeenth century. As Araki Kengo repeatedly points out in his works on Confucianism and Buddhism in the late

Ming, "it may not be wrong to state that for the development of the School of Wang Yangming Buddhism was necessary and for the popularization of Buddhism the School of Wang Yangming was indispensable." According to Araki, the evolution of Chan Buddhism in the late Ming had not only "kept pace with" the development of Wang Yangming's learning of the mind but also "owed much to Wang Yangming's theory of innate knowledge."[98]

Similar to Araki, I regard the impact of Wang Yangming's intellectual movement in Chan communities as one of the impetuses for the reinvention of Chan Buddhism.

However, readers must bear in mind that, during this period, there were no full-fledged Chan communities or eminent Chan teachers who actively promoted such an intellectual discourse. Rather, the Chan craze in the literati culture was largely a product of the prevailing publishing culture that catered to the taste of a reading public, among whom a shared view about Chan was formed and spread further within various communities connected by reading, writing, and publishing Chan texts. As I will further elaborate in chapter 10, these communities were largely textual communities in which a shared hermeneutical view was commonly held to interpret Chan texts. Some Buddhist monks, as members of these communities, accepted such a view as well and developed their monastic communities based on this view, which was largely imaginative and rhetorical. As I have shown in this chapter, the early Chan communities emerged in Eastern Zhejiang, where the literati promoted the Chan masters they favored.

Here, the issue of religious reading looms large because the literati's understanding of Chan was largely a romantic imagining based on their leisure reading of Chan texts. Some of these Confucian literati, without serious interest in everyday monastic routines, such as liturgical services, observance of precepts, and ordination, envisioned Chan as iconoclastic and antinomian, exactly as the authors of numerous Chan texts wanted their readers to believe. Evidence shows that some members of Wang Yangming's movement played pivotal roles in nurturing Chan ideals in monastic communities. I tend to call the religious experience generated purely from reading and writing religious texts "textual spirituality" to distinguish it from a more devotion-oriented type of religiosity.

In the next chapter, I will demonstrate the full-fledged recovery of the Chan tradition, characterized by clear sectarian identities and the practice of dharma transmission in a more strict sense.

3

The Rise of Chan Buddhism

As demonstrated in previous chapters, Chan Buddhism did not become a full-fledged movement until the 1630s. Some late Ming literati, such as Huang Zongxi, whose observation on the rise of Chan was quoted in chapter 1, witnessed the growth of Chan and were startled to see such a sudden surge because a few decades before there were very few active Chan masters. Chen Danzhong (*jinshi* 1643), a lay disciple of the Caodong master Juelang Daosheng and an accomplished seal carver and painter, also saw a surprising increase in the number of Chan masters, as he stated in the following in his "*Xixiebian* yin" (Introduction to *Xixiebian*):

> During the Wanli period, [Chan Buddhism] was transmit-
> ted in an obscure way and the Chan style was not greatly
> promoted. Even the three great masters Daguan (Zibo
> Zhenko), Lianchi (Yunqi Zhuhong), and Hanshan [Deqing],
> whose practice and understanding corresponded to each
> other, did not hold the white stick and ascend to the
> patriarch seat. This is because they were prudent. The "old
> Buddha" Shouchang (Wuming Huijing) came to be known
> in the world in Jiangxi and the monk Boshan (Wuyi
> Yuanlai) at Dongyuan succeeded him. Meanwhile, the
> masters Yunmen (Zhanran Yuancheng) and Tiantong
> (Miyun Yuanwu) also rose in Eastern Zhejiang. Then,
> Chan Buddhism became prominent. . . . In the recent

twenty years, within the Buddhist world, there are as many as six to
seven hundred people who claimed that they have been offered
whisks (*fuzi*, that is, the token for dharma transmission).[1]

Because the author wrote this comment shortly after 1654, the recent
Chan boom to which he referred must have occurred between the 1630s and
1650s. He observed that in the late Ming, eminent monks such as Zibo
Zhenke, Yunqi Zhuhong, and Hanshan Deqing intended to revive Chan by
advocating a joint practice of Chan and Pure Land. However, after these masters died, the Chan revival entered into a new phase and a group of new Chan
figures, amounting to 600–700 people, according to Chen Danzhong, dominated the Buddhist world.

The Chan revival cut across the Ming-Qing transition. To a large extent,
the dynastic change from Ming to Qing did not interrupt the development of
Chan Buddhism. During this period, Chan Buddhism continued to grow and
its connection with society was even strengthened. Buddhist institutions became sanctuaries for disheartened literati, and many Ming loyalists, either
deliberately or having been forced, chose the life of Buddhist monks to avoid
the embarrassment of surrendering to the culturally "inferior" Manchu rulers. For most of them, the ideal of withdrawal in Buddhism, as Timothy Brook
has aptly pointed out, fit perfectly into the imagined world of Confucian eremitism, a justified alternative for ambitious Confucians who had failed to fulfill their own social and cultural ideals. Thus, some dejected literati were ordained and accepted dharma transmission from either Caodong or Linji. There
is no doubt that this new wave of conversion, regardless of these literati's motivation, boosted Chan Buddhism in the seventeenth century. These literati
monks further strengthened the ties between Chan Buddhism and society
and brought new changes into Chan communities.

In the seventeenth century, Chan masters in the Linji and Caodong lineages became prominent in the Buddhist world through spreading their
dharma transmissions. Some famous Chan masters attracted many followers
and by bestowing their dharma transmission, these followers extended their
teachers' influence in the same way. At the end of the century, the two Chan
lineages, especially Linji, were well established in southwest, southeast, and
north China. In this chapter, I will introduce influential Chan masters in both
the Linji and Caodong lineages and through them track the growth of Chan
Buddhism from a regional network to a national one. Being aware of the motives and intentions of some hagiographical modes of description in monks'
standard biographies, I have consulted other sources, such as chronological
biographies, monks' autobiographies, and monastic gazetteers, to recount the

lives of these monks. My intention is not to provide standard biographies for these monks. Rather, I hope that by introducing these figures I can reveal the process of Chan growth and the success of an idealized Chan style.[2] In addition, it is important to introduce these figures because they were the major protagonists in the controversies I focus on in this book.

The Rise of the Linji School

Most Buddhist controversies in the seventeenth century were related to the Linji school, whose transmission line belonged to the Yangqi branch that developed during the Northern Song.[3] This branch was greatly promoted by the Song master Yuanwu Keqin's two heirs Dahui Zonggao and Huqiu Shaolong in the Southern Song. Although Dahui was much more famous, the dharma transmissions of most Linji monks in the seventeenth century derived from Huqiu Shaolong, leaving Dahui's lineage a collateral branch. During the Yuan, Huqiu Shaolong's transmission was once again greatly expanded by Zhongfeng Mingben (1263–1323), who revived and promoted the Linji school as the orthodox tradition.[4]

This line of Linji transmission became obscure again in the early and mid-Ming until during the Wanli reign the Linji master Xiaoyan Debao claimed that he held the unbroken transmission in this lineage. One of his dharma heirs was Huanyou Zhengchuan,[5] from whom three prominent Linji masters derived and greatly promoted the Linji transmissions. They were Tianyin Yuanxiu, Xuejiao Yuanxin, and Miyun Yuanwu. Tianyin Yuanxiu's influence was largely expanded through his disciples Ruo'an Tongwen (?–1655) and Yulin Tongxiu (1614–1675). Yulin Tongxiu was summoned by the Shunzhi emperor in 1658 and was bestowed with honorary titles. Tianyin Yuanxiu's lineage was also called the Panshan transmission.[6] Xuejiao Yuanxin was influential among the literati, and he compiled the *Wujia yulu*, in which he collected the recorded sayings of five Chan masters in the late Tang and the Five Dynasties. However, his dharma transmission was controversial because he claimed to be descended from the Yunmen school, which was defunct in the late Ming. He left no dharma heirs according to some genealogies.[7]

In addition to these two figures, Miyun Yuanwu was a pivotal figure. Not only did his dharma heirs significantly outnumber those of other lineages, but his dharma heirs also composed many influential Chan historical works, such as the *Wudeng yantong* and *Wudeng quanshu* (The complete genealogy of the five Chan schools). Since Miyun Yuanwu's Chan lineage became multibranched as a result of dharma transmission, it is impossible to trace the development of

all of his descendants. In this section, I introduce him, along with several influential disciples who were involved in the controversies.

Miyun Yuanwu

According to his chronological biography compiled by Feiyin Tongrong, Miyun Yuanwu was born in the Jiang family in Yixing county of Changzhou
prefecture. He attended a village school at the age of six but disliked studying
Confucian classics. At eight, he began to recite the Buddha's name without
instructions from anybody. When he was fifteen years old, he was forced to
take up farming and fishing to support himself. He married at sixteen. The
moment of revelation came when he was twenty-one. After reading the *Platform Sūtra*, he was immediately attracted by Chan teaching. In 1594, at twenty-
nine, he abandoned his wife and family to join the Buddhist order.

After he was ordained, he closely followed his master Huanyou Zhengchuan and gradually gained his trust. He was appointed as the manager of Yuwang monastery in Changzhou after his master traveled to Beijing in 1603.
During this time, he reached sudden enlightenment when he passed Mount
Tongguan.[8] Later, he was summoned to Beijing to help his teacher there. The
turning point of his career occurred in 1607 when he visited Zhou Rudeng
and Tao Wangling, who admired his iconoclastic Chan style.

As I introduced in the previous chapter, in the early seventeenth century,
Zhou Rudeng and Tao Wangling were active in Eastern Zhejiang as leaders of
Wang Yangming's movement. They organized various kinds of lecture meetings, to which Buddhist monks were often invited. Miyun's chronological biography records that in 1607, after serving his master in Beijing for two years, Miyun
returned to the south and traveled to many famous monasteries. On his way to
Mount Tiantai in Zhejiang, he visited Zhou Rudeng in Shaoxing, the birthplace
of Wang Yangming. The welcome he received was unexpected. Not only did
Zhou Rudeng express his admiration, but Miyun also became acquainted with
other renowned literati, such as Tao Wangling. In the following year, he was invited to live at Tao's private temple, called the Chapel of Preserving Life (*Husheng
an*). At this time, although Miyun had not become Huanyou Zhengchuan's formal dharma heir, his fame as an authentic Chan master had spread widely.

The reason for this unprecedented welcome was that Miyun had demonstrated an idealized Chan style that Zhou and Tao, as proponents of Wang
Yangming's teaching, deeply admired. In addition to the story about his unusual encounter with Zhou Rudeng, which I described in the previous chapter, here is another example of his teaching. When Miyun lived in Tao Wangling's private cloister in 1608, a celebrated patron visited him. When this

patron saw that Miyun was reading the *Analects* and *Mencius*, he scolded Miyun, saying, "They are none of your business." On hearing this, Miyun immediately slapped his face. Of course, the patron was irritated. He was not pacified until Tao Wangling explained to him that Miyun was treating him in a Chan Buddhist way and that no offense was meant.[9]

When Miyun's master Huanyou Zhengchuan came back from Beijing, he gave Miyun the dharma robe and recognized him as his dharma heir. Miyun's career after 1607 was extremely successful. After observing the three-year mourning period for his master's death, he succeeded to the abbacy of Yuwang monastery in Mount Longchi in 1617; in 1624, he moved to Mount Jinsu; in 1630, he became the abbot of Mount Huangbo; and in 1631, he was invited to Ayuwang monastery. In the same year, he moved to Tiantong monastery; in 1641, he was granted the honorific purple robe by the imperial court and was appointed abbot of Bao'en monastery, a famous institution in Nanjing, although he declined the appointment later. At his death in 1642, he had about 300 disciples ordained through him and twelve certified dharma heirs.

In addition to his excessive use of beating and shouting as training methods, his success lay in his superb talent for monastic administration. His talent was demonstrated in a series of projects he undertook to revive Tiantong monastery. As Timothy Brook has documented, before Miyun Yuanwu was invited to Tiantong, the monastery was in terrible shape as the result of a great flood in 1587. Miyun Yuanwu first produced a monastic gazetteer, which was published in 1633, to restore the popular faith in this famous Chan monastery. From 1635 to 1641, Tiantong was completely rebuilt. As the late Ming literatus Zhang Dai (1597–1689) observed in 1638, the total population of both clergy and craftsmen at Tiantong amounted to 1,500 people, and they were well organized and well supervised.[10] Zhang's observation is confirmed by the existence of some relics in Tiantong monastery from his time. For example, figure 3.1 shows a huge iron wok named the "Wok for a Thousand Monks" (*qiansengguo*), which was cast in 1641, according to its inscription.

While the number of residents swelled, the amount of land owned by the monastery increased as well. To a large extent, Miyun Yuanwu, whose successors continued his work of renovation, created the layout of the present-day Tiantong monastery. (Figure 3.2 shows the entrance hall of Tiantong monastery, whose name was handwritten by Miyun in 1635.) As Ishii Shūdō points out, from 1631 to 1724, Miyun Yuanwu and his dharma heirs controlled the monastery by appointing abbots from within their lineage.[11] In this sense, Miyun was interested in expanding and perpetuating his influence, and recruiting qualified dharma heirs became one of his major concerns. (Because his heir Feiyin Tongrong's disciple Yinyuan Longqi became the founder of the Japanese Ōbaku school, Miyun was

FIGURE 3.1. "Wok for a Thousand Monks" in Tiantong monastery, cast in 1641. Photograph by Jiang Wu, June 2006.

worshiped in Manpukuji in Uji, Tokyo. Figure 3.3 is his portrait painted by a Japanese painter.) During the seventeenth century, influential Linji Chan branches were derived from the following dharma heirs of Miyun Yuanwu.

Hanyue Fazang

Hanyue was born into a literati family in Wuxi. His chronological biography records that his decision to join the Buddhist order was triggered by his reading of Zhuhong's essay on releasing animals when he was only nine years old.[12] At fifteen, he became a novice in the local Deqing monastery. By twenty-three, he was famous as a Buddhist monk with excellent knowledge of Confucian classics. However, at twenty-eight, Hanyue realized that the study of Confucian classics could never lead him to enlightenment, and from then on, he became eager to achieve enlightenment through self-cultivation and studying with renowned Buddhist masters. His first enlightenment experience finally came in 1613 during a hundred-day intensive solitary confinement (*biguan*) when he was forty years old. At that time, Hanyue's fame was already widespread, and famous literati like Qian Qianyi had inquired of him about spiritual issues. He was also a celebrated poet.[13] Confucian scholars such as Gu Xiancheng (1550–1612) and Qian Yiben (1539–1610), who were associated with the political circle of the Donglin school, admired him. At Yushan in Suzhou, he attracted a large number of literati followers.

FIGURE 3.2. The entrance hall of Tiantong monastery. The plaque "Tianwang Hall" was written by Miyun Yuanwu in 1635. Photograph by Jiang Wu, June 2006.

FIGURE 3.3. Portrait of Miyun Yuanwu. Detail. Original 109.3 cm × 50.5 cm. Painted by Kita Genki. Reprint from *Ōbaku Ingen* (Uji: Manpukuji, 1992), p. 7. Courtesy of Manpukuji.

Because his views about Chan principles and practice differed from Mi-yun's, he sought for and received Miyun's dharma transmission in the 1630s with some reluctance. (His clash with Miyun is the main topic of chapter 4.) After Hanyue's death in 1635, his lineage continued to grow, and among his disciples, Jiqi Hongchu (1605–1672) became most prominent. It should be also noted that within Hanyue's lineage, many female disciples, such as Qiyuan Xinggang (1597–1654), Yikui Chaochen (1625–1679), Baochi Jizong (b. 1606), and Zukui Jifu, became his second- or third- generation dharma heirs.[14]

Hanyue's lineage took a dramatic turn in the early eighteenth century when the Yongzheng emperor revived the controversy between Miyun and Hanyue and condemned Hanyue's lineage. As a result, Hanyue's dharma descendants were not allowed to be abbots. However, according to Hasebe Yūkei's study, after the emperor died in 1735, Hanyue's lineage was restored.[15]

Muchen Daomin

Starting in the Shunzhi reign (1644–1661), some of Miyun Yuanwu's dharma heirs managed to receive unprecedented imperial patronage from the new rulers. Muchen Daomin, one of Miyun Yuanwu's leading dharma heirs, was granted the title of national preceptor by the Shunzhi emperor and was allowed personal audiences with the emperor in 1659.[16]

Muchen Daomin (secular name: Lin Li) was a native of Dapu in Guang-dong. Though a Confucian student in his youth, he was determined to become a monk against his parents' will. Finally, he was ordained in Lushan and later received complete ordination from Hanshan Deqing. Because of his literary skills and education as a Confucian student, he served Miyun as literary scribe (*shuji*) for almost ten years and exerted his own influence in many of Miyun's writings. After Miyun's death, Muchen Daomin managed to control Mount Tiantong, the center of Chan Buddhism in south China at that time. In addition to his tenure there, he served as abbot in several other monasteries.[17]

The turning point of Muchen Daomin's career occurred in 1659 when he was summoned to Beijing by the Shunzhi emperor, who received various kinds of religious influences, including Christianity through Jesuit missionaries like Adam Schall von Bell (1592–1666). During intimate conversations with Muchen Daomin, the emperor showed tremendous interest in Chan Buddhism, as recorded in Muchen's book *Beiyou ji* (Collections of northern excursion).[18] Delighted with Muchen's responses, the emperor honored a portrait of Muchen Daomin's teacher, Miyun Yuanwu, and allowed Miyun's recorded sayings to be included in the imperial canon.[19] Muchen Daomin was bestowed with honorary titles and his disciples were appointed as abbots in big monasteries in Beijing.

After his short stay in the capital, he returned to the south with the emperor's blessing. He also brought back some calligraphic works by the emperor. As shown in figure 3.4, one of them, written as *jingfo* (Revering the Buddha), was inscribed on a stele and was erected in Tiantong monastery.

Shortly after the fall of the Ming, Muchen Daomin showed great sympathy toward the lost Ming cause and befriended many Ming loyalists. However, after his audience with the emperor, he became a supporter of the new regime and publicly boasted of his close relationship with the emperor. His ostentatious display of royal patronage brought him into conflict with other literati followers and monks who still clung nostalgically to the lost Ming dynasty. Such self-promotion incurred resentment from the imperial government as well. In 1735, the Yongzheng emperor condemned him for exposing the personal life of the former emperor and banned his book *Beiyou ji*. Only Yongzheng's admiration for his teacher, Miyun Yuanwu, and the Shunzhi emperor's interest in him prevented Muchen's lineage from being eliminated.[20] Because Muchen Daomin turned quickly from a loyalist monk to a national preceptor in the Manchu regime, his fellow Buddhists denounced him as a "Buddhist sinner."

Muchen Daomin's role in the controversies to be discussed was decisive. As Miyun's personal scribe, he often wrote essays and personal correspondence

FIGURE 3.4. Calligraphy by the Shunzhi emperor in 1660, Tiantong monastery. Photograph by Jiang Wu, June 2006.

on Miyun's behalf and thus became directly involved in many conflicts with other monks. The *Chandeng shipu,* for example, nominally authored by Miyun but actually edited by Muchen Daomin, was one of the early works that kindled the controversy about the two Daowus.

Feiyin Tongrong

Feiyin Tongrong was a native of Fuqing county, where Huangbo monastery was located. Unlike Miyun, whose career as a Buddhist monk started when he entered adulthood, Feiyin became a monk when he was fourteen. After his parents died, his relatives sent him to a local monastery. Although he later became a Linji master, he first studied with the Caodong masters. From the time he was eighteen, Feiyin was a student of Caodong monks, such as Zhanran Yuancheng, Wuming Huijing, and Wuyi Yuanlai.[21]

Although Feiyin favored the antinomian Chan style, his interest in performing kōan did not blend with the Caodong teaching very well, and his fellow Caodong monks, who favored solid practice in meditation, incantation, and doctrinal studies, often opposed and ridiculed him. For example, Feiyin used to study with a renowned monk whom he believed to have reached enlightenment. During their conversation, this monk asked Feiyin about the meaning of the seamless pagoda (*Wufengta*).[22] Feiyin responded with hand clapping, imitating some kōan stories. This monk then warned him: "Try to learn to be honest!" However, Feiyin replied: "Considering that you are elderly, I will just give you thirty blows!" Feiyin thus left him with disappointment.[23]

After about ten years of Chan practice under Caodong masters, Feiyin left the Caodong lineage and turned to Linji. In 1621, Feiyin read Miyun's recorded sayings and was immediately drawn to Miyun, greatly admiring his teaching because it reflected an understanding of Chan literature similar to his own. Later, Feiyin visited Miyun and thus had a meaningful encounter with Miyun. During their encounter, no discursive dialogue was involved. Shouts and blows, though appearing a little bit violent, conveyed their understanding of Chan.[24] When he studied with Caodong masters, Feiyin never experienced such a feeling of a "match" and approval. After their meeting, Feiyin burned all of the doctrinal essays he had written and began to concentrate solely on Chan literature.[25] He admired Miyun so much that he was determined to request Miyun's dharma transmission.

After following Miyun Yuanwu for several years, Feiyin finally received Miyun's transmission in Huangbo monastery during Miyun's brief residence there.[26] In 1631, Miyun arrived in Fuqing county by the sea. In the seventh month of that year, Miyun conferred on Feiyin the certificate of dharma transmission, a whisk, and a robe during a public ceremony. When Miyun left in

FIGURE 3.5. Portrait of Feiyin Tongrong. Detail. Original 109.3 cm × 50.5 cm. Painted by Kita Genki. Reprint from *Ōbaku Ingen* (Uji: Manpukuji, 1992), p. 8. Courtesy of Manpukuji.

the eighth month, Feiyin was invited to Mafeng cloister in Fujian. But in 1633, he was invited back to Huangbo monastery as abbot.

After his three-year tenure in Huangbo monastery, Feiyin Tongrong's career was extremely successful. In 1638, he was invited to Jinsu monastery in Zhejiang; in 1647, he was invited to Tiantong. In 1650, he presided over Fuyan monastery. It seems that during the 1650s Feiyin's career reached its height. He traveled among famous Chan centers in Zhejiang and exerted his influence on clerical affairs. It was exactly at this time that he planned the polemical book *Wudeng yantong*, which later caused turmoil in the Buddhist world and led to his failure and frustration. He died in 1662 and left sixty-four certified dharma heirs. Because his dharma heir Yinyuan Longqi established himself in Japan, Feiyin was also revered in the Japanese Ōbaku school. Figure 3.5 shows his portrait by a Japanese painter.

The Rise of the Caodong School

The Caodong monks in the seventeenth century claimed that their transmissions could be traced back to the Song master Furong Daokai and his disciples.[27] This lineage was active in both north and south China when the north was occupied by Kitans and Jurchens. In the north, Wansong Xingxiu, in particular, received royal patronage from the nomad rulers. One of his disciples, Xueting Fuyu, was appointed abbot of the famed Shaolin monastery and greatly promoted the Caodong school. Since then, despite the decline of Buddhism during the early and mid-Ming, the Caodong transmission in Shaolin monastery is believed to have been maintained without disruption.

In the late Ming, the Caodong monks in Shaolin became active again, and their transmissions were sought after. Most Caodong lineages in the seventeenth century were derived from two figures who received their transmission from Shaolin: Zhanran Yuancheng and Wuming Huijing. These two masters attracted a large number of followers, especially among the literati. They were acclaimed by these literati as revivers of the Chan spirit that was rarely seen in Chan communities before. By conferring dharma transmissions on capable disciples, the Caodong lineage grew rapidly in Zhejiang, Fujian, and Guangdong.

Although both Linji and Caodong monks boasted of their capability of performing encounter dialogues spontaneously, the revived Caodong tradition was often more conservative than Linji, if we compare the two. For example, with regard to the use of dharma transmission as a means to expand the lineage, the Caodong masters maintained a much smaller group of dharma heirs and offered dharma transmission more cautiously and selectively to candidates. This is probably why the Caodong lineage, largely confined in the southeast, was not spread as far as the Linji lineage was. However, the Caodong tradition did benefit from such a selective policy: Its dharma heirs were often accomplished in doctrinal studies, and many erudite literati were attracted to the tradition.

A number of Caodong monks were involved in the dispute over Feiyin Tongrong's *Wudeng yantong*, as I will explain in detail in part III. In addition to this controversy, these Caodong masters engaged in various internal disputes over dharma transmission with their fellow monks, as I document in appendix 2.A. In this section, I will provide brief introductions to some major Caodong figures.

Zhanran Yuancheng and His Lineage

Zhanran Yuancheng was born in Kuaiji county of Shaoxing prefecture in Zhejiang. He received precepts from Yunqi Zhuhong and studied with many Chan masters. When he was thirty years old, he had an enlightenment experience, which was later acknowledged as a genuine one by Zhuhong. Similar to Miyun Yuanwu, his rise in the Zhejiang area was also closely connected with such famous literati as Zhou Rudeng and Tao Wangling, who promoted Chan Buddhism.

As a Caodong master, Zhanran was famous for using "words of true color" (*benseyu*) to train students.[28] These words refer to his teaching of kōan stories during the ceremony of ascending the hall. During these ceremonies, Zhanran often explained the meaning of a kōan story. Sometimes, he interacted sponta- neosly with students. For example, when a monk visited him, he asked: "How do you understand your pilgrim tour?" The monk drew a perfect circle on the ground. Zhanran scratched the circle and the monk knocked on the table three times. Then, Zhanran also drew a perfect circle, and the monk knocked the table twice. Again, Zhanran drew three circles, and the monk wiped them out with his hands. Zhanran said: "Beyond this, please say a sentence [to explain]!" When the monk was about to speak, Zhanran gave a shout.[29]

Zhanran Yuancheng rebuilt Yunmen monastery at Kuaiji with help from the Qi family. He left eight dharma heirs who were active in the Zhejiang area. Among them, Shiyu Mingfang (1593–1648), Sanyi Mingyu (1599–1665), and Ruibai Mingxue (1584–1641) were the most famous. To some extent, all of them were involved in the controversy of 1654 by writing essays critical of Feiyin Tongrong's stance on dharma transmission. Eventually, they brought the case to the local government. Shiyu Mingfang's heir, Weizhong Jingfu, was particu- larly active in the polemics. He wrote *Famen chugui* to refute Feiyin Tongrong and the *Wudeng quanshu*, compiled by Linji monks. He also compiled a contro- versial new genealogy for the entire Caodong lineage, *Zudeng datong* (The great compendium of ancestral lamps), causing a dispute among the Caodong monks. (I will briefly discuss the content of this book in appendix 2.A.)

Wuming Huijing and His Lineage

Another famous Caodong master was Wuming Huijing (1548–1618). Accord- ing to his biography written by Hanshan Deqing, when he was twenty-one, Wuming Huijing was determined to leave his family after reading the *Dia- mond Sūtra*. In order to achieve enlightenment, he lived in solitude for three years. He was finally enlightened at the age of twenty-seven, and he spent the next twenty-four years living in the mountains by farming, obviously model- ing his monastic practice on Baizhang Huaihai (720–814), who was believed to have started a self-reliant labor tradition (*nongchan*) in Chan communities. Only when he was fifty-one years old, in 1598, did he accept the invitation from Baofeng monastery to become its abbot. Since he had never left his hometown to travel, as a Chan monk usually did, he decided to begin his pilgrimage tour of China. During his trip, he met many famous monks, including Zibo Zhenke. His biography records that he had studied with the Caodong master Yunkong Changzhong (1514–1588).[30]

After returning to the south, he began to claim himself a Caodong master publicly. Under his leadership, Shouchang monastery in Xincheng of Jianchang prefecture in Jiangxi was revived. This reconstruction, however, was not like the usual one under the sponsorship of literati patrons. Rather, he completed the project through the communal labor of the Chan monks living in the monastery. Wuming Huijing maintained this tradition, resonating with Baizhang's work ethic, even when he was in his sixties. The revival of this tradition won him the sobriquet "the ancient Buddha of Shouchang monastery."[31]

Wuming Huijing's Chan teaching was praised as "singly lifting upwards" (*danti xiangshang*). His recorded sayings are full of encounter dialogues with students. For instance, during one session of the ceremony of ascending the hall, the rector announced: "Please contemplate the supreme meaning!" Wuming Huijing shouted, "Do the masses understand the supreme meaning? If not, please turn to the secondary meaning." Again, he shouted.[32]

Within his lineage, Chan masters were prudent in selecting dharma heirs. Unlike Miyun Yuanwu and his disciples, who often had dozens of dharma heirs, the number of Wuming Huijing's disciples was limited. Among his four dharma heirs, Wuyi Yuanlai, Huitai Yuanjing, and Yongjue Yuanxian were active in Jiangxi and Fujian. Yongjue Yuanxian and his only heir, Weilin Daopei (1615–1702), were instrumental in reviving Gushan monastery in Fuzhou, which became an important Buddhist center in southeast China. Gushan's influence on monastic practice in mainland China and Taiwan can be felt even today.[33]

One of Huitai Yuanjing's dharma heirs, Juelang Daosheng (1592–1659), was particularly active in the seventeenth century. As a thinker well versed in both Buddhism and Confucianism, he intended to construct a philosophical system based on Buddhist teaching and Confucian thought in *The Book of Changes*.[34] Emphasizing the role of "fire" among the "five natural agents" (*wuhang*) as the ontological substance of the universe, he believed that during the Ming-Qing transition, in order to put the disrupted society in order one had to rely on the power of fire to rectify people's minds and to transform the "rancor" (*yuan*) toward the status quo into positive forces. He was also one of the plaintiffs who sued Feiyin Tongrong in 1654. In addition, the lineage of Wuming Huijing's disciple Wuyi Yuanlai also enjoyed great popularity in Jiangxi and Guangdong areas, as we will see in the next section.

The Further Spread of Chan Buddhism

The Chan masters introduced in the previous two sections were often revered as the "renaissance patriarchs" (*zhongxing zi zu*) of the lineages they started. After several generations of dharma transmission, Chan Buddhism moved beyond its original birthplaces and quickly spread to other areas. Also notable were the Chan missions overseas. Meanwhile, after the fall of the Ming, a number of celebrated literati joined the Buddhist order and received dharma transmissions from established Chan masters.

From Regional to National to Overseas

The spread of Chan shows a clear pattern of expansion from regional to national and then to overseas. After Miyun's death in 1642, his lineage enjoyed unparalleled growth throughout the rest of the seventeenth century. The spread of his lineage took advantage of the internal migration of the population and Chinese emigration overseas, which was forced by the Manchu conquest.

In Fujian, Miyun Yuanwu's lineage had a strong presence because two of his disciples, Feiyin Tongrong and Yinyuan Longqi, were natives of Fuqing, where Mount Huangbo was located. In 1630, Miyun was invited to be the abbot at Mount Huangbo. After he left, eight months later, Feiyin succeeded him, and after Feiyin his dharma heir Yinyuan Longqi took the position. With Mount Huangbo as a base, Feiyin's and Yinyuan's dharma heirs took control of many local temples in Fujian.

While the Southern Ming government gradually retreated from the southeast coast to the southwest after 1644, Chan Buddhism also spread from southeast to southwest, quickly occupying and revitalizing major local monasteries. Among all of the lineages, Miyun Yuanwu's lineage flourished in Sichuan, Yunnan, and Guizhou through the efforts of his dharma heir Poshan Haiming (1577–1666),[35] who revived Chan Buddhism in southwest China. After becoming Miyun's first dharma heir in 1627, Poshan Haiming returned to Sichuan in 1633 and lived in Taiping monastery in Liangshan. Following Miyun's Chan style of beating and shouting, he attracted a great number of followers. During the periods of Zhang Xianzhong's (1606–1646) peasant rebellion and the Manchu conquest, his influence continued to grow, and through the efforts of his disciples, such as Zhangxue Tongzui (1610–1693) and Xiangya Xingting (1598–1651), his lineage spread to the entire southwest. The Chinese scholar Chen Yuan conducted meticulous studies of Buddhism in Yunnan and Guizhou during the late Ming and early Qing. According to his statistics, in southern Guizhou alone, among 121 Chan masters, 110 belonged to Poshan Haiming's lineage.[36]

To the north, the influence of Chan Buddhism reached Beijing and drew attention from the young Shunzhi emperor, who had great interest in Buddhism.[37] At that time, Feiyin Tongrong's second-generation dharma heir Hanpu Xingcong (1610–1666) was in Beijing. During a hunting trip in 1657, the emperor met him and became attracted to Chan Buddhism. In 1658, the emperor asked Hanpu Xingcong to recommend famous Chan masters in the south to the court. Thus, the Manchu emperor's interest in Chan brought Linji Chan Buddhism from the south to the north: Yulin Tongxiu, a dharma heir of Miyun Yuanwu's dharma brother Tianyin Yuanxiu, was summoned to Beijing in 1659 and was rewarded with honorary titles. Meanwhile, Miyun Yuanwu's dharma heir Muchen Daomin was also invited to Beijing. The disciples of these two masters were appointed to be abbots in monasteries of national prestige.

The Caodong lineage was more popular in Guangdong due to the effort of Wuyi Yuanlai's dharma heir Zongbao Daodu (1600–1661), who attracted some young literati such as Zuxin Hanke (hao. Shengren; secular name: Han Zonglai, 1611–1659), who was ordained in 1639. After the fall of the Ming, Zuxin Hanke remained defiant of the new regime. He was thus persecuted in a literary inquisition and was sent into exile to Mount Qianshan in Liaoning.[38] Another Zongbao Daodu's dharma heir, Tianran Hanshi (1608–1685), further extended his teacher's influence in Guangdong. He resided in Guangxiao monastery in Guangzhou in 1649.[39] In addition to Daodu's lineage, his dharma brother Liji Daoqiu (1586–1685) and Daoqiu's disciple Zaisan Hongzan (1611–1681) developed Mount Dinghu in Zhaoqing as a new Buddhist center. Although they continued Wuyi Yuanlai's Caodong dharma transmission, Liji Daoqiu and his followers were famous for observing strict Vinaya rules and spreading proper ordination procedures.[40]

Among all of the Caodong teachers in Guangdong, Shilian Dashan (1633–1702) was perhaps the most famous. He claimed to have received Juelang Daosheng's transmission, but he was never officially acknowledged as such in Chan genealogies. He was prominent in Guangzhou and Macau not only as a Caodong master but also as a skillful painter and garden designer. Residing in Changshou monastery in Guangzhou, he attracted a group of Ming loyalists, such as Qu Dajun (1630–1696). Following his teacher Juelang Daosheng, Shilian Dashan also joined the debate by writing several polemical essays, which I will briefly discuss in chapter 9.

It is clear that after the Manchu conquest, Chan Buddhism continued to grow in China. Miyun's Linji lineage in particular achieved prestige at the national level. More notable, Chan Buddhism further extended to Vietnam and Japan along with a new wave of Chinese emmigration resulting from the political turmoil of the Ming-Qing transition.

The Linji lineage was brought to Vietnam by Shouzun Yuanzhao (1647–1729), a dharma heir of Muchen Daomin's disciple Kuangyuan Benkao. He came to Vietnam in 1665 and founded the Nguyên-Thiêu tradition within the Lâm-Tê (Chinese: Linji) school in Vietnam. According to Thich Thien-An, Shouzun Yuanzhao was ordained at nineteen. In 1665, he sought refuge in

Vietnam after the Manchu conquest of China. He arrived in Bình-Đinh province and founded the Thâp-Tháp Di- Đà monastery. Later, he settled in Hué, the capital of the Nguyên regime, and built Hà-Trung monastery and Quôc-Ân monastery. He is regarded by the Vietnamese Buddhist tradition as the founder of the Nguyên-Thiêu school of Thiên (Chinese: Ch'an; Japanese: Zen) because the two lineages derived from him dominated the Vietnamese Thiên tradition. The Lâm-Tê tradition which he transmitted from China to Vietnam is the largest Buddhist order in the country.[41]

The Caodong lineage also became influential in Vietnam during Shilian Dashan's visit in 1695. Shilian Dashan sailed to central Vietnam in 1695 at the request of the Vietnamese ruler, Nguyên Phúc Chu (1674–1725), who had based his government at Hué. Shilian Dashan not only offered the Triple Platform Ordination Ceremony for Vietnamese Buddhist monks but also converted the Vietnamese king and named him the thirtieth-generation Caodong dharma heir.[42]

Taking advantage of the frequent trade connection between Nagasaki and the southeast coast of China, monks arrived in Japan in the early seventeenth century. After 1644, more and more established Chan masters with dharma transmissions came to Japan and spread their lineage. Among them, Feiyin's second-generation dharma heir Daozhe Chaoyuan (1599–1662) stayed in Japan briefly from 1651 to 1658 and befriended the Japanese Zen monk Bankei Yōtaku (1622–1693).[43] Feiyin Tongrong's first dharma heir, Yinyuan Longqi, was perhaps the most famous because he arrived in Nagasaki in 1654 and founded the Japanese Ōbaku school. Figure 3.6 shows his portrait by a Japanese painter.

Regarding Yinyuan's departure from China, there are still some speculations about his motives and the real reason. Most scholars believe that his loyalty to the Ming regime was a major factor in his decision. But some speculated that his emigration must have been related to the lawsuit aimed at his master Feiyin Tongrong about the *Wudeng yantong* in 1654.[44] Although Yinyuan's departure in the same year had nothing to do with the lawsuit, he did publish the *Wudeng yantong* in Japan and found some other evidence in Japanese sources. In this sense, he brought this dispute to Japan and exerted a certain influence on Japanese Buddhism. (I will discuss the impact of this book in Japan in chapter 9.)

The Caodong lineage had no presence in Japan until one of Juelang Daosheng's disciples, Xinyue Xingchou (1639–1695), also known as Donggao Xinyue, landed in Nagasaki in 1677. Because he belonged to the Caodong lineage, he was not welcomed by Yinyuan Longqi's disciples, who had firmly established themselves since 1654. He was later invited to Mitō and started the Jushō tradition within the Japanese Sōtō school.[45]

FIGURE 3.6.   Portrait of Yinyuan Longqi. Detail. Original 138.4 cm x 60.2 cm. Painted by Kita Genki. Reprint from *Ōbaku bunka* (Uji: Manpukuji, 1972), p. 6. Courtesy of Manpukuji.

The Literati "Escaping into Chan"

Chan Buddhism could not have achieved such a wide spread in China without the literati's support. Some of them were not only patrons but also became ordained monks and even dharma heirs under certain circumstances. Within the Confucian world, this eremitic gesture of withdrawal from public service was euphemized as "escaping into Chan" (*taochan*). This was, however, not a unique cultural phenomenon that only occurred after 1644.

As early as 1550s, because Wang Yangming's movement opened the door for Buddhism to be part of the Confucian discourse of self-cultivation, some inspired literati deliberately shaved their head and lived as monks. Among them, the most famous literati-monk was Deng Huoqu (1489–1578?) from Sichuan, who used to be Wang Yangming's follower Zhao Zhenji's disciple. Claiming to have an enlightenment experience in 1539, he felt that even Wang Yangming's teaching could not reach the ultimate truth. Thereafter, he read Buddhist works, especially Chan texts, and practiced meditation. In 1548, he decided to shave his head and become a monk, believing that in order to "seek the true nature" he had to cut off connections with the mundane world. However, as a monk, he continued to associate with the literati and actively participated in various kinds of lecture meetings organized by Wang Yangming's followers. In his semi-autobiography *Nanxun lu* (Records of inquires in the south), he described himself as a person whose character combined the straightforwardness of the Song Confucians, the spirit of freedom of the Neo-Taoists, and the transcendental poetic thinking of the Tang poets.[46] Although he did don the Buddhist robe and travel as a monk, his *Nanxun lu* shows that he was still an outcast member of the literati class: He was inspired by Wang Yangming but became too obsessed with the spiritual question of reaching enlightenment. Because of his radical behavior as a monk, he was considered by some of his literati friends as one of the strange people in his time.

About four decades after him, Taizhou scholar Li Zhi also shaved his head and resided in a Buddhist cloister, as mentioned in the previous chapter. Although both Deng and Li claimed to "have left family," none of them observed the conventional Buddhist disciplines seriously and to a large extent retained their identities as marginalized Confucian literati. Therefore, as outcasts from the Confucian world, their iconoclastic behavior was not approved by society: Deng died miserably in obscurity, and Li committed suicide.

The trend of literati turning to monks became a noticeable social phenomenon in the late Ming and the dynastic change simply spurred more *jinshi* degree holders into the Buddhist order. According to Timothy Brook's study, Yunqi Zhuhong was perhaps the first literatus with the licentiate degree to become a serious monk in 1560. Xinglang Daoxiong (1598–1673), ordained in 1637, was identified by Brook as the first *jinshi* degree holder who formally turned to Buddhism.[47]

This trend was also testified by Muchen Daomin and Yulin Tongxiu's disciple Maoxi Xingsen (1614–1677) when they had an audience with the Shunzhi emperor in 1659. When the emperor asked why Muchen Daomin chose to become a monk, Maoxi Xingsen explained that, during the past thirty years (ca. 1629–1659), in Guangdong province alone there were more people from the literati family to join the Buddhist order, and Buddhism in Guangdong flourished even more than in the traditional Buddhist areas in Zhejiang.[48]

For the vast majority of the literati, who were highly educated but not successful in their official careers, monastic life offered a different kind of distinction. Many of them were influenced by a deeply rooted Buddhist culture and the prevalent intellectual penchant for Chan teaching. Some of them were acquainted with Buddhist teaching through reading Buddhist scriptures and were determined to join the Buddhist order. These literati converts were more than welcomed in Chan communities. Because of their literary skills, they were often appointed as secretary (*shuji*) of the master and were responsible for drafting correspondence, correcting mistakes in the master's writings, or even serving as ghost writers sometimes. Their careers as Chan monks were usually more successful than those of less-educated clergy because of their close associations with the teacher and their outstanding educational backgrounds.

Muchen Daomin's career represents the path of distinction of a literary monk. In his chronologically arranged autobiography, titled *Shanweng Min chanshi suinian zipu* (Muchen Daomin's chronological autobiography), which he never published, he detailed his conversion from a young Confucian student to a celebrated Chan master.[49] Although the record is not complete, it reveals that Muchen Daomin disliked Confucian teaching despite his status of a licentiate in his youth, and was attracted to the ascetic Buddhist life. Without success in persuading his parents to allow him to be ordained, he escaped twice from his home to live in monasteries. Eventually, he was ordained in Guizong monastery in Lushan. In his understanding, Buddhist life required devotion and diligent even ascetic practices, such as vegetarian fasting and disciplines. Along this line of thinking, he reasoned that the literary skills he acquired through Confucian education had no influence on his enlightenment.

However, when he decided to completely abandon his literary career, his master persuaded him that literary accomplishment did not impede the effort of reaching enlightenment. Beginning in 1628, Muchen Daomin became Miyun's literary assistant and secretary for almost ten years. He played an active role in monastic affairs and in securing Miyun's support among literati followers. Because of his literary talent, he had broad connections in the literati circle. Miyun Yuanwu's ascendancy in Eastern Zhejiang, for example, can be attributed to Muchen Daomin's friendship with Huang Duanbo.[50] His autobiography also suggests that he was responsible for composing replies to all correspondences addressed to Miyun Yuanwu, including the polemical letters.[51] If this assertion is true, some of Miyun's essays might be actually authored by Muchen Daomin.

Muchen Daomin eventually received Miyun's dharma transmission and distinguished himself with his literary accomplishments. When he had audiences with the Shunzhi emperor in Beijing, their topics of discussion were not confined to religious matters. Rather, their conversation, as documented in his *Beiyou ji*, covered topics ranging from Confucian philosophy, calligraphy, painting, poetry, and literature, to popular novels and dramas.

The Literati Becoming Monks after the Fall of the Ming

After the fall of the Ming, especially after the fall of several Southern Ming regimes, more *jinshi* degree holders and famed literary men were forced to consider Buddhism as an alternative to serving the Manchu rulers if they didn't want to commit suicide.[52] Among them, some of the best intellectuals became Chan masters.

In the early Qing, Hanyue Fazang's lineage was known for accommodating Ming loyalists in its monasteries. For example, Xiong Kaiyuan (dharma name: Bo'an Zhengzhi, 1599–1676) was one of the most famous Southern Ming officials in his lineage. Xiong received the *jinshi* degree in 1625 and was appointed supervising secretary of the Office of Scrutiny for Works and junior vice censor in chief in the Longwu court of the Southern Ming. He met Hanyue Fazang for the first time in 1629 and was attracted by his teaching. After failed attempts of resisting the Manchu invasion, he was ordained in 1646 and later received dharma transmission from Hanyue's disciple Jude Hongli (1600–1667).[53]

Another literatus, Huishan Jiexian (*zi*. Yuanyun, 1610–1672), also became Jude Hongli's dharma heir after the Manchu conquest. A lay Buddhist in his youth, he was ordained in Mount Baohua when he was thirty-five. In 1649, he received dharma transmission from Jude Hongli. Famous for his literary talent, he was regarded as a monk-poet.[54] As I will demonstrate in chapter 9, he played a crucial role in the early 1670s in rekindling the debate about dharma transmission.

More famous were the four monk-painters who received dharma transmission from various Chan masters. Shitao Yuanji (1630–1708), a Ming royal descendant,[55] received dharma transmission from Muchen Daomin's heir Lü'an Benyue (?–1676). Kuncan (1612–1673, dharma name: Zutang Dagao) joined the Buddhist order in 1638. In 1658, he became Juelang Daosheng's dharma heir.[56] Bada Shanren (dharma name: Ren'an Chuanqing, 1626–1705), also a descendant of the Ming royal family, joined the Buddhist order in 1648 and received the Caodong transmission from Wuyi Yuanlai's dharma heir Xueguan Dao'an's (1585–1637) disciple Yingxue Hongmin (1606–1671).[57] Another painter, Jianjiang Hongren (1610–1664), joined the order in northern Fujian in 1646 after a failed uprising against the Manchu conquerors. He received dharma transmission from one of Wuyi Yuanlai's dharma heirs, Guhang Daozhou (1585–1655).[58]

Jin Bao (1614–1680), a former Southern Ming official, became Tianran Hanshi's disciple and adopted the dharma name Dangui Jinshi.[59] Jin Bao acquired the *jinshi* degree in 1640 and served as a local prefect in Shandong. After 1644, he served several Southern Ming regimes. Before his ordination in 1650, he served in the Yongli court (1647–1661) as supervising censor and was deeply involved in factional court politics because of his sharp criticism of his political rivals.[60] After he was persecuted as a member of the political clique "Tiger Five" in 1650, he decided to become a monk. He later became Tianran Hanshi's disciple in 1652 and received his dharma transmission in 1668. As a monk, he was famous for his poems and essays, which expressed a nostalgic feeling for the lost Ming dynasty. For this reason, his works were banned in 1775. As I will show in chapter 9, he was also involved in the controversy about dharma transmission because he wrote a short essay to express his opinion. In addition to Jin Bao, Qu Dajun, another famous literati in Guangzhou, was ordained temporarily under Tianran Hanshi in 1650 and was given the name Yiling Jinzhong. He later disrobed and became critical of Buddhism.[61]

Because the Southern Ming government retreated to Guizhou and later to Yunnan, many court officials, after being defeated, refused to surrender or to serve the Qing government. To remain loyalists, they chose to become Buddhist monks. Chen Yuan has studied twenty-seven such literati figures in Yunnan and Guizhou areas. One of the most famous among them was the monk Dacuo, whose secular name was Qian Bangqi (1602–1673). Qian obtained the *jinshi* degree during the Wanli reign. At the end of the Ming, he was the traveling surveillance governor in Yunnan. After the fall of the Ming, Qian continued to serve the Yongli court of the Southern Ming as the traveling surveillance governor of Guizhou. When Guizhou was conquered by the Qing army, Qian left the Southern Ming court. However, Qing officials pressured him to serve the new government. Qian had no choice but to ordain as a monk.[62] Another local literatus, Tang Tai (1593–1673), was also ordained after 1644 under the name Dandang Tonghe.[63]

Among all literati monks, Fang Yizhi (1611–1671) is perhaps the most famous and influential intellectual who took refuge in Buddhism. Fang obtained his *jinshi* degree in 1640 and was an active participant in a literati political organization called Fushe. After the fall of the Ming, he took part in the resistance movement. When all attempts to serve the Southern Ming government failed, he dressed as a Buddhist monk in 1650 to avoid further persecution from the Manchu regime. In 1653, he received full ordination from the Caodong master Juelang Daosheng, who enjoyed the reputation of a loyalist monk during the Ming-Qing transition and gained a following of Ming loyalist literati. Fang Yizhi's dharma name was Wuke Dazhi, and he was also known as the monk Moli or Yaodi.[64] Fang was offered Juelang Daosheng's dharma transmission as well and thus began his career as abbot in several monasteries, one of which was Mount Qingyuan.

Mount Qingyuan, the original place of Qingyuan Xingsi's monastery, was first revived by Wang Yangming's followers after 1534 as the site for Confucian gatherings. In 1615, the leaders of these gatherings decided to withdraw from this Buddhist monastery. They rebuilt it and returned it to the monks. After serving several monasteries as abbot in Jiangxi, Fang Yizhi succeeded Xiaofeng

Daran (Ni Jiaqing, 1589–1659, *jinshi* 1622) as abbot of Mount Qingyuan in 1664.[65] Throughout his life, Fang remained a productive author whose works ranged from philosophy, etymology, orthography, geography, astronomy, and medicine to the knowledge of Western science. Inspired by his teacher, Juelang Daosheng, he developed what the eminent Chinese Marxist historian Hou Wailu calls "the philosophy of fire."[66] Willard Peterson praises him as a representative of the first generation of Qing thinkers, together with Huang Zongxi and Gu Yanwu (1613–1682). His sudden death in 1671 intrigues Ying-shih Yü, who speculates that his death was a planned suicide. Unlike many literati who temporarily wore monks' robes in the turmoil of the Manchu conquest and later returned home as scholars in retirement, Fang did not resume his literati identity. Instead, he was committed to being a serious Caodong master. He stayed in Mount Qingyuan for the last seven years of his life. Not only did he rebuild the monastery, he also attracted a group of followers. In addition to his academic works, he initiated a new edition of the monastic gazetteer to document the revival of the monastery and left a collection of his recorded sayings.[67]

Chan Buddhism within Seventeenth-Century Chinese Society

In this part of my book, I have described the transformation of Chan Buddhism as a reinvention, which revived certain ancient forms of Chan practice in the Tang and the Song. My argument is that although the Chan tradition appeared to be faithful to its predecessors in earlier periods, it actually originated from the most recent intellectual and social milieu of the seventeenth century. When considering the transformations within Chan communities, we should beware that the reinvented Chan tradition was deeply rooted in seventeenth-century Chinese society and was constantly shaped by various intellectual and social forces. In part, I am trying to delineate the trajectory of Chan growth in the seventeenth century. What I have discovered is a clear path of Chan revival from obscurity to prominence. It shows that the growth of Chan Buddhism was embedded in seventeenth-century Chinese culture and society. Here, I summarize some of the most important findings in this part.

The Path of Chan Revival

The Chan tradition was reinvented amid the revival of Buddhism in the late Ming and early Qing, which can be divided into several stages. The Wanli reign, in which the thought and practice of the three eminent monks Yunqi Zhuhong, Hanshan Deqing, and Zibo Zhenke dominated the Buddhist world, can be considered the first stage. Meanwhile, doctrinal studies flourished and lectures on popular Buddhist scriptures were welcome. In this period, the three eminent monks represented a much more syncretic teaching than the Chan masters in later times did, combining Chan with Pure Land practice, doctrinal studies, and meditation on "critical phrases" (*huatou*). For them, the role of dharma transmission was downplayed; the simplistic reenactment of kōan stories was criticized; and enlightenment through gradual and arduous self-cultivation was appreciated. As I showed in chapter 1, in this initial stage of Buddhist revival, Chan Buddhism had not yet reacquired its unique character and identity: Monks claimed dharma transmission without personal confirmations from their teachers, and they were free to teach their own versions of Chan teaching.

After 1620, the last two decades of the Ming can be viewed as the second stage of the Buddhist revival because all three eminent monks passed away around that time. Dramatically, Chan masters from the Linji and Caodong lineages replaced the three eminent monks and dominated the Buddhist world. Simple methods of beating and shouting were used profusely in Chan monasteries, and "authentic" dharma transmission was increasingly emphasized in Chan communities in response to the chaotic situation of "false" claims. During this time, various controversies about Chan understanding and lineage affiliation began to develop.

The Manchu conquest marked the beginning of the third stage, which lasted until the early eighteenth century. I regard 1733 as a turning point because the Yongzheng emperor intervened in Buddhist affairs by publishing his *Jianmo bianyi lu* and publicly denouncing Hanyue and his lineage. After this event, Chan communities lost vitality: No new eminent teachers emerged; few books of recorded sayings were published; and few Chan genealogies were compiled. During the third stage, Chan Buddhism continued to grow, however, uninterrupted by the dynastic change. Chan institutions were well established, and Chan masters were patronized by the Manchu court. However, disputes initiated in the late Ming degenerated into nasty controversies that no longer reflected genuine interest in Chan practice. Rather, the apparent flourishing of Chan Buddhism foreshadowed its decline.

Shortly after the seventeenth century ended, the revived Chan Buddhism quickly foundered, leaving little trace in historical memory. This can be seen from the rate of literary production of Chan literature, which is an important index to the development of Chan Buddhism. The emphasis on producing Chan recorded sayings of living masters and updating genealogies stopped around the turn of the eighteenth century. The enthusiasm for controversy resurged at the end of the seventeenth century briefly and then completely disappeared after the compilation of the *Zhengming lu* around 1694. Timothy Brook also noticed that the publication of monastic gazetteers, which proliferated in the 1590s–1640s, declined steadily after reaching its peak around 1690–1710.[68]

Chan Buddhism as an Extension of Intellectual and Social Transformations

My account of the rise of Chan Buddhism shows clearly how social, cultural, and intellectual changes profoundly influenced the growth of Chan. It might not be an exaggeration to claim that this reinvented tradition originated from the broader intellectual and social changes as one of their extensions. This view helps to explain the rise and fall of Chan Buddhism in a particular time period: When the intellectual and social environment conducive to the promotion of Chan rhetoric and to the development of Chan communities no longer existed, Chan Buddhism retreated from the historical scene. In the following, I summarize some of the most significant changes that configured the transformation of Chan Buddhism as seen in this process.

The first was the notable movement of Wang Yangming's learning of the mind, which fostered an intellectual craze for Chan thought. As I documented in chapter 2, Wang Yangming's followers, favoring the Chan spirit of spontaneity, considered Wang's teaching of the direct comprehension of moral knowledge as resonating with the Chan rhetoric of sudden enlightenment. Inspired by Wang's teaching, they studied Chan texts extensively and purposefully interpreted Chan Buddhism as the embodiment of the antinomian rhetoric. They also sought like-minded Chan monks who would match their anticipation of a true master as in the Chan texts they read.

The second factor was the booming print culture that facilitated the spread of Chan texts and ideas. Social historians observe that, during this time, private libraries were erected and commercial printing houses flourished. The simplicity and affordability of woodblock printing technologies enabled many individuals and private institutions such as Buddhist monasteries to become publishers and distributors of printed materials. A general reading public also took form and had access to cheaply priced books. As Kai-wing Chow correctly calls it, all of these activities that were related to "book production, materialization, distribution, generic classification, and reading" formed a "semantic field of the book," "presenting to the reader a great variety of ways in which meaning [could] be constructed."[69] In this period, Chan anthologies authored by the literati and Confucian commentaries using Buddhist, especially Chan, terminologies were welcomed by readers. Around 1590, a visible Chan craze can be detected in the popular print culture.

The third factor was the increased gentry patronage of Buddhist institutions during this period as a result of resurging local activism. Social historians reveal that, due to economic growth and political changes, local gentry were particularly active in creating their domain of influence independent of state control through activities such as patronizing Buddhist monasteries. Statistics also indicate that the late Ming and early Qing period was one of the most active periods of temple construction in Chinese history. These studies show that the reinvented Chan Buddhism had deep-rooted economic and institutional bases in local society.

Finally, the political change from Ming to Qing also had an impact on Chan Buddhism because some literati joined the Buddhist order. For most of them, becoming a Buddhist monk was a justifiable alternative to serving the new Manchu rulers. Some notable scholar-officials, such as Fang Yizhi, Xiong Kaiyuan, Jin Bao, etc., received dharma transmission and participated in the debates in varying degrees. There is no doubt that this new wave of escapism, regardless of its motivation, boosted Chan Buddhism at that time. These literati-turned-Chan-monks further strengthened the ties between Chan Buddhism and the society and brought new changes into Chan communities.

First, the literati and Chan monks forged an even more closely knit community in which eminent Chan masters became gentrified. Even those monks without sophisticated educational backgrounds had to devote themselves to learning literary crafts, such as poetry writing, painting, calligraphy, etc., in order to communicate with the literati. In this sense, eminent Chan monks were another kind of literati, only they had donned Buddhist robes. Second, these literati-monks, even after being ordained, continued to pursue their Confucian learning and thus brought the most recent intellectual changes directly into the Buddhist world. Finally, as both Chan masters and literati, these literati-monks felt free to interpret Chan texts and to represent Chan's past according to their views. As a result, textual authority—acquired through literary education—and spiritual authority—received from dharma transmission—became a seamless unity.

The Ming-Qing transition also accelerated the already-begun process of the internal migration of the population and the Chinese diaspora overseas, which facilitated the spread of Chan Buddhism. On the one hand, along with the shift of battlefields and the retreat of the Southern Ming regime from the southeast coast to southwest China, Chan Buddhism also spread from the southeast to the southwest as some defeated Ming scholar-officials donned monks' robes. Miyun Yuanwu's lineage, which was the most prominent in the late Ming, flourished in Sichuan, Yunnan, and Guizhou. On the other hand, the Manchu conquest along the southeast coast forced some of the population to relocate to overseas Chinese enclaves in Japan, Vietnam, and Malaysia. Chan monks traveled with refugees and merchants, spreading Chan transmissions and Chinese-style monasticism.

The Qing court also showed a great deal of interest in all kinds of Buddhism, including Chan Buddhism. The first Qing emperor, Shunzhi, brought Miyun Yuanwu's dharma heir Muchen Daomin and his dharma nephew Yulin Tongxiu to Beijing, according them with national prestige. Although the emperor had a personal interest in Chan teaching, his stance can be viewed as part of a systematic cultural strategy to win the favor of the literati population in the south who had close connections to Chan masters and communities. In contrast to the relatively lax religious policy in the late Ming, the Qing court tightened ideological controls over Buddhism. As I will detail in chapter 6, the Yongzheng emperor, proclaiming himself an enlightened Chan person, was directly involved in the debate between Miyun and Hanyue.

The reinvention of Chan Buddhism was shaped and conditioned by a variety of intellectual, social, cultural, and political circumstances. It shows that the revival of Chan Buddhism was a complex phenomenon. Along this line of thinking, Chan Buddhism can be viewed as a product and an extension of the intellectual, social, and cultural transformations of the seventeenth century. Yet, this does not mean that Chan Buddhism was not important in seventeenth-century China. On the contrary, because all of these factors were connected by Chan Buddhism, it became the center of various kinds of social relationships. Although this book focuses on the internal transformations of Chan Buddhism, some of its unique characteristics simply reflected the society and culture that nourished its growth and shaped its trajectory of development.

Conclusion

It is not an exaggeration to say that seventeenth-century Chinese Buddhism was a world dominated by Chan masters. Within Chan communities, beating and shouting were widely accepted as the hallmark of Chan practice; and dharma transmission was considered a serious matter that was subject to verification. Chan students, seeking enlightenment from eminent Chan monks, traveled throughout the country and congregated in large Chan centers. After attaining enlightenment and receiving official acknowledgment from their masters, they became qualified to receive students and to live in monasteries as abbots. The growth of Chan accelerated after the fall of the Ming, as some literati and loyalists joined the Buddhist order. Meanwhile, the new Manchu emperor was interested in patronizing Chan Buddhism.

In this chapter, I have provided detailed accounts of some of the most important figures in Chan Buddhism. As we will see in my study of the two controversies, many of them contributed in different ways. Because the monastic world was becoming increasingly congested with so many ostensibly enlightened masters, whose understanding of some fundamental spiritual issues varied significantly, they questioned the authenticity of their rivals' enlightenment experiences and argued against each other about the meaning of Chan principles, which is the focus of the next part of this book.

PART II

The Principle of Chan

4

Clashes among Enlightened Minds

The rise of Chan Buddhism was accompanied by various kinds of controversies. The eminent Chinese scholar Chen Yuan, thoroughly studying the Buddhist disputes at this time, summarizes four different kinds of controversy that marked seventeenth-century Chan Buddhism. He laments the deplorable moral debasement of Buddhists as follows:

> Controversies are misfortunes to the Buddhist world. But
> from the perspective of evidential historians, they show the
> vitality of Buddhism. Before the Jiajing reign (1522–1566)
> and the Longqing reign (1567–1572), the Buddhist world was
> silent and no controversy could even be sought. The rise of
> controversies started from the Chongzhen reign 1628–1644
> when Hanyue Fazang wrote *Wuzong yuan* and Miyun
> Yuanwu refuted it. This was a first-rate controversy because
> it was about principles and doctrines. During the Shunzhi
> reign (1644–1661), Feiyin Tongrong wrote *Wudeng yantong*
> and Sanyi Mingyu sued him. This is a second-rate contro-
> versy because it is about sectarian strife. There were also
> controversies out of emotion and power, which are lower.
> There were controversies about cemeteries and land rev-
> enue, which are lowest of all.[1]

Chen Yuan has identified the dispute between Miyun Yuanwu and Hanyue Fazang as the first of the many Buddhist controversies in the late Ming and early Qing periods. Unlike other debates, which concerned the pursuit of secular interests, this dispute between master and disciple displayed a high level of polemical sophistication.[2]

The two antagonists, Miyun Yuanwu and Hanyue Fazang, were bound by a master-disciple relationship resembling the father-son relationship in secular Chinese lineage organizations. A master "fathers" a disciple through dharma transmission, and the disciple has the responsibility to uphold the same dharma that his master has given to him. Therefore, in theory, this relationship of dharma transmission necessitates a sense of consistency in Chan teaching and practice. But the formation of the master-disciple relationship between these two, as I will show, was from the beginning a process of negotiation. On the one hand, Hanyue wanted the orthodox Linji transmission from Miyun but wished to reserve the right to develop his own Chan teaching; on the other hand, Miyun was eager to have a famous monk such as Hanyue, who was as senior as Miyun himself, as his disciple. As a result, Miyun granted transmission to Hanyue and also gave him permission to follow his own Chan style; Hanyue, therefore, conditionally accepted the transmission and paid public homage to Miyun to indicate his subordination. Their initial reluctance and reservation undoubtedly sowed the seeds for later disputes. After Hanyue published his book *Wuzong yuan* (Origins of the five Chan schools), in which he articulated his unique Chan teaching and indirectly criticized Miyun, several rounds of polemical letters were published almost immediately after they were written. Nor did these disputes end after Hanyue died in 1635. Determined to save Chan Buddhism and to defend his master's honor, Hanyue's disciple Tanji Hongren (1599–1638) wrote the *Wuzong jiu* (Rescuing the five Chan schools). This book provoked Miyun's fierce rebuttal, *Pi wangjiu lueshuo* (Outlined refutation of the vain rescue), which was published in 1638.

Part II includes three chapters. In this chapter, I focus on Miyun Yuanwu and Hanyue Fazang's understanding of Chan and introduce various polemical essays. In chapter 5, I will discuss the areas in dispute thematically. Finally, I will focus on the Yongzheng emperor's involvement in the dispute.

Hanyue Fazang's Distinction between Tathāgata Chan and Patriarch Chan

Hanyue Fazang's chronological biography indicates that he achieved enlightenment primarily through his own study. During this process, the works of two early Chan masters, Juefan Huihong (1071–1128) and Gaofeng Yuanmiao (1238–1295), played decisive roles in the formation of his thought. Hanyue even imitated Gaofeng Yuanmiao by setting up a "solitary confinement" (*biguan*) to achieve enlightenment. Yuanmiao's use of the perfect circle (*yuanxiang*, or a drawing, O, in Hanyue's writing), the symbol of perfect enlightenment for Chan Buddhists, also stimulated Hanyue's understanding of the origins of Chan Buddhism. Juefan Huihong's work *Linji zongzhi* (The principle of the Linji school), which centers on Fenyang Shanzhao's (947–1024) elaboration of Linji Yixuan's teaching of the "three mysteries and three essentials," directly inspired Hanyue to formulate his views on principles, which I will explain in detail later. Another work elaborating the concept of the three mysteries and three essentials, Juefang Huihong's *Zhizheng zhuan* (Records of wisdom and realization), became Hanyue's favorite text for teaching his students. In 1616, he read the *Zhizheng zhuan* and started to use it in his teaching. In 1620, his disciples compiled his remarks about the *Zhizheng zhuan* into a separate book, *Zhizheng zhuan tiyu* (Suggestions and remarks about the *Zhizheng zhuan*).[3]

One of Hanyue's unique views is his division of Chan Buddhism into Patriarch Chan (*Zushi Chan*) and Tathāgata Chan (*Rulai Chan*).[4] The concept of Tathāgata Chan appeared in early Chan history without much discussion. In Huineng's biography composed in 803, when the emperor's envoy Xue Jian asked Huineng's view on meditation, Huineng replied by extolling Tathāgata Chan:

> The Way is enlightenment through the mind. How could it rely on
> sitting? The *Diamond Sūtra* says: "If someone says that the Tathāgata
> appears sitting or reclining, this person does not understand the
> meaning of my words." The so-called Tathāgata is therefore named
> Tathāgata because he comes from nowhere and heads toward nowhere.
> Coming from nowhere is called "arising;" heading toward nowhere is
> also called "extinguishing." If there is no arising or extinguishing,
> that is the pure Chan of Tathāgata (*rulai qingjing chan*).[5]

Obviously, Huineng advocated Tathāgata Chan as the highest Chan teaching, transcending the conventional practice of seated meditation. This teaching was also widely used among Huineng's disciples. For example, according to the *Lidai fabao ji*, once a month, Shenhui "preached at the altar to establish Tathāgata Chan."[6] Shenhui's disciple Zongmi also intended to systematize the theory of Tathāgata Chan, which is supreme among the five types of Chan.[7] According to him:

> If one's practice is based on having suddenly awakened [to the
> realization that] one's own mind is from the very beginning pure, that

the depravities have never existed, that the nature of the wisdom that is without outflows is from the very beginning complete, that this mind is Buddha, and that they are ultimately identical, then it is *dhyāna* of the Highest Vehicle. This type is also known as pure *dhyāna* of the Tathāgata, one-mark *samādhi*, and the Tathāgata *samādhi*. It is the root of all *samādhi*.[8]

It is clear that, for Zongmi, Tathāgata Chan represents the supreme teaching. In the late Tang, however, Tathāgata Chan became a derogatory term in Chan communities. Instead, Patriarch Chan represented the most profound Chan teaching because it completely negates the existence of buddhahood and embodies the most extravagant Chan rhetoric of transcendence. The term "Patriarch Chan" first appeared in Guishan Lingyou's recorded sayings, in which Yangshan Huiji (808–883) used this concept to distinguish his understanding from that of his study mate Xiangyan Zhixian (?–898). Guishan Lingyou records the following encounter, which begins with a verse by Xiangyan:

> "The poverty in last year is not poverty, but the poverty in this year is poverty. Last year I was poor, but I still had a place to erect a gimlet. This year I am poor, but I don't even have a gimlet."
> Yangshan answered, "You are only allowed to understand Tathāgata Chan. Patriarch Chan won't be seen even in a dream."
> Xiangyan presented a verse again: "I have an opportunity and I look at you with blinking eyes. If you don't understand, I will call another monk." Yangshan reported to his master Guishan: "I am really happy that Brother Xiangyan has understood Patriarch Chan."[9]

Despite the vagueness of their dialogue, Yangshan and Xiangyan clearly agree that Patriarch Chan is superior to Tathāgata Chan. In my opinion, the reason Yangshan judged Xiangyan's first verse as representing Tathāgata Chan is that Xiangyan indicated only a gradual process of enlightenment by alluding to a period from last year to this year. However, in the second verse, he succeeded in indicating that Chan teaching is understood as an instantaneous insight. Consequently, Yangshan regarded the second verse as the expression of Patriarch Chan. This encounter became a famous kōan story frequently alluded to by Song Chan Buddhists, such as Yuanwu Keqin and Dahui Zonggao, to indicate the distinction between Tathāgata Chan and Patriarch Chan. However, the exact meaning of Patriarch Chan has never been fully explained.[10]

In the seventeenth century, Hanyue Fazang resurrected this topic and used it as a polemical tool to promote his understanding of Chan Buddhism. He said, "Chan contemplation values the determination of Patriarch Chan and Tathāgata Chan first. Patriarch Chan transcends the ten dharma realms without falling into the rank of Tathāgata. Therefore, it is called 'beyond the frame' (chuge)."[11]

For Hanyue, Tathāgata Chan transcends nine dharma realms but stays at the top of the tenth realm without transcending all realms completely. This form of Chan teaching, thought to be the highest of the ten realms, still employs language and symbolic actions such as beating and shouting. Therefore, it is simply "within the frame" (genei), meaning within the confinement of the various realms. Patriarch Chan, however, represents the supreme Buddhist teaching because it is not restricted by mundane phenomena such as the linguistic expressions of "literary Chan" or the devices of beating and shouting advocated by the Linji school. Hanyue Fazang believed that he represented Patriarch Chan while his contemporaries, including his master, Miyun Yuanwu, had fallen into the realm of Tathāgata Chan.

The meaning of "frame" (ge) in Hanyue's works is difficult to determine because he tends to use examples to illustrate his point by analogy. However, Hanyue's distinction between Tathāgata Chan and Patriarch Chan can be clarified by turning to an example he used in his preface to the Wujia yulu, compiled by Xuejiao Yuanxin and Guo Ningzhi.

In this preface, Hanyue speaks in a mystical way about his understanding of Chan teaching: He uses the image of a nine-story timber stūpa to symbolize Buddhist teaching. According to him, the stūpa was built to store Śākyamuni's relics. This nine-story timber structure of several hundred arm spans "falls from the sky like a gimlet" and both bottom and top can be seen from any corner of the stūpa. Here Hanyue refers to the entire stūpa body as the "frame" and the finial structure above it as "beyond the frame." He continues to describe the finial of the stūpa, to which several rounds of "jewel discs" (baopan) are added. Beyond these discs, a sharp "golden tip," which emits the light of five colors, points directly to the sky, illuminating human minds and stopping cognitive thinking. For Hanyue, the image of such a giant stūpa has a special symbolic meaning: The nine-story stūpa body symbolizes the Buddha's doctrinal teachings in the five different periods; the top of the stūpa is the Tathāgata Chan. However, this is not the highest Buddhist teaching. As he describes it, Patriarch Chan "turns around toward outside the frame" (xiang gewai zhuanshen), meaning that it has transcended all Buddhist establishments. The pointed "golden tip" thus represents the sharpness and directness of Patriarch Chan, which eliminates all set patterns and conventions. For him, the five kinds of light symbolize the five Chan schools. While praising the five schools, Hanyue despises the critics of Chan Buddhism and chastises them as not "yet escaping from the nine stories."[12] This analogy vividly shows Hanyue's creative and iconoclastic understanding of Chan Buddhism.

Hanyue Fazang's Encounter with Miyun Yuanwu

Although he was confident about his Chan understanding, Hanyue worried about his dharma transmission because he believed that a legitimate Chan teacher must have proper transmission. He sought out Hanshan Deqing to continue his dharma but soon realized that under Hanshan "the style of doctrinal studies prevails and the principle of Chan Buddhism is seldom heard."[13] What troubled Hanyue was the traditional notion of *yinke*, or the seal of the recognition of enlightenment, usually a formal recognition by acknowledged Chan masters. Without such verification, enlightenment cannot be ascertained as genuine. The reception of dharma transmission is thus a token of verification from enlightened persons.

Among contemporary Chan masters, Miyun Yuanwu, who presented himself as the most authentic descendant of the Linji school because he had revived the practice of beating and shouting, had a special appeal for Hanyue: The two masters whom Hanyue most admired, Juefan Huihong and Gaofeng Yuanmiao, were also from the Linji lineage.

Miyun Yuanwu was revered as a Chan master in the Linji school because he was considered to have embodied Linji's teaching style and possessed the authentic dharma transmission. In addition, he was famous for his performance of beating and shouting. As Huang Duanbo praised him, "He uses beating and shouting alternatively and thus students have no chance to open their mouths. There is no one who does not follow him. He is regarded as the second coming of Master Linji."[14]

Unlike learned scholar-monks in the late Ming, who often based their teachings on the exegesis of scriptures, Miyun seldom lectured on the profundities of Buddhist philosophy. As Noguchi Yoshitaka observes, even the prevailing synthesis of Chan and Pure Land did not appear in his teaching. Rather, Miyun Yuanwu displayed a "pure" version of Chan teaching, which was characterized by blows and shouts.[15] As he himself explained, his advocacy of this simple method may have had something to do with his insufficient education both before and after he joined the Buddhist order. When he succeeded to the abbacy of Yuwang monastery in Longchi, he confessed this lack of education:

I am not an outsider from other places. I was simply a woodcutter on Mount Nanyu of this county. Since my family was poor when I was a layperson, I did not have the opportunity to read Confucian books, classics, and histories. Because I left the mundane world so late, again I did not attend as many lectures [about Buddhist doctrines].[16]

While Miyun Yuanwu's reputation was growing in the Buddhist world, he was increasingly concerned about recruiting qualified dharma heirs to perpetuate his lineage and influence. Unlike some Chan masters, who were stingy in giving out transmission certificates, Miyun Yuanwu, comparatively generous in offering dharma transmission, had twelve dharma heirs. Thus, he was accused by the Caodong master Juelang Daosheng of "bestowing [dharma transmission] indiscriminately on unqualified people" (lanfu feiren).[17] His dharma heirs had even more dharma descendants: Feiyin Tongrong had more than fifty and Yinyuan Longqi had more than twenty. (Because of this quantitative increase of Chan masters, part of the later debate was written on how it was possible to have an impressive number of heirs while still maintaining the quality and solemnity of dharma transmission.) While the number of Chan masters rose through dharma transmission, the candidate pool of truly qualified disciples dwindled relatively. Thus, it became extremely hard for Chan masters to find a widely acknowledged candidate. This is why Miyun Yuanwu was more than happy when Hanyue Fazang, an established Chan monk, came to him and indicated his willingness to receive Miyun's dharma transmission.

Hanyue Fazang first met Miyun Yuanwu in 1624 in Jinsu monastery. At this time, Hanyue was already fifty-two years old and had become famous earlier than Miyun. Therefore, this visit was considered a compliment to Miyun Yuanwu. However, from the very beginning, their relationship was uneasy and contentious.

The modern scholar Lian Ruizhi has thoroughly studied their relationship. According to Lian, their encounter was not harmonious since they did not share a basic understanding of Linji's Chan teaching. However, since Hanyue was such a popular candidate, Miyun did not hesitate to give him his official recognition. According to a letter Hanyue wrote to Miyun, although Miyun had kindly bestowed the certificate and other credentials on him, Hanyue refused to accept them immediately. He stated arrogantly that he completely understood the principle of the Linji school without any more doubts since he had reached enlightenment by listening to the sound of bamboo cracking in 1613.[18] He believed that his Chan method transcended the mere use of beating, shouting, and cognitive understanding. At the end of this short letter, he challenged Miyun:

> I request you respectfully to instruct me what kind of dharma the "three mysteries and three essentials" are ultimately. Only if your dharma corresponds to mine, I dare to receive your transmission. If there is no correspondence, I will bow to you nine times to decline [your offer]. This is a great matter for the Buddhist dharma and I wish that you wouldn't treat the Buddhist dharma as though it were a matter of human sentiment (*yi Fofa wei renqing*).[19]

Dissatisfied with Miyun's simplistic Chan teaching, Hanyue rejected the transmission but his disciples secretly kept the certificate.

Only three years later, after Hanyue had failed to obtain other transmissions elsewhere, he accepted Miyun's transmission on the condition that Miyun would allow him to pursue his own understanding of Linji Chan. As Lian shows, Hanyue's reception of Miyun's dharma transmission was full of tension and compromise.[20]

The process of dharma transmission from Miyun to Hanyue was initially awkward and conditional. Since he already had his own monastic network based in Wuxi and was widely known among literati followers, Hanyue wanted nothing from Miyun except the token of dharma transmission. Miyun, on the other hand, was eager to have Hanyue as his dharma heir even though this meant that he had to compromise what he considered to be the essential Chan teaching and to grant Hanyue the liberty to follow his own understanding. Miyun Yuanwu's flexibility in the matter of dharma transmission was later castigated by Hanyue's disciples as "treating the Buddhist dharma as though it were a matter of human sentiment."[21]

This uneasy transmission no doubt overshadowed their relationship in later times. As Miyun Yuanwu's dharma heir, Hanyue Fazang was supposed to hold fast to his master's teaching. However, Hanyue publicly expressed his distinctive, even heretic, understanding of Chan Buddhism, to which Miyun responded with a series of polemical letters.

The controversy started with the publication of Hanyue's *Wuzong yuan* in 1625. In this book, Hanyue argued that all five Chan schools have their distinctive principles that Chan masters should not neglect. In so arguing, he intimated that his dharma master, Miyun Yuanwu, who performed only beating and shouting without reference to "the three mysteries and three essentials" of the Linji school, did not follow the authentic Chan practice. More important, Hanyue Fazang developed his own theory on "the perfect circle," which he regarded as the origin of the universe and the source of all Buddhist teachings.

Exchange of Polemical Essays

As a convention, polemical essays were usually not included in a Chan master's recorded sayings. In Miyun's recorded sayings, there were no traces that he had engaged in so many nasty controversies. Rather, he put all of his polemical essays in a separate collection called *Tiantong zhishuo,* which was not circulated widely nor known to people outside a small circle. I have retrieved this separate collection from Japan, and figure 4.1 shows the first page of fascicle 1. Through reading his polemical essays, it becomes very clear how the controversy proceeded.

To summarize, the controversy was first kindled by Hanyue's work *Wuzong yuan.* Although Hanyue sent a copy to Miyun, Miyun did not read it and thus had no idea about its content. Meanwhile, Hanyue also sent a letter to Miyun's dharma brother Tianyin Yuanxiu to share his understanding of the Chan principle. Yuanxiu immediately pointed out that Hanyue's opinion had departed from the standard understanding of Linji Chan. While writing a letter to repudiate Hanyue, he briefed Miyun about Hanyue's essays. Then, Miyun started to read Hanyue's work seriously. He found that Hanyue intended to theorize the principle of Linji Chan by conceptualizing some frequently mentioned words in

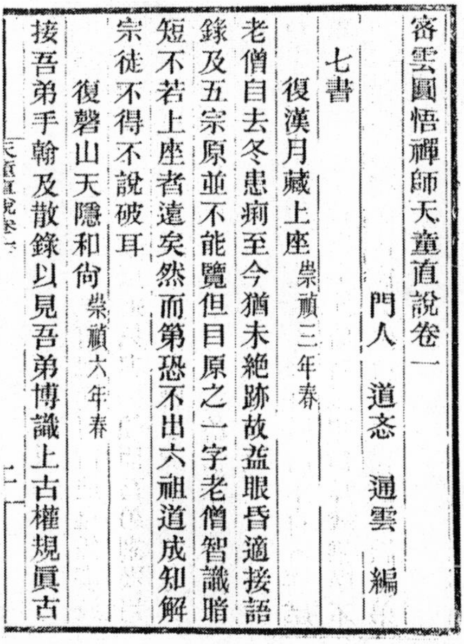
密雲圓悟禪師天童直說卷一
門人 道忞 通雲 編
七書
復漢月藏上座 崇禎三年春
老僧自去冬患痢至今猶未絕跡故益眼昏適接語錄及五宗原並不能覽但目原之一字老僧智識暗短不若上座者遠矣然而第恐不出六祖道成知解宗徒不得不說破耳
復磬山天隱和尚 崇禎六年春
接吾弟手翰及散錄以見吾弟博識上古權規眞古

FIGURE 4.1. First page of *Tiantong zhishuo,* ca. 1642–1643. Rare book in Tōhō Bunka Gakuen Tōkyō Kenkyūshō. Originally from Zhejiang Provincial Library. Photocopy from Komazawa University Library.

the *Linji lu*, such as "the three mysteries and three essentials." This attempt deviated from Miyun's spontaneous use of beating and shouting, which he saw as the only expression of enlightenment. Miyun then wrote seven letters to refute Hanyue and his disciples. After this round of attack, Miyun and his disciples composed several other essays in response to Hanyue's rebuttals. After Hanyue died in 1635, the controversy did not abate. Rather, it was escalated by Hanyue's disciple Tanji Hongren's *Wuzong jiu*. Miyun immediately responded by ordering his disciples to compile a lengthy book called *Pi wangjiu lueshuo* in ten fascicles. Since the controversy was marked by the publication of dozens of polemical works, I discuss their contents below in chronological order. [22]

Hanyue Fazang: Wuzong yuan

The current edition of the *Wuzong yuan* preserved in the Japanese supplementary canon is the epitome of Hanyue's thought on Chan Buddhism. [23] This work outlines his views on the principles of the five Chan schools and on the controversial concept of the perfect circle, which was regarded by him as the origin of all five schools. As Hanyue stated in the preface, he wrote this short essay in response to questions from a group of followers in Sheng'en monastery. The questions themselves were about a phenomenon prevalent in his times: Some Chan masters solely focused on the ineffable meaning of Chan symbolized in actions such as Śākyamuni's legendary smile to Kāsyapa, ignoring the principles of the five Chan schools. Here the reference to "those Chan masters" could be easily associated with Miyun Yuanwu because it was he who advocated the method of sudden enlightenment without reference to principles.

In response, Hanyue refuted such an "error" by emphasizing the importance of principles. For him, principle was the seal of dharma transmission, without which no one could be tested for their enlightenment experience. To illustrate his point, he invoked the simile of a "tally" in the Chinese military system: A general must have the matched "tally" bestowed by the emperor as proof of his right to command his army. If the two sides of the tally do not match each other, the holder must be an imposter. In fear of the loss of principle and the wrong claim of dharma transmission by sinister people, Hanyue was willing to clarify the principles of the five schools for his disciples. [24]

The main text starts with the Linji school, to which he officially belonged, and proceeds to a discussion about other schools. In the beginning, he puts forward his idea about the perfect circle, which became the most disputed concept in later controversies. He remarks:

> I have seen in the *Huishi jiatu* (Paintings and illustrations of lineages) [25] that the origin of the seven Buddhas was the *Weiyinwang fo*

(Sanskrit: Bhīṣma-garjita-ghoṣāsvara-rāja, the king with the awe-inspiring voice) who was only painted as a perfect circle. After the [creation] of the circle, the seven Buddhas have their own respective discursive teachings in linguistic forms. Although these teachings differ from each other, the principles of their transmission poems are contained within.[26]

Here, Hanyue has not clearly articulated the creation of the circle and the seven Buddhas, and nowhere in his writing does he specifically explain the origin of the universe. Not surprisingly, this ambiguity later became a target of Miyun Yuanwu's and the Yongzheng emperor's criticisms. (As I will explain in the next chapter, Hanyue resorted to an esoteric understanding of the Rite of Releasing the Hungry Ghosts to bridge the gap.) Moreover, Hanyue thought that the circle contained the principles of the five Chan schools as well. The different aspects of the circle, he argued, represent the different schools. The first lineage derived from the circle was the Linji school, which was regarded as the orthodox tradition by Hanyue Fazang; the second was the Yunmen school, and then the Guiyang, Fayan, and Caodong schools.

Hanyue's antagonists were right about the vagueness and ambiguity of this text because his essay, which is hardly expository, presents no argument. His main strategy was to excerpt all passages he deemed to be relevant from Chan literature and to list them together without further explanation. For example, to prove that Linji's three mysteries and three essentials is the principle of the Linji school, he searched all of the encounter dialogues of Chan masters in the Linji school for references to the number three and put them together. (I will analyze his analogical use of the number three in chapter 5.) His discussions about Yunmen, Guiyang, and Fayan are rather short and truncated, merely alluding to some famous sayings of Chan masters. Because of the prominence of the Caodong masters at that time, Hanyue included a lengthy discussion of the principle of the Caodong school. He stated that the principle of the Caodong lineage lay in the "Five Ranks between Monarch and Subject" (junchen wuwei). Employing the same analogical strategy, he reiterated that this principle was derived from the perfect circle.

Hanyue Fazang's Letter to Tianyin Yuanxiu

Although Hanyue delivered a copy of his Wuzong yuan to Miyun Yuanwu, Miyun did not take the book seriously. Instead, Hanyue's letter to Miyun's dharma brother Tianyin Yuanxiu triggered the debate. In this letter, Hanyue repeated his understanding of the principle of the Linji school as the three mysteries and three essentials and lamented the disappearance of this principle among his contemporary Chan fellows. At the beginning of this letter, he stated:

> Since the Weiyin Buddha has no appearance and the one O (the perfect circle) is the ancestor of thousands and millions of Buddhas, the seven Buddhas, by "connecting the two ends into one" (shuang-tou dujie) and "intertwining the four methods together" (sifa jiaojia), created the secret seal without words. And what Mahakāsyapa transmitted to the twenty-eight patriarchs is no more than verification of the mind with the dharma. This dharma cannot be extinguished. It is indeed important![27]

Once again, as his many opponents pointed out, Hanyue used very obscure language to describe a mysterious process of evolution.

While praising Linji's three mysteries and three essentials as the true embodiment of the "secret seal without words," Hanyue criticized the Chan method that he despised as "a wild fox's slobber, which resembles the Chan teaching of one wooden stake" (yijuetou xiangsi yehuxian). Although Hanyue did not explain the meaning of these words, this phrase is clearly derogatory.[28] All of Hanyue's opponents interpreted this phrase as directly slandering his teacher Miyun Yuanwu's simple Chan practice.

In this letter, he continued to complain that the principle of three mysteries and three essentials had gradually lost its place in the Linji school after Zhongfeng Mingben (1263–1323). According to him, after Wanfeng Shiwei and Baozang Zongchi, no one had heard about this principle. Hanyue was particularly critical of one of his dharma great-grandfather Xiaoyan Debao's disciples, Sanji Guangtong,[29] who, according to Hanyue, intended to eliminate the five lineages after the sixth patriarch Huineng. He criticized Sanji Guangtong's emphasis on the phrase "Originally not a single thing existed" (benlai wu yiwu), the third line of Huineng's famous verse in the Platform Sūtra.[30] According to Hanyue, a one-sided emphasis on emptiness entailed another kind of attachment to an illusionary object. Although Hanyue did not intentionally criticize Huineng, his opponents viewed his work as a direct attack on the sixth patriarch.[31]

Tianyin Yuanxiu's Reponses

Miyun Yuanwu's dharma brother Tianyin Yuanxiu was perhaps the first person to respond to the Wuzong yuan. He wrote several letters to Hanyue and also criticized Hanyue in a sermon.[32] In his first reply to Hanyue, Tianyin Yuanxiu warned that Hanyue should be more prudent about his argument because in Tianyin Yuanxiu's view the Chan school is consistent with "the method of one mind" without further division into principles. He worried as well that the introduction of concepts such as the perfect circle and principles would become an actual entity and a new "set pattern" to which Chan students would attach. Tianyin Yuanxiu also disagreed completely that the Linji lineage was in decline.[33]

Hanyue Fazang must have replied to this letter because Tianyin Yuanxiu's recorded sayings preserve another letter refuting his arguments. Apparently, Hanyue's reply, which defended himself and challenged Tianyin Yuanxiu's criticism, angered Tianyin Yuanxiu. Marking Hanyue's letter with sarcastic remarks such as "wrong," "ignorant," and "slandering," he straightforwardly rejected Hanyue's interpretation of the perfect circle and principles as nonsensical and false ideas.[34] In his sermon, Tianyin Yuanxiu once again denounced Hanyue's theory as "attaching to three and discarding one" (zhisan quyi), meaning that Hanyue wrongly adhered to the three mysteries and three essentials but eliminated the one mind.

Shortly after these unpleasant communications with Hanyue, Yuanxiu wrote a letter to alert Miyun Yuanwu. In this letter, he briefed Miyun about the incident with Hanyue and pointed to some critical references to Miyun's Chan teaching. In particular, he exaggerated Hanyue's opinion of the phrase "Originally not a single thing existed" as criticizing the sixth patriarch as a "heretic" (waidao; Sanskrit: tīrthika).[35]

Miyun Yuanwu: "Seven Letters"

Yuanxiu's letter directed Miyun Yuanwu's attention to Hanyue's work, which he did not take seriously when he first received it. His first response was the writing of a series of letters between 1633 and 1634, later published as the "seven letters" (qi shu), commonly known as the "seven refutations" (qi pi).[36] Four of these letters were replies to Hanyue Fazang regarding the Wuzong yuan. Of the rest, one was to Miyun's dharma brother Tianyin Yuanxiu, who was the whistle-blower; one was to Hanyue's disciple Dingmu Hongche (1588–1648), regarding the monk Ruiguang's recorded sayings; and one was to Liu Daozhen, a literati follower of Hanyue.[37]

In these letters, Miyun tried hard to control his anger and maintain the courtesy and respect owed to Hanyue Fazang. Wanting Hanyue to abandon his ideas, he intended to persuade him to be consistent with his master's teaching and not to "have separate teaching in private."[38] In one of the letters, he candidly admitted that he was not as learned as Hanyue, but he also pointed out that Hanyue's problem was his self-conceit and his tendency of "boasting about his learning for fame."[39] Miyun was much harsher to Hanyue's disciple Dingmu Hongche, his dharma grandson. Completely rejecting Dingmu Hongche's reading of the three mysteries and three essentials, Miyun derided Dingmu Hongche's blind following of his teacher's interpretation. For him, the supreme Chan teaching cannot be further divided into categories, such as the "three mysteries and three essentials" or "the host and guest."[40] Miyun also wrote a lengthy reply to Hanyue's lay disciple Liu Daozhen, commenting critically on Liu's work *Sheng'en wendao lu* (Records of inquiring into the Way at Sheng'en monastery), which detailed Hanyue's sermons but is no longer extant.[41] Feeling that these letters had not completely expressed his resentments, Miyun wrote another letter to Hanyue Fazang in the winter of 1634, directly responding to Hanyue's criticism of his use of beating and shouting.[42]

Miyun Yuanwu: "Follow-up Records"

Hanyue must have read all of these letters, which had been distributed publicly. He wrote a response letter and asked a Chan monk called Jichang to deliver it to Miyun.[43] According to Miyun's account, Hanyue showed no remorse over his ideas and continued to accuse Miyun of eliminating the principles of the five schools. After reading Hanyue's rebuttal letter, Miyun immediately replied and then published his letter under the title *Houlu* (Follow-up records), together with his three replies to Xu Guanfu,[44] another of Hanyue's followers, and to Qi Junjia, son of Qi Chenghan and brother of Qi Biaojia. In these letters, Miyun largely repeated his previous criticisms. However, Hanyue died in 1635 without a chance to respond to these letters.[45]

Miyun Yuanwu: The "Third Record"

The third polemical collection, which was often referred to as *Sanlu* (Third record), was published soon after in response to the rebuttals from Ruibai Mingxue[46] and Dingmu Hongche, who continued Hanyue's teaching. After reading Ruibai's recorded sayings in two fascicles, Miyun felt that Hanyue's disciples had not completely returned to the correct teaching. Rather, they had "attached [themselves] to the words of ancient times." The debate continued to focus on the understanding of the three mysteries and three essentials.

This collection also includes *Boyu* (Discourse of rebuttal),[47] which was composed after Hanyue died in 1635. This essay comments in detail on the letter Hanyue wrote to Tianyin Yuanxiu and on his *Wuzong yuan*. In this essay, Miyun focuses on Hanyue's criticism of the practice of beating and shouting and the concept of the perfect circle.

Muchen Daomin's Response

Hanyue's *Wuzong yuan* incurred responses from his dharma brother Muchen Daomin immediately. Muchen wrote the *Wuzong pi* (Refuting the *Wuzong yuan*) to repudiate Hanyue's work. Although this essay is no longer extant, according to his contemporary Dong Han, Muchen Daomin's work was extremely critical of Hanyue and his disciples. As a result, it provoked Tanji Hongren's writing of the *Wuzong jiu*.[48]

Tanji Hongren Defending Hanyue Fazang

Hanyue Fazang's death did not end the controversy. The confrontation was escalated when Hanyue's disciple, Tanji Hongren, wrote a book titled *Wuzong jiu* in 1637 to reaffirm Hanyue Fazang's teaching and to repudiate Miyun Yuanwu's accusations of his master.

The background of Tanji Hongren is not known. He appears to have been a monk from Sichuan who studied with Hanyue Fazang. Later, he lived in Anyin monastery where Hanyue was the abbot. Among Hanyue's disciples, Tianji Hongren was famed as an eloquent debater.[49] According to Tanji Hongren's preface to the *Wuzong jiu*, this ten-fascicle book was his response, written on behalf of his late master Hanyue Fazang, to Miyun Yuanwu's polemical essays (the "Third Record" in Miyun's literary collection, mentioned earlier) that were published after his master's death. Tanji Hongren's book, in appearance, resembles a Chan genealogy that outlines the transmission lines and gives brief introductions to Chan patriarchs. It primarily focuses on the transmissions in the Linji lineage and represents a single retrospective transmission line.

The first fascicle of this book includes three essays by Tanji Hongren entitled "General Remarks." The next three fascicles are devoted to the standard Chan mythology, starting with the seven Buddhas and twenty-eight Indian patriarchs and ending with the Tang master Huangbo Xiyun, who was Linji Yixuan's master. In fascicles 5–8, he provides a detailed account of the patriarchs in each generation of the Linji school. He briefly discusses the other four schools, giving only sketchy biographical accounts for the first several patriarchs. After each entry, Tanji Hongren states his own opinions, commenting particularly on figures crucial to the Linji tradition. His comments on Linji Yixuan and his master, Hanyue Fazang, reflect his discontent with Miyun Yuanwu's judgmental remarks about his master.

Despite this apparent similarity to conventional Chan genealogies, Tanji Hongren's work is pointedly polemical. The book's arrangement highlights his master's interpretation of the biography of each patriarch, as contrasted with

Miyun Yuanwu's. In fascicle 8, which is devoted to the relationship between Miyun Yuanwu and Hanyue Fazang and the origin of their divergent interpretations of Chan Buddhism, Tanji Hongren quotes passages from Miyun Yuanwu's polemical essays and responds to them directly. This work provoked more serious responses from Miyun and later from the Yongzheng emperor.

Miyun Yuanwu's Pi wangjiu lueshuo

This time, Miyun Yuanwu reacted vehemently and ordered his disciples to compile a book entitled *Pi wangjiu lueshuo* in 1638. It is not a simple repetition of Miyun's former essays. Instead, it is a new compilation largely following the structure of Tanji Hongren's book, which outlines the transmission lines of the Linji school. It incorporates almost all accounts of major Chan figures, supplemented with Miyun Yuanwu's comments. As the text indicates, it must have been edited by Miyun's disciple Zhenqi (?–1641).[50] Miyun probably only wrote the preface.

The division of the book into ten fascicles appears to have been a direct response to Tanji Hongren's book: Miyun's book also starts from the seven Buddhas and the twenty-eight patriarchs in India but ends with Hanyue Fazang without reference to the other four Chan schools. After a brief biography of each patriarch, Miyun's remarks appear. The crucial sections are fascicle 5 on Linji Yixuan, fascicle 9 on Miyun Yuanwu himself, and fascicle 10 on Hanyue Fazang.

In his preface to this work, Miyun Yuanwu summarizes the process of this debate. Citing Hanyue's letter to Yuanxiu, Miyun states that he had noticed Hanyue's dangerous ideas but had not taken action, hoping that Hanyue could change for the better. However, when he saw the works written by Hanyue's disciples Dingmu Hongche and Liu Daozhen, he could not remain silent: He reread Hanyue's *Wuzong yuan* and published the "Third Record." Tanji Hongren's work *Wuzong jiu*, which continued his master's "erroneous views," also necessitated this lengthy rebuttal. Miyun says in this preface:

> Because Hanyue did not rely on himself as the principle to point
> directly to all people, he found instead alternatives in the *Huishi jiatu*
> and in the Weiyin Buddha in the beginning of the seven Buddhas.
> [He also considered] the single O (the perfect circle), which has no
> historical records and no evidential proof, as the ancestor of thou-
> sands and millions of Buddhas. In addition, he said that each of the
> five lineages was derived from one aspect of the O (the perfect circle)
> and that the only orthodoxy is Linji. Therefore, he falsely recognized
> such names as "three mysteries and three essentials" as the principle,

forcibly citing "three strikes and three shakes" (*sanji sanhan*)[51] and similar things to match it. Buddha's teachings have been transmitted from previous [patriarchs]. Hasn't the crystal-clear great meaning been confused and destroyed by Hanyue? . . . They talked about dreams to each other, and, like demons, they bewitched children of other people. Now, these two have died, but I am more afraid that descendants of other houses may continue to fall into their dens and cheat each other in turn so that students in later times would falsely recognize the single O (the perfect circle) without achieving enlightenment by oneself. Thus, the fault of eliminating Buddhas and patriarchs and the fate of wisdom began with Hanyue. If I sit here and watch without rescuing them, then it is also my fault. Therefore, I have no choice but to briefly summarize the main points, rescuing Tanji by refuting what he [wanted to] rescue falsely.[52]

As Miyun succinctly points out in this writing, Hanyue and his disciples misinterpreted Chan Buddhism in three ways: First, they believed that the perfect circle was the origin of the five Chan lineages; second, they falsely regarded the phrase "three mysteries and three essentials" as the principle of the Linji lineage; third, they arrogantly claimed that they were the only ones who possessed true dharma eyes. According to Miyun, even though Hanyue and Tanji Hongren are dead, their evil ideas should be repudiated to forestall their spread among later generations.

The Antagonism between Miyun's and Hanyue's Lineages

Miyun Yuanwu may have claimed certain victory. At any rate, Hanyue Fazang and Tanji Hongren died in 1635 and 1638, respectively. Hanyue's other disciples, such as Jiqi Hongchu, did not carry on the debate. Literati followers like Qi Junjia proposed that Hanyue Fazang's book be burned in order to conclude the dispute gracefully.[53] According to the *Zongtong biannian* (Chronology of Chan lineages and transmissions), after the mediation of the literati, Miyun Yuanwu announced in 1641 the end of the controversy as well as his intention to reunite his lineage.[54]

Although Hanyue's dharma heirs continued to revere Miyun Yuanwu as their patriarch, the schism between his disciples and Miyun's lineage can be palpably felt. In the early Qing dynasty, occasional disputes between these two groups continued to erupt. However, these disputes concerned sectarian interests and ecclesiastic status rather than spiritual attainment.

Miyun's leading heir, Feiyin Tongrong, was the most aggressive in defending his teacher. Because his dharma brother Chaozong Tongren (1604–1648) was sympathetic with Hanyue's view, Feiyin attacked him relentlessly. In the meantime, because Miyun's other leading heir, Muchen Daomin, was unfriendly to Hanyue's major disciple, Jiqi Hongchu, the two had skirmishes as well. Although their disputes were about trivial issues and personal animosity, the tension between their teachers lingered in the background. In addition, Miyun's disciple Muyun Tongmen also contributed essays to attack Hanyue and his disciples in the late 1680s. The antagonism between the two groups even spread to their literati patrons. When Qian Qianyi was asked to write Miyun's epitaph, he made unfavorable comments about Hanyue. In retaliation, Hanyue's disciples immediately asked Qian's rival Huang Zongxi to write Hanyue's epitaph, in which Huang praised Hanyue and denounced Miyun's Chan style. I describe these events as follows.

Feiyin Tongrong against Chaozong Tongren

Hanyue's fame won him many sympathizers within Chan communities. Miyun Yuanwu's dharma heir Chaozong Tongren was one of them. Chaozong Tongren first studied with Hanyue in 1627 and later turned to Miyun in 1640 and received his dharma transmission. Because Tongren was influenced by Hanyue, he tended to intellectualize the Linji principle of the three mysteries and three essentials. In 1634, Miyun wrote him a letter, criticizing him for his "wrong" tendency.[55]

Apparently, Chaozong Tongren did not change his opinion. Not only did he applaud Hanyue's interpretation of the three mysteries and three essentials, he also criticized some of Feiyin Tongrong's remarks on Chan kōans, especially his *Yuanliusong* (Eulogy of the lineage; this was a standardized encomium composed by dharma heirs upon receiving *yuanliu*, that is, the transmission certificate), published in 1634.[56] In addition, he showed great admiration for Dahui Zonggao and wished to inherit his dharma transmission. On behalf of his master, Feiyin Tongrong strongly denounced Chaozong Tongren.[57] In 1640, he wrote the *Jinsu pimiu* (Feiyin's refutation of errors),[58] which detailed his dispute with Chaozong Tongren.

In this essay, Feiyin views Chaozong Tongren's tolerance of Hanyue as indirectly slandering Miyun and himself. Regarding Chaozong Tongren's praise of Dahui Zonggao, Feiyin points out that Dahui Zonggao did not belong to the orthodox transmission, which derived from Zonggao's dharma brother Huqiu Shaolong. Rather, his was only a collateral lineage. Thus, Tongren was foolish to abandon the orthodox transmission from Huqiu Shaolong, to which

Miyun belonged. When Chaozong Tongren fought back with a series of essays, Feiyin responded in 1644 with two additional essays, "Gui miujian zhanglao" (Persuading the teacher with erroneous views) and "Zai gui miujian zhanglao" (Persuading again the teacher with erroneous views).[59]

Disputes over Miyun's and Hanyue's Epitaphs

After Miyun's death, how to write an epitaph to evaluate his life appropriately became an issue within the Linji lineage. According to Chen Yuan's study, two controversies occurred about Miyun Yuanwu's epitaph. The first one occurred immediately after his death, when Muchen Daomin bestowed his teacher's dharma transmission on several study mates who did not have the chance to get Miyun's recognition when he was alive. However, Feiyin disputed him on the basis of his strict rule of dharma transmission and insisted on inscribing the names of Miyun's twelve official dharma heirs in his epitaph. (I briefly recount this dispute in appendix 2.C.). The second dispute happened around 1659, when Muchen Daomin invited the famous literatus Qian Qianyi to write a new epitaph for Miyun.

Qian Qianyi (1582–1664) was the most prominent literary man in the Jiangnan area.[60] Throughout his life, his writings, regardless of their literary merit, had documented many aspects of the Buddhist revival. Many of them demonstrate his extensive connections with such Buddhist masters as Zibo Zhenke, Yunqi Zhuhong, Hanshan Deqing, Ouyi Zhixu, and Xuelang Hong'en. Among these monks, he regarded Hanshan Deqing as his true teacher. In the last years of his life, he became even closer to Buddhism and devoted himself to the publication of Hanshan Deqing's complete works and the study of the *Śūraṃgama Sūtra*.[61] He also kept a close relationship with the Caodong masters, especially Wuming Huijing's dharma descendants, such as Juelang Daosheng and Tianran Hanshi, who showed clear loyalist sentiment toward the Ming dynasty.[62]

Preferring sophisticated doctrinal studies, Qian Qianyi was very critical of contemporary Chan practices like beating and shouting, which he scornfully labeled as "faked Chan" (*weichan*), "crazy Chan" (*kuangchan*), "demonic Chan" (*mochan*), and "blind Chan" (*mangchan*). Probably for this reason, he was particularly hostile toward Hanyue, whose Chan teaching he listed as one of the "three evils" of the day.[63] However, after the Manchu conquest, he maintained good relationships with Miyun's heir Muchen Daomin and Hanyue's heir Jiqi Hongchu.[64]

Qian Qianyi accepted Muchen Daomin's request to write a new epitaph for Miyun. However, because he personally loathed Hanyue Fazang, he mentioned him unfavorably in Miyun's epitaph. Qian's comments incurred unpleasant responses from Hanyue's disciples, such as Jiqi Hongchu and Bo'an Zhengzhi (Xiong Kaiyuan), who were influential in Zhejiang. To counter Qian Qianyi, whose surrender to the Manchu army severely tarnished his reputation, Jiqi Hongchu invited his rival, the Ming loyalist Huang Zongxi, to write a new epitaph for Hanyue.[65] Because Huang was particularly close to Hanyue's lineage, his new epitaph praised Hanyue with the highest regard.[66]

Muchen Daomin against Jiqi Hongchu

In the early Qing, the controversy between Miyun Yuanwu and Hanyue Fazang evolved into sectarian hostility between the two lineages. As a result, tension developed between Muchen Daomin and Jiqi Hongchu, their two leading disciples. There were two such incidents. The first one concerns a rare book in the Shanghai Library, Jiqi Hongchu's *Shuquan ji* (Collections of master Shuquan), compiled between 1651 and 1652. In 1651, an anti-Manchu uprising in Zhoushan of Ningbo was suppressed and many Ming loyalists died. Because Muchen Daomin and Jiqi Hongchu had close ties with these loyalists, the court summoned them for questioning. For personal reasons, the two could not get along. Therefore, when Jiqi Hongchu published his *Shuquan ji*, in which he labeled himself a "true Buddha," Muchen Daomin condemned Hongchu as "arrogant" and "shameless."[67]

The fuse for the second incident was even more trivial. According to Chen Yuan, the dispute started with a plaque hanging in Jinsu monastery in Haiyan county. When Feiyin Tongrong was abbot there, a literatus wrote the phrase *Miyun mibu* (Thick cloud spreads all over) on the plaque. Because this phrase contained Miyun's name, it was regarded as a perfect pun, which promoted Miyun's lineage. However, when Hanyue Fazang's disciple Jiqi Hongchu succeeded to the abbotship in 1661, he replaced the original phrase with a new one, imprinting it with the seal *Sanfeng zhenzi* (A true son of Sanfeng) to declare his identity as Hanyue's dharma heir. To some of Miyun's heirs, this change indicated a serious challenge to Miyun's authority: The plaque had to be removed. Muchen Daomin took the lead by writing "Jinsu fanzheng lu" (Records of returning to the right in Jinsu) and "Duni shuo" (Discourse on eliminating traitors) to refute Hongchu.[68]

Muyun Tongmen's Involvement

In the late seventeenth century, the publication of five polemical essays rekindled the debate. One of Miyun Yuanwu's twelve dharma heirs, Muyun Tongmen (1599–1671), wrote these highly acrimonious essays first around 1662, and his disciples printed them in 1671.[69] According to Chen Yuan, these essays targeted both Hanyue and his disciple Jiqi Hongchu. Muyun Tongmen claimed that even after Miyun Yuanwu denounced Hanyue Fazang, Jiqi Hongchu still followed his teacher and belittled his patriarch, Miyun Yuanwu. Therefore, he regarded both Hanyue and Jiqi as demons.

Muyun Tongmen wrote the essays and Tianli Xingzhen (1624–1694) published them. Tianli Xingzhen belonged to the Linji master Tianyin Yuanxiu's lineage[70] and he could not get along with the monks of Hanyue's lineage, especially with Yushan Shangsi (1630–1688).[71] They engaged in a dispute about how to understand certain kōans. Tianli Xingzhen thus wrote "Duxie shuo" (Discourse on eliminating heresies), and Yushan Shangsi wrote "Zhengbian lu" (Record of right argument) to refute him.[72]

Because of this unpleasant relationship, when Muyun Tongmen's five essays were printed, many of Hanyue's disciples believed that Tianli Xingzhen had forged them to attack his enemies. For instance, in 1690, Bo'an Zhengzhi's (Xiong Kaiyuan) lay disciple Qian Lucan (1612–1698) wrote *Bianmo xuzhi lu* (The record of necessary information for discerning demons) to spread such a hypothesis.[73] Qian accused Tianli Xingzhen of fabricating the five essays and attributing them to Tongmen. More important, because Tianli Xingzhen was ordained by Hanyue's disciple Dingmu Hongche, he actually belonged to Hanyue's tonsure lineage. According to Qian Lucan, by rekindling the attack on Hanyue, Tianli Xingzhen was "demonically" impugning his own ancestor. Because these essays were so detrimental, their printing blocks were destroyed on the twenty-third day of the fifth month of 1688, according to Qian's record.

Conclusion

Reading these voluminous polemical texts is a challenging task. They were not written in an elegant literary style, nor were they arranged to support a central thesis. Instead, they are largely responsive essays targeting specific points raised by their opponents, even very trivial ones, in order to rebut them. The structure of their opponents' works also constrains these polemical texts because the "art" of debate consists of attacking every word written by the enemy.

Miyun Yuanwu and his disciples were certainly masters of this art. They often embellished their polemical essays with detailed citations from Chan literature. Their opponents' trivial mistakes also provoked pages of response from them. Another feature of these polemical texts is repetition. Although they did not go so far as to repeat the wording literally, the authors reiterate the same points throughout the debate, making it difficult to comprehend their full meaning.

Nevertheless, to discard these polemical works as worthless would be to disregard their value as demonstrations of the common character of the Chan masters who claimed to have achieved enlightenment at that time. All of them believed that an enlightened mind generates tremendous spiritual authority, which not only prompts a monk to claim access to the most correct understanding of Chan but also enables him to judge, evaluate, and criticize other monks' interpretations of Chan. As a result, their polemical works are rife with acrimonious language, senseless accusations, and shameless self-promotion. It will not be an exaggeration to point out that an aspect of seventeenth-century Chan Buddhism was the arrogance of the enlightened mind, which led to polemics, disputes, and even deliberate alterations of conventional genealogies of dharma transmission. More important, careful readings of these "boring" materials reveal the most pointed concerns of Buddhists at that time. In the next chapter, I will examine the issues that emerged from the debates.

5

The Divergence
of Interpretation

The essential point in the debate between Miyun and Hanyue is the verification of Chan enlightenment. That is, on what grounds could a Chan master judge someone's enlightenment, a subjective human experience, to be authentic? In seventeenth-century Chan Buddhism, this verification question was especially meaningful because Miyun Yuanwu had reintroduced encounter dialogue, a spontaneous exchange of nondiscursive verbal communication and bodily action between master and disciple, as the way to sudden enlightenment. This method sought immediate comprehension of the truth and, according to Miyun Yuanwu, was effective when both master and disciple applied shouts and blows to eliminate all cognitive thinking. For Hanyue Fazang, however, shouts and blows were meaningful only when the student fully understood the principle of Linji Chan. Therefore, the dispute centered on the issue of the principle of the Chan teaching of Linji Yixuan, the founding patriarch of the Linji school.

In this chapter, I focus on three points of contention in the debate: First, how should one evaluate the subjective experience of enlightenment by using observable standards, such as the Chan principle? Second, how should one understand the meaning of the perfect circle as proposed by Hanyue? Third, when beating and shouting are applied in encounter dialogues, how can consensus be reached about its meaning between teacher and student?

Objectifying the Subjective Experience of Enlightenment

The enlightenment experience to which Chan Buddhists referred was fundamentally a private and subjective experience that denied public access through
direct observation. When a monk made such a claim in public, his enlightenment experience had to be presented in a way that could be observed and
evaluated by members of the community. Then the question arose about the
appropriate criteria for judging the validity of the enlightenment experience.
For Miyun Yuanwu, the criterion is a mysterious sense of "match" (qi) between master and disciple, which is manifest in the performance of the encounter dialogue. Moreover, in his opinion, all five Chan lineages share one
single principle without further distinction. For Hanyue Fazang, however,
the ultimate way to ascertain genuine enlightenment is principle, and each
Chan lineage has its unique principle, which can not be confused with
another.

The Principle of Linji Chan

The primary issue between Miyun Yuanwu and Hanyue Fazang was the principle of the Linji school, which was attributed to its founder, Linji Yixuan, who
was supposed to have had fully displayed the antinomian spirit.[1] Within Miyun Yuanwu's lineage, Linji's recorded sayings, *Linji lu* (Recorded sayings of
Linji), played an important role in shaping Chan teaching and practice. Miyun
Yuanwu found the *Linji lu* to be the best expression of his Chan teaching. This
emphasis on early Chan texts also influenced his dharma heirs. For example,
when Yinyuan Longqi arrived in Japan, the Japanese monks immediately observed that Yinyuan's Chan teaching, largely inherited from Miyun Yuanwu
and Feiyin Tongrong, relied heavily on the reading of the *Linji lu* rather than
on the Song collection *Biyan lu* (Blue cliff records).[2]

   The *Linji lu* is among the earliest recorded sayings and has had a great influence on the development of recorded sayings as a literary genre.[3] Linji's
Chan style, demonstrated in the records, was characterized by the extensive
use of beating and shouting, which was intended to stop conventional thinking and to induce an immediate apprehension of the truth. This sort of Chan
spirit defies any doctrinal articulations of the principle of his teaching. However, Linji left a trace of a possible interpretation of the principle. In an instruction session, Linji made the following remark without further explanation: "One sentence should have three gates of mystery and each mystery
contains three essentials."[4] This teaching, later referred to as the "three mys-

teries and three essentials" (*sanxuan sanyao*), was developed by his followers as the principle of the Linji school.

Fenyang Shanzhao (947–1024) and Juefan Huihong were among those who regarded the three mysteries and three essentials as the principle.[5] Feng-yang Shanzhao, renowned in Chan history for his pioneering use of kōans to instruct students, wrote the "Songgu baize" (One hundred eulogies of the ancient stories) to comment on many famous episodes of encounters recorded in Chan texts. He especially elaborated on Linji Yixuan's three mysteries and three essentials, which he believed could not be understood as theory. Rather, the principle could only be contemplated as a means of achieving enlightenment. He remarked as follows:

> The matter of the three mysteries and the three essentials is difficult to discern;
> One who can get the meaning and forget the words is easily intimate with words/paths;
> This one sentence brightly illuminates all the myriad forms;
> On the ninth day of Chongyang [festival] the chrysanthemums' blossoms are new.[6]

Based on Fenyang Shanzhao's elaboration, Huihong wrote the *Linji zong-zhi* (The principle of Linji) to describe his understanding of this crucial teaching. He accused some Chan teachers of ignoring the principle of each individual Chan school. For him, "mysteries" and "essentials" could not be divided into a sequence through which a practitioner progresses. Rather, this teaching was a device to test students.[7]

Hanyue's Understanding of the Chan Principle

As noted earlier, Hanyue Fazang was deeply influenced by Juefan Huihong's work on the principle of the Linji Chan teaching and aspired to promote what he regarded as the principle. His purpose, as he indicated, was to provide a standard by which to test students. He worried about a tendency among his contemporaries to take the enlightenment experience for granted and to erase the principle entirely. According to the popular view among his contemporaries, a true practitioner of Chan should go back directly to the sixth patriarch and the Śākyamuni Buddha himself to attain true enlightenment.[8] For Hanyue Fazang, however, the division of the five schools and the variety of principles provided students with the necessary entrance to ultimate enlightenment.

Hanyue divided the Chan transmission into two aspects: the personal enlightenment of the mind and the transmission of the dharma by the master. As he remarked, "The mind is obtained by oneself while the dharma is obtained through a master."[9] In distinguishing between these two aspects, Hanyue rejected the need for the master as the source of enlightenment. For him, the master simply devised the principles to confirm the student's enlightenment. However, two kinds of wrong practices may occur. The first would be to take the token of transmission as the only way to achieve enlightenment and thus lose the opportunity to realize one's own enlightened mind. The other wrong tendency would be to rely solely on one's own enlightenment experience and neglect the transmission of the dharma through testing in accordance with Chan principles. As Hanyue complained, "In the latter days [of the dharma], those with exceptional abilities in obtaining enlightenment through their own [cultivation] of mind want to simply erase the principles and just hold on exclusively to their own understanding [of the Buddhist truth] achieved through enlightenment."[10] In other words, dharma transmission must be awarded in accordance with Chan principles. However, Hanyue lamented that, in his day, dharma transmission and the apprehension of principles had been separated.

Hanyue clarified this distinction in a short appendix to the *Wuzong yuan* titled "Chuanyifa zhu" (Notes on transmitting the robe and the dharma). In this work, Hanyue pointed out that the transmission of the dharma robe as a symbol of the transmission of principles had been discontinued after the sixth patriarch. He quoted early Chan historiographers, who recorded that when Śākyamuni bestowed the "treasure of the true dharma eye" on Mahākāśyapa in front of the Pagoda of Many Sons, he also entrusted the robe to him. This record, probably invented by the author of the *Tiansheng guangdeng lu* (Extensive records of lamp transmission in the Tiansheng reign, compiled in 1036),[11] appeared in many Chan historical works, indicating the role of the robe as a symbol of dharma transmission. However, Hanyue also noted that when the fifth patriarch Hongren transmitted the dharma to Huineng as recorded in the *Platform Sūtra*, the dharma robe was no longer important. As Hongren explained to Huineng,

> When Great Master [Bodhi]dharma came to this land long ago,
> people did not yet come to rely upon him. Therefore he transmitted
> this robe as the embodiment of reliance [upon him]. It has been
> handed down for generation after generation. . . . . . . The robe
> [however] has become the focus of conflict, and beginning with you
> it should not be transmitted. If you transmit this robe, your life
> expectancy will be like a hanging thread.[12]

This passage indicates a controversy about the transmission of the robe in early Chan history, as many scholars have noted.[13] Here, however, Hanyue

FIGURE 5.1.   Yinyuan Longqi's transmission certificate, 1637. Reprint from *Ōbaku bunka* (Uji: Manpukuji, 1972), p. 32, no. 20. Courtesy of Manpukuji.

imbued the dharma robe with new meaning. For him, it symbolized the principle. He singled out Bodhidharma's words as proof: "Inside, I transmitted the seal of the dharma to verify the mind; outside, I entrust the *kariya* (robe) to determine the principle."[14]

This distinction between the mind and the principle corresponds to Hanyue's views on the attainment of enlightenment by the mind and the transmission of the dharma by principle. However, he noted that, in later generations, when many monks attained enlightenment by themselves, the transmission of the dharma robe was not continued, as he believed it should have been. By reemphasizing the role of the robe, Hanyue opposed the widespread use of the transmission certificate, literally "origin and stream" (*yuanliu*),[15] which records only a string of personal names, without any symbolic reference to the principle. To validate Hanyue's charges, an actual copy of the *yuanliu* can be seen in figure 5.1, which shows Yinyuan Longqi's transmission certificate issued by Feiyin Tongrong in 1637.

A parable related by his disciple Tanji Hongren further illustrates Hanyue's view of the relation between dharma transmission and Chan principles. Tanji Hongren told a story about a dying man who had many sons, which I have paraphrased below:

> Before he died, he showed some tallies to his sons: "I have more sons who are young and wandering in the world. Only these tallies can verify their identities [as my sons]. They are my genuine sons only if they match these tallies." Receiving their father's order, the sons set out to find those wandering brothers, but they mistakenly entrusted their house to a neighbor who not only assumed ownership of the house when they left but also burned all the tallies belonging to the lost sons. When the sons returned home from afar, they were denied entry to their own home. But no one in the neighborhood was bothered. "Why was this the case?" Tanji Hongren asked. "[Because the true sons] left for a long time without returning and [their origin] was

concealed. The principle of the Linji school is the tally and the transmission certificate from the patriarchs is the house. From Xinghua
[Cunjiang] to Xueyan [Zuqin] and Gaofeng [Yuanmiao], the patriarchs
of about twenty generations were the sons who went out to verify the
other sons and my deceased master Sanfeng (Hanyue Fazang) was the
true son who traveled afar and then returned. Alas! Who was the
neighbor? I am not hardhearted enough to speak out [his name]."[16]

This disgraceful neighbor obviously refers to Miyun Yuanwu, the most
famous Linji teacher of the time, who was in a position to offer transmission
certificates. As Hanyue Fazang and his disciple Tanji Hongren explained, true
authority lay in the principle of the Linji school rather than the mere token of
certification. Only the combination of the two could legitimize the transmission. This unique interpretation perfectly integrates two aspects of Chan Buddhism: the personal enlightenment experience and the mediation through the
master's transmission. Through the master's testing, which they believed
should be in line with the principle corresponding to each Chan school, Chan
practitioners could set an objective standard for testing and avoid the danger
of relativity and subjectivity.

Hanyue's Criticism of Miyun and Miyun's Responses

Hanyue's elaborate interpretation, however, implicitly attacks his dharma master Miyun Yuanwu's Chan as "one-stake rigid Chan" (yi juetou yingchan) because Miyun, throughout his career, advocated only the use of beating and
shouting and ignored other, more sophisticated teaching methods. When
Hanyue used this term in a letter to his dharma uncle Tianyin Yuanxiu, Tianyin Yuanxiu spotted the reference and wrote a letter of rebuttal.[17] To my knowledge, Hanyue is the only person in Chan history to use this term with certain
meaning. On another occasion, he used this phrase with reference to the enlightenment experience of two Chan masters in the Tang, Luofu and Xinghua.
As Hanyue commented, before these two people were "tamed" by their teachers, Jiashan Shanhui and Dajue, they had displayed exactly the symptoms of
what he called yijue yingchan: They "always responded to questions with shouts"
and believed that this method was the true Chan teaching.[18]

In this reference, the term yijue yingchan has a more definitive meaning
than yi juetou yingchan. It refers to a Chan teaching that uses the method of
shouting superficially without discriminating various circumstances. By
searching Chan texts, we find that Chan teachers often used the phrase yijue
as a derogatory term for a one-sided understanding of Chan teaching. To my

knowledge, Xuedou Chongxian (980–1052) was the first to use this term, as recorded in the *Blue Cliff Records* (*Biyan lu*). Commenting on Yunmen Wenyan's answer to "What is the Buddha's teaching?" Xuedou added, "The old man Shaoyang obtained one stake" (*Shaoyang laoren de yijue*).[19] Yuanwu Keqin adopted this phrase, using it frequently to refer to those who had not yet understood the highest teaching. Here, *yijue* means a broken piece of wood that looks like a stick or stake.[20] Hanyue's coinage of the terms *yijue chan*, *yijue ying-chan*, and *yijuetou chan* is obviously consistent with this use.

Because Hanyue quoted frequently the "three mysteries and three essentials" in Linji's recorded sayings, Miyun Yuanwu tried to explain away this reference. He regarded this reference as a "provisional means" that Linji had devised to teach Chan practitioners. However, according to him, principles should not be used as a means to attain enlightenment.[21] The real goal is to reach the ultimate, or what Miyun Yuanwu often referred to as "the original color" of the self. His use of shouting was also provisional. As he quoted Linji Yixuan, "a shout is not used as a shout,"[22] meaning that shouts have many more nuances than the utterance, and, in a similar vein, the three mysteries and three essentials should not be taken as real principles.

Miyun's most serious accusation of Hanyue Fazang is that of being a disciple of cognitive understanding (*zhijie zongtu*). In Chan history, the term *zhijie zongtu* refers to the adherents of a type of "incorrect" understanding of Chan Buddhism. The followers of cognitive understanding do not apprehend the meaning of Chan as a separate transmission outside doctrinal studies. They try to use ordinary cognition to understand the ineffable dharma. These followers tend to overtheorize Chan, which in essence defies all explanations. Despite their significant contributions to the development of Chan Buddhism, Shenhui (684–758) and his follower Zongmi (780–841) were identified by many later Chan teachers as followers of cognitive understanding because of their emphasis on the role of *zhi* (awareness) in Chan practice.[23] This characterization is a distortion because, for Zongmi, *zhi*, the word that he chose to represent the function and essence of the true Buddha nature (*tathāgatagarbha*), means "awareness" rather than "knowledge."[24] However, Zongmi's opponents not only created this stereotype of *zhijie zongtu* but codified it in the Zongbao edition of the *Platform Sūtra*, in which Huineng reprimands Shenhui as "a follower of cognitive understanding."[25] The association of this term with Shenhui and Zongmi shows the shifting of religious topography in the late Tang when the so-called Hongzhou school, which upheld the Chan discourse of sudden enlightenment most fervently, replaced Shenhui's lineage as the new orthodoxy.[26]

From the perspective of this orthodox Chan discourse, which privileges the immediate enlightenment experience, Hanyue Fazang had indeed shown a strong inclination to systematize and theorize Chan teaching. For example, he was extremely fond of using the number three to synthesize disparate parts of Chan teaching. Many previous Chan patriarchs had used numerology to explicate the ineffable meaning of Chan. In the *Linji lu*, for example, the number three appears frequently: Linji Yixuan followed Huangbo Xiyun for three years without participating in encounter dialogues; when he had three interviews with Huangbo Xiyun, he was beaten three times. Later, Linji was enlightened at Dayu's place and gave Dayu three punches in the ribs with his fist. Moreover, Linji taught his students about the three mysteries and three essentials.[27] All of these appearances of the number three seem to have been meaningful to Hanyue Fazang, probably because his courtesy name, Sanfeng (three peaks), also contains the number three and thus seems to presage his succession to the Linji school.

Both the Chinese tradition and the Buddhist tradition use numbers as a convenient way to arrange knowledge. In the Buddhist Abhidharma tradition, scholars seeking to classify intricate Buddhist doctrines find numbers extremely useful. This numerical arrangement of Buddhist knowledge reemerged in the Ming and seems to have been very popular.[28] Numerical classification was also widely used in the Chinese scholarly tradition, especially in relation to *The Book of Changes*, which provides rich resources for using numbers and diagrams. Hanyue's fascination with numbers and symbols, such as the perfect circle, which he also used extensively to construct a new interpretation of Chan Buddhism, may have derived from his study of *The Book of Changes*.[29] But the most conspicuous reference to the number three in Buddhism is the symbol of the Sanskrit syllable ī, often written as three dots (*sandianyi* or *yizi sandian*) and representing *dharmakāya* (*fashen*), *prajñā* (*bore*), and *vimokśa* (*jietuo*), according to the *Mahāparinirvāna Sūtra*.[30] Although Hanyue did not invoke this symbol in his own work, his disciple Tanji Hongren used it lavishly in his *Wuzong jiu*.[31]

In his critique of Hanyue, Miyun noticed Hanyue's obsession with numbers. Both Miyun and, later, the Yongzheng emperor took Hanyue Fazang's frequent references to the number three as a sign of a farfetched imagination: They believed that expedient means such as the use of numbers by Chan masters were situational and spontaneous and could not be used to systematize interconnected ideas. Along the same line, Miyun criticized Hanyue for his promotion of Juefan Huihong's *Zhizheng zhuan*. As he lamented, "The Linji lineage has been greatly transformed by my disciple. It has become a place of lecturing."[32] For Miyun, only one thing was important for a Chan practitioner, that is, the "transcendent upward lift" (*xiang shang yi zhuo*). Any other theories or speculations about principles were useless.

Objectivity versus Subjectivity

The controversy between Miyun and Hanyue on the Chan principle demonstrates fully that Chan Buddhism is a paradoxical tradition and a tradition based on paradox. On the one hand, the rhetoric of denial, a hallmark of Chan, often entails a greater risk of self-contradiction because a total rupture with the existing Buddhist conventions, such as doctrinal studies and ritualism, is almost impossible. On the other hand, it becomes even more problematic for Chan Buddhists to claim complete realization or enlightenment, whether gradual or sudden, within this lifetime because the demand for the verification of a subjective experience defies the legitimacy of any such claim. In this sense, the master plays a crucial role in testing the validity of a claim of enlightenment. However, even this method, which places the burden of legitimization on the master's authority, does not solve the issue entirely because the witty verses and symbolic actions, considered to be demonstrations of enlightenment, lack observable and objective standards for verification. In other words, the formality of the spiritual test could easily slip into a kind of relativism, which opens the door to the abuse of dharma transmission.

To supplement and support the enlightenment experience with gradual and rigorous procedures of cultivation might solve the problem partially, but the anxiety of the lack of objectivity bothered many Chan thinkers throughout history. In the seventeenth century, this issue became extremely important because, on the one hand, the transmission of the dharma was a prerequisite for the position of abbacy in a monastery; on the other hand, the proliferation of Chan lineages had created a large number of Chan masters with certificates or other credentials that symbolized the attainment of enlightenment. Therefore, there was a great need for verification of the authenticity of the original enlightenment experience that Chan masters claimed to have attained. The demand for objectivity in the process of testing was even more keenly felt by Chan masters because enlightenment and its test were no longer a private matter between master and disciple. The public interest in Chan had brought the subjectivity of the Chan experience into the public domain through Chan masters' publicizing their own enlightenment experiences in the form of circulated recorded sayings and chronological biographies. In this sense, the private and subjective experience suddenly became "observable" and was subject to public scrutiny. Under these circumstances, it was meaningful for Chan masters to discuss the "principle" of Chan Buddhism.

However, the controversy about the principle of Linji Chan Buddhism reveals that it is almost impossible to determine any "objective criteria" to ascertain a genuine enlightenment experience. From Hanyue Fazang's perspective, the principle of the three mysteries and three essentials seemed to have set a new "objective" standard. But he failed to offer an operative method to achieve his goal. All he could do was to appeal to mystical experience in the esoteric practice of releasing the hungry ghosts and to match kōan stories with his principle of the three mysteries and three essentials in a farfetched way. From Miyun Yuanwu's perspective, the ultimate principle remains ineffable; he rejected any attempt to articulate it in a discursive way. In this respect, he correctly pointed out that Hanyue Fazang's efforts at theorizing the principles ran against the Chan rhetoric of sudden enlightenment.

The perfect transmission from mind to mind is obviously an ideal in the Chan tradition. Chan literature never fully reveals the actual process nor offers a standard to objectify the subjective enlightenment experience. In the seventeenth century, when this ideal was intended to be put into practice, the struggle between objectivity and subjectivity was never solved successfully.

The Mystery of the Perfect Circle: Hanyue Fazang's Esotericism

The most disputed aspect of Hanyue Fazang's creative Chan theory is his extensive use of the perfect circle, not only as a symbol but also as the ontological origin of all beings, including the five Chan schools.

Hanyue's use of the perfect circle is, however, not unique to him. Chan masters have frequently employed a circle to symbolize the pure mind or full enlightenment. Nanyang Huizhong (?–775) was perhaps the first to use the circle as a metaphor for the enlightened mind. Yangshan Huiji, the founder of the Guiyang school, was also skillful at using the circle, and through him the use of the circle became a characteristic of the Guiyang school. Other Chan schools used this symbol to refer to the pure Buddha nature or Buddha mind. For example, Zongmi employed the circle as the symbol of enlightenment.[33] Among later Chan masters, Gaofeng Yuanmiao, whom Hanyue greatly admired, was renowned for his use of the circle.

However, most polemicists did not understand Hanyue Fazang's obsession with the perfect circle. Tianyin Yuanxiu, for example, was puzzled by the derivation of the five schools from different aspects of the perfect circle as Hanyue claimed. He questioned Hanyue: "Which school was derived from which aspect? How do I see one or another aspect of a perfect circle?"[34] In fact, Hanyue intimated that this symbol had an esoteric connection that he was not revealing publicly: a direct link to an esoteric tantric practice. The particular form of the tantric ritual from which Hanyue Fazang drew inspiration is the Preta Food Bestowal Ritual or the Rite for Releasing the Hungry

Ghosts, which uses the perfect circle as the basis for meditation and visualization. In the seventeenth century, due to the popular demand for this ritual, many Buddhist clergy, including Chan monks, learned to perform the rite as a source of income. To understand Hanyue's position on esotericism, we should first review briefly the new development of this rite in the seventeenth century.

The Esoteric Rite for Releasing the Hungry Ghosts in the Seventeenth Century

The particular type of esoteric ritual that Hanyue intended to connect with Chan teaching was the so-called Rite for Releasing the Hungry Ghosts (shishi), commonly referred to as "releasing flaming mouth" ritual (fang yankou). In Buddhist cosmology, the term "hungry ghosts," preta in Sanskrit, refers to the creatures who live in the lower rung of the six rebirth realms within the realm of desire. They are imagined as creatures with huge bellies and tiny necks. As a result of their evil acts in previous lives, the hungry ghosts suffer from insatiable hunger but are unable to eat because food delivered to them is transformed into disgusting substances, such as pus and blood. Through performing the Rite for Releasing the Hungry Ghosts, however, food can be transformed into something edible to them.

The early version of the rite can be certainly traced back to the emergence of esoteric Buddhism in the Tang, which was a significant event in Chinese Buddhism. The process of busting hell open and destroying sins as depicted in Hanyue's ritual manual corresponds roughly to the actual ritual procedures for performing mantra and mudrā described in the Fo shuo jiuba yankou egui tuoluoni jing (The Buddha's discourse on the scripture of the spell for saving the burning-mouth hungry ghost), translated by Amoghavajra (705–774).[35] Although it is still debatable if the three Tang esoteric masters Śubhakarasiṃha (637–735), Amoghavajra, and Vajrabodhi (671?–741) actually intended to construct a separate institution of the esoteric Buddhist school as the Japanese pilgrim Kūkai did in Japan,[36] there is no doubt that since the Tang the spread of esoteric rituals had left distinctive marks in Chinese Buddhism, largely in a diffused fashion and without an institutional basis independent of the existing monastic structure. That is to say, Chinese Buddhist rituals had been tantricized through the conspicuous use of esoteric elements such as mantra, mudrā, and visualization. Chan monastic rituals, for example, were particularly influenced by esoteric elements as evidenced in Chan Pure Regulations and daily liturgical manuals, such as the Chanmen risong (Daily liturgy in Chan monasteries), which were largely an amalgam of Chan mythology,

patriarch veneration, Vinaya rules, the Pure Land aspiration, and more aston-
ishingly, esoteric tantrism. The Rite for Releasing the Hungry Ghosts, which
flourished during the Ming and Qing dynasties, was also incorporated into
Chan monastic codes compiled during the seventeenth century.

Although there had been certain contacts between Chan monks in the
Northern school and the esoteric masters in the Tang, there were few fruitful
communications resulting from these early contacts.[37] In Ming China, esoteric ritual performance for the dead was supported by the state. The Ming
founder even created a separate sectarian division called *jiao* (that is, esoteric
ritual performance) within the Buddhist monastic system and designated it as
an institution solely devoted to esoteric ritual performance. Monks in this
kind of monastery were required to master various kinds of esoteric ritual performance based on standardized manuals, and they served the local communities based on a fee schedule stipulated by the state.[38] In addition, many Ming
emperors were fervent supporters of Tibetan tantric Buddhism, which was
largely patronized as a court religion serving the emperor's interests.[39] While
eminent Tibetan lamas received royal titles and resided in designated monasteries in Beijing, there is evidence suggesting that many more less-prominent
Tibetan monks were wandering in the country and maintained contacts with
Chinese monks and local elites in south China.[40] Although the Tibetan influence on esoteric Buddhism in China proper is still under investigation, it is
evident that, in late imperial China, esoteric Buddhism was still alive in Buddhist communities and evolved with some new characteristics.[41] For example,
Robert Gimello has discovered that the esoteric cult of Cunti (Zhunti) was extremely popular among the populace and the elite. [42]

Among all esoteric rituals popular in late imperial China, the Rite for Releasing the Hungry Ghosts, as Charles Orzech observes, was in great demand,
and many editions of the ritual manual were published. Representing different
styles and methods of performance, these manuals teach the correct way of
holding esoteric ceremonies.[43] During the Ming, this form of ritual developed
rampantly on the basis of an anonymous ritual manual, *Rites from the Essentials
of the Yoga Teachings for Distributing Food to Burning-Mouths* (*Yuqie jiyao yankou
shishi yi*). According to this text, the ritual begins with the preparation of the
altar and the distribution of food and culminates in busting hell and releasing
the hungry ghosts. With their sins being destroyed, the hungry ghosts are
made to accept the Three Jewels. *Dhāraṇi* chanting, *mudrā* maneuvers, and visualization characterize the whole process and indicate an unmistakable esoteric tone.[44]

Although the Rite for Releasing the Hungry Ghosts as an esoteric ritual
was popular in late imperial China, there has been little evidence suggesting a

conscious effort to synthesize Chan and esotericism together. Here, Hanyue's attempt to connect the two traditions provides a unique approach to reinterpreting the relationship between them.

Hanyue's Synthesis of Esotericism and Chan Buddhism

Hanyue systematically elucidated his understanding of the Rite for Releasing the Hungry Ghosts in a short essay entitled *Yumi shen shishi zhigai* (The general principle of food bestowal by Yumi [Hanyue Fazang]), which was published in 1626.[45] As Hanyue stated in a short note appended to this writing, he wrote this manual when he realized that in his youth he took a vow to perform a hundred ceremonies of releasing the hungry ghosts but would never be able to fulfill it. He admitted that he learned how to perform the ritual when he was young. But later he set his mind on Chan Buddhism and ignored this esoteric practice. Because his vow was not fulfilled, Hanyue was afflicted by ghosts' frequent visits in his dream. To pacify these hungry ghosts, Hanyue began to study different versions of performance and composed his own manual. Lamenting the formulaic style of performance that mimicked the singing and acting styles in popular drama, he focused his work completely on contemplation and visualization, which he regarded as the source of power of esoteric ritual performance.[46]

In this work, Hanyue shows that he was aware that this ritual belonged to the esoteric tradition, which he interprets as "correspondence." That means, "the three deeds of body, mouth, and mind correspond to the dharma that one has penetrated." Hanyue thus describes the whole ritual as characterized by the correspondence of visualization (mind), *mantra* (mouth), and *mudrā* (body) at each of its stages.

To summarize, according to Hanyue, visualization begins with the basic esoteric contemplation of the moon-disc (*yuelun*), represented by him simply as a circle. Although Hanyue did not labor to explain this first step, it serves as a fundamental metaphor with which he attempted to integrate Chan and esoteric Buddhism. In most of his writings, he simply uses the drawing of a circle to convey the meaning of the "perfect circle." As I have shown, he regarded this circle as the essential substance of all beings and the source of the five Chan schools. From his perspective, this mysterious origin of the Chan tradition had to be understood through tantric meditation on a moon-disc.

Because Hanyue did not further explain this basic practice, Amoghavajra's description may help us to understand it:

> All Buddhas are so compassionate as to preach this extremely
> profound esoteric *yoga* with their brilliant wisdom. They ask the

practitioners to visualize a white moon-disc in their minds. To start
the contemplation from this, one illuminates one's original mind,
which is clearly clean and pure like moonlight spreading through
space without distinction. It is also called enlightenment, the pure
dharmadhātu, the ocean of the real mark of *prajñā*, which can
contain enormous treasures and [in which] *samādhi* is just like the
purely white and bright full moon.[47]

This basic contemplation serves as the background for more complex
kinds of esoteric meditation, including the popular meditations on the "seed"
(*bīja*) syllables, such as *hrīḥ*, *oṃ*, and *raṃ* within the moon-disc. This practice
might be similar to the so-called *Ajikan*, the contemplation of syllable A
against the background of the full moon-disc, in Japanese Shingon Buddhism.[48]

It should be noted here that the compilers of the Japanese supplementary
canon reprinted the syllables in Hanyue's text with Siddham scripts. I suspect
that those scripts were originally written in the Lantsa style. This is because
while Siddham scripts were dominant in Tang esoteric sources, the Lantsa
scripts, a more angular and decorative style than Siddham, gradually replaced
Siddham in late imperial China due to the influence of Tibetan Buddhism.[49]
Figure 5.2 shows a syllable chart of Lantsa scripts that were often used in late
imperial China.

Based on a series of *bīja* contemplations, Hanyue urges the practitioners
to purify the universe (*dharmadhātu*). As he explains, because the entire *dharmadhātu* is derived from the perfect circle, namely, the moon-disc, a monk
should first visualize the creation of the Buddhist cosmos that centers on
Mount Meru[50] and then transform himself into the Ratnasaṃbhava Buddha
as preparation for conducting the ritual. However, at this point, Hanyue regards it as essential to clear away the intention of food bestowal, which consti-
tutes an obstruction to emptiness. Even the notion of emptiness should be
eliminated with visualized fire and fierce *vajra* fists.

Here, Hanyue seizes the opportunity to add his Chan interpretation. He
thought that this process of elimination was identical to the Chan practice,
which fully demonstrates Linji Yixuan's spirit of "killing Buddhas and patriarchs." In other words, just as Linji Yixuan wanted to destroy the very notion
of Buddhas and patriarchs, so esoteric masters sought to eliminate the notion
of emptiness through visualization. Here, Hanyue alludes to a famous remark
made by Linji Yixuan. According to the *Linji lu*, when a student asked about
the final enlightenment, Linji informed him that the true way is to "kill" their
teachers: "Kill Buddhas when you see Buddhas; kill patriarchs when you see

FIGURE 5.2.   Lantsa scripts used in esoteric ritual performance
during the late Ming. From Yunqi Zhuhong, *Yuqie jiyao shishi yigui*
(1606), Z no. 1080-A, 59: 25.

patriarchs; kill parents when you see parents; and kill relatives when you see
relatives."[51] On this occasion, Linji advocated an immediate enlightenment
without the mediation of Buddhas and patriarchs. Interestingly, Hanyue found
that Linji's thought resonated with the tantric use of *vajra* fists and the visualization of fire to destroy illusions.

   After a series of complicated visualizations of the syllables *hrīḥ, ā,* and *huṃ*
in coordination with certain *mudrās,* the *dharmadhātu* is said to be completed.
At this point, the performer is advised to identify with Avalokiteśvara and to
assume the position of Mahāvairocana. Reciting the *Heart Sūtra* invites all
Buddhas to come. The text goes on with a series of visualizations of seed syllables. After positioning oneself as Avalokiteśvara, one begins the crucial process of empowerment (Sanskrit: *adhiṣṭhāna*; Chinese: *jiachi*). By assuming the
position of Avalokiteśvara and Mahāvairocana, the practitioner can empower
his own body by visualizing different syllables. Once the empowerment is

effected, the practitioner, now the powerful Avalokiteśvara, breaks open hell, releases the hungry ghosts, and invites them to enter the altar. Since all of the sins emerge when hell is broken open and then accumulate into a mountain of sins, the practitioner lets out a great shout, which smashes this mountain into tiny motes of dust.

Hanyue's ritual continues by spreading the sweet dew to the ghosts, again with a series of visualizations of Siddham or Lantsa syllables. Through this, all ghosts, even the ghosts who have obstructed the Food Bestowal Ritual, take the three refuges and return to the original perfect circle that is the source of all beings.

This description is only a brief outline of Hanyue's text. But the text clearly demonstrates Hanyue's attempt to synthesize Chan and tantrism based on the perfect circle. For him, Chan contemplation is compatible with esoteric rituals. Taking the meditation on the moon-disc as his root metaphor, he even speculated at the end of his text that the secret principle of contemplation, as manifested in the perfect circle, had later been transmitted from Central Asia to the Chan patriarchs Nanyang Huizhong (?–775) and Yangshan Huiji, both of whom frequently used the perfect circle to symbolize ultimate enlightenment. He remarked as follows:

> Nevertheless, this principle [of food bestowal] originated from the Western Region (Central Asia) and was transmitted by patriarchs. Being brought to the East, it was handed down to the National Master Nanyang Huizhong and after three transmissions, it became transformed into Yangshan Huiji's (807–883) teaching, which contains ninety-seven phases of the perfect circle. Thus, one knows that the method of food bestowal reflects succinctly the function of correspondence (that is, esoteric teaching) and the principle of Chan contemplation. Shouldn't this be a great matter in the world of cause and effect? I thought that this method [of food bestowal] had been [performed] without its principle for a long time. I came across it because I studied the teachings of the five Chan lineages. [52]

Here, Hanyue Fazang clearly intended to interpret the meaning of this esoteric ritual in light of Chan teaching. He regarded the Rite of Releasing the Hungry Ghosts as the great "function" (yong), while arguing that Chan teaching is its "essence" (ti). By using the philosophical categories ti and yong, Hanyue considered his understanding of the close connection between the two traditions as a great discovery, which could have been attributed to his study of Chan Buddhism. Hanyue also speculated that, in history, esoteric teaching had been assimilated into Chan teaching as embodied in Chan masters' use of the perfect circle. However, Hanyue's idea deviated most significantly from orthodox Chan ideology. By the seventeenth century, the separate transmission of the Chan tradition to China had been canonized and was indisputable. Chan was widely accepted as a separate Buddhist teaching transmitted through the twenty-eight Indian patriarchs and received unbroken by Chinese patriarchs. Hanyue, however, offered a strikingly different version of Chan transmission to China: He regarded Nanyang Huizhong and Yangshan Huiji as the patriarchs who actually received transmission from Central Asia. Although he did not specify the Central Asian patriarchs who introduced the dharma to China, the only prominent Buddhist transmission from India and Central Asia at that time was the esoteric tradition brought by Śubhākarasiṃha, Vajrabodhi, and Amoghavajra. Both Nanyang Huizhong and Yangshan Huiji lived in a period when esoteric Buddhism enjoyed remarkable imperial support.[53] Although there is no clear historical evidence to confirm the interaction between the Chan tradition and esoteric Buddhism, Hanyue apparently felt emboldened to suggest that the esoteric masters had transmitted the secret meaning of the perfect circle to Chan patriarchs.

Neither Miyun Yuanwu nor the Yongzheng emperor were aware of this esoteric dimension of the perfect circle because Hanyue's esoteric writings were not widely known in the Chan circle. To rebut Hanyue Fazang, Miyun Yuanwu argued that the Weiyin Buddha within the perfect circle, the cosmic source of all beings, simply resides in everyone's true nature and is beyond human thinking. In Miyun's view, Hanyue took the name literally and, in so doing, had fallen into the "realm of demons." Moreover, Miyun Yuanwu argued that Hanyue Fazang's attribution of the origin of Chan Buddhism to the perfect circle was idiosyncratic since there were no historical sources to prove the validity of either the perfect circle or the Weiyin Buddha. Obviously, Miyun's attack did not match Hanyue's sophistication.

The Encounter Dialogue in Question

If Miyun Yuanwu and Hanyue Fazang disagreed over so many aspects of Chan teaching, why did Miyun confer dharma transmission on Hanyue in the first place and why did Hanyue accept it? On the surface, a process of testing based on encounter dialogue legitimized the transmission process. In 1624, Hanyue visited Miyun at Mount Jinsu and engaged in a lively encounter dialogue that was not only transcribed in their recorded sayings but also later became a focal point of controversy. According to both participants, although Miyun granted dharma transmission to Hanyue, the original encounter dialogue showed no agreement between their respective understandings of Chan. The following account not only illustrates their divergent interpretations of the same event but also provides a valuable glimpse of Chan practice in the seventeenth century.

The Encounter between Miyun and Hanyue

Tanji Hongren offers the most detailed account about this encounter, which is translated as follows:

> Sanfeng Zang (Hanyue Fazang) came for an interview. He [first] asked [Miyun Yuanwu] to ascend to the seat and to illuminate the origin of the principle of the Linji school. Master [Miyun Yuanwu] raised the case of Baizhang's second interview with Mazu and Huangbo's showing of his tongue. [Miyun told the story:] "Baizhang said, 'In the future are you going to inherit Mazu's transmission?' Huangbo replied: 'No. Today, because you raise the case, I have a chance to see the great function of Mazu's expedient means. Moreover, I don't know Mazu personally. If I receive Mazu's transmission, I will lose my heirs in the future.' Therefore, [later, when] Linji inquired about the essential meaning of the Buddhist dharma, Huangbo only replied with three fist-blows. When Linji started to teach, he only introduced people by beating and shouting without asking how and what. He simply valued the straightforward method, as sharp as a knife."
>
> [On hearing this,] Sanfeng (Hanyue) stepped forward from the assembly and bowed. He uttered a shout immediately after he rose up. Master [Miyun] remarked: "What a good shout!" Sanfeng shouted again. The master asked: "Will you try another shout?" [But] Sanfeng bowed again and then returned to the assembly. Master [Miyun] turned to Hanyue and raised another case: "A monk asked a venerable master, 'What about the time when a bright moon is shining in the sky?' This master replied, 'You are still a person falling below the rank.' The monk said, 'Master, please introduce me to [what is] above the rank.' This venerable master replied, '[Let's] see each other after the moon sets.'" [After introducing this case,] Master Miyun Yuanwu said, "Now, please tell me, after the moon sets, how do they see each other?" Hanyue at once left the hall [without replying].
>
> The second day, in the assembly hall, Hanyue was appointed the head of assembly. He stepped out and said [to Miyun], "The sea

moves and the cloud follows / The benevolent rain is falling from the sky. I don't want to ask about the appearance of the jumping and flying dragon, but what does the phrase 'driving the thunder and pulling the flash' mean?" Master [Miyun] gave a shout at once. Hanyue asked further, "Why is the flower at Mount Jinsu blossoming but at Baolin monastery the fruits have ripened?" Master [Miyun] shouted again. Hanyue bowed and returned to the assembly.

Miyun raised his stick and said, "I can only raise one instead of two. If I miss the first one, I have to pick up the second." He then threw his stick on the ground. "I have to go to pick up the second one, but how can I raise the first one?" He then left his seat. Hanyue immediately took the stick and followed. When Miyun returned to his seat, Hanyue presented the stick [to Miyun] and said, "This is the stick that beats all people in the world. Today I return it to you." Miyun took the stick and then hit Hanyue, saying, "Let me give you a blow first." Hanyue replied, "I am honored to receive your blow." Master [Miyun] said, "Do you still feel it is not enough?" And then he struck Hanyue several more times.

[Later,] Hanyue asked, "Skipping the trivial issues at the gate of the Linji school, what is the essential thing inside the central hall?" Master Miyun replied, "Where are you right now?" Hanyue answered, "This is still a trivial issue." Master Miyun showed him the seat and said, "Now, be seated." Hanyue said, "Why (yi)?"[54]

These scenes are vivid depictions of the performance of encounter dialogue and thus deserve our close attention. The record shows that the encounter between Miyun and Hanyue lasted for several days and was composed of several interconnected episodes. On the first day, Hanyue had an interview with Miyun. The location of this meeting was not specified. But because the record says later that Hanyue "stepped from the assembly," it is very likely that this encounter occurred during the ceremony of ascending the hall. The record even mentions in passing that Hanyue was allowed to be seated, showing Miyun's great respect for him.

Hanyue started with his question about the principle of the Linji Chan with a clear intention to challenge Miyun. Miyun first immediately raised the kōan stories about the three early Chan patriarchs who contributed to the formation of the Linji school: Baizhang Huaihai, Huangbo Xiyun, and Linji Yixuan. Here, Miyun deliberately selected those words and phrases insinuating the importance of dharma transmission and the use of beating and shouting.

He singled out Huangbo's refusal to accept Mazu's transmission, emphasizing that the reason was, as Huangbo confessed, the absence of a personal encounter with Mazu. Both Miyun and Hanyue must have known what this meant: It had been widely known before Hanyue approached Miyun that Hanyue admired Juefan Huihong and Gaofeng Yuanmiao and even considered claiming their dharma transmission by means of remote succession. Obviously, Miyun was hinting here that Hanyue should consider a living Chan master, such as him, to be his teacher. Immediately after raising this kōan story, Miyun shifted to Linji and accentuated that beating and shouting were the quintessential characteristics of the Linji school. Once again, by citing Linji, Miyun referred to himself as the true heir of the Linji school because of his emboldened use of beating and shouting.

After hearing Miyun's talk, Hanyue responded with shouts without any verbal reply. It is hard to know exactly what he thought about Miyun's answer to his question. But judging from our knowledge about Hanyue's consistent view about the principle of the Linji school, it is safe to assume that Hanyue shouted with dissatisfaction because Miyun failed to comment on the most significant phrase that loomed large in his mind: the "three mysteries and three essentials." Miyun probably didn't know what was behind Hanyue's formulaic shout. So he praised Hanyue and pressed him to shout again. Hanyue gave another shout but returned to his seat when Miyun asked the second time.

Then, it was Miyun's turn to test Hanyue. He alluded to an anecdote from Caoshan Benji's recorded sayings, in which a master points to his disciple's insufficiency in training and suggests a meeting after moonset. It is obviously an impossible meeting because in the dark without the moonlight, no one can see the other clearly. By posing this dilemma, Miyun wanted to see how Hanyue responded. Miyun must have been pleased because Hanyue did not reply at all, showing his reluctance to conceptualize his thought. Instead, he walked away without turning around.

During the first day of their encounter, it was Hanyue who displayed the antinomian Chan spirit to the full extent. Here, we must bear in mind that, although Hanyue disagreed with Miyun, he did not oppose the use of beating and shouting. Rather, his difference from Miyun only lies in the question of whether one should employ the method with a proper understanding of the principle of the Linji school or one simply uses it randomly at will without a clear purpose. He thought that, without principle, even if Miyun could perform beating and shouting, he was not a true Chan master with the spirit of spontaneity. For him, because of his adherence to the Linji principle, he could use beating and shouting in a more meaningful way.

The encounter continued on the second day when Tanji Hongren's record clearly indicates that an assembly was called. Hanyue was dutifully honored as the leader of all monks, a position that was reserved for the abbot's favorite disciple, who was usually the candidate for the next dharma transmission. Obviously, the person in this position was expected to initiate the conversation. Thus, Hanyue first presented a poem composed in literary Chinese. (I assume this is his own work because I could not find a reference to this verse in digitized Chan texts.) As he clearly indicated, the first three lines are irrelevant and only the last line contains the core meaning of the poem. He asked for Miyun's reply, and Miyun simply shouted. Hanyue asked another question, and Miyun shouted again. Without further question, Hanyue returned to the assembly.

Then, Miyun threw the ball to Hanyue. This time, Miyun used his stick as a prop. He first pointed to his stick, indicating he could only hold one stick in his hand at a given time. Then, he threw the stick onto the ground, wondering how he would pick up the stick on the ground while having the stick previously in his hand at the same time. This is once again a mission impossible, because the stick in the past and the stick at the present are simply the same object that is located in two temporal frameworks. There was basically only one stick, but by mentioning two sticks here, Miyun was referring to the one in the past moment and to the one on the ground as two separate entities. He was wondering, if he went to pick up the one on the ground, where was the stick from a moment ago? (This reasoning resonates with Sengzhao's sophistry in his *Things Do Not Shift*.) The most enigmatic aspect is that Miyun then left his seat. Here, the meaning of the game should be understood in this way: Miyun emptied his seat, awaiting a capable candidate to succeed him. This person must be able to raise the stick on the ground, which symbolizes Miyun's spiritual authority. Hanyue must have seen this clearly: He immediately picked up the stick and returned it to Miyun. But Miyun hit him with the stick. Miyun even scolded Hanyue for not having enough of his beating.

If I understand correctly, when Miyun left his seat, Hanyue should have picked up the stick on the ground and made a bold movement to take the empty seat, indicating his willingness to accept the dharma and succeed Miyun's position. Instead, he must have surprised Miyun when he returned the stick, a symbolic rejection of Miyun's offer. Even after Miyun hit him several times—probably for real—Hanyue still wasn't "awakened."

It became clear that Hanyue felt reluctant to accept Miyun's dharma transmission when he asked Miyun again the essential teaching of the Linji school in the last episode. Miyun once again pointed to the empty high seat and urged Hanyue to look at his surroundings in search of the true dharma. But

Hanyue bluntly responded with an exclamatory *yi* (why?), questioning the necessity of accepting Miyun's offer.[55]

During this encounter, the questions and responses of Miyun and Hanyue centered on the meaning of several kōans or verses articulated in a highly literary fashion, and the attention was always directed to the meaning of one essential phrase in the story. For readers who are familiar with Chan kōan stories, Miyun's and Hanyue's language and behaviors show clear traces of imitation. Their use of words and actions shows similarities with the situations in encounter dialogues in Chan texts, as I have pointed out. From critics of Chan in the sixteenth and seventeenth centuries, such as Yunqi Zhuhong and Hanshan Deqing, we learn that a significant number of Chan monks believed that authentic Chan teaching should resemble this example.

Two Different Interpretations

This encounter dialogue appears to be a perfect embodiment of the spirit of Linji Chan. No explanation is involved; shouts are uttered at junctures when ordinary cognition might be used to answer questions; the remarks by Miyun and Hanyue are too puzzling to be understood immediately by an outsider, if at all; and the stick is used symbolically as a token of patriarchal power. The encounter, which tested a student's qualifications, seemed to have accomplished its objective since Miyun Yuanwu finally granted the transmission certificate to Hanyue Fazang. However, as the later controversy reveals, this performance failed to achieve its ultimate goal, because the mutual agreement (*qi*), which is the prerequisite for dharma transmission, did not take place at that time.

Although I have offered a tentative analysis of their encounter from the perspective of a modern scholar, we must listen to how the two protagonists evaluated each other afterward. Miyun complained that Hanyue, judging from his reaction in the encounter, did not understand his teaching and that Hanyue's response showed his ignorance of the essential meaning of Chan teaching. Pointing to the last episode of their exchange, when Hanyue asks about the "essential things in the central hall" and Miyun replies by asking, "Where are you right now?" Miyun states that "the central hall" refers to the place where the "master" (*zhuren*) resides. (Miyun commonly used "master" to signify one's true self.) Therefore, his reply was intended to point directly to Hanyue Fazang's own self. However, Hanyue totally missed the point and regarded this question as a "trivial thing." Miyun comments: "I pointed to the fundamental [nature] of his existence, but Hanyue still avoided it by moving outwards. Isn't he obsessed with karmic consciousness without any ground to stand on? Isn't this why he does not understand the meaning of my words?"[56]

Hanyue was equally dissatisfied with Miyun's reply to his inquiry about principles. According to his disciple Tanji Hongren, Hanyue once asked about the essential teaching of the Linji school. Miyun kept silent for a long time and then said, "Principles are too complicated. The transmission of a principle is more difficult than [the transmission] through human beings. It would be better to stop talking about it. Moreover, my master did not mention it." Hanyue was not happy with this answer. He declared:

> People in ancient times established the principle. Even if it is
> extremely firm and solid, there are still people who broke it and
> falsely claimed the dharma, thus confusing the true principle. As a
> master, if your dharma is not clear, there will be no way to test
> students, and meaningless shouts and aimless blows will be used
> outrageously. How disgraceful our lineage is![57]

It should be noted that this disagreement was not about the use of beating and shouting as a means of training students. Both Miyun Yuanwu and Hanyue Fazang employed this method extensively. However, Hanyue felt that the purpose or intention of these blows and shouts must be elaborated and articulated; otherwise, they would lose their meaning. For Miyun, everything depended on spontaneous responses that were supposed to emerge from one's own true enlightened self. This divergence of interpretation was the main reason for Hanyue Fazang's reluctance in accepting Miyun Yuanwu's transmission. Clearly, the dharma transmission between the two was not the result of a successful encounter dialogue but rather of pragmatic considerations: the perpetuation of a lineage and the need for legitimization.

Encounter Dialogues in the Seventeenth Century

The plethora of historical records from seventeenth-century Chan Buddhism allows us to unearth a series of events through Chan monks' polemical essays. It is certain that, at least in the seventeenth century, encounter dialogues were not merely a literary genre. To be specific, for Chan monks in that period, enlightenment was widely believed to be attainable through sudden experience and encounter dialogue, which was a real performance involving master and disciple. It had become the way for Chan masters to induce the enlightenment experience in their students. My study of the controversies shows that when encounter dialogues were enacted, beating and shouting, two kinds of action that were of a performative nature, were regarded by Chan Buddhists as the hallmark of the "authenticity" of their tradition.

The episode I examined above was typical in that time. In seventeenth-century Chan Buddhism, historical records indicate that Chan masters were prone to enact encounter dialogues. Many Chan masters such as Miyun Yuanwu were recognized as authentic teachers because they were capable of performing encounter dialogue by their frequent use of beating and shouting as devices. (Other tricks might include leaving the room without replying, smiling and holding a fan, turning a somersault, etc.) However, all of these encounter dialogues, characteristic of the Chan revival at that time, had some similar problems, as some of Miyun's critics pointed out.

First, even though masters and disciples did their best to perform encounter dialogues as if they were spontaneous, their performances were often criticized as forced and faked demonstrations of spontaneity. This is because in their performances there were clear traces of imitations based on existing kōan stories preserved in Chan texts. In this sense, the performances, seemingly creative and spontaneous, lacked originality and sometimes appeared to be awkward imitations and silly parodies. The renowned Caodong master Zhanran Yuancheng, for example, observed critically the performance of encounter dialogues in his book *Kaigu lu* (Records of lamenting the past), which was written in 1607. According to him, Chan masters of his time could only "talk about Chan by following the texts" (*yiben tanchan*). As performers, they "resembled greatly actors in theaters" (*dasi xichang youren*). Thus, Chan teaching became extremely easy: After listening to the lectures about these texts, upon which their master commented, Chan students could claim that they "understood" Chan. However, in antiquity, Chan enlightenment only came after years of great effort and exertion. Therefore, Zhanran Yuancheng concluded, "People today who are fond of talking about Chan are actually possessed by demons."[58]

What is clear to us is that during this time through a much more literal understanding of Chan literature, a textualized performance was enlivened. However, to make this revived Chan tradition appear to be authentic, Chan masters had to repeat or imitate what had been recorded in Chan texts. In this sense, repetition and imitation helped to recreate an imagined past and a sense of authenticity.

Second, as Zhanran Yuancheng correctly pointed out, encounter dialogue, when performed, resembles the performance of a drama. From the viewpoint of the spectator, the encounter dialogue as performed by Miyun and Hanyue during the ceremony of ascending the hall certainly had theatrical features. Based on the account of this event, we can imagine the following theater-like performance taking place in a monastery: Monks wearing colorful robes assemble in the hall where a central space is clearly marked by its setting and alignment. Miyun, the Chan master, sitting in the central seat, holds his stick, which symbolizes patriarchal power but can also be viewed as a prop. A monk steps out from the line, entering the central space, and recites a passage of highly literary prose, probably in a high-pitched voice. The ensuing exchange is composed of words drawn from the existing kōan literature, which may serve as a kind of script. Instead of answering the monk's question, the Chan master suddenly lets out a shout at which the monk who asked the question shouts in reply. The whole event culminates when the monk grabs the master's stick, runs away from the hall, and only returns later.

The entire process was clearly characterized by several salient theatrical features: a clear sense of stage, formal and stately movements, highly stylized voices, the use of props, and a plot structure that ends with a dramatic climax. A hundred years later, when the Yongzheng emperor read Tanji Hongren's record of the encounter dialogue between Miyun and Hanyue in the *Wuzong jiu*, he immediately associated this encounter with popular dramas. Miyun Yuanwu and Hanyue Fazang, wrote the emperor, were "putting on a *Zaju* drama (*banyan zaju*)." In the emperor's eyes, beating, shouting, and imitated conversations between master and disciple made them "a pair of marionettes (*yishuang kuilei*)."[59]

Qian Qianyi, a famous literatus in the seventeenth century who favored the scholarly pursuit of Buddhist teachings such as Tiantai and Huayan, disparaged this kind of Chan practice. The most salient criticism was that this kind of performance was extremely artificial and no different from a theatrical performance. The following comment by Qian Qianyi in 1634 was possibly made with Miyun Yuanwu in mind:

> The present-day Chan is not Chan. It is no more than kōan and
> beating and shouting. Master Hedong (Hanshan Deqing) [once]
> commented on Master Miyun: "Chan is only one of the six *pārami-
> tās*. How can it include all [Buddhist] laws? Chan is not a law and
> thus cannot be preached according to laws; it is not doctrine and
> thus cannot be taught like a doctrine. How could it be sought by
> following fixed tracks? Speaking of the Chan school, if a smile is
> called for, just smile; if wall-gazing is called for, just gaze at a wall; if
> beating and shouting are called for, just shout and beat. These are
> the so-called 'no-teaching and no-laws without traceable tracks.'"
> Today, [Chan masters] draw analogies freely and lecture to whom-
> ever. *The demonstration in the dharma hall is like actors ascending the
> stage; paying homage and offering certification of enlightenment are simi-
> lar to a drama acted out by little boys. . . .* [emphasis mine]. They boast

to each other about the number of their followers, the extent of their fame, and the wealth of their profits and patronage.[60]

In Qian Qianyi's eyes, the Chan Buddhism of his day, instead of reviving ancient practices, was in a state of degeneration. Chan had lost the ethos of spontaneity and tended to be ritualized on occasions such as the ceremony of ascending the dharma hall.

To some audiences, especially Chan followers and the literati with similar Chan mindsets, the performance of encounter dialogue was distinctively real because through the manipulation of religious symbols and the reenactment of textualized encounter scenes, a "performatively created reality" corresponded with the collective imagination of the past among the audience. In this sense, the reinvention of encounter dialogue was successful on the condition that Chan ideals occupied the thoughts of the audience. If this condition were removed, however, the reinvented performance would appear no different from the somehow "vulgar" popular dramas, which forced an impression of reality. Ironically, as I have indicated above, immediately after the emergence of this recreated Chan style, some opponents of Chan, such as Qian Qianyi, identified the glaring discrepancy between the represented past and the reality: The sense of the real presence of the ideal of antiquity as "acted out" was forced and faked.

In the seventeenth century, Chan monks' lively performances were indeed identified as "putting a popular drama on stage." Such an explicit association between Chan encounter dialogue and popular drama indicates a certain kind of failure of encounter dialogue as a legitimate way of attaining enlightenment: A ritual performance became controversial if it appeared to be deliberately staged as a theatrical performance because the aura of reality created by the manipulation of religious symbols was thus dispelled, and the audience clearly sensed that the performance was a stylized representation rather than a "real" happening. (In ritual studies, this kind of situation is identified as "ritual failure" and is extremely useful for the study of the dynamic of ritual performance and the inner construction of the experience of reality.) The Chan performance of encounter dialogue in the seventeenth century, to a large extent, failed to communicate to some audiences a sense of reality because it was largely a reinvented practice based on imitations of similar performances textualized in Chan literature.

Indeed, soon after the seventeenth century, the lively performance of beating and shouting completely disappeared from the mainstream monastic world. In other words, the success was only temporary because, as seen from other sources such as the monastic codes, the performance of beating and shouting became less and less important, and in modern Chinese Buddhism, as Holmes Welch observes, it largely withdrew from the monastic scene without a trace.[61]

Conclusion

Polemical texts are revealing exactly because they allow different voices to speak, which have been consciously or unconsciously suppressed in more normative writings. In these materials, we see disparate understandings of common Chan practices at that time.

To distinguish Chan masters with genuine enlightenment experience from imposters, Hanyue wanted to use the principle to enforce an objective standard to test Chan students. Miyun, however, rejected such a concept because for him any attempt to theorize the principle contradicts the meaning of enlightenment, which transcends any human knowledge and thus cannot be objectified. Hanyue's esoteric understanding of the perfect circle, which appears to be idiosyncratic to most Chan Buddhists, is definitely a creative synthesis of Chan and esotericism in Chan history. Meanwhile, it reveals the prevalence of esoteric rituals in monastic reality: Even the most famous Chan masters were adepts of this kind of ritual performance.

In addition, the dispute between Miyun and Hanyue shows that encounter dialogue was transformed from a textual ideal into a live performance. This transformation brought to prominence a series of hermeneutic issues: What is enlightenment? How does one seek objectivity within a subjective experience in order to ascertain a claim of enlightenment? What criteria could a Chan master use to examine and test his students' spiritual achievement? Could sudden enlightenment itself justify and guarantee the attainment of buddhahood?

Although these questions occupied the minds of serious Chan practitioners in the seventeenth century, the debate about the validity of sudden enlightenment gradually subsided because Chinese Chan Buddhists had already solved these problems in some degree, concluding that Chan aspiration must be supplemented by various gradual practices, such as doctrinal studies, Pure Land invocations, and intensive meditation. Guifeng Zongmi, Yongming Yanshou, and Yunqi Zhuhong justified this "syncretic" orientation as compatible with the spiritual ideal of Chan, at least in theory. In contrast to this consensus among Chan practitioners, Miyun Yuanwu and his followers represented a radical, essentialist, and uncompromising version of Linji Chan.

6

The Yongzheng Emperor
and Imperial Intervention

The controversy between Miyun and Hanyue did not end with the deaths of the two major antagonists. With the ascendancy of Chan Buddhism in the Qing court, its ripples extended far beyond the Buddhist community in south China. Later, a self-proclaimed Chan master, the Yongzheng emperor, emerged. During his thirteen-year rule, he not only consolidated the Manchu political rule of China but also exerted great ideological control of the intellectual world. Among a series of interventions in monastic affairs, Yongzheng was best known for the refutation of Hanyue Fazang found in his eight-fascicle book, *Jianmo bianyi lu* (Records of pointing out demons and discerning heterodoxy).[1] His personal involvement in Buddhist affairs cannot be understood simply in terms of political power, for the emperor was deeply religious. Therefore, the judgments made by this emperor add an extra dimension to the controversy between Miyun and Hanyue.

Yongzheng's Journey to Chan Enlightenment

The Qing emperors were skillful manipulators of religious discourses. They maintained a diverse and multilayered belief system involving Confucianism, Tibetan Buddhism, Chan Buddhism, Taoism, and their native shamanism. In this way, they sought to recreate a symbolic representation of a multicultural empire centering on the power, both spiritual and political, of self-proclaimed enlightened monarchs.

The first Qing emperor, Shunzhi, while still a teenager, showed tremendous interest in Chan Buddhism. At the recommendation of Feiyin Tongrong's disciple Hanpu Xingcong, he summoned Muchen Daomin and Yulin Tongxiu to the court and promoted their lineages. The Kangxi emperor, during his tours of the south in 1684 and 1689, visited many Chan monasteries, such as Tianning monastery in Yangzhou, Sheng'en monastery in Suzhou, and Lingyin monastery in Hangzhou. Kangxi presented these monasteries with new plaques and his calligraphy. He also summoned eminent Chan monks, most of whom were Miyun Yuanwu's descendants, to his court.[2] Among the early Qing emperors, Yongzheng and his son Qianlong were the two most zealous autocrats who engaged deeply in religious affairs, especially in Chan Buddhism.[3] They read Chan literature extensively, organized their own Chan training sessions in the court, and associated themselves with favored Chan monks. Not simply monarchs but also supposedly enlightened Chan masters, they actively interfered with monastic business by writing polemical essays and issuing imperial edicts to promote the masters they liked and to denounce those they detested.

Yongzheng's Support of Buddhism

As the third emperor of the Qing dynasty, Yongzheng was a diligent and powerful ruler who contributed to the consolidation of the Manchu rule of China. Beyond his political accomplishments, his immersion in Buddhism, especially Chan Buddhism, has intrigued many historians.[4] During his reign, Yongzheng exerted great influence on the Buddhist world. He befriended the second lCang-skya Khutuγtu Ngag-dbang-blo-bzang-chos-ldan (Chinese: Zhangjia hutuketu Awangluosangquedan, 1642–1714) when he was still a prince and invited the third lCang-skya master Rol-pa'i-rdo-rje (Chinese: Ruobiduoji, 1717–86) to Beijing immediately after he was enthroned in 1723.[5] Both Tibetan masters played significant roles in court politics. As I will explain later, the second lCang-skya master tested his enlightenment experience and the third lCang-skya master, who was educated under Yongzheng's tutelage, became a leading monastic official and translator of various versions of the Buddhist canon.

Yongzheng and his successors maintained a special relationship with Bailin monastery (not to be confused with Bailin monastery in Hebei where Zhaozhou Congshen [778–897] lived), which was close to Yonghegong palace, Yongzheng's former residence. This is because Yongzheng befriended the abbot of the monastery Jialing Xingyin (1671–1726) and practiced meditation with monks in Bailin monastery in 1712.

Jialing Xingyin hailed from a prominent family in Shenyang, Liaoning province. He joined the Buddhist order when he was twenty-four and went south to Li'an monastery (also referred to as Nanjian) in Hangzhou. In 1707, his teacher Meng'an Chaoge (1639–1708) was invited to be abbot in Bailin monastery in Beijing. In the following year, when his teacher died, Jialing Xingyin assumed his teacher's position. Officially, he belonged to Miyun Yuanwu's dharma brother Tianyin Yuanxiu's lineage. Because of the location of this monastery, it became one of Yongzheng's favorite places for meditation when he was a prince.

Yongzheng's patronage was also extended to Li'an monastery in Hangzhou where Jialing Xingyin and his teacher came. In 1714, after learning from Jialing Xingyin that Li'an monastery was in poor condition and one of its abbots Yuejian Chaoche (1659–1709) was even starved to death, Yongzheng, still a prince at that time, petitioned to his father Kangxi to grant fund and imperial titles to revive the monastery. Since then, both Bailin monastery in Beijing and Li'an monastery in Hangzhou formed a special relationship with the imperial house: Most abbots in Bailin monastery were selected from eminent monks in the lineage of Li'an monastery, which received tremendous royal patronage in the mid-Qing. For example, during his southern tours, the Qianlong emperor visited Li'an in 1751, 1757, 1762, and 1780 respectively.[6]

Not only did Yongzheng patronize Buddhist institutions, as many monarchs did, he also initiated important projects and policies. For example, starting in 1734, he ordered the compilation of the so-called Dragon Edition of the Buddhist canon (Longzang), which his son Qianlong completed in 1738.

His policies also significantly weakened the official ordination system. When the Qing dynasty came to power in 1644, the new regime attempted to restore the traditional control over the issuance of ordination certificates and to curb the practice of private ordination by requiring all ordained monks to purchase the certificates. In 1660, the Shunzhi emperor changed the law, allowing monasteries to issue ordination certificates without charge and thus greatly increasing the number of clergy. Later, he permitted ordination certificates to be handed down from master to disciple provided that no new certificates were issued. Yongzheng also paid attention to the ordination system. He greatly promoted the Vinaya tradition in Mount Baohua by organizing an imperial ordination ceremony in 1733. Vinaya master Wenhai Fuju (1686–1765) was invited to administer the ceremony, and various writings on the Triple Platform Ordination were incorporated into the imperial canon.[7] During the late years of the Yongzheng reign, the emperor realized that ordination certificates had become a mere formality. In the twelfth month of 1735, he issued a decree to invite open discussions about the official ordination system and even suggested abolishing the system.[8] Although he died soon afterward without taking action, the ordination system was officially abolished in 1754 by his son

Qianlong. This unprecedented move in Chinese history was conditioned by two factors: First, Yongzheng adopted a tax reform to incorporate the labor-service tax into the land tax. Thus, since the state's revenue relied on the acreage of land rather than on population, there was no need to continue to control the monastic population.[9] Second, as I described in chapter 1, because the Triple Platform Ordination Ceremony developed during the late Ming had been offered freely by all major monasteries, it was impossible for the state to regulate ordination again.[10] This means the Qing government finally gave up the idea of setting up official ordination platforms and monks then could offer the Triple Platform Ordination Ceremony legally and freely.

Not only did he lavishly support Buddhism, but Yongzheng was perhaps the only Chinese emperor who claimed to have attained enlightenment. His son, the Qianlong emperor, praised his father's supreme understanding of Buddhism in an inscription he wrote in 1744:

> Our August Father has from the beginning devoted himself to the highest doctrines. He has realized *Nirvāṇa-samādhi* and reached the highest enlightenment (*anuttara-samyak-sambodhi*) and so extended blessings to all sentient beings and conferred benefits upon aeons [innumerable as] dust. As King Śākyamuni, powerful and benevolent, he has manifested himself in his real shape; all beings take their refuge in (owe their lives to) Him.[11]

David Farquhar considers this description a "fulsome example of Buddhist hyperbole." In my opinion, Qianlong may have been simply telling the truth about his father as he perceived it. As an active member of Yongzheng's Chan association at the court, Qianlong had witnessed his father behaving as an enlightened Chan master. As Farquhar correctly points out, "Ch'ien-lung (Qianlong) is suggesting that his father became a Buddha through his own spiritual efforts—something both more and less than being a Bodhisattva by imperial prerogative."[12] Indeed, in this hyperbolic claim of enlightenment, Qianlong implies that Yongzheng did not empower himself through the usual pattern of direct identification with a bodhisattva. Instead, he earned his achievement by dint of his own spiritual exertions and, more specifically, through Chan enlightenment.

Yongzheng's Chan Enlightenment

Yongzheng's interest in Chan Buddhism began when he was still a young prince. Pei Huang, a scholar of Yongzheng's life, describes him as harboring a deep sense of inferiority to his half brothers because of his mother's humble origins.[13] As a consequence of this deeply rooted insecurity, Pei Huang states, the prince developed a "personality of introversion" that led him to the intensive study of philosophical thought, particularly Chan Buddhism. According to Yongzheng's own account, at an early age, he was fond of reading Buddhist scriptures and later even hired people to be ordained on his behalf. He also collected his favorite accounts of Chan enlightenment into an anthology called *Yuexin ji* (Essays that entertain the heart), in which he expressed a desire to escape the mundane world. Because his palace, now the famous lamaist temple Yonghegong, was close to Bailin monastery, he began to practice seated meditation with the monks there in 1712.

According to his own account, the sign of enlightenment appeared soon after the young prince began to meditate. On the twentieth day of the first month of 1712, the prince sat for only about the burning time of two incense sticks. The next night, when the third incense stick was lit, the prince felt that he had reached the ultimate realization. The famous Chan master residing in Bailin monastery was Jialing Xingyin.[14] Usually, according to the Chan tradition, the authenticity of a Chan enlightenment experience must be tested by a Chan master. However, the young prince did not trust Jialing Xingyin, the local Chan master, who acknowledged the validity of the prince's ultimate realization of Buddha nature. Later, a lama, the second ICang-skya Khutuɣtu Ngag-dbang-blo-bzang-chos-ldan (Chinese: Zhangjia hutuketu Awangluo-sangquedan, 1642–1714), a "living Buddha" from Amdo serving the imperial court, ultimately confirmed the validity of the prince's Chan enlightenment.

Yongzheng felt that something was uncertain about his enlightenment because, during his encounter with Jialing Xingyin, he had been unable to arouse a single doubt, the prerequisite to ultimate enlightenment. Days after the meditation session, his uneasiness led him to the second ICang-skya master, who gave him the following advice:

> What Your Highness has seen is like peeking at the sky from a hole
> poked in the window paper with a needle. Although the sky can be
> said to have been seen, the whole sky is vast. Wouldn't we say that
> the view from a needle-hole is a partial view? The Buddhist dharma
> is endless, and you should be diligent in your practice for more
> progress.[15]

Following this Tibetan monk's instruction, Yongzheng resumed seated meditation on the eleventh day of the second month of the same year. During his meditation session three days later, he suddenly began to sweat all over his body and experienced unity with all Buddhas and sentient beings. Again, he asked the second ICang-skya master about his experience. The master said:

What Your Highness has seen, although advancing one step forward, is like viewing the sky from within the compound of the inner quarter. But the whole sky is endless and has never been perceived in its entirety. The substance of the Buddhist dharma is immeasurable and you should make progress even more forcefully.[16]

When Yongzheng asked for the Chan master Jialing Xingyin's opinion about the second ICang-skya master's remark, Jialing Xingyin simply replied that the Tibetan monk was playing the lamaist trick of *huitu* (the way of returning).[17] However, Yongzheng doubted Jialing Xingyin's understanding of Chan. Trusting his Tibetan master, Yongzheng continued to practice. On the twenty-first day of the first month of 1713, when he was meditating, he suddenly realized the unity between the self and all beings. Afterward, when Yongzheng was about to ask the second ICang-skya to test his experience, this Tibetan master, without waiting for Yongzheng's question, remarked: "Your Highness has obtained the Great Freedom" (*Dazizai*). Therefore, Yongzheng regarded the second ICang-skya master, a Tibetan lama from Amdo, as the master who had tested his Chan enlightenment.

The Chan Society at the Imperial Court

It is still unclear how Yongzheng's Chan experience affected his personality and indirectly contributed to his ascendancy to the throne. It is well known that Kangxi, Yongzheng's father, had initially named his older son Yinreng (1674–1725) as the heir-apparent. However, Kangxi gradually recognized Yongzheng's talent and maturity. He often praised him for his Chinese scholarship and calligraphy and for being modest, sincere, and filial.[18] In the end, he chose Yongzheng to be his successor.

As Pei Huang notes, Yongzheng was unique in Chinese history. He was "a strong person, with a sense of being 'called' to the throne," and his introspective character provided the self-examination that the empire needed. More important, Yongzheng assumed his position as the Son of Heaven in several unique ways:

He made inspirational and emotional appeals to reorient his officials and subjects. He also applied coercive measures to remove opponents and command obedience from bureaucrats. Since he carried on his policies vigorously, his administration was marked by religious zeal. He changed the governmental structure handed down from his father and grandfather to fit his ideal and improved the general condition of the people to fulfill his imperial duty. Besides, he published works to promote Ch'an Buddhism and even claimed attainment of sudden enlightenment, the final stage pursued by Ch'an monks. In the last years of the Yung-cheng period, he organized a seminar group to study Ch'an Buddhism. He concentrated not only political but religious authority in his person.[19]

As Pei Huang has pointed out, Yongzheng's interest in Chan Buddhism did not abate after his enlightenment, and he even summoned a small group to study Chan. In fact, Yongzheng had been acting as a Chan master in such kind of study group for a long time. In the summer of 1712, in the summer palace of Jehol (Rehe), Yongzheng, still a prince, began his own Chan teaching by organizing a small Chan association consisting of monks and his attendants. The conversations conducted during the meetings of the association, including his systematically articulated viewpoints about Chan training and meditation, were later published in the *Yuanming jushi yulu* (Recorded sayings of layman Yuanming), which was incorporated later in his *Yuxuan yulu* (Imperial selection of recorded sayings).

Yongzheng's Understanding of Chan

Yongzheng's Chan teaching reflected his experience of enlightenment. He emphasized the role of true insight and opposed any Chan teaching mediated by literary forms or superficial discourses. True insight, according to him, is the understanding of the meaning of emptiness, not only the emptiness of the external world, but also that of the mind and the self. For him, the line between the enlightened and the deluded lies in the attainment of the mental state of no-mind. The practice of Chan meditation was therefore divided by him into three stages, or "passes," through which a practitioner must travel. Although various Chan masters in Song China had used the term "three passes," Yongzheng was perhaps the first to systematize its meaning.[20] According to him, after successfully navigating through the first pass, a beginner may experience the penetration of all truths. Yongzheng remarked:

> When a Chan student embarks upon the path of liberation, because he first removes the sufferings caused by his actions, he will feel that rivers, mountains, and the earth, together with the space of the ten directions, disappear completely. Without being deceived by those learned people in antiquity, he realizes that the human body is no more than [the elements] of earth, water, fire, and air. It is by nature ultimate purity, and not the slightest bit contaminated. This is what

is called the first pass of penetrating the truth and breaching of past and future.[21]

Nonetheless, the emperor felt that a beginner is easily deceived into regarding this experience as the attainment of full enlightenment, which in fact requires much more effort. The proper way, then, is to give rise to the feeling of doubt toward this experience and to aspire to advance upward. By the second pass, according to Yongzheng, the practitioner should realize that the true emptiness of all beings and all forms of delusion and attachment have been completely eliminated. At this point, the doubts should cease, and the practitioner should be able to respond to the world spontaneously and insightfully. Yongzheng remarked:

> After the first penetration of the truth, [he] will know that mountains are mountains; rivers are rivers; the earth is the earth; and the space of ten directions is the space of ten directions. Earth, water, fire, and wind are earth, water, fire, and wind. Even delusions are delusions; vexations (*fannao*; Sanskrit: *kleśa*) are vexations; color, sound, fragrance, and the sense of touch are colors, sound, fragrance, and the sense of touch. They are all the true self and nirvāna. There is not a single being that is not contained within my own body and not a single being that belongs to me. The external world and wisdom are mutually penetrated; beings and emptiness have no obstruction. The great freedom is obtained without moving. This is called "the penetration of the second pass."[22]

The practitioner, however, Yongzheng continued, must still go through the third pass, in which the enlightened mind is embodied in daily life. Using the traditional Chinese metaphysical categories, "substance" (*ti*) and "function" (*yong*), Yongzheng held that every aspect of life is the unity of substance and function. Finally, Yongzheng warned practitioners that the penetration of the three passes is also a kind of skillful means, and that ultimately there is actually nothing to be penetrated.

Teaching Chan at Court

Yongzheng's fascination with Chan continued after he was enthroned, especially in the last several years of his life. He was able to develop a small Chan community consisting of courtiers and relatives who were devoted to Chan training. In their Chan meditation sessions, Yongzheng was confident enough to act as a Chan master himself. Although some Buddhist monks and Taoist priests were also invited to join the meetings, most of them played only marginal roles. The following Buddhist and Taoist clergy are recorded as having attended the meetings:

Xuehong Yuanxin (1664–1750): An heir of Huaiguang Can, he was sent by the emperor to Mount Tiantong in 1733.

Chuyun Minghui (1664–1735): He was summoned to Beijing in 1733.

Ruoshui Chaoshan: A Linji master residing in Wanshou monastery in Beijing, he received the purple robe and was in charge of compiling the imperial canon.

Yuxuan Chaoding: A Linji master residing in Nianhua monastery in Beijing, he also transmitted Huayan teaching.

Ruchuan Chaosheng: A dharma heir of Yulin Tongxiu's disciple Maoxi Xingsen (1614–1677), he received the purple robe in 1733.[23]

Lou Jinyuan (1689–1776): A Taoist "heavenly master" from Mount Longhu, he accompanied his teacher Zhang Xilin (the fifty-fifth-generation heavenly master) to Beijing in 1727 and became a close associate of the emperor. Despite his role as a Taoist priest, he practiced Chan sessions together with the emperor, and his recorded sayings were included in Yongzheng's collection of recorded sayings.[24]

In addition to these monks and priests, this exclusive Chan group included the following regular members:

Zhang Tingyu (1672–1755): A native of Tongcheng, Anhui province, he was the son of the grand secretary, Zhang Ying. He earned his *jinshi* degree in 1700. During Yongzheng's reign, he was appointed tutor to the imperial princes, minister of rites, minister of revenue, and chancellor of the Hanlin Academy. In 1729, he was promoted to the position of grand councillor (*junji dachen*).[25]

E'ertai (1680–1745): A son of Oboi (Aobai), he was a Manchu banner man who was appointed as governor of Yunnan, Guizhou, and Guangxi.[26]

Fupeng (?–1748): A Manchu aristocrat, he was appointed general of pacifying the frontier and was charged with suppressing the Eleuths' rebellion.[27]

Yinlu (1695–1767): Kangxi's sixteenth son and Yongzheng's brother, he held the post of minister of interior affairs.[28]

Yinli (1697–1738): Kangxi's seventeenth son and Yongzheng's brother, he apparently held no important posts.

Hongli (1711–1799): Yongzheng's son, he later became the Qianlong emperor.[29]

Zhang Zhao (*jinshi* 1709): He was appointed subchancellor of the grand
secretariat.[30]

The members of this group were all persons whom Yongzheng trusted,
and the relationships fostered through Chan practice undoubtedly strengthened the ties among them. They had formed such an intimate relationship
that, in the most secret memorials, they discussed spiritual issues of Chan
enlightenment.[31] Yongzheng even gave up all formalities between monarch
and subject, addressing his official-disciples intimately as "my dear old disciples" (*laotudi*). The posts to which its members were appointed indicate that
Pei Huang is correct in viewing this group not simply as a spiritual community but also as a "political advisory committee."[32] However, the political involvement of this Chan group in the Yongzheng reign is beyond the scope of
this book, and my discussion will concentrate on its religious significance.

Yongzheng's Chan remarks and his exchanges with his courtiers have
been recorded in *Yuanming jushi baiwen* (A hundred questions of layman Yuanming) and *Dangjin fahui* (Contemporary dharma assembly).[33] Within this Chan
group, Yongzheng played the role of an enlightened Chan master who wanted
to help his followers to attain enlightenment. The Chan sessions took the form
of questions and answers. Usually, the emperor would first distribute a meaningful Chan "turning phrase" (*zhuanyu*) in the form of a pivotal sentence to his
courtiers, and then his courtiers would submit their answers, often in the form
of a poem or a phrase, for the emperor's comments. For example, Yongzheng
once posed the following question: "Among all the generations of Buddhas and
patriarchs, there is one person who transcends all Buddhas and patriarchs.
Please say who he is." Here are the answers that were submitted:

Zhang Tingyu: "He is the Buddha."
E'ertai: "An anonymous person."
Fupeng: "A clod of earth."
Yinlu: "One hand points to the heaven and the other points to the earth.
The Way does not distance itself from humans."[34]

In this session, Yongzheng's question was not about a particular Buddha or
patriarch but rather referred to the dharma body of the Buddha in relation to his
enjoyment body and transformation body. According to the Trikāya theory, only
the dharma body remains constant and permanent. However, the rule of the
Chan encounter dialogue is not to respond directly to the question. Students
should also present their understanding in indirect but illuminating ways that
convey the meanings of their answers effectively. Zhang Tingyu's reply, for example, showed that he understood the unity of Buddha and the dharma body.

E'ertai demonstrated that he considered humans and Buddhas to be of equal status. Fupeng's realization that Buddha nature is identical with all things, even with a clod of earth, indicated a deeper understanding. Yinlu's reply was, however, more subtle because he alluded to both Buddhism and Confucianism. His first sentence obviously referred to the Buddha's birth. His second sentence, however, was taken from Confucius' *Analects*. If we associate the meanings of these two sentences together, Yinlu could have intimated that the Śākyamuni Buddha is the person who transcends all Buddhas and patriarchs. Yet, because according to Confucian teaching, the transcendent Way is also immanent in all human beings, there is no difference between Buddhas and human beings. Eventually, to answer that the Buddha is the superior being is equal to saying that every sentient being transcends all Buddhas and patriarchs.

Yongzheng's Works on Buddhism

During his reign, Yongzheng empowered himself as the supreme Chan master in the nation. To impose his Chan teaching, he even meddled with Chan literature and Buddhist scriptures in order to create a standardized Buddhist canon for all Buddhists.

Yongzheng's Chan Historiography

As the monarch and an ostensibly enlightened person, he considered it his duty to rewrite Chan history and to apply his standard of Chan enlightenment. Dissatisfied with popular Chan anthologies, which included dialogues from all Chan masters without careful selection, Yongzheng compiled the *Yuxuan yulu* (Imperial selection of recorded sayings) in 1733. In this work, the emperor, without being constrained by various Chan sectarian considerations, intended to select the writings of Chan people according to his own standard. In this sense, Yongzheng's compilation breached many accepted conventions in the genre of Chan literature.

The arrangement of this anthology is unique. The main collection (*zhengji*) contains the works and sayings of fifteen "Chan" monks selected according to the emperor's criteria. These monks included Yongjia Xuanjue (665–713), Weishan Lingyou, Yangshan Huiji, Zhaozhou Congshen, Yunmen Wenyan, Yongming Yanshou (904–975), Xuedou Chongxian (980–1052), and others. Curiously, Yongzheng chose Sengzhao as the first "Chan master" on his list. A few poet-monks, such as Hanshan and Shide, were also included. The only contemporary Chan masters whose recorded sayings the emperor incorporated were Yulin Tongxiu, his disciple Maoxi Xingsen, and Yongzheng himself. Regarding himself as the number one Chan teacher in the empire, Yongzheng put his *Recorded Sayings* (*Yuanming jushi yulu*), compiled when he was still a prince, in fascicle 12.

Most extraordinary is the inclusion of the sayings of the Taoist master Zhang Boduan (987–1082) in this Chan anthology. This is because Yongzheng highly appreciated Zhang's works, such as the *Wuzhen pian* (Essay on understanding the truth), which embodies the highest understanding of Chan teaching according to the emperor. Although Yunqi Zhuhong combined Chan with Pure Land and thus was not a pure Chan master, Yongzheng included his selected works in fascicle 13, entitled "External Collection" (*waiji*), justifying his decision by praising Zhuhong as a person with "correct knowledge and correct views." Clearly, the emperor acknowledged Zhuhong as a true Chan master even though this judgment disagreed with many Chan genealogies compiled in the seventeenth century, which excluded Zhuhong completely from Chan lineages because of his lack of dharma transmission.

Fascicles 14 and 15 are "The Early Collection" (*qianji*), which includes the sayings of 156 Chan masters whose understanding Yongzheng regarded as slightly inferior to the Chan figures listed in the main collection. Absent from this collection are some famous names in Chan history, including Deshan Xuanjian, Xinghua Cunjiang, Fenyang Shanzhao, Dahui Zonggao, Juefan Huihong, and Gaofeng Yuanmiao. This is because these so-called Chan masters did not meet Yongzheng's standard of enlightenment. For example, he loathed Danxia Tianran's (738–824) and Deshan Xuanjian's (782–865) teachings in particular because their antinomian actions, such as burning the Buddha statue, implied a serious challenge to the established hierarchy.[35] With regard to the two monks named Daowu in the Tang, which was central to the debate over dharma transmission, the emperor included some of Tianwang Daowu's sayings in his "Early Collection," suggesting that he might have accepted the two-Daowu theory.[36] To supplement the "Early Collection," Yongzheng compiled the "Later Collection" (*houji*, fascicles 16, 17, and 18), which incorporates passages he selected from later Chan anthologies, such as *Jiaowai biechuan* (Separate transmissions outside doctrine) and *Chanzong zhengmai* (True transmissions of the Chan lineage). The final document in this collection (fascicle 19) contains records of his *Dangjin fahui* (Contemporary dharma assembly), in which Yongzheng played the role of Chan master and supervised Chan training sessions with his courtiers.

Such an unconventional and arbitrary collection reflects Yongzheng's version of the unity of the three teachings. In his eyes, no sectarian boundary should be set among the three teachings, and a Chan thinker should be judged by his understanding of the ultimate truth, regardless of the conventional

fame ascribed to him. His view of the unity of the three teachings can be illustrated by the emperor's favorite metaphor. At the end of his imperial edict
banning the works of Hanyue and his disciple, Yongzheng proposed to use the
relationship among the sun, the moon, and a star to analogize the relationship
among the three teachings: All three celestial objects share the quality of light
yet retain their individuality. Likewise, the three teachings, though functioning differently, share the same substance. Without contradiction, all teachings
contribute to the great Way, or, in other words, the only Way that an "enlightened sovereign" had laid out.[37]

Yongzheng's Study of Buddhist Doctrines and Scriptures

While promoting Chan Buddhism, Yongzheng did not forget Buddhist doctrines. After his enlightenment, he realized his neglect of Buddhist scriptures
and consciously read a broad range of classics. The result of his efforts was the
compilation of two anthologies of doctrinal studies. In 1734, he compiled the
Yulu Zongjing dagang (Imperially recorded essentials of *Records of the Source
Mirror*), which condensed Yongming Yanshou's *Zongjing lu* (Records of the
source mirror) from one hundred fascicles to twenty fascicles. In 1735, he compiled the *Yulu jinghai yidi* (Imperially recorded one drop in the sea of scripture)
in thirteen fascicles, which features passages he deemed to be important from
twenty scriptures.

Apparently, the emperor had indulged in scriptural studies and thereby
exposed himself to the criticism of "cognitive understanding." However, in the
preface to his collections, the emperor defended his effort, claiming that scriptural studies and true enlightenment are not contradictory because scriptures
are expedient expressions of the Buddha's teaching. He used Yongming Yanshou's *Zongjing lu* as an example because Yongming Yanshou had been criticized by Hanyue's disciple Tanji Hongren as a monk of exegesis. The emperor
defended scriptural studies on Yongming Yanshou's behalf and questioned
the antinomian style of Chan teaching:

> If the *Zongjing lu* can be called a work of exegesis, then Buddha's
> canon with twelve sections are entirely works of exegesis. Further-
> more, in this world, every single word and character, every single dot
> and stroke, is exegesis without exception. Then what is not exegesis?
> Should waving fists and erecting whisks, raising eyebrows and
> winking eyes, and crazy shouts and wild blows, be non-exegesis? If
> these were understood in this way, it is the fault of exegesis. Further-
> more, not explaining the meaning equals madness and stupidity.

Besides, the sayings spoken by Chan masters in antiquity are no more than selected phrases and words from the scriptures that were chosen to respond to situations for students. How do they ever detach from a single word of the scriptures? These selected phrases and words are not exegesis, but the complete chapters and entire verses are then rejected as exegesis. How could this be? If these are all exegeses, then how could Chan Buddhists from the past to now ascend the hall and preach the dharma?[38]

This passage shows Yongzheng's conciliatory attitude toward scriptural studies. Not only did he regard scriptures as compatible with Chan training, he even viewed encounter dialogues between master and disciple as originating from quoting scriptures. Thus, for the emperor, those so-called Chan masters who fully displayed the spirit of antinomianism and disdained scriptural studies had not even comprehended the meaning of Chan teaching. Yongzheng's view on the role of scriptural studies in Chan practice was consistent with his position in the *Yuxuan yulu*, which excludes many antinomian Chan masters.

The Emperor's Polemical Writing

Yongzheng's view toward Chan masters was ambiguous and selective. While patronizing some masters he favored, Yongzheng was hostile to some famous Chan teachers whom his predecessors had patronized, and one by one he removed their and their disciples' honorary titles and privileges. In 1733, he issued a series of decrees concerning Buddhism. He first denounced Miyun's leading dharma heir, Muchen Daomin, whom the Shunzhi emperor had welcomed to Beijing warmly. This is because Yongzheng was upset when he read Muchen Daomin's account of his audience with Shunzhi. The emperor thought that these records revealed too much information about the royal family. Because Shunzhi was only eighteen and was not politically mature, as Yongzheng was, Yongzheng deemed that he should correct his ancestor's mistake by depriving Muchen Daomin of the honorary title given by Shunzhi. In the same year, he also ordered the arrest of two disciples of Yulin Tongxiu, the Linji master who had been well received by Shunzhi, because they were found, on their return from Beijing to the south, to be raising the dragon flag, showing off the imperial patronage they had received. The two unfortunate monks committed suicide as they were being transported to Beijing.[39] The most dramatic event, however, was Yongzheng's direct intervention in the debate between Miyun and Hanyue.

In 1733 Yongzheng wrote an eight-fascicle book entitled *Jianmo bianyi lu*, which was devoted solely to a discussion of the controversy between Miyun and Hanyue. For the significance of this book in Chan history, a similar book authored by the emperor can serve as a reference framework. The *Dayi juemi lu* (The awakening from delusion), which has been studied by Jonathan Spence, was published three years earlier than the *Jianmo bianyi lu*. According to Spence, the *Dayi juemi lu* was based on the trial of Zeng Jing between 1728 and 1736. Zeng Jing was a follower of the Ming loyalist Lü Liuliang (1629–1683), whose writings, according to the government's account, were replete with anti-Manchu sentiment. Implicated in a rebellious plot, Zeng Jing was arrested and tried by the government for propagating his anti-Manchu ideas. This case, which was related to the legitimacy of Manchu rule in China, concerned Yongzheng. Through exchanges of written texts, the emperor and the prisoner conducted a series of discussions about a wide range of forbidden topics, such as racial concepts in Chinese history, the politics at court, the issue of governance, and local administration. These "conversations" transformed the "traitor" Zeng Jing into a "renewed person." The emperor decided that these materials, together with his edicts concerning this case, should be published as required texts for government officials and students in Confucian schools. After Yongzheng died, however, his son, the Qianlong emperor, rescinded the book and destroyed the circulated copies.

The style of the *Dayi juemi lu* is extremely personal. As Spence notes, the book is full of "tantalizing personal details on the members of the imperial family and the emperor himself, and the virulence and personal intimacy of the charges."[40] The *Jianmo bianyi lu* has the same character. It begins with the emperor's decree issued in the fifth month of 1733, which lays out his reasons for writing this book. He states that he first came to know of the controversy between Miyun and Hanyue through reading some polemical essays found in the recorded sayings of Miyun Yuanwu and Tianyin Yuanxiu, in which references to Hanyue's understanding of the Chan principle had been made. Hanyue's deluded view shocked him, the emperor notes, and it was clear to him that Hanyue neither understood the essence of Chan nor appreciated his master Miyun's enlightenment experience. More heinous was his disciple Tanji Hongren's *Wuzong jiu*, which was written to disseminate his teacher's heterodox views. As a person possessing both virtue and authority, Yongzheng decided to eliminate the delusions represented by these demonic figures forever.[41]

All eight fascicles are responses to about eighty extracted passages from Tanji Hongren's *Wuzong jiu*. The passages selected for criticism are printed in a smaller font, followed by the emperor's comments in a larger font. Unlike Miyun Yuanwu's *Pi wangjiu lueshuo*, the *Jianmo bianyi lu* does not adhere to the structure of the *Wuzong jiu*. Rather than arranged the fascicles according to the genealogical sequences of ancient Chan patriarchs, Yongzheng juxtaposed his own comments with quotations from Tanji Hongren's book. Before each quotation, the phrase "Demon [Hong]ren said" was added to indicate the heretical nature of Tanji Hongren's remarks.

Yongzheng agreed with Miyun that Hanyue and his disciples represented a "cognitive understanding" of Chan. According to him, the Chan principle, which they regarded as "subtle" and "esoteric," was an example of their errors. The emperor commented that, in Chan Buddhism, there is only separate transmission but no "esoteric" transmission. He apologetically defended Miyun's use of beating and shouting as expedient means to induce enlightenment although he was critical of this style of Chan training. In Yongzheng's view, the true Chan should be as follows:

> The Way of Buddhas and patriarchs takes the enlightenment of one's own mind as fundamental. Whatever confirms this teaching is the true knowledge and true insight. . . . The so-called way of heretics (*waidao*) and the way of demons (*mo*) also have their understandings. Because they falsely identify consciousness and [attachment to] death and life as the fundamental and ultimate Buddha nature, they slander the Buddhist cultivation. Therefore, they are called heretics and demons.[42]

In Yongzheng's eyes, a Chan master must conform to the rhetoric of immediate enlightenment of the mind and his failure to do so made him no different from a demon. Hanyue's interpretation of the perfect circle, with the implication of a possible synthesis of Chan and tantrism, clearly did not meet this standard of Chan teaching, which transcends all concepts and principles.

According to the emperor, Hanyue eventually created a set pattern of the perfect circle. He traced Hanyue's use of the perfect circle to the encounter story between Yangshan Huiji and his early teacher Danyuan. In this story, the Chan teacher Danyuan transmitted Nanyang Huizhong's ninety-seven images of the perfect circle to Yangshan Huiji. When Yangshan saw these images, he immediately burned them but later recreated the complete set of images from memory.[43] On another occasion, when Yangshan was still an attendant of Guishan Lingyou, Yangshan drew an image of the perfect circle on the ground but immediately wiped it out. Guishan burst into laughter.[44] In these encounters, the perfect circle was used as a vehicle to induce the enlightenment experience. In Hanyue's references to the perfect circle, however, the emperor noted that he focused only on the means they employed rather than on the facts that Yangshan eventually wiped out the image and Guishan burst into laughter. This shows that the ultimate truth transcends images and symbols, which must be cast away. Moreover, the emperor did not believe that the use of the perfect circle was unique. If needed, as he proclaimed, he could immediately draw countless circles and alter them as he wanted.[45]

For the emperor, Hanyue's and Hongren's faults lay in their literal interpretations of many symbolic actions of ancient patriarchs. Their fascination with the three mysteries and three essentials is a good example. The emperor asked: "The Buddhist teaching cannot be divided into two. How could [Hanyue] hold steadfast to 'three' and 'four,' and even have the secretly transmitted principle of 'three' and 'four'?"

To prove his point, the emperor quoted various famous kōan stories freely. His writing style was authoritative, extravagant, and pungent, fully displaying his erudition in Chan literature. Chinese and Buddhist idioms, most of them sardonic, were quoted frequently, adding weight to the emperor's criticism. For example, to denigrate Hanyue's and Tanji Hongren's vain attempts to impugn their master, Miyun Yuanwu, the emperor alluded to a famous simile in the *Scripture in Forty-two Sections*: "[They] faced up to the sky and spat toward the clouds, but in reverse [they] smeared their own faces." To berate the followers of cognitive knowledge, the emperor likened Hanyue and his disciple to Śākyamuni's attendant Ānanda, the protagonist of the *Śūraṃgama Sūtra*, who is helplessly seduced by the prostitute Mātaṅgī despite his superb memory of various kinds of knowledge.[46]

As I have shown in the previous chapter, Hanyue's fascination with the perfect circle had an esoteric connotation because he was also a practitioner of the esoteric ritual of Feeding the Hungry Ghosts. Because Hanyue's esoteric writing was not widely circulated and he did not mention his esoteric connection in his Chan writings, it is certain that the emperor did not and could not understand this background.[47] For example, Yongzheng mentioned Hanyue's preface to a book called the *Wuzong lu* (Records of the five lineages).[48] In his preface, Hanyue considered Patriarch Chan superior to Tathāgata Chan. Meanwhile, in a mysterious way, the five kinds of light emitted from the stūpa symbolize the five Chan lineages.[49] As I explained in chapter 4, Hanyue used the stūpa structure as an example to illustrate the relationship between Patriarch Chan and Tathāgata Chan. However, without any background knowledge about Hanyue's analogical thinking, the emperor was deeply puzzled by these words.

The most striking difference between the emperor's argument and Miyun's is the ethical criticism of Hanyue's lineage. The fact that Hanyue Fazang, while criticizing Miyun Yuanwu, was still willing to receive Miyun's dharma transmission is intrinsically ironic because, according to the emperor, it is unfilial for a "son" to denounce his "father."[50] More important, according

to the emperor, Hanyue had slandered the sixth patriarch, Huineng, by referring to Huineng as "falling into the [rank] of heretics [who believe in] absolute
nothingness."[51]

Hanyue's most heinous crime, according to the emperor, was the violation
of the Buddhist Vinaya rules. Yongzheng listed the following sins of Hanyue
Fazang and his disciples: no meditation, no summer or winter retreats, drinking wine and eating meat, and engaging in literary compositions as a means to
flatter the literati. The last charge, according to the emperor, placed them in the
same category as prostitutes.[52] We have no specific evidence to substantiate the
emperor's various charges about the moral corruptions in Hanyue's Chan community. But we do know that Hanyue and his disciples kept close relationships
with the literati. Some scholars thus speculate that by alluding to Hanyue's
connection with the literati, the emperor referred to the interaction between
Ming loyalists and Chan communities. Hasebe Yūkei, for example, thinks that
the persecution of Hanyue's lineage was related to the Zeng Jing case because
Zeng Jing's teacher, Lü Liuliang (1629–1683), was a close friend and relative of
Huang Zongxi, who wrote Hanyue's epitaph. (Lü's daughter married a son of
Huang's brother.) Although these specific charges in Yongzheng's edict remain unverified, his criticism of Hanyue's monastic practice divulged the emperor's secret political agenda: The vice of Hanyue's Chan Buddhism lies not
only in his heterodox ideas but also in his broad and close connection with the
literati. For the emperor, the popularity of Hanyue and his lineage among the
literati posed a severe threat to the established social order, especially considering that many literati associated with Hanyue were Ming loyalists.

Yongzheng ordered all works written by Hanyue Fazang and Tanji Hongren to be removed from the Buddhist canon and destroyed. They were to be
replaced by the emperor's refutation of the *Wuzong jiu*, which all were required
to read. The dharma transmissions of Hanyue Fazang's heirs were to cease
completely, and none of his dharma heirs would be allowed to preside over any
monastery. However, the emperor made what he considered a benevolent gesture at the end of his decree:

> If there are people in his lineage who still adhere to his demonic
> teaching, who regard his understanding as corresponding to the
> meaning of the separate transmission and as receiving the Linji
> transmission without errors, and people who do not feel completely
> convinced or are not awakened from the state of dreaming and being
> drunk, please let them see me. I will let them speak to me directly. I
> will use the sacred laws of the Buddha to argue with them. If their
> insights indeed surpass mine and their arguments are superior to

mine, I will rescind my decree and allow the Sanfeng school (*sanfeng zongpai*, that is, Hanyue Fazang's lineage) to continue as an independent sect. If they use up all their tricks but are still unconvinced and plead with the laws of the secular world instead, I will use the secular laws to punish them severely. Please do not regret [the punishment].[53]

This verdict illustrates the continuity between this case and the earlier Zeng Jing case. The emperor enjoyed arguing with his opponents and persuading them by means of his wisdom and reasoning rather than by sheer political power. As in the Zeng Jing case, the emperor chose to publicize his personal views and to share them with his subjects regardless of social status. Moreover, his own enlightenment experience must have convinced him that human beings can be transformed or awakened from delusions. This basic conviction of the perfectibility of human beings may explain why Yongzheng was so eager for personal engagement with "deluded" criminals, such as Zeng Jing, and the "demons" in the Buddhist world, such as Hanyue Fazang and Tanji Hongren.

Although the emperor had deep personal interest in the debate between Miyun and Hanyue, it is undeniable that Yongzheng harbored an omnipresent political and ideological agenda disguised behind his proclaimed neutrality. If we put this work in the context of Yongzheng's rule in the early eighteenth century, together with the *Dayi juemi lu*, this book reveals the emperor's deep concern over the rebellious literati in the newly conquered south. Although the Manchu regime ruled the south successfully in political and military terms, the occasional disobedience manifested in literary writings reminded the "foreign" rulers that they had not yet conquered the hearts and minds of the Chinese literati. And this was exactly what Yongzheng wanted to achieve: He pretentiously suspended the use of any coercive force to combat his rivals and assumed the role of a moral persuader. Believing that defiant "criminals" could eventually be converted wholeheartedly, he deigned to take part in the messy controversy.

His political intention in the debate, as far as I can see, was to create a religious orthodoxy within a Buddhist world that was directly under his control, not influenced by the literati, especially some of the most dangerous dissidents. In this way, his intervention prevented Chan Buddhism from becoming a spiritual safe haven for the disobedient literati. Yongzheng at least partially achieved this goal. By promoting Miyun's teaching as a new Chan orthodoxy, he elevated himself as the greatest of all Chan masters, who was capable of judging other people's Chan teachings and enlightenment experiences.

FIGURE 6.1. Yongzheng's calligraphy in praise of Miyun Yuanwu, 1733. The plaque reads *Ciyun mibu* (Benevolent cloud spread thickly). It is hung in the Buddha hall of Tiantong monastery. Photograph by Jiang Wu, June 2006.

Because of this, the emperor's presence in the Buddhist world has been formidable and long lasting. Even today, a sign board that Yongzheng bestowed in honor of Miyun is still hanging in Tiantong monastery, as figure 6.1 shows. The emperor's personal involvement in this controversy also gave rise to a myth within the Buddhist community: Yongzheng was none other than the reincarnation of Miyun Yuanwu because he had repudiated Hanyue Fazang on behalf of Miyun Yuanwu.[54]

Conclusion

The Yongzheng emperor's intervention in this controversy is interesting but difficult to interpret. By writing an eight-fascicle book to condemn Hanyue Fazang's heterodoxy, the emperor was using political power to support Miyun Yuanwu's argument and to suppress Hanyue's. However, if political expediency were the major consideration for the writing of this book in 1733, this controversy would not seem to merit the emperor's full attention because by that time the controversy had been over for a hundred years. Nevertheless, the Yongzheng emperor's embrace of Chan Buddhism added a new political dimension to the revival of Chan Buddhism.

Yongzheng's intervention not only concluded the controversy between Miyun and Hanyue but also changed the nature of the polemic. The controversial spiritual issues regarding the criteria of enlightenment carried a political connotation after Yongzheng's intervention. The Yongzheng emperor's engagement with Chan Buddhism thus suggests a new pattern of legitimization of political power. Perhaps for the first time in Chinese history, an emperor could claim to have achieved enlightenment, at least according to his own standards, and empower himself as a judge of religious affairs within Buddhist communities.

Yongzheng's involvement in this controversy reveals that the implicit power structure of enlightenment can easily be translated into the political realm. This finding helps to explain the interconnection of the two themes of the debate: enlightenment and dharma transmission. Both are crucial components in a power structure established through the master-disciple relationship: Enlightenment empowers the master and dharma transmission establishes a hierarchy among his followers to dispense spiritual power. If the legitimacy of enlightenment is contested, the authority of dharma transmission becomes equally controversial. Following this reasoning, part III of this book exposes the prolonged and vicious ideological war initiated by Feiyin Tongrong over the strict definition of dharma transmission.

PART III

Lineage Matters

7

The Debate about Tianhuang Daowu and Tianwang Daowu in the Late Ming

In 1654, Xiao Qiyuan, the provincial governor of Zhejiang, was presented with an unusual lawsuit: The Caodong master Sanyi Mingyu was suing the Linji master Feiyin Tongrong. The case went far beyond disputes over material interests, such as those involving land and monastic ownership. Rather, it was peculiar because this case was an intellectual dispute: Feiyin Tongrong, Miyun Yuanwu's dharma heir, was accused of deliberately changing the accepted genealogy and listing certain Caodong masters under the category of "lineage unknown" in his new Chan genealogy, *Wudeng yantong*.

Feiyin's unconventional arrangement of dharma transmission, which changed the lineage affiliations of many historical figures and mostly affected contemporary Caodong masters, hinged on a new theory about the identities of two monks: Tianhuang Daowu and Tianwang Daowu in the Tang dynasty. In contrast to the earlier dispute documented in the previous chapters, the dharma transmission controversy escalated in scope and intensity, largely because Feiyin Tongrong intended to examine the entire Chan lineage to determine the authenticity of its dharma transmissions.

In the following sections, I examine the background of this unusual lawsuit against Feiyin's work *Wudeng yantong* and some initial debates about the two Daowus in the late Ming. I focus on the investigation of the identity of Tianhuang Daowu and Tianwang Daowu to demonstrate how evidence, either textual or epigraphic, was used by Buddhist monks to verify or disprove the ambiguous dharma transmission. In this chapter, I will first introduce the issue in dispute and summarize the relevant evidence from both sides. Then, I will focus on the early stage of the controversy in the late Ming, when the literati first discovered the issue of the two Daowus and made subsequent changes in Chan anthologies they compiled. Soon after, Miyun and his disciples followed by altering dharma transmission lines in their genealogical works. These audacious moves elicited fierce responses from Huang Duanbo, a pro-Chan local official in Ningbo. In chapter 8, I will focus on the lawsuit against Feiyin and in chapter 9 on the aftermath of the lawsuit after 1654.

The Myth of the Two Daowus

This chapter concentrates on one particular case: the dispute over the identity of the two Daowus in the Tang dynasty. This dispute constituted the core of the lawsuit against Feiyin Tongrong's *Wudeng yantong*, which fundamentally altered the commonly accepted Chan historiography represented in the *Jingde chuandeng lu*. This reorganization was based on the discovery of a Tang dynasty Chan monk named Daowu. According to the *Jingde chuandeng lu*, the transmission after the sixth patriarch, Huineng, was divided into two major branches, represented by Qingyuan Xingsi and Nanyue Huairang, respectively. Qingyuan Xingsi transmitted the dharma to Shitou Xiqian, and one of Shitou Xiqian's disciples named Daowu, who lived in Tianhuang monastery in the capital city of Jingzhou (now Jiangling county), transmitted the dharma to Longtan Chongxin. Longtan Chongxin nourished the formation of two Chan schools, Yunmen and Fayan, which were attributed to his fourth-generation heir Yunmen Wenyan (864–949) and sixth-generation heir Qingliang Wenyi (885–958). This official version of lineage transmission is illustrated in chart 7.1.

For a long time, this official version was widely accepted in the Buddhist world. Its acceptance did not mean a lack of serious challenges, however. Feiyin Tongrong, for example, considered the identity of Daowu problematic and transmissions from Daowu in need of complete revision. He found an inscription, supposedly written by an obscure Tang official called Qiu Yuansu (or Qiu Xuansu),[1] of a monk also named Daowu and claimed that this new Daowu was actually Mazu Daoyi's dharma heir. According to this inscription, Longtan Chongxin was the dharma heir of this Daowu rather than the Daowu who belonged to Shitou Xiqian's line. Therefore, the two Chan lineages originally attributed to Qingyuan Xingsi should be changed to Mazu Daoyi's line because Longtan Chongxin was the dharma heir of this Daowu rather than the Daowu who lived in Tianhuang monastery. Interestingly, Feiyin Tongrong

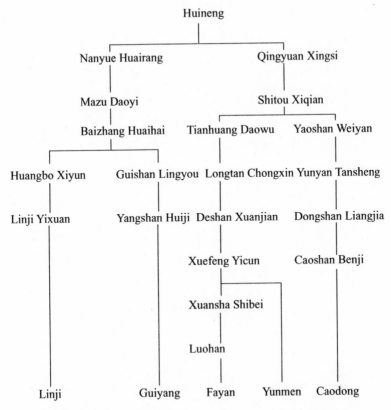

CHART 7.1. Diagram of Chan Dharma Transmissions according to Daoyuan, *Jingde chuandeng lu*

discovered that, according to the inscription, this new Daowu was active in the same city but lived in Tianwang (King of Heaven) monastery on the west side of the city.

In short, there were two monks named Daowu. One was Tianhuang Daowu, to whom two schools, Fayan and Yunmen, were traditionally attributed; the other was Tianwang Daowu, whom Feiyin Tongrong believed to be the real master of Longtan Chongxin, meaning that the two schools derived from him, Fayan and Yunmen, should be changed back to Mazu Daoyi's line of transmission. Feiyin Tongrong's reorganization of the Chan lineage, which was based on this new inscription, is shown in chart 7.2. In general, monks affiliated with Miyun's Linji lineage favored the new theory that there had been two Daowus, while the Caodong monks opposed it strongly. Both sides dug into Chan history and combed through historical sources to find new evidence to validate or falsify this theory.

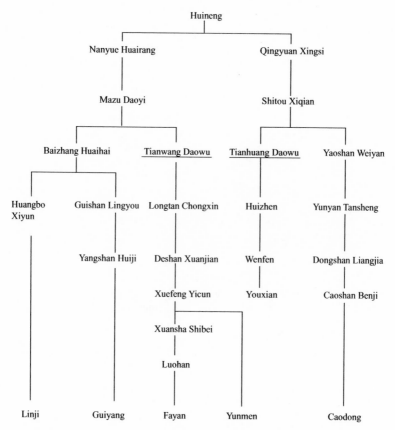

CHART 7.2. Diagram of Chan Dharma Transmissions according to Feiyin Tongrong, *Wudeng yantong*

Summary of Major Evidence

The controversies over dharma transmission are by nature disputes about Chan historiography and textual criticism. In various polemical essays, Chan monks marshaled a plethora of evidence through their investigation of Chan historical sources. In the previous section, I introduced briefly the issue of the two Daowus without reviewing some key evidence, which should be of interest to scholars of early Chan history. This is because these pieces of evidence show that, after the controversy between the Southern and Northern Chan schools subsided, the disputes began to center on the transmissions of later Chan masters in the Hongzhou school in the late Tang dynasty. Since the arguments in this debate involve many easily confused people's names, place names, and complex relationships, I list all of the evidence in appendix 3, which has been prepared for specialists. Here, I only summarize a few areas of contention, which are seemingly trivial but extremely important.

The new theory was first of all established on the existence of Tianwang Daowu's inscription authored by Qiu Yuansu, which stated clearly that Tianwang received Mazu's dharma transmission and his dharma heir was Longtang Chongxin. In this document, Qiu's title has been recorded as "the military governor of Jingzhou." Miyun's followers also found that the information contained in this inscription was further corroborated by a note recorded in Juefan Huihong's work *Linjian lu* (Records of Chan grove). Juefan Huihong not only confirmed the existence of this Tianwang Daowu but also described his biography in a way similar to the inscription. Moreover, he provided his source of information: His teacher Daguan Tanying's (989–1060) Chan genealogy *Wujia zongpai* (Lineages of the five houses), which is no longer extant, first recorded Tianwang based on the inscription. At the end of this record, Huihong offered a list of evidence from the Tang that all suggested the existence of a second Daowu.

Miyun's followers discovered that, at least in the Northern Song, the two-Daowu theory had been raised by literati patrons, such as Zhang Shangying (1043–1121) and his friends. Zhang supported the two-Daowu theory and according to an obscure source Zhang had seen the hard copy of Tianwang's inscription from Daguan Tanying. In addition, supporters of this new theory tried to prove it by looking for inconsistent or even contradictory statements of Chan masters' lineage affiliations in their favor. After combing through Chan recorded sayings and genealogies after the Tang, they found that in the records of some renowned Chan masters, such as Xuedou Chongxian (980–1052), who has been conventionally put in Shitou's transmission line, there were clues suggesting that they belonged to Mazu's line. For example, although the *Jingde chuandeng lu* listed him as a descendant of the Yunmen school, in Weibai's *Jingzhong jianguo xu denglu* (Supplementary lamp records of the Jingzhong jianguo reign), he was listed as the ninth-generation heir in Mazu's line, which was confirmed by Xuedou Chongxian's epitaph written by Lü Xiaqing. For Miyun's supporters, the only possible explanation is that Xuedou Chongxian was actually derived from Mazu's line through Tianwang Daowu rather than through Tianhuang Daowu. Although these masters knew clearly their own lineage affiliations, the compilers of Chan genealogies placed their lineage affiliations erroneously.

It seems that the two-Daowu theory had been established firmly on the ground of epigraphic evidence, and it became a difficult job to disqualify it. The Caodong monks, however, using the same skills of precise scholarship, studied Chan historical sources even more thoroughly in order to counter this new hypothesis. Their strategy was to scrutinize the evidence that their rivals presented and to check it against historical background materials in order to identify their spurious nature. They discovered that there were flaws in the following five areas.

Juefan Huihong's Record

First, the earliest textual record of Tianwang's biography is from Huihong's *Linjian lu*. Although this record was Huihong's own writing, the Caodong monks found that Huihong collected it largely as an anecdote or even a joke. Thus, Huihong was not serious about his new theory. Then, some Caodong monks surmised that the origin of this false claim must have been Daguan Tanying, who concocted all of the "evidence." Others pointed to the connection of this theory to Zhang Shangying, who was a lay patron but who had a tarnished reputation as a supporter of Wang An'shi's (1021–1086) reformative policy. They also identified an anachronism between Daguan Tanying's and Zhang Shangying's life spans and proved eloquently that it was impossible for Zhang to have met Daguan Tanying and thus he could not have acquired Tianwang's inscription from him. While acknowledging that Zhang was indeed involved, the Caodong monks blamed Zhang for promoting such a false theory. Considering Zhang's blemished political reputation, they reasoned that he must have intended to use this theory to promote the Linji sect and to suppress its rivals, such as the Yunmen school in the Northern Song.

Inscriptions of Tianhuang and Tianwang

Second, the Caodong monks focused on the two inscriptions that weighed so much in the argument. After careful studies, they easily discounted the importance of the two inscriptions because both of them appeared no earlier than the Yuan dynasty as appendixes or notes to a new edition of the *Wudeng huiyuan*. (They were later erroneously included in the *Quan Tang wen* [Complete collections of Tang prose] compiled in the Qing dynasty as texts of Tang origins without critical inquiries.) Because they were not credible early sources derived from the Tang, they could not be used to prove the existence of a Tang master. Even for Tianhuang Daowu's biography, some Caodong masters considered Zanning's account in the *Song gaoseng zhuan* (Song biographies of eminent monks) much more reliable than the commonly used inscription in standard Chan genealogies.

The Caodong monks also scrutinized the content of Tianwang's inscription in order to find internal evidence that might point to its spuriousness. They identified one passage about the master's deathbed remarks that was completely plagiarized from another monk's biography in the *Jingde chuan-*

deng lu. (This monk also lived in Jingzhou.) For the Caodong monks, this convinced them that Tianwang's inscription was a complete forgery. They even pointed to a Chan monk in the Yuan as the possible culprit for forging the inscription, although some literati such as Huang Zongxi argued later that, based on the presented evidence, it was still not conclusive which author of these two records was the actual plagiarizer.

The Identity of Qiu Yuansu

Although Tianwang's inscription was proved useless, the Caodong monks did not let go of this easy target. They then examined the official career of its author, Qiu Yuansu, who was referred to as the "military governor of Jingzhou." A quick check in the *Tang Fangzhen nianbiao* (Chronicles of Tang governors) produced no information about this figure. Thus, the Caodong monks claimed that the alleged author, Qiu, was simply a fabrication: There had been no such governor in Jingzhou.

This hasty conclusion incurred criticisms from some literati scholars who had done more extensive research in history. These scholars found that mid-Tang politics were extremely confusing and that the existing records about Tang administrators were not complete. As for Qiu's identity, some found that his name had been recorded in early Song sources. Ouyang Xiu (1007–1072), for example, saw that Qiu's name was inscribed on the cliff in the Three Gorges and made a note in his collection of epigraphic records.

The Existence of Tianwang Monastery

The evidential research in this dispute also involves historical geography. While Tianhuang monastery was a well-established Buddhist institution in Jingzhou city, some Caodong monks found that there were no traces of Tianwang monastery in historical records. They checked local gazetteers, which had nothing to say about Tianwang monastery. Not convinced by textual records, some Linji monks, such as Shuijian Huihai (1626–1687), actually visited the city and found a site that was reported by local people as a cloister called Tianwang. They then rebuilt the monastery and claimed it was presided over by Tianwang in the Tang.

Lineage Affiliations of Later Generations

The testimony from later Chan masters about their dharma transmissions could also serve as powerful evidence. If the two-Daowu theory were true, there must be traces in many Chan masters' recorded sayings that would show that the changes were justified. While the Linji monks found some evidence in their own favor, the Caodong monks also read these records carefully and discovered that the current lineage affiliations outlined in the *Jingde chuan-deng lu* could be justified. For example, if the lineage affiliation of Chan masters formerly attributed to Tianhuang's descendants must be changed to Tian-wang's, the Yunmen master Deshan Xuanjian should now be put under Mazu. However, the Caodong monks detected that, in Deshan Xuanjian's descendant Xuefeng Yicun's record, Xuefeng Yicun clearly stated in front of the king of the Min state that his teacher belonged to Shitou's lineage. This simply contradicts the new arrangement of Deshan Xuanjian's lineage. For the Caodong monks, this proved that the new theory was not logically consistent.

The Use of Evidence in the Debate

In the previous section, I outlined the major evidence presented in the debate, omitting many details. To historians of Chan Buddhism, debates about dharma transmission have been the least valuable subject for research because their worth was reduced by the ubiquitous ideological agendas behind them. The tedious and argumentative style of these polemical essays written in the seventeenth century indicates their inferior intellectual quality in comparison to the essays produced by sophisticated Buddhist thinkers. However, these controversies are extremely informative for us to understand the intellectual orientation of Buddhist clergy at that time. For example, the style of the arguments, which varied piece by piece, bears the intellectual hallmark of that particular century. Here, it is the way in which Buddhists argued with each other that is most interesting: What were the spiritual issues that concerned them? How did they prove a correct thesis, and what evidence did they bring to support their arguments? Moreover, controversies provided a new impetus for Chan monks to explore new areas of learning, including those that did not belong to Buddhist knowledge but were available for all learned scholars at that time. In the controversy pertaining to dharma transmission, evidential scholarship was widely used by clergy as a powerful intellectual apparatus.

This intellectual phenomenon appears to have been new in Buddhist scholarship. Previously, Buddhist scholars, though engaging in historiographical writings, never handled historical and textual evidence in such a meticulous way. In fact, if we consider the phenomenon in the broader intellectual milieu of the seventeenth century, it is clear that the extensive use of evidential research in the debates had an obvious connection to Confucian evidential scholarship, which flourished in the seventeenth and eighteenth centuries. Signifying an intellectual transition away from philosophical speculation and moral cultivation, Confucian evidential scholarship emphasized a different set of scholarly activities, such as text recovery, forgery detection, collation, and examination of text editions. Disregarding the metaphysical questions of neo-Confucianism and Wang Yangming's philosophy of the mind, evidential scholars demonstrated what Ying-shih Yü has called "intellectualism."[2] The rise of this type of scholarship, as Benjamin Elman shows, was foreshadowed in the seventeenth century and became a "shared epistemological perspective" in literati communities in the eighteenth century.[3]

As shown in the Buddhist controversies, the intellectual changes occurring within the Confucian tradition made a clear mark on the Chan debates about dharma transmission that resulted from the interactions between Buddhist clergy and the literati in the seventeenth century. However, the motivation for monks to engage in this kind of learning was quite different from that of the Confucian scholars whose precision and sensitivity to sources embodied the spirit of scholarly professionalism. In the context of the Buddhist controversies, evidential scholarship had an ideological agenda that guided the use of this new scholarly apparatus. To be specific, the principle of strictness about dharma transmission as articulated by Feiyin Tongrong became the primary motive for monks to investigate the vast sources of Chan historiography.

In the polemical works I have examined, Buddhist monks handled the sources in a seemingly professional way: All Chan historical sources pertaining to dharma transmission were carefully examined; full attention was given to epigraphic findings; and by juxtaposing sources from different editions, scholar-monks were able to reach their conclusions by induction and to pinpoint logical inconsistencies inherent in a particular version of dharma transmission. Similar to Confucian evidential techniques, "forgery detection" (bianwei) became the primary task because the claimed "new" inscriptional texts were often derived from obscure sources and contained significant textual alterations, interpolations, and manipulations. In order to strengthen their arguments, Buddhist monks even planned field investigations to sites of ancient monasteries in the hope of finding new epigraphic sources to verify the textual evidence.[4]

Such an extensive use of evidence was, however, ephemeral in the Buddhist world because it directly served the controversies about dharma transmission. When the debates ceased, evidential learning did not have a lasting effect on the Buddhist scholarly tradition. Unlike Confucian evidential scholarship, which has left visible marks on modern archaeology and philology, Chan evidential scholarship failed to sustain itself as a continuous scholarly tradition in the Buddhist world. However, modern Chan historiography should not overlook the evidence unearthed in the course of the debate because under the monks' scrutiny of historical sources, an obscure segment of Chan history was illuminated.

The Role of the Confucian Literati

In the seventeenth century, evidential scholarship emerged as a new fashion of textual practice, and Buddhist monks were also able to assimilate it into Buddhist learning. For Buddhist monks, evidence represented a special kind of authority based on the investigation of texts. However, when they undertook evidential scholarship, they had transgressed into another territory and entered a new kind of scholarly world that was not derived from the Buddhist textual tradition. This is because evidential scholarship was basically an intellectual apparatus that was developed among Confucian scholars within the Chinese textual tradition. In this sense, the textual authority of Buddhist monks was subject to the ultimate authority of Confucian scholars. This means that controversies about dharma transmission were not monopolized by Buddhist clergy and only through the works of the Confucian literati could evidence have come to light and been accepted.

To a large extent, evidential scholarship was not the clergy's traditional training, and Buddhist monks, unless they had received Confucian education before entering the Buddhist order, were amateur evidential scholars. Only the Confucian literati who were well versed in classical knowledge were able to provide fuel for the debate. The political and scholarly reliance on the Confucian literati can be seen in the compilation of Feiyin Tongrong's *Wudeng yantong*: Although this book was actually compiled by two monks, Feiyin Tongrong and his disciple Baichi Xingyuan (1611–1662), in the beginning of the *Wudeng yantong*, Feiyin Tongrong unprecedentedly listed fifty-eight literati followers as collaborators. The names of Feiyin Tongrong and his disciple Baichi Xingyuan, as the only two clergymen, were listed at the end.[5]

In this sense, the use of evidence in the debate was dependent on the Confucian pursuit of evidential scholarship because Confucian scholars could easily apply the tools of evidential research to religious matters that were also within their domain of control. Throughout history, Chinese Buddhists had tried to bridge the gap between the clergy and the literati by consciously approximating Confucian cultural ideals through refining their literary skills. As early as the Song, they consciously pursued the Confucian ideal of *wen*, an embellished literary tradition. Accordingly, the literati's intellectual orientation and textual practice were absorbed into the Buddhist culture.[6] Thus, when evidential investigation of ancient relics and inscriptions took shape in Ouyang Xiu's *Jigu lu* (Records of collecting relics), printed in 1061, Buddhist historians also became serious about collecting Buddhist relics and inscriptions. For instance, Zanning, a Buddhist *wen* master, as Albert Welter calls him, was a prominent Buddhist historiographer with Confucian training on textual practice. His *Song gaoseng zhuan*, for example, was based on his collection of epitaphs and inscriptions.[7] In late imperial China, because Buddhist history had merged into the Chinese historical tradition, Confucian scholars had equal interest in epigraphs related to Buddhism, and these interests contributed to the formation of evidential scholarship in the Qing.

Although most scholars of Chinese intellectual history attribute the rise of evidential scholarship in the Qing dynasty to the internal transformation of the Confucian tradition in the Jiangnan area, religious disputes and controversies might have, to some extent, stimulated these Confucian scholars' interest in evidential research. During the late Ming, the study of inscriptions became fashionable, and discussions about forgery were the harbinger of the later intellectual movement of evidential scholarship. Besides the debate about the inscription of Tianwang Daowu, there were two other debates about inscriptions that deeply influenced late Ming Chinese intellectuals. The first was the so-called stone inscription of the ancient version of the *Great Learning*, which was soon proved to be a forgery.[8] Another was the discovery of the Nestorian inscription in Xi'an, which proved that, as early as the Tang, one denomination of Christianity had spread to China.[9] The authenticity of both inscriptions was debated among the literati. In both cases, the key issue was the possible forgery of the inscriptions.

The investigations of the inscriptions of the ancient version of the *Great Learning* and the Christian Nestorian stele are beyond the scope of this study. But the debate over the identity of the two Daowus demonstrates the extent to which literati-scholars had become involved in Buddhist controversies. Confucian scholars played such a crucial role that many important pieces of evidence about Tianwang Daowu were actually discovered by them rather than by Buddhist monks.

The Literati's Initial Discovery of the Two Daowus

During the late Ming, many Confucian literati were attracted by Chan Buddhism and became involved in Buddhist controversies. Because they had acquired superb abilities in evidential scholarship through rigorous training in classics and history, they often discovered some significant discrepancies in

Chan records first, and then Chan monks started to follow their lead and to compile new genealogies. The evidence about Tianwang Daowu, for example, was one of these discoveries by the literati. In the following sections, I will introduce a number of works on this issue produced by the literati.

Qu Ruji's Discovery of Tianwang Daowu

The rediscovery of the two Daowus in the late Ming was first made public by the famous literatus Qu Ruji, who compiled the Chan anthology Zhiyue lu in 1602.[10] In fascicle 9 of this work, a special section documents the undetermined dharma transmissions of Tianhuang Daowu and Tianwang Daowu, including two inscriptions in their entirety and listing all relevant sources.[11] Although Qu was skeptical about the Jingde chuandeng lu, he did not dare to change the official genealogy according to the two-Daowu theory. Rather, he invented a unique way to accommodate both Daowus. Because the generations after Daowu might belong to either Tianhuang or Tianwang, after each name, Qu simply wrote the Chinese character tian, the same initial of both Tianhuang and Tianwang, with a number to indicate the generation. For example, to avoid the dispute about Longtan Chongxin's lineage affiliation, Qu marked tian yi, meaning the first generation after the Tian master, after Longtan Chongxin's name and tian er, meaning the second generation of the Tian master, after Longtan Chongxin's disciple Deshan Xuanjian's name. By so doing, Qu avoided the dilemma of naming either "Tianwang" or "Tianhuang."

Judging from the early date of this Chan anthology, Qu Ruji must have been the first person who systematically examined the issue, and his research provided fodder for later debates. Qu's leading role in the discovery of the two Daowus is confirmed in an introductory preface to the rebuilt Tianhuang monastery. Also called Qianming, Tianhuang monastery was built in the Tianjian reign of the Liang kingdom (502–519). In the early Ming, this monastery was rebuilt and was named Huguo monastery. In the early seventeenth century, it was rebuilt again, and Qu was asked to write a new inscription. In this writing, he stated that there were actually two Daowus living in Jingzhou but in different monasteries.[12] He criticized the Jingde chuandeng lu for confusing the two as one and falsely tracing Longtan Chongxin's lineage back to Qingyuan Xingsi through Tianhuang Daowu. He proudly declared that Yuan Hongdao (1568–1610) was correct in saying, "People know that Buddhism can bless Confucianism but do not know that Confucianism can actually protect Buddhism."[13] Qu intended the quotation to suggest that Confucian scholars could use their expertise to untangle the confused dharma transmission and thus protect Buddhism. In this case, the Confucian literati indeed helped to clarify obscure dharma transmissions in Chan history.

Guo Limei's Change of Chan Genealogy

Like Qu Ruji, Guo Limei, a little known literatus who also used the name Guo Ningzhi, publicly supported the two-Daowu theory in a new history of lamp transmission, *Jiaowai biechuan* (Special transmissions outside the doctrine). Organized into sixteen fascicles and published in 1631, this work, based on the *Wudeng huiyuan*, recorded the Chan genealogy from the Śākyamuni Buddha to the seventeenth generation of Nanyue's transmission and to the fifteenth generation of Qingyuan's. Guo Limei intentionally redefined Tianwang Daowu as a legitimate heir of Mazu Daoyi, changing the transmission lines accordingly.[14]

Both Miyun Yuanwu and Hanyue Fazang endorsed this view by writing prefaces to this collection. In a highly rhetorical style, Miyun emphasized that a Chan person should transcend all Buddhas and patriarchs. He warned Chan students that patriarchs' recorded sayings were not words at all. Rather, one "[should] not be entangled by mysterious and sophisticated reasoning." If some students insisted on seeking truth from written words, Miyun said, he would use his stick to awaken them. Hanyue also praised Guo Limei as a Confucian gentleman who had attained the highest understanding of Buddhism. He considered the key to Chan Buddhism to be the comprehension of "separation" because the essential Chan teaching transcended written words.[15]

Guo Ningzhi (Guo Limei) Redefined Chan Transmissions

In the late Ming, Xuejiao Yuanxin and his lay disciple Guo Ningzhi, the same author of the previous writing but using a different name, compiled and published the recorded sayings of five Chan masters (*Wujia yulu*) in 1632. These masters were Guishan Lingyou, Yangshan Huiji, Dongshan Liangjia, Caoshan Benji, and Fayan Wenyi. At the beginning of this work, Guo Ningzhi inserted a "Chart of the Transmission of the Five Lineages" (*Wuzong yuanliu tu*) that lists Tianwang Daowu as Mazu Daoyi's dharma heir and switches Longtan Chongxin to his lineage, at the same time eliminating Tianhuang Daowu's name. As Guo Ningzhi noted, this chart, which he made after consulting Miyun Yuanwu and Xuejiao Yuanxin, was based on the appended notes about Tianwang Daowu in the *Wudeng huiyuan*.[16]

Tianwang Daowu in Zhu Shi'en's Genealogy

Zhu Shi'en's *Fozu gangmu* (Essential outlines for Buddhas and patriarchs), a genealogical work in forty-one fascicles, was another effort by literati followers to reformulate Chan transmissions. According to Zhu Shi'en's preface, he spent more than twenty years (from 1610 to 1631) researching and writing this book. Zhu's effort was praised by the famous artist Dong Qichang (1553–1636), who wrote a preface for this work. (According to this preface, Zhu's work was printed in 1634.) As a Confucian scholar, Zhu had been diligent in collecting evidence to clarify every ambiguous dharma transmission. He strongly supported the existence of Tianwang Daowu, not only listing every piece of evidence he could find, but also boldly changing the dharma transmission lines accordingly.[17]

The Dispute about Muchen Daomin's *Chandeng shipu*

As I have shown, the issue of the two Daowus was first brought up by the literati who were interested in Chan literature. They read Chan genealogies with critical eyes and with professional judgments concerning textual matters. As early as 1602, Qu Ruji spotted the discrepancy about the two Daowus in Chan records and made the earliest attempt to amend the problem. However, at that time, there were not many full-fledged Chan communities that were interested in dharma transmission. As I have pointed out repeatedly in this study, Chan communities such as Miyun's only came to maturity during the 1630s. When the claim of dharma transmission became important for establishing Chan monks' identities, they started to look for textual supports in Chan literature.

The early discovery of the two Daowus evolved into a controversy when Muchen Daomin published the *Chandeng shipu* in 1632 on Miyun's suggestion. In this work, Muchen Daomin rearranged dharma transmissions based on the two-Daowu theory. He also confessed that, regarding the issue of the two Daowus, he was advised by a local literatus from Fuqing. Because this new compilation not only altered the traditional lines of dharma transmission but also denied some Caodong masters' dharma transmissions, the local official Huang Duanbo in Ningbo first praised this work and then publicly denounced it. Miyun Yuanwu and his lay disciples responded immediately, and his relationship with Huang deteriorated. Below, I provide a detailed account of this controversy by introducing several important polemical works.

Muchen Daomin's Chandeng shipu

Muchen Daomin was perhaps the first monk to compile a Chan genealogy supporting the two-Daowu theory. His *Chandeng shipu*, composed under Miyun's direction and published in 1632, publicly sanctioned the two-Daowu theory. According to Muchen Daomin's postscript, he composed this new version of the genealogy when he accompanied Miyun Yuanwu to Mount Huangbo in Fujian. At Mount Huangbo, Muchen Daomin obtained a copy of the local literatus Wu Tong's work of Chan genealogy and revised it by collating it with sources in the Ming Buddhist canon. He lamented that the existing histories of lamp transmission were all biographical rather than genealogical. Thus, excluding recorded sayings and encounter dialogues, Muchen arranged the whole Chan genealogy into a continuous chart that lists the names of Chan masters without ambiguous lineage affiliations.[18]

The second fascicle of the *Chandeng shipu* officially lists Tianwang Daowu as Mazu's dharma heir and attributes Longtan Chongxin to his lineage. Qiu Yuansu's inscription was also appended.[19] Similarly, the ninth fascicle, which describes Qingyuan Xingsi's line, lists Tianhuang Daowu, attached with an abbreviated version of the inscription written by Fu Zai. More provocative was the attribution of some monks in the contemporary Caodong lineage to the category of "lineage unknown."[20]

Huang Duanbo's Criticism

Literati followers not only identified obscure sources but also played a vital role in intensifying the Buddhist controversies. Huang Duanbo, a famous Ming loyalist and scholar-official who was instrumental in promoting Miyun Yuan-wu's rise in Zhejiang, became a decisive figure in this series of controversies. At first, Huang supported the theory of the two Daowus and considered it a breakthrough in Chan historiography.

When the *Chandeng shipu* was first published, Huang was asked to write a preface to it. In this preface, Huang praised Muchen Daomin's effort and expressed his will to reconcile the uneasy relationship between Linji and Caodong. As a former student of the Caodong master Wuming Huijing, he recalled that Wuming Huijing had once told him that his enlightenment was actually attested to by the Linji master Ruifeng, who was Xiaoyan Debao's disciple. Based on this information, Huang Duanbo argued that Wuming Huijing was also a legitimate descendant of the Linji lineage and his attribution to

Caodong was simply nominal. Huang Duanbo was delighted by his discovery that the two lineages apparently did not conflict.[21]

However, when he sensed Miyun's intention of denying the legitimate status of other transmissions, he publicly opposed this theory. On the thirteenth day of the fifth month of the tenth year of the Chongzhen reign (July 4, 1637), in Xuedou monastery of Fenghua county, Huang Duanbo posted a public notice, often referred to as "Huang sili kaoding zongpai gaoshi" (Public notice about the investigation and correction of dharma transmissions), accusing Miyun of slandering former worthies and elevating the Linji sect by eliminating the Caodong transmission.[22] He declared his attitude in the beginning of this notice:

> I read the *Jingde chuandeng lu*, which clearly records that Tianhuang Daowu received the dharma from Shitou [Xiqian] and [the lineages] of Yunmen and Fayan are all listed under Qingyuan [Xingsi]. This is indeed an ironclad case. Then, the *Wudeng huiyuan* makes another claim that there had been two Daowus in Jingzhou: One resided in Tianwang monastery at the west of the city and the other in Tianhuang monastery at the east of the city. [Its author] thus doubts that Longtan [Chongxin] was the dharma heir of Tianhuang [Daowu] and quotes epigraphs and inscriptions to prove this view. However, he adds only a brief note [to the main text] without daring to change their lineage affiliation arbitrarily because heirs of the Yunmen and Fayan lineages never recognized Mazu as their patriarchal ancestor.[23]

Huang directly pointed out that in the *Chandeng shipu*, Miyun Yuanwu and Muchen Daomin changed the name Tianhuang Daowu to Tianwang Daowu, thus shifting the Yunmen and Fayan lineages to Mazu's line. This notice explicitly denounced Miyun Yuanwu's intention to eliminate the Caodong lineage in order to promote his own Linji transmission. (I have translated Huang's notice in appendix I.A.)

Huang singled out the *Jingde chuandeng lu* as the orthodox version of dharma transmission and questioned Miyun's arbitrary insertion of Tianwang Daowu in the *Chandeng shipu*. However, as he stated, he did not find any solid evidence to refute Miyun until he read the *Xuefeng guanglu* in 1637. Huang pointed to the conversation between Xuefeng Yicun and the king of the Min kingdom. In their conversation, Xuefeng Yicun mentioned that he was a disciple of Deshan Xuanjian and Shitou Xiqian, meaning that Deshan Xuanjian's teacher, Longtan Chongxin, belonged to Shitou's lineage. Accordingly, he must be Tianhuang Daowu's heir. Huang considered this new discovery the strongest evidence against the altered version of dharma transmission. Furthermore, he analyzed the validity of both inscriptions. Comparing them with Tianhuang Daowu's and Longtan Chongxi's biographies in the *Song gaoseng zhuan*, Huang concluded that Tianhuang Daowu's inscription was more credible than Tianwang's because it corresponded with the records in Zanning's work. Huang also expressed his resentment of Miyun's bias toward Qingyuan Xingsi's lineage. He pointed to Miyun's verses concerning Qingyuan Xingsi as examples. In these verses, Miyun commented on Qingyuan's enlightenment experience unfavorably and mocked his partial understanding of Chan teaching. He viewed Qingyuan Xingsi as still having "emotional residue."

Referring to Miyun's dispute with Hanyue, Huang derided Miyun's ignorance of the principle of the Linji school. After reading Miyun's recorded sayings, Huang sensed that Miyun intended to provoke controversies with other monks and to slander ancient patriarchs. As a local authority, Huang had been prepared to invite Miyun to be the abbot of Xuedou monastery before the dispute. However, because of this incident, Huang declared publicly that he had changed his mind. Although Huang had befriended Miyun and promoted his lineage, this public announcement signified the end of their relationship.[24]

Yu Dacheng's Letter to Huang Duanbo

Huang's sharp criticism of Miyun was applauded by his friend Yu Dacheng (*zi.*. Jisheng), who was a Ming official and follower of the Caodong masters Wuming Huijing and Wuyi Yuanlai. In a letter addressed to Huang, Yu expressed his strong opposition to Muchen Daomin's arbitrary addition of Tianwang Daowu. He was appalled by the lack of evidence for this alteration, regarding both inscriptions included in the *Wudeng huiyuan* as spurious. Instead of trusting these false documents, he suggested to examine the evidence from Tianhuang Daowu's descendants, who were not far from him. For example, he identified Xuefeng Yicun's claim that he was a disciple of Shitou's line as a strong piece of evidence. In addition, in the preface and postscript to *Gushan xuanyao guangji* (Extended collection of mysteries and essentials of Gushan), he found the statement that the Chan master Shenyan received dharma transmission from Xuefeng Yicun and belonged to the sixth generation of Shitou Xiqian's line.[25] If this self-proclaimed genealogy was valid, Yu reasoned, Longtan Chongxin must have inherited the dharma from Tianhuang Daowu, who was Shitou Xiqian's dharma heir.

Moreover, Yu Dacheng gave tremendous weight to Qisong's *Chuanfa zhengzong ji* (Records of the orthodox transmissions), which he regarded as the most authoritative Chan historiography produced in the Song. Qisong's work reserved no place for Tianwang Daowu. In Yu's view, it was wrong to alter genealogical works whose authority had been established in the imperial Buddhist canon.[26]

Wang Gu's Response to Huang Duanbo

A lay disciple of Miyun Yuanwu, Wang Gu, wrote his *Zongmen zhengming lu* (Record of the rectification of names in Chan lineages) in 1637 to respond to Huang Duanbo.[27] Claiming that his master simply copied the historiography of the *Fozu lidai tongzai* (Records of successive generations of Buddha) and the *Shishi jigu lue* (Outlined investigation of Buddhist history), he disputed Huang Duanbo's accusation of Miyun Yuanwu. With regard to Xuefeng Yicun's claim that his teaching came from Deshan Xuanjian and Shitou Xiqian, Wang Gu countered that Xuefeng Yicun had not mentioned this as proof of his dharma transmission. Rather, in his youth, Xuefeng Yicun had often visited Caodong masters Touzi Datong and Dongshan Liangjia. Therefore, it was possible for him to mention the Caodong masters as his former teachers rather than as his dharma masters. In addition, Wang Gu pointed out that Xuefeng Yicun's Chan teaching was closer to that of Deshan Xuanjian than to that of the Caodong lineage, suggesting that Xuefeng Yicun belonged to Mazu's line. Recent scholarship shows that Xuefeng Yichun's Chan style was indeed similar to Mazu's.[28]

Miyun Yuanwu's Response

On the night of the seventh day of the twelfth month of 1637, Miyun Yuanwu heard about Huang Duanbo's notice in Xuedou monastery and reacted with disbelief. According to his own account in the *Tiantong zhishuo*, he immediately went to the monastery to see it with his own eyes. Having seen it in person, he wrote "Pan Huang Yuangong Tianhuang Daowu chanshi kao" (Judging Huang Duanbo's investigation of Chan master Tianhuang Daowu) to defend himself. In this rebuttal, he commented on Huang Duanbo's argument point by point. Insisting on the accuracy of his own views on the two Daowus and the new dharma transmission lines he had approved, Miyun laughed at Huang Duanbo's narrow-mindedness and claimed that Huang himself embodied the accusations he had made about Miyun Yuanwu. Repudiating several letters that Huang had written to him and others, Miyun Yuanwu seemed confident enough to claim victory in this round of the debate.[29]

Conclusion

The disputes about dharma transmission in the seventeenth century displayed different characteristics from those in earlier periods. If the purpose of engaging in disputes in early periods was to construct a new transmission line, the primary concern of seventeenth-century Chan monks was to reconstruct the existing dharma transmissions and to reclaim orthodoxy and legitimacy. The source for their reconstruction was the large amount of Chan literature that had accumulated through the centuries. These sources provided inspirations and clues for Chan monks to clarify obscure lineage affiliations and the identities of Chan masters in early periods, to verify unclear transmissions, and to make suggestions about possible alterations of the existing transmission chart. Because the overwhelming number of Chan texts became the focus of the debates over dharma transmission, the way that Buddhist monks argued with each other was largely influenced by the prevalent textual culture in the seventeenth century, which had cultivated a penchant for collecting ancient relics, such as inscriptions, and for verifying existing historical records with these relics. Therefore, the controversies over dharma transmission were an impressive display of the plethora of textual evidence and the monks' abilities in historical criticism.

According to these pieces of evidence, it is clear that early debates about the identities of the twenty-eight Indian patriarchs and the struggles between the Southern and Northern schools were no longer the focal points. Rather, the disputed area gradually moved to the formative period of the five denominations in the late Tang. In existing Chan historiographies, the identity of crucial figures like Tianhuang Daowu and Tianwang Daowu remained ambiguous, leaving room for further debate in the seventeenth century. Although the contexts and focal points of the debate changed, the motivation behind the impressive display of evidence was the same: Alterations of dharma transmission in Chan history meant the redistribution of power and authority in existing Chan communities.

8

The Lawsuit about Feiyin Tongrong's *Wudeng yantong* in the Early Qing

The Manchu conquest of China in 1644 disrupted the debate. Miyun Yuanwu died in 1642, and Huang Duanbo, refusing to surrender at the fall of Nanjing, was executed in 1645. When the situation was stabilized, the debate resurfaced. Miyun Yuanwu's leading disciple, Feiyin Tongrong, published his book containing the altered dharma transmission lines based on the two-Daowu theory and immediately incurred a lawsuit, arousing what Chen Yuan calls "a great fracas of the two lineages in 1654 and 1655" (*jiayi liangzong dahong*) in his famous book *Qingchu sengzeng ji*.

The trial of Feiyin Tongrong was an extreme case among all of the disputes over dharma transmissions. The central issues in these disputes are similar: Monks wrote new books about their discoveries of new evidence about the dharma transmission of a particular Chan master, usually one from whom the mainstream dharma transmissions of Chan schools were derived. Altering this master's dharma transmission was controversial because it would change the lineage affiliations of contemporary Chan monks.

In this chapter, I will unfold the intricacies of the controversy through examining various polemical essays written by monks and literati followers concerning Feiyin's *Wudeng yantong*. In particular, I will reconstruct the lawsuit in light of the newly discovered *Hufa zhengdeng lu*, according to which, the lawsuit was started by the literati's petitions from four neighboring prefectures in Eastern Zhejiang. After reviewing the case, the provincial authority ruled against Feiyin, and a public warrant was thus issued to arrest Feiyin and to burn his book.

The Publication of the *Wudeng yantong*

After Miyun Yuanwu died in 1642, his dharma heirs continued to grow by multiplying themselves at a fast pace through the practice of dharma transmission. This sizable group of monks quickly took control of many famous Chan institutions in south China and transformed them into dharma transmission monasteries under their control. The development of Chan Buddhism was thus based on the form of a lineage modeled on the prevailing Chinese lineage organization but reproduced itself through the continuity of dharma transmission. In this respect, the importance of dharma transmission as a tool of institutionalization to define and perpetuate Chan Buddhism was emphasized by Chan monks. One way of doing so was to compile new editions of Chan genealogies that demanded the authentication of all Chan masters, including those who were widely respected, as proven spiritual leaders. As a result, this strict sense of dharma transmission brought about contestations and resentments in the Buddhist world because commonly accepted transmission lines were being altered and famous masters were excluded because of a lack of evidence.

Inspired by his teacher, Miyun, Feiyin had been ruminating on an ambitious genealogical work for many years. Like his master, Feiyin was conscious about his identity as a Chan master and often provoked debates with other monks. In his little known separate collection of polemical essays entitled *Feiyin chanshi bieji*, he was actually involved in almost all of the controversies at that time. (Figure 8.1 shows the first page of fascicle 4.) Feiyin was particularly sensitive to any attempts that would challenge his and his teacher's orthodox position in Chan communities. The direct impetus for him to finish the *Wudeng yantong* was the publication of the Caodong master Yuanmen Jingzhu's (1604–1654) Chan genealogy, which elevated the status of Caodong over that of Linji. Feiyin's work is therefore, first of all, a response to his Caodong counterpart.

Yuanmen Jingzhu's *Supplement to the* Wudeng huiyuan

Feiyin's work was initially a response to the *Wudeng huiyuan xulue* (Outlined supplements to the *Wudeng huiyuan*) by the Caodong master Yuanmen Jingzhu,[1] who was Shiyu Mingfang's dharma heir. Lamenting the lack of records of Chan masters during the Ming, he planned this work to be a supplement to the

FIGURE 8.1. First page of fascicle 4 of *Feiyin chanshi bieji*, preface dated 1648. Rare book in Komazawa University Library, Japan. Photocopy from Manpukuji.

Wudeng huiyuan. Completed in 1644 and printed in 1648, it focused on the Linji and Caodong lineages only because, according to him, both Guiyang's and Fayan's lineages had died out, and no reliable sources could be found for the Yunmen lineage. As a supplement to the *Wudeng huiyuan*, it delineates a clear line of transmission from the late Song to the seventeenth century. The first fascicle lists the Caodong lineage from the fifteenth generation of Qingyuan to the thirty-sixth generation. Many of Yuanmen Jingzhu's teachers and contemporaries, such as Wuming Huijing, Zhanran Yuancheng, Wuyi Yuanlai, Yongjue Yuanxian, and Juelang Daosheng, are included. Fascicles 2–4 record the Linji lineage from the sixteenth generation of Nanyue to the thirty-fourth.

Although Yuanmen Jingzhu provided valuable sources for Chan dharma transmissions, he listed the Caodong lineage first, followed by the Linji. For Feiyin, this sequence implied the superiority of Caodong over Linji. Moreover, he regarded the uninterrupted transmission of the Caodong lineage as suspicious because of the lack of evidence.

Feiyin Tongrong: Wudeng yantong

Among the Chan genealogies produced in the seventeenth century, Feiyin Tongrong's *Wudeng yantong* was the most controversial because it advocated a strict definition of dharma transmission and applied it to Chan historiography. Not only did he change dharma transmissions according to the two-Daowu theory, he also intended to correct two kinds of widespread practice of dharma transmission: transmission by proxy (*daifu*) and transmission by remote succession (*yaosi*). As I described in the introduction, transmission by proxy means that a monk transmits the dharma on behalf of another master, who may have died. Remote succession means that a monk, without a chance to see a master who lived in earlier times, declares himself to be the master's legitimate dharma heir based on his own admiration of that master's teaching. Rejecting these two popular practices, Feiyin Tongrong emphasized one's personal encounter with the master as the only valid criterion for dharma transmission.

The current preserved edition of the *Wudeng yantong*, which contains twenty-five fascicles, was a 1657 reprint by Feiyin's leading dharma heir, Yinyuan Longqi, in Japan.[2] Five prefaces were included: the first two by relatively unknown officials, two by Feiyin's lay disciples Xu Changzhi[3] and Li Zhongzi, and one by Feiyin himself. The prefaces are followed by "Editorial Principles" in which Feiyin outlined his views about dharma transmission and the major changes he made. Then, Feiyin listed seven pieces of evidence regarding Tianwang Daowu to support his alteration of the lineages. (I examine this evidence in appendix 3.)

The main content of the book, which will be briefly summarized below, follows the conventions of a typical Chan genealogy.[4] Readers should bear in mind that because Feiyin believed in the existence of Tianwang Daowu, this book departed from the arrangement of the standard Chan genealogy in fascicles 7, 8, 10, 15, and 16, in which Chan masters' generation should be marked as belonging to "Qingyuan" rather than "Nanyue."

Fasc. 1: seven Buddhas, Indian patriarchs, and early Chinese patriarchs

Fasc. 2: the collateral lineage derived from the fourth patriarch, Daoxin, down to the eighth generation; the collateral lineage derived from the fifth patriarch, Hongren, down to the fourth generation; and the lineage from Huineng down to the fifth generation

Fascs. 3 and 4: the lineage of Nanyue Huairang down to the fifth generation

Fascs. 5 and 6: the lineage of Qingyuan Xingsi down to the seventh generation

Fascs. 7 and 8: the lineage of Tianwang Daowu from the second generation of Nanyue Huairang's lineage to the ninth generation (before the
formation of the Yunmen and Fayan schools)

Fasc. 9: the lineage of the Guiyang school from the third generation of
Nanyue Huairang's lineage to the eighth generation

Fasc. 10: the lineage of the Fayan school from the eighth generation of
Nanyue to the twelveth generation

Fascs. 11 and 12: the lineage of the Linji school from the fourth generation of Nanyue to the fifteenth generation

Fascs. 13 and 14: the lineage of the Caodong school from the fourth
generation of Qingyuan to the thirty-fourth generation

Fascs. 15 and 16: the lineage of the Yunmen school from the sixth
generation of Nanyue to the sixteenth generation

Fascs. 17 and 18: the lineage of the Huanglong branch of the Linji school
from the eleventh generation of Nanyue to the seventeenth generation

Fascs. 19–24: the lineage of the Yangqi branch of the Linji school from
the nineteenth generation of Nanyue to the thirty-fourth generation

Fasc. 25: the lineage of the Caodong school in the thirty-fifth and thirty-
sixth generations

Feiyin's work updated the Chan genealogy to include his contemporaries
at the end but with serious revisions of the early transmission lines. As he declared in the "Editorial Principles," the motive for compiling a new Chan genealogy was to prevent the two above-mentioned false practices because most
unfounded claims of dharma transmission were based on them. Feiyin argued that the only acceptable transmission was "transmission through personal acquaintance" (*mianbing qincheng*). Thus, if a disciple had no chance to
meet the master in person, the claim of transmission was invalid. Concerned
that these self-proclaimed transmissions could be confused with true transmission personally conferred and certified by a master, Feiyin attempted to
clarify the already-chaotic lines of transmission and to eliminate false claims
by writing the *Wudeng yantong*. Not only did he question the dharma transmissions of contemporary Caodong masters, he also suspected that the whole
Caodong transmission after Tiantong Rujing had become baseless because of
the lack of recorded sayings and the scarcity of evidence in extant inscriptions
of Chan patriarchs.[5]

Feiyin placed those contemporary Chan masters who failed this strict criterion of dharma transmission in the category of "lineage unknown" (*sifa
weixiang*), which is a special section appended to the end of fascicle 16 in the
Wudeng yantong. Historically, this category was to accommodate those Chan

masters whose dharma transmissions were still undetermined after a thorough investigation. It first appeared in the *Jiatai pudeng lu* (1204) and then in the *Wudeng huiyuan* (1252). Because Chan figures in this category were usually not prominent, it had never attracted much attention among Chan historians. In many Chan genealogies composed in the seventeenth century, such a list of Chan monks, which customarily included the three eminent late Ming monks Zibo Zhenke, Yunqi Zhuhong, and Hanshan Deqing, usually did not cause serious problems. However, Feiyin's use of this category became problematic because he placed the famous Caodong masters Wuming Huijing and his heir Wuyi Yuanlai into this category. This arrangement was resented by the Caodong monks.[6]

Feiyin Tongrong challenged the claim of dharma transmission in the Chan genealogy compiled by the Caodong monks. What made him uncomfortable was the designation of Wuming Huijing as the official dharma heir of Yunkong Changzhong (1514–1588), then an acknowledged Caodong dharma heir. Citing his own experience with Wuming Huijing, Feiyin contended that he had seldom heard Wuming Huijing or even Zhanran Yuancheng discuss their dharma transmissions. According to him, Wuming Huijing was indeed ordained by Yunkong Changzhong; however, he belonged only to Yunkong Changzhong's tonsure line but not to his dharma transmission line.[7] Following the arrangement of the Caodong genealogies would open the Chan lineage to remote succession and transmission by proxy, which often worked hand in hand. The danger of this arbitrary claim, as Feiyin saw it, was to confuse legitimate transmissions with self-proclaimed false transmissions. Therefore, Feiyin listed Wuming Huijing as "lineage unknown." Although he acknowledged that Wuyi Yuanlai was Huijing's dharma heir, he completely dismissed Wuming Huijing's other heirs, such as Yongjue Yuanxian, as illegitimate. He listed Zhanran Yuancheng as a legitimate Caodong master with genuine dharma transmission. But he questioned if Zhanran Yuancheng truly benefited from his teacher. The implication of such an arrangement for the Caodong lineage was obvious: If the status of the dharma transmission of the masters, from whom the whole lineage was supposedly derived, was questionable, the subsequent dharma heirs would no longer be considered legitimate.

Feiyin Tongrong applied his principle of strict transmission even to his fellow dharma heirs. He was particularly dissatisfied with Muchen Daomin, who tried to confer Miyun Yuanwu's transmission on a monk of his acquaintance who otherwise had no opportunity to receive Miyun's transmission.[8] In a letter sent in the summer of 1644 to the layman Xu Zhiyuan (*zi.* Xinwei),

Feiyin complained that Muchen Daomin's epitaph of their master, Miyun Yuanwu, which was composed shortly after his teacher died in 1642, mentioned only the number of dharma heirs without actually listing their names, providing Muchen an opportunity to cheat other dharma heirs and to legitimize the transmissions he had conferred by proxy.[9] Feiyin's obstinacy was so extreme that when he mourned Miyun's death in Tongxuan monastery at Mount Tiantai in 1642, he publicly burned the remaining whisks that had once belonged to his master and destroyed his seals to prevent any false claims of dharma transmission from Miyun.[10] He feared that if his master's seals and other belongings were preserved, they might be used by others as credentials to falsely claim Miyun's dharma transmission.

In the *Wudeng yantong*, Feiying took issues with Yuanmen Jingzhu's *Wudeng huiyuan xuelue* because it included a Linji monk called Puming Miaoyong (1586–1642) as a dharma heir of Nanming Huiguang (1539–1620), whose master was Wuhuan Xingchong (?–1611), a contemporary of the Chan master Xiaoyan Debao, from whom Feiyin's own lineage was derived. Feiyin denied Puming Miaoyong's legitimate status as a Linji dharma heir because of a lack of evidence. In his *Wudeng yantong*, he simply put him in the category of "lineage unknown."[11] By doing so, he meant to eliminate the transmissions from other Linji lineages and to make an exclusive claim to the Linji orthodoxy.

Feiyin Tongrong's stringent criteria for dharma transmission raise a question of priority in the Chan tradition: Should one judge true spiritual insight based on the authenticity of dharma transmission? In other words, what is the prime spiritual quality that defines a Chan master? The following examples clearly illustrate Feiyin Tongrong's attitude toward these issues.

In 1652, when he resided at Mount Jingshan, one layman asked about the *Wudeng yantong*, on which Feiyin had been working for some years. This literati follower suggested that many present-day clergy had excellent understandings of Buddhist teaching. Therefore, the book should record those outstanding masters with supreme enlightenment experiences rather than those who only possessed dharma transmissions. He suggested that if Buddhist masters were judged only by transmission, the book would not be worth writing. Feiyin replied stubbornly, "The tradition transmitted from the previous time has its own lineage. If there is no root, even those enlightened people are not worthwhile."[12] Clearly, for Feiyin Tongrong, lineage meant exclusivity. Weighing the supreme understanding of the Buddhist dharma against dharma transmission, Feiyin preferred legitimate transmission as the criterion for excellence.

Accusations and Responses

While the alteration of dharma transmission became one focus of dispute, the excessive use of "lineage unknown" by Chan monks such as Feiyin Tongrong to categorize accomplished Chan masters irritated the followers of those masters. The plaintiffs in the 1654 lawsuit against Feiyin Tongrong's book were leading dharma heirs of Zhanran Yuancheng and Wuming Huijing, whose dharma transmission had been questioned by Feiyin. Such a response from the Caodong side was to be expected: If a master's dharma transmission was questioned, how could his dharma heirs continue to claim the legitimacy of their transmission? A group of Caodong monks led by Sanyi Mingyu launched the first round of attacks, and in response Feiyin Tongrong and Muchen Daomin had to explain themselves.

Rebuttal Essays by the Caodong Monks

When Feiyin Tongrong's *Wudeng yantong* was published in 1654, the Caodong monk Sanyi Mingyu led the opposition. Sanyi Mingyu received Zhanran Yuancheng's transmission in 1623 and was entrusted with the management of the Caodong lineage. Together with Yuanmen Jingzhu, he wrote three essays: *Mingzong zhengwei* (Clarifying lineages and correcting forgery), *Zhaiqi shuo* (A discourse on selecting scams), and *Pimiu shuo* (A discourse on refuting errors). In addition, Xiaofeng Daran wrote *Xixie bian* (Discussion of eliminating heterodoxy). Although these works have not survived, Feiyin's refutation preserves some of their points.[13] According to Feiyin's account, the Caodong monks accused Feiyin of changing the officially acknowledged genealogy preserved in the imperial canon and thus committing "treason." Listing most of the evidence, the Caodong masters argued that all of the epitaphs of the two Daowus could have been forged with no historical basis.

These Caodong masters' rebuttals must have obtained their literati followers' strong support, as indicated by some of the extant prefaces they wrote for the clergy's polemical works. For example, Qi Xiongjia, one of Qi Chenghan's sons, prefaced the essay *Mingzong zhengwei* and lamented that Feiyin Tongrong's skepticism about ancient classics and history came close to "belittling ancestors and defaming sages."[14] Wang Wei, a follower of the Caodong school, compared Feiyin Tongrong's idea to the famous heterodoxy of ancient Confucian heretics Yang Zhu and Mozi and to what Buddhists referred to as heretics and demons. He singled out three crimes that he believed Feiyin Tongrong had committed: disrupting the genealogy, destroying ancestors, and eliminating Chan lineages.[15]

Feiyin Tongrong Defending his Wudeng yantong

In response to these criticisms, Feiyin composed the *Wudeng yantong jiehuo pian* (Essay explaining doubts about the *Wudeng yantong*) around 1655 to defend his *Wudeng yantong*.[16]

In the main text, Feiyin declared that his theory had sufficient support from texts in the imperial canon. In response to the Caodong masters who had accused him of ignoring imperial authority by contradicting the conventional Chan genealogies, Feiyin clarified that his source was the *Wudeng huiyuan*, which was included in the imperial canon. In his eyes, the *Wudeng huiyuan* was superior to other genealogical works that did not delineate the sequences of dharma transmission and the superiority of different lineages clearly. Another reason for Feiyin's reliance on this work is that it was the first to append the inscriptions of the two Daowus.

In this essay, Feiyin first singled out the Caodong masters Sanyi Mingyu and Yuanmen Jingzhu's works *Mingzong zhengwei*, *Zhaiqi shuo*, and *Pimiu shuo* as his targets for refutation. As he stated, these Caodong monks complained about his change of lineage affiliations based on Tianwang Daowu's inscription and charged him with "altering the imperial canon and making the mistake of ignoring the emperor." Feiyin countered that his views were strongly supported by the literati patrons because the authors of Tianwang's and Tianhuang's inscriptions were all reputable Confucian gentlemen in the Tang dynasty. Moreover, according to Feiyin, inscriptional evidence carried more weight in comparison to other textual records. In addition, all of this evidence had been incorporated into the *Fozu lidai tongzai*, which could be found in the imperial canon. Thus, he further accused his critics of not respecting the imperial canon. He said, "You are too arrogant and reckless to mention and somehow lack fear and scruple. Refutations and slanders like these are not only disrespectful to the imperial canon but also destroy and defame the imperial edict. Thus, how about the crime of ignoring the emperor?" (Z 81:317a)

To explain why he did not follow the traditional lineage chart in the *Jingde chuandeng lu*, Feiyin argued that, as an author, he had the right to investigate and examine the previous works on Chan genealogy and to correct the mistakes. More important, the government never prohibited doing so. He gave two examples to prove his case. First, the Song Chan historiographer Qisong, the author of the *Chuanfa zhengzong ji*, did exactly what Feiyin did by rejecting false claims and correcting wrong attributions and mistakes regarding the ages, generations, and encounter dialogues of Chan masters.

The second example to which Feiyin referred was the repeated efforts to update Chinese history, such as the *Annals of Spring and Autumn* in the Confucian tradition. Down to the Ming, official historians had written seventeen dynastic histories in total. However, according to Feiyin, that did not mean that these official histories could not be criticized and amended. Actually, many Confucian scholars had attempted to revise the previous historical publications. One of the most popular such works was Lü Zuqian's (1137–1181) *Shiqi shi xiangjie* (Detailed and abridged histories of seventeen dynasties), which tailored the official histories according to his standard. Even the neo-Confucian thinker Zhu Xi wrote a historical work called *Tongjian gangmu* (Outline of the compendium), without mentioning Sima Guang's monumental historical work *Zizhi tongjian* (Compendium for aiding governance). All of these authors, Feiyin claimed, added and deleted content. He urged his opponents to purchase one of these editions from the bookstores to gain some perspective. Feiyin stated sarcastically:

> These authors had consulted the editions in imperial libraries. But since they were never criticized for their values and faults, why should I be accused of "altering the Great Canon"? If I have stolen the printing blocks from imperial libraries and altered them arbitrarily by myself, then my crime lies in risking death. Without the order of prohibition, I write essays and interpret the meaning [of previous versions of Chan genealogies] to amend their insufficiency and to supplement what is beyond their authors' reach. So, is this "altering the Great Canon"? Then, the above-mentioned monks, Confucians, and eminent people with knowledge and insight also relied on the Buddhist canon without exception to write books and to establish words, to distinguish and explain in particular, and to discuss mixed evidence. All could have been punished for their crimes, couldn't they?[17]

Here Feiyin pretended to be innocent and naïve about the importance of his work. Both he and his opponents must have been aware that the critical matter was not scholarly criticism but the actual institutional power reified in the abbot succession system in dharma transmission monasteries.

After defending his rights as an author, Feiyin returned to the topic of Chan historiography. He selected three famous Chan histories to compare in order to show the different editorial preferences of the authors. These three works are Daoyuan's *Jingde chuandeng lu*, Qisong's *Chuanfa zhengzong ji*, and

Dachuan's *Wudeng huiyuan*. In terms of editorial principles, Feiyin saw great differences among the three. For instance, Feiyin said that the *Jingde chuandeng lu* lists 1,434 people after the sixth patriarch while the *Chuanfa zhengzong ji* has 1,496 people. The *Jingde chuandeng lu* gives information about generations and biographies about those Chan masters, while the *Chuanfa zhengzong ji* simply describes dharma transmissions and generations. In common, these two works did not further divide sublineages according to their Chan principles and teaching styles. According to Feiyin, these two works are not perfect because of this. In his eyes, only does the *Wudeng huiyuan* provide a model for Chan historiography.

He praised highly the Southern Song master Dachuan, the author of the *Wudeng huiyuan*. He saw that Dachuan's contribution lies in his effort to determine the sequence of priority of the lineages derived from Nanyue and Qingyuan. In Feiyin's understanding, making Nanyue the first and Qingyuan the second shows the superiority of Nanyue's lineages. Furthermore, in addition to providing names, generation information, and encounter dialogues, as the *Jingde chuandeng lu* and the *Chuanfa zhengzong ji* did, Dachuan delineated the Chan lineages into five houses, which settled further disputes and arguments. "Since the five schools are determined and their branches are divided clearly," Feiyin praised him admiringly:

> Even if there are thousands and millions of descendants after
> billions of generations, all can see their affiliated lineages
> and branches, from the beginning to the end. [Dachuan] revised and
> collected all kinds of documents and made one single great book as
> the final history of the Chan school. His merit is not below that of
> [the great sage-king] Yu. Therefore, since it has been circulated for
> more than five hundred years, no one does not praise it as a great
> classical work.[18]

Feiyin's reliance on the *Wudeng huiyuan* shows the popularity of the work in late imperial China. More important, Tianwang Daowu's inscription and other related evidence were first recorded in the Yuan edition of the *Wudeng huiyuan*. At the end of this essay, Feiyin pleaded with the literati patrons:

> I humbly wish all gentlemen and officials to use the correct eyes of
> humans and gods to sincerely bestow your support and protection
> without tolerating one man to receive your protection in particular. If
> so, all Chan monks in the empire would praise and pray for all great
> dharma protectors, [wishing them] to receive the dharma offerings
> of the wisdom of the great perfect mirror together with the first

Chinese patriarch [Bodhidharma]. Since you have planted the cause of being a Buddha or patriarch, and we all live in the three realms of the world, the retribution of cause and effect will not deviate by so much as a hair's breadth. If I had a slight bit of selfish mind, how could I not bear its results and run away? As to the compilation of the *Wudeng yantong*, books of rebuttal written by those people were published without restraint, [but] there have been established opinions in the empire long ago.[19]

The *Wudeng yantong jiehuo pian* also incorporated two letters that Feiyin wrote to literati followers in the Hangzhou and Yuezhou areas. These letters explained his reasons for classifying such Caodong masters as Wuming Huijing and Wuyi Yuanlai and the Linji master Xuejiao Yuanxin as "lineage unknown": As a monk familiar with these masters, he had seen no evidence of their dharma transmissions. At the end of this short work, he appended a postscript listing once again the pieces of evidence he deemed important.

Muchen Daomin Defending His Chandeng shipu

Because the addition of Tianwang Daowu and the relegation of Wuming Huijing and other Caodong masters into "lineage unknown" started with his own book *Chandeng shipu*, Muchen Daomin felt the need to explain his position in the controversy. In 1654, he wrote a short postscript to his *Chandeng shipu*, published twenty-two years earlier.[20] He admitted that Feiyin Tongrong had largely followed his arrangement of Chan lineages in the *Chandeng shipu*, but he emphasized that his intention had not been to spark disputes between the two lineages. Rather, he argued, the affiliation of Tianwang Daowu would not change the greatness of either lineage, and thus the dispute concerning this monk was meaningless. For him, placing the Caodong masters into the category of "lineage unknown" was a temporary solution necessitated by the lack of evidence at that time.

The Intervention of Local Authorities

In the sphere of Chinese religion, political power often intervened in sectarian debates. The Yongzheng emperor, for example, finally judged the controversy between Miyun Yuanwu and Hanyue Fazang. Unlike the former case, the trial of 1654 never reached the imperial court. In the court of Zhejiang province, Feiyin lost the lawsuit. In 1654, when the new Manchu regime was still consolidating the conquered land in the south, local governments seemed to continue to follow the Ming legal codes. As these codes stipulated, religion should be put under constant surveillance for any violations of secular laws, such as the restrictions on building temples and on initiating novices. However, the circumstances of governmental intervention, as stated in legal codes, remained limited, not mentioning mediating sectarian disputes over a Chan genealogical book. It seems that there were no compelling reasons for local authorities to review this case. In fact, this lawsuit, as the following records indicate, was started by local literati followers, who had influenced local authorities.

As previously mentioned, the result of this controversy was a notorious lawsuit. However, scholars have not yet looked into the process of litigation because of the lack of sources. The newly discovered book *Hufa zhengdeng lu* (Records of protecting the dharma and rectifying lamp transmissions), written circa 1655, provides a detailed account of how the government was involved.

To my knowledge, the *Hufa zhengdeng lu* was never mentioned in any historical studies. Chen Yuan's and Hasebe's research on early Qing Buddhist controversies, for example, contain no citation for it. However, during a visit to the Shanghai Library in the summer of 2001, I accidentally came across this book, which shed new light on the development of the controversy over dharma transmission. The current edition is a reprint of the original book published in Zhejiang. The preface by Lin Zhifan, a follower of the Caodong master Yongjue Yuanxian, stated that it was reprinted in Fujian out of the fear that Feiyin's followers might spread his theory of dharma transmission there. Lin condemned Feiyin Tongrong's book as an "apocryphon" and defined his own job as correcting the "incorrect," or more directly, "eliminating heterodoxy."[21] The actual years of compilation and reprinting are not clear, but I suspect that this book was compiled immediately after 1654 and reprinted a few years later in Fujian. The reference to "Feiyin's followers" in Fujian may allude to Yinyuan Longqi and his disciples at Mount Huangbo because Mount Huangbo was widely known as a stronghold in Miyun Yuanwu and Feiyin Tongrong's monastic network.

The *Hufa zhengdeng lu* contains fifteen essays and documents directly related to the controversy, including public notices issued by local government officials, prefaces to polemical essays, the local literati's petitions, and the warrant to arrest Feiyin Tongrong. Because this work highlights the role of literati followers and officials, it omits the original polemical texts written by Buddhist clergy. In addition to listing evidence to repudiate Feiyin Tongrong's speculations about the two Daowus, it depicts Feiyin and his followers as advocating a new heterodoxy from both Confucian and Buddhist vantage points.

I display part of the table of contents of this rare collection in figure 8.2 and translate all titles in this work as follows:

Huang Duanbo: "Fa Xuedou gaoshi" (Public notice issued at Xuedou monastery)

Yu Dacheng: "Fu Huang Sili shu" (Reply to Judge Huang)

Qi Xiongjia: "Mingzong zhengwei xu" (Preface to the *Mingzong zhengwei*)

Wang Wei: "Zhaiqi shuo xu" (Preface to the *Zhaiqi shuo*)

Xing Jixian: "Pimiu shuo xu" (Preface to the *Pimiu shuo*)

Chen Danzhong: "Xixie bian yin" (Introduction to the *Xixie bian*)

Weiyuzi: "Shuoyuan wen" (Inquiry on *Tracing the Origins*)

Clerk Wei: "Can Chiyan ben" (Memorial of accusing [the monk] Chiyan)

"Sijun hufa xiangshen shang Fu Si Dao zhugongzu qi" (A Petition to officials in the county, prefecture, and province, submitted by Buddhist dharma protectors in four prefectures)

"Gejun hufa shang Fu Si Dao gongcheng" (Public petition submitted by dharma protectors from several prefectures)

Surveillance Commissioner Lü (Li Rifang): "Jinchi Yantong weishu kanyu" (Investigative remarks on banning the spurious book *Wudeng yantong*)

Provincial Governor Xiao (Xiao Qiyuan): "Xiangyun piyu" (Comments of approval)

"Zongbuting gaoshi" (Public Notice by the Bureau of Police Chief)

Magistrate Dai of Yuhang county (Yuhang xian Dai): "Gaoshi" (Public notice)

"Minzhong zhu hufa gongxi" (Public memorial by all dharma protectors in central Fujian)

According to these sources, the litigation had been building up since the end of the Ming dynasty. Yu Dacheng and Huang Duanbo discovered the "evil" influence of the *Chandeng shipu* compiled by Miyun Yuanwu and Muchen Daomin. As the local judge of Mingzhou prefecture, Huang Duanbo publicly denounced the two-Daowu theory and the subsequent alteration of dharma transmission. (Because this event occurred in the late Ming, I have introduced Yu's and Huang's writings in the previous chapter.)

In the early Qing dynasty, this case was brought up again by Feiyin Tongrong's *Wudeng yantong*. As evidenced in the *Hufa zhengdeng lu*, the Caodong masters wrote a series of essays to refute Feiyin, which I discussed earlier. More seriously, the debate escalated to a legal dispute, and various petitions written by the literati on behalf of the Caodong monks were submitted to the local mag-

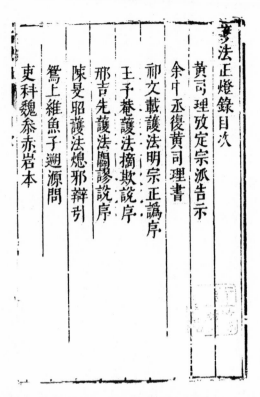

護法正燈錄目次

黃司理攷定宗派告示

余中丞復黃司理書

祁文載護法明宗正譌序

王子蒸護法摘欺說序

邢吉先護法闢診說序

陳旻昭護法熄邪辯引

鴛上維魚子遡源問

吏科魏泰赤岩本

FIGURE 8.2. Table of contents of the *Hufa zhengdeng lu*, ca. 1654. Photo-copy from the Shanghai Library.

istrate, showing the broad support that the Caodong monks had marshaled. One petition from Zhejiang lists the names of more than a hundred literati in four prefectures: thirty-five signed petitioners from Hangzhou, thirty-seven signed petitioners from Jiaxing, twenty-two signed petitioners from Huzhou, and eighteen signed petitioners from Shaoxing. Another petition from Fujian lists the names of forty-five local gentry. These petitions unanimously accused Feiyin Tongrong and his disciple Baichi Xingyuan, the two leading compilers of the *Wudeng yantong*, of "belittling the emperor" and disturbing the "familial relationship" within Buddhist lineages. These petitions suggested that the book be burned and the printing blocks destroyed.[22] Another petition equated Feiyin Tongrong's book with the words of demons.[23]

In 1654, in the court of Zhejiang province, Feiyin lost the lawsuit. As these records indicate, the lawsuit was started by local literati followers and finally reviewed by local authorities.[24] The governor of Zhejiang province reviewed the case based on the literati's petitions. It seems that this case involved no serious trial. Instead, the local government issued a decree banning Feiyin Tongrong's book. The presiding officials of this case were Xiao Qiyuan, who served as the provincial governor of Zhejiang province from 1646 to 1655, and Li Rifang, who served as the regional surveillance commissioner of Zhejiang in 1654.[25] The situation was very unfavorable for Feiyin Tongrong, and eventually Xiao and Li arrived at the following verdict, which has been translated in full in appendix 1.B:

> Feiyin stubbornly adheres to his own opinion and it is difficult to pardon him by the law. The printing blocks of the *Wudeng yantong* should be retrieved and burned; all printed copies must be recalled and strictly prohibited [for circulation]. Since Feiyin has fled, he will be severely punished when captured.[26]

This legal action was a heavy blow to Feiyin Tongrong. At least in Jiaxing prefecture and Yuhang county in Hangzhou, public warrants were posted, condemning him and listing him as a wanted man.

I have translated one such warrant issued by the police chief of Jiaxing prefecture in appendix 1.C. Written by police chief Wang, this warrant elevates a sectarian dispute to a struggle between orthodoxy and heterodoxy that threatened national security. Adopting the rhetoric of unification between Confucianism and Buddhism, Wang defended the traditional dharma transmission in the *Jingde chuandeng lu*, arguing that Feiyin and his disciple Baichi Xingyuan had changed this accepted convention without clear evidence. This warrant also revealed a related case that had alerted higher officials. Police chief Wang mentioned a monk named Chiyan, who claimed to be a disciple of Feiyin.[27] He traveled to Beijing to solicit writings from officials supporting his teacher's compilation of the *Wudeng yantong*. Chiyan was arrested, and Wang wanted to arrest Feiyin as well.[28]

Although there was no serious attempt to arrest him, the printing blocks, which amounted to about 800,[29] were indeed destroyed, not through government coercion but by other Linji monks through negotiations with the Caodong monks. As his chronological biography indicates, in the tenth month of 1654, Feiyin visited Hangzhou, where the local literati of both Hangzhou and Shaoxing were divided in their opinions on the *Wudeng yantong*. Feiyin again showed them the evidence he had marshaled and said, "If I did not make the point correctly, you could change the printing block. . . . Why should you press [me] by relying on official authority?"[30] Jiqi Hongchu, a leading dharma heir of Hanyue Fazang, eventually sent the printing blocks to Lingyan monastery and had them burned.[31] This source suggests that monks from Feiyin's own lineage, who had expressed the desire for pacification, carried out these arrangements voluntarily.

Conclusion

The dispute involving Feiyin Tongrong in 1654 marks a turning point in seventeenth-century Chan Buddhism: Controversies became more sectarian and pragmatic about such mundane interests as lineage affiliation and abbot succession. In the controversy over Feiyin's book, evidential scholarship, a dominant intellectual apparatus in Confucian learning, became the primary means through which Chan monks constructed or deconstructed a line of transmission. Chan monks' diligent evidential research on early Chan historiography in Tang and Song times, despite its sectarian motivation, reveals astonishing and valuable findings not yet fully utilized by modern scholars of Chan history. In my opinion, the unease that this dispute brought to Buddhists largely resulted from the disgraceful lawsuit against Feiyin Tongrong because local authorities had been introduced to judge a religious affair, disclosing that the seemingly "transcendent" monastic Buddhism was just as mundane as the secular world.

The controversies about dharma transmission reveal more about Chan Buddhism in seventeenth-century China than we expected. Not only did the will to orthodoxy manifest itself in voluminous polemical writings, but the process of the construction of a new form of orthodoxy, which was basically a reconstruction of the power structure in Chan Buddhism, was also unveiled through the surrounding events of the 1654 lawsuit.

9

The Aftermath

The controversy over the *Wudeng yantong* involved many eminent monks from the two lineages, and its impact lingered in the Buddhist world even after the lawsuit. Some of Feiyin's followers continued to adhere to his theory and to his editorial principles when compiling new Chan genealogies. One of them even added an extra aura of actuality onto the questioned Tang figure Tianwang Daowu by rebuilding Tianwang monastery in Jingzhou, claiming that it was the original site where this monk had resided in the Tang. More significantly, the publication of the *Wudeng quanshu*, the most comprehensive Chan genealogy, in 1693 rekindled the debate about the *Wudeng yantong* because it revived Feiyin's theory in a different fashion. All of these efforts by Feiyin's followers met with severe criticisms from the Caodong monks, who never gave up their efforts to falsify the theory through evidential research. During the course of the debate, the Confucian literati continued to intervene as both observers and participants.

The Rebuilding of the Dubious Tianwang Monastery

Although Feiyin lost the legal case in 1654, his revision of Chan genealogy continued to inspire his followers. After his death, some of his dharma heirs held fast to the views expressed in his ill-fated book and sought every opportunity to rehabilitate their master's reputation.

One example was the rebuilding of Tianwang monastery by Feiyin's follower Shuijian Huihai, who visited Jingzhou city and selected an obscure place as the site of this dubious monastery. Shuijian Huihai's audacious action involved the famous literatus-monk Huishan Jiexian, who wrote an inscription for the newly erected monastery without fully understanding its implication in the debate about the two Daowus. After being reminded by some Caodong monks, Huishan Jiexian was persuaded to retract his writing.

Shuijian Huihai Rebuilt Tianwang Monastery

Shuijian Huihai studied with both Miyun Yuanwu and Feiyin Tongrong. He eventually received transmission from Feiyin's dharma heir Duguan Xingjing (1613–1672). When he studied with Miyun, Miyun had once expressed the expectation that Shuijian Huihai would someday renovate Tianwang Daowu's monastery in Jingzhou.[1] Keeping Miyun's words in mind, Shuijian Huihai fulfilled his wish when he was invited to Iron Buddha monastery (Tiefosi) in Jingzhou in 1658. Believing that he had found the original site of Tianwang monastery, he reported:

> In the summer of the Wushu year of the Shunzhi reign (1658), I began to search [Tianwang monastery's] original site in Jingzhou. I found an iron lump that had not belonged to anybody for seven hundred years and thought that the place where the military commander threw [Tianwang Daowu] into the water should be at the riverside. Again, I visited twenty shrines within ten miles and they also claimed to be on the site of Tianwang Hall.[2]

Shuijian Huihai "therefore dragged [the iron lump] to [his] monastery and wrote a plaque, which read 'The Relics of Tianwang' and ordered craftsmen to carve it with diamond chisels. Those who came to watch were like [going to] the market."[3] Thus, Shuijian Huihai's discovery aroused a new round of debate.

Huishan Jiexian's Inscription

Shuijian Huihai's revival of Tianwang monastery put the famous monk Huishan Jiexian on the spot because in 1662 he was asked to write an inscription to commemorate the event. This inscription, entitled "Jingzhou Tianwangsi zhongxing beiji" (Inscription on the revival of Tianwang monastery in Jingzhou) was written at the suggestion of Shuijian Huihai and claimed the existence of Tianwang Daowu and praised Shuijian Huihai's effort to revive the monastery. However, this inscription incurred immediate critical responses from such Caodong masters as Weizhong Jingfu and Shichao Daning (?–1720). Admitting that he had been deceived by Shuijian, Huishan Jiexian showed his regret and tried to prevent his writing from being inscribed. However, in 1684, twelve years after Huishan Jiexian's death, Shuijian Huihai finally erected a stele with Huishan's inscription.[4]

Caodong Monks' Continuing Efforts to Falsify the Two-Daowu Theory

After claiming victory in the lawsuit against Feiyin, the Caodong monks kept alert to any new attempt to revive the two-Daowu theory. In order to settle the case permanently, they continued to search for new evidence and to write new essays to synthesize their findings. Among these works, Weizhong Jingfu's *Famen chugui* was the most systematic writing to refute the two-Daowu theory.

Weizhong Jingfu's Contribution

Weizhong Jingfu's 1667 work *Famen chugui* (Eliminating traitors within the dharma gate) presented the Caodong argument in a systematic way.[5] As the Caodong master Shiyu Mingfang's dharma heir, Weizhong Jingfu was an active monk-historian who had written several works on Chan historiography. Based on his careful study of Chan history, he authored a historical work entitled *Zudeng bian'e* to clarify historical mistakes in Chan records. His views were reflected in his Chan genealogy, *Zudeng datong*, caused a dispute in the Caodong lineage. (See my discussion in appendix 2.A.)

The current surviving edition of the *Famen chugui* is a Japanese reprint from 1690. It includes prefaces by Ruoshen Daoren, Weizhong Jingfu, and Shichao Daning. Shichao Daning's extremely long and polemical preface cites Qisong's *Chuanfa zhengzong ji* and Daoyuan's *Jingde chuandeng lu* as evidence to refute the two-Daowu theory, arguing that Tianwang Daowu's inscription was a forgery written by Qiu Yuansu in order to flatter Zhang Shangying. Moreover, he claims that no Tianwang monastery existed in Jingzhou. He even pinpoints a Yuan monk, Yehai Ziqing, as the person who inserted this inscription into a reprinted edition of the *Wudeng huiyuan* in 1364.[6] Weizhong Jingfu's main text summarizes the major arguments against the two-Daowu theory, which I discuss in appendix 3.

Weizhong Jingfu provides evidence that casts significant doubts on the existence of Tianwang Daowu. For example, he points out that parts of Tianwang Daowu's inscription are identical to Baima Tanzhao's life stories and that Tianhuang Daowu's descendants all claimed to belong to Qingyuan's line. Weizhong Jingfu cites Zanning's *Song gaoseng zhuan* to show that there was indeed a Tianhuang Alley in Jingzhou where Longtan Chongxin lived and met Tianhuang Daowu. Furthermore, he demonstrates that Zhang Shangying could not have obtained Tianwang Daowu's inscription from Daguan Tanying because Zhang was too young when Daguan Tanying died. [7]

Because Shuijian Huihai had rebuilt Tianwang monastery in Jingzhou and rekindled the debate, the *Famen chugui* includes two letters exchanged between the Caodong monk Jiansou Kongzheng (1593–?) and Huishan Jiexian from 1668 and 1669. As noted earlier, after Jiansou Kongzheng criticized Huishan Jiexian's involvement in the debate, Huishan Jiexian withdrew his support for Shuijian Huihai.

Yongjue Yuanxian's Admission of the Existence of the Two Daowus

Although Yongjue Yuanxian was a prominent Caodong master, his view on the two-Daowus controversy was not in line with that of his fellow monks, who vehemently opposed Feiyin Tongrong. During the controversy, he accepted the evidence presented in Juefan Huihong's *Linjian lu* and admitted that there were indeed two Daowus. However, he thought that Longtan Chongxin should be Tianhuang's heir rather than Tianwang's heir as the inscription stated. His evidence was the same as that collected by Yu Dacheng (*zi.* Jisheng), whose position was introduced in chapter 7.

According to Yongjue Yuanxian, Chan masters such as Xuefeng Yicun and Shenyan all claimed to be descendants of Tianhuang Daowu. Because these masters lived in the Five Dynasties period, which was not far from the Tang, Yongjue Yuanxian regarded their testimony as reliable. In addition, he cited Zanning's biography of Longtan Chongxin in his *Song gaoseng zhuan*, which clearly recorded that Longtan Chongxin was ordained and enlightened by Tianhuang Daowu rather than by Tianwang Daowu. According to Yongjue Yuanxian, the false claim that Longtan Chongxin was Tianwang's heir must have been interpolated into Tianwang's inscription to provoke dispute and controversy.[8]

Dangui Jinshi's Eclectic View

Dangui Jinshi's (Jin Bao) "Wudeng shifei liangqian shuo" (Essay that dismisses both right and wrong arguments about the five lamps) was probably written in the mid-1670s since Dangui Jinshi stated that he wrote the piece twenty years after the controversy took place in 1654.[9] Without unearthing any new evidence, Dangui Jinshi intended his essay to provide a new perspective on the controversy, which he believed was caused by confusion between the public and the private. According to Dangui Jinshi, although Feiyin Tongrong appeared to argue for the public good, he had a private interest in the debate, that is, to elevate Linji and to downplay Caodong. Ultimately, Jinshi argued, the enlightenment experience of true Chan monks never relied on their masters, and the struggle for orthodoxy could no longer guarantee the flourishing of one's lineage. In fact, as Jinshi pointed out, all of the contemporary lineages were derived from collateral lineages rather than from the orthodox one. For example, the contemporary Linji lineage was derived from Huqiu Shaolong rather than from Dahui Zonggao and the Caodong lineage from Yunju rather than from Caoshan Benji. For Dangui Jinshi, this showed that dharma transmission was less important than genuine enlightenment experience.

Responses from Juelang Daosheng's Disciples Xiaofeng Daran and Wuke Dazhi (Fang Yizhi)

Within the Caodong lineage, Juelang Daosheng and his dharma heirs participated in the controversy actively. His disciple Xiaofeng Daran (Ni Jiaqing), for example, wrote *Xixie bian*, which is not extant. Based on the account of its contents in Weizhi Zhikai's *Zhengming lu*, we learn that his work examined the institutional history of the Tang and proved that Qiu Yuansu was not one of the military commissioners.[10] Xiaofeng Daran also drafted the *Chuandeng zhengzhong* (Orthodox lineage of lamp transmission) under the direction of his master, Juelang Daosheng. The content of this book is not known. According to some sources, Xiaofeng Daran had not finished it when he died. Later, his dharma brother Wuke Dazhi (Fang Yizhi) completed this work, and Shilian Dashan finally published it in 1676.[11]

The Debate over the *Wudeng quanshu*

In the early seventeenth century, the Linji monks from Miyun's lineage controlled many monasteries in south China. After the fall of the Ming, they quickly embraced the new regime and received royal patronage from the Shunzhi and Kangxi emperors. This advantage gave Feiyin's sympathizers an opportunity to promote the two-Daowu theory. In 1693, under the aegis of the Kangxi emperor, two Linji monks compiled the monumental *Wudeng quanshu* and thus caused another controversy.[12]

The Publication of the Wudeng quanshu

The *Wudeng quanshu* in 120 fascicles is perhaps the most comprehensive Chan historiography. Compiled by Jilun Chaoyong and collated by Lun'an Caokui (both were Miyun Yuanwu's third-generation dharma heirs) in 1693, it was presented to the Kangxi emperor and published by the court. Its main contents can be briefly described as follows.[13] Readers should note that starting from fascicle 13, the Guiyang, Yunmen, and Fayan lineages were listed under Tianwang Daowu, an arrangement similar to that of the *Wudeng yantong* but different from the conventional transmission chart.

> Fascs. 1–5: seven Buddhas; Indian patriarchs and their collateral lineages; the six Chinese patriarchs and their collateral lineages
>
> Fascs. 6–8: the lineage of Nanyue Huairang from the first generation to the sixth
>
> Fascs. 9–12: the lineage of Qingyuan Xingsi from the first generation to the seventh
>
> Fascs. 13–16: the lineage of Tianwang Daowu from the second generation of Nanyue to the ninth
>
> Fasc. 17: the lineage of the Guiyang school from the third generation of Nanyue to the eighth
>
> Fascs. 18–20: the lineage of the Fayan school from the eighth generation of Nanyue to the fourteenth
>
> Fascs. 21–25: the lineage of the Linji school from the fourth generation of Nanyue to the fifteenth
>
> Fascs. 26–30: the lineage of the Caodong school from the fourth generation of Qingyuan to the seventeenth
>
> Fascs. 31–36: the lineage of the Yunmen school from the sixth generation of Nanyue to the sixteenth
>
> Fascs. 37–40: the lineage of the Huanglong branch of the Linji school from the eleventh generation of Nanyue to the seventeenth
>
> Fascs. 41–60: the lineage of the Yangqi branch of the Linji school from the eleventh generation of Nanyue to the thirty-first
>
> Fascs. 61–63: the lineage of the Caodong school from the eighteenth generation of Qingyuan to the thirty-sixth
>
> Fascs. 64–108: the lineage of the Yangqi branch of the Linji school from the thirty-second generation of Nanyue to the thirty-seventh
>
> Fascs. 109–118: the lineage of the Caodong school in the thirty-seventh generation of Qingyuan
>
> Fascs. 119–120: monks with "unknown lineage"

Based on the previous Chan genealogical compilations, this book includes more than 7,000 Chan figures in thirty-seven generations after Nanyue and Qingyuan. In particular, it updates Chan development in the early Qing and presents a complete picture of Chan dharma transmissions in the seventeenth century. About half of the book (fascs. 61–118) was devoted to Chan monks active in the seventeenth century.

Its "Editorial Principles" outline major issues that call for readers' attention. Most of them are related to determining the correct dharma transmission of newly updated Chan figures. However, on the most crucial issue of the two Daowus, the authors decided to follow the argument advanced in Feiyin's *Wudeng yantong* and regarded the existence of Tianwang Daowu as a settled case. Therefore, its structure resembles the *Wudeng yantong*, listing all masters in the Yunmen and Fayan schools under the lineage of Nanyue Huairang. In the crucial fascicle 13, where Tianwang Daowu's record appears, Tianwang is listed as Mazu's heir. It shows that the authors of this book largely based their account of Tianwang on Qiu Yuansu's inscription. In addition, the authors added a brief encounter dialogue between Tianwang and Longtang Chongxin as evidence for their relationship of dharma transmission. This short dialogue, however, was actually adopted from the *Wudeng huiyuan* and was originally attributed to Tianhuang Daowu.[14] The authors also put a note after their account of Tianwang, listing all the pertinent evidence.

Although the authors did not list Feiyin's *Wudeng yantong* as one of their references, this new compilation was clearly influenced by Feiyin's work. The authors must have been aware of the debate about the *Wudeng yantong* several decades before. More important, the authors themselves belonged to the Linji school and shared the same sectarian concern as Feiyin did. However, these two authors did tone down Feiyin's critical attitude toward the Caodong lineage. In this new work, unlike Feiyin's *Wudeng yantong*, the Caodong master Wuming Huijing and his dharma heirs were fully reinstated as legitimate Caodong masters without further doubts. For the records of contemporary Caodong monks, the authors carefully stated that they followed the available sources compiled by the Caodong masters to avoid further disputes.

Shilian Dashan's Role in the Controversy

Because the *Wudeng quanshu* continued to follow the error in the *Wudeng yantong*, the Caodong monks responded immediately. For instance, Juelang Daosheng's alleged disciple Shilian Dashan wrote several polemical essays, such as *Zhengwei lu* (Record that proves falsity), *Bugan buyan* (Not daring not to speak), and *Yuanliu jiuzheng* (Rectification of origins and streams), attacking both the

Wudeng yantong and *Wudeng quanshu* because these works were based on the spurious inscription of Tianwang Daowu. In his *Zhengwei lu*, he pointed to four pieces of internal evidence to prove that the inscription was a forgery:

1. The name Quan Yuansu was not in the Tang history.
2. According to Juefan Huihong, in Nanyue Huairang's epitaph, Daowu's name was listed as Nanyue Huairang's dharma grandson, meaning that when this epitaph was written, Tianwang Daowu must have been acknowledged as his descendant. However, Nanyue Huairang died in the third year of the Tianbao reign (744), when Tianwang Daowu was only eighteen. Therefore, Shilian Dashan argued, if Tianwang Daowu had no chance to meet Nanyue Huairang, how could he be listed as a dharma grandson when Nanyue Huairang's epitaph was written?
3. The spurious inscription indicates that Tianwang should have been born in 727 and visited Mazu in 760, when he was thirty-four years old. However, at that time, Mazu was not born yet. (We must note here that Mazu was commonly known as born in 709 and passed away in 788, except that the *Quan Tang wen* edition of his stele cites his death year as 786. There must be another source about Mazu's biography upon which Shilian Dashan based his argument. Or, Pen Lei's account of Shilian Dashan's view was wrong.)
4. According to Juefan Huihong's record, Zhang Shangying acquired the two inscriptions from Daguan Tanying. However, when Daguan died in 1060, Zhang Shangying was only a teenager, without any knowledge of dharma transmission in Buddhism.[15]

Weizhi Zhikai's Zhengming lu

The evidential research on the two-Daowu issue culminated in Weizhi Zhikai's *Zhengming lu* in fourteen fascicles, which provides the most comprehensive survey and summary of the debate.[16] In the Shanghai Library, I found a reprinted version from the Puhui canon published in 1945. (Figure 9.1 shows the cover page of this rare source.) This book, compiled in 1694, collects several essays the author had previously written. It tackles all of the issues covered in seventeenth-century debates about dharma transmission. Although little is known about its author, Weizhi Zhikai, it is clear that he hailed from Hengyang in Hunan and was Weizhong Jingfu's disciple, as he often refers to himself as such throughout the book.

As the title *Zhengming lu* suggests, Weizhi Zhikai borrowed the Confucian theory of the "rectification of names," which asks for a correspondence between

大藏經

正

名

錄

普慧大藏經刊行會校印

FIGURE 9.1.   Cover page of the *Zhengming lu*, 1694. Reprint, 1945.
Photocopy from the Shanghai Library.

words and reality. Embodying a critical attitude toward dharma transmission, all of its fascicles were titled "investigation." Using a massive array of historical sources and inscriptional evidence, Weizhi Zhikai demonstrated remarkable skills in evidential research, convincingly illustrating that when the principle of strictness of dharma transmission is taken to the extreme, even the legitimacy of Miyun Yuanwu's and his predecessors' transmissions become questionable.

Targeting the monumental *Wudeng quanshu*, which largely followed Feiyin's rearrangement of dharma transmission, Weizhi Zhikai attempted to clarify dharma transmissions that he considered dubious. To summarize, Weizhi Zhikai disagreed with the authors of the *Wudeng quanshu* in three crucial areas.

First, according to Weizhi Zhikai, regarding the disputed identities of the two Daowus, the *Wudeng quanshu* largely accepted Miyun's and Feiyin's position and switched the Yunmen and Fayan schools to Nanyue Huairang's lineage. The first four fasicles of the *Zhengming lu* investigated this issue, providing all kinds of evidence pertaining to the origins of the two branches of Chan transmissions derived from Nanyue Huairang and Qingyuan Xingsi. This part gave full attention to the dispute over the two Daowus. Zhikai believed that, regarding this crucial issue, the authors of the *Wudeng quanshu* were not much different from Feiyin. Thus, for him, the newly printed *Wudeng quanshu* was simply a reprint of the *Wudeng yantong*.[17]

The second area in dispute was the treatment of the Caodong transmission lines in the *Wudeng quanshu*. As I mentioned above, in order to avoid conflicts with the Caodong monks, the authors of the *Wudeng quanshu* had deliberately followed several of the most popular genealogies compiled by famous Caodong monks, such as Yongjue Yuanxian and Yuanmen Jingzhu. However, the authors of the *Wudeng quanshu*, deliberately or not, failed to consult a controversial Chan genealogy entitled *Zudeng datong*, authored by the Caodong master Weizhong Jingfu, who was Weizhi Zhikai's teacher. In Weizhong Jingfu's work, the significant change he made was the elimination of five generations of the Caodong patriarchs between Furong Daokai and Lumen Zijue, claiming that the confusion over a Northern Song Caodong master's identity caused the error. He found that this master was originally considered to be a dharma heir of Tiantong Rujing. But actually he was an heir of Furong Daokai, who was five generations earlier than Tiantong Rujing. (I discuss this dispute in detail in appendix 2.A.) The authors of the *Wudeng quanshu* did not adopt this change probably because this new theory was opposed by some influential Caodong monks. Weizhi Zhikai, as Weizhong Jingfu's disciple and a participant in his teacher's research, felt the need to promote his teacher's new discovery. Fascicles 5–7 of his book thus deal with this issue.

The third area that Weizhi Zhikai felt was inadequately addressed in the *Wudeng quanshu* was the transmission in the Linji lineage. As the two authors stated in the beginning of their "Editorial Principles," the *Wudeng quanshu* reconstructed the Linji transmission line in the Ming according to the identity of an early Ming monk: Haizhou Yongci rather than Haizhou Puci. Here, the two authors referred to a new controversy about the Linji dharma transmission in the early Ming. Previously, Miyun Yuanwu and his disciples believed that their transmission passed through a monk called Haizhou Puci. But later, due to the discovery of a new inscription, they changed their position and believed this monk should be Haizhou Yongci. However, Weizhi Zhikai pointed out poignantly that this change of position was simply the Linji monks' attempt to cover up errors in counting their own transmissions.[18] (See my discussion in appendix 2.B.) In addition, he charged that the Linji transmissions, especially those in the Ming, were full of confusion and inaccurate information. Even Miyun Yuanwu's and his master Huanyou Zhengchuan's transmissions were doubted.[19] However, the authors of the *Wudeng quanshu*, due to their sectarian bias, were not willing to examine their Linji dharma transmissions critically. Weizhi Zhikai investigated these problematic Linji transmissions in fascicles 8–14 in his book.

Weizhi Zhikai's critical examination of various lineage disputes made references to several polemical works that are no longer extant today. As he indicated, before the compilation of the *Wudeng quanshu*, he had composed the *Weideng lu* (Records of defending the lamp) in ten fascicles. The *Zhengming lu* also includes a work by Zhuo'an Zhipu (Zhanran Yuancheng's third-generation dharma heir), entitled *Cuncheng lu* (Records of preserving sincerity), which expresses similar concerns about the *Wudeng quanshu*.[20] Weizhi Zhikai incorporated evidence mentioned in the *Cuncheng lu* into the beginning of his book. In addition, he quoted frequently the Caodong monk Xiaofeng Daran's *Xixie bian*, which examined the institutional history of the Tang, in order to prove that Qiu Yuansu was not one of the military commissioners.[21]

The debate about Feiyin's *Wudeng yantong* received the most extensive review in Weizhi Zhikai's work, which also marked the end of the controversy. After the publication of this work at the end of the seventeenth century, no significant work was ever written regarding the disputes about dharma transmission. Apparently, monks lost interest in such debates, and Weizhi Zhikai's book suggests that many contemporary Chan monks, who were born in the early Qing and belonged to a new generation, had been deeply confused by the intricacy of these debates initiated in the late Ming. As Weizhi Zhikai pointed out, they often made obvious mistakes about important figures and events. Such a sharp decline in the production of polemical essays indicates that, at the end of the seventeenth century, a precise investigation of dharma transmission began to have less significance in Chan communities.

The Literati's Involvement

The continued debate in the early Qing could not have been sustained without the literati's support. Many eminent monks who joined the debate, such as Xiaofeng Daran (Ni Jiaqing), Wuke Dazhi (Fang Yizhi), and Dangui Jinshi (Jin Bao), were established Confucian scholar-officials before their ordination. In addition, other literati such as Huang Zongxi also joined the debate directly or indirectly by writing their opinions about the two-Daowu issue. Some literati scholars tended to side with Feiyin because he possessed equally powerful evidence to support the two-Daowu theory.

Huang Zongxi's Defense of Qiu Yuansu and Tianwang Daowu

The conclusion of the lawsuit did not end the controversy. On the contrary, it attracted increasing numbers of Confucian scholars to conduct in-depth research. Huang Zongxi, for example, offered his opinion in a letter to a recluse called Wang Weimei. In this letter, which is entitled "Da Wang Weimei wen Ji Dong liangzong zhengduan shu" (Reply to Wang Weimei, who asked for a correct judgment of the Linji and Caodong lineages), he rebutted the popular view that Qiu Yuansu was not a true historical figure, citing Ouyang Xiu's epigraphic record about this person. While acknowledging the similarity between the account of Tianwang Daowu's death in Qiu's inscription and the account of Baima Tanzhao's death in the *Jingde chuandeng lu*, he indicated that the author of the *Jingde chuandeng lu* must have plagiarized Tianwang Daowu's inscription rather than vice versa. Thus, he was inclined to believe the authenticity of Tianwang Daowu's identity.

He also questioned the accuracy of Tianhuang Daowu's inscription because of its author's misreading of personal names. (See my detailed discussion in appendix 3.) In his conclusion, however, he expressed his deep skepticism about the whole Buddhist religion, stating that even if the inscriptions were real, the miraculous story it recorded was unbelievable.[22]

Liu Xianting's Note about the Two Daowus

Liu Xianting (*zi*. Jizhuang, 1648–1695) was a learned man interested in history and geography.[23] In the late 1680s, he was recruited to work in the Ming History Office in Beijing. In addition to his historical works, he recorded random jottings about his observations or opinions about things around him. His miscellaneous notes in five fascicles became a source of information about events and figures in the Ming-Qing transition. As a literatus with many social connections, Liu did not fail to document the great controversy regarding the two Daowus. He wrote a short paragraph, entitled "Tianhuang Tianwang kao" (Investigation of Tianhuang and Tianwang), in which he recounted the history of the debate and provided a list of relevant evidence. Among them, he mentioned two rare sources from the Ming, Gongchen's *Zuyuan tongyao* (Essential history of ancestral origins) and the "Shaolin lianfang beiji" (Inscription of linked flowers of Shaolin). He also mentioned Wu Ding's *Dingzu tu* (Determined lineage chart of patriarchs) and the *Yi hua wuye tu* (Chart of one flower and five leaves), preserved in the Da Xingshan monastery in Beijing. According to him, these sources list Tianwang Daowu as an heir of Mazu Daoyi.[24] Apparently independent of Huang Zongxi's research, Liu discovered the inscriptional record of Qiu

Yuansu collected in a postscript of Ouyang Xiu's *Jigu lu*. Judging from the sources he presented, Liu was sympathetic about Feiyin's position. From his perspective, the debate was far from being conclusive.

Pan Lei Argued against Shilian Dashan

Shilian Dashan's views, mentioned earlier, are actually reconstructed from Pan Lei's rebuttal essay, "Tianwang bei kao" (Investigation of Tianwang's inscription). Pan Lei (1646–1708) was a literatus who first befriended Shilian Dashan in Guangzhou and later denounced him for his extravagant lifestyle and his trip to Vietnam.[25] He was selected in 1678 as a "scholar of extensive learning," an examination category created for learned Ming loyalists, and worked in the Ming History Office at the court.[26] He was demoted and retired in 1684. Because his relationship with Shilian Dashan deteriorated for some personal reason, in 1699 he composed and printed the *Jiukuang bianyu*, which included several letters and essays by Qu Dajun, Weilin Daopei, and himself to attack Dashan. Dashan countered with his essay "Xi e cao" (Draft essay on pitying the moth), which is not extant.[27]

Pan Lei's "Tianwang bei kao" in his *Jiukuang bianyu* targeted Shilian Dashan's *Zhengwei lu*. After briefly reviewing the debate over the two Daowus, Pan Lei focused on the falsity of Dashan's four points, which I mentioned earlier. Regarding Qiu Yuansu's official title, "military commissioner of Jingnan," Dashan claimed that the place name "Jingnan" was used only in the Song rather than in the Tang. Pan Lei, however, while boasting his historical knowledge and belittling monks' ignorance of the imperial administrative system, discovered that the office of the military commissioner of Jingnan, established in 757, commanded an area of ten prefectures with its administrative seat at Jingzhou. It was abolished in 832 but was reinstated in 838. Pan Lei believed that during its 150 years of existence, there might have been a commissioner called Qiu Yuansu. Regarding the anachronism of Tianwang Daowu and Mazu Daoyi, Pan Lei suggested that Shilian Dashan should accept Tianwang Daowu's death year of 818 as recorded in Juefan Huihong's *Linjian lu* rather than 808, as recorded in the *Wudeng huiyuan*. Thus, Tianwang Daowu's life span would fit perfectly with Mazu Daoyi's career. With regard to Shilian Dashan's question about listing Daowu's name in Nanyue's inscription by Guideng, Pan Lei ridiculed Shilian Dashan for not knowing the convention of inscription writing: An inscription erected many years after the death of a master could refer to events that happened after the master's death.

Shilian Dashan's last question about Tianwang Daowu's inscription repeats Weizhong Jingfu's point in the *Famen chugui*, which claimed that Zhang

Shangying had no chance to meet Daguan Tanying and to acquire the two inscriptions from him. Pan Lei, considering that Shilian Dashan had misread Juefan Huihong's (actually, Juemengtang's) preface to Daguan Tanying's *Wujia zongpai*, believed that the relevant passages about the acquisition of the inscriptions did not mean that the two men had personal contact. Instead, the text suggests that Zhang Shangying obtained the inscription by reading works composed by Daguan Tanying. Pan Lei admitted that the almost-identical deathbed remarks of Baima Tanzhao and Tianwang Daowu caused confusion.[28] However, he suggested that inscriptions are more reliable than other sources and that some sources had probably confused people's names and place names in their transcriptions. In the end, he suggested a more judicious solution to avoid future controversy: counting generation sequences from the sixth patriarch without further division into the lines of Nanyue and Qingyuan. Meanwhile, all pieces of evidence about the two Daowus should be preserved in new genealogical writings.[29]

The Debate about the Two Daowus in Japan

Although the original printing blocks of the *Wudeng yantong* were destroyed in China, the new edition found its way into Japan with Yinyuan Longqi, who arrived in Nagasaki in 1654. A theory about Yinyuan's emmigration, supported by Ōbaku's critics in Japan, such as Keirin Sūshin (1652–1728), claims that Yinyuan's move to Japan resulted from his master Feiyin Tongrong's defeat in the lawsuit.[30] The truth is that the lawsuit took place in the tenth month of the year, but Yinyuan Longqi had already left Mount Huangbo for Japan in the sixth month. Although Yinyuan knew that his master was undertaking a major historic work about Chan genealogy, he had no chance to participate in the later debate because he had left China. What he was able to do was to reprint his master's work in Japan and to send the copies back to China.

The reprints came out in 1657, when Yinyuan lived in Fumonji monastery of Setsushu prefecture. Yinyuan's postscript to this Japanese edition declares that he was motivated by his own sense of responsibility rather than by his master's request. When he saw a Chan poem that Feiyin gave to Yiran Xingrong (1601–1668), who had arrived in Japan earlier, he sensed that it was a secret message for him to spread the dharma. Together with Yiran Xingrong and other patrons, Yinyuan Longqi finished the reprint within a hundred days.[31]

After he left China, Yinyuan kept contact with his master, Feiyin, and the Manpukuji has preserved five letters from Feiyin to Yinyuan from 1652 to 1660. In a letter to Yinyuan written in 1660, Feiyin Tongrong asked Yinyuan to send back copies of the new reprints: "If the *Wudeng yantong* is to be sent back to the mainland several dozens of copies every year, my disciple's virtue is more than enormous."[32] He was even proud about the fact that his book was printed overseas, boasting to his critics:

> Master Longqi of Mount Huangbo accepted the invitation by the Japanese emperor. When the emperor saw the *Wudeng yantong*, he was extremely delighted and thus ordered it to be printed for circulation in Japan. To him is a bright destiny entrusted! And on him does the ancestral lamp rely for its transmission![33]

Obviously, Feiyin Tongrong was exaggerating the reception of his book in Japan because Yinyuan did not mention the role of the Japanese government in its publication.[34] Nevertheless, the impact of the publication of the *Wudeng yantong* on Japanese Buddhism may have been far reaching. For example, Yanagida Seizan considers the publication of Feiyin Tongrong's book in Japan significant in the spread of Ōbaku Buddhism because this book publicized the Ōbaku claim of *Rinzai shōshū*. According to Yanagida, this claim of orthodoxy, as articulated in Feiyin Tongrong's work *Wudeng yantong*, was attractive to Ōbaku's Japanese followers because it reflected Japanese expectations of Zen Buddhism. He remarks:

> Japanese people pursue orthodoxy and love purity and unity. This disposition of thinking conforms to Feiyin's and Yinyuan's claim. Sometimes, Japanese people are more eccentric than Chinese people are, and their habit of mind tends to slip into a narrow rigidity. This must have something to do with modern Japanese Buddhism, which began with Yinyuan. The Japanese preference for "one-stream transmission" reveals one of the secrets of the indigenization of Ōbaku culture in Japan.[35]

The impact of the *Wudeng yantong* on Japanese Buddhism is beyond the scope of this discussion. However, Yinyuan Longqi found important evidence from Japanese sources to validate his master's views on dharma transmission, especially the two-Daowu theory. He discovered that the Japanese Rinzai master Kokan Shiren (1278–1346) wrote an essay entitled *Goke ben* (Discerning the five houses), which supported his master's views.[36] Kokan never studied in China, but his literary talent and knowledge of Chinese Chan Buddhism were exceptional. Kokan's view, summarized by a Japanese monk named Nichi'an Itto (?–1486) around 1485,[37] was even more radical than that of Feiyin Tongrong. Not only did Kokan Shiren wholeheartedly accept the authenticity of the two inscriptions about Daowu and thus assign Longtan Chongxin to Mazu's line, he also

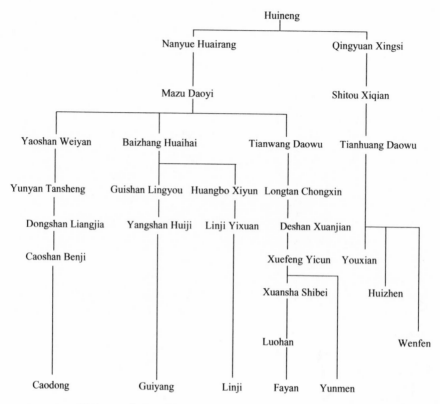

CHART 9.1. Diagram of Chan Dharma Transmissions according to Kokan Shiren, *Goke ben*

regarded the whole Caodong lineage as belonging to Mazu Daoyi rather than to Shitou Xiqian.

His argument was based on another inscription collected in the *Fozu lidai tongzai,* which claimed that Yaoshan Weiyan (751–834), a Caodong ancestor, also belonged to Mazu Daoyi's line. According to this inscription, written by Tang Shen in 836, Yaoshan Weiyan had studied with Mazu Daoyi for almost twenty years, and his enlightenment experience was actually tested by Mazu Daoyi rather than by Shitou Xiqian.[38] Thus, according to Kokan Shiren's reading of this inscription, all later Chan lineages were actually derived from Mazu's line, and Qingyuan Xingsi's transmission after Tianhuang Daowu was simply extinguished during the Tang.[39] Chart 9.1 illustrates Kokan's radical alteration of Chan dharma transmission.

This fundamental change advocated by Kokan Shiren in Japan must have had its origins in China because some Buddhist historiographies compiled in the Song and Yuan sanctioned this new change. For instance, Zuxiu, in his *Longxing biannian tonglun* (General annals of Buddhism compiled in the Longxing reign, 1163–1164), supported the claim that Yaoshan Weiyan was a disciple of Mazu Daoyi as recorded in the inscription composed by Tang Shen. His reasoning was that Tang Shen's inscription was written only eight years after Yaoshan Weiyan's death and was thus highly reliable.[40] Benjue, in his *Shishi tongjian* (Compendium of Buddhist history), recorded only Tianwang Daowu's lineage, completely ignoring Tianhuang Daowu's transmission.[41] Kokan's views, echoing these Chan monks in China, show that the impact of the sectarian debate had been extended to Japan as early as the thirteenth and fourteenth centuries, when Kokan Shiren was active.[42]

Conclusion

In this chapter, it has become clear that the debate over the *Wudeng yantong* was a definitive event in seventeenth-century Chan Buddhism. Not only was the 1654 trial sensational, but its aftermath in Chinese Buddhism and the repercussions in Japan also highlight its significance. To a large extent, it shows that Chan monks in the late Ming and the early Qing shared the same kind of collective consciousness of Chan identity as defined by dharma transmission.

One of the issues behind the numerous pieces of evidence is the struggle for authority. It is obviously pointless to simply display an array of evidence of doubtful origins and showcase one's skill in evidential scholarship, unless one has an ideological agenda. Because the controversy over Feiyin's work *Wudeng yantong* occurred in three contexts—Chan lineages, local government, and the prevailing textual culture—three kinds of "authority" were intertwined: patriarchal authority that was derived from Chan masters' qualification as holders of dharma transmission, legal authority within the secular world, and textual authority that was based on expertise in handling Chan texts and conducting historical criticism. Although patriarchal authority and legal authority appeared to be decisive in the controversy, textual authority was equally important in the settlement of the case.

The controversy over Feiyin Tongrong's *Wudeng yantong* also indicates that the patriarchal authority of Chan masters was in deep crisis. This crisis manifested itself in Chan monks' quest for their own historical origins and in their challenge to the legitimacy of other monks' transmissions. However, no such patriarchal authority existed in general terms: The domain of authority was in constant flux and the ways to define authority varied. Here, we must reconsider how patriarchal authority was historically constructed and the sources of its strength and meaning as well. In the context of seventeenth-century Chinese Buddhism, I suggest that a very specific form of authority was introduced by Chan monks to resolve the crisis of patriarchal authority: Textual authority, which had been valid in the Confucian world, played the decisive role in this controversy. In other words, through the exercise of textual authority and the manipulation of textual evidence, Chan masters established themselves as a new orthodoxy.

PART IV

Critical Analysis

IO

Explaining the Rise and Fall of Chan Buddhism

As I have shown in this book, by the end of the seventeenth century, Chan monks' enthusiasm for debates had ebbed to a low point, and no serious works were written in the eighteenth century. The decline in textual production indicates a corresponding conclusion of monastic expansion. In modern times, the memory of these controversies seems to have been completely erased from monks' collective consciousness, and pressing threats to monastic existence have necessitated a different kind of revival that is headed toward a new direction. However, the fact that seventeenth-century Chan Buddhism has fallen into oblivion in modern times requires an explanation. Certainly, modern Buddhist historians have not deliberately suppressed the account of the rise of Chan Buddhism in this period. The most obvious reason for the apparent neglect is that seventeenth-century Chan monks were involved in too many controversies that were nasty, notorious, and detrimental to the harmony of the Buddhist world. In addition, these voluminous but poorly written polemical essays made little contribution to solving Buddhist doctrinal issues.

Seventeenth-century Chan Buddhism has been indeed neglected, but for a reason. In this chapter, I will try to explain its rise and fall. The departure point of my reasoning is my observation of the textual nature of the debates I have studied: All of them were based on the reinterpretation and manipulation of ancient Chan texts. These Chan texts, including recorded sayings and Chan genealogies, contained textualized Chan ideals that were not fully grounded in monastic reality. In this sense, the reinvented Chan Buddhism was actually textually constructed. Because of the textual nature of the Chan tradition, the literati, who were skillful in textual matters, were allowed to play a significant role in the Chan revival. Their favorable attitude toward Chan tilted the balance of various traditions in monastic communities and influenced the collective mentality of the clergy.[1] Because both the literati and Chan clergy shared a common interest in Chan texts and attempted to reshape the Chan tradition jointly, it can be said that they created in concert various kinds of Chan textual communities in which an iconoclastic type of Chan was brought into reality out of the imagination of Chan textual ideals. However, because some practices, such as spontaneous beating and shouting and strict dharma transmission, were mere ideals, Chan monks could not sustain them in the routinized monastic reality. Thus, Chan Buddhism rose on the high tide of Wang Yangming's movement and fell at the juncture of the intellectual transition in the early eighteenth century.

Textual Ideals and Monastic Reality

China is renowned as "the empire of the text."[2] Based on a unique writing system developed in the early stage of Chinese civilization, written words and textual practice associated with literary manipulation created a formidable tradition that privileged the use of texts as the primary means of communication. Moreover, the maturity of writing, at least in early Chinese history, created what Mark Lewis calls a "textual double" of reality, meaning that a parallel reality, created through writing, mirrored the actual world and served as a model for regulating the Chinese empire. In this sense, those who controlled this textual world necessarily acquired authority that was derived from their ability to write and to interpret texts.[3]

Chan Buddhism became part of Chinese civilization by creating its own textual tradition and carefully crafted a "textual double" for itself. Although this double was parallel to the monastic reality and to some extent should have represented the monastic world faithfully, evidence shows that there was a glaring gap between the two: The textual double was truly idealized while the monastic routine operated on another plane.

The rise and fall of seventeenth-century Chan Buddhism demonstrates that this reinvented tradition was not firmly grounded in actual Chan training and practice. It was largely an imagined tradition because the historical distance between past and present allows the human mind to assume continuity with antiquity through adopting a creative hermeneutic stance. Without actually experiencing the ancient Chan Buddhist practice, the Chan monks filled the gap in their knowledge with their own romantic imagination of the past. Such a romantic perspective was, however, not entirely baseless or ahistorical. On the contrary, historical consciousness, as manifested in the controversy over Feiyin Tongrong's ill-fated genealogy book, rose to an unprecedented level. As shown in this controversy, evidential investigations of dharma transmissions were grounded firmly in the Chan textual tradition, which contains what Gregory Schopen calls "carefully contrived ideal paradigms."[4] Therefore, Chan texts became the ultimate source for invention and imagination because texts were supposed to be a faithful representation of the past. As the European historian Brian Stock remarks, "[T]hrough the text, or, more accurately, through the interpretation of it, individuals who previously had little else in common were united around common goals."[5]

To resume the continuity with the past, Chan monks had to rely on the reinterpretation of Chan texts created in previous times. Despite the Chan rhetoric of "not establishing written words," these Chan texts had been produced and reproduced in great numbers. Among these, two types of Chan texts were essential in Chan Buddhists' reinterpretation of the past: recorded sayings and histories of lamp transmissions, which present iconoclastic Chan ideals that were seldom seen as monastic routines in the majority of Chinese monasteries.

As many scholars of early and medieval Chan Buddhism point out, Chan Buddhism, though claiming to be iconoclastic, was deeply ritualistic in monastic practice. In reality, there had been few traces of the kind of radical iconoclasm portrayed in Chan literature.[6] The same was true in the seventeenth century. Because full-fledged Chan communities came into existence only after the revival of other Buddhist traditions, such as doctrinal studies and the ordination ceremony, the newly reformed monasteries occupied by Chan monks assimilated virtually all of the available monastic practices into their routines. In addition, many Chan monks, when they were young, were well trained in scholastic studies, esoteric ritual performance, and Vinaya rules. However, under the influence of the prevailing intellectual discourse at that time, they chose to present themselves as authentic and iconoclastic Chan monks without emphasizing their virtuosity in conventional Buddhist training. Hanyue Fazang, for example, was simultaneously a master of Chan, Vinaya, and esoteric rituals. As he confessed, he learned to perform esoteric rituals when he was a young monk and later concentrated on studying Vinaya when he was twenty-nine. However, in his forties, he became a Chan teacher.[7] But in his writings, he opted for portraying himself as a member of the Chan lineage. Even in his biography, his followers did not mention his engagement in reinventing the Triple Platform Ordination Ceremony and performing the esoteric Rite for

Feeding the Hungry Ghosts. Although the iconoclastic Chan style of spontaneous beating and shouting was indeed enacted publicly in monasteries, it was soon ritualized and only retained its symbolic meaning. In contrast to this gradual disappearing of Chan ideals, we find that Chan monks largely followed a synthesized Buddhist tradition that was highly syncretic. As I will discuss in the next chapter, one of the many legacies of seventeenth-century Chan Buddhism is the spread of Buddhist ritual performance. Chan monks in the seventeenth century, in addition to embodying the Chan spirit in the public eye, routinely performed the Triple Platform Ordination Ceremony and various kinds of rituals. But Chan monks, who were referred to as Chan masters and recognized by the literati as such, had to show that their practices conformed to the imagined ideals that could only be read in Chan texts.

As I have pointed out, Chan texts served as the source of new interpretations and inventions for Chan monks and the literati. Their religiosity is therefore a type of textual spirituality, as I called it in chapter 2, because it is largely textually based and nourished by activities such as reading and writing. Along with the rise of such textual spirituality was a conscious search for a new hermeneutic strategy to approaching texts. Depending on the hermeneutic strategy that was chosen, the meanings of these texts could be understood in different ways: A metaphorical reading could regard all occurrences recorded in Chan texts as if "real" or, in other words, as "pedagogical devices" to induce enlightenment experiences for students of these texts. Or, as Bernard Faure suggests, Chan texts are basically products of a "writing-act," which follows the rule of textual production and thus must "be read as [a] *self-referential* literary work" (Faure's emphasis).[8] A more literal understanding, however, could lead one to the belief that the events, or textual precedents, created in Chan texts were distinctively "real." The implication of this reading is that the idealized events are considered performable and realizable.

This literal hermeneutic strategy became the way that Chan masters recreated reality.[9] The fact that Chan Buddhism in the seventeenth century lacked any spiritual innovations comparable to those in early periods shows exactly that Chan Buddhism intended to be loyal to Chan's past as reflected in Chan texts. The controversies reveal that, in the seventeenth century, Chan monks advocated exactly this literal mode of interpretation, which considered the events recorded in Chan literature to be real and practical. For example, encounter dialogue, a seemingly real occurrence, was imitated and repeated; a strict definition of dharma transmission, based on the principle of face-to-face instruction and authentication by evidence, was put into practice. In short, the Chan monks read Chan texts literally and intended to revive an imagined past in the present.

In light of this perspective, the controversies I examine in this study resulted from divergent interpretations of the textual ideals of Chan Buddhism. As I have demonstrated throughout this book, these controversies teemed with quotations and references from ancient Chan texts, which were considered to be "evidence" for supporting a particular interpretive stance. To a large extent, these debates were conducted by a series of textual manipulations, such as reading, writing, and interpreting, without ever leaving a carefully constructed textual realm. Chan masters who engaged in these controversies had immersed themselves in this textual world to such an extent that they intended to live the ideals described in Chan texts even though their behaviors appeared ridiculous to bystanders who lacked a sympathetic appreciation of these textual ideals. For example, as I mentioned in chapter 5, some literati's observations of the performance of encounter dialogues found that these performances resembled popular drama in many ways and were awkward imitations of Chan encounter stories. In short, the extensive use of Chan texts reveals the distinctive textual nature of these controversies in the seventeenth century. In my view, these textually based controversies are indicators of the reinvention of Chan Buddhism. Moreover, Chan masters' frequent reference to Chan's past as textualized in written words signals a greater degree of discontinuity than continuity.

The Formation of Chan Textual Communities: Monks and the Literati

In my study, it is telling that the romantic imagination of Chan textual ideals was most conspicuously favored by the literati who gained access to the Chan tradition, or even to the entire Buddhist religion, primarily through reading texts. Although scholars have shown convincingly that the reality of Chan institutions in the Song was not as Chan Buddhists claimed in their rhetoric of purity and authenticity, it is revealing to note that according to Mark Halperin's study, most Song literati largely accepted the Chan rhetoric of uniqueness because many of them were attracted to Buddhism through reading the fashionable new Chan genre of recorded sayings.[10] This shows that Chan Buddhists, despite practicing monastic routines contrary to their rhetoric, had been successful in ingraining a romantic perception of Chan in the minds of the literati by using writing. To compare the degree of literati participation in the Song, and the late Ming and the early Qing, the literati in the late Ming and early Qing became more active in participating in the process of Chan reinvention through reinterpreting and recreating Chan texts, even through engaging directly in Chan debates. For example,

Mark Halperin notes that the Song literati generally took no heed of the arguments among Chan monks, like the one about kōan study and silent meditation between Daihui Zonggao and Hongzhi Zhengjue (1091–1157).[11] In contrast, the literati in the seventeenth century often responded to debates rapidly and followed their development closely, showing their unprecedentedly close relationship with the clergy and their deep involvement in monastic affairs.

The close relationship between the literati and Chan monks has been also demonstrated in Albert Welter's book *Monks, Rulers, and Literati,* in which he documents in great detail the triangular relationship of the three in the Northern Song. He shows convincingly that, during that period, Chan Buddhism, especially the Linji faction, was aided by the cultural and literary elite in their ascendancy to the political center. Chan Buddhists, searching for a national identity, sought to organize their dharma transmissions in a multifactional way, and they gained recognition first from regional rulers in southeast China during the Five Dynasties period and later from the Northern Song court. For Song authorities, the promotion of Chan Buddhism fit into a political agenda of uniting the empire under the Buddhist religion. More important, since the Northern Song court delegated its authority largely to the civil bureaucracy controlled by the literati, the literati's interest in Chan Buddhism greatly influenced the political status of Chan Buddhism in the court and even shaped its literary representation in Chan literature by directly involving themselves in the compilation of Chan lamp histories. According to Welter, the Song literati, cherishing the cultural ideal of *wen,* or civilization, might have been attracted to Chan Buddhism, especially Linji Chan, by its antinomian characteristics because, in actions such as shouting and beating, "the Chan masters present[ed] dynamic authority, unbounded by convention, completely free to dispense 'justice' in accordance with their own enlightened nature[s]."[12]

Welter's conclusion can be certainly extended to the seventeenth century. In my study, I have shown the intricate relationship among Chan monks, the literati, and the Qing rulers. As I have demonstrated, promoted by a special intellectual and cultural interest in Chan thought, the literati patronized Chan monks and helped to foster early Chan communities. The Chan monks, under the influence of these literati, consciously or unconsciously adjusted their teaching to adopt an imagined style of iconoclastic Chan practice. In this sense, jointly, the literati and Chan monks reinvented the Chan tradition.

There were many bonds that linked Chan monks and the literati together. Here, I want to once again stress the role of texts in binding their relationship because Chan texts were the ultimate sources of the reinvention of textual ideals.

As I hinted in the introduction and the end of chapter 3, in the seventeenth century, the thriving print culture provided the opportunity for direct encounters between readers and texts. This booming textual culture certainly influenced Buddhists, who actively participated by focusing on reprinting and distributing Buddhist texts. The most ambitious Buddhist printing project was the publication of the Jiaxing canon, which lasted for a hundred years. Independent of government funding, its operation was run on a commercially sustainable model. In addition, many printing houses affiliated with monasteries were dedicated to printing and distributing Buddhist texts. All of these efforts greatly increased the availability of Buddhist literature. Most well-established monasteries could now afford to purchase an entire canon and build their own collections of essential texts. In general, Chan monks and the literati lived in a shared textual culture that regarded Buddhist texts, especially Chan texts, as part of a textually constructed antiquity. It is no wonder, then, that the debates drew responses from both Chan monks and the literati, who had a common interest in Chan texts. The discovery of ancient texts and inscriptions, motivated by a penchant for the rare Song and Yuan editions, also spurred intellectual discussions and debates. Because of the literati's superior literary skills, some of the most important textual evidence crucial to the debates, such as that pertaining to the issue of the two Daowus, first brought to light by Qu Ruji, was actually discovered by the literati. Moreover, during the course of the debates, the literati continued to provide fodder by adding new evidence and texts gleaned from their reading.

It is clear that, for both Chan Buddhists and the literati, a body of Chan texts, composed of recorded sayings, histories of lamp transmission, etc., constituted a shared textual tradition in which an idealized past could be identified through reinterpretation. Based on a common textual tradition and a similar hermeneutics of reading, the literati and Chan monks formed distinctive textual communities, from which a collective Chan mentality emerged.

As mentioned above, I borrow the concept of textual communities from the European historian Brian Stock to explain the construction of a public domain defined by textual communications. An expert in medieval European history, Stock employs the idea of textual communities to describe the formation of dissenting religious groups in eleventh-century Europe as a result of the rising literacy rate. According to him, the emergence of various kinds of textual communities in the eleventh century resulted from the rise of a more literate society. In these communities, the study of texts led to behavioral changes in individual members. He argues that authoritative texts and literate interpreters of them helped to constitute new religious groups, often small and heretical, which were distinguished by their dismissal of beliefs and practices not legitimized through texts. According to Stock, in eleventh-century Europe, textual authority became a new form of spiritual authority.[13]

In the context of seventeenth-century Chinese Buddhism, I find that Chan monks and the literati also lived in various kinds of textual communities that centered around reading, writing, and distributing Buddhist texts as ways of seeking spiritual authority. These Chan textual communities were not necessarily confined in monasteries or Confucian academies. They even did not have to be in the form of a religious association in which members met regularly. Although members of these communities might have lived separately without regular meetings, their communities were kept alive through various kinds of extended networks by means of communication such as letter writing, printing, and publishing. For instance, in the late sixteenth century, an intellectual community surrounding the Confucian iconoclast Li Zhi was formed through intensive networking. Li Zhi first met Jiao Hong in Nanjing in 1569 and they became good friends. In 1572, the active Confucian leader Geng Dingli (?-1584) came to Nanjing and joined this fellowship. After Li Zhi retired from his office in 1581, he immediately moved to live with Geng Dingli and his brother Geng Dingxiang in Huang'an in Hubei province. Many other friends such as Guan Zhidao came to visit him and discuss Confucian and Buddhist teachings with him. In Huang'an, the monk Wunian Shenyou became his disciple and often traveled on his behalf to deliver letters to friends in Beijing, Nanjing, and other places. In 1589, Li Zhi sent Wunian Shenyou to Beijing to meet Jiao Hong and through Jiao Hong, Wunian Shenyou was introduced to the three Yuan brothers who were also sojourning in Beijing at that time. In 1591, after learning more about Li Zhi through Wunian Shenyou, Yuan Hongdao visited Li Zhi in Zhifo cloister in Hubei for the first time and was immediately attracted by him. Since then, he became Li Zhi's follower and they kept close relationship. This network was further extended to Eastern Zhejiang when Yuan Hongdao was appointed the magistrate of Wu county in Jiaxing prefecture in 1594. During his short stay, he befriended the Taizhou scholars Guan Zhidao and Tao Wangling. Although these intellectuals did not see each other very often, close ties were maintained through frequent correspondences as evidenced in their literary collections. Among these associates, not a few were monks. After Li Zhi died in 1602, the center of this community gradually shifted to Eastern Zhejiang where Zhou Rudeng and Tao Wangling became active leaders. Both of them patronized Chan monks in particular. As I have explained in chapter 2, they met Zhanran Yuancheng in 1588 and Miyun Yuanwu in 1607 and both of them became influential Chan patriarchs, from whom dharma transmissions of both Linji and Caodong were revived.

Despite the mobility and fluidity of their membership, the impact of such visible or invisible communities could be tangibly felt in the course of the debates as I studied their works. To a large extent, the polemical essays were all products of collective literary efforts by clergy and the literati who supported them. In other words, joining a Chan controversy by writing polemical letters or essays was an internal literary transaction within a textual community, whose contours became clear when the writers and readers of Chan texts emerged in the same "communications circuit," as Robert Darnton terms it.[14] Although a variety of means of communication existed in seventeenth-century China, links by textual methods such as reading, writing, and publishing remained essential. More important, any educated monks and literati could participate in this kind of community at will, and they defined their spiritual authority through textual investigations. In these communities, a common hermeneutics was shared by all: Chan ideals were extracted from Chan texts and imagined to be true. In reality, inspired by these ideals, some Chan monks tried to perform according to them and thus recreated an imagined world that had to be sustained by continuous efforts in textual manipulation and reproduction, such as publishing new recorded sayings and genealogies of dharma transmission.

Because literacy and a cultivated literary taste were crucial in establishing membership in such Chan textual communities, it was common in the seventeenth century that Chan monks were motivated to engage in the secular learning of Confucian classics, history, and literature. Some practical skills that marked elite status, such as poetry writing, letter writing, painting, and calligraphy, were viewed as highly desirable. (For example, both Miyun Yuanwu and Feiyin Tongrong, despite their low social origins, were accomplished calligraphers, as shown in figures 10.1 and 10.2. Their disciple Yinyuan Longqi and his followers brought the Ming elite art style to Japan and created the so-called Ōbaku culture.) Some monks even joined Confucian students to practice writing examination essays. All of these efforts showed that in Chan textual communities a high level of textual skill was crucial, and monks tried to match the high-level literacy that the literati had acquired. As I indicated in some of the biographical accounts of eminent literati-monks in chapter 3, monks with literati background often quickly rose to prominence in Chan communities by serving their masters as literary secretaries. Hence, all communications and writings by their masters were actually filtered and edited by these literati-monks. In this sense, lacking comparable professional training in literary skills, the clergy achieved a high level of collective literacy by soliciting literary assistance from the literati.

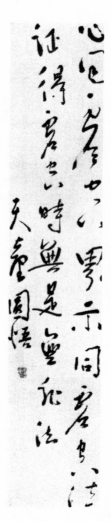

FIGURE 10.1. Miyun Yuanwu's calligraphy. Original 176 cm × 35.9 cm. Reprint from *Ōbaku bunka* (Uji: Manpukuji, 1972), p. 31, no. 19. Courtesy of Kōfukuji, Tokyo.

If we consider Chan communities as basically textual communities, this view will open a completely new area of Chan studies that involves research on the production, proliferation, and manipulation of Chan texts.[15] Here, my immediate goal is to employ this concept to understand the rise and fall of Chan Buddhism in the seventeenth century. Based on the evidence I have shown in this book, it is certain that Chan Buddhism, prior to becoming an institutional system, first started to take shape in the form of textual communities, in which both the literati and inspired Chan monks participated. Through active

FIGURE 10.2. Feiyin Tongrong's calligraphy, written for Yinyuan in 1655. Original 29 cm x 134.5 cm. Reprint from *Ōbaku bunka* (Uji: Manpukuji, 1972), pp. 32–33, no. 21. Courtesy of Manpukuji. Legend says that, because his right hand was cut off by bandits at the fall of the Ming, Feiyin used his left hand to create a unique calligraphic style.

reading, writing, and interpreting, a mentality of Chan spontaneity gradually grew prominent in the minds of the members of these groups, some of whom even became famous by enacting the written records of oral discourses and by performing encounter dialogues publicly. In these communities, oral discourse, written words, and performance interacted to create a sense of reality from a romantic imagination of the past.[16]

It must be noted here that Chan textual communities were only one kind of Buddhist textual community that took form in the late Ming. Many other smaller communities focused on doctrinal texts. For example, learned monks often organized lectures on Buddhist sūtras and dedicated themselves to writing commentaries on these sūtras. However, Chan textual communities, because of their effective use of dharma transmission as an organizing principle, eventually evolved into a more institutionalized fellowship of Chan monks who were able to take over many famous Buddhist institutions. It can be said that Chan arose because of the thriving of such communities. However, when the literati lost interest in Chan texts and ideals, such Chan textual communities could no longer be sustained. This is because, after the turmoil of the seventeenth century, Confucian intellectuals and scholars once again demanded a redefinition of the meaning of Confucian learning in theory and practice. Gradually, Wang Yangming's subjectivism was no longer in vogue, and Zhu Xi's thought regained the status of state orthodoxy. Meanwhile, a restoration of Confucian learning led to the rise of evidential scholarship that emphasized different kinds of scholarly activities, such as text recovery, forgery detection, collation, and the examination of text editions. There had been no attempt to address the issue of moral cultivation in the style of lecturing and discussing, which was a typical way of learning among Wang Yangming's followers. This transition was characterized by Benjamin Elman as "from philosophy to philology."

Leaders of this new movement of intellectualism disparaged Chan Buddhism, which was believed to have corrupted authentic Confucian learning. Without the literati's intellectual support, the iconoclastic Chan style was doomed to disappear. The fact is that, corresponding to this intellectual change in the Confucian world, in the eighteenth century, Chan communities stopped their expansion, and the literati withdrew their active participation in monastic affairs. Several signs indicated this change: Few Chan monks were seriously interested in beating and shouting as the characteristic Chan practice; fewer Chan genealogies were compiled; and fewer Chan recorded sayings were produced.

Drawing the Boundary: Monks and Emperors

In light of the close relationship between Chan monks and the literati in textual communities, Qing rulers' intervention to sever the ties between them was another factor that contributed to the demise of Chan Buddhism. During the early Qing, Chan Buddhism, especially Miyun's lineage, enjoyed unprecedented patronage from the court. Although the Qing rulers certainly had deep personal interest in Chan, their involvement in Buddhist affairs often pointed to more complicated motives.

Ever since the introduction of Buddhism to China, Chinese Buddhists had been seeking ways to ally themselves with political power. The most convenient way for Buddhists to link up with political power was to employ the Buddhist notion of *cakravartin*—"the king of kings or the wheel-ruler"—to religiously legitimize political power. As early as 419 A.D., the emperor of the Northern Wei was declared by the monk Faguo to be the Tathāgata Buddha. Emperor Wu of the Liang (r. 502–49), a pious Buddhist devotee, was called "the Bodhisattva Son of Heaven" or "Emperor Bodhisattva." This notion was later promoted by Esoteric Buddhism during the Tang dynasty. According to Charles Orzech's study, the Buddhist notion of the *cakravartin*, in terms of the esoteric master Amoghavajra's interpretation, coincided neatly with the Confucian ideal of the sage-king. The logical connection here is the direct identification of the emperor with the *cakravartin*.[17] In later periods, however, according to David Farquhar's study, Chinese rulers seldom identified themselves as Buddhas or Bodhisattvas officially. Unofficially, however, the identification with Bodhisattva Mañjuśrī, the special protector of China, was frequently used. For instance, the Manchu emperor Huang Taiji (15921–643) was recognized by the fifth Dalai Lama as "Mañjuśrī-Great Emperor" in 1640. The later Manchu emperors, including Yongzheng, continued to support this political ideal in an unofficial way.[18]

In my examination of Yongzheng's intervention in Chan controversies, I have shown that Yongzheng, assuming the role of an enlightened Chan master, attempted to judge the enlightenment experience of all Chan teachers. For him, political and spiritual authorities mingled together without distinction because he was simultaneously the monarch of the Chinese empire and the teacher above all religious teachers. By denouncing Hanyue, whose lineage was closely associated with the literati, the emperor implicitly expressed his concern over the close ties between monks and the literati.

The emperor's concern was justified by the fact that, in the first several decades of Manchu rule, the literati in the south had not been fully subdued. As Benjamin Elman points out, the Qing government intervened in the literati's scholarly life on a large scale in the seventeenth and eighteenth centuries in order to "depoliticize Chinese literati and mobilize them in support of the state." They tried to achieve this by imposing literary inquisition occasionally and initiating grandiose literary projects, such as the compilation of the *Ming History* (*Mingshi*) in 1679–1699 and the *Complete Collection of Four Treasures* (*Siku quanshu*) in 1772–1782, which attracted the best literati scholars in the south.[19] Yongzheng's effort in the Buddhist realm was certainly in tune with this general policy. To isolate the literati and conquer their minds, the emperor cleverly chose Chan Buddhism as his target: While exerting authority over Chan Buddhism, with which the literati often found alliance and refuge, the emperor successfully delinked them by joining the debate between Miyun and Hanyue and creating a favorable situation for the policy of "divide and rule."

In this sense, the emperor's ideal type of religion was a tightly controlled ideological and institutional existence that was isolated from the rest of society, especially from the cultural and literary elite, who were the emperor's reserved bureaucrats but also potential challengers if let loose. He wanted to see himself as the absolute leader of both groups while keeping the two separate. In Yongzheng's eyes, the ideal type of Chan monks was not represented by monks like Hanyue Fazang, who allied themselves with the literati and officials. In an imperial edict issued on December 30, 1726, to commemorate the death of Jialing Xingyin, the former abbot of Bailin monastery, where he practiced meditation as a prince, Yongzheng praised him as the paragon of all Buddhist monks because he not only strictly observed disciplines and precepts but also consciously secluded himself from the secular society, even concealing his special relationship with the emperor. Yongzheng appreciated Jialing Xingyin's voluntary retreat from the capital after he was enthroned because the emperor did not want his subjects to gossip about his indulgence in Buddhism. Even when Jialing Xingyin died in Lushan, no local officials knew that he was actually one of the emperor's closest associates.[20] Clearly, this monk met Yongzheng's expectation. In sharp contrast, Yongzheng excluded some eminent Chan masters such as Dahui Zonggao from his Chan anthology partially because of their close relationship with the literati.

While continuing to patronize Buddhism, the Qing rulers, since the 1680s, had revived the orthodox neo-Confucian discourse to lure the literati back to the track of the state agenda. Clearly, a united front between Chan clergy and the literati threatened the emperor's control over China's best minds. In this sense, Yongzheng's attitude was similar to the Ming founder Zhu Yuanzhang's, who regulated the Buddhist world and forbade monks' contacts with his officials and the rest of the society. This general policy of isolation helps to explain the fall of Chan from another perspective: While Chan Buddhism was elevated to the national level, a limit was also explicitly or implicitly set for its growth.

Institutional Implications of Dharma Transmission

The power of Chan teaching lies in its rhetoric of immediacy, which propounds the transcendence of all means of mediation, such as words, doctrines, and any possible spiritual authorities. In reality, however, as part of Buddhist monasticism, Chan Buddhism had to negotiate with various forms of mediation because the institutional life was sustained by a mediating power structure. Dharma transmission provided such a power structure for Chan Buddhism: Patriarchs dispensed spiritual authority and legitimacy through the hierarchy of an imagined lineage. This became especially important when a new Chan orthodoxy, such as Miyun Yuanwu's lineage, took shape.

In the seventeenth century, a great deal of energy was spent on the issue of dharma transmission as the controversies discussed here have shown. Such an unprecedented effort reflected the institutional demand for rationalizing the system of abbot succession. Miyun Yuanwu and his disciples followed an idealized principle of the strict practice of dharma transmission. The core value, as formulated by Feiyin Tongrong in his *Wudeng yantong*, was true transmission through personal encounter without ambiguous claims, such as remote succession (*yaosi*) or transmission by proxy (*daifu*). In addition, according to these masters, a Chan monastery, if truly embodying the Chan spirit, should always be headed by masters with dharma transmissions from one single lineage.

This means that the debates of dharma transmission had a clear institutional implication. Although scholars of early Chan history have realized the possible institutional function of the Chan lineage system, they have not yet fully explored the correlation between the surge of Chan genealogical writings and the institutional changes in Buddhist monasteries.[21] In the seventeenth century, as I have shown elsewhere, the plethora of sources in monastic gazetteers informs us that while the debates of dharma transmission were full-fledged, a quiet institutional revolution was under way: Chan monks implemented the practice of strict dharma transmission in order to organize the so-called dharma transmission monasteries.[22]

However, this principle of dharma transmission was truly idealized because it entailed insurmountable difficulties to be realized, and in practice dharma transmission monasteries could not sustain themselves as genuine embodiments of the principle that Chan monks were supposed to endorse. In other words, as shown from the practice of dharma transmission in later generations, dharma transmission monasteries were doomed to be eroded by various compromised forms of transmission. For example, ideally, one disciple could only receive dharma transmission from one master. But in reality, many capable monks had more than one transmission from multiple teachers. More ironically, contrary to the principle of the strict practice of dharma transmission, Chan monks adopted exactly the practices against which Miyun and Feiyin had fought so hard: remote succession and transmission by proxy.

First of all, a strict form of dharma transmission, as idealized by Miyun's and Feiyin's followers, is mathematically impossible after several generations because dharma transmission, as a mechanism of reproduction, will exhaust the candidate pool in a given time period and force Chan masters to compromise the principle of transmission from one single master. This conclusion is based on a simple mathematical calculation, considering the amazing reproduction rate of dharma heirs of Chan masters, especially the Linji masters, in the seventeenth century. For example, Miyun had twelve dharma heirs, who constituted the first generation after him. Each of them reproduced prolifically. The three most productive among them were Poshan Haiming (ninety heirs), Muchen Daomin (eighty-four heirs), and Feiyin Tongrong (sixty-five heirs). On average, each of Miyun's twelve dharma heirs produced forty-one heirs.[23]

If the reproduction of dharma heirs maintained this momentum, we can imagine a calculation as follows: Starting from Miyun, if each of his twelve heirs produced forty heirs, and each of these masters kept the same rate of reproduction, the second generation would amount to 480; the third generation to 19,200; the fourth generation to 768,000; and so on. This is simply impossible because, according to the Qing census of the monastic population, the number of Buddhist clergy was about 118,907 in 1667 and about 294,897 during the period between 1736 and 1739.[24] Down to the fourth generation, Miyun's lineage would have exceeded the total number in the monastic population. In addition, considering that other Chan lineages, such as the Caodong, were also offering transmission at the same time, within a few generations, it would have become very difficult to find suitable candidates to accept transmission because every capable monk would have been given at least one transmission.

In other words, offering dharma transmission unrestrictedly for the purpose of lineage development would lead to the situation that there were more masters who would be willing to offer transmission than qualified monks who would wish to receive the transmission. Obviously, the idealized principle of transmission from a single master must be compromised either by dramatically reducing the number of dharma heirs or by allowing any single candidate to receive multiple transmissions. This is exactly what happened in later generations: Many Chinese monks in modern times have more than one transmission certificate, and the number of certified heirs of each master has been reduced to a single digit.

Second, even if a strict practice of dharma transmission were temporarily in place, it would erode after several generations due to the increasing demand for transmissions from famous Chan masters. Miyun Yuanwu and his followers, in particular, were adamant opponents of the prevailing practices of remote succession and transmission by proxy, as articulated in Feiyin Tongrong's *Wudeng yantong*. From their perspective, these practices would adulterate the purity of a lineage, allowing fraud and deception. But in reality, there must have been compelling reasons to support the practices, which occurred when a monk considered himself or was considered to be a qualified candidate to be the heir of a certain master but had no chance to receive transmission from that master personally. For instance, in a Chan community, transmission to a highly capable student was usually expected in the near future. But sometimes, because of unforeseen reasons, such as the master's sudden death, the transmission could not be completed. In this case, a proxy had to be introduced to transmit the dharma. Although in principle, the Linji masters upheld the ideal of dharma transmission firmly; in practice, their later generations had to compromise the principle when circumstances necessitated the relaxing of the rule of face-to-face transmission.

Actually, a case of transmission by proxy occurred immediately after Miyun's death in 1642. Because of his death, some of his disciples, who had served and studied with him for many years, simply lost the hope of receiving dharma transmission from him. To assuage their disappointment, Miyun's heir Muchen Daomin showed flexibility regarding dharma transmission: He claimed that, besides the twelve certified dharma heirs who were publicly known, there were dozens of other heirs to whom Miyun had offered transmission secretly. In addition, he personally offered dharma transmission to one of his fellow monks on behalf of his deceased master. Feiyin Tongrong, who was the most adamant follower of the strict practice of dharma transmission, immediately attacked Muchen on the ground that he had violated the rule of transmission. Feiyin insisted that the names of all twelve legitimate heirs be inscribed on his teacher's stone inscription and his teacher's seals be effaced to prevent possible abuses.[25] Within Huangbo monastery in China and Manpukuji in Japan, Feiyin's leading dharma heir, Yinyuan Longqi, seemed to have followed his master's rule without transgression. However, after his death in 1673, his dharma heirs in later generations, especially Gaoquan Xingdun (1633–1695), the fifth abbot of Manpukuji in Japan, reluctantly opened the door for the corruption of dharma transmission. His more flexible attitude inevitably resulted in disputes.[26]

Finally, a strict practice of dharma transmission as an organizing principle of Buddhist institutions incurred strong opposition from local patrons. Ideally, if a Chan lineage continued to grow by building more dharma transmission monasteries across the region, it might have been organized into a more institutionalized form, preparatory to becoming a sect, as Buddhist institutions did in Japan. However, dharma transmission monasteries in China never evolved into independent sects because the development of these monasteries was based on the practice of dharma transmission, implying that a transregional monastic network tended to threaten the control of monasteries by local gentry.

The institutional framework implied in dharma transmission monasteries is a vertical structure that is superimposed on the local society where each individual monastery is located.[27] Dharma transmission forms a hierarchy that links numerous local monasteries. In this vertical structure, these local monasteries, meeting the needs of local people, would be administratively controlled by a headquarters. While such a vertical monastic structure was possible in seventeenth-century Japan, as demonstrated by the success of the Ōbaku school, which developed a monastic system covering all Japanese territory, in China, such an idea contradicted the local gentry's interests. This is because, as social historians inform us, during the sixteenth and seventeenth centuries, Chinese monasteries, without any internal hierarchy to regulate themselves, were largely the territory of the local elite. Timothy Brook's observation is a truism about the existence of Chinese monasteries:

> Ming Buddhism existed as a congeries of little institutions dispersed randomly across the country, without hierarchy, internal organization, or any regulatory body other than what the state supplied. With the exception of limited ties among sister monasteries and linked pilgrimage sites, Buddhist institutions did not participate in a larger

institutional framework at any level. Unlike European Christianity, Ming Buddhism was not woven into the net of secular power.[28]

Because Buddhist institutions were largely locally based, the local gentry were able to reclaim these monasteries as their sphere of influence. This means that, due to the local gentry's involvement in temple-building activities, monasteries in the seventeenth century were increasingly localized, indicating that the local gentry had more control of monastic affairs. For the local gentry, if the practice of dharma transmission led to the subjection of a monastery's leadership to a religious force outside the locality, they would oppose it fiercely.

I have come across one such case of opposition in my study. This incident occurred around 1640, when Miyun's influence extended to both Tiantong monastery in Ningbo and Jinsu monastery in Haiyan county. When Miyun left Jinsu monastery for Tiantong, his dharma heir Feiyin Tongrong became the succeeding abbot, just as he should have in a dharma transmission monastery. Thus, at the same time, Feiyin was the abbot of Jinsu and Miyun was the abbot in Tiantong. Both monasteries used to be among the five prestigious Chan institutions in China and were completely independent from each other. However, the close ties between Miyun and Feiyin gave rise to a rumor among the local patrons of both monasteries about a possible institutional change that was going to be implemented: Because Miyun and his dharma heir controlled these monasteries at the same time, it was possible that Jinsu monastery would become a subtemple of Tiantong.

The local gentry's reaction demonstrated clearly their fear of a translocal monastic hierarchy that might jeopardize their control of a local monastery. Eventually, according to Xu Changzhi's record, Miyun had to come to Jinsu monastery personally to explain away any doubts about the status of this institution, reassuring the gentry that no such change would occur.[29] (Because of both masters' strong will to orthodoxy, I assume that Miyun and Feiyin actually did plan to bring the two institutions more closely together.) In this sense, although dharma transmission monasteries could have been more tightly connected by their abbots' relationship of dharma transmission, they had to remain local institutions, and the institutional implications of dharma transmission were thus limited.

Conclusion

In this chapter, I have offered an explanation for the rise and fall of Chan Buddhism in the seventeenth century. I have identified some factors: the overwhelming reliance on textual manipulation, the imagination of textual ideals, close associations with the literati, the formation of Chan textual communities, and the internal contradiction of dharma transmission. To summarize, I believe that the very nature of seventeenth-century Chan Buddhism as a reinvented tradition explains its neglect because it was created out of Chan monks' romantic imagination of an obscure past recorded in a linguistically paradoxical way. The records of these ideals entail contradictions and ambiguities. When the social and cultural milieu that gave rise to such an imagination vanished, this reinvented tradition simply disappeared and was replaced by a more standardized form of Buddhist monasticism.

II

The Pattern of Buddhist
Revival in the Past

At the end of our exploration of seventeenth-century Chan Buddhism, it is now the time to ask some questions that can help us to understand Chinese Buddhism in general. First, if Chan Buddhism was a mere reinvention in the seventeenth century, did it leave any legacies in the Buddhist world from which we can still evaluate the importance of this tradition? Second, if the iconoclastic style of Chan Buddhism was only popular in certain periods of Buddhist history in China, why is it important and what is the role of Chan in the history of Chinese Buddhism? Finally, if the reinvention of the Chan tradition was part of the larger Buddhist revival, can we discover a general pattern of Buddhist revival in which Chan played a role?

Legacies of Seventeenth-Century Chan Buddhism

As I have reiterated, the reinvented Chan tradition in the seventeenth century was based on romanticized textual ideals created in Chan texts. When the aura of these ideals faded away, mechanical imitations of beating and shouting and the voluminous reproduction of dharma transmission appeared to be senseless and out of context. For some Buddhists, the seemingly sincere but meaningless debates I have revealed in this study only provided amusement for the Confucian literati and later generations. Although Miyun and Feiyin, the two major protagonists in the controversies, have been largely

FIGURE II.I. "Dharma-spreading Spring" (*Hongfa quan*) in Tiantong monastery. Legend says that Miyun dug the spring, and the Shunzhi emperor named it upon Muchen Daomin's request. Photograph by Jiang Wu, June 2006.

forgotten in modern Chan history, they are still commemorated in local traditions. In today's Tiantong monastery, as shown in figures 11.1 and 11.2, Miyun has been enshrined as a patriarch, and the relics from his time testify to the glory of Tiantong in the seventeenth century. In the rebuilt Huangbo monastery, as shown in figures 11.3 and 11.4, Feiyin Tongrong's pagoda has been restored and a memorial pavilion was built by Japanese pilgrims. Despite these remaining symbols, however, it might seem that the reinvention of the Chan tradition in the seventeenth century was an ephemeral phenomenon that left no positive impacts on the Buddhist world. On the contrary, as I will show below, the legacies of the reinvented Chan Buddhism are profound and far reaching.

Holmes Welch's study of Chinese Buddhism in modern times provides an excellent retrospective angle because, through his study, we can tell that the legacies of the reinvented Chan tradition still lingered in the monastic world more than 200 years later. According to Welch, Buddhism still functioned between 1900 and 1950 in Chinese society despite some biased claims that Buddhism was in a state of financial instability and moral decadence. His interviews with monks in exile reveal that Chinese Buddhist institutions were basically localized without any central governance. Each monastery took care of its own business without outside interference. Among 10,000 temples, according to a census in 1930, the majority were hereditary monasteries with a few monks in residence. In these small institutions, ownership of the monas-

FIGURE II.2. Inscription of rebuilding the "Dharma-spreading Spring" in 1836, inlaid on the back wall of the Buddha hall at Tiantong monastery. Photograph by Jiang Wu, June 2006.

tic property was handed down from master to disciple based on their tonsure relationship. In contrast, there were a number of much larger institutions where traveling monks congregated. In these monasteries, monastic property was not held privately, and monastic rules were usually well established and strictly observed. The abbots were selected publicly and often based on the dharma transmissions of the candidates. Welch observes that most monasteries, even those nominally belonging to the Tiantai, Huayan, or Pure Land traditions, were technically Chan institutions because their abbots had either Linji or Caodong dharma transmissions, among which Linji transmissions were most widely spread. In practice, however, there were few sectarian divisions because these monasteries largely followed a uniform routine symbolically attributed to the Tang Chan master Baizhang Huaihai but supplemented by more specific rules and codes devised by individual monasteries. Monks were ordained according to the Triple Platform Ordination Ceremony though the duration of the ceremony varied in different regions. Among the mortuary rites that monks performed for profit, the tantric Rite for Releasing the Hungry Ghosts was extremely popular.[1]

Welch does not venture to trace the historical roots of these practices to earlier periods. Actually, Chinese Buddhist practice in modern times has deep roots in the seventeenth century. Certainly, in the eighteenth century, the spontaneous performance of beating and shouting in public was gone; only a few Chan masters had serious interests in compiling recorded sayings that were full of stock phrases and strange allusions; dharma transmissions became nominal since every qualified candidate would eventually receive one or even more certificates because too many Chan masters were eager to offer the devalued titles due to their excessive issuance. By simply calculating the

FIGURE 11.3. Feiyin Tongrong's longevity pagoda, built in 1641, in Huangbo monastery, Fuqing, Fujian province. Photograph by Jiang Wu, June 2001.

number of dharma heirs and the publications of Chan lamp histories, we can see that both numbers dropped significantly after the seventeenth century. This indicates the conclusion of an era of expansion, intensive networking, and reintegration.

It is these three aspects of seventeenth-century Chan Buddhism that I regard as the lingering legacy that laid the foundation for the sustained development of Chinese Buddhism in later times. I suggest that great institutional changes took place under the disguise of the rhetoric of enlightenment. When Chan masters took control of monasteries in the name of a pure and iconoclastic Chan teaching, they transformed these institutions by assimilating all available Buddhist heritages and ritual elements.

First, seventeenth-century Chan Buddhism was a great expansion, more than a revival that simply restored Buddhist institutions to a previous level. It transgressed the boundaries normally delimited by state laws and social conventions: Monasteries were rebuilt and refurnished on a large scale; Chan monks became celebrities and participated in social affairs together with their

FIGURE 11.4. Feiyin Pavilion (*Feiyin ting*) in Huangbo monastery, built by Japanese pilgrims in 1999. Photograph by Jiang Wu, June 2001.

literati patrons; and the Chan way of thinking penetrated literary and artistic expressions. Eventually, Chan Buddhism became the refuge of the dispirited elite, who were caught between the reality of the Manchu conquest and the nostalgic longing for a lost cultural identity. Because of the appeals of Chan Buddhism, many historically famous Chan monasteries were rebuilt on a grandiose scale and today still stand intact as silent witnesses to the glory of Chan Buddhism in the seventeenth century.

Second, this expansion was based upon a movement of intensive network-ing that connected the once-disparate and localized Buddhist institutions to-gether. Within this monastic world, dharma transmission, as I suggested in the previous chapter, became a powerful tool to extend the institutional net-work, which included most of the prominent Buddhist centers in China. It is clear that the practice of dharma transmission led to the formation of an insti-tutional network of dharma transmission monasteries. This network connected a group of locally based monasteries by abbots' dharma transmissions but was much weaker than a formally established sect or denomination. In modern Chinese Buddhism, this network of dharma transmissions still exists. Accord-ing to Welch's study, in the Republican era (1912–1949), dharma transmission continued to be practiced in major Buddhist centers. In some areas, dharma transmission was closely tied to the abbot succession system, as it was in the seventeenth century. Although the abbot system varied regionally, dharma transmission played an important part in selecting abbots. Welch believes that it might serve as a potential bond that could eventually unite Chinese Buddhism.[2] He remarks, "All these networks of affiliation were superimposed one upon the other, loosely and haphazardly binding together in different combinations, the hundreds of big monasteries and tens of thousands of small temples in China." For him, this kind of relationship is more natural than the superimposed National Buddhist Association created by reformers. On the basis of this observation, he predicts in the same discussion that these links of dharma transmission "might grow stronger if circumstances [are] favorable."[3]

The third legacy is that, through creating a regional or even national monastic network, a set of commonly shared values and practices was disseminated and accepted within a much more integrated Buddhist world. In this sense, the rise of Chan Buddhism led to the reintegration of the whole Buddhist world because, behind their discourse of sudden enlightenment, Chan masters assimilated and reconfigured all Buddhist heritages through institutionalizing tools, such as the compilation of monastic codes and liturgical manuals that are still followed by modern Buddhists. In this process, Buddhist rituals and routine practices were systematized and codified. Moreover, Chan Buddhists spread these new rules through their extensive monastic networks.

For instance, several ritual ceremonies that are common in today's Chinese monastic setting were all reformulated during the seventeenth century and were promoted by Chan monks. One of them is the Triple Platform Ordination Ceremony, which is no longer a monopoly by Vinaya masters. This significant change occurred in the early seventeenth century, and in the following decades it was offered by major Chan monasteries and administered by Chan monks frequently. As I briefly described in chapter 1, this ritual was an expedient invention in response to the close-down of official ordination platforms in the late Ming. In the process of reformulating and propagating the newly invented Triple Platform Ordination Ceremony, Chan monks were deeply involved. For example, Hanyue Fazang, one of the protagonists in this study, was also renowned for standardizing this new ordination ritual.[4] Based on his work, his dharma nephew Yinyuan Longqi published the *Hongjie fayi*, the same title as Hanyue's ordination manual, in Japan as the guideline for performing this new ordination ceremony, which was essential to the perpetuation of the new Ōbaku school.[5] Chan monks' active role in offering ordination can be also seen from the testimony of the Caodong monk Dangui Jinshi (Jin Bao), who criticized Chan monks for offering the ordination ceremony in lieu of those by Vinaya masters.[6] His criticism simply shows that in the seventeenth century it became widespread for Chan monks to perform ordination ceremonies. Although some scholars have noted that as early as Tang times, some Vinaya masters had close ties with Chan Buddhism and the creation of

Huineng's *Platform Sūtra* might be related to Chan monks' effort to use ordination ceremonies to propagate their teaching, the interaction between Chan and Vinaya in late imperial China was unprecedented.[7]

Another example that suggests continuity in ritual performance is the esoteric Rite for Releasing the Hungry Ghosts. In my study of Hanyue Fazang's interpretation of the perfect circle from the esoteric perspective, I have suggested that his understanding was based on his performance of this rite. Although it was not new for Chan monks to incorporate esoteric ritual elements into their practice, it was novel that Chan institutions were instrumental in reinforcing these tantric influences and even included them in their liturgical service. For example, one version of this esoteric ritual was entitled "Mengshan Rite for Releasing the Hungry Ghosts" (*Mengshan shishi yi*). Attributed to an Indian monk called Budong, who was prominent in the Tangut court and later resided in Mengshan along the Sino-Tibetan border,[8] this ritual demonstrates that the predominant influence of esoteric rituals in later imperial China had penetrated the monastic world. Still performed in today's Chinese monasteries, this rite was formally incorporated into the Chan liturgical manual in the seventeenth century.

In contemporary monastic settings, Chinese Buddhists commonly use a liturgical manual called *Chanmen risong* for morning and evening services.[9] Among its various versions, the Tianning edition is the most popular. Comparing different versions of existing liturgical manuals, Chen Jidong traces the origin of the contemporary agenda of morning and evening services to the eighteenth century.[10] Although Zhuhong compiled a manual called *Zhujing risong* (Scriptures for daily chanting), it is still significantly different from the modern version. In fact, the modern liturgical tradition in Chinese monasteries took shape in the seventeenth century, as evidenced in a rare source, *Chanlin kesong* (Japanese: *Zenrin kaju*; Daily liturgies in Chan groves), printed in 1662 in Kyoto, Japan. (Figure 11.5 shows the first and last pages of this rare source.) This text must have been brought to Japan by Yinyuan Longqi because this title appears in the catalog of Mount Huangbo's printing house in China. A comparison between this version and the popular Tianning edition of the *Chanmen risong* shows that the Tianning edition was developed from the *Chanlin kesong*. This means that, during the seventeenth century, the Buddhist liturgy for morning and evening services had been reformed, and *Chanlin kesong*, as a synthesized new version, was promoted by Chan monks such as Yinyuan Longqi, who even brought it to Japan.

The systemization of Buddhist rituals can be also seen in Chan monks' efforts to create new versions of monastic rules. During the sixteenth and seventeenth centuries, the revival of Buddhist monasticism created an

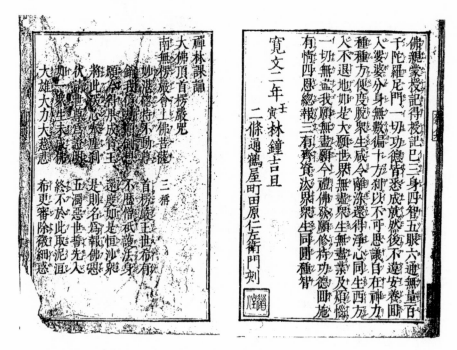

FIGURE 11.5. (A) First page of the *Chanlin kesong*, 1662. (B) Last page of the *Chanlin kesong*. Both photocopies from Komazawa University Library.

unprecedented demand for new rules to regulate the growing monastic population. For instance, in 1600, Hanshan Deqing presided over Caoxi monastery in Guangdong and compiled ten articles of rules for the meditation hall
in the monastery.[11] These rules, rather than regulating the proper monastic
ritual life, emphasized the administrative aspect of a public monastery. Miyun and Feiyin also formulated their own rules to administer their monasteries.[12] The most complete version of monastic regulation produced in the seventeenth century was Yinyuan Longqi's *Huangbo qinggui*, or *Ōbaku shingi* in
Japanese (Ōbaku pure regulations). This version of a monastic code, though
finalized in Japan in 1673, can be seen as a systematic presentation of monastic practices in Chinese monasteries.[13]

Chan monks' interests in compiling liturgical manuals and monastic
codes simply show the overwhelming demand for a routinized monastic life
and regulated daily services, rather than for the spontaneous performance of
beating and shouting. This is because routinization can provide an enduring
paradigm for spiritual cultivation. Yet, as the dominant Buddhist tradition in
China, Chan Buddhism systemized all available ritual elements under its
name. These ritual elements were the accumulated legacies of Chinese Bud-

dhism through centuries. The result of this process was not the desired "purity," as the Chan rhetoric suggests. Instead, Chan monastic practice in China was undeniably a mixture of meditation, esotericism, and Pure Land.[14]

On the surface, Chan Buddhism as reinvented in the seventeenth century was "rhetorical" in its hyperbolic style of the performance of beating and shouting and in its unreasonable emphasis on the strictness of dharma transmission. Beneath it, Chan Buddhists had a deeper concern about institution building. They were extremely talented in managing monastic affairs and initiating new construction and renovation projects. This characteristic thus differentiated them from the four eminent monks in the late Ming, who set their minds on scholasticism and meditation without interest in expanding their influence on monastic institutions. In this sense, Chan masters in the seventeenth century were not original thinkers. Instead, they were "entrepreneurs," whose contributions to monasticism were even more far reaching.

The Place of Chan in the History of Chinese Buddhism

If Chinese Buddhism is basically nonsectarian and syncretic, as many scholars observe, why are most modern Chinese monasteries titled "Chan institutions," and why is the Linji lineage particularly popular in tonsure ordination and dharma transmission? If the Chan rhetoric of antinomianism has nothing to do with actual monastic practice, why in some historical periods, did many inspired and talented Buddhists want to uphold the rhetoric and display the Chan spirit in action? As I have discussed in the previous section, the role of Chan masters in synthesizing monastic rituals seems to point to a possible answer to these questions. That is, the rise of Chan Buddhism was not only meaningful for the Chan tradition only. Rather, because Chan Buddhism had the advantageous position in Chinese society and culture, it served as a unique linkage between the monastic world and the secular society and among the various Buddhist traditions. Therefore, Chan rhetoric has a special place in the history of Chinese Buddhism, and to some extent it became a survival strategy for Chinese Buddhists in several critical moments of history. In light of this observation, the study of the Chan revival does not simply concern Chan Buddhism.

In order to understand Chan's special place in Chinese Buddhism, we need to gain perspective about the actual existence of Buddhist institutions in China. As I have cited previously, Timothy Brook observes that within Chinese Buddhism there were no functional power structures comparable to those in European Christianity that could supervise and discipline the monastic routines. Because of this, in order to maintain a level of moral standards and disciplinary rigor, a unifying force, which Chan Buddhism would provide, was much needed.

Brook is not the first to notice this characteristic of the Chinese monastic world. According to Eric Zürcher, since the introduction of Buddhism into China in the first century, Buddhist institutions have existed as individual local monasteries without any organized way of connecting with each other. In Zürcher's comparison between the missionary strategy of the Jesuits in seventeenth-century China and that of early foreign Buddhists in Han China, he finds that these two religions represent two different modes of religious dissemination. The spread of Buddhism was achieved through spontaneous contact with each locality; in other words, without central leadership, Buddhism was able to be absorbed and assimilated as part of the local tradition. However, the Jesuits in seventeenth-century China adopted a strategy of "guided transmission" that put the administration of local churches under the management of a central ecclesia that was controlled by a group of foreigners directed by the papal bureaucracy in Rome.[15]

Both observations, one from the early stage of Chinese Buddhism and the other from a later period, reveal an aspect of Buddhism in Chinese society: Buddhist institutions were merely local institutions without any hierarchy to connect them. The various kinds of state bureaucracy that were superimposed on Buddhism by the state only passively carried out state policies regarding Buddhist institutions. The implication of this institutional characteristic is that the practice and teaching of Chinese Buddhism should have been as diverse as the number of local communities. However, despite regional differences, Chinese Buddhism shows a great level of homogeneity in monastic practices and doctrinal trainings. This demonstrates that, within Chinese Buddhism, there must be a unifying force that periodically renews the spiritual aspiration for the goal of enlightenment, reintegrates the gradually diversified and localized practices, and reconnects the once-disparate local institutions. Based on this study, I surmise that, historically speaking, Chan Buddhism fulfilled such a role by using dharma transmission as an organizing principle to integrate individual monasteries in disparate localities and by providing a sinicized rhetoric of iconoclasm that bridged the gap between the Buddhist religion and Chinese culture, especially the elite literati culture. Let me explain further.

First, Chan Buddhism provided a unifying force within the discrete monastic world by organizing a power structure through dharma transmission and by reformulating monastic codes as monks' behavioral standards. As I have shown, Chan's legacies in monastic building were not really about Chan rhetoric, and the reformulation of monastic rituals was not aimed at maintaining an antinomian spirit. Rather, Chan monks' efforts in institution building were entirely geared toward restoring routine monasticism by assimilating all aspects of Buddhist practice, such as doctrinal studies, esotericism, meditation, and Pure Land devotion. This process is similar to that which occurred in the Northern Song, as Griffith Foulk points out: Most monasteries simply changed their plaques to those of Chan institutions by royal decree. However, these so-called Chan institutions maintained syncretic practices after the conversion.[16] It is true that, in this process, Chan monasteries lost their unique character. Therefore, it was justifiable to claim that there were actually no Chan monasteries at all. But if viewed from an opposite perspective, Chan Buddhism became significant to the healthy development of the entire monastic world: While Chan monasteries lost their uniqueness, Chinese monasteries acquired their characteristics. This is because, by taking advantage of a favorable intellectual and social movement, Chan Buddhism provided a mechanism for Chinese Buddhist monasteries to organize themselves internally and to integrate disparate practices into a somewhat unified code of behavior shared by all. Therefore, Chan's organizing role is particularly important for Chinese Buddhism.

Second, Chan Buddhism provided a literarily polished rhetoric that was easily accepted by China's cultural elite and thus helped the entire Buddhist world to elevate its social, cultural, economic, and political status. Often sponsored by their literati patrons, Chan Buddhists took advantage of their secular support and reintegrated the disparate Buddhist institutions under the structure of dharma transmission while synthesizing monastic practices from all existing traditions.

From the perspective of the seventeenth century, to determine the role of Chan Buddhism in the history of Chinese Buddhism, we need to look at Chan Buddhism both synchronically and diachronically. Synchronically, along with the promotion of the Chan discourse of spontaneity in the literati's intellectual life, Chan communities took shape. As a result, a series of monastic reforms took place under the guise of Chan rhetoric. Diachronically, due to the changes in the intellectual and political climate, Chan Buddhism, which was closely knit into the elite culture, was doomed to decline. However, the results of its efforts to reintegrate Chinese Buddhism remained.

Finally, Chan Buddhism provides a lineage model of monastic existence based on dharma transmission. This model tends to expand through the network of dharma transmission and to integrate the entire Buddhist world. It is in contrast to the local model that Zürcher and Brook have identified. According to this local model, individual monastic institutions were largely locally based without a superimposed power structure.[17] In light of the lineage model, however, the controversies over dharma transmission, as I have shown in this study, expressed the clergy's cry for a more integrated and organized Buddhist world.[18] This lineage model allowed Chan monks to arrange themselves into a hierarchy of authority within which patriarchal power was established.

However, this doesn't mean that the lineage model would eventually replace the local model and move toward a more aggressive sectarian model that would bond various kinds of Buddhist institutions more closely. In fact, while the lineage model prevailed in certain times and certain regions, the local model remained strong in most of the history of Chinese Buddhism as the fundamental mode of monastic existence. The debates over dharma transmission, accompanied by a process of institutionalization of dharma transmission monasteries whose leadership had to be controlled within a lineage, show the strongest urge toward a lineage-based structure. However, after dharma transmission was indeed introduced to a local monastery that was annexed into a larger network of transmission, it gradually lost its significance in the local context. The so-called dharma transmission monasteries were again drawn back to the status of local monasteries by various kinds of local forces. This doesn't mean, however, that dharma transmission completely disappeared from monastic life. Rather, it demonstrates that the introduction of dharma transmission had to be negotiated with various kinds of local forces to remain meaningful. In this sense, the actual existence of Chinese Buddhism was the interplay between both models.

In light of this transition between these two models, the Chan debates I have studied here can be viewed as an attempt at reconstructing power structures through building a rationalized lineage model of dharma transmission. However, this attempt was not successful because the debates, by scrutinizing evidence and revealing inconsistencies in dharma transmission, actually devastated the stability of a structured lineage-based hierarchy. Unconsciously, Chan monks who were deeply involved in these debates helped Buddhism to move toward a mode of existence based on the local model, which is exactly what happened after the seventeenth century.

The Meaning of Buddhist Revival Revisited

At the end of Holmes Welch's book *The Buddhist Revival in China*, he questions the meaning of Buddhist revival because he finds in his research that the term was a creation in Western literature and was used most frequently by missionaries and Buddhist reformists, such as Taixu (1890–1947). This process is better referred to as "revitalization," and according to Welch, Chinese Buddhists did not restore Buddhism to the level of the early stages, such as that during the Tang. Instead of a restoration of the past, the movement was "a series of innovations" or "a redirection from the religious to the secular."[19] Welch's doubt about the meaning of Buddhist revival needs to be addressed here because my study also deals with a similar religious phenomenon, which I have sometimes referred to as "Buddhist revival" or "Chan revival."

The rise and fall of Chan Buddhism, as I have described in this study, indicates the existence of a cyclical pattern in the growth of Chan Buddhism. Such a pattern is conventionally referred to as "revival" and "decline." Although these terms are indeed convenient to describe the state of Buddhism, and I did use them throughout this study to refer to the observable rise and fall of Chan Buddhism, we should realize that these characterizations do not describe the reality accurately. When such terms are used, people tend to view the "revival" positively and the "decline" undesirably, showing their wish for the growth and lament for the decline. Therefore, researchers pay more attention to the period of revival.

However, as Welch points out correctly, despite some biased observations of monastic decline, the monastic communities functioned well in the Republican era. In other words, the Buddhist tradition was alive even before the so-called revival, and there was no need to revive anything.[20] Rather, it can be viewed as a phase of innovation and revitalization, which was only temporary. In my opinion, it is incorrect to assume that before the so-called Buddhist revival in history, the monastic world was completely in ruin or had declined to a deplorable state. For example, in my study, I have cited many historical records that show the so-called decline of Buddhism in the mid-Ming. However, these records were largely retrospective recollections written by some eminent and highly educated monks from southeast China a hundred years later. In some other sources, however, we learned that it is certainly not true that Buddhism had completely disappeared from the public scene. Yu Qian's *Supplementary Biographies of Eminent Monks* (*Xinxu gaoseng zhuan siji*) compiled in the Republican era, for example, offered a dramatically different picture from the one portrayed in Chan genealogies. Documenting many less known monks in late imperial China, Yu Qian's work shows that even in the early and mid Ming, Buddhist monks still maintained a traditional style of practice focusing on doctrinal studies, pious devotion, and pilgrimage rather than on dharma transmission, encounter dialogue, and literary composition. Because the Ming founder Zhu Yuanzhang had successfully severed the ties between clergy and the literati, monks' activities did not have traces in literati's writing. Only after the mid-sixteenth century, when the literati were once again interested in Buddhism, some records of monks' activities surfaced in their literary collections. However, not all monks wanted to be associated with the literati and the secular world. Qu Ruji, for example, wrote a biography for the monk Biechuan Huizong (1489–1569), who often shunned away from invitations and fled from his monastic posts arranged by the literati. After he became famous for his devotional activities in Mount E'mei, he was invited by the Taizhou scholar Zhao Zhenji. However, Biechuan simply left and continued the life of an ascetic. Later, he was invited to Qu's hometown Changshu by the retired prime minister Xu Jie (1494–1574). Even when he was awarded with prestige and patronage, he soon left again for pilgrimage.[21] The image of this type of Buddhist hermits stands in sharp contrast to that of later Chan Buddhists who deliberately sought after literati's support and emulating literati's textual practice.

Obviously, even during the period of the so-called Buddhist decline, some official Buddhist institutions still carried out duties the government assigned to them. For example, the Japanese monk Sakugen Shūryō (1501–1579), during his diplomatic missions to Ming China in 1539–1540 and 1548–1549, stayed in many famous Chinese monasteries and did not complain about the decline of Buddhism there.[22] He arrived in Ningbo and traveled to Beijing along the Grand Canal. Because he was a Buddhist monk, he paid special attention to Chinese Buddhism and left records about his visits to monasteries in his travelogues. He visited several monasteries in Ningbo, including the famed Tiantai center, Yanqing monastery, which was renovated several times in the Ming. Along his way to the north, he also stopped at some monasteries in Hangzhou and Suzhou. Except for complaining about the dilapidated condition of Baoshu pagoda, he had positive impressions about Buddhism in southeast China. After crossing the Yangtse River in Zhenjiang, he visited the famed Jinshan monastery and noticed that the Buddhist monastery, Taoist temple, and Confucian academy were built side by side without interference. He also recorded his visits to monasteries in the north. For example, in Cangzhou, a transportation hub along the Grand Canal in Hebei, he visited Jishan monastery, which was built by a eunuch in 1492. In Beijing, he stayed in official monasteries, such as Da Xinglong monastery, which boasted a monastic population of as many as 3,000.[23] Sakugen's records show that, under the patronage of the state and the imperial house, Buddhist institutions in major cities did not have obvious signs of decline.

During his trips, he did not visit famed Chan monasteries in Ningbo, such as Tiantong and Ayuwang, because they were located in the mountainous suburbs. It might be true that these traditional Chan centers, which were far away from cities, suffered from dwindled state support. More conspicuously absent in Chan genealogies and recorded sayings produced in the seventeenth century were records about Buddhism in the north, especially in Beijing. However, through Susan Naquin's study of Buddhist monasteries in Beijing, we learn that despite the so-called Chan revival in the south, Buddhism in the capital existed in a different mode, enjoying patronage from the royal family and the eunuchs. More important, Buddhism in the north seemed to have more popular support from the uneducated masses and tended to intermingle with sectarian movements.[24] Therefore, when we use concepts such as "revival" and "decline" to describe a historical cycle of Buddhist activities, we need to keep in mind that they represent two different modes of existence: One was a spontaneous intellectual and spiritual movement that was only temporary because it was limited by social and cultural conditions, and the other, though under the aegis of state sponsorship and locally based, was perhaps more enduring and fundamental.

In my opinion, it seems that Buddhist revivals in history should be viewed as anomalies and extensions of the significant social and cultural changes that gave rise to these revivals. This is because an invisible boundary has been set for the growth of Buddhism: Within the boundary, as long as Buddhist monasteries functioned as service providers for local people and fulfilled their fiscal duties assigned by local magistrates, they would be left alone without interference from the authorities.

In my study of the Buddhist revival characterized by the rise of Chan Buddhism in the seventeenth century, such a boundary can be palpably felt, and the debates I have studied can be viewed as one of the means through which Buddhists negotiated an acceptable place in Chinese society. It seems to me that there were several social factors that prevented the further growth of Buddhism and constantly pushed Buddhism back behind the invisible boundary.

First, the state did not want to see Buddhist institutions crossing the boundary. For example, the Yongzheng emperor, representing the attitude of the state, did not want to see Chan Buddhism grow to the extent that the literati's loyalty to the state would be weakened by their alliance with Buddhism. Second, as I explained in the previous chapter, the local literati patrons didn't want to see the monasteries they supported be controlled by a large monastic structure that was lineage-based. Finally, the Buddhist rhetoric of the unity of Confucianism and Buddhism could be viewed as a challenge to the dominant Confucian ideology by conservative literati, and periodically these conservatives had to attack an overly extended Buddhism to maintain the purity of Confucian ideology. In this sense, Buddhist monasteries had to be kept as individual local religious institutions without connections to other institutions outside the locality.[25]

However, the Buddhist revival in the seventeenth century transgressed the boundary in all areas: Not only did it form a closer relationship with the literati, it also grew outside the local sphere and moved toward the formation of a translocal network by extending dharma transmissions. On the one hand, the most salient slogan "Unity of Buddhism and Confucianism" was a legitimate excuse for the literati to embrace Chan teachings. On the other hand, for the Buddhists, promoting such an syncretic approach was a sign of Buddhist transgression into the literati's territory: Such a saying was ideologically aggressive because it implied that Buddhism had gained social status on a par with its Confucian counterpart.[26] However, the Buddhist revival gradually subsided along with the intellectual and social transformation of Chinese society. In this sense, the cycle of revival and decline, rather than being gauged by the intensity of Buddhist activities, should be rephrased as expansion beyond and retreat behind the boundary set by the society. Therefore, such an expansion was always temporary and doomed to be resisted by the state and by the local society.

Echoing Welch's explanation of the meaning of Buddhist revival, I concur that this concept is only a convenient description that indicates the increased presence of Buddhist activities in public and closer ties with cultural elites and national politics. It is problematic to believe that Buddhism before the revival was in complete decline as Buddhist reformers would like to depict. However, it is clear to me that the so-called Buddhist revival is less enduring than the routine form of Buddhist practice during the quiet period of the so-called Buddhist decline. Because more historical sources about the period of revival survive, our attention was unevenly drawn to it.

In Search of a Pattern

In my view, to figure out the pattern of Buddhist revival in China is more important than interpreting the meaning of Buddhist revival because, by establishing a historical pattern of Buddhist revival, we can perhaps predict the future of Chinese Buddhism in the evolving Chinese society. If we look closely at several cases of Buddhist revival in history, we can detect a general pattern of Buddhist revival in which Chan Buddhism played a significant role.

The Buddhist revival in the seventeenth century, as I see it, can be divided into several stages. In the first stage, the state relaxed control over Buddhism, and the royal family led the efforts to rebuild the monasteries for their personal spiritual needs. Meanwhile, a general interest in Buddhism, especially Chan Buddhism, emerged in elite culture, and the flourishing publishing industry disseminated Buddhist texts in the country. A private edition of the Buddhist canon, for example, was produced based on a commercial model. There was also a great demand among the laity to acquire knowledge of Buddhism and to receive guidance from Buddhist clergy. Under this circumstance, various kinds of Buddhist textual communities, largely dominated by the literati, were formed, and the Chan textual community was simply one of them.

In the second stage, more monasteries were rebuilt but remained locally based. Meanwhile, monastic Buddhism responded to the literati's religious interests by providing education for monks through traditional training in scholastic traditions, such as Tiantai, Huayan, and Yogācāra, in order to enable the monks to become active members in these literati-dominated textual communities. In this stage, Chan Buddhism as a monastic establishment remained obscure. But some monks inspired by Chan ideals through their reading began to reenact the scenes of kōan stories, and their performances were greatly welcomed by the literati as a demonstration of the Chan spirit of spontaneity.

In the third stage, Chan Buddhism began to gain momentum by upholding the iconoclastic Chan rhetoric and the practice of dharma transmission, through which they organized themselves into strictly defined lineages and controlled the abbot succession in many monasteries. In the fourth stage, Chan Buddhists continued to expand their influence in the Buddhist world, and the ties between the clergy and the laity were greatly strengthened. At the same time, however, disputes regarding all kinds of issues surfaced. Because the mobility of Chan monks was greatly increased, numerous local monasteries were integrated into a complicated, multilayered network through which major monastic routines and ritual practices were standardized and propagated.

In the final stage, various levels of government officials stepped in and redrew the boundary between Buddhism and the secular world. The expansion of Chan Buddhism stopped, and popular interest in Chan rhetoric and dharma transmission dwindled. Buddhism retreated to its normally assigned place in Chinese society but in a stronger position because, during its expansion, the economic condition of Buddhist institutions had been greatly improved and standard monastic routines reestablished.

This pattern shows that (1) the impetus for change in the Buddhist world first came from outside, (2) the initial stage of revival was characterized by intense activities in printing and monastic education about doctrine, (3) a Buddhist style of teaching, such as Chan rhetoric, which was appealing to the elite, dominated the Buddhist world, and institutions embodying such teachings had the leadership position to reorganize the monastic structure, and (4) such a popular form of Buddhism eventually lost its glory when the social and intellectual climate changed.

When I look beyond the seventeenth century, I find that Buddhist revivals in different periods seem to follow a similar pattern. For example, we find this familiar picture of Buddhist revival in the Northern Song (960–1127), in which Chan Buddhism played a significant role. Although a thorough study of the institutional changes during this time is still needed, some signs indicate that it followed roughly the pattern I have delineated: The Song literati's interests in Buddhism fostered an elite culture favorable for the growth of Buddhism, and Buddhist clergy responded by embracing the Confucian cultural ideal of *wen*.[27] Buddhist scholasticism, such as Tiantai teaching, was revived. Chan Buddhism, entering the national scene from the southeast as local and regional factions, became prominent by positing a "lettered" version of its rhetoric, catering to the taste of the literati. As a result, various kinds of classical Chan genealogies were composed with the editorial help of the literati. Meanwhile, taking advantage of its political gains through winning the minds of the literati, Chan Buddhism aggressively expanded its influence in Buddhist institutions: By imperial decrees, monasteries were converted to Chan and accepted abbots with Chan dharma transmissions. Meanwhile, monastic routines in these Chan institutions were standardized in Pure Regulations, which preserved existing monastic heritages. As Robert Gimello aptly points out, during the Northern Song, the "conservative impulse," a tendency to reject the outdated radical Chan as a separate establishment and to accommodate conventional doctrinal studies and devotional practice, prevailed in Chan communities. Moreover, as Gimello puts it, because Chan monks' active efforts to synthesize all Buddhist traditions, "Ch'an had become, precisely by virtue of its preeminence, the guardian and husbander of the whole Buddhist heritage."[28]

The late Qing and early Republican periods, roughly the years between 1850 and 1937, saw another wave of intensive Buddhist activities, as Holmes Welch has documented in great detail. The results of his research show even more clearly that a similar pattern of Buddhist revival can be detected. Welch succinctly summarizes his findings as follows:

> The Buddhist revival began, I believe, as an effort by laymen to reprint the scripture destroyed in the Taiping Rebellion. It gathered momentum as the discovery of Western Buddhist scholarship stimulated the need for Chinese Buddhist scholarship, and as the invasion of China by Christian evangelists and missionaries led to

the idea of training Buddhist evangelists and sending missionaries to India and the West. Up to this point only laymen were involved. The monks, isolated and secure in their monasteries, carried on as usual. But in the last decade of the Ch'ing dynasty, when moves were made to confiscate their property for use in secular education, the monks began to organize schools and social-welfare enterprises as a means of self-defense. They too began to be aware of the need to counter the denigration of Buddhism, to which Christian missionaries had added a new dimension.[29]

Welch's observation resembles that of Chan Buddhism in the seventeenth century in many ways. As he details in his study, the Buddhist revival in modern China actually started with the efforts of the layman Yang Wenhui (1837–1911), who was greatly stimulated by foreign missionaries and friends, both Christians and Buddhists, such as Joseph Edkins (1823–1905), Timothy Richard (1845–1919), Anagarika Dharmapala (1864–1933), and Nanjio Bunyū (1849–1927). He initiated a press in Nanjing to disseminate Buddhist scriptures and an educational program in which he became a teacher of Buddhism, especially of the sophisticated Yogācāra thought, for both monks and laypeople, among whom Taixu and Ouyang Jingwu (1871–1943) later became leaders of Buddhist reform. Unaware of the literati's extensive influence on monks, as I described in chapter 2, Welch claims that Yang's instruction about Buddhist doctrines to monks "appears to have been the first time in Chinese history that monks studied Buddhist texts under a lay teacher."[30] It is clear that, according to Welch, the impetus for Buddhist revival came from outside the Buddhist world, started with Buddhist publishing as a lay movement, and then was followed by the clergy themselves reforming monastic education and organizing national Buddhist associations. Conspicuously missing in this picture is the rhetoric of the iconoclastic Chan spirit, which was replaced by the so-called Buddhist scientism, as embodied in the long-neglected Yogācāra teaching. This is because, under the circumstances of the early twentieth century, this doctrine apparently represented a Buddhist version of rationality that matched its Western counterparts. Clearly, the Chan rhetoric of spontaneity, not being able to satisfy the nationwide cry for science and modernity, lost its context.

Conclusion

So far, scholars have obtained clear pictures of Chan Buddhist revival in several periods of Chinese history: the rise of the Northern school in early Chan history, the emergence of the Hongzhou school in the late Tang, the ascendancy of Chan in the Northern Song, and the revitalization of Chan Buddhism in the seventeenth century, as described in this book. In most cases, scholars find a similar pattern: Chan started locally, then expanded to regional influence, and finally to national; Chan Buddhists maintained close relationships with the literati; and the actual Chan practices were not as unique as Chan Buddhists often claimed. These phenomena show that the rise of Chan has been part of a general movement of Buddhist revival in which Chan Buddhists often played a leading role. If we have such knowledge of the past, can we use it to project the future of Chinese Buddhism in mainland China? When economic reform brings wealth and prosperity to Chinese people, is that the moment to expect another wave of intensive Buddhist activities that might merit the term "Buddhist revival"?

To answer these questions, we must keep in mind that, as I articulated in the beginning of this study, Chinese Buddhism has been synchronized with the changes of Chinese culture and society. By "synchronization," I mean that any significant intellectual and social changes are almost immediately extended to the realm of Buddhism and have significant impact on its existence. For example, starting from the Tang, Chinese society has undergone profound changes that have been characterized by Chinese historians as "localist turn[s]" that occur periodically. Peter Bol summarizes this view as follows:

A localist turn following an era of statist policies is something of a pattern in Chinese history. Dynastic periods can often be divided into two parts: an era of state building, centralization, and efforts at social control, followed by an era of government withdrawal (or incompetence) and the rise of local elites. In the Song dynasty case the localist turn followed a period of institutional centralization, aggressive foreign policy, attempts to create ideological unity, and intervention in the economy and society that began in the 1040s and culminated in the New Policies regimes (1070–85, 1093–1124). In the Han the strong state building and military expansion that peaked in Wudi's reign in the Western Han (and again in Wang Mang's New Dynasty) was followed by the rise of "Confucian magnates" in the Eastern Han. Tang state expansion and its control over land and labor was halted by the An Lushan rebellion of 755, which ushered in the era of local military governors and the breakdown of controls over land ownership and commerce. The Qing divides into a similar two halves in the early nineteenth century. The history of the People's Republic arguably divides with the "opening up" after 1978.[31]

Clearly, in this general picture, Buddhist revivals, especially Chan revivals, can be viewed as expressions of such localist turns in Chinese history. It is arguable that most Buddhist revivals happened in the periods when state control was weakened and local society flourished. Following this line of thinking, it is predictable that when the People's Republic of China adjusts its policies and power structures to accommodate the growth of local societies, Buddhism will rise again along with other social and intellectual forces.[32]

Although the future is hard to predict, based on our knowledge of Buddhist revival in history, it might be safe to point out that the Buddhist revival in mainland China will probably follow the general pattern I have laid out. This means that the following factors may characterize this new movement of Buddhist revival. First, the impetus for such a revival may come from outside the monastic world, and a particular type of Buddhist teaching will be especially favored by the educated populace. Second, an early sign of the revival may initially appear in active publishing activities that will aim at reproducing Buddhist texts, such as a new edition of the Buddhist canon by the private sector. In terms of publishing in the information age, the Internet may play a significant role. Following this, various kinds of textual communities, or even online communities, will take shape and devote themselves to interpreting Buddhist texts. At this stage, these activities might still be confined in the secular world and promoted by intellectuals. Third, some Buddhist clergy will respond to this new intellectual and spiritual interest in Buddhism by positioning themselves as embodying this particular type of Buddhist teaching and by greatly expanding the monastic education programs. This new gesture will be welcomed by the public, and this type of Buddhism will gain a significant following. Fourth, a monastic reform will follow or occur at the same time. As a result, each individual monastery will be interwoven into a regional or national network that is independent of state agencies. Although these networks will bring Buddhist institutions much closer and through them monastic practices will be unified and integrated, each monastery will retain its independence in its own locality. Finally, there will be a series of dramatic events that bring the Buddhist revival to an end: A new boundary will be drawn, and Buddhism will retreat from the public view.

Concluding Remarks

My objective in this book has been to explore the changes in Chan Buddhism in seventeenth-century China by investigating a series of controversies that indexed religious, cultural, and social transitions at various levels. On the surface, Buddhist controversies in the seventeenth century appeared nasty and trivial because they were motivated by the pursuit of power and authority. However, such controversies indicate religious transformations complicated by social and cultural changes.

I have used the term "reinvention" to characterize the transformation in Chan communities and to highlight the discontinuity between seventeenth-century Chan Buddhism and its antecedents in the Tang and Song Chan traditions. Rather than maintaining an unbroken institutional connection, Chan Buddhism in the seventeenth century was a conscious recreation of a series of Chan ideals imagined to be the real Chan tradition during the Tang. The purpose of this characterization is neither to prove nor to disprove the authenticity of a revived tradition. Rather, I have tried to underscore the historicity of this reinvention and the issues emerging from the process of an ideological reconstruction.

A methodological pitfall that I try to avoid is the simplistic and positivistic use of terms like "invention" and "imagination," which entail the danger of reducing new creations to literary fabrications, pitting truth against falsity, separating myth from reality, and debunking the advocacy of ancient ideals as wearing "the emperor's new clothes." In my opinion, the emergence of a rhetoric or a reinvention should be considered creative and be treated as a legitimate force in the historical process of religious transformation. In seventeenth-century China, the Chan masters not only convinced themselves that their teaching and practice genuinely revived the past but also persuaded their audiences, such as the Confucian literati, to believe in the authenticity of their teaching and the legitimacy of their authority. This collective remaking of the Chan tradition had significant historical consequences: Chan Buddhism expanded from local to national influence and spread from southeast China to other parts of East Asia, such as Japan and Vietnam.

My observations presented here remain suggestive, not conclusive, given the scope and depth of the sources with which I am dealing. The validity of these observations must be left to further studies to determine. However, as I have demonstrated in this book, no matter in what direction the future studies of Chan history may go, it has become imperative for Chan scholars to study the broader intellectual, social, and cultural milieu in order to understand the transformation of the tradition. This is because the development of Chinese Buddhism has synchronized with the transformations of Chinese culture and society. Therefore, when investigating Chan Buddhism in late imperial China, it is no longer meaningful to discuss the issue of the sinification of Buddhism. Instead, we should pay close attention to this synchronization effect.

As I stated in the introduction, I entered the field of seventeenth-century Chan Buddhism through a focused study on controversies. Because of the limitations of these polemical sources, my study has not yet covered some important aspects of Chan Buddhism in this period. These aspects, some of which were briefly discussed in part IV, include the formation of Chan monasteries as local institutions, the systemization of Buddhist rituals, other forms of Chan practice such as meditation on key phrases, Buddhist nuns' Chan experience, etc. Because the Linji monks were the most active participants in the controversies, they were disproportionately represented in the polemical sources. Thus, my study has focused more on these Linji monks. It should be noted here that it is equally important to understand the Caodong tradition in this period, although the number of Caodong masters was fewer, and they tended to emphasize a more balanced Chan practice that was supplemented by doctrinal studies, meditation, and Confucian learning.

Through my study, it is clear that the rise of Chan Buddhism was rooted in the general intellectual and cultural climate of the seventeenth century, which favored a direct and subjective way of apprehending the ultimate truth of the universe. This hermeneutical approach resonated with the Chan rhetoric of immediacy and inspired a more intuitive understanding of Chan's textualized past. The romantic imagination of Chan's past, however, was not invented by Buddhists themselves. Rather, it was fermented among the Confucian literati and then reintroduced into the Buddhist world under the patronage of those Chan-minded elites. If we follow this line of thinking, it won't be an exaggeration to claim that, to some extent, Chan Buddhism became an extension of the literati culture.

However, the consequence of such a close alignment with the literati culture was that when this literati culture changed its basic orientation, a reinvented Buddhist tradition fostered by it could not find its place in a syncretic monastic environment. This transformation indeed occurred in the eighteenth century when intellectualism embodied in rigorous evidential scholarship was the dominant mentality among the literati, and the Chan spirit of spontaneity was condemned as "frantic" and as the direct cause of the fall of the Ming. In this sense, I tend to describe the rise and fall of seventeenth-century Chan Buddhism as an intrusion in Buddhist history: It came from outside the Buddhist world, and it disappeared together with an exciting but turbulent century.

Appendix 1: Translation of Official Documents

A. Huang Duanbo: "Public Notice Issued by Judge Huang Yuangong [Duanbo] at Xuedou Monastery"[1]

"Huang Sili Yuangong fa Xuedou gaoshi"

[Written by] Judge Huang of Hangzhou prefecture for the matter of investigating Chan lineages.

The thirteenth day of the fifth month of the tenth year of the Chongzhen reign (July 4, 1637)

I read the *Jingde chuandeng lu*, which clearly records that Tianhuang Daowu received the dharma from Shitou Xiqian and [the lineages] of Yunmen and Fayan are all listed under Qingyuan Xingsi. This is indeed an ironclad case. Then, the *Wudeng huiyuan* makes another claim that there had been two Daowus in Jingzhou: One resided in Tianwang monastery at the west of the city and the other in Tianhuang monastery at the east of the city. [Its author] thus doubts that Longtan Chongxin was the dharma heir of Tianhuang Daowu and quotes epigraphs and inscriptions to prove this view. However, he adds only a brief note [to the main text] without daring to change their lineage affiliation arbitrarily because heirs of the Yunmen and Fayan lineages never recognized Mazu as their patriarchal ancestor.

Recently, I read Master Miyun's newly printed *Chandeng shipu*, in which he directly changed Tianhuang Daowu to Tianwang Daowu and the lineages of Yunmen and Fayan were all listed as those of

Nanyue Huairang. I doubted it in my mind but had no [evidence] to challenge him. During the first ten days of the fourth month of 1637, Miyun sent to me the *Xuefeng guanglu* (Extensive records of Xuefeng) in one fascicle. Without anything to do in my boat, I opened and read it until the end of the text. When I read the passage about Xuefeng Yicun's and Xuansha Shibei's reply to the king of Min, inside, it is claimed that "I, a mountain monk, have been transmitting this secret dharma gate since the [time] of our former [patriarchs] Deshan Xuanjian and Shitou Xiqian." After reading this, I believe that the *Jingde chuandeng lu* indeed relies on evidence. If Tianhuang were indeed Mazu's heir, why wouldn't Xuefeng go ahead and claim "since former [patriarchs] Deshan and Mazu?" On the contrary, he said instead "since former [patriarchs] Deshang and Shitou."

I have investigated Tianwang Daowu's inscription by Qiu Yuansu in detail. The text claims that after Tianwang Daowu studied with Mazu, he built a grass hut at Jingmen (Jingzhou). The military commissioner was angry about the narrow road that obstructed his way and thus threw the master into the river. When he returned with flying flags, the entire government compound was on fire. Only a sound from the sky was heard: "I am God, the Heavenly King!" The military commissioner thus provided support for him in the west of the city and the plaque of his monastery bore the name "Tianwangsi." This is the whole story of Tianwang Daowu. The inscription by Fu Zai claims that after Tianhuang studied with Shitou and attained enlightenment, he lived as a recluse in Zilingshan of Dangyang. Lingjian invited him to reside at Tianhuang monastery on the east side of the city. It also claims that on the east side of Jingnan (Jingzhou) city, there remained an alley named Tianhuang. I investigated accounts of Chan master Longtan Chongxi's encounter stories, [which say that] in the beginning the monk Daowu was invited by Lingjian to reside at Tianhuang monastery. Longtan Chongxin, whose family was located at the entrance of the alley, presented baked pastries to him (Tianhuang Daowu) everyday. This agrees with the account that Lingjian invited him and there was a Tianhuang alley in the east of the city. Tianhuang also bestowed the name Chongxin on the master. The whole story [of Tianhuang Daowu] is detailed. It is certain that Longtan was an authentic heir of Tianhuang. This is why the two elders Xuefeng and Xuansha proclaimed themselves as originating from Shitou. Heirs of the Yunmen and Fayan lineages also said that they derived from Qingyuan and Shitou. Because there were only two generations between Xuefeng and Tianhuang, Xuefeng inherited Tianhuang's dharma personally and clearly stated it. Although Lü Xiaqing and Zhang Wujin (Zhang Shangying) doubted that Daowu was Mazu's heir, Chan communities regarded this as a mistake. This is a fair argument indeed.

Now, Miyun wants to change [the lineages] arbitrarily [based on] his own opinion. He can only achieve this by simply obliterating the *Xuefeng guanglu.* Moreover, only after the stories recorded in the five lamp histories about Lingjian's invitation of [Tianhuang Daowu] to Tianhuang monastery, the master's (Longtan Chongxin) residence at the alley beside the monastery, the gift of pastries, and the bestowal of the name, were omitted arbitrarily, could Miyun's theory be proved. Because Miyun recognizes Yunmen and Fayan as belonging to the lineage of Nanyue, he slandered Qingyuan by saying that [his verses] "goes ahead with mutual independence" and "words should avoid complete accomplishment" (*huihu dangtou yuji shicheng*) are not comparable to the sixth patriarch's face-to-face interaction and to Nanyue's [teaching] that "what kinds of things come by what kinds of means." Miyun commented on Qingyuan as follows:[2]

> He does not acquire the holy truth and does not step down from the
>   stage.
> He still holds emotional residue to abandon the two ends.
> Only if the reclining dragon understands [the meaning] of the lion's
>   somersault can he then be completely promoted to the company of
>   enlightened ones.

In addition, he says:[3]

> Master Qingyuan always eats meals from Luling.
> He does not seem to know the cause of the price of rice.
> Exactly what great significance do we see from him?
> Please don't fail to live up to the two lines of your eyebrows (a
>   reference to being a man).

Therefore, I know that Miyun smears and impugns former worthies with the mind of birth and death and right and wrong. What a pity! What a pity! Gentleman Yu Jisheng (Yu Dacheng) says, "Miyun's own intention is no more than eliminating the lineage of Caodong and one-sidedly elevating Linji." He thus drags and pulls Yunmen and Fayan as Nanyue's lineage and slanders Qingyuan with irrelevant talk about cultivation and practice. He not only falsely accused Caoxi (Huineng) but also [spoke] useless words with cognitive knowledge. Alas! Miyun unwarrantedly claims himself as an heir of Linji, but he does not understand the principle of the Linji lineage. Hanyue and Dingmu [Hongche] have mentioned this. How could he neglect ancient masters in order to deceive scholars in our times? I don't know what kind of intention this old man has. [Descendants of] Yunmen and Fayan do not recognize Mazu as belonging to their own lineages, but Miyun alters it arbitrarily with his own opinion. Whom would he deceive?

I read his *Tiantong quanlu*,[4] in which he loves to refute other people and to boast of his own skills. Masters such as Shouchang (Wuming Huijing), Yunmen (Zhanran Yuancheng), and Kongdong have all been smeared openly. As to the debates and disputes with Sanfeng (Hanyue Fazang), Ruiguang, and Shouzhao, people who know these disputes cannot bear to hear about them. However, unexpectedly, even ancient masters are belittled and slandered! Masters such as Qingyuan and Caoshan are defamed as well. What kind of intention is this? Originally, I prepared to invite Miyun as abbot of Xuedou Chan monastery. However, Moming and Mingjue are all heirs of Yunmen and Fayan.[5] Since Miyun has slandered the patriarchs of these two houses, this place is of course not where he would be happy to live. I publicize this especially on the right to let it be known.[6]

B. Surveillance Commissioner Lü (Li Rifang): "Investigative Remarks on Banning the Spurious Book *Wudeng yantong*"[7]

"Anchasi Lü jinchi Yantong *weishu kanyu"*

With regard to the five houses of the Chan school, there are only the two lineages of Linji and Caodong. The *Wudeng yantong* printed by Feiyin, however, intends to make Linji the single practice within the Buddhist world. He lives after many generations but ignores people before him. He reveres the patriarchs of one house but denounces those who belong to the different lineage. He follows his own mind with arrogance and holds his own view obstinately, so he has incurred anger from the masses. Since books such as lamp transmissions are all preserved in imperial canons and for hundreds and thousands of years they have remained authentic and verifiable, why is it necessary to create another transmission of lineage separately? Furthermore, after the establishment of the five lineages, both Linji and Caodong can be continued, why is it necessary to eliminate Caodong completely and singly make Linji the orthodox lineage in the Buddhist world?

These two houses have preserved their respective genealogies and Chan teaching styles separately. Private opinions and narrowed minds are indeed garrulous. The book [*Wudeng yantong*] should be prohibited without circulation, not letting it confuse people's view and arouse strife. According to the trial based on the monk Xingyi's confession, Feiyin has been away from his monastery for a long time and there is no way that he can be questioned and interrogated. We have obtained eighty-five original printing blocks of the

Wudeng yantong and they have been stored in the government warehouse. The presented documents by the literati represent their own views. But finally, since the original book has been banned, [their opinions] can be put in silence. Drafting and summarizing [this case], I present it to you humbly.

COMMENTS OF APPROVAL BY GOVERNOR XIAO [QIYUAN]
Feiyin follows his own mind and stubbornly adheres to his own opinion. It is difficult to pardon him by the law. Since the printing blocks of the *Wudeng yantong* have been retrieved, the debate about it can be put down. All remaining blocks must be recalled completely and the original copies be strictly prohibited [for circulation]. Since Feiyin has fled, his case can wait until the date when he is captured for further investigation and conclusion.[8]

C. "Public Notice by the Bureau of Police Chief"[9]

"Zongbuting gaoshi"

Police Chief Wang of Jiaxing prefecture, in order to observe imperial edicts and orders, is seriously capturing heinous criminals and eliminating their followers and conspirators. I strengthen the law and regulation to stop malefactors, refute heterodox teachings, and to support the cause of the sagely teaching. I know clearly that the Way of Indian Buddhism teaches people to promote the good and eliminate the evil. Therefore, it supports and assists the rule of the emperor, and Confucianism and Buddhism have been practiced jointly without contradiction. This has a long history. Furthermore, the three teachings of Chan Buddhism, Doctrinal Studies, and Vinaya are at their height, and Chan learning is particularly revered. However, the Chan school has been divided into five lineages: Fayan, Yunmen, Guiyang, Caodong, and Linji. Three of these lineages died out long ago, and therefore Caodong and Linji have been prominent together up to this day. Transmissions from teachers continue and descendants reproduce and multiply themselves. They have their own right places respectively and exist peacefully without disputation.

Suddenly, the heinous monk Feiyin, hiding a criminal mind and unfathomable evils, plotted to singly promote one lineage and cut off the patriarchs of the other lineage completely. For this reason, he fostered many supporters and the poisons flowed to his fellows not lightly. Without reading books with his own eyes, he falsely usurped the name "author"; without acquainting [himself] with people in person, he carved [their names] in the list of collators and proofreaders. This is why every Confucian gentleman is angry and words [of complaint] are everywhere. I was appalled to hear that he even had an evil accomplice named Baichi Xingyuan, who was regarded as the rebirth of [the great historian] Dong Hu.[10] Arrogantly exercising his authority to write and edit, Baichi deceived his lineage and eliminated his ancestors with the biased opinion of a son of a wolf. In addition, a monk called Chiyan, claiming to be a dharma heir of Feiyin, clandestinely sneaked into the capital with the secret intention to conduct surreptitious things. He begged prefaces for this book and tried to secure strong support. Under the emperor's chariot (meaning, in the capital), how can it be tolerated! Chiyan has been arrested according to imperial edicts and will be punished according to the law. For this reason, the literati have public assaults; the gentry have complete rebuttals; and my superior wants to abide by the law and arrest Feiyin. We must eliminate this [nuisance] and then have breakfast.

Unexpectedly, the fox has hidden his traces without notice. [However,] circumstances make it difficult to change his face and to hide cleverly. He should be captured and verified as the real person. People who hide and retain him must be prosecuted. Even though Chiyan is an accomplice who follows, the emperor does not tolerate him with pardon. Thus, Feiyin is the principal criminal of this treacherous plot. How could he be allowed to escape? My bureau is in charge of criminal investigation. We are extremely angry and share the same hatred. What we honor is to follow our superior's order that cutting branches must get rid of their root and capturing criminals must eliminate all their followers. It should be noticed in public and let it be known that if any military servicemen and civilians capture the prime culprit and his followers, awards should be given with special honors. If [people] let them go free or allow them to stay, a joint punishment will be applied to them and their family members. Perhaps he is hiding in some cloisters and chapels, trying to find out the situation and to bribe officials. I allow the head monks of these chapels or cloisters to grab him to my office. I will investigate and punish him according to the law. This affair concerns the refutation of heterodoxy, support of Confucian teaching, rectification of the law, and the elimination of evils. It is not comparable to ordinary affairs. Even a three-inch space should not be ignored carelessly. I thus issue the order especially.

Appendix 2: Major Controversies in the Seventeenth Century

In addition to the two controversies I examined in the main text, there are many similar disputes that were equally important. To some extent, a history of seventeenth-century Chan Buddhism is a history of these controversies. In this appendix, I will turn to the Caodong school and introduce the debate over the "five superfluous generations" (*wudai diechu*) of Caodong masters in the Song, which some monks believed should be eliminated from Chan genealogy because of a newly discovered inscription. Then, I focus on the debate over Haizhou Ci, a crucial Linji figure in the early Ming from whom Miyun Yuanwu's lineage derived. Finally, I will give brief accounts of various other minor controversies in which the Linji monks played the dominant role. These disputes reveal how divided and contentious the Buddhist world had become.

A. The Debate over the "Five Superfluous Generations" in the Song Caodong Lineage

Within the Caodong lineage, the need to redefine dharma transmission and to legitimize the existing dharma masters was also keenly felt. The genealogical sources about the Caodong school were often inconsistent in listing the generations of the Caodong masters. In some sources, Zhanran Yuancheng was recorded as belonging to the twenty-sixth generation and in others as belonging to the thirty-first generation of the Caodong lineage. Comparing these two versions, there is a five-generation difference. This inconsistency resulted from a seventeenth-century debate about the elimination of five generations of Caodong transmission in the Song.

Like the two-Daowu dispute, which was discussed in part III, the Caodong dispute about dharma transmission was related to two monks with the same name. In 1672, Weizhong Jingfu compiled his version of the genealogy, *Zudeng datong*, in ninety-eight fascicles.[1] In this work, he intentionally eliminated five generations of Caodong masters in the Song, including Dōgen's master, Tiantong Rujing, from the accepted transmission lines. Weizhong Jingfu argued that, according to traditional Chan histories, there were two different monks who had the same name, Zijue, but lived in different monasteries, Jingyin and Lumen. However, according to Jingfu, they were actually the same person. The result was that the five generations before Zijue were eliminated, and all Caodong masters who accepted this version of dharma transmission would be five generations closer to the founder of the lineage.

The accepted Caodong lineage in the Song begins with Furong Daokai (1043–1118), followed by Danxia Zichun (1064–1117), Zhenxie Qingliao (1089–1151), Tiantong Zongjue (1091–1162), Xuedou Zhijian (1105–1192), and Tiantong Rujing (1163–1228). After Rujing, the lineage derives from Dōgen (1200–1253), who brought the Caodong transmission to Japan, and from Rujing's other dharma heir, Lumen Zijue.[2] However, Weizhong Jingfu noted that one of Furong Daokai's dharma heirs, who was often called Jingyin Zijue, also lived in Lumen monastery.[3] For this reason, he speculated that these two monks, Jingyin Zijue and Lumen Zijue, were the same person. (Readers might want to refer to chart 1.1 to see how Weizhong Jingfu revised the traditional transmission lines.) He considered the five generations on the right side as superfluous and the two masters, Jingyin Zijue and Lumen Zijue, as one person. As a result, all Caodong masters after the Song could be moved back five generations after the elimination of the misidentified Caodong masters.

Weizhong Jingfu claimed that the following inscription of Zijue's dharma heir Qingzhou Yibian (1081–1149) validated his speculation:

During the Zhenghe reign (1111–1118), [Qingzhou Yibian] studied with Lumen Zijue at Xiangzhou prefecture. [Lumen Zijue] asked him to see Furong Daokai. Passing Dengzhou prefecture, he had a chance to meet Danxia [Zi]chun. During the Xuanhe reign (1119–1126), he lived in Tianning monastery in Qingzhou prefecture and afterwards filled the vacancy in Huayan monastery. In his later years, he moved to Yangshan monastery. In the Gengshen year of the Tianjuan reign [of the Jin or Jurchen dynasty] (1140), he again presided over Wanshou monastery. In the eighth day of the twelfth month of the ninth year of the Huangtong reign (1149), he wrote the inscription himself and on the twelfth day, he died in the watch of Hai (9–11 p.m.) at night.[4]

According to the traditional Caodong genealogy, if Lumen Zijue were Tiantong Rujing's disciple, his dharma heir Qingzhou Yibian should have been active in the mid- and late thirteenth century. However, according to Qingzhou Yibian's inscription cited above, he was active in the first half of the twelfth century in the north. In the beginning of this inscription, his teacher Lumen Zijue even suggested that he study with Furong Daokai, indicating Daokai was still alive. This shows that Furong Daokai, Lumen Zijue, and his disciple Qingzhou Yibian all lived around the same time. Based on this inscription, Weizhong Jingfu assumed that Lumen Zijue was Furong Daokai's dharma heir because they were contemporaries. Thus, Lumen Zijue must actually be the same person as Jingyin Zijue and not Tiantong Rujing's disciple, as he was erroneously assumed to be. Accordingly, the later Caodong transmission should leap over the five generations after Furong Daokai and go back directly to Furong Daokai himself.

Weizhong Jingfu's alteration of the Caodong transmission line sparked new angst in the Chan world. Some Caodong masters, such as Juelang Daosheng and his dharma heirs, promoted Weizhong Jingfu's view on dharma transmission. But some, such as Yongjue Yuanxian and his disciple Weilin Daopei (1615–1702), opposed it. They doubted Qingzhou Yibian's epitaph discovered by Weizhong Jingfu and thought it was simply a forgery.[5] Influenced by Jingfu's new theory, however, some writers of Chan genealogical works adopted his version of the Caodong genealogy. However, more influential Chan histories, such as the *Wudeng quanshu*, still adhered to the original version of the Caodong dharma transmission. As a result, the generation numbers of the Caodong masters in the seventeenth century became very confusing.

Jingfu's capable disciple Weizhi Zhikai made efforts to defend his teacher. In his *Zhengming lu*, he marshaled all kinds of evidence to prove that the two Zijues were actually one person. He also repudiated skeptical authors who wrote essays against his teacher. He advanced the following arguments in his writing:[6]

1. Weizhi Zhikai assured his readers that the inscriptions that he and his teacher presented were genuine and credible. As he related, his teacher first dispatched his disciple Huaiyi to north China. After two years, Huaiyi brought back Qingzhou Yibian's epitaph. Then, his teacher asked Weizhi Zhikai to start a new search. He departed from Zhejiang and Jiangsu, heading toward Hunan and Hubei. After touring historically important monasteries there, he turned north to Henan. From there, he crossed the Yellow River. However,

because of a severe illness, Weizhi Zhikai had to turn back to Nanjing. In the spring of 1693, Weizhi Zhikai traveled again to the north, passing through Shandong, Hebei, Beijing, Shanxi, and other northern provinces. It took him two years to finish the second tour. During his extensive travels, he gathered much inscriptional evidence that had been previously unavailable to writers of Chan genealogies.[7]

2. Regarding the dispute of the two Zijues, Weizhi Zhikai identified many anachronisms in the conventional version of the Caodong dharma trans-mission. If the old version were correct about Zijue being Tiantong Rujing's dharma heir, then all dharma heirs after Zijue, including Qingzhou Yibian, Zizhou Bao (1114–1173), Wangshan Ti, Xueyan Man (?–1206), and Wansong Xingxiu (1166–1246) would have received their dharma transmissions much later. However, according to the newly discovered epitaph of Qingzhou Yibian, he and his master, Zijue, were contemporaries of Furong Daokai and were ac-tive during the end of the Northern Song. In contrast, Tiantong Rujing was active during the time close to the end of the Southern Song. It was impossible for Zijue to have received Rujing's transmission. In addition, Weizhi Zhikai examined the biographies of Caodong patriarchs after Zijue down to Wansong Xingxiu and found that most of them became renowned Chan teachers before Tiantong Rujing received his dharma transmission. Among them, Wansong Xingxiu, active in north China, which was controlled by the Jurchen state, was Tiantong Rujing's contemporary. If the conventional Caodong transmission line were correct, it would be absurd to see a patriarch and his sixth-generation dharma heir become prominent at the same time but under two regimes hos-tile to each other. Weizhi Zhikai surmised that the mistake occurred because most Chan histories were compiled in the south and thus collected more de-tailed information of Chan masters who lived in the south. Due to the lack of communication between the north and the south in the Southern Song, Chan historiographers erroneously inserted five generations of Caodong patriarchs into the actual transmission line.

3. The third kind of evidence Weizhi Zhikai used was the numerous in-scriptions concerning the dharma transmission of Caodong masters in the Ming. In most of these inscriptions, the Caodong patriarchs often made clear to which generation they belonged. If the generation they claimed was five generations earlier than they should be in the conventional transmission line, this shows that in the actual process of transmission, Caodong patriarchs were never aware of these five generations. Weizhi Zhikai collected more than a hundred pieces of such epigraphic evidence: All of them counted their genera-tions without the five generations. He thus demonstrated that there must have been five superfluous generations in the conventional transmission chart.

Weizhi Zhikai showed convincingly that, in some of the most influential compilations of Chan genealogies, the transmission lines of the Caodong lineage were not documented correctly. More important, his evidential research brought to light many epigraphic materials that had never been examined before. Further research following Weizhi Zhikai's work on this issue might illuminate the Caodong history after the Tang.

B. The Debate over the Two Linji Monks Named Haizhou Ci in the Early Ming

Linji monks' involvement in the numerous controversies shows clearly their exclusive positions toward their rivals, especially the Caodong lineage. Feiyin Tongrong's *Wudeng yantong* is one such work that challenged the Caodong lineages by critically examining Caodong masters' dharma transmissions. Those who failed his strict standards should be expelled from established genealogies and relegated to the category "lineage unknown." Although Feiyin described his method as strict, as the title of his book suggests, he was lenient toward his fellow Linji patriarchs, especially those in the previous generations from whom he inherited the dharma. If the strict standard were to be applied to the Linji dharma transmissions, even Feiyin's ancestors could not be spared from the charges of remote succession (*yaosi*) and transmission by proxy (*daifu*).

The Linji transmission at issue concerns one of the crucial Chan figures in the early Ming from whom Miyun Yuanwu's lineage derived. According to Miyun, his lineage came from the Song Chan master Yuanwu Keqin's leading dharma heir, Huqiu Shaolong (Nanyue 16). (Because the Linji monks customarily counted their generations from Nanyue Huairang, I provide generation numbers for the figures in dispute. Readers might want to refer to chart 1.2 for a visual presentation of the dispute.) There was little dispute about this line of transmission in the Southern Song and Yuan, which includes famous teachers such as Mi'an Xianjie (1118–1186, Nanyue 19), Wuzhun Shifan (1178–1249, Nanyue 20), Gaofeng Yuanmiao (1238–1295, Nanyue 22), and Zhongfeng Mingben (1263–1323, Nanyue 23). This line of transmission was brought into the Ming by Wanfeng Shiwei (1313–1381, Nanyue 25), followed by Baozang Puchi (Nanyue 26), Dongming Huichan (1372–1441, Nanyue 27), Haizhou Ci (Nanyue 28), Baofeng Xuan (Nanyue 29), Tianqi Benrui (?–1503, Nanyue 30), Wuwen Cong (Nanyue 31), Xiaoyan Debao (1512–1581, Nanyue 32), and Huanyou Zhengchuan (1549–1614, Nanyue 33). From Huanyou Zhengchuan, Miyun received his dharma transmission and thus became the patriarch in the thirty-fourth generation after Nanyue Huairang.

Here, I must call attention to the identities of three monks in the line. First, in the 1630s, Haizhou Ci (Nanyue 28) was commonly regarded by Miyun's lineage as referring to Haizhou Puci. But decades later, a newly discovered inscription showed that there was another Haizhou Ci, named Haizhou Yongci. Second, the patriarch after Haizhou Ci was Baofeng Xuan (Nanyue 29), who was often referred to as Baofeng Mingxuan but was later changed to Baofeng Zhixuan and then to Yufeng Zhixuan because of the discovery of new evidence. Third, Wuwen Cong (Nanyue 31) was commonly regarded as referring to Wuwen Zhengcong. However, after further investigation, there were at least six other monks named Wuwen Cong who lived about the same time, and three of them received dharma transmission from Tianqi Benrui (Nanyue 30). As I will explain below, these similar names became the source of confusion in many Chan genealogies.

The transmission line I just described is the actual lineage chart delineated in the transmission certificates (*yuanliu*) used in Miyun Yuanwu's lineage. However, problems occurred when Chan monks looked at other sources to examine this line in the early Ming. People found that two names in the line, Baozang Puchi (Nanyue 26) and Dongming Huichan (Nanyue 27), were not mentioned at all in some Linji monks' dharma transmissions. These sources suggest that Haizhou Ci (Nanyue 28) was actually Wanfeng Shiwei's (Nanyue 25) dharma heir. This means that, in Miyun's official lineage chart, two generations were mistakenly added by his teacher Huanyou Zhengchuan. If this theory were true, it would have been a great embarrassment for Miyun Yuanwu and his dharma heirs because all of their transmission certificates were wrong, and as claimants of the orthodox Linji transmission, they could not even clarify their own dharma transmissions. We can imagine that Miyun's followers would do whatever they could to defend their dharma transmissions even they were proven wrong. Below, I reconstruct this controversy from Weizhi Zhikai's *Zhengming lu*, which detailed the provenance and evolution of this controversy.[8]

Basically, the controversy escalated through several stages. In the first stage, the controversy was started within Miyun Yuanwu's lineage by his dharma heir and rival, Hanyue Fazang, in the late Ming, who first cast a suspicious look at the transmission of Haizhou Ci. After receiving dharma transmission from Miyun Yuanwu, Hanyue did careful research on every patriarch in the transmission line in order to write his eulogy of the transmission (*Yuanliu song*). He noticed that in Wanfeng Shiwei's (Nanyue 25) recorded sayings, Haizhou Ci (Nanyue 28) was actually listed as his leading dharma heir. This means that the transmission certificate Hanyue had received from Miyun was wrong about this. However, he did not dare to challenge the version of dharma transmission he had received. He simply suspected that there might be two

Haizhou Cis who had different transmissions and thus caused the problem. He hoped that a future discovery of Haizhou Ci's epitaph and recorded sayings would solve the mystery.

Hanyue's disciple Tanji Hongren, more than echoing his teacher's view in the *Wuzong jiu* published in 1637, was so audacious as to point out straightforwardly that the version of dharma transmission that Miyun had handed down was wrong about Hanzhou Ci and had erroneously inserted two unrelated Chan masters into the line of transmission. The new evidence upon which he relied was Wuwen Zhengcong's (Miyun believed that he and Wuwen Cong were the same person) recorded sayings, which were newly discovered by a literati family and reprinted by Miyun himself. In this work, the line of transmission was clearly delineated from Wanfeng Shiwei to Haizhou Ci, meaning that all patriarchs after Haizhou Ci would move ahead two generations. Tanji Hongren also strongly suggested that there must be a second Haizhou Ci, who had formed a different line of transmission, which was confused with Miyun's lineage. This was a significant change that Miyun simply could not accept.

The controversy entered into the second stage when Miyun responded to Tanji Hongren in his *Pi wangjiu lueshuo*, published in 1638, in which he defended the version of transmission he had offered by citing a new discovery in Dongming monastery in Hangzhou, where both Dongming Huichan and Haizhou Ci had lived. This new evidence was presented by one of Tianyin Yuanxiu's dharma heirs, Shanci Tongji (1608–1645), who became abbot of Dongming monastery in 1635. Shanci Tongji claimed that he accidentally discovered in a pile of waste paper Dongming Huichan's and Haizhou Puci's epitaphs and encounter dialogues. Together with other sources, he published this alleged new discovery in the *Dongming yilu*.[9] (For the first page of this rare source, see figure 1.1.)

In the *Dongming yilu*, many biographical details of the two masters were supplied. In particular, in Haizhou Puci's epitaph, he was described as first studying with Wanfeng Shiwei and then after about thirty years of living as a hermit, he accepted Dongming Huichan's dharma transmission. This important piece of evidence gave Miyun much-needed relief because now he could explain away the discrepancy between his version of the transmission and alternative versions in other sources. He claimed that because Haizhou Puci first studied with Wanfeng Shiwei, he was mistaken as Wangfeng Shiwei's dharma heir. However, as his epitaph showed, Haizhou Puci actually received the dharma transmission from Dongming Huichan, which corresponded to the transmission certificates Miyun had issued. Following Miyun Yuanwu, in newly compiled Chan genealogies such as *Chandeng shipu* (1632), *Wudeng huiyuan xulue* (1648), and *Wudeng yantong* (1654), Miyun's theory about Haizhou Puci was adopted.

The controversy could have been put to rest if an inscription about another Haizhou Ci were not discovered in Yishan monastery in Nanjing in 1657 by one of Muchen Daomin's disciples. This new discovery thus moved the controversy into the third stage. On the front side of a stone stele, which was erected in 1461, the epitaph of a monk called Haizhou Yongci was carved. On the back, a decree appointing Haizhou Yongci as abbot of Yishan monastery, issued by the Ministry of Rites in 1445, could be seen. According to this new inscriptional evidence, this Haizhou Yongci was a completely different person from Haizhou Puci. He was born in 1394 and studied with Dongming Huichan in his youth. Later, sponsored by a eunuch, he was appointed as the founding abbot of Yishan monastery in 1437. He received Dongming Huichan's dharma transmission ten years after his teacher died in 1440. Haizhou Yongci died in 1466.

The discovery of this inscription was sensational because it proved that Hanyue Fazang's and his disciple Tanji Hongren's conjecture of a second Haizhou Ci was correct. It was at the same time another embarrassment for Miyun Yuanwu and his followers because Haizhou Puci's alleged epitaph in the *Dongming yilu*, upon which he had relied to explain away the doubts about his transmission line, was clearly a forgery. Since the discovery of this new inscription, Miyun's surviving followers unanimously changed their position about Haizhou Ci: Now they endorsed the theory that this Haizhou Yongci was actually the monk commonly referred to as Haizhou Ci in their transmission certificates, and the Haizhou Puci they used to accept became an insignificant figure in a collateral lineage. By so doing, the integrity of their transmissions was maintained.

This sudden change of position, however, left many holes that needed to be mended. If this Haizhou Yongci were to be the Hanzhou Ci in the official transmission line, he ought to be the teacher of the next patriarch in line, who was Baofeng Xuan, commonly believed to be Baofeng Mingxuan. However, in Haizhou Yongci's epitaph, Baofeng Mingxuan's name was not clearly mentioned. Yet, his epitaph did mention that his leading dharma heir was named Baofeng and his twenty-fifth dharma heir Zhixuan. This gave Miyun's followers a new hope to concoct a theory about this Baofeng Xuan. They believed that Haizhou Yongci's leading dharma heir Baofeng actually referred to Baofeng Mingxuan, whose real name should be Zhixuan and who should be listed as Haizhou Yongci's twenty-fifth dharma heir. Then, it became logical to assume that Miyun's transmission line passed from this Haizhou Yongci rather than from Haizhou Puci.

Miyun's opponents, such as Weizhong Jingfu and his disciple Weizhi Zhikai, soon found discrepancies in this theory because, after examining the actual stone inscription carefully, it became clear that the leading dharma heir Baofeng mentioned in the stele referred to Haizhou Yongci's first disciple,

Zhiren, and according to other sources, the Zhixuan mentioned as Yongci's twenty-fifth dharma heir was actually referred to as "Yufeng" instead of "Baofeng." This showed that Haizhou Yongci's lineage, though derived from Dongming Huichan, actually passed through this Baofeng Zhiren and then became obscure in the seventeenth century.

However, despite protests about their manipulation of Haizhou Yongci's inscription, some of Miyun's followers adopted this new theory of the transmission from Haizhou Yongci to Baofeng Zhixuan. Subsequently, all new compilations of Chan genealogies, such as the *Wudeng quanshu*, simply replaced Haizhou Puci's biography with Haizhou Yongci's and grafted the accounts of Baofeng Mingxuan's life almost verbatim under Baofeng Zhixuan's name because they believed that Baofeng Mingxuan and Baofeng Zhixuan were actually the same person.

Some Caodong monks could not tolerate this conspicuous cover-up of a serious mistake about dharma transmission. As Weizhi Zhikai's *Zhengming lu* shows, the critical examination of the two Haizhou Cis was soon expanded to other patriarchs in the line. In addition to Haizhou Ci, the next patriarch singled out for public debate was Wuwen Cong (Nanyue 31), whose teacher was Tianqi Benrui (Nanyue 30) and whose dharma heir was Xiaoyan Debao (Nanyue 32). Careful readers found in Tianqi Benrui's recorded sayings that, among a list of more than three hundred dharma heirs, there were three named Wuwen Cong, whose differences were clearly marked by the original places from which they hailed. However, the current account of Wuwen Zhengcong, who was undoubtedly Xiaoyan Debao's dharma master, did not match any of those three. This shows that this Wuwen Zhengcong was not Tianqi Benrui's official dharma heir, and he must have claimed to be Tianqi Benrui's dharma heir by remote succession without a personal encounter with the master. However, as Weizhi Zhikai pointed out, almost all authors of recent Chan genealogies were confused about these four Wuwen Congs and combined their life stories haphazardly into the biography of one person.

The third patriarch who became a target was Miyun's immediate dharma teacher, Huanyou Zhengchuan, who was widely acclaimed as the leading dharma heir of Xiaoyan Debao. When readers checked Xiaoyan Debao's recorded sayings, however, Huanyou Zhengchuan's name could not be found in the list of Xiaoyan Debao's six official dharma heirs.

Critics also cast doubts toward earlier patriarchs in the Linji's transmission lines. The most problematic, according to Weizhi Zhikai, was the patriarch Xinghua Cunjiang (830–888, Nanyue 6), who was after Linji Yixuan (Nanyue 5). According to his biography in the *Jingde chuandeng lu*, he was actually enlightened by Sansheng Huiran and Weifu Dajue, not by Linji Yixuan. Only reluctantly, he chose to continue the Linji dharma transmission. In addition, Xueyan Zuqin's (1215–1287, Nanyue 21) dharma transmission from Wuzhun Shifan (1178–1249, Nanyue 20) also became problematic because of a lack of evidence.

These critical investigations of Miyun Yuanwu's line of transmission were largely instigated by his followers' aggressive attitudes toward other lineages as evidenced in Feiyin's *Wudeng yantong*. The results of these controversies demonstrate that when the strict standards of dharma transmission advocated by Miyun's followers were applied to themselves, no one could stand the test of evidential examination. This is exactly what John McRae said in the third rule of Zen studies: "Precision implies inaccuracy. "[10] Chan monks intended their genealogy to be as precise as possible. However, their efforts only revealed how problematic their transmissions were as historical facts.

C. Other Controversies Related to the Linji Monks

As Chen Yuan's work has shown, most of the controversies were related to Miyun Yuanwu and his lineage. Miyun was a highly controversial figure even in his lifetime. His simple understanding of Chan often involved him in various disputes with his fellow monks and lay patrons. This can be seen from a rare source, *Tiantong zhishuo*, which collects all of his polemical works. Another rare manuscript entitled *Feiyin chanshi bieji* preserves almost all of Feiyin's notorious polemical works. This valuable source, unlike his recorded sayings, is straightforward, sharp in language, and revealing about clerical strife. It tells us that Feiyin had willingly involved himself in various disputes with his fellow monks within and outside his lineage.[11]

Based on these sources, it is now clear that Linji monks initiated most of the controversies in the seventeenth century. Some notable controversies are summarized as follows.

Miyun's Debate with Daoheng concerning Sengzhao's Things Do Not Shift

This debate was an extension of the lively discussion of Sengzhao's *Things Do Not Shift* initiated by the Huayan master Kongyin Zhencheng. Miyun Yuanwu's teacher Huanyou Zhenchuan participated in this debate and refuted Kongyin Zhencheng's claim that Sengzhao did not employ Buddhist logic correctly.[12] Following his master's suit, Miyun's polemical essay, entitled

"Jupingshuo" (Essay commenting on [Sengzhao's work])," was primarily targeted at a monk named Daoheng, who wrote *Wubuqian zhengliang zheng* (Validation of [Zhencheng's] "Inference of *Things Do Not Shift*") to support Kongyin Zhencheng.[13] Miyun wrote this rebuttal to defend his teacher. His polemical essay, probably written in 1629, and some letters about the dispute were reprinted in the fifth fascicle of the *Tiantong zhishuo*.

Miyun's Debate with Ruibai Mingxue about the Meaning of "the Master"

This debate concerns how to understand Gaofeng Yuanmiao's enlightenment experience. Gaofeng Yuanmiao's recorded sayings became popular after Yunqi Zhuhong reprinted them in 1599. According to this work, Yuanmiao's enlightenment was triggered by a conversation with his teacher Xueyan Zuqin about the meaning of the phrase "the master" (*zhurengong*).[14] Concerning this episode, both Zhanran Yuancheng and Miyun Yuanwu wrote verses to praise Gaofeng Yuanmiao. However, the crucial difference between the two was whether Gaofeng Yuanmiao had had one or two enlightenment experiences. Zhanran Yuancheng tended to interpret Yuanmiao's experience as two separate events involving a gradual progression to ultimate enlightenment while Miyun Yuanwu insisted that Yuanmiao had only one sudden enlightenment experience. Both sides exchanged polemical essays from 1636 to 1638. Zhanran's dharma heir Ruibai Mingxue defended his teacher, and Miyun Yuanwu thus had a debate with him.[15] Tianyin Yuanxiu's disciple Yulin Tongxiu also joined the debate, writing the *Bianmo shuo* (Discourse on refuting the demon) to refute Ruibai Mingxue.[16]

Miyun's Debate with the Jesuits

In the late Ming, Jesuit missionaries, led by Matteo Ricci, were actively propagating Christianity in China. Adopting the policy of "uniting with Confucianism and resisting Buddhism," the growing Christian movement posed serious threats to Buddhism. Famous monks, such as Zhuhong in 1615 and Ouyi Zhixu (1599–1655) in 1643, responded to the challenge.[17] Miyun Yuanwu also participated in the anti-Christian movement. In 1635, at the request of a literatus, Huang Zhen, Miyun wrote three essays on the meaning of heaven (*Biantian sanshuo*) to challenge the Christian church at Hangzhou. These essays were collected in fascicle 6 of the *Tiantong zhishuo* and reprinted in the *Shengchao poxie ji* (Collected essays for destroying heterodoxy in the holy dynasties).[18]

Feiyin Tongrong's Dispute with Muchen Daomin concerning
the Legitimacy of Miyun's Dharma Heirs and the Succession of Abbots
at Tiantong Monastery

After Miyun Yuanwu's death in 1642, Feiyin Tongrong became a central figure among Miyun's dharma heirs. He had been influential and controversial
because he was always critical of his contemporaries and acted as a censor
within his master's lineage. He would evaluate other monks' understanding
of Chan according to their recorded sayings, which publicized their enlightenment experiences. His dharma brother Muchen Daomin, later prominent in
the Qing court, was Feiyin Tongrong's enemy. Feiyin's *Separate Collection*
(*Feiyin chanshi bieji*) reveals that strong personal conflicts between the two
centered on the issues of abbot succession in Tiantong monastery and the
abuse of dharma transmission that occurred in 1643.[19]

According to Feiyin, this dispute started when all of Miyun Yuanwu's
dharma heirs gathered in Tiantong monastery to attend their master's funeral.
Making use of this opportunity, Muchen Daomin declared himself to be the
successor of Miyun Yuanwu as abbot of Tiantong. In addition, Muchen Daomin
distributed Miyun Yuanwu's remaining personal belongings, such as robes and
whisks, to several dozen monks who had studied with Miyun but never received
dharma transmission. Muchen claimed that these monks had received secret
transmissions and that he only acted on behalf of his master to acknowledge
these monks after Miyun's death. Feiyin then accused Muchen Daomin of ma-
nipulating his fellow monks to elect him as abbot of Tiantong rather than following the usual practice of lot drawing. Feiyin also criticized Muchen for conferring dharma transmission to other monks by his master's proxy, a practice
that Feiyin viewed as a threat to the legitimately established dharma heirs personally certified by Miyun. To avoid any future confusion, Feiyin insisted on
writing the names of all twelve legitimate dharma heirs into Miyun's epitaph.

Feiyin Tongrong's Dispute with Ruibai Mingxue concerning
the Principles of Caodong and Linji

Feiyin Tongrong was particularly belligerent toward the Caodong monks who
had formerly been his study mates. For example, when he found that the Caodong master Ruibai Mingxue also used shouts and blows to teach students,
he felt threatened because he believed that the shouts and blows were derived
from the Linji school rather than from the Caodong. For him, the principles of
Linji and Caodong were separate and distinctive. He thus picked a fight with

this Caodong monk in 1634 and accused him of "plagiarizing" the Linji method of shouts and blows.[20]

Feiyin Tongrong's Dispute with the Jesuits

Following his master closely, Feiyin Tongrong also joined the anti-Christian movement in northwest Fujian. At the request of the local gentry, he wrote four essays under the title *Yuandao pixie shuo* (Treatise on the origins of the Way and the refutation of heresies). He also compiled an anthology in 1636 with the same title and collected polemical essays written by him and his disciples. In 1639, at the request of Miyun Yuanwu and Feiyin Tongrong, Feiyin Tongrong's lay disciple Xu Changzhi (1582–1672) compiled the most comprehensive anti-Christian anthology, which is known today from its Japanese reprint, *Shengchao poxie ji*.[21]

Feiyin's Disputes with Other Chan Masters

Feiyin had conflicts with many Chan masters. In addition to the disputes already mentioned, in 1642 and 1643, he wrote several essays to criticize other Chan masters whose Chan understandings were deemed by him as "crazy." For example, he joined his teacher, Miyun Yuanwu, in the debate about Gaofeng Yuanmiao's enlightenment experience; he also argued with his dharma brother Yulin Tongxiu about the meaning of beating and shouting; and he criticized the Caodong master Yongjue Yuanxian's remark about his simple Chan style.[22]

Controversy over Xuejiao Yuanxin's Stūpa at Yunmen Monastery

Xuejiao Yuanxin was popular among the literati and his two literati followers, Huang Duanbo[23] and Xu Qirui, were listed as his only dharma heirs. (Both men became martyrs in the anti-Manchu resistance movement.) However, having been enlightened by reading Yunmen Wenyan's recorded sayings, Xuejiao Yuanxin considered himself a dharma heir of the Yunmen school. For this reason, Muchen Daomin eliminated him from the Linji lineage in his *Chandeng shipu*. Yet, the new Manchu ruler, Shunzhi, was extremely interested in Xuejiao Yuanxin and even questioned his omission from Chan genealogies during an interview with Muchen Daomin in 1659. Thus, in the current edition of the *Chandeng shipu*, Xuejiao was added as a Linji heir. Later, the emperor allotted money to repair Xuejiao Yuanxin's memorial pagoda in Yunmen monastery. Muchen Daomin was assigned the job and used it as an opportunity to attack Hanyue Fazang's disciple Jude Hongli.

Muchen Daomin accused Jude Hongli and his disciple Sanmu Zhiyuan of neglecting the emperor's edict and destroying Yunmen monastery, where Xuejiao's pagoda was located. As Chen Yuan correctly points out, this dispute was simply Muchen Daomin's latest attempt to increase his influence in the Buddhist community.[24]

Controversy over the "Tower of Emperor's Handwriting" at Pingyang Monastery

After Muchen Daomin was called to Beijing, he became the new national preceptor of the Manchu regime. To increase his influence in the Buddhist world, he frequently engaged in disputes and competed with his rivals, such as Tianyin Yuanxiu's dharma heir Yulin Tongxiu, who was also summoned to Beijing to receive honorary titles. After Muchen returned to the south, he built a new monastery called Pingyang in Kuaiji to store the emperor's calligraphic works that had been given to him. However, Yulin Tongxiu did not do the same with the emperor's writings that he received. Thus, Muchen wrote "Baokui shuo" (Essay on the precious royal writings) in 1670 to criticize Yulin Tongxiu. He argued that Tongxiu should have erected a similar building to house the emperor's writings as he did. But by not doing so, Yulin Tongxiu had obtained fame as transcending worldly interests. According to Muchen Daomin, this was one of Yulin Tongxiu's faults.[25]

Controversy over Monastic Property at Shanquan Monastery

Shanquan monastery was located in Yixing county and was revived by Zhanran Yuancheng's heir Baiyu Jingsi (1610–1665) in the early Qing. In 1671, Baiyu's disciple Hansong Zhicao (1626–1686) became abbot. However, the newly appointed national preceptor, Yulin Tongxiu, intended to usurp this property because the memorial pagoda of his patriarch Huanyou Zhengchuang's tonsure master was located there. In the name of protecting this pagoda, Tongxiu expelled Hansong Zhicao and gained control of the property in 1673. Yulin Tongxiu appointed his heir Baisong Xingfeng (1612–1674) as the new abbot. Hansong Zhicao wrote the *Zhimi pushuo* (General discourse on pointing to the deluded) to criticize Yulin Tongxiu.[26] The dispute became bloody when Baisong Xingfeng wanted to expand the property by incorporating the neighboring lineage shrine of the Chen family. The Chen lineage could not endure the oppression and set fire to the monastery in 1674. Baisong Xingfeng was killed in the fire. As Chen Yuan laments, the disputes in the seventeenth century had degenerated into a struggle for secular interests.[27]

Appendix 3: Survey of Evidence Concerning the Issue of Two Daowus

In the following, I glean evidence from various polemical works about the issue of the two Daowus and present them in chronological order. The textual records are listed as evidence according to the polemicists' standards. From the perspective of modern historians, however, some pieces of "evidence" are obviously legends or myths.

A. Evidence Supporting the Two-Daowu Theory

Evidence from the Tang Period

Although there was no dispute about the two Daowus in the Tang dynasty, all later debates pointed to some early sources of Tang origin. This section lists some of the most important pieces of evidence, both extant and missing, that were frequently cited by the polemicists.

THE PROPHECY ABOUT MAZU DAOYI AND HIS LINEAGE. The acceptance of Tianwang Daowu implies that Mazu's line is more prominent than Qingyuan's because if Longtan Chongxin were Tianwang Daowu's heir, his entire lineage would have belonged to the line of Nanyue Huairang and Mazu Daoyi. Thus, the transmissions derived from Mazu would outnumber those from Qingyuan.

One reason in particular led Feiyin and his followers to believe firmly in the existence of Tianwang Daowu. That is, a prophecy had been made by the mythical Indian Chan patriarch Prajñātāra before Bodhidharma's trip to China. Feiyin Tongrong interpreted this prophecy as suggesting the superiority of Nanyue Huairang's line.

From the perspective of modern historians, these prophecies contained in Chan histories, deliberately concocted for ideological purposes, can hardly be seen as evidence. For Chan followers in the seventeenth century, however, the predictions proclaimed by an Indian patriarch and recorded in many Chan historiographies were beyond reasonable doubt. These prophecies had appeared as early as the ninth century in proto-Chan genealogical works such as the *Baolin zhuan* (Baolin records), compiled in 801. Two such prophecies are relevant to the debate. The first was about Bodhidharma. Before his departure for China, when he asked the venerable Prajñātāra, the twenty-seventh patriarch, about his future in China, Prajñātāra predicted that there would be two "tender branches" in China, symbolizing both Mazu's and Shitou's lineages, and Mazu would assume the leadership. His verse continues as follows:

> Traveling on land and crossing waters, [you] will meet a goat.
> Alone, [you] will cross the [Yangzi] river sadly and secretly.
> Under the sun, there is a pitiful pair of elephant and horse.
> Two tender branches will flourish forever.[1]

The first line of this prediction indicates Bodhidharma's arrival at Guangzhou, "the city of the goat." The second line suggests that Bodhidharma, after his unpleasant meeting with the Wu emperor of the Liang state, would leave for north China and eventually settle at Mount Song. The meaning of the last two lines is much more obscure and consequently subject to different interpretations. In the third line, "elephant" and "horse" may refer to Huineng and Shenxiu. For Feiyin Tongrong, however, the "two tender branches" clearly represent the lineages of Linji and Caodong, and the word *ma* in the third line refers to Mazu Daoyi, thus establishing the superiority of Mazu's line.[2]

The second prediction articulated by the sixth patriarch, Huineng, had been recorded in both Deyi and Zongbao editions of the *Platform Sūtra*.[3] Citing the prophecy of Prajñātāra in India, Huineng predicted that, under Nanyue Huairang's lineage, a pony would come out and sweep the world. "The pony" serves as a pun here: It refers to Mazu Daoyi, whose name contains the character *ma*.[4] As Huineng said to Nanyue Huairang, "A pony will come from beneath your feet, and will stamp to death people in the world." Because the earliest extant Dunhuang edition does not contain this phrase, modern historians recognize this saying as a later interpolation.[5]

ZONGMI'S "CHAN CHART". One of the earliest pieces of evidence to which the polemicists appealed is Zongmi's *Zhonghua chuanxindi Chanmen shizi chengxitu* (Chart of the master-disciple succession of the Chan gate that transmits the mind ground in China), often abbreviated as the "Chan Chart."[6] In the current edition of this text, preserved in the Japanese supplementary canon, a Daowu was indeed listed as Mazu's heir. Because Zongmi's documentation of early Chan history is highly reliable, it is certain that Mazu had a disciple who resided in Jiangling and had the name Daowu. Feiyin Tongrong and his followers regarded this as the most compelling evidence supporting the existence of Tianwang Daowu. Curiously, however, a note was added to Zongmi's record of Daowu, stating that he was also an heir of the national preceptor Faqin (714–792) in Jingshan.[7] This note contradicts Tianwang Daowu's biography, which says nothing about his study with Faqin. As some Caodong masters pointed out, it does fit in Tianhuang Daowu's biography, which states that he studied with Faqin in his youth.

GUIDENG'S INSCRIPTION OF NANYUE HUAIRANG. Guideng, a Tang official active during the Zhenyuan reign (708–805),[8] wrote the inscription of Chan master Nanyue Huairang. The complete text of this inscription is not extant. In the *Song gaoseng zhuan*, Zanning (919–1001) wrote a biography for Nanyue Huairang based on Guideng's inscription but without any reference to Huairang's disciples.[9] According to Zanning's account, Guideng unquestionably wrote an epitaph for Nanyue Huairang during the Yuanhe reign (806–820). However, Juefan Huihong, who apparently had seen the original inscription, indicated that this inscription actually listed several dharma grandsons after him, among whom was Daowu. Daowu, therefore, belonged to Nanyue's lineage.

QUAN DEYU'S EPITAPH OF MAZU DAOYI. Quan Deyu (759–818) was a famous official of the Tang who was befriended by Mazu Daoyi. He composed Mazu's inscription in 791.[10] This inscription listed Daowu as Mazu's disciple.[11] Modern scholars of Mazu Daoyi have hypothesized that this Daowu must have been Tianhuang Daowu, who may have studied with Mazu during his stay in Kaiyuan monastery from about 770 to 778. For the polemicists in the seventeenth century, however, this reference was additional evidence for a second Daowu because they believed this Daowu must be Tianwang Daowu.

HUANG ZONGXI'S DISCOVERY OF QIU YUANSU'S IDENTITY. Qiu Yuansu was the Tang official who allegedly wrote Tianwang Daowu's epitaph. According to this epitaph, which has not been determined as a genuine text created in the Tang, he had been the military governor of Jingnan (*Jingnan jiedushi*). However, many polemicists diligently searched Tang history but failed to discover his name and title. Thus, some Caodong monks concluded that Qiu Yuansu was nonexistent, and, accordingly, Tianwang Daowu's inscription must be a forgery.

Nonetheless, Huang Zongxi, a famous historian in the early Qing, believed in the authenticity of Tianwang Daowu's inscription because he discovered the identity of Qiu Yuansu from inscriptional sources.

Huang Zongxi's opinion is worth mentioning because of his prominent status in Chinese intellectual history. He discovered the name Qiu Yuansu in Ouyang Xiu's collection of inscriptions. In his postscript to the *Jigu lu* (Records of collecting antiquity), Ouyang Xiu made the following entry:

THE POEMS ABOUT THE SHENNÜ (SPIRIT LADY) SHRINE: THE
FOURTEENTH YEAR OF THE ZHENYUAN REIGN (798)
On the right are the poems on the Shennü Shrine, written by Li Jifu,
Qiu Yuansu, Li Yisun and Jing Qian. When I was appointed as magistrate of Yiling, I took a boat [ride] along the Yellow Cow Gorge
(*Huangniu xia*) to visit this shrine and drink water from the foggy Fu
River. I watched the river and mountain standing out steep and alone
but only regretted that I could not see the exotic beauty of Mount Wu.
Every time I read the poems written by these people, I loved their
diction and style and thus made a record.[12]

The record of Qiu Yuansu's poem can be also seen in Chen Si's collection of inscriptions. Chen Si added that Qiu Yuansu was the military commissioner of Kuizhou (today, Sichuan).[13] Although Ouyang Xiu and Chen Si compiled their works during the Song, the inscriptions they recorded were all written in previous dynasties. Both claimed to have seen many of these inscriptions in person. Based on these Song records, Huang Zongxi concluded that Qiu Yuansu was indeed a contemporary of Daowu and had served as a military officer in the Sichuan area.

Evidence from the Song

Apparently, the evidence just cited did not arouse any controversies in the Tang because the division of the five Chan lineages had not yet emerged.

During the Song, however, the dispute about the two Daowus began to surface as a critical response to the officially sanctioned *Jingde chuandeng lu*.

DAGUAN TANYING'S *WUJIA ZONGPAI*. The first person who posited the existence of Tianwang Daowu was Daguan Tanying (989–1060), a Linji Chan master active in the Northern Song. He allegedly wrote the no-longer extant *Wujia zongpai* (The lineages of five Chan houses). Many later sources pointed to his work as the first that contains information about the two Daowus, especially about Tianwang Daowu. As the following record provided by Juefan Huihong indicates, the two inscriptions were first in Daguan Tanying's possession.[14]

JUEFAN HUIHONG'S ACCOUNTS OF THE TWO DAOWUS. One of the most important sources to which Feiyin Tongrong could refer regarding the existence of the monk Tianwang Daowu was a short note in Juefan Huihong's miscellaneous collection *Linjian lu*, which raised the possibility of the existence of two monks named Daowu. I translate this note as follows:

> The *Jingde chuandeng lu* records the following information about Chan master Daowu in Tianhuang monastery in Jingzhou:
>
> Daowu received the dharma from Shitou Xiqian. The temple he resided in was called Tianhuang. He was from Dongyang in Wuzhou with the surname "Zhang." At the age of fourteen, he left his household and was tonsured by an eminent monk in Mingzhou (Ningbo). At the age of twenty-five, he received the complete ordination in Zhulin monastery in Hangzhou. He first visited Master Guoyi (Faqin) at Mount Jingshan and served him diligently for five years. During the Dali reign (766–780), he arrived in Zhongling to visit Master Mazu. After two summers, he finally visited Shitou Xiqian. He died in the fourth month of the Dinghai year of the Yuanhe reign [807] at the age of sixty and had joined the saṅgha for thirty-five years.
>
> I have read Chan master Daguan Tanying's collection *Wujia zongpai*, which says that Daowu is an heir of Mazu. [This source] quotes Qiu Yuansu's inscription of Daowu, which amounts to several thousand words. Abbreviated as below, it says: The master's name is Daowu, a Zhugong (Jiangling) person with the surname of Cui, and he is Ziyu's descendant. At fifteen, he left the household after receiving tonsure from Master Tanzhu. At twenty-three, he visited the Vinaya master at Mount Song and was ordained. He also visited Shitou Xiqian and studied with him for two years but had no perfect

awakening. He then went to Chang'an to visit the national preceptor, Huizhong. At thirty-four, returning to the south with the attendant Yingzhen, he visited Master Mazu and achieved the great enlightenment upon hearing [Mazu's teaching]. [Mazu] prayed [for him]: "In the future, do not leave your original place." Thus, he returned to Zhugong (Jiangling). In the beginning of the fourth month of the thirteenth year of the Yuanhe reign (818), he became ill and died on the thirteenth day at the age of eighty-two and had been a monk for sixty-three years.

After examining these two biographies, [I found] that they look like exactly two different people. But Qiu Yuansu recorded that he (Tianwang Daowu) had one dharma heir named Chongxin, who lived in Longtan monastery in Fengzhou. "The Inscription of Chan Master Nanyue Huairang" written by the famous gentleman Guideng of the Tang listed several dharma grandsons after him, among whom there was Daowu's name. The *Da Pei xiangguo zongqu zhuang* (Reply to Prime Minister Pei Xiu on Chan teaching) written by Zongmi lists six dharma heirs of Mazu and the first name is Daowu of Jiangling. The note under the name says: "[He is] also Jingshan's (Guoyi's) heir." Nowadays, one can laugh at those who erroneously took the Yunmen and Linji schools as rivals.[15]

Juefan Huihong's record was the first written source to quote Tianwang Daowu's inscription. Here, Huihong never stated that his account was an exact replica of the inscription. Rather, according to Huihong, the actual inscription, which was in Daguan Tanying's possession, was several thousand words long. This detail certainly contrasts with the short inscription of Tianwang Daowu popular in later Chan histories, which is less than two hundred words. Juefan Huihong suggested that, in the Northern Song, the Yunmen school and the Linji school seemed to be in competition. However, he believed that if there were indeed two Daowus and Longtan Chongxin did belong to Tianwang Daowu's lineage, both the Yunmen school and the Linji school would belong to Mazu's line. Thus, for Huihong, the rivalry between Yunmen and Linji was laughable. In addition to providing a biographical sketch of the two Daowus, Huihong listed the early sources from the Tang that contained evidence favorable to the new Tianwang Daowu. (I have already examined some of these early sources.)

ZHANG SHANGYING'S INVOLVEMENT. Daguan Tanying's *Wujia zongpai* is no longer extant. However, Juemengtang's preface to this work provides more information about the relation between the "sudden" appearance of Tianwang Daowu's biography and Zhang Shangying (1043–1121), Daguan Tanying, and Juefan Huihong.[16] Written for a recollated version of the *Wujia zongpai*, this preface first targets the delineation of dharma transmissions in the *Jingde chuandeng lu* and argues for the existence of Tianwang Daowu. The author suggests that the two schools derived from Longtan Chongxin should be changed to Mazu's line. He points to the fact that Daoyuan, the compiler of the *Jingde chuandeng lu*, could not consult the existing epigraphic sources personally, and the authenticity of his collection was thus suspicous. The author of this preface also provided some new information about the relation between this dispute and Zhang Shangying:

> Nowadays, all people in the world are taking the *Jingde chuandeng lu* as evidence. Even those who hold positions in big monasteries and lineages are not able to discern clearly. Only two virtuous men, Prime Minister layman Wujin (Zhang Shangying) and Lü Xiaqing,[17] often discussed affairs in the Chan lineage whenever they met. They said: "Shitou had Yaoshan (Weiyan) and Yaoshan developed the Caodong school. His teaching, principle, practice, and accomplishment were demonstrated in a delicate and tactful way. And also from Tianhuang Daowu came a *vajra* Zhou (*Zhou jingang*, referring to Deshan Xuanjian). He chastised [people] like the wind and cursed like the rain. Even Buddhas and patriarchs did not dare to test his sharpness. It may be wrong that he derived from Tianhuang." The venerable Master Jiyin (Juefan Huihong) also doubted it and remarked: "It seems that there were two people named Daowu." Later Wujin (Zhang Shangying) obtained the epitaph of Tianhuang Daowu written by Fu Zai of the Tang from Daguan Tanying and again received the epitaph of Tianwang Daowu written by Qiu Xuansu. [Zhang Shangying] carried them and showed them to all people, saying: "I have doubted if Deshan Xuanjian and Dongshan Liangjia were all derived from Shitou: Why were their approaches fundamentally different? Now I have proved it with Qiu's and Fu's records, and it is crystal clear. I thus realize that I was not mistaken in selecting [Chan] methods and testing people."[18]

According to this record, Zhang Shangying proved the theory of two Daowus. He first doubted that Deshan Xuanjian belonged to Tianhuang Daowu's transmission line. Then, he borrowed Tianwang Daowu's inscription from Daguan Tanying and compared it with the existing inscription of Tianhuang Daowu. Zhang Shangying was thrilled because Tianwang Daowu's

inscription listed Longtan Chongxin, from whom Deshan Xuanjian was derived, as Tianwang Daowu's heir, and thus his transmissions belonged to
Nanyue Huairang's line.

XUEDOU CHONGXIAN'S LINEAGE AFFILIATION. Records of later Chan masters' lineage affiliations also provided some clues to the identities of the two
Daowus. By tracing their family trees as they were claimed, Longtan Chongxin's teacher can be ascertained. One such record comes from Weibai's *Jingzhong jianguo xu denglu* (Supplementary lamp records of the Jingzhong jianguo reign), compiled in 1101. This book is a genealogical work written after the
Jingde chuandeng lu by a monk of the Yunmen lineage. It records the biographies of the Śākyamuni Buddha and thirty-three patriarchs in Chan history.

The seventeenth-century polemicists regarded the so-called evidence from
this work not as direct support for the two-Daowu theory but rather as an inference based on the attribution of Xuedou Chongxian's (980–1052) lineage
affiliation and generation number. According to Weibai, Xuedou Chongxian
was Mazu's ninth-generation dharma heir.[19] However, this record contradicts
that in the *Jingde chuandeng lu*, which states that Xuedou Chongxian, as a patriarch of the Yunmen school, should be Shitou Xiqian's descendant. Because
it was indisputable that Xuedou Chongxian was derived from Longtan
Chongxin, Xuedou Chongxin's affiliation to Tianhuang Daowu or Tianwang
Daowu became crucial. If Xuedou Chongxian's lineage affiliation could be
traced back to Longtan Chongxin and then to Tianhuang Daowu, it meant that
Xuedou Chongxian belonged to Shitou's line as the *Jingde chuandeng lu* indicated. However, if he was indeed a descendant of Mazu's line, then Longtan
Chongxin could not be Tianhuang Daowu's heir. The only possibility, according to later polemicists, was that Longtan Chongxin was Tianwang Daowu's
heir and thus could be traced back to Mazu.

Because Weibai was also a monk in the Yunmen lineage, his own account
of his patriarch's lineage affiliation carried a certain weight. Such evidence
can be also found in the Song Chan master Gongchen's *Zuyuan tongyao* (Outlines and essentials of the origins of patriarchs) in thirty fascicles. Gongchen
was a dharma heir of Daguan Tanying and resided in Xiyu monastery. Because of his relationship with Daguan Tanying, it was natural for him to adopt
the two-Daowu theory.[20]

Polemicists found further evidence about Xuedou Chongxian's lineage affiliation from his epitaph written by the Song official Lü Xiaqing, which clearly
states that Xuedou was one of Mazu's ninth-generation dharma heirs.[21] As
mentioned earlier, in Juemengtang's preface to the *Wujia zongpai*, Lü Xiaqing,
together with Zhang Shangying, supported the two-Daowu theory strongly.

Thus, it is not surprising to find his account of lineage affiliation consistent with the two-Daowu theory.

Evidence from the Yuan Dynasty

The theory of the two Daowus gained momentum in the Yuan, when the epitaphs of both Tianhuang Daowu and Tianwang Daowu were officially incorporated into Chan historiographies. Some Chan historiographers even publicly sanctioned such a theory and altered the transmission lines delineated in the *Jingde chuandeng lu*. The following sources attempted to establish the existence of Tianwang Daowu and to perpetuate the two-Daowu theory.

TWO INSCRIPTIONS IN THE *WUDENG HUIYUAN* AND *FOZU LIDAI TONGZAI*. The complete records of the two inscriptions appeared only in the Yuan dynasty. In the Yuan edition of the *Wudeng huiyuan*, printed in the fourth year of the Zhi-yuan reign (1267) when the Southern Song still controlled south China, a long annotation included the full text of the two inscriptions for the first time, and they appeared under the entry for Tianhuang Daowu.[22] The Yuan edition of the *Jingde chuandeng lu* added a note about the two Daowus without changing its main text and official lineage affiliations. In the Yuan work *Fozu lidai tong-zai* (Records of successive generations of Buddha), the two inscriptions became the main text, annotated with Juefan Huihong's records (translated earlier in this appendix).[23] All of these works were included in the imperial canon in the Ming, reinforcing Feiyin Tongrong's argument.

A comparison of the two inscriptions illustrates their parallel structure and the similar accounts of the two monks. Fu Zai, the chief musician of the Court of Imperial Sacrifice (*Xielülang*), wrote Tianhuang Daowu's inscription. Tianwang Daowu's inscription was written by Qiu Yuansu, the military governor of Jingnan (Jingzhou). I translate both biographies as follows.[24] First, here is Tianhuang Daowu's inscription by Fu Zai:

> Daowu, surnamed Zhang, was a man from Dongyang county in
> Wuzhou prefecture. At fourteen, he renounced the household life
> and became a disciple of an eminent master in Mingzhou prefecture
> (Ningbo). At twenty-five, he received full precepts at Zhulin monas-
> tery in Hangzhou. He first studied with Master Guoyi (Faqin) and
> served him for five years. In the eleventh year of the Dali period
> (776) he lived as a recluse at Mount Damei. In the first year of the
> Jianzhong period (780), he visited Mazu in Jiangxi. In the second

year (781), he studied with Shitou and thus achieved the great
awakening. Thereupon, he lived as a recluse in Mount Ziling in Dangyang and later went to Jingnan (Jingzhou). There was a monastery
called Tianhuang in the east part of the city. Because it was destroyed in a recent fire, the monk Lingjiang intended to restore it. He
said. "If we can invite Chan master Daowu as the fund-raiser, he will
certainly bless us." At that time, Mr. Pei, prefect of Jiangling and vice
director of the right, humbly inquired [Master Daowu] about the
[Buddhist] teaching. He was welcomed [into the monastery] with the
utmost politeness. Because the master never [went out] to welcome
or send off his guests regardless of their social status, he sat there
and bowed to all of them. Mr. Pei therefore revered him even more.
Because of this, the Way of Shitou Xiqian became prominent.

The master suffered from backpain. When he was about to die,
the assembly came to visit him. The master suddenly summoned the
cook to his nearby. He asked: "Do you understand?" [The cook]
replied: "I don't understand." After picking a pillow and threw it on
the ground, the master died. He lived for sixty years and had been a
monk for thirty-five years. He had three generations of dharma
heirs, who were Huizhen, Youxian, and Wenfen. [Daowu died] on
the thirteenth day of the fourth month of the second year of the
Yuanhe reign (807).

Here is Tianwang Daowu's inscription by Qiu Yuansu:

Daowu, a man from Zhugong (Jiangling) and surnamed Cui, was a
descendant of Ziyu. At the age of fifteen, he renounced the house-
hold life under the Vinaya master Tanzhu of Changsha monastery
(later Tianhuang monastery). At twenty-three he received full
precepts at Mount Song. At thirty-three he went to study with Shitou.
Although he received Shitou's instructions and suggestions frequently, he did not have a single moment of satisfaction. Then, he
visited the national preceptor Huizhong (?–775). At thirty-four,
together with Yingzhen, an attendant of Huizhong, he returned to
the south to visit Mazu. Mazu said, "[You must] realize that your
own mind is originally the Buddha. Without relying on the gradual
sequence and cultivation, your own original substance is itself the
Absolute Reality with myriad perfect virtues." The master immediately attained the great awakening upon hearing these words. Mazu
told the master: "If you are to head a monastery, return to the place
you come from." Following this instruction, Daowu returned to

Jingzhou, where he built a grass hut not far away from the city. Later, because the military commissioner asked his attendants about this monk and he was told stories about him, the commissioner came to visit Daowu in person to inquire about the Way. He saw the road [leading to the grass hut] was so narrow that horses and carriages had difficulty in getting through. As far as the eyes could see there was only wild forest that was not trimed and cleared up. Seeing this, the commissioner became so angry that he had the master arrested and thrown into a river. When his entourage with banners and canopies just returned to office, they saw that the entire office compound was on fire. Both inside and outside were flames and intense heat; and no one could get close to it. Only a voice was heard in the sky: "I am the god of the Heavenly King! I am the god of the Heavenly King.!" The commissioner repented and paid homage to the god. Then, the fire and smoke were all gone, and everything was just as it was before. He then went to the riverbank and saw that the master was still in the water and his cloth was not even wet. Express-ing his repentance again, the commissioner invited the master to come to live in the government compound. The commissioner built a temple in the western part of the city [of Jingzhou] and named it officially "King of Heaven" (Tianwang).

The master often said, "Happy! Happy!" When he was about to die, he shouted "Painful! Painful!" He also said, "King Yama is coming to grab me." The abbot asked, "When you were caught by the commissioner and thrown into the water, you were so calm. Why do you behave like this right now?" The master raised the pillow and said, "Can you tell me whether I was right at that time or I am right now?" The abbot could not even reply. Thereupon, the master entered nirvāna. It was on the thirteenth day of the tenth month of the third year of the Yuanhe reign (808). He was eighty-two years old and had spent sixty-three summer retreats. He has one dharma heir, whose name was Chongxin, the master of Longtan.[25]

These two biographies show surprisingly similar structures and informa-tion. Having the same name, both monks lived in Jiangling, but one was in the Monastery of the Emperor of Heaven (Tianhuang) in the eastern part of the city and the other was in the Monastery of the King of Heaven (Tianwang) in the western part of the city. They both had studied with Mazu Daoyi and with Shitou Xiqian although they claimed to have received different trans-missions: Tianhuang Daowu received transmission from Shitou Xiqian and

Tianwang Daowu from Mazu Daoyi. Each master had connections with a local official who played a decisive role in the monk's career. The significant difference between the two biographies is that, among the three disciples listed in Tianhuang Daowu's inscription, there is no mention of Longtan Chongxin. However, Tianwang Daowu's biography records Longtan Chongxin as his only dharma heir. Such an astonishing similarity and such a glaring difference in their dharma transmissions suggest strongly that the authenticity of at least one biography is questionable. Equally important, these two inscriptions, though frequently mentioned in Song sources, never appeared until the Yuan. No account is provided, either, about how these two inscriptions were handed down to monks in the Yuan. The authenticity of these inscriptions was consequently an issue in later debates.

BENJUE'S BUDDHIST HISTORY. The monk Benjue compiled *Shishi tongjian* (Compendium of Buddhist history) in twelve fascicles in 1270. Imitating the Confucian historical work *Zizhi tongjian* (Compendium of history) by Sima Guang (1019–1086), Benjue's work chronicled events from 970 B.C. to 960 A.D. Based on various historical records, it provides a clear account of Buddhist history and has very high scholarly value. However, in this historical work, he supported the authenticity of Tianwang Daowu's identity. In the entry of the third year of the Yuanhe reign of the Tang (808), he recorded: "On the thirteenth day of the tenth month, the Chan master Daowu of Tianwang monastery in the west of Jingnan city entered nirvāna, aged eighty-two, [having] sixty-three summer retreats. He was Mazu's heir and his heir was Longtan Chongxin."[26] In this entry, Benjue added a note about Juemengtang's preface to the recollated edition of Daguan Tanying's *Wujia zongpai*, upon which Benjue apparently relied. Benjue's position on the issue shows that the existence of Tianwang Daowu had been acknowledged by some Buddhist scholars, and the legend of Tianwang Daowu was even incorporated into newly compiled historical works.

YUNHE RUI'S CHAN GENEALOGY. At the end of the Southern Song and the beginning of the Yuan dynasty, Chan Buddhism remained active, and some Chan masters, accepting the two-Daowu theory, started to compile new supplementary histories of lamp transmission based on the altered lineage affiliations. Many later polemicists pointed to Yunhe Rui's *Xindeng lu* (Records of the lamp of mind) as the first attempt to completely revise the conventional dharma transmission lines. This work, according to some sources, was finished between 1341 and 1368, though a later source pinpointed it to the year

1277, which was still during the Southern Song.[27] Regardless of its origins, this book was lost, and even during the seventeenth century, polemicists had no chance to read it. All references to this book come from a preface to the Yuan edition of the *Wudeng huiyuan* written by the monk Tingjun (?-1368) in 1364.[28] In this preface, Tingjun praised the compilation of the *Wudeng huiyuan* and specifically mentioned the writing of the *Xindeng lu*. He singled out the *Xindeng lu* because he believed that this work was the most comprehensive among all genealogical works. However, Tingjun regretted that such a work did not circulate widely because it had adopted the inscription of Tianwang Daowu and thus changed the conventional transmission lines. Although this book was no longer extant, this reference was enough for later polemicists to cite it as a precedent for their alteration of Chan genealogy.

JUE'AN'S BUDDHIST HISTORY. Another Buddhist history that publicly adopted the theory about Tianwang Daowu was the *Shishi jigu lue* (Outlined investigation of Buddhist history). Compiled by Jue'an (1286-?) in 1354, this work in four fascicles was a comprehensive record of important events in Buddhist history. Modeled on Benjue's *Shishi tongjian*, it arranged various records according to the chronology of the succession of dynasties and emperors. By juxtaposing political events and Buddhist history, this work detailed the relationship between the Chinese empire and the development of Buddhism. Broadly consulting various kinds of historical sources, it was especially rich in data about translations, monastic construction, and numbers of ordained monks. However, as Chen Shiqiang points out, it had numerous historical errors.[29]

Fascicle 3 contained information about Tang Buddhism. In the entry for 807, Jue'an recorded Tianhuang Daowu's biography based on Fu Zai's inscription. In the entry for 808, he recorded Tianwang Daowu's biographical information based on the reprinted *Wudeng huiyuan*. Explicitly referring to Qiu Yuansu's inscription, whose authenticity he seemed to have completely accepted, he recorded Longtan Chongxin as Tianwang Daowu's only dharma heir.[30] As he noted, he had consulted the *Wudeng huiyuan*. Obviously, his source about Tianwang Daowu was based on the inscription appended in the *Wudeng huiyuan* reprinted in the Yuan dynasty. However, paradoxically, under the entry for 827, he entered Longtan Chongxin as Tianhuang Daowu's heir.[31] This is obviously contradictory to his early record about Tianwang Daowu. As he noted, this time, he based his information on the *Jingde chuandeng lu*. From these contradictory entries, we can see again the confusion about the identities of the two Daowus in the Yuan dynasty.

B. Evidence against the Two-Daowu Theory

Seventeenth-century supporters of the two-Daowu theory based their argument primarily on the sources listed above. It seems that the thesis of the existence of the two Daowus had been firmly established. However, the Caodong monks' counterarguments pointed directly to the spuriousness of Tianwang Daowu's inscription written by Qiu Yuansu. In the following sections, I introduce the evidence deemed to be important by the Caodong monks.

Evidence from Major Chan Historical Writings

Although evidence supporting the two-Daowu theory shed new light on Chan history, opponents gained a clear upper hand by citing numerous Chan historiographies that mentioned only Tianhuang Daowu. Among them, Zanning's *Song gaoseng zhuan* was the most important and detailed account about Tianhuang Daowu and Longtan Chongxin.

ZANNING'S BIOGRAPHIES OF TIANHUANG DAOWU AND LONGTAN CHONGXIN. The strongest evidence against the two-Daowu theory was the biographies of Tianhuang Daowu and Longtan Chongxin included in Zanning's *Song gaoseng zhuan*. This work, which was not a Chan historiography, divided monks into ten traditional categories. An eminent monk could be included in the biographies if he had made considerable contributions to the Buddhist religion as a translator, exegete, thaumaturge, practitioner of meditation, elucidator of Vinaya, aspirant to the next life, *sūtra* chanter, benefactor, hymnodist, or proselytizer.[32] Zanning, in his *Song gaoseng zhuan*, grouped many Chan patriarchs, such as Bodhidharma, under the category of "practitioner of meditation" despite some Chan monks' protest.[33]

In fascicle 10, Zanning provided a detailed account of Tianhuang Daowu's life. According to Zanning, Daowu was determined to leave his family at fourteen and was ordained in Mingzhou. At twenty-five, he received the full ordination in Zhulin monastery in Hangzhou. Later, he went to study with the Chan teacher Guoyi at Jingshan. After serving for five years, he received his certification (*yinke*). Then, in 776, he went to Mount Damei at Yuyao and lived as a recluse for three or four years. In the early years of the Jianzhong reign (780), he visited Mazu at Zhongling. In 781, he visited Shitou. Here, Zanning did not mention from which Master Daowu eventually received dharma transmission. Instead, he praised Daowu for studying with all three Chan masters. According to this biography, Daowu first lived in Fengyang and then in Jingkou. Eventually, he settled in Mount Chaizi at Dangyang, which was close to the regional metropolis of Jingzhou. Earlier, however, because the famous Tianhuang monastery had recently burned down, the abbot of Chongye monastery, Lingjian, invited Daowu to live there. Thus, a dispute about the master's final residence erupted. At that time, the magistrate of Jingling and vice director of the right (*Jiangling yin youpuye*), a man surnamed Pei, was attracted by Daowu and completely devoted himself to him. Zanning's account shows that, in 807, Daowu suffered back pain and, in the last day of the fourth month, he died at the age of sixty after a total of thirty-five summer retreats. On the fifth day of the eighth month, he was buried on the east side of the city.[34]

Zanning's chronology of Daowu provided much detailed information, even mentioning the master's height and physical features. Besides documenting Daowu's life, Zanning provided a glimpse of his Chan thought. According to him, Daowu's practice was based on the scripture of *Pusa yingluo benye jing*, and he relied on the *Avataṃsaka Sūtra* for inspiration. His teaching was sharp and powerful. Zanning quoted one passage from him: "Defilements and Purity exist together, and water and wave share the same substance. Contact with objects causes attachment and delusion; and one completely forgets to return to the root. The three worlds are equal and originally pure. If a single instant of thought does not arise, one will see the Buddha mind immediately." Judging from this short verse, Daowu's thought was consistent with the rhetoric of the Southern school. At the end of this biography, Zanning mentioned that his disciples were prominent and collectively known as "the style of Tianhuang's lineage" (*Tianhuang menfeng*).[35] Zanning listed his two disciples, Huizhen and Wenfen.[36] Zanning also mentioned that Fu Zai had written essays (not an inscription) to praise Daowu. (Although Zanning did not speak about the source of his account, I suspect that he may have based his information on Fu Zai's essays.)

Zanning did not mention Longtan Chongxin among Daowu's disciples. However, immediately after rewriting Daowu's biography, he provided a brief account of Chongxin and his relationship with Daowu. According to him, Longtan Chongxin was the son of a baker of Central-Asian-style pastry in Zhugong (Jiangling). His house happened to be in the alley where Tianhuang monastery was located. Every day, Chongxin would bring pastries to Daowu. But after Daowu ate, he always returned one piece to Chongxin and said, "I bequeath it to you to benefit your descendants." Longtan Chongxin was greatly puzzled because this piece was from the cakes he had brought to the master. When he questioned the master, Daowu replied, "It is you who brought them to me. Then, what is wrong with you?" Thus, Daowu encouraged Chongxin to join the Buddhist order and named him Chongxin. Later, Chongxin went to live at Longtan monastery in Fengyang. Because of Prime Minister Li Ao's (772–836) promotion, he became famous, and his disciple Deshan Xuanjian made Longtan Chongxin's Chan teaching prominent.[37]

Obviously, although Zanning did not mention explicitly that Chongxin was Daowu's dharma heir, the juxtaposition of both biographies in one section suggests the relationship of master and disciple. Because Zanning's work was compiled in 988, earlier than all other accounts of Tianhuang Daowu, it may have provided an archetype for abbreviated accounts of Daowu's life, including his inscription, which appeared much later.[38]

TIANHUANG DAOWU'S RECORD IN THE JINGDE CHUANDENG LU. The Caodong masters also cited Daoyuan's Jingde chuandeng lu because it contained no information about Tianwang Daowu.[39] In fascicle 14, only Tianhuang Daowu was recorded clearly as Shitou Xiqian's dharma heir. Unlike Zanning's record, Daoyuan added an encounter dialogue between Shitou and Tianhuang and clearly stated that Tianhuang reached enlightenment because of it. Furthermore, Daoyuan said that, after Tianhuang was invited to Jingzhou, Shitou's dharma flourished there. In addition, Longtan Chongxin was listed as Tianhuang's dharma heir. The majority of lamp histories, such as Qisong's Chuanfa zhengzong ji and even Huihong's Chanlin sengbao zhuan, followed the Jingde chuandeng lu, rejecting the hypothetical existence of Tianwang Daowu.

Interpolations in the Records about the Two Daowus

With regard to the emergence of Tianwang Daowu in some lamp histories, opponents of the two-Daowu theory found that these references were later interpolations. Although Huihong mentioned the anecdotes about Tianwang Daowu, information about the two Daowus was added only to the Yuan edition of the Jingde chuandeng lu and the Wudeng huiyuan.[40] For example, as the Caodong master Weizhi Zhikai pointed out, in the twenty-fourth year of the Zhizheng reign (1364), when the Wudeng huiyuan was reprinted by Yehai Ziqing of Kaiyuan monastery in Yuezhou, the two inscriptions were incorporated as notes, following Yunhe Rui's Xindeng lu.[41]

Fabrication by Zhang Shangying

Juemengtang's preface to Daguan Tanying's Wujia zongpai was an important piece of evidence, providing the most detailed account of the involvement of literati figures, such as Zhang Shangying. However, the Caodong monks, after reading this preface carefully and checking its contents against historical facts, claimed that this preface or the information provided in this preface must be false because there was an apparent anachronism. As this preface stated, Zhang Shangying requested the inscriptions from Daguan Tanying. However, the Caodong masters argued, Zhang Shangying and Daguan Tanying never met in their life time. Daguan Tanying died sixty-three (actually sixty-one according to our calculation) years earlier than Zhang Shangying did and when he died, Zhang Shangying was still a student taking civil service exams. Moreover, the current biography of Zhang Shangying indicated that in his early years, he was a radically anti-Buddhist Confucian scholar and even intended to compose an essay titled *Wufolun* (Discourse on the nonexistence of the Buddha). If so, their encounter could not have occurred as recorded in Juemengtang's preface.[42]

The Dubious Existence of Qiu Yuansu and Tianwang Monastery

The authenticity of Tianwang Daowu's inscription was one of the foci of the debate. If this inscription were proved to be false, the two-Daowu theory would naturally collapse. Opponents asserted that the author of this inscription was a fake, and Tianwang monastery never existed at all. According to some Caodong masters, in existing Tang sources and dynastic histories, there was no such official named Qiu Yuansu. The Caodong monk Xiaofeng Daran (Ni Jiaqing) authored an essay called *Xixie bian*, which examined the institutional history of the Tang. He proved that Qiu Yuansu was not one of the military commissioners in Jingzhou.[43] (As I indicated earlier, Xiaofeng Daran's claim was wrong, based on Ouyang Xiu's and Chen Si's inscriptional records.) In addition, in the preface of Weizhong Jingfu's *Famen chugui*, Xiaofeng Daran's dharma brother Shichao Daning added that, even in the local gazetteers of Hubei province, there was only Tianhuang monastery and no trace of Tianwang monastery.[44]

Plagiarized Contents of Tianwang Daowu's Inscription

The strongest internal evidence cited by the Caodong masters is the fact that the encounter story recorded in Tianwang Daowu's inscription was plagiarized from the chapter on Baima Tanzhao in the *Jingde chuandeng lu*. Baima Tanzhao was Nanquan Puyuan's disciple and lived in White Horse monastery (Baima si) in Jingnan, the same city where the two Daowus had lived.

Baima Tanzhao's biography contains the same story as Tianwang Daowu's biography does: He was thrown into the river in Jingzhou by a military commissioner. The following passage in Baima Tanzhao's biography is almost identical to Tianwang Daowu's inscription:

> The Chan master Baima Tanzhao in the south of Jingzhou often said "Happy! Happy!" But when he was about to die, he started to shout painfully. He also said that King Yama was going to grab him. The abbot asked: "When you were thrown into the river by the military commissioner, why did your complexion not change? Why are you behaving like this now?" [Baima Tanzhao,] holding the pillow, replied: "Can you tell whether I was right at that time or whether I am right now?" The abbot had no reply.[45]

Because of this similarity, the Caodong masters concluded that the inscription of Tianwang Daowu had been produced by someone who intended to flatter Zhang Shangying, the most prominent Buddhist patron at that time.

Internal Contradictions in the Two Inscriptions Discovered by Weizhi Zhikai and Huang Zongxi

In addition to finding external sources to invalidate Tianwang Daowu's inscription, the Caodong monks discovered some internal discrepancies within the texts of Tianwang Daowu's inscription. For example, the Caodong monk Weizhi Zhikai pointed out that, although most accounts of Tianwang Daowu say that he first visited Shitou Xiqian at age thirty, the *Fozu lidai tongzai* recorded that he was thirty-three when he met Shitou Xiqian.[46] For his death year, the *Wudeng huiyuan* and the *Zhiyue lu* had "the third year of the Yuanhe reign" while the *Linjian lu* and the *Fozu lidai tongzai* recorded "the thirteenth year of the Yuanhe reign." Weizhi Zhikai also spotted an anachronism that occurred when Song place names were used for Tang places. For example, he noted that Qiu Yuansu, the author of Tianwang Daowu's inscription, was recorded as the military commissioner of "Jingnan," a Song place name for a city that had been called "Jiangling" in the Tang. These discrepancies were regarded as strong internal evidence for the spurious nature of Tianwang Daowu's inscription.[47]

Internal evidence in Tianhuang Daowu's inscription also conflicted with Zanning's biography of eminent monks. Huang Zongxi represented this view based on his close reading of Zanning's *Song gaoseng zhuan*. The inscription of Tianhuang Daowu that appeared later did not add to the information that Zanning provided, except for a small discrepancy caught by Huang Zongxi.

Regarding Tianhuang Daowu's disciples, Zanning made the following record: "Monks Huizhen, and Wenfen are all serene and gentle in nature (*chanzi youxian*) and have entered [Daowu]'s chamber to receive the awakening."⁴⁸ The received inscription of Tianhuang Daowu, however, listed the disciples as follows: "His teaching has been transmitted through three generations by Huizhen, Youxian, and Wenfen." Here, the word *youxian*, meaning "being serene and gentle," was taken as a monk's name. Huang Zongxi saw this as an indication that Tianhuang Daowu's inscription was also forged:

> The so-called *Chanzi youxian* refers to Huizhen and Wenfen, meaning that their character is serene and gentle. The appended note [of *Wudeng huiyuan*] changes it to "there were three dharma heirs, namely Huizhen, Wenfen, and Youxian." Since the euphemism *youxian* was distorted to be a person's name, those who made this note did not understand the [Chinese] grammar.⁴⁹

Huang Zongxi, therefore, doubted strongly the authenticity of Tianhuang Daowu's inscription because the author read Zanning's record incorrectly and took an epithet to be a person's name. This internal evidence pointed to the possibility that Fu Zai's inscription may have been forged on the basis of Tianhuang Daowu's biography written by Zanning.

The Discovery of Deshan Xuanjian's Inscription in the Late Ming and Xuefeng Yicun's Testimony

In this debate, the lineage affiliation of Longtan Chongxin was crucial to later generations. One effective strategy for demonstrating that Longtan Chongxin was Tianhuang's heir rather than Tianwang's was to look at how Longtan Chongxin's descendants viewed their own origins: If the dharma heirs close to his era claimed that they belonged to the lineage of Qingyuan Xingsi rather than to that of Nanyue Huairang, this proved that Longtan Chongxin was Tianhuang Daowu's heir. The Caodong monks indeed found many such testimonies from historical sources. For example, Deshan Xuanjian's inscription explicitly stated that his lineage could be traced back to Tianhuang Daowu in Jingzhou.⁵⁰ However, this inscription was only discovered in 1615 at the ancient site of Mount Deshan, and its origins may not be reliable. An abbreviated inscription from the *Zhengming lu*, written by the monk Wenxue, is translated as follows:

> From Caoxi (Huineng) to Master [Xing]si of Jizhou, Shitou of Nanyue, Tianhuang of Jingzhou, and Longtan of Fengzhou, my

former master [Deshan] Xuanjian [received the dharma]. He heard
that Master Longtan was in Fengzhou and he was the second generation of Shitou's [lineage]. He packed his clothes and went [to Longtan.]
When he saw Longtan, he exclaimed, "Exhausting all mystical
arguments is equal to a tiny piece of hair in the vast space."[51]

This new piece of evidence was discovered in Wuling in the spring of 1615
by a local man named Yang He (?–1635) and his son. They visited the ancient
site of the monastery and found a discarded stele in the bushes. Although
most of the characters were corrupted, they were able to read the passage
translated above. The remaining part clearly stated that Longtan Chongxin
was Tianhuang Daowu's heir.

In addition to this new evidence, Xuefeng Yicun (822–908), another descendant of Deshan Xuanjian, claimed that he belonged to Qingyuan's line.
An episode in Xuefeng Yicun's extensive records documented a conversation
between Xuefeng and the king of the Min state in which he admitted that Deshan Xuanjian belonged to Shitou's lineage. Thus, Deshan's teacher, Longtan
Chongxin, must belong to Tianhuang Daowu.[52] Such evidence, meticulously
recorded in the *Zhengming lu*, is plentiful in Chan records composed during
the Song.[53]

C. Modern Scholarship on the Two-Daowu Theory

In modern scholarship on Chan history, the dispute about the two Daowus in
the seventeenth century has caught the attention of Chinese and Japanese
scholars, who have apparently reached a consensus that the inscription of
Tianwang Daowu should be dismissed as spurious.[54] For example, Nukariya
Kaiten marshals as many sources as possible to prove the falsity of Tianwang
Daowu's inscription. Most of his sources were mentioned in the seventeenth-
century debate. As a Sōtō priest, he readily accepts the Chinese Caodong masters' arguments, especially those posited by Weizhong Jingfu. For him, all
disputes originated from Daguan Tanying, who was ignorant about Buddhist
history, biased regarding sectarian differences, and "shameless" in making
false claims. For those Linji monks, such as Miyun Yuanwu and his followers,
who supported the two-Daowu theory, Nukariya's remarks and reprimands
are harsh and derogatory, revealing once again the sectarian nature of the debate even after three centuries.[55]

Ui Hakuju also examined this issue briefly and his view has influenced
other Japanese Sōtō scholars, such as Abe Chōichi, Suzuki Tetsuo, and Ishii

Shūdō.[56] Ui identifies several problems with Tianwang Daowu's inscription. First, although Huihong mentioned Tianwang Daowu in the *Linjian lu*, he did not accept the account as true history. In his *Chanlin sengbao zhuan* (The biographies of Chan monks), published later, Juefan Huihong still insisted on the original version of the genealogy in the *Jingde chuandeng lu*. Second, although both Guideng and Zongmi mentioned Daowu as Mazu's leading disciple, this does not mean that this Daowu refers to Tianwang Daowu. Rather, it only shows that Tianhuang Daowu had studied with both Mazu and Shitou. Third, there was a textual discrepancy between Juefan Huihong's account and Tianwang Daowu's inscription: Huihong reported that Tianwang Daowu died in the thirteenth year of the Yuanhe reign, while the inscription stated that he died in the third year of the Yuanhe reign.[57] This shows, according to Ui, that Tianwang Daowu's inscription must be false. Finally, Ui notices that Zanning's biographies of Tianhuang Daowu and Longtan Chongxin appeared earlier than Daguan Tanying's work *Wujia zongpai* and Juefan Huihong's *Linjian lu*. This means that the fabrication of Tianwang Daowu may have been a reaction to Zanning's *Song gaoseng zhuan*. Similar to Nukariya, Ui relies on Weizhong Jingfu's *Famen chugui*, which I introduced in chapter 9.

Ishii Shūdō also investigates this issue briefly. Largely based on Nukariya's and Ui's research, Ishii rejects the authenticity of Tianwang Daowu's inscription and criticizes Kokan Shiren, who supported the two-Daowu theory. Based on the fieldwork of the Sixth China Tour of Komazawa University on September 7, 1984, Ishii confirms that Tianhuang Daowu formerly lived in Mount Ziling in the Mount Caizi region of Dangyang county.[58]

Chen Yuan also examines this controversy, and his conclusion has influenced most Chinese historians. As he points out, the central piece of evidence, the inscription of Tianwang Daowu, was baseless, and Juefan Huihong's account of Tianwang Daowu should be read as an anecdote that reflected the struggle between the Linji school and the Yunmen school rather than as a serious account of history. He suspects that even Huihong did not believe in the existence of Qiu Yuansu's inscription because in his preface for his Chan genealogy, *Chanlin sengbao zhuan*, published later than the *Linjian lu*, Huihong still insisted on the original version of the genealogy in the *Jingde chuandeng lu*. According to Chen Yuan, Feiyin's error was that he relied too much on the dubious *Fozu lidai tongzai* compiled in the Yuan, which contained so much incorrect information.[59]

Qiu Yuansu's identity is crucial to this debate. However, modern historians have done no better job than Ouyang Xiu and Huang Zongxi. No historians have found any firm evidence that Qiu was indeed the military commissioner of Jingzhou. Whether or not he was the commissioner in Kuizhou, as

Ouyang Xiu and Chen Si found, is still under investigation.[60] In addition, some scholars suspect that the official Pei mentioned in Tianhuang Daowu's inscription may be Pei Zhou (?–803), who served as military commissioner of Jingnan from 792 to 803.[61] In mainland China, a new archaeological discovery has confirmed only the identity of Tianhuang Daowu. In the 1950s, Tianhuang Daowu's memorial pagoda built in the Tang was discovered in the suburb of Shashi in Hubei province. According to a short archaeological report, Tianhuang Daowu's name was carved on the pagoda, but no inscription or epitaph was discovered.[62] Based on these pieces of evidence, it is safe for modern scholars to accept Tianhuang Daowu's identity.

The most telling textual evidence may come from the earliest Chan anthology, *Zutang ji* (Patriarch hall collections), compiled in 952. This early collection of biographies contained no records about Tianwang Daowu, but Tianhuang Daowu was clearly recorded as a dharma heir of Shitou Xiqian. The record stated that he lived in Jingnan and his name was Daowu. Other than recording his encounter dialogues with Shitou, his record provided no further information. More important, his biographers stated clearly that they had not yet read his epitaph or official biography.[63] Although the *Zutang ji* did not record Longtan Chongxin's biography immediately after Tianhuang's, as Zanning did, he was recorded as Tianhuang Daowu's heir in fascicle 5. According to this record, Longtan Chongxin lived in Fenglang (a misprint for Fengzhou) prefecture. Before he entered the Buddhist order, he lived in the Tianhuang alley and baked pastries as his profession. At that time, Tianhuang Daowu practiced seated meditation in the monastery, and no one could approach him except Chongxin, who always brought ten pastries to serve Daowu. Each time, Daowu left one piece for Chongxin to bless his descendants. Later, Chongxin was converted by Daowu and reached great awakening. Despite some textual variations, these detailed accounts are similar to those in Zanning's record.[64]

Glossary

Ai Rulue 艾儒略 (Giulio Aleni, 1582–1649)
Ajikan 阿字觀
Amoghavajra 不空 (705–774)
Anchasi Lü 按察司呂, see Li Rifang
Anchasi Lü jinchi Yantong weishu kanyu 按察司呂禁飭嚴統偽書勘語
Anyin 安隱
Ayuwang (Sanskrit: Aśoka) 阿育王
Azhali jiao 阿吒力教

Bada Shanren 八大山人 (a.k.a. Zhu Da 朱耷; dharma name: Ren'an Chuanqing 仁庵傳綮, 1626–1705)
Baicheng ji 百城集
Baichi Xingyuan 百痴行元 (1611–1662)
Bailin 柏林
Baima 白馬
Baima Tanzhao 白馬曇照

Baisong Xingfeng 白松行豐 (1612–1674)
Baiting Xufa 柏亭續法 (1641–1728)
Baiyu Jingsi 百愚淨斯 (1610–1665)
Baizhang Huaihai 百丈懷海 (720–814)
Bankei Yōtaku 盤珪永琢 (1622–1693)
banyan zaju 搬演雜劇
Baochi Jizong 寶持繼總 (1606–?)
Bao'en 報恩
Baofeng 寶峰
Baofeng Mingxuan 寶峰明瑄
Baofeng Xuan 寶峰瑄
Baofeng Zhixuan 寶峰智瑄
Baohua 寶華
Baokui shuo 寶奎說
Baolin 寶林
Baolin zhuan 寶林傳
baopan 寶盤
Baoshu pagoda 保淑塔

Baozang Puchi 寶藏普持

Baozang Zongchi 寶藏總持

Baozhi 寶志

Baqiu Pavilion 八求樓

Beiyou ji 北游集

beizi 輩字

Beizong ren Nanzong fa 北宗人南宗法

Beizong wushiliu zi 北宗五十六字

Benjue 本覺

benlai wu yiwu 本来無一物

benseyu 本色語

Bianmo shuo 辯魔說

Bianrong Zhenyuan 偏融真圓
  (1506–1594)

Biantian sanshuo 辯天三說

bianwei 辨偽

Bie'an Xingtong 別庵性統

Biechuan Huizong 別傳慧宗
  (1489–1569)

biguan 閉関

biqu tiaoli 避趨條例

Biyan lu 碧岩錄

Bo'an Zhengzhi, see Xiong Kaiyuan

bore 般若

Boshan 博山, see Wuyi Yuanlai

Budong 不動

Bugan buyan 不敢不言

Cai Maode 蔡懋德 (1586–1644)

Cai Runan 蔡汝南

Can Chiyan ben 參赤岩本

can 參

Cangxue Duche 蒼雪讀徹
  (1588–1656)

Cangzhou 滄州

Cao Yinru 曹胤儒 (*hao*. Luchuan 魯川,
  zi. Ruwei 汝為)

Cao'an Weng'ao 草庵翁媼

Caodong 曹洞

Caoshan Benji 曹山本寂 (840–901)

Caoxi zhongxing lu 曹溪中興錄

Ch'oe Pu 崔溥 (1454–1504)

Chaizi 柴紫

Chan 禪

Chandeng shipu 禪燈世譜

Changqing 長青

Changsha 長沙

Changshou 長壽

Changshu 常熟

Changzhou 常州

chanku 禪窟

Chanlin kesong 禪林課誦

Chanlin sengbao zhuan 禪林僧寶傳

Chanmen risong 禪門日誦

chanyue 禪悅

chanzi youxian 禪子幽閑

Chanzong zhengmai 禪宗正脈

Chao Jiong 晁迥 (951–1034)

Chaozong Tongren 朝宗通忍
  (1604–1648)

Chen Danzhong 陳丹衷 (*jinshi*
  1643)

Chen Jidong 陳繼東

Chen Si 陳思

Chen Yuan 陳垣 (1880–1971)

Chen Zhichao 陳智超

Chenghua reign 成化 (1465–1487)

Chengzong, emperor 成宗 (r.
  1295–1307)

Chiyan 赤岩 (dharma name:
  Tongyuan 通淵)

Chongye 崇業

Chongzhen reign 崇禎 (1628–1644)

Chouzu 讐祖

Chushi Fanqi 楚石梵琦 (1296–1370)

Chuandeng zhengzong 傳燈正宗

chuanfa conglin 傳法叢林

Chuanyifa zhu 傳衣法注

chuge 出格

Chuiwan Guangzhen 吹萬廣真
  (1582–1639)

Chushan Shaoqi 楚山紹琦
  (1403–1473)

Chuyun Minghui 楚云明慧
  (1664–1735)

Cisheng 慈聖 (Madame Li, 1546–1614)

ciyun mibu 慈云密布

Cizhou Fangnian 慈舟方念 (?–1594)

Conglin Yaoshi fayu 叢林藥石法語

Conglin shixun tiaogui dayue 叢林師
  訓條規大約

Cui 崔

Cuncheng lu 存誠錄

Da Pei xiangguo zongqu zhuang 答裴
相國宗趣狀

Da Wang Weimei wen Ji Dong
  liangzong zhengduan shu 答汪魏
  美問濟洞兩宗正段書

Da Xinglong 大興隆

Da Xingshan 大興善

Da Zhuangyan jing lun 大莊嚴經論

Da'an 大庵

Dachuan 大川

Dacuo 大錯 (secular name: Qian
  Bangqi 錢邦豈, 1602–1673)

Daguan, see Zibo Zhenke

Daguan Tanying 達觀曇穎
  (989–1060)

Dahui Zonggao 大慧宗杲
  (1089–1163)

daifu 代付

daifu jiken 代付事件

daifu ronsō 代付論爭

Dajue 大覺

Dali reign 大歷 (766–780)

Damei 大梅

Dangjin fahui 當今法會

Dangui Jinshi, see Jin Bao

Dangyang 當陽

danti xiangshang yilu 單提向上一路

Danxia Tianran 丹霞天然 (738–824)

Danxia Zichun 丹霞子淳 (1064–1117)

Danyuan 眈源

Daoheng 道衡

Daowu. See Tianhuang Daowu and
  Tianwang Daowu

Daoyuan 道原

Daozhe Chaoyuan 道者超元
  (1599–1662)

Dapu 大埔

Daqi 打七

Daqian Putong 大千普同

dasi xichang youren 大似戲
  場優人

Datian Tongli 達天通理 (1701–1782)

Daxue qianlü 大學千慮

Dayang Jingxuan 大陽警玄
  (943–1027)

Dayi juemi lu 大義覺迷錄

Dayu 大愚

Dayuan 大圓

Dayi Yuanlai, see Wuyi Yuanlai

Dazizai 大自在

Deng Huoqu 鄧豁渠 (1489–1578?)

dengshi 燈史

Dengzhou 鄧州

Deqing 德慶

Deqing, see Hanshan Deqing

Deshan 德山

Deshan shutan 德山暑譚

Deshan Xuanjian 德山宣鑒
  (782–865)

Deyi 德異

Dinghai 丁亥

Dinghu 鼎湖

Dingmu Hongche 頂目弘徹
(1588–1648)
Dingzu tu 定祖圖
Dodo. See Duoduo
Dōgen 道元 (1200–1253)
Dong Han 董含 (*zi*. Rong'an 榕庵)
Dong Hu 董狐
Dong Qichang 董其昌 (1553–1636)
Donggao Xinyue. See Xinyue
Xingchou
Donglin 東林
Dongming 東明
Dongming Huiri 東溟慧日
(1291–1379)
Dongming Huichan 東明慧昌
(1372–1441)
Dongshan Liangjia 洞山良价
(807–869)
Dongyang 東陽
Dongyuan 東苑
Dufeng Jishan 毒峰季善 (1443?–1523)
Duguan Xingjing 獨冠行敬
(1613–1672)
Dumen 度門
Duni shuo 杜逆說
Duoduo 多鐸 (1614–1649)
duowen 多聞
dushuren 讀書人
Duxie shuo 杜邪說
Duyuan Xiao 都院蕭, see Xiao
Qiyuan
Duzhan Xingying 獨湛性瑩
(1628–1706)

E'ertai 鄂爾泰 (1680–1745)
E'jiao 惡狡
E'mei 峨嵋
Er'mi Mingfu 爾密明澓
(1591–1642)

Fa Xuedou gaoshi 發雪竇告示
Fadeng Murong 法燈慕容
Faguo 法果
Fahai 法海
Fahua jing wenju 法華經文句
fajuan 法卷
Famen chugui 法門除宄
Fang Yizhi 方以智 (dharma name:
Wuke Dazhi 無可大智 or Hongzhi
弘智; *hao*. Moli 墨歷 or Yaodi 藥地
1611–1671)
fang 房
fangseng 房僧
fangtou 房頭
fangyankou 放焰口
fannao 煩惱
Fanwang jing 梵網經
Faqin 法欽 (714–792)
Faqing 法慶
fashen 法身
Fayan 法眼
Fayan Wenyi 法眼文益 (885–958)
Fayu Zhongguang 法雨仲光
(a.k.a. Rusong 如嵩, *hao*. Foshi
佛石, 1569–1636)
Fayuan 法遠
Fazang 法藏 (643–712)
Fazhou Daoji 法舟道濟 (1487–1560)
Feiyin ting 費隱亭
Feiyin Tongrong 費隱通容
(a.k.a. Mingmi 明密, Jingshan
Rong 徑山容, 1593–1662)
Feiyin chanshi bieji 費隱禪師別集
Feng Ji 馮楫 (?–1153)
Feng Fang 丰坊 (1493–1566)
Fenghua 奉化
Fenglang 灃朗
Fengyang 灃陽
Fengzhou 灃州

Fenyang Shanzhao 紛陽善昭
   (947–1024)

Fofa zhenglun 佛法正輪

Foyan Qingyuan 佛眼清遠

Fozu gangmu 佛祖綱目

Fozu lidai tongzai 佛祖歷代通載

Fu Dashi 傅大士 (497–569)

Fu Huang sili shu 復黃司理書

Fu, prince 福王 (Zhu Yousong 朱由
   崧, 1607–1646)

Fu Zai 符載

Fu River 涪江

Fuqing 福清

Fumonji 普門寺

Fupeng 福彭 (?–1748)

Furong Daokai 芙蓉道楷 (1043–1118)

Fushe 復社

Fuyan 福嚴

fuzi 拂子

Gao Qizhuo 高其倬 (1676–1738)

Gaofeng Yuanmiao 高峰原妙
   (1238–1295)

Gaoming 高明

Gaoquan Xingdun 高泉性潡
   (1633–1695)

Gaoshi 告示

Gaoyuan Mingyu 高原明昱 (fl. 1612)

Gejun hufa shang Fu Si Dao
   gongcheng 各郡護法上撫司道公呈

geliang 格量

genei 格內

Geng Dingli 耿定理 (?-1584)

Geng Dingxiang 耿定向 (1524–1596)

Gengshen 庚申

Genxin Xingmi 亙信行彌
   (1603–1659)

gewu 格物

Goha itteki zu 五派一滴圖

Goke benshō 五家辨正

Goke ben 五家辨

Gomizunoo 後水尾 (1596–1680)

Gong'an 公安

Gongchen 拱辰

Gu Xiancheng 顧憲成 (1550–1612)

Gu Yanwu 顧炎武 (1613–1682)

Guan Zhidao 管志道 (1536–1608)

Guangrun 廣潤

Guangshan 廣善

Guangxiao 光孝

Guhang Daozhou 古航道舟
   (1585–1655)

Gui miujian zhanglao 規繆見長老

Guideng 歸登

Guifeng 圭峰, see Zongmi

Guishan Lingyou 溈山靈祐 (771–853)

Guiyang 溈仰

Guizong 歸宗

Gulin 古林

Guo Limei 郭黎眉 (a.k.a. Guo
   Ningzhi 郭凝之; *hao.* Tiandi di
   zhuren 天地地主人)

Guo Ningzhi, see Guo Limei

Guoqing 国清

Guoyi 国一

Gushan Shenyan 鼓山神宴 (862–938)

Gushan xuanyao guangji 鼓山玄
   要廣集

Gushan 鼓山

Guxin Ruxin 古心如馨(1541–1615)

Guzupai 古祖派

Hai 亥

Haiyan 海鹽

Haiyin 海印

Haizhou Ci 海舟慈

Haizhou Puci 海舟普慈
   (1393–1461)

Haizhou Yongci 海舟永慈
  (1394–1466)
Hangzhou 杭州
Hanlin 翰林
Hanpu Xingcong 憨樸性聰
  (1610–1666)
Hanshan Deqing 憨山德清
  (1546–1623)
Hanshan 寒山
Hansong Zhicao 寒松智操
  (1626–1686)
Hanyue Fazang 漢月法藏 (*zi.* Yumin
  於密, 1573–1635)
Hà-Trung 河中
He Xinyin 何心隱 (1517–1579)
Hengyang 衡陽
Hong Chengchou 洪承疇
  (1593–1665)
Hongfa quan 弘法泉
Hongjie fayi 弘戒法儀
Hongli 弘厲. See Qianlong
Hongren 弘忍 (600?–674?)
Hongzhi reign 弘治
  (1488–1506)
Hongzhi Zhengjue 宏智正覺
  (1091–1157)
Hongzhou 洪州
houji 後集
Houlu 後錄
Huaiguang Can 懷光燦
Huaiyi 懷誼
Huang Duanbo 黃端伯 (*zi.* Yuan-
  gong 元公, *hao.* Hai'an Daoren 海
  岸道人, 1579–1645)
Huang Ming gaoseng jilue 皇明高
  僧集略
Huang sili kaodig zongpai gaoshi
  黃司理考訂宗派告示
Huang sili Yuangong fa Xuedou
  gaoshi 黃司理元公發雪竇告示

Huang Taiji 皇太極 (Abahai,
  1592–1643)
Huang Yuangong. See Huang
  Duanbo
Huang Yuqi 黃毓祺 (1579–1649)
Huang Zhen 黃貞
Huang Zongxi 黃宗羲 (1610–1695)
Huangbo 黃檗
Huangbo Xiyun 黃檗希運
  (776–856)
Huanglong Huinan 黃龍慧南
  (1002–1069)
Huangniu xia 黃牛峽
Huangtong reign 皇統 (1141–1149)
Huanxiu Changrun 幻休常潤
  (a.k.a. Daqian 大千, ?–1585)
Huanyou Zhengchuan 幻有正傳
  (1549–1614)
huatou or *hua-t'ou* 話頭
Huayan 華嚴
Huayue 華岳
Hué 順化
Hufa zhengdeng lu 護法正燈錄
Huguo 護國
Huiguang Benzhi 慧光本智
  (1555–1605)
huihu dangtou yuji shicheng 回互當頭
  語忌十成
Huiji Yuanxi 晦机元熙 (1238–1319)
Huilin 慧林 (*hao.* Wansong 萬松,
  1482–1557)
Huineng 慧能 (638–713)
Huishan Jiexian 晦山戒顯 (*zi.*
  Yuanyun 愿雲, 1610–1672)
Huishi jiatu 繪事家圖
Huitai Yuanjing 晦臺元鏡
  (1577–1630)
huitu 回途
Huixin 惠昕
Huizhen 慧真

Huizhong 慧忠, see Nanyang
 Huizhong
huochang 火場
Huqiu Shaolong 虎丘紹隆
 (1077–1136)
Husheng an 護生庵

ICang-skya Khutuɤtu Ngag-dbang-
 blo-bzang-chos-ldan, see Zhangjia
 hutuketu Awangluosangquedan

jiachi 加持
Jiajing reign 嘉靖 (1522–1566)
Jialing Xingyin 迦陵性音
 (a.k.a. Chuiyu 吹餘, 1671–1726)
Jianchang 建昌
Jianfu Chenggu 薦福承古
 (970–1045)
Jiang 蔣
jiang 講
Jiang Yueguang 姜曰廣
jianghui 講會
Jiangling yin youpuye 江陵尹右僕射
Jiangling 江陵
Jiangnan 江南
jiangxi pingchang 講習評唱
Jianjiang Hongren 漸江弘仁
 (1610–1664)
Jianmo bianyi lu 揀魔辨異錄
Jiansou Kongzheng 劍叟空晟 (1593–?)
Jianyue Duti 見月讀體 (1601–1679)
Jianzhong reign 建中 (780–801)
jiao 教
Jiao Hong 焦竑 (1540–1620)
Jiaoshan 焦山
Jiaowai biechuan 教外別傳
Jiaoyou lun 交友論
Jiashan Shanhui 夾山善會
Jiatai pudenglu 嘉泰普燈錄
jiawu 甲午

Jiaxing 嘉興
jiayi liangzong dahong 甲乙兩宗大哄
Jichang 濟昌
jietuo 解脫
Jigu lu 集古錄
Jilun Chaoyong 霽崙超永
Jin 晉
Jin Bao 金堡 (dharma name: Dangui
 Jinshi 澹歸今釋, 1614–1680)
Jin Sheng 金聲 (zi. Zhengxi 正希,
 1598–1645)
Jinchi Yantong weishu kanyu 禁飭嚴
 統偽書勘語
Jing Qian 敬騫
Jingchao, see Qi Junjia
Jingde chuandeng lu 景德傳燈錄
jingfo 敬佛
Jingkou 景口
Jingling 竟陵
Jingnan Jiedushi 荊南節度史
Jingshan 徑山
Jingyin Zijue 淨因自覺
Jingzhong jianguo xudeng lu 靖中建國
 續燈錄
Jingzhou 荊州
Jingzhou Tianwangsi zhongxing
 beiji 荊州天王寺中興碑記
Jinling facha zhi 金陵梵刹志
Jinshan 金山
jinshi 進士
Jinsu fanzheng lu 金粟反正錄
Jinsu 金粟
Jiqi Hongchu 繼起弘儲 (hao.
 Tuiweng 退翁, 1605–1672)
Jishan 集善
Jiukuang bianyu 救狂砭語
jiyuan wenda 機緣問答
Jizong songyu 濟宗頌語
Jizhou 吉州
Jizu 雞足

Jubo Jiheng 巨渤濟恆 (1605–1666)

Jude Hongli 具德弘禮 (1600–1667)

Juding 居頂 (?–1404)

Jue'an 覺岸 (1286–?)

Juefan Huihong 覺範慧洪 (1071–1128)

Juelang Daosheng 覺浪道盛 (hao. Zhangren 杖人, 1592–1659)

Juemengtang 覺夢堂

junchen wuwei 君臣五位

junji dachen 軍機大臣

Juping shuo 劇評說

juren 舉人

Jushō 壽昌

Kaigu lu 慨古錄

Kaiō Hōkō 晦翁寶曷 (1635–1712)

kaitang shuofa 開堂説法

Kaixian 開先

Kangxi reign 康熙 (1662–1692)

Keirin Sūshin 桂林崇琛 (1652–1728)

Keizuiji 慶瑞寺

Kita Genki 喜多元規

kōan or gong'an, k'ung-an 公案

Kokan Shiren 虎關師鍊 (1278–1346)

Kongdong 崆峒

Konggu Jinglong 空谷景隆 (1387–1466)

Kongyin Zhencheng 空印鎮澄 (1547–1617)

Kuaiji 會稽

kuangchan 狂禪

Kuangyuan Benkao 鑛圓本犒

Kuizhou 夔州

Kuncan 髡殘 (dharma name: Zutang Dagao 祖堂大杲, 1612–1673)

lanfu feiren 濫付非人

Lanzhai houji 嬾齋后集

Lao 嶗

laotudi 老徒弟

Laozi 老子

Lengyan guanjian 楞嚴管見

Lengyan huijie 楞嚴會解

Lengyan 楞嚴

li 理

Li'an 理安 (a.k.a. Nanjian 南澗)

Li Ao 李翱 (772–836)

Li Jifu 李吉甫 (758–814)

Li Madou 利瑪竇 (Matteo Ricci, 1552–1610)

Li Rifang 李日芳

Li Tongxuan 李通玄 (a.k.a Zhaobai 棗柏, or Fangshan 方山, 647–740)

Li Yisun 李貽孫

Li Zhi 李贄 (a.k.a. Longhu 龍湖 or Wenling 溫陵, 1527–1602)

Li Zhongzi 李仲梓

Li Zhushan 李朱山

Li Zicheng 李自成 (1605–1645)

Lianchi 蓮池, see Yunqi Zhuhong

Liangshan 梁山

liangzhi 良知

lianmochan 煉魔場

Liji Daoqiu 離際道丘 (1586–1685)

Lin Li. See Muchen Daomin

Lin Zhifan 林之蕃

Linggu 靈古

Lingyin Dachuan 靈隱大川

Lingyin Huishan Xian heshang quanji 靈隱晦山顯和尚全集

Linji lu 臨濟錄

Linji Yixuan 臨濟義玄 (?–867)

Linji zhengzong 臨濟正宗

Linji zongzhi 臨濟宗旨

Linjian lu 林間錄

Liu Daozhen 劉道貞 (zi. Moxian 墨仙)

Liu Shisong 劉詩嵩 (1940–2002)

Liu Xianting 劉獻庭 (zi. Jizhuang 繼莊, 1648–1695)

Liu Zongzhou 劉宗周 (1578–1645)

Longchang 龍場

Longchi 龍池

Longhu 龍湖

Longhu 龍虎

Longqing reign 隆慶 (1567–1572)

Longtan Chongxin 龍潭崇信

Longwu reign 隆武 (1645–1646)

Longxi 龍溪

Longxing biannian tonglu 隆興編年通論

Longzang 龍藏

Lou Jinyuan 婁近垣 (1689–1776)

Lü 呂. See Li Rifang

Lü Liuliang 呂留良 (1629–1683)

Lü Xiaqing 呂夏卿

Lü Zuqian 呂祖謙 (1137–1181)

Lü'an Benyue 旅庵本月 (?–1676)

Lümen zuting luizhi 律門祖庭匯誌

Lüzong dengpu 律宗燈譜

Lu, regent 魯監国 (Zhu Yihai 朱以海, 1618–1662)

Lu'an Putai 魯庵普泰 (a. k. a. Lushan 魯山, fl. 1511)

Luling 廬陵

Lumen Zijue 鹿門自覺 (?–1117)

Lun'an Chaokui 輪庵超揆

Luo Rufang 羅汝芳 (1515–1588)

Luofu 洛浦

Luohan 羅漢

Luoyang 洛陽

lupan 露盘

Lushan 廬山

Luzhou 瀘州

Ma Shiqi 馬世奇 (1584–1644)

Ma Shiying 馬世英

Ma'anshan 馬鞍山

Macheng 麻城

Mafeng 馬峰

mangchan 盲禪

Manpukuji 萬福寺

Maoxi Xingsen 茆溪行森 (1614–1677)

Mazu Daoyi 馬祖道一 (709–788)

Meng'an Chaoge 夢庵超格 (1639–1708)

Mengshan 蒙山

Mengshan shishi yi 蒙山施食儀

Mengtang Tan'e 夢堂曇噩 (1285–1373)

Mi'an Xianjie 密庵咸傑 (1118–1186)

mianbing qincheng 面秉親承

Miaofeng Zhenjue 妙峰真覺 (*hao.* Baisong 百松 1537–1589)

Miaoxinsi (Myōshinji) 妙心寺

Min 閩

Mingjue 明覺

Mingmi. See Feiyin Tongrong

Ming shi 明史

Ming shilu 明實錄

Mingzhou 明州

Mingzong zhengwei 明宗證偽

Mingzong zhengwei xu 明宗證偽序

Minyu 憫愚

Minzhong zhu hufa gongxi 閩中諸護法公檄

Mitō 水戶

miyun mibu 密雲彌布

Miyun Yuanwu 密雲圓悟 (a.k.a. Tiantong 天童 or Mizu 密祖, 1566–1642)

mochan 魔禪

Moming 末明

Mozi 墨子

Mu Konghui 穆孔暉 (*jinshi* 1505)

Muchen Daomin 木陳道忞 (Lin Li 林蕊, 1596–1674)

Muyun Tongmen 牧雲通門 (1599–1671)

Nanjio Bunyū 南條文雄 (1849–1927)
Nanming Huiguang 南明慧廣 (?–1620)
Nanquan Puyuan 南泉普愿 (748–834)
Nanshan zhengzong 南山正宗
Nanshan zongtong 南山宗統
Nanxun lu 南詢錄
Nanyang Huizhong 南陽慧忠 (?–775)
Nanyue Huairang 南岳懷讓 (677–744)
Nguyên Phúc Chu 阮福週 (1674–1725)
ni 譨
Nianhua 拈花
Nichi'an Itto 日庵一東 (?–1486)
Ningbo 寧波
nongchan 農禪

Ōbaku. See Huangbo
Oboi 鰲拜 (Aobai, ?–1669)
Ouyang Jingwu 歐陽竟無 (1871–1943)
Ouyang Xiu 歐陽修 (1007–1072)
Ouyi Zhixu 藕益智旭 (Zhong Shisheng 鈡始聲 or Zhong Sheng 鈡聲, 1599–1655)

Pan Huang Yuangong Tianhuang Daowu chanshi kao 判黃元公天皇道悟禪師考
Pan Lei 潘耒 (1646–1708)
Pan Zenghong 潘曾纮 (*jinshi* 1616)
Panshan 盤山
Panshi 判師
Panyu 判語
Pei 裴
Pei Zhou 裴冑 (?–803)
Pimiu shuo xu 闢謬說序
Pimiu shuo 闢謬說
Pingyang 平陽
Pi wangjiu lueshuo 闢妄救略說
Poshan Haiming 破山海明 (1577–1666)
Prajñātāra 般若多羅
Puhui 普慧
Puji 普寂 (651–739)
Puming Miaoyong 普明妙用 (1586–1642)
Pusa yingluo benye jing 菩薩瓔珞本業經
Puyang 普仰

qi 契
Qi Bansun 祁班孫 (dharma name: Zhoulin Ming 咒林明, 1632–1673)
Qi Biaojia 祁彪佳 (a.k.a. Shipei 世培 or Huzi 虎子, 1602–1645)
Qi Chenghan 祁承㸁 (written as [火業], 1565–1628)
Qi Junjia 祁駿佳 (*zi*. Jichao 驥超, dharma name: Jingchao 淨超)
qi pi 七闢
qi shu 七書
Qi Xiongjia 祁熊佳
Qi Zhijia 祁豸佳
Qian Bangqi, see Dacuo
Qian Lucan 錢陸燦 (1612–1698)
Qian Qianyi 錢謙益 (*zi*. Muzhai 牧齋, 1582–1664)
Qian Sule 錢素樂 (1606–1648)
Qian Yiben 錢一本 (1539–1610)
qianji 前集
Qianlong 乾隆 (1711–1799, r. 1736–1795)
Qianming 乾明
qiansengguo 千僧鍋
Qianshan 千山

Qianzi wen 千字文

qinggui 清規

Qingchu sengzheng ji 清初僧諍記

Qingliang Wenyi 清涼文益
(885–958)

Qingyuan 青原

Qingyuan Xingsi 青原行思 (?–740)

Qingzhou 青州

Qingzhou Yibian 青州一辯
(a.k.a. Xibian 希辯, 1081–1149)

Qingshan 磬山. See Tianyin Yuanxiu

Qisong 契嵩 (1007–1072)

Qiu Yuansu 丘元素 (a.k.a. Qiu
Xuansu 丘玄素)

Qiyuan Xinggang 祇園行剛
(1597–1654)

Qu Dajun 屈大均 (dharma name:
Yiling Jinzhong 一靈今种,
1630–1696)

Qu Ruji 瞿汝稷 (1548–1610)

Qu Shigu 瞿式穀 (1593-?)

Qu Shisi 瞿式耜 (1590–1651)

Quan Deyu 權德輿 (759–818)

Quan Tang wen 全唐文

Quanzhou 泉州

Quôc-Ân 國恩

Rehe 熱河

R'yohae-rok 漂海錄

Rinzai shōshū 臨濟正宗

Risshō Kōseikai 立正佼成會

rixia 日下

Rol-pa'i-rdo-rje, see Ruobiduoji

Ruchuan Chaosheng 如川超盛

Ruibai Mingxue 瑞白明雪 (1584–1641)

Ruifeng 瑞峰

Ruiguang 瑞光 (dharma name:
Faxiang 法祥, 1533–1610)

Ruiyan Guanglei 銳嵒廣鐳
(1369–1481)

Rujin 如岑 (1425–?)

Rulai Chan 如來禪

Rulai qingjing Chan 如來清淨禪

Runing 汝寧

Ruo'an Tongwen 箬庵通問
(1604–1655)

Ruobiduoji 若必多吉 (1717–1786)

Ruomei Zhiming 若昧智明
(1569–1631)

Ruoshen Daoren 若深道人

Ruoshui Chaoshan 若水超善

Ryōkei Shōsen 龍溪性潛 (1602–1670)

Sakugen Shūryō 策彥周良
(1501–1579)

San chun ji 三蠢記

San xiansheng yishu 三先生逸書

sandianyi 三點伊

Sanfeng zhenzi 三峰真子

Sanfeng zongpai 三峰宗派

Sanji Guangtong 三際廣通

sanji sanhan 三擊三撼

sanjiao heyi 三教合一

sanlu 三錄

Sanmu Zhiyuan 三目智淵

Sanshan Denglai 三山燈來
(1614–1685)

Sansheng Huiran 三聖慧然

santan fangbian shoushou 三壇方便
授受

Sanmei Jiguang 三昧寂光
(1580–1645)

sanxuan sanyao 三玄三要

Sanyi Mingyu 三宜明愚 or 盂
(1599–1665)

Seng lu si 僧錄司

Sengzhao 僧肇 (384–414)

Setsushu 攝州

Shanci Tongji 山茨通際
(1608–1645)

Shandao 善導 (613–681)

Shangcheng 商城

shangtang 上堂

Shanhu lin 珊瑚林

Shanquan 善權

Shanweng Min chanshi suinian zipu
山翁忞禪師隨年自譜

Shaolin lianfang bei 少林聯芳碑

Shaoxing 紹興

Shaoyang laoren de yi jue 韶陽老人
得一橛

Shaozhou 韶州

She county 歙縣

She Changji 佘常吉 (zi. Yongning
永寧)

Shemo 攝魔

Shen Defu 沈德福 (1578–1642)

Shen Yiguan 沈一貫 (1531–1615)

Shengchao poxie ji 聖朝破邪集

Sheng'en wendao lu 聖恩問道錄

Sheng'en 聖恩

Shenyang 瀋陽

shengyuan 生員

Shenhui 神會 (684–758)

Shennü 神女

Shenxiu 神秀 (606?–706)

Shenyan 神宴. See Gushan Shenyan

Shi can chan qie yao 示參禪切要

Shichao Daning 石潮大寧 (?–1720)

Shide 拾得

Shilian Dashan 石濂大汕 (1633–1702)

Shiqi shi xiangjie 十七史詳節

Shishi jigu lue 釋氏稽古略

Shishi tongjian 釋氏通鑒

Shitao Yuanji 石濤元濟 or Daoji 道濟
(a.k.a. Kugua Heshang 苦瓜和尚,
1630–1708)

Shitou Xiqian 石頭希遷 (700–790)

Shiyu Mingfang 石雨明方
(1593–1648)

Shizong 世宗. See Yongzheng

Shongjiang 松江

Shou'an Zhong 守庵中

Shouchang 壽昌

Shoujie bian 授戒辯

Shoulengyan jing 首楞嚴經

Shouzhao 受昭 (*zi.* Dacheng 達澄)

Shouzun Yuanzhao 壽尊源昭
(Vietnamese: Tho Tôn Nguyên-
Thiêu, 1647–1729)

Shu *Chandeng shipu* hou 書禪燈世
譜后

Shuangtou dujie 雙頭獨結

shuangxiangma 雙象馬

Shuijian Huihai 水鑑慧海
(1626–1687)

shuji 書記

Shunzhi 順治 (Fulin 福臨, 1638–
1661, r. 1644–1661)

Shuoyuan wen 鎁原問

Shuquan ji 樹泉集

sifa jiaojia 四法交加

sifa weixiang 嗣法未詳

siguan 死関

Sijun hufa xiangshen shang Fu Si
Dao zhugongzu qi 四郡護法鄉紳上
撫司道諸公祖啟

Siku quanshu 四庫全書

Sima 駟馬

Sima Guang 司馬光 (1019–1086)

Siming Zhili 四明知禮 (960–1028)

sishu 嗣書

Songgu baize 頌古百則

Song 嵩

Song gaoseng zhuan 宋高僧傳

Su'an Zhenjie 素庵真界 (1519–1593)

Śubhakarasiṃha 善無畏 (637–735)

Ta-hui, see Dahui Zonggao

Taiping 太平

Tairu Minghe 汰如明河 (1588–1640)

Taixu 太虛 (1890–1947)

Taiyuan 太原

Taizhou 泰州

Tan Yuanchun 譚元春 (1585–1637)

Tang Fangzhen nianbiao 唐方鎮年表

Tang Shen 唐伸

Tang Tai 唐泰 (dharma name:
  Dandang Tonghe 擔當通荷 or
  Puhe 普荷, 1593–1673)

Tangzong 談宗

Tanji Hongren 潭吉弘忍
  (1599–1638)

Tanjing jielu or *Liuzu tanjing jielu* 壇
  經節錄 or 六祖壇經節錄

Tanzhe 潭柘

Tanzhu 曇翥

Tao Shiling 陶奭齡 (?–1640)

Tao Wangling 陶望齡 (*zi.* Zhouwang
  周望, *hao.* Shikui 石簣,
  1562–1609)

Thâp-Tháp Di-Đà 拾塔彌陀

ti 體

Tian er 天二

Tian yi 天一

Tianbao reign 天寶 (742–756)

Tianhuang Daowu 天皇道悟
  (748–807)

Tianhuang menfeng 天皇門風

Tianhuang Tianwang kao 天皇天
  王考

Tianjian reign 天監 (502–519)

Tianjie 天界

Tianjuan reign 天眷 (1138–1140)

Tianli Xingzhen 天笠行珍
  (1624–1694)

Tianning 天寧

Tianqi Benrui 天奇本瑞 (?–1503)

Tianran Hanshi 天然函昰
  (1608–1685)

Tianru Weize 天如惟則 (1276–1354)

Tiansheng guangdeng lu 天聖廣燈錄

Tiantong 天童

Tiantong quanlu 天童全錄

Tiantong Rujing 天童如淨
  (1163–1228)

Tiantong zhishuo 天童直說

Tiantong Zongjue 天童宗珏
  (1091–1162)

Tiantongsi seng 天童寺僧

Tianwang Daowu 天王道悟 (737–818
  or 727–808)

Tianxi Shoudeng 天溪受登 (*zi.*
  Jingchun 景淳, *hao.* Huanyi 幻依,
  1607–1675)

Tianyi 天衣

Tianyin Yuanxiu 天隱圓修
  (1575–1635)

Tianzhu Manxiu 天柱滿秀 (?–1568)

tichi 提持

Tiefosi 鉄佛寺

Tieqin tongjian lou 鐵琴銅劍樓

Tingjun 廷俊 (*zi.* Yongzhang 用彰;
  hao. Lanweng 嬾翁; ?–1368)

Tongcheng 桐城

Tongguan 銅官

Tonghe 通荷, see Tang Tai

Tongji, see Shanci Tongji

Tongjian gangmu 通鑑綱目

tongxin 童心

Tongxuan 通玄

Touzi Datong 投子大同 (819–914)

Touzi Yiqing 投子義青 (1032–1083)

Tu Long 屠隆 (1542–1605)

Vajrabodhi 金剛智 (671?–741)

waidao 外道

waiji 外集

Wanfeng Shiwei 萬峰時蔚 (1313–1381)

Wang An'shi 王安石 (1021–1086)

Wang Daokun 汪道昆 (1525–1593)

Wang Gen 王艮 (1483–1540)

Wang Gu 王谷

Wang Guocai 王國才

Wang Ji 王畿 (1498–1583)

Wang Wei 王罍

Wang Weimei 汪魏美

Wang Weizhang 王維章

Wang Yangming 王陽明 (1472–1529)

Wangshan Ti 王山體

Wanli reign 萬曆 (1573–1620)

Wanshou 万壽

Wansong Xingxiu 萬松行秀 (1166–1246)

Wei, clerk 吏科魏

Wei Qu 韋璩

Weibai 惟白

weichan 偽禪

Weideng lu 衛燈錄

Weifu Dajue 魏府大覺

Weilin Daopei 為霖道霈 (1615–1702)

weixin jingtu 唯心淨土

Weiyinwang fo 威音王佛

Weiyuzi 維魚子

Weizhi Zhikai 惟直智楷

Weizhong Jingfu 位中淨符 (a.k.a. Baiyan 白巖)

wen 文

Wenfen 文賁

Wenhai Fuju 文海福聚 (1686–1765)

Wenjue 文覺

Wenxiu 文琇 (1345–1418)

Wenxue 文學

Wu 巫

Wu county 吳縣

Wu Dechang 吳德常 (*zi.* Shizheng 世徵)

Wu Ding 吳定

Wu, emperor of the Liang dynasty 梁武帝

Wu Shaoyao 吳紹堯 (1939–1985)

Wu Tong 吳侗

Wu'ai Puzhi 無礙普智 (?–1408)

Wubian 無邊

Wubuqian 物不遷

Wubuqian zhengliang lun 物不遷証量論

Wubuqian zhengliang zheng 物不遷証量証

wudai diechu 五代叠出

Wudeng huiyuan 五燈會元

Wudeng huiyuan xulue 五燈會元續略

Wudeng shifei liangqian shuo 五燈是非兩遣說

Wudeng yantong 五燈嚴統

Wudeng yantong jiehuo pian 五燈嚴統解惑篇

Wufengta 無縫塔

Wufolun 無佛論

wuhang 五行

Wuhuan Xingchong 無幻性冲 (1539–1611)

Wuji Mingxin 無極明信 (1512–1574)

Wuji Zhenghui 無跡正誨 (?–1628)

Wujia yulu 五家語錄

Wujia zongpai 五家宗派

Wujin Chuandeng 無盡傳燈 (1554–1628)

Wuke Dazhi. See Fang Yizhi

Wulin chongxiu Baoguoyuan ji 武林重修報國院記

Wuling 武陵

Wulou Chuanping 無漏傳瓶 (1565–1614)

Wulun 五論

Wuming Huijing 無明慧經 (1548–1618)

Wunian Shengxue 無念勝學 (1326–1406)

Wunian Shenyou 無念深有 (1544–1627)

wushizhi 無師智

Wuwen Cong 無聞聰

Wuwen Zhengcong 無聞正聰

Wuwen Mingcong 無聞明聰 (?–1543)

Wuxi 無錫

Wuyi Yuanlai 無異元來 (a.k.a Dayi 大艤, 1575–1630)

Wuyue 吳越

Wuzhen pian 悟真篇

Wuzhou 婺州

Wuzhun Shifan 無準師範 (1178–1249)

Wuzong jiu 五宗救

Wuzong lu 五宗錄

Wuzong pi 五宗闢

Wuzong yuan 五宗原

Wuzong yuanliu tu 五宗源流圖

Xi'an 西安

Xi'e cao 惜蛾草

xiang gewai zhuanshen 向格外轉身

xiang shang yi zhuo 向上一著

Xiangya Xingting 象崖性挺 (1598–1651)

Xiangyan Zhixian 香嚴智閑 (?–898)

Xiangyun piyu 詳允批語

Xiangzhou 襄州

Xiangzong bayao 相宗八要

Xiansheng 顯聖

Xiao Qiyuan 蕭起元

Xiaofeng Daran 笑 (嘯) 峰大然 (Ni Jiaqing 倪嘉慶, 1589–1659, *jinshi* 1622)

Xiaoshan Zongshu 小山宗書 (*zi.* Dazhang 大章, 1500–1567)

Xiaoyan Bao zu nanbei ji 笑嚴寶祖南北集

Xiaoyan Debao 笑嚴德寶 (*zi.* Yuexin 月心, 1512–1581)

Xielülang 協律郎

Xifeng Shen 西峰深

Xincheng 新城

Xindeng lu 心燈錄

Xing Jixian 邢吉先

Xinghua 興化

Xinghua Cunjiang 興化存獎 (830–888)

xingju 性具

Xinglang Daoxiong 星朗道雄 (1598–1673)

Xingtong 行通 (1097–1165)

Xingyi 行義 (*zi.* Poyun 破雲)

Xinxu gaoseng zhuan siji 新續高僧傳四集

xinxue 心學

Xinyue Xingchou 心越興儔 (a.k.a. Donggao Xinyue 東皋心越, 1639–1695)

Xiong Kaiyuan 熊開元 (dharma name: Bo'an Zhengzhi 檗庵正志, 1599–1676)

Xiong Shili 熊十力 (1885–1968)

Xishan jietai si 西山戒台寺

Xixia 西夏

Xixie bian yin 熄邪辯引

Xixie bian 熄邪辨

Xiyu 西余

Xiyun 西雲

Xu Changzhi 徐昌治 (*hao.* Jinzhou 覲周, dharma name: Tongchang 通昌, a.k.a. Wuyi Daoren 無依道人, 1582–1672)

Xu chuandeng lu 續傳燈錄

Xu Fuyuan 許孚遠 (*zi.* Jing'an 敬庵, 1535–1604)

Xu Guanfu 徐觀復

Xu Jie 徐階 (1494–1574)

xu lian fang 續聯芳

Xu Guangqi 徐光啓 (1562–1633)

Xu Qirui 徐啓睿

Xu Wei 徐渭 (1521–1593)

Xu Zhiyuan 徐之垣 (*zi.* Xinwei 心韋, *jinshi* 1625)

Xuande reign 宣德 (1426–1435)

Xuanhe reign 宣和 (1119–1126)

Xuansha Shibei 玄沙師備

Xudeng zhengtong 續燈正統

Xue Cai 薛寀 (1598–1665)

Xue Jian 薛簡

Xuedou 雪竇

Xuedou Chongxian 雪竇重顯 (980–1052)

Xuedou Zhijian 雪竇智鑑 (1105–1192)

Xuefeng guanglu 雪峰廣錄

Xuefeng Yicun 雪峰義存 (822–908)

Xueguan Dao'an 雪關道闇 (1585–1637)

Xuehong Yuanxin 雪鴻圓 (元) 信 (1664–1750)

Xuejiao Yuanxin 雪嶠圓信 (*hao.* Yufeng 語風, 1570–1647)

Xuelang Hong'en 雪浪洪恩 (*zi.* Sanhuai 三懷, 1545–1608)

Xueting Fuyu 雪庭福裕 (1203–1275)

Xueyan Man 雪巖滿 (?–1206)

Xueyan Zuqin 雪巖祖欽 (1215–1287)

Yan county 剡縣

Yan Jun 顏鈞 (1504–1596)

Yan Diaoyu 嚴調禦

Yang He 楊鶴 (?–1635)

Yang Wenhui 楊文會 (1837–1911)

Yang Yi 楊億 (974–1020)

Yang Qiyuan 楊起元 (*zi.* Zhenfu 貞復; *hao.* Fusuo 復所, 1547–1599)

Yang-ming, see Wang Yangming

Yangming Chan 陽明禪

Yangshan Huiji 仰山慧寂 (807–883)

Yangshan Xueyan 仰山雪巖, see Xueyan Zuqin

Yangshan 仰山

Yang Zhu 楊朱

Yanqing 延慶

Yaoshan Weiyan 藥山惟儼 (751–834)

yaosi 遙嗣

Yefu 冶父

Yehai Ziqing 業海子清

yi 咦

yi Fofa wei renqing 以佛法為人情

Yi hua wuye tu 一花五葉圖

yi juetou yingchan 一橛頭硬禪

Yi zhuanyu 一轉語

yiben tanchan 依本談禪

yichou 乙丑

Yijiang Zhenfeng 一江真灃 (1501–1572)

yijue ying chan 一橛硬禪

yijue 一鐰

yijuetou xiangsi yehuxian 一橛頭相似 野狐涎

Yikui Chaochen 一揆超琛 (1625–1679)

Yiling 宜陵

Yinajue 依那爵

Yingxue Hongmin 穎學弘敏 (1606–1671)

Yingzhen 應真

Yingzong reign 英宗 (1064–1067)

yinke 印可

Yinli 胤禮 (1697–1738)

Yinlu 胤祿 (1695–1767)

Yinreng 胤礽 (1674–1725)

Yinyuan Longqi 隱元隆琦 (1592–1673)

Yinzhen 胤禛, see Yongzheng

Yiran Xingrong 逸然性融
(1601–1668)

Yishan 翼善

yishuang kuilei 一雙傀儡

Yixing 一行 (685–727)

Yixing 宜興

Yiyu Tongrun 一雨通潤
(1565–1624)

yizi sandian 伊字三點

Yonghegong 雍和宮

Yongjia Xuanjue 永嘉玄覚
(665–713)

Yongjue Yuanxian 永覺元賢
(1578–1657)

Yongle reign 永樂 (1403–1424)

Yongli reign 永曆 (1647–1661)

Yongming Yanshou 永明延壽
(904–975)

Yongqing 永慶

Yongzheng 雍正 (1678–1735,
r. 1723–1735)

You pankuangjie 又判狂解

Youning 佑寧

Youxi 幽溪

Youxian 幽閑

Yu 禹

Yu, prince 豫王, see Duoduo

Yu Dacheng 余大成 (*zi*. Jisheng 集生,
dharma name: Daoyu 道裕)

Yu Qian 喻謙

yuan 怨

Yu'an Changzhen 玉庵常鎮 (?–1581)

Yuan Hongdao 袁宏道 (1568–1610)

Yuan Zhongdao 袁中道 (1570–1624)

Yuan Zongdao 袁宗道 (1560–1600)

Yuandao pixie shuo 原道闢邪說

Yuanhe reign 元和 (806–820)

Yuanliu jiuzheng 源流就正

yuanliu 源流

Yuanliusong 源流頌

Yuanmen Jingzhu 遠門淨柱
(1604–1654)

Yuanming jushi baiwen 圓明居士百問

Yuanming jushi yulu 圓明居士語錄

Yuanwu Keqin 圓悟克勤 (1063–1135)

yuanxiang 圓相

Yuejian Chaoche 越鑑超徹
(1659–1709)

yuelun 月輪

Yueting Mingde 月亭明德 (*hao*. Qian-
song 千松, 1531–1588)

Yuexin ji 悅心集

Yuezhou 越州

Yufeng 玉峰

Yufeng Zhixuan 玉峰智瑄

Yuhang xian Dai 余杭縣戴

Yulin Tongxiu 玉琳通琇 (1614–1675)

yuqie jiao 瑜伽教

Yuqie jiyao yankou shishi yi 瑜伽集要
焰口施食儀

Yumi shen shishi zhigai 於密滲施食
旨概

Yungu Fahui 雲谷法會 (1500–1579)

Yunhe Rui 雲壑瑞

Yunju 雲居

Yunkong Changzhong 蘊空常忠
(1514–1588)

Yulu jinghai yidi 御錄經海一滴

Yulu Zongjing dagang 御錄宗鏡大綱

Yunmen 雲門

Yunmen Wenyan 雲門文偃
(864–949)

Yunqi Zhuhong 雲棲袾宏 (1535–1615)

Yunyan Tansheng 雲巖曇晟

Yuquan 玉泉

Yushan 虞山

Yushan Shangsi 雨山上思
(1630–1688)

Yuwang 禹王

Yuxuan Chaoding 玉鉉超鼎

Yuxuan yulu 御選語錄
Yuyao 余姚
Yuzhi Faju 玉芝法聚 (1492–1563)

Zai gui miujian zhanglao 再規繆見長老
Zaisan Hongzan 在犙弘贊 (1611–1681)
Zanning 贊寧 (919–1001)
Zeng Jing 曾鯨 (1568–1650)
Zengji xu chuandeng lu 增集續傳燈錄
Zenrin shūhei shū 禪林執弊集
Zhaiqi shuo xu 摘欺說序
Zhaiqi shuo 摘欺說
Zhang Boduan 張伯端 (987–1082)
Zhang Dai 張岱 (1597–1689)
Zhang Juzheng 張居正 (1525–1582)
Zhang Qiran 張歧然 (a.k.a. 秀初, dharma name: Ren'an Jiyi 仁庵濟義, 1599–1664)
Zhang Shangying 張商英 (1043–1121)
Zhang Tingyu 張廷玉 (1672–1755)
Zhang Xianzhong 張獻忠 (1606–1646)
Zhang Xilin 張錫麟
Zhang Ying 張英 (?–1708)
Zhang Yue 張說 (667–731)
Zhang Zhao 張照 (*jinshi* 1709)
Zhangjia Hutuketu Awangluosangquedan 章嘉呼圖克圖阿旺羅桑卻丹 (a.k.a. Awangluosangquedian 阿旺羅桑曲殿,, 1642–1714)
Zhangxue Tongzui 丈雪通醉 (1610–1693)
Zhanran Yuancheng 湛然圓澄 (*hao.* Sanmu 散木, 1561–1626)
Zhao Zhenji 趙貞吉 (*hao.* Dazhou 大洲, 1508–1576)
Zhao Mengfu 趙孟頫 (1254–1322)

Zhaoqing 昭慶
Zhaozhou Congshen 趙州從諗 (778–897)
Zhending 真定 (?–1582)
Zheng Chenggong 鄭成功 (1624–1662)
Zhengbian lu 正辯錄
Zhengzong xinyin houxue lianfang 正宗心印後續聯芳
Zhenghai 正海
Zhenghe reign 政和 (1111–1118)
zhengji 正集
Zhengtong reign 正統 (1436–1449)
Zhengwei lu 証偽錄
Zhenqi 真啟 (?–1641)
Zhenxie Qingliao 真歇清了 (1089–1151)
Zhenyuan reign 貞元 (708–805)
Zhenzhou 鎮州
zhi 知
Zhifo 芝佛
Zhihuan Daofu 知幻道孚 (a.k.a. E'tou zushi 鵝頭祖師 or Fengtou zushi 鳳頭祖師, 1401–1456)
zhijie zongtu 知解宗徒
Zhimi pushuo 指迷普說
Zhiren 智忍
zhisan quyi 執三去一
Zhixin bian 直心編. See *Fofa zhenglun*
Zhixuan 智瑄
Zhiyi 智顗 (538–597)
Zhiyuan reign 至元 (1264–1294 or 1335–1340)
Zhizheng reign 至正 (1341–1370)
Zhizheng zhuan 智証傳
Zhizheng zhuan tiyu 智証傳提語
Zhong Xing 鍾惺 (1574–1624)
Zhong Yuchang 鐘宇淐
Zhongfeng Mingben 中峰明本 (1263–1323)

Zhonghua chuanxindi chanmen shizi chengxitu 中華傳心地禪門師資承襲圖

Zhongling 鈡陵

Zhongshan Guangzhu 鈡山廣鑄 (1248–1341)

Zhongtian Zhengyuan 中天正圓 (1537–1610)

zhongxing zi zu 中興之祖

Zhou Jingang 周金剛, see Deshan Xuanjian

Zhou Rudeng 周汝登 (*hao.* Haimen 海門, 1547–1629)

Zhu Geng 朱庚 (*hao.* Jinting 金庭, 1535–1608)

Zhu Shanren 朱山人

Zhu Shi'en 朱時恩

Zhu Xi 朱熹 (1130–1200)

Zhu Yuanzhang 朱元璋 (1328–1398)

zhuanyu 轉語

Zhuangzi 莊子

Zhugong 渚宮

Zhuhong. See Yunqi Zhuhong

Zhujing risong 諸經日誦

Zhulin 竹林

Zhunti 準提 (Sanskrit: Cunti)

Zhuo'an Zhipu 拙庵智樸 (1636–?)

Zhurengong 主人公

Zibo Zhenke 紫柏真可 (1543–1603)

Zijue 自覺, see Lumen Zijue and Jingyin Zijue

Ziling 紫陵

Zining 子凝

Ziyu 子玉

Zizhi tongjian 資治通鑒

Zizhou Bao 磁州寶 (a.k.a. Daming Bao 大明寶, 1114–1173)

Zongbao Daodu 宗寶道獨 (1600–1661)

Zongbuting gaoshi 總捕聽告示

Zongjing guangshu 宗鏡廣樞

Zongjing shelu 宗鏡攝錄

Zongmen bubi kaijie shuo 宗門不必開戒說

Zongmen zhengming lu 宗門正名錄

Zongmi 宗密 (780–841)

Zongtong biannian 宗統編年

zongzhi 宗旨

Zou Yuanbiao 鄒元標 (1551–1624)

Zudeng datong 祖燈大統

Zudeng bian'e 祖燈辨訛

Zukui Jifu 祖揆繼符

Zushi Chan 祖師禪

Zushi tu 祖師圖

Zutang ji 祖堂集

Zuxin Hanke 祖心函可 (Secular name: Han Zonglai 韓宗騋, *hao.* Shengren 剩人, 1611–1659)

Zuxiu 祖琇

Zuyuan tongyao 祖源通要

Abbreviations of Dictionaries and Collections

DMB	*Dictionary of Ming Biography, 1368–1644*
ECCP	*Eminent Chinese of the Ch'ing Period (1644–1912)*
JXZ	*Mingban Jiaxing dazang jing*
T	*Taishō shinshū daizōkyō*
XZJ	*Wanzi xu zang jing*
Z	*Shinsan dai Nihon Zokuzōkyō*
ZFR	*Zhongguo Fojiao renming dacidian*
ZFS	*Zhongguo Fosi zhi congkan*
ZH	*Zhonghua dazang jing di er ji*

Notes

INTRODUCTION

1. For a recent critique of "normative Buddhism," see Sharf, *Coming to Terms with Chinese Buddhism*, pp. 12–17. For the Buddhist discourse of decline, see Nattier, *Once upon a Future Time*.

2. The term "seventeenth-century crisis," first used by European historians, has been applied to East Asia as well. See Adshead, "The Seventeenth-century General Crisis"; Atwell, "Some Observations on the 'Seventeenth-century Crisis' in China and Japan"; and Wakeman, "China and the Seventeenth-century Crisis."

3. See Chün-fang Yü, "Ming Buddhism," p. 927. For an overview of the study of Buddhism in the Qing dynasty, see Qiu, "Qingdai Fojiao yanjiu xianzhuang" and *Yizhi duxiu*.

4. These five collections of recorded sayings have been compiled into modern Buddhist canons under separate titles. For the prefaces to the *Wujia yulu*, see Z no. 1326, 69: 21a–23a. According to Xuejiao Yuanxin's preface, his lay disciple Guo Ningzhi (a.k.a. Limei) collected the sayings of these masters from Chan texts and compiled them into a single work.

5. The source data are based on Hasebe, *Min Shin Bukkyō kyōdanshi kenkyū*, pp. 382–86.

6. The source data are cited from ibid., pp. 343–44. I have omitted Xuejiao Yuanxin's transmission line because Hasebe's record lists only two of his dharma heirs. See also Shengyan's discussion of major Chan figures in the late Ming in his *Mingmo Fojiao yanjiu*, pp. 1–84.

7. In addition, they engaged in a controversy with Jesuit missionaries. For a detailed study, see my dissertation, "Orthodoxy, Controversy, and the

Transformation of Chan Buddhism," chapter 4. See also my article "Buddhist Logic and Apologetics in Seventeenth-century China."

8. See Spence, *Treason by the Book*, and Yongzheng, *Jianmo bianyi lu*, Z no. 1281, 65: 191–254.

9. For a recent study of this process, see Welter, *Monks, Rulers, and Literati*.

10. See McRae, "Encounter Dialogue and the Transformation of the Spiritual Path in Chinese Ch'an," p. 340.

11. See Hasebe, *Min Shin Bukkyō kyōdanshi kenkyū*, pp. 286 and 368.

12. See my article "Building a Dharma Transmission Monastery."

13. Here I largely follow Eric Hobsbawn's use of this term. See Hobsbawm and Ranger (eds.), *The Invention of Tradition*.

14. Hobsbawm, "Introduction: Inventing Traditions," in *The Invention of Tradition*, p. 1.

15. This phrase is based on an inscription composed in the Yuan dynasty. In 1295, the Chengzong emperor (Termür Öjeitü, r. 1295–1307) of the Yuan bestowed a jade seal inscribed with "the Seal of the *Linji zhengzong*" (*Linji zhengzong zhi yin*) on the Linji master Xiyun and ordered the famous calligrapher Zhao Mengfu (1254–1322) to write an inscription for it. The imperial decree stated that Master Xiyun was appointed to manage monastic affairs within the Linji school. See Zhao Mengfu, *Zhao Mengfu ji*, p. 202. The first appearance of the combination of "Linji" and *zhengzong* may be traced back to Yuanwu Keqin (1063–1135). In 1129, Yuanwu Keqin wrote a short essay entitled *Linji zhengzong ji* (A record of *Linji zhengzong*) and sent it to his disciple Dahui Zonggao (1089–1163), who was a secretarial scribe (*shuji*) at that time. In this essay, Keqin examined the Linji transmission since Mazu Daoyi and Huangbo Xiyun and summarized the basic principle of the three mysteries and three essentials (*sanxuan sanyao*) and the method of shouting used frequently by Linji Yixuan. See Yuanwu Keqin, *Yuanwu Keqin Foguo chanshi yulu*, fasc. 15, T no. 1997, 47: 783a.

16. For some of the critiques of Chan Buddhism along this line, see Elman, *From Philosophy to Philology*, pp. 50–53.

17. See Brook, *Praying for Power*, p. 57.

18. In Holmes Welch's *The Practice of Chinese Buddhism*, Miyun is mentioned only in a footnote. See Welch, *The Practice of Chinese Buddhism*, p. 523 n8. Modern Chinese monks seem only to remember him as the master who revived Tiantong monastery. See Chen-hua, *In Search of the Dharma*, p. 170.

19. The revival of this doctrinal teaching can be traced to a small seminary established by Ouyang Jingwu (1871–1943). For a brief account, see Welch, *The Buddhist Revival in China*, pp. 117–120.

20. For example, the most prominent Buddhist journal *Haichao yin*, founded by Taixu and influential in the Buddhist reform during the Republican era, never cited Miyun Yuanwu's name. I make this statement based on a search of the index prepared for a reprint of the volumes of this journal published between 1920 and 1949. See *Haichao yin*. For a study of Taixu, see Pittman, *Towards a Modern Chinese Buddhism*. I visited Tiantong monastery in June 2006 and found that, although some inscriptions and plaques are still attributed to him, Miyun is not prominently revered as one of the revivers of the monastery.

21. See Lan, "Jiaxing dazangjing de tese jiqi shiliao jiazhi," p. 263.

22. Timothy Brook has noticed the value of these sources. See his *Praying for Power* and *Geographical Sources of Ming-Qing History*.

23. Rather than simply dismissing normative discourses, Buddhist scholars such as Jan Nattier have attempted to develop sophisticated reading strategies to highlight their descriptive value. See Nattier, *A Few Good Men*.

24. See *Riben Huangboshan Wanfusi cang lü Ri gaoseng Yinyuan Zhongtu laiwang shuxin ji*.

25. I use a microfilm copy from Tōhō Bunka Gakuen Tōkyō Kenkyūsho. This collection was compiled by Miyun's disciple Muchen Daomin, ca. 1642–1643. I am grateful to Harvard-Yenching Library for ordering this rare source for me.

26. This collection, compiled by his disciple Yinyuan Longqi, most likely in Japan, is the property of the Keizuiji in Osaka. I obtained one copy from the Manpukuji archive.

27. The version I use is a photocopy from the Puhui canon published in 1945. This copy has been reprinted in *Dazangjing bubian*, 24: 445–501.

28. I will briefly discuss this work in appendix 2.

CHAPTER I

1. For their works on Ming Buddhism, see the bibliography.

2. After the founding of the Ming dynasty, Zhu Yuanzhang vigorously promoted a syncretic version of the state religion. For details, see Langlois and Sun, "Three Teachings Syncretism and the Thought of Ming T'ai Tsu."

3. See Tatsuike, "Mindai no Yūga kyōsō."

4. Huanlun, *Shishi jigu lue xuji*, fasc. 2, XZJ 133: 254b–55b.

5. Ibid., 259b–260b.

6. See Brook, "At the Margin of Public Authority."

7. See He Xiaorong, *Mingdai Nanjing siyuan yanjiu*, p. 7. See also Mano, "Mindai no Bukkyō to Minchō," pp. 243–334.

8. Brook, "At the Margin of Public Authority," p. 175. For statistics about these events, see He, *Mingdai Nanjing siyuan yanjiu*, pp. 43–44.

9. For statistics on the Ming prohibition on temple building, see He, *Mingdai Nanjing siyuan yanjiu*, pp. 13–14.

10. He was exiled to the remote frontier of Hainan island. For a brief account in English, see Hsu, *A Buddhist Leader in Ming China*, pp. 75–84.

11. See *Ayuwang shan zhi*, fasc. 16, ZFS 90: 895–906.

12. See Eberhard, "Temple-Building Activities in Medieval and Modern China," pp. 264–318.

13. Brook, *Praying for Power*, p. 93.

14. For Tibetan Buddhism in the Ming, see Toh, "Tibetan Buddhism in Ming China."

15. *Da Zhaoqing lüsi zhi*, ZFS 71: 31–32.

16. For Cisheng's biography, see DMB, 856–59. For an account of her Buddhist activities, see Naquin, *Peking: Temples and City Life*, pp. 156–61.

17. For a brief review of Ming Buddhist canons in English, see Long, "A Note on the Hongwu Nanzang."

18. For Zibo Zhenke's involvement in compiling the Jiaxing canon, see Guoxiang, *Zibo dashi yanjiu.*

19. There are many discussions about this sūtra in Japanese and Chinese. For a recent discussion in English, see Benn, "Another Look at the Pseudo-*Śūraṃgama Sūtra*." I wish to thank Dr. Benn for sharing his manuscript with me. See also my article "Knowledge for What?" and my unpublished paper "The Commentarial Tradition of the *Śūraṃgama Sūtra*."

20. Most of these commentaries can be found in XZJ, vols. 16–25 and 89–91. According to Qian Qianyi (1582–1664), who devoted his later life to writing a comprehensive commentary on the *Śūraṃgama Sūtra*, the exegetical tradition of this text derived from the Yuan and survived in large monasteries in Beijing. Qian noted that commentators in both north and south China strictly followed the exegetic tradition originating from Tianru Weize's *Lengyan huijie* (ten fascicles). See Qian Qianyi, *Lengyan jing shujie mengchao*, XZJ 21: 84b.

21. According to Chikusa Masaaki, doctrinal schools such as Huayan and Yogācāra flourished in Beijing under the patronage of the Liao, Jin, and Yuan dynasties. See Chikusa, "Enkin Daitō no Kegonshū: Hōshūji to Sūgokujiso tachi."

22. See Naquin, *Peking: Temples and City Life*, p. 219.

23. *Qingliang shan zhi*, ZFS 9: 161–62.

24. Qian Qianyi believed that his work *Lengyan guanjian* challenged Tianru Weize's *Lengyan huijie* and thus started a new era for the interpretation of the *Śūraṃgama Sūtra*. See Qian Qianyi, *Lengyan jing shujie mengchao*, XZJ 21: 85a.

25. See Hanshan Deqing, *Hanshan dashi mengyou ji*, fasc. 30, Z no. 1456, 73: 676c–679a. For a detailed study of the rise of Yogācāra in the late Ming, see Zhang Zhiqiang, "Weishi sixiang yu wanming weishixue yanjiu." See also Liao, "Xuelang Hong'en chutan." For Xuelang Hong'en's other extant work, see his *Xuelang ji* and *Xuelang xuji* in *Chanmen yishu xubian*, vol. 12. See also Shenyan's discussion of Yogācāra scholars in the late Ming in his *Mingmo Fojiao yanjiu*, pp. 187–238. It should be noted here that although Xuelang Hong'en was renowned as a Buddhist scholar, in his later years he became increasingly drawn to Chan Buddhism.

26. For Cangxue Duche's chronological biography, see Chen Naiqian, *Cangxue dashi xingji kaolue*. See also Sun Changwu, "Shiseng Cangxue."

27. For an overview of Huayan studies in the late Ming and early Qing, see Guo Peng, *Mingqing Fojiao*, pp. 337–38; and Wei, *Zhongguo Huayan zong tongshi*, pp. 276–301.

28. See Araki Kengo's discussion of Li Tongxuan in the late Ming in his *Chūgoku shingaku to kodō no Bukkyō*, pp. 141–184. Robert Gimello has also noted the popularity of Li's work in post-Tang Chinese Buddhism. See Gimello, "Li T'ung-hsüan and the Practical Dimensions of Hua-yen."

29. See Miaofeng Zhenjue's epitaph in *Tiantai shan fangwai zhi*, ZFS 81: 560–62. For short biographies of Yueting Mingde and Miaofeng Zhenjue, see ZFR, pp. 371

and 557. Some Chinese scholars trace Yueting Mingde's Tiantai lineage back to Huilin (1482–1557), Wu'ai Puzhi (?–1408), and Dongming Huiri (1291–1379). See Pan and Wu, *Zhongguo Tiantaizong tongshi*, pp. 714–20.

30. For some studies of Siming Zhili in English, see works by Brook Ziporyn, Dan A. Getz, and Daniel Stevenson listed in the bibliography.

31. *Youxi biezhi*, ZFS, supplement, 9, pp. 198–99.

32. For Wujin Chuandeng's and Wulou Chuanping's biographies, see ibid., pp. 445–53. See also Wulou Chuanping's epitaph written by Shen Yiguan in *Ayuwang shan zhi*, ZFS 89: 376–80.

33. See Guo Peng, *Ming Qing Fojiao*, p. 337, and Pan and Wu, *Zhongguo Tiantaizong tongshi*, pp. 720–41.

34. For details, see Jiang Canteng's discussion about the late Ming debate over Sengzhao's *Wubuqian* in his *Mingqing Minguo Fojiao sixiang shilun*, p. 106, and his *Wan Ming Fojiao conglin gaige yu Foxue zhengbian zhi yanjiu*, pp. 203–300.

35. See Shen Defu's (1578–1642) description in his *Wanli yehuo pian*, pp. 687–88. Translated in Chün-fang Yü, *The Renewal of Buddhism in China*, pp. 169–70.

36. Chün-fang Yü, *The Renewal of Buddhism in China*, pp. 157–58.

37. See Qu Ruji's preface written for appointing the monk Dayuan as abbot of Tanzhe monastery in his *Qu Jiongqing ji*, fasc. 6, *Siku quanshu cunmu congshu*, 187: 180a. Qu expressed the same concern in his preface written for monks seeking full precepts from Yunqi Zhuhong. See his *Qu Jiongqing ji*, fasc. 6, *Siku quanshu cunmu congshu*, 187: 183b.

38. *Xishan Jietai si* was first built in 622. During the Liao dynasty (907–1125), an ordination platform was constructed. During the Ming, it was rebuilt in 1434 and became the official ordination platform under government control. Zhihuan Daofu was first called "Phoenix Head Patriarch" (Fengtou zushi), but he changed his title to "Goose Head Patriarch" (Er'tou zushi). He became a monk when he was thirty years old and lived for eighty-five years. His imperial title was "Ten Thousands Longevity" (Wanshou), which was also the official name of Xishan Jietai monastery. For his biography, see Fuju, *Nanshan zongtong*, fasc. 2, pp. 16–17; Yuanliang, *Lüzong dengpu*, p. 39.

39. See the veritable records of the Jiajing reign, fasc. 313, *Ming shilu*, 84: 4a. Translation from Overmyer, *Folk Buddhist Religion*, p. 171.

40. See the veritable records of the Jiajing reign, fasc. 64, *Ming shilu*, 73: 1477.

41. See Zhanran Yuancheng, *Kaigu lu*, Z no. 1285, 65: 368c. Some monastic gazetteers also mention this event. For example, the gazetteer of Zhaoqing monastery records that near the end of the Jiajing reign, ordination was prohibited by the court because some "vagabonds" were ordained through the ordination platform at Ma'anshan. See *Da Zhaoqing lüsi zhi*, ZFS 71: 38.

42. Hanyue Fazang, "Shoujie bian," *Hongjie fayi*, ZH 116: 48874. The essay "Shoujie bian" does not appear in another version of the *Hongjie fayi* collected in JXZ no. 397, 37: 735–43.

43. Ibid. For the use of monks in these military campaigns, see Shahar, "Ming-period Evidence of Shaolin Martial Practice."

44. See the veritable records of the Wanli reign, fasc. 2, *Ming shilu*, 96: 22.

45. See the veritable records of the Jiajing reign, fasc. 276, *Ming shilu*, 83: 5405 and the veritable records of the Wanli reign, fasc. 84, *Ming shilu*, 100: 1761–2. See also *Ming shilu leizuan*, pp. 1007 and 1023.

46. Zhuhong called his novice precept the "ordination of peace and compassion" (*xici jie*). See Chün-fang Yü, *The Renewal of Buddhism in China*, pp. 196–202. According to Hanyue's biography written by Tanji Hongren, Hanyue did received precepts from Zhuhong, but this biography does not specify if Zhuhong's ordination offered novice or full precepts. See *Dengweishan Sheng'en si zhi*, ZFS 44: 114.

47. For Hanyue's ordination experience, see Hanyue Fazang, "Sanfeng Zang chanshi nianpu," JXZ no. 299, 34: 205a–b.

48. Hasebe Yūkei questioned whether Guxin Ruxin received proper ordination from Su'an Zhenjie. See Hasebe, "Min Shin jidai ni okeru Zen Ritsu ryōshū kōka no dōkō," pp. 194–96.

49. See the full biography of Guxin Ruxin in Fuju, *Nanshan zongtong*, fasc. 2, pp. 17–20; Yuanliang, *Lüzong dengpu*, fasc. 1, pp. 40–42; and *Lümen zuting huizhi*, pp. 8–10. Guxin Ruxin's lineage was usually referred to as the "Guzupai." See Hasebe, "Kosoha no sho ritsuso gyōgō kiryaku."

50. *Qingliang shan zhi*, ZFS 9: 145.

51. For details about the spread of this ceremony, see Hasebe, "Chūgoku kindai ni okeru gukai hogi."

52. Hanyue Fazang's work was reprinted in JXZ no. 397, 37: 735–44. Yinyuan Longqi also wrote a version of the *Hongjie fayi* based on Hanyue's work. For a textual analysis of these two works, see Hasebe, *Min Shin Bukkyō kenkyū shiryō*, pp. 95–100. Hanyue Fazang's *Hongjie fayi* was the first work to outline the procedure for the Triple Platform Ordination Ceremony. For a detailed study of this and other similar works on the invention of the ordination ceremony in the Ming and Qing dynasties, see Hasebe, *Min Shin Bukkyō kyōdanshi kenkyū*, pp. 157–68; and Baroni, *Obaku Zen*, pp. 94–98.

53. See Hanyue's epitaph written by Huang Zongxi in his *Nanlei wen'an*, fasc. 2, in *Lizhou yizhu huikan*, p. 16.

54. See the monk Wubian's epitaph written by Qu Ruji in his *Qu Jiongqing ji*, fasc. 11, *Siku quanshu cunmu congshu*, 187: 268b.

55. See Zibo Zhenke's epitaph written by Hanshan Deqing in *Hanshan dashi mengyou ji*, fasc. 27, Z no. 1456, 73: 652b-655b. Because of his tragic death, he never completed this work.

56. For a brief account of their biographies, see Chün-fang Yü, "Ming Buddhism," pp. 922–27.

57. The function of this monastic system in the Ming remains unknown. Since we know that, during the early Ming consolidation of monasteries, many small temples tended to be incorporated into larger ones instead of being destroyed as illegal buildings, it is reasonable to surmise that this system was adopted to address the situation in the much-enlarged monastic communities. This also explains why dharma transmission was no longer important for selecting abbots. In my reading, I found that even when dharma transmission was reintroduced into these monasteries,

the abbot and his entourage kept separate from the house monks who were the original residents. There were obvious tensions between these two groups of monks. For the early Ming effort to consolidate Buddhist monasteries, see Brook, "At the Margin of Public Authority." Welch observes in his study of modern Chinese Buddhism that, in large hereditary monasteries, several houses were divided by the abbot's disciples. For his brief account of this modern practice, see *The Practice of Chinese Buddhism*, pp. 166–67.

58. See Brook, *Praying for Power*, p. 257.

59. See *Da Zhaoqing lüsi zhi*, ZFS 71: 323–24.

60. Hanshan Deqing's effort to revive Caoxi monastery has been recorded in "Caoxi zhongxing lu" (Record of the revival of Caoxi). See Hanshan Deqing, *Hanshan dashi mengyou ji*, fasc. 50, Z no. 1456, 73: 807–15. It should be noted here that Hanshan Deqing was only able to control the meditation hall. It seems that the rest of the monastery was not involved in the reform. Eventually, Hanshan Deqing was expelled from Caoxi.

61. See Dachuan, *Wudeng huiyuan*, fasc. 14, Z 80: 289b.

62. Feiyin Tongrong, *Wudeng yantong jiehuo bian*, Z 86: 318c. Ironically, Xuejiao Yuanxin returned to the Linji lineage when he desired to retire in a temple assigned by Miyun Yuanwu's disciples. He was readmitted in Chan historiography as Huanyou Zhengchuan's heir because the Shunzhi emperor questioned Muchen Daomin about his exclusion. See Chen, *Qingchu sengzheng ji*, pp. 63–65; and Muchen Daomin's *Beiyou ji*, fasc. 3, JXZ no. 180, 26: 294c–95a.

63. Mount Yuquan was located in Dangyang county, Hubei. The revival of Mount Yuquan was one of Timothy Brook's case studies of gentry patronage in the late Ming. See Brook, *Praying for Power*, pp. 278–310.

64. See Wuji Zhenghui's biography in *Yuquan zhi*, fasc. 3, ZFS 14: 340–49. A short note was added stating that the so-called fifty-six characters were carved on the back of Zhang Yue's (667–731) inscription for Shenxiu. However, according to this note, because the stele had been damaged, this verse could not be deciphered completely. The verse is transcribed as follows:

弘神普一修無學　　念持三昧不思議　　湛然瑩徹佛子燈
耀見靈源全杲日　　彌滿正乘法界廣　　徧知性相圓覺鈔
禪師權實淨光明　　行願力深心自遠

Apparently, the first few characters correspond to the early Northern school teachers. According to modern scholarship, although evidence shows that the Northern school was active in Tibet and the Nanzhao kingdom in Yunnan, there is no conclusive evidence of its dharma transmission to corroborate this verse. For the development of the Northern school, Shenxiu's biographical sources, and eminent disciples of Shenxiu, see McRae, *The Northern School and the Formation of Early Ch'an Buddhism*, pp. 44–46 and 61–72.

65. Through careful reading, I have deduced that this text was derived from an obscure Chan community led by Chan masters Zhending (?–1582) and Da'an, who

may have lived in Beijing. Because this text mentioned Zhongtian Zhengyuan (1537–1610), who later revived Huangbo monastery by requesting the bestowal of a complete Buddhist canon, I determined that this Chan community was active at the end of the sixteenth century. In this community, monks appeared to have engaged in active encounters with the masters to induce their enlightenment experiences.

66. Shanmi, *Zhengzong xinyin houxu lianfang*, XZJ 148: 369–84.

67. For Xueting Fuyu's dharma transmission in Shaolin monastery, see Wu Limin et al., *Chanzong zongpai yuanliu*, pp. 458–74.

68. See Huanxiu Changrun's epitaph by Wang Daokun (1525–1593) in *Shaolin si zhi*, ZFS 6: 162, and also the dharma transmission of the Caodong lineage in ZFS 9: 192–93.

69. Chuiwan Guangzhen was a Chan monk in Sichuan. His claim was opposed by other Chan masters. His lineage was greatly promoted by his disciple Sanshan Denglai (1614–1685). Sanshan Denglai's dharma heir Bie'an Xingtong wrote the *Xudeng zhengtong* in forty-two fascicles to legitimize Guangzhen's lineage. See Chen, *Mingji Dian Qian Fojiao kao*, p. 52. However, Guangzhen's claim was dubious because one of his dharma masters, Wunian Shenyou, had no claim of dharma transmission. See his epitaph in *Chuiwan chanshi yulu*, JXZ no. 239, 29: 553–54a. See also Hasebe, "*Zokutō shōtō* to Shūōn Tsuiman homon."

70. For this dispute, see my discussion in appendix 2.B.

71. See Weizhi Zhikai, *Zhengming lu*, fascs. 8 and 9, pp. 102–41.

72. See Tianzhu Manxiu's biography in Yu Qian, *Xinxu Gaoseng zhuan siji*, pp. 1549–50.

73. See his epitaph by Hanshan Deqing in *Hanshan dashi mengyou ji*, fasc. 22, XZJ 127: 265c.

74. Noguchi, "Minmatsu Kokyūha no genryū," pp. 121–40. See also Noguchi, "Minmatsu ni okeru shūjingo ronsō," pp. 164–67.

75. For a brief account of Yungu Fahui's meditation practice, see Chün-fang Yü, "Ming Buddhism," pp. 926–27.

76. In addition to Mount Wutai, many Chan aspirants went to Mount Funiu to practice meditation. Renowned in the late Ming as "a place to subdue demons" (*lianmochan*) or "the place of fire" (*huochang*), it was largely forgotten in later times.

77. See Chün-fang Yü, *The Renewal of Buddhism in China*, pp. 29–63.

78. See Hanshan Deqing, *Hanshan dashi mengyou ji*, JXZ no. 115, vol. 22. Translation is adapted from Hsu, *A Buddhist Leader in Ming China*, p. 130.

79. See Hanshan Deqing's prefaces for the dharma transmissions in Jiaoshan and Huayue monasteries in JXZ 22: 496c–97a and 496a–b. In this work, Hanshan Deqing lamented that dharma transmission had become nominal.

80. Cleary, *Zibo*, p. 11.

81. See Zhuhong's essay "One turning phrase" ("Yi zhuanyu"), in his *Yunqi fahui*, JXZ no. 277, 33: 41c. Translation adopted from Yü, *The Renewal of Buddhism in China*, p. 173.

82. Hanshan Deqing, "Shi can chan qie yao," in *Hanshan dashi mengyou ji*, fasc. 6, Z no. 1456, 73: 499. Translation is adopted from Hsu, *A Buddhist Leader in Ming China*, p. 131.

83. See Zibo Zhenke's epitaph by Hanshan Deqing in *Hanshan dashi mengyou ji*, fasc. 27, in Z no. 1456, 73: 655.

84. See Chen Yuan, *Qingchu sengzheng ji*, p. 15; and Chün-fang Yü, *The Renewal of Buddhism*, p. 35.

CHAPTER 2

1. See Brook, *Praying for Power*, p. 182.

2. As Chikusa Masaaki observes, from the Song forward, Buddhist institutions were in steady decline in terms of their economic status. See Chikusa, "Sōdai Fukken no shakai to jiin," pp. 181–87. Other studies of Buddhist institutions in the late Ming confirm Chikusa's conclusion. As T'ien Ju-k'ang notes, Buddhist monasteries in Fujian in the late Ming and early Qing were in a deplorable condition and could not be compared to their glory in the Tang and Song. T'ien regards the moral degeneration of Buddhism and the secularization of Buddhist monks as the main cause for its decline. See T'ien, "The Decadence of Buddhist Temples in Fukien in Late Ming and Early Ch'ing," pp. 83–101.

3. Eberhard, "Temple-Building Activities in Medieval and Modern China," pp. 264–318.

4. Brook, *Praying for Power*, pp. 137–84.

5. Ibid., p. 257.

6. For a study of Wang Yangming's thought, see Tu, *Neo-Confucian Thought in Action*.

7. For a study of Guan Zhidao, see Araki, *Minmatsu shūkyō shisō kenkyū*. For a study of Zhao Zhenji, see Araki's discussion in his *Chūgoku shingaku to kodō no Bukkyō*, pp. 99–140. Legend says that Zhao recommended the *Śūraṃgama Sūtra* to his students in particular.

8. Mu Konghui obtained his *jinshi* degree during the Hongzhi reign (1488–1506). He was a follower of Wang Yangming and was interested in Buddhism. For his official career, see his literary collection *Mu Wenjian gong huangao*. (In this collection, however, he rarely mentioned his relationship with Wang Yangming and Buddhism except in fasc. 1, p. 33.) He wrote a commentary entitled *Daxue qianlü*, in which he quoted Zhiyi's *Fahua jing wenju* and *Da Zhuangyan jing lu* to interpret the crucial concept of *gewu* (investigation of things). According to him, the word *ge* should be understood as *geliang* (measuring). See his *Daxue qianlü*, in *Siku quanshu cunmu congshu*, 156: 633b–34a.

9. Edward Ch'ien claims that this syncretic approach was based on the model of noncompartmentalization, which intermingles the three teachings as a unity. Jiao Hong, a Taizhou scholar, represents such syncretic thinking. According to Edward Ch'ien, for Jiao Hong, "they (the three teachings) were 'one' not in the sense that they were united as differentiated parts of a composite assemblage but in the sense that they had the fused integrity of a single entity and were mutually identified and indistinguishable." See Ch'ien, *Chiao Hung and the Restructuring of Neo-Confucianism*, p. 119.

10. See de Bary, *Learning for One's Self* and *The Liberal Tradition in China*.

11. For Li Zhi's family background, see Hok-lam Chan (ed.), *Li Chih*, pp. 41–77.

12. Legend says that Li did not shave his head for serious ordination. Rather, he first did it to escape the summer heat and later gradually became used to it. In 1589, he even thought about keeping his hair again and living with Jiao Hong in Nanjing. See Lin Haiquan, *Li Zhi nianpu kaolue*, pp. 185 and 209.

13. See his biography in DMB, pp. 1349–55.

14. See his biography in ibid., pp. 513–15. See also Dimberg, *The Sage and Society*.

15. The discovery of Yan Jun's literary collection (1856) in the 1990s sheds new light on this crucial Taizhou figure. See *Yan Jun ji*.

16. See Li, "The Rhetoric of Spontaneity in Late-Ming Literature," p. 48. Yan Jun's literary collection was recently discovered in mainland China and was reprinted. See his *Yan Jun ji*. The incident I quote is from Wai-yee Li's essay and was not included in Yan's collection.

17. See Qian, *Yuan Hongdao ji jianjiao*, pp. 1225–26.

18. See Huang Zongxi's account about the Taizhou school in his *Mingru xue'an*, p. 703. The translation is adapted from *The Records of Ming Scholars*, p. 165. I added the pinyin transliterations of persons' names in parentheses.

19. This concept became the central idea that defined Hanyue Fazang's Chan thought. See my detailed explanation in chapter 4.

20. Historians have noticed that, due to the significant increase in exam candidates and the low success rate in the exam, many low-level literati had to seek other professions, such as professional writer, publisher, teacher, doctor, office clerk, etc., to support themselves. See Hymes, "Not Quite Gentlemen?" and Elman, *From Philosophy to Philology*, pp. 130–38. See also Chow, *Publishing, Culture, and Power in Early Modern China*, chapter 3, pp. 90–148. For the success rate in the exam, see Bol, "The Sung Examination System and the Shih"; Lee, *Education in Traditional China*; and Elman, *A Cultural History of Civil Service Exam in Late Imperial China*.

21. Veblen, *The Theory of the Leisure Class*, pp. 33–79, especially 46–48.

22. I borrow this phrase from the title of a chapter in a Ming connoisseur book. See Clunas, *Superfluous Things*, p. 18.

23. For some studies, see Li Yu, "A History of Reading in Late Imperial China"; and Lee, "Books and Bookworms in Song China." See also Cherniack, "Book Culture and Textual Transmission in Sung China"; and Clunas, "Books and Things."

24. See Griffiths, *Religious Reading*, p. 40.

25. Chao was a high official and had a sizable collection of books that one of his grandsons used to compile a famous bibliography of Chinese books. Several works of his miscellaneous reading notes were printed during the late Ming. See Chen Yuan, *Zhongguo Fojiao shiji gailun*, pp. 129–131. For details of Chao's works, see Gimello, "The Buddhism of a 'Confucian' Scholar." For the lineage of the Chao family, see Bol, *This Culture of Ours*, pp. 59–73.

26. Chao Jiong, *Fazang suijin lu*, fasc. 9. Translation is adopted from Robert Gimello, "The Buddhism of a "Confucian' Scholar." p. 875.

27. Ibid. fasc. 2. Translation is adopted from Robert Gimello, "The Buddhism of a "Confucian' Scholar," p. 876.

28. For details, see Welter, "Literati Influences on the Compilation of Chan Records," in his *Monks, Rulers, and Literati*, pp. 161–207. For the production of Chan texts as literary works, see also McRae, *Seeing through Zen*, pp. 99–100; Maraldo, "Is There Historical Consciousness with Ch'an?" The most famous example of literati involvement in editing Chan texts would be the role of the scholar-official Yang Yi (974–1020) in the formation of the *Jingde chuandeng lu*.

29. See Halperin, *Out of the Cloister*, p. 4.

30. See my article "Knowledge for What?"

31. Tu Long, *Suoluo guan qingyan*, p. 1. Quoted in Brook, *Praying for Power*, p. 67.

32. Juelang Daosheng, *Tianjie Juelang Sheng chanshi quanlu*, JXZ no. 311, 34: 652a.

33. See Zhuhong,*Zhuchuan suibi*, JXZ no. 277, 33: 33a.

34. For details, see my article "Knowledge for What?" and "The Commentarial Tradition of the *Śuraṃgama Sūtra*;"Araki, "Mindai ni okeru *Ryogonkyō* no ryūkō," pp. 245–274, especially p. 264.

35. See Yuan Hongdao, *Jinxie bian*. He claimed in the preface that he selected seventy-two passages but the text only contains sixty-eight passages. I want to thank Charles Jones for sharing the copy of the original Naikaku bunko edition with me. An original print preserved in the Beijing National Library was reprinted in *Xuxiu siku quanshu*, series 3 (*zibu*), vol. 1131, pp. 56–74. The year of compilation is determined according to his biography in the gazetteer of Gong'an county. See Ren Fangqiu, *Yuan Zhonglang yanjiu*, p. 127. According to the Chinese scholar Wang Guichen, this work, together with Yuan's *Shanhu lin* and *Liuzu tanjing jielu*, were published in the 1617 edition of *San xiansheng yishu* (Lost works of three masters), which collects lost works by Xu Wei, Li Zhi, and Yuan Hongdao. See Wang Guichen, "Ji Ming Wanli keben *Liuzu tanjing*."

36. For his biographies written by Ye Xianggao and Qian Qianyi, see Qu Ruji, *Qu Jongqing ji*, fasc. 14, *Siku quanshu cunmu congshu* 187: 328–29. According to some Christian sources, however, such a famous Buddhist follower was finally converted to Christianity by Matteo Ricci (Li Madou, 1552–1610). The Christian sources have detailed records about his contact with Ricci and other Jesuits. He was among the first group of the literati who were attracted to Ricci. He first met Ricci in Shaozhou in 1589 and advised him to dress up like the Confucian literati rather than Buddhist monks. In 1599, he wrote a preface for Ricci's work *On Friendship* (*Jiaoyou lun*). One reason for their enduring friendship was that Ricci prayed for the birth of a boy on behalf of Qu when Qu was forty-three and his wife forty-two. Qu Ruji was finally baptized on March 25, 1605 and was named "Ignatius" (Yinajue), after Loyala Ignatius (1491–1556), the founder of the Order of the Jesuits. In 1607, his son Qu Shigu (1593–?) was also baptized and was named "Matteo" (Madou) to commemorate Matteo Ricci. Qu's newphew Qu Shisi (1590–1651), one of the most famous Ming loyalists and Southern Ming officials, was also baptized by the Jesuit Giulio Aleni (Ai Rulue, 1582–1649) around 1624. For the Christian biographies of Qu Ruji, Qu Shigu, and Qu Shisi, see Fang Hao, *Zhongguo Tianzhujiaoshi renwu zhuan*, vol. 1, pp. 274–83.

37. See Qu Ruji's preface to the *Zhiyu lu*, Z no. 1578-A, 83: 396c–7a.

38. Ouyi Zhixu lamented the negative impact of the *Zhiyue lu* in particular. See Araki, "*Shigetsu roku* no seritsu," especially p. II.

39. For the popularity of the *Zongjing lu* in the late Ming, see Araki, "Minmatsu ni okeru Enmei Enjū no eizō."

40. According to his brother Yuan Zhongdao's preface to a printed edition of this work, Yuan Hongdao started to read the *Zongjing lu* in 1603. He selected essential passages from the text and asked his attendants to transcribe them. After his death, his friend published this collection. See Qian Bocheng, *Yuan Hongdao ji jianjiao*, pp. 1707–8; Araki, *Minmatsu shūkyō shisō kenkyū*, p. 452.

41. See Yuan Hongdao, *Tanjing jielu*, p. 4. Conspicuously missing in his rearrangement, for example, were all the references to the military governor Wei Qu, who was the most significant patron of Huineng. Yuan must have thought that events related to him were not historically true.

42. This attitude can be seen in his remark in the *Shanhu lin*, in *Sango rin*, no. 80, p. 208. My observation of his consistent commitment to Chan teaching was confirmed by Charles Jones in an e-mail to author, June 11, 2007. I thank Charles Jones for sending me a rare copy from the Naikaku bunko in Japan. A copy from the Beijing Library was reprinted in *Xuxiu siku quanshu*, series 3 (*zibu*), vol. 1131, pp. 1–55. See also Araki's Japanese translation in *Sango rin*.

43. A selected version approved by Yuan Hongdao was first published as *Deshan shutan* and the complete record entitled *Shanhu lin* was published after his death. For *Deshan shutan*, see Qian Bocheng, *Yuan Hongdao ji jianxiao*, fasc. 44, pp. 1283–1300.

44. See Yuan Hongdao, *Shanhu lin*, in *Sango rin*, no. 59, p. 205; nos. 138 and 141, p. 216.

45. Ibid., no. 111, p. 212, no. 264, p. 234.

46. See Xilin's biography written by Hanshan Deqing in *Hanshan dashi mengyou ji*, fasc. 30, Z 73: 672.

47. Juelang Daosheng, *Tianjie Juelang Sheng chanshi quanlu*, JXZ 34: 652a.

48. See Benzhi's biography written by Hanshan Deqing in *Hanshan dashi mengyou ji*, fasc. 30, Z 73: 679a–80b.

49. For a thorough study of this debate, see Araki, *Unsei Shukō no kenkyū*, pp. III–21 and also the Chinese translation of Araki's book, *Jinshi Zhongguo Fojiao de shuguang*, pp. 163–190. Other literati such as Zhou Rudeng also criticized Zhuhong. See Araki, *Unsei Shukō no kenkyū*, pp. 158–9 and also the Chinese translation *Jinshi Zhongguo Fojiao de shuguang*, pp. 252–54.

50. Quoted from Chün-fang Yü, *The Renewal of Buddhism in China*, p. 61.

51. Strict observance of Buddhist precepts had become an issue of debate among the literati around 1600. Zhou represents a radical position. Other literati such as Yuan Zhongdao, following Zhuhong, argued that Buddhist mind cultivation must be based on the observance of precepts. For details of the debate, see Eichman, "Spiritual Seekers in a Fluid Landscape," pp. 45–100.

52. See Zhou Rudeng's collection of discussions in *Zhou Haimen xiansheng wenlu*, pp. 198–99.

53. Williams, *Mahayana Buddhism*, p. 88.

54. Kusumoto, *Ō Yōmei no Zen teki shisō kenkyū*.

55. See Chan, "How Buddhist Is Wang Yang-ming?"

56. See Tu, *Neo-Confucian Thought in Action*, pp. 63–72.

57. For a detailed study of his relation with Wang Yangming, see Araki, "Zensō Gyōkushi Hōshū to Yomei gakuha."

58. See Yuzhi Faju's biographies by Xue Wei and Cai Runan in Jiao Hong (ed.), *Guochao xianzheng lu*, fasc. 118, pp. 942–44.

59. Araki, "Zensō Gyōkushi Hōju to Yomei gakuha," p. 90.

60. All these correspondences are collected in Wunian Shenyou's *Huangbo Wunian chanshi fuwen*, JXZ no. 98, vol. 20. He kept close relationship with Yuan Hongdao as well, who knew him through Li Zhi. Yuan's two poems translated by Jonathan Chaves show that Yuan practiced meditation and studied Buddhist scriptures under him. See Chaves, *Pilgrim of the Clouds*, pp. 42 and 68. For detailed discussions about Wunian's thought, see Araki, "Minmatsu no Zensō Munen Shinyō ni tsuite."

61. See Wunian's biography in *Huangbo Wunian chanshi fuwen*, fasc. 6, ZH 79: 32592 and JXZ no. 98, 20: 526–27.

62. Juding, *Xu Chuandeng lu*, fasc. 29, T no. 2077, 51: 671b.

63. Li Zhi, *Fenshu*, fasc. 3, in *Li Zhi wenji*, vol. 1, p. 136. He wrote this piece of work in 1593. See Lin Haiquan, *Li Zhi nianpu kaolue*, p. 280.

64. See Yang Qiyuan's biography in Peng Shaosheng, *Jushi zhuan*, fasc. 44, Z 88: 261c–62a.

65. She Changji, "Yongqing dawen," in *Li Wenling waiji*, pp. 43–58. This collection also includes Li Zhi's conversations about historical figures and contemporary thinkers.

66. See Jiao Hong's preface to She Changji's "Yongqing dawen" in *Li Wenling waiji*, p. 41.

67. *Yunmen Xiansheng si zhi*, ZFS 4: 112.

68. Because of its nominal nature, Zhanran Yuancheng may have not mentioned his dharma transmission in front of his disciples. This is perhaps why Feiyin Tongrong, who studied with Zhanran Yuancheng for many years, claimed that he had never heard about his former teacher's dharma transmission and thus put him in the category of "lineage unknown" in his work *Wudeng yantong*. See chapter 8 for details.

69. This has been corroborated by some observations in the seventeenth and eighteenth centuries. See Brook, *Praying for Power*, pp. 61 and 64.

70. For a study of intellectuals in Eastern Zhejiang, see He Bingsong, *Zhedong xuepai suyuan*.

71. Meanwhile, inspired by Zhuhong's teaching of non-killing, these literati also participated in a charitable activity called "releasing animals." See Smith, "Liberating Animals in Ming-Qing China." For the relationship between Wang's followers and Buddhist monks, see Shengyan, *Mingmo Fojiao yanjiu*, pp. 253–56.

72. The records of various lectures that Zhou organized have been preserved in a collection of discussion remarks in Yan county. See *Zhou Haimen xiansheng wenlu*. For studies of Zhou Rudeng, see Araki, "Shū Kaimon no shisō," in his *Mindai shisō kenkyū*, pp. 227–64; Zhao, "Chou Juteng (1547–1629) at Nanking."

73. Zhou Rudeng, *Fofa zhenglun*, in *Meiguo Hafo daxue Hafo Yanjing tushuguan cang zhongwen shanben huikan*, vol. 33, p. 113.

74. Zhou Rudeng, *Zhou Haimen xiansheng wenlu*, in *Siku quanshu cunmu congshu*,165: 140.

75. See Peng Shaosheng, *Jushi zhuan*, fasc. 44, Z no. 1646, 88: 262a–63a.

76. See Huang Zongxi's account of the Taizhou school in his *Mingru xue'an*, fasc. 36, p. 869. The translation is adapted from Brook, *Praying for Power*, p. 82. See also Julia Ching's translation of this entire section in *The Records of Ming Scholars*, pp. 165–201. For a detailed study of the rise of Chan Buddhism in Eastern Zhejiang, see Sun, "Mingmo Chanzong zai Zhedong xingsheng zhi yuanyou tantao."

77. See Miyun's encounter dialogues (*wenda jiyuan*) in Miyun Yuanwu, *Miyun chanshi yulu*, fasc. 5, ZH 37: 15458 and JXZ no. 158, 10: 28c.

78. See Zhanran's biography in his *Kuaiji Yunmen Zhanran Cheng chanshi yulu*, JXZ no. 172, 25: 664b–c.

79. See Huang Duanbo's brief account of his career in *Yaoguang ge waiji*, pp. 294b–95a. For his Chan thought, see Noguchi, "Minmatsu no Bukkyō koji Ō Tanhaku o megutte," pp. 117–18. In some Chan histories, he was recorded as a dharma heir of either Xuejiao Yuanxin or Wuming Huijing.

80. See Noguchi, "Minmatsu no Bukkyō koji Ō Tanhaku o megutte," pp. 122–25.

81. See Qi Biaojia's biography in DMB, pp. 216–20. See also Smith, "Gardens in Ch'i Piao-chia's Social World."

82. Qi Chenghan designed a garden that embodied his artistic taste. He also built a private library and collected a large number of rare and ancient books. This library became one of the four renowned private libraries in the late Ming Jiangnan area. There is evidence that the Qi family's private library was available for monks to conduct research on disputed historical issues. According to Feiyin Tongrong's record, in 1642 Miyun Yuanwu retired from Tiantong monastery and retreated to Tongxuan monastery at Mount Tiantai. When Miyun felt the need to consult some books, he immediately sent his disciples to the Qi family in Shaoxing to borrow books for the purpose of "investigation and refutation." The Qi family must have done Miyun a special favor because Qi Chenghan prohibited his family members from lending books. It is rumored that, after 1644, the Qi family's private collection was dispersed into monasteries, especially Yunmen monastery, which was likely the Qi family's private chapel initially.

83. For their Buddhist activities, see my discussion below.

84. See his biography written by Qi Xiongjia in Qi Biaojia, *Qi Biaojia ji*, p. 237.

85. Feiyin Tongrong, "Miyun chanshi nianpu," ZH 37: 15578.

86. See Feiyin Tongrong's brief account of this event in his *Feiyin chanshi bieji*, pp. 7–8.

87. See his preface to Shiyu Mingfang's recorded sayings in *Qi Biaojia ji*, p. 26; his letter inviting Master Mingfang to Xiansheng monastery in ibid., p. 53; and Er'mi Mingfu's epitaph he wrote in ibid., p. 61.

88. See *Hufa zhengdeng lu*, pp. 6 and 22.

89. Huang Zongxi, *Mingru xue'an*, vol. 2, p. 1369. All these people died for resisting the Manchu invasion except Cai Maode and Ma Shiqi. Cai admired Wang

Yangming's teaching and was attracted to Buddhist teaching. As governor of Shanxi province, he committed suicide when Taiyuan was captured by Li Zicheng's (1605–1645) rebel troops in 1644. Ma Shiqi committed suicide when Beijing was captured by Li Zicheng. For their biographies in the *Ming History*, see *Ming Shi*, fasc. 266, biography, no. 151 and 154. For details of Cai Maode's martyrdom, see Wen Bing, *Shanxi xunfu Cai Yunyi xiansheng xunnan shimo zhuan*, in *Xijian Mingshi shiji jicun*, vol. 17, pp. 1–11.

90. Huang Yuqi was listed as Miyun Yuanwu's dharma heir in Bie'an Xingtong, *Xudeng zhengtong*, fasc. 33, Z no. 1583, 84: 596b. See also his biography in Peng Shaosheng, *Jushi zhuan*, fasc. 51, Z no. 1646, 88: 281c. For Huang Yuqi's efforts at resistance, see Xu Zi, *Xiao tian ji zhuan*, fasc. 46, pp. 470–71; Chen Yinke, *Liu Rushi biezhuan*, pp. 882–905; and Wakeman, *The Great Enterprise*, vol. 2, p. 878; and He Lingxiu, "Huang Yuqi de Fu Ming huodong ji Huang Yuqi an."

91. Jin Sheng obtained his *jinshi* degree in 1628. He was first influenced by Wang Yangming's thought and later became a devout Buddhist. He studies with the Caodong masters Zongbao Daodu and Julang Daosheng. His best friend was Xiong Kaiyuan, who became a Caodong monk after the fall of the Ming. After the fall of the Ming, he organized a strong army in the south to resist the Manchu invasion. His efforts to resist the Manchu troops are detailed in *Mingji liechen zhuan*, in *Xijian Mingshi shiji jicun*, vol. 29, pp. 217–23; Wen Ruilin, *Nanjiang yishi*, fasc.14, pp. 96–7; and in Xu Zi, *Xiao tian ji zhuan*, pp. 46–7. For his resistance effort and his encounter with Hong Chengchou, see Chen-main Wang, *The Life and Career of Hung Ch'eng-ch'ou*, pp. 157 and 227. For his Buddhist thought and biography, see Peng Shaosheng, *Jushi zhuan*, fasc. 52, Z 88: 283a–84c; Araki, ""Kin Shōki to Yō Gyozan." However, some Christian scholars claim that he was actually converted to Christianity because he befriended the famous Chinese Christian Xu Guangqi (1562–1633) and showed his sympathy to the Christian religion. See the Christian version of Jin Sheng's biography in Fang Hao, *Zhongguo Tianzhujiao shi renwu zhuan*, vol. 1, pp. 240–6.

92. Qian Sule was finally buried at Mount Huangbo by Yinyuan Longqi in 1654. See my article "Leaving for the Rising Run," p. 107n53. For Qian Sule's role in the Southern Ming, see Xu Zi, *Xiao tian ji zhuan*, fasc. 40, pp. 388–94; Wen Ruilin, *Nanjiang yishi*, fasc. 32, pp. 223–25.

93. See Huang Duanbo's reply to Chen Gongyu in his *Yaoguang ge waiji*, fasc. 1, in *Siku quanshu cunmu congshu*, 193: 294b–95a, especially 295a. For a short discussion of his Chan thought, see Noguchi, "Minmatsu no Bukkyō koji Ō Tanhaku o megutte," pp. 117–18. Noguchi seems to have worked from a different edition of Huang's *Yaoguang ge waiji*.

94. Huang Duanbo's heroic martyrdom shows an apparent link between Huang's loyalism and his Chan learning. However, his contemporary Huang Zongxi, though admiring his sacrifice, objected such an easy conclusion. He commented on those Chan-minded martyrs as follows.

All these gentlemen left their fame of loyalty and righteousness in the world. Because in Chan Buddhism, there is no good and no evil and both aspects of principles and phenomena are dismissed without attaching to [the categories] of being and nothingness, the myriad of things are dissolved like tiles cracking [into pieces]. When some [evil-doers], hiding these notorious names, entered into Chan communities, they enjoyed themselves and thus had no shame and remorse. [However], these gentlemen's loyalist and righteous [deeds] resulted from their natural temperament that was not thawed by the Chan teaching style. Therefore, this should not be called "knowing the [Buddha] nature." People in later times see that loyalty and righteousness came from these followers of Buddhist teaching and thus thought they (loyalty and righteousness) are inherent in Buddhist teaching. Some Confucians also said accordingly that Buddhist teaching does not obstruct the [Confucian virtues of] loyalty and righteousness. They don't know that clearly this is where their natural temperament can not be hidden. Please do not misidentify the true seeds of our Confucians because of these gentlemen's [indulgence in Chan Buddhism]." (See Huang Zongxi, *Mingru xue'an*, p. 1369.)

Here, Huang Zongxi, unsympathetic of the hyperbolic Chan teaching, tried to draw the boundary between Confucianism and Buddhism and to explain away the possible Chan influence on these martyrs' choices of sacrifice. He acknowledged that Chan teaching did destroy the dualistic distinction between good and evil and thus could have encouraged a nihilistic attitude toward everything. However, as Huang mentioned, under the name of nondualism, evil-doers could also have no scruples. Rather, he saw these men as true Confucians: Although they were deeply immersed in Chan teaching, their moral character was still derived from Confucian teaching. Although Huang Zongxi was biased against Buddhism, his analysis was probably true because as I have delineated in this chapter, some Confucian literati were inspired by Wang Yangming and developed the discourse of nonduality within the literati culture and only found expressions of such a discourse in Chan teaching. For them, Chan teaching fit in a broader intellectual discourse of the ultimate moral truth that transcended the distinction of good and evil. Peng Shaosheng, the author of *the Jushi zhuan*, noted Huang's above comments and quoted them when he discussed these Ming martyrs. But he disputed Huang's judgment from the Buddhist perspective and believed that their Buddhist cultivation was the source of their courage. See Peng Shaosheng, *Jushi zhuan*, fasc. 52, Z 88: 285c.

95. See Wakeman, *The Great Enterprise*, vol. 1, pp. 585–86. Huang Duanbo's death was recorded in many late Ming sources. For some of the references, see Wen Bing, *Jiayi shi'an*, fasc. 2, *Siku jinhuishu congkan*, series 2 (*shibu*), 72: 96b; Shi Dun, *Tong yu zaji*, in *Siku jinhuishu congkan*, series 2 (*shibu*), 72: 120a–b; *Mingji liechen zhuan*, in *Xijian Mingshi shiji jicun*, vol. 29, p. 122; Xu Zi, *Xiao tian ji zhuan*, fasc. 16, pp. 183–84; Wen Ruilin, *Nanjiang yishi*, fasc. 10, pp. 75–6; Zha Jizuo, *Guo shou lu*, pp. 47–8.

96. Spence, *Return to Dragon Mountain*, pp. 205–6. For Qi Biaojia's efforts to reorganize the Southern Ming defense, see *Mingji liechen zhuan*, in *Xijian Mingshi shiji jicun*, vol. 29, pp. 132–39; Wen Ruilin, *Nanjiang yishi*, fasc. 11, pp. 81–3; Xu Zi, *Xiao tian ji zhuan*, fasc. 15, pp. 176–79; Zha Jizuo, *Guo shou lu*, pp. 44–5.

97. Qi Biaojiao's sixth son, Qi Bansun (1632–1673), became a monk after being implicated in an uprising against the Manchu rule. He later became the abbot at

Ma'anshan monastery in Nanjing and was known as Zhoulin Ming. See Xu Zi, *Xiao tian ji zhuan*. fasc. 15, pp. 179–80. Chen Yuan cites Huang Zongxi's observation of the dispersion of the Qi collection into Buddhist monasteries. See Chen Yuan, *Qingchu sengzheng ji*, p. 38.

98. See Araki, "Confucianism and Buddhism in the Late Ming," p. 54. In a series of later works, Araki continues to develop his argument along this line. His recent articulation of this argument can be found in his work on Zhuhong. See his *Unsei Shukō no kenkyū*, pp. 12–41 and its Chinese translation, *Jinshi Zhongguo Fojiao de shuguang*, pp. 57–90.

CHAPTER 3

1. See Chen Danzhong's preface in *Hufa zhengdeng lu*, p. 12.

2. While I introduce these masters according to their relationships of dharma transmission, I am fully aware of the "string of pearls" fallacy, as John R. McRae calls it. However, as McRae points out, descriptions based on lineage successions cannot be avoided completely because Chan Buddhism is genealogically constructed. For details, see McRae, *Seeing through Zen*, pp. 9–11.

3. Some of the Linji transmissions that I summarize below were disputed in the seventeenth century. For details, see appendix 2.B.

4. For a detailed study of this important master, see Chün-fang Yü, "Chung-feng Ming-pen and Ch'an Buddhism in the Yüan."

5. Huanyou Zhengchuan and Yunqi Zhuhong were study mates under Xiaoyan Debao, but Yunqi Zhuhong left later. Although Huanyou Zhengchuan was widely acknowledged as a dharma heir of Xiaoyan Debao, his transmission was questioned in later sectarian debates. See Weizhi Zhikai, *Zhengming lu*, fasc. 14, pp. 209–27, and my discussion in appendix 2.B. For Huanyou Zhengchuan and Xiaoyan Debao, see Chün-fang Yü, "Ming Buddhism," p. 926; and Noguchi, "Minmatsu Kokyūha no genryū."

6. See Guo Peng, *Ming Qing Fojiao*, pp. 322–29. I didn't determine why Guo Peng calls Tianyin Yuanxiu's lineage as the Panshan tradition. Panshan might be a misprint for Qinshan, which is Tianyin Yuanxiu's literary name.

7. For a study of his influence, see Liao, "Diyideng toulan shamen."

8. Feiyin Tongrong, "Miyun chanshi nianpu," in *Miyun chanshi yulu*, JXZ no. 158, 10: 77c.

9. Ibid., 78c.

10. See Zhang Dai's observation of monks in Tiantong monastery in his *Tao'an mengyi*, p. 172.

11. Ishii, "Minmatsu Shinsho no Tendōzan to Mitsuun Engo."

12. Hanyue Fazang, "Sanfeng Fazang chanshi nianpu," JXZ no. 299, 34: 204a. Lynn Struve notes in her research on Xue Cai's (1598–1665) journal that, in his youth, Hanyue stayed with Xue's family and studied medicine initially. Xue was eventually ordained by Hanyue's leading dharma heir, Jiqi Hongchu, in 1646. See Struve, "Ancestor *Édité* in Republican China" and "Dreaming and Self-search during the Ming Collapse." I thank Professor Struve for sharing her papers and the relevant pages of Xue Cai's journal with me before their publication.

13. Liao, "Wanming sengren shanju shi lunxi."

14. For studies of these female dharma heirs, see Beata Grant's articles listed in the bibliography.

15. According to the governor of Suzhou Gao Qizhuo's (1676–1738) memorial on the eighth day of the eighth month of 1735, Yongzheng's edict was carried out thoroughly. See Zhang Wenliang, *Yongzheng yu Chanzong*, pp. 116–18. However, according to Hasebe Yūkei, Hanyue Fazang's lineage managed to survive the persecution and lasted until the Republican era in the 1940s. See his "Sanhō ichimon no ryūtai," I–VI.

16. For the best studies of Muchen Daomin and early Qing politics, see Chen Yuan's "Yulu yu Shunzhi gongting" and "Tang Ruowang yu Muchen Min." For a study of government policies toward Buddhism, see Zhou Shujia, *Qingdai Fojiao shiliao jigao.*

17. For a brief account of Muchen Daomin's career, see Rao, "Qingchu seng Daomin jiqi *Bushuitai ji.*"

18. This summary is based on Chen Yuan, "Tang Ruowang yu Muchen Min."

19. The portrait, presented by Muchen Daomin, was painted by Zeng Jing. Shunzhi kept the original and returned a copy to Muchen. For the relation between Zeng Jing and the Ōbaku portraiture tradition, see Sharf, "Ōbaku Zen Portrait Painting and Its Sino-Japanese Heritage." According to Sharf, Ōtsuki Mikio and Mishigami Minoru identified several passages in Muchen Daomin's recorded sayings related to this portrait. See also *Tiantong si zhi*, ZFS 84: 268. According to this record, two portraits were copied by Wang Guocai, and the emperor claimed that he painted the sleeve area by hand with ink.

20. See Yongzheng, "Qing Shizong guanyu Foxue zhi yuzhi," pp. 1–4.

21. According to Feiyin's own account, he was actually ordained by Zhanran Yuancheng and was given the tonsure name "Mingmi," which must have been changed to the current name after Feiyin was converted by Miyun Yuanwu. See Feiyin Tongrong's comment on this issue in *Feiyin chanshi bieji*, fasc. 12, p. 12.

22. The story about the seamless pagoda is often used as a kōan to train students. It originated from the Chan master Nanyang Huizhong, who asked the Tang emperor to build a "seamless pagoda" after his death. See Daoyuan (ed.), *Jingde chuandeng lu*, T no. 2076, 51: 245a.

23. Feiyin Tongrong, "Fuyan Feiyin Rong chanshi jinian lu," in *Feiyin chanshi yulu*, JXZ 26: 183a.

24. See Feiyin Tongrong, "Fuyan Feiyin Rong chanshi jinian lu," in *Feiyin chanshi yulu*, JXZ 26: 184b and ZH 101: 42120.

25. One of Feiyin Tongrong's early works, *Bore Xinjing zhuolun jie*, has survived. See XZJ no. 451, vol. 41; and Z no. 548, vol. 26. Feiyin was actually a good student of doctrinal studies under the training of the Caodong masters. Although he seldom showed off his knowledge of Buddhist doctrine, his polemical essays arguing against Matteo Ricci demonstrate that he was skillful in using Buddhist syllogism to refute Christianity. See my article "Buddhist Logic and Apologetics in Seventeenth-century China."

26. Feiyin's chronological biography reveals that he was actually instrumental in introducing Miyun to Mount Huangbo because Feiyin was a Fuqing native. Accord-

ing to this record, in 1630, Feiyin returned to Fuqing for half a year and introduced Miyun Yuanwu to the local literati. Through Feiyin Tongrong's negotiation, Miyun accepted the position. See Feiyin Tongrong, "Fuyan Feiyin Rong chanshi jinian lu," JXZ no. 178, 26: 185b.

27. There was a dispute about the early Caodong transmission in the Song. For details, see appendix 2.A.

28. See Zhanran's epitaph written by Tao Shiling and collected in Zhanran's recorded sayings in JXZ no. 172, 25: 663b.

29. See Zhanran Yuancheng, *Kuaiji Yunmen Zhanran Cheng chanshi yulu*, fasc. 6, JXZ 25: 631b.

30. However, no explicit reference to his dharma transmission can be found. Therefore, based on the lack of evidence, Feiyin Tongrong listed Wuming Huijing as a monk of "lineage unknown" in his *Wudeng yantong*.

31. See Wuming Huijing's epitaph written by Hanshan Deqing in Wuming Huijing, *Shouchang Wuming heshang yulu*, JXZ no. 173, 25: 683b–84c.

32. Wuming Huijing, *Shouchang Wuming heshang yulu*, JXZ 25: 670c.

33. For Yongjue Yuanxian's life and thought, see Lin Ziqing, "Yuanxian chanshi de 'Gushan chan' jiqi shengping."

34. For Juelang Daosheng's life and thought, see Araki, *Yūkoku rekka Zen*.

35. See Chen Yuan, *Mingji Dian Qian Fojiao kao*; and Wang Luping, *Guizhou Fojiao shi*.

36. See Chen Yuan, *Mingji Dian Qian Fojiao kao*, chapter 3. In Yunnan, Mount Jizu was the most active Buddhist center. It seems that dharma transmissions there were developed independently from those in the southeast. See Hou Chong, "Yunnan Jizushan de jueqi jiqi zhuyao Chanxi."

37. Shunzhi's interest in Buddhism reached such an extreme that he considered becoming a monk in his later years. Some legends even claim that he abdicated the throne and was ordained in Mount Wutai. For refutations of this myth, see Chen Yuan, "Shunzhi huangdi chujia," in his *Chen Yuan shixue lunzhu xuan*, pp. 482–90. See also Meng Sen's and Peng Guodong's works listed in the bibliography.

38. Zuxin Hanke's exile was related to the famous early Qing official Hong Chengchou (1593–1665), a former Ming governor who surrendered to the Manchus. According to Chen-main Wang, Zuxin Hanke was trapped in Nanjing when the Manchu army captured the city in 1645. Because Zuxin Hanke's father, a former minster of rites in the Ming, was Hong Chengchou's teacher, he asked Hong, who led the Manchu army to Nanjing, to issue a pass for him to leave the city. Unfortunately, he was detained at a check point after his anti-Manchu writings were discovered from his belongings. A year later, Zuxin Hanke was put into exile. See Chen-mian Wang, *The Life and Career of Hung Ch'eng-ch'ou*, pp. 167–68. See also Wakeman, *The Great Enterprise*, vol. 2, pp. 759–60; Yim, "Political Exile, Chan Buddhism Master, Poetry Club Founder"; Xie, "Qingchu Dongbei liuren kao"; Wang Zongyan, *Mingji Shengren heshang nianpu*; and Yang Haiying, *Hong Chengchou yu Ming Qing yidai yanjiu*, pp. 239–48.

39. See Wang Zongyan, *Tianran chanshi nianpu*.

40. Timothy Brook conducts a case study of Mount Dinghu in his *Praying for Power*, pp. 137–58.

41. However, there is very little scholarship about this master. Most sources list his name as 源 or 元. According to Muchen Daomin's original transmission verse, the character was initially written as *xuan* 玄. Because the Kangxi emperor's name contains the character *xuan*, all appearances of this character were subsequently changed. Details of his life in China are not clear, but the Vietnamese sources provide some biographical information about him. For Yuanzhao's biography, see Thich, "Nguyen-Thieu Zen School: A Sect of Lin-chi Tradition Contemporary with Japanese Ōbaku Zen," in his *Buddhism and Zen in Vietnam*, pp. 148–61. A short English biography of Yuanzhao (Nguyên-Thiêu), which is based on Thich Thien-An's account, can be found in John Power's *The Concise Encyclopedia of Buddhism*, p. 150.

42. Shilian Dashan left a travelogue entitled *Haiwai jishi*.

43. See Baroni, *Obaku Zen*, pp. 34–35. Daozhe Chaoyuan was Feiyin's disciple Genxin Xingmi's (1603–1659) dharma heir.

44. As I have clarified elsewhere, his migration to Nagasaki was carried out under unique social circumstances, including a new wave of Chinese emigration to Japan and Ming loyalist Zheng Chenggong's (1624–1662) desperate attempt to request Japanese military aid. For details, see my article "Leaving for the Rising Sun."

45. In the 1930s, Van Gulik noticed the importance of this monk. Donggao Xinyue was also an accomplished musician who was especially instrumental in introducing the Chinese zither to Japan. See Van Gulik, *Mingmo yi seng Donggao chan shi ji kan*; and Chen Zhichao (ed.), *Lü Ri gao seng Donggao Xinyue shi wen ji*. See also Nagai, "Tōkō Shin'etsu kenkyū josetsu."

46. See Deng Huoqu, *Nanxun lu*, no. 101, p. 408–9. For detailed discussion of Deng's life and thought, see Araki, *Chūgoku Shingaku to kodō no Bukkyō*, pp. 261–96.

47. See Brook, *Praying for Power*, pp. 119–26. Xinglang Daoxiong hailed from a prosperous family in Longxi in Zhejiang. His surname was Lin. He studied with both Miyun Yuanwu and Zhanran Yuancheng and received dharma transmission from Wuyi Yuanlai. He resided in Mount Yefu in Luzhou, Sichuan, beginning in 1647. See his short biography in ZFR, pp. 819–20.

48. See Muchen Daomin, *Beiyou ji*, fasc. 3, JXZ no. 180, 26: 296c-297a.

49. This autobiography, covering the major events in his life from his birth in 1596 to 1640, may have been written in the thirteenth year of the Shunzhi reign (1657), when he was sixty.

50. In his autobiography, Muchen Daomin claimed that he played a role in these invitations. As early as 1627, when he was studying in Kaixian monastery at Mount Lushan with his master, Ruomei Zhiming (1569–1631), he was already acquainted with Huang Duanbo, who later became an official in Ningbo and invited Miyun to Ayuwang and Tiantong. According to Muchen, because of his good relationship with Huang, he persuaded Huang to invite Miyun.

51. Several important polemical works attributed to Miyun Yuanwu were actually either composed or edited by Muchen Daomin. For example, in the autumn of 1634, Miyun was involved in a dispute with Hanyue Fazang. Muchen confessed that he actually wrote the polemical essays. He also edited Miyun's anti-Christian essay *Biantian sanshuo*. See Muchen Daomin, *Shanweng Min chanshi suinian zipu*, p. 300. An early edition of the *Biantian sanshuo* with Muchen Daomin's preface was

discovered in the Shanghai Library. It shows that Muchen Daomin was responsible for compiling these essays on Miyun's behalf. This preface was absent in the popular edition of the *Shengchao pixie ji* compiled by Xu Changzhi. This is why scholars assume that Miyun was the author of these essays.

52. For a brief discussion about literati-turned-monks during the Ming-Qing transition, see Zhao Yuan, *Ming Qing zhiji shidafu yanjiu*, pp. 289–308; Liao, "Mingmo Qingchu yimin tao Chan zhi feng yanjiu."

53. Xiong was a good friend of Jin Sheng, who died as a martyr. He also kept close relationship with Jiqi Hongchu although he eventually received Jude Hongli's dharma transmission. For his role in the resistance movement, see Xu Zi, *Xiao tian ji zhuan*, fasc. 248–49; Wen Ruilin, *Nanjiang yishi*, fasc. 28, pp. 197–8. For his short biography and works, see Struve, *Ming-Qing Conflict*, p. 264; Araki, "Kin Shōki to Yō Gyozan."

54. See Lin Yuanbai, "Huishan heshang de shengping jiqi *Chanmen duanlian shuo*." For his biography in detail, see Noguchi, "Iminsō Kaizan Kaiken ni tsuite" and "Kaizan Kaiken nenpu kō." Noguchi's paper is based on *Lingyin Huishan Xian heshang quanji* (twenty-four fascicles), a rare book preserved in Tōkyō daigaku Tōyō bunka kenkyūjo.

55. For a comprehensive study of Shitao, see Hay, *Shitao*.

56. See Xue and Xue, *Kuncan*.

57. Barnhart and Wang, *Master of the Lotus Garden*.

58. For a study in English, see Kuo, *Austere Landscape*.

59. Jin Bao has attracted some scholarly attention. See Liao, "Kin Hō *Hengyōdō shū* ni ryōru Minmatsu Shinsho Kōnan bunjin no seishin yōshiki no saikentō" and "Jin Bao de jieyi guan yu lishi pingjia tanxi." See Wu Tianren, *Dangui chanshi nianpu*. For Qianlong's imperial decree banning Jin Bao's work, see Zhou Shujia, *Qingdai Fojiao shiliao jigao*, p. 141. For his detailed biography in English, see Struve, *Ming-Qing Conflict*, pp. 26–27, 301; ECCP, p. 166.

60. For his political career in the Yongli court, see Struve, *The Southern Ming*, pp. 132–35.

61. He disrobed in 1662 and resumed his Confucian identity. See Tan, *Lingnan Chan wenhua*, pp. 138–41. For Qu Dajun's connection with Buddhism, see Cai, *Qingchu Lingnan Fomen shilüe*, pp. 73–98; and Struve, *Ming-Qing Conflict*, p. 340.

62. For Qian Bangqi's role in the Southern Ming, see Xu Zi, *Xiao tian ji zhuan*, pp. 320–22. For a short introduction to his work in English, see Struve, *Ming-Qing Conflict*, pp. 295–96.

63. Because he visited Zhanran Yuancheng in his youth, he claimed to be a dharma heir of Zhanran Yuancheng and thus changed his original name from Puhe to Tonghe. See Chen, *Mingji Dian Qian Fojiao kao*, pp. 200–203.

64. For a brief biography of Fang Yizhi in English, see ECCP, p. 864b; also see Ren, *Fang Yizhi nianpu*; Peterson, *Bitter Gourd*; Ying-shih Yü, *Fang Yizhi wanjie kao*.

65. Xiaofeng Daran joined the Buddhist order in 1645 and lived in Mount Qingyuan in Jiangxi after receiving Juelang Daosheng's dharma transmission in 1648. See his biography in *Qingyuan zhilüe*, ZFS 18: 106–12.

66. See Hou Wailu, *Zhongguo sixiang tongshi*, vol. 4, part II, pp. 1121–88.

67. Wuke Dazhi, *Qingyuan Wuke Zhi chanshi yulu*, JXZ no. 331, vol. 34. For Yü's speculation about Fang's possible suicide, see his *Fang Yizhi wanjie kao.*

68. See Brook, *Praying for Power*, p. 182.

69. See Chow, *Publishing, Culture, and Power*, pp. 154–56. For recent studies in this field, see also Brokaw and Chow (eds.), *Printing and Book Culture*; Chia, *Printing for Profit*; McDermott, *A Social History of the Chinese Book.*

CHAPTER 4

1. Chen Yuan, *Mingji Dian Qian Fojiao kao*, p. 48.

2. Ibid., p. 275.

3. This book is not extant. For a discussion of Hanyue Fazang's use of the *Zhizheng zhuan*, see Hasebe, "Sanhō ichimon no ryūtai," II, pp. 109–11.

4. For this division in Chan history, see the works by Mou Zongsan, Dong Qun, Hong Xiuping, and Zhang Wenliang listed in the bibliography.

5. See the collated biography of Huineng in *Enō kenkyū*, p. 45. This paragraph has been completely incorporated into the Zongbao edition of the *Platform Sūtra*. See Zongbao (ed.), *Liuzu dashi fabao tanjing*, T no. 2008, 48: 359c.

6. See *Lidai fabao ji*, p. 154.

7. See Broughton, "Tsung-mi's Zen Prolegomenon," pp. 11–52.

8. Zongmi, *Chanyuan zhu quanji duxu*, T 48: 399b. Translation adapted from Jeffrey L. Broughton's "Kuei-feng Tsung-mi," pp. 93–94.

9. Guishan Lingyou, *Tanzhou Guishan Lingyou chanshi yulu*, T no. 1989, 47: 580b.

10. Yuanwu's and Dahui's comments have been incorporated into Guishan Lingyou's recorded sayings. See T 47: 580b.

11. Hanyue Fazang, *Sanfeng Zang heshang yulu*, fasc. 6, JXZ 34: 154c.

12. See Hanyue Fazang's preface to the *Wujia yulu* in XZJ 119: 848 and Z no. 1326, 69: 21a–c. Hanyue's analogy was criticized by the Yongzheng emperor. See my discussion in chapter 6. For some references on Chinese pagodas, see Chang, *Zhongguo guta de yishu licheng*. See also Steinhardt (ed.), *Chinese Traditional Architecture*, pp. 109–20.

13. Tanji Hongren, *Wuzong jiu*, in *Zhongguo Fojiao congshu*, 6: 823. Because Tanji Hongren's work became the target of the Yongzheng emperor's criticism, the emperor ordered it to be destroyed, and consequently the original edition is difficult to identify. The editor of the current edition did not specify the origin of this book. I suspect that it may be a reprint of an early edition. For a description of various editions, see Hasebe, "Sanhō ichimon no ryūtai," IV, pp. 40–44. Huang Zongxi mentioned that the *Wuzong jiu* was largely composed by the literatus Zhang Qiran (1599–1664), commonly known as Ren'an, who was ordained after 1644. See Chen Yuan, *Qingchu sengzheng ji*, p. 127. See also Zhang Qiran's epitaph written by Huang Zongxi in his *Nanlei wending qianji houji sanji (xia)*, pp. 53–55.

14. See Huang Duanbo's preface to Miyun's recorded sayings, JXZ no. 158, 10: 1a.

15. Noguchi, "Minmatsu ni okeru shūjinko ronsō," p. 164. Miyun's negative attitude toward Zhuhong's Pure Land practice can be seen from his sarcastic comment on Zhuhong in his *Miyun chanshi yulu*, fasc. 12, JXZ no. 158, 10: 66a-b.

16. Miyun Yuanwu, *Miyun chanshi yulu*, ZH 37: 15401. Miyun Yuanwu may have exaggerated his ignorance of Buddhist doctrines. His polemical essays show that he was at least familiar with contemporary doctrinal debates, such as the one over Sengzhao's (384–414) *Things Do Not Shift* (*Wubuqian*) between Kongyin Zhencheng (1547–1617) and other scholar-monks, including Miyun Yuanwu's dharma master, Huanyou Zhengchuan. Judging from his existing collection *Tiantong zhishuo*, he had demonstrated his proficiency in tathāgatagarbha and Madhyamaka thought and even in Buddhist logic. See Miyun Yuanwu, *Tiantong zhishuo*, fasc. 5.

17. It was recorded by Weizhi Zhikai that when Miyun Yuanwu was invited to Mount Huangbo, the Caodong master Juelang Daosheng sent a letter to Miyun and criticized him for recruiting dharma heirs indiscriminately. In response, Miyun Yuanwu ordered Feiyin Tongrong and Muchen Daomin to compile a new Chan genealogy, *Chandeng shipu*. Zhikai regarded this incident as the trigger for later debates about dharma transmission. See Weizhi Zhikai, *Zhengming lu*, fasc. 14, p. 210.

18. Hanyue's enlightenment story was widely known through the publication of his chronological biography, which states that on the fifth day of his practice, after feeling sleepy and dizzy, he was suddenly awakened by a loud cracking sound outside his chamber when two monks were chopping bamboo. See Lu K'uan Yü's (Charles Luk) translation of this episode in his *The Secrets of Chinese Meditation*, pp. 78–79.

19. See Hanyue's letter to Miyun in *Sanfeng Qingliang chansi zhi* (1892 edition), ZFS 40: 335. In another letter to Miyun, Hanyue expressed similar opinions. See *Sanfeng Qingliang chansi zhi* (1892 edition), ZFS 40: 335–36. This letter was also preserved in *Sanfeng Zang heshang yulu*, fasc. 14, JXZ 34: 190a.

20. Lian, "Hanyue Fazang (1573–1635) yu wan Ming Sanfengzongpai de jianli." Hanyue explained his motive for accepting Miyun's transmission in a letter, in which he delineated some ideas that he developed in his later *Wuzong yuan*. See Hanyue's second reply to Miyun, *Sanfeng Qingliang chansi zhi* (1892 edition), ZFS 40: 336–37. This letter was also included in *Sanfeng Zang heshang yulu*, fasc. 14, JXZ 34: 190a–b.

21. See Miyun Yuanwu, *Tiantong zhishuo*, fasc. 3, p. 30.

22. It must be noted here, however, that most works allegedly authored by Miyun might have been significantly edited by his leading disciple Muchen Daomin, then Miyun's private secretary. As Muchen Daomin confessed in his autobiography, during the fall of 1633, his master published several polemical essays, and he often took his teacher's idea and composed them. He mentioned especially Miyun's *Tiantong zhishuo* and his role as an editor in the process of compilation. See Muchen Daomin, *Shanweng Min chanshi suinian zipu*, p.300

23. There are three editions of this text. The first is preserved in the supplementary canon as an independent title; the second can be found in Hanyue Fazang's recorded sayings (fasc. 11, JXZ 34: 175c–80b), and the third, an abbreviated version, is contained in *Sanfeng Qingliang chansi zhi* (1892 edition), fasc. 6, ZFS 40: 155–68. I rely on the first edition in the supplementary canon. For a comparison of these versions, see Hasebe, "Sanhō ichimon no ryūtai," IV, pp. 37–39.

24. Hanyue was not the only person to use the metaphor of a "tally." Before him, this metaphor had been widely used in Chan literature. Zongmi, for example, was

also fond of it. However, I did not find evidence of Zongmi's influence on Hanyue's thought. For Zongmi's use of "tally," see Broughton, "Tsung-mi's Zen Prolegomenon," pp. 16–17.

25. The background of this book is not known.

26. Hanyue Fazang, *Wuzong yuan*, Z 65: 102.

27. See Tianyin Yuanxiu, *Tianyin heshang yulu*, fasc. 11, JXZ no. 171, 25: 574c.

28. The term *yehu yan* derived from the famous kōan story of a wild fox in Baizhang Huaihai's recorded sayings and referred to a kind of shallow teaching. For this kōan, see *Baizhang yulu*, T 48: 231c–32b; *Shinpan Zengaku daijiten*, p. 1236. This passing remark was singled out for criticism in the later debate. See my discussion in chapter 5.

29. He was Xiaoyan Debao's disciple and compiled his teacher's literary collection *Xiaoyan Bao zu nanbei ji*.

30. One significant difference between the Dunhuang edition and the later popular editions, such as the Zongbao edition, is the alteration of Huineng's verses. In the Dunhuang edition, two verses were recorded, but the later editions only contained the first one, and the third line was changed to "Originally not a single thing existed." For a comparison of this verse in different editions, see *Enō kenkyū*, p. 284.

31. Noguchi suggests that the real targets of Hanyue's criticism may have been Hanshan Deqing and Zibo Zhenke, whose thought was similar to Sanji Guangtong's. For details, see Noguchi, "Honrai mu ichi butsu wa gedō no hō."

32. For this sermon, see his *Tianyin heshang yulu*, fasc. 11, JXZ no. 171, 25: 575c–77b.

33. See Tianyin Yuanxiu's reply to Hanyue in his *Tianyin heshang yulu*, JXZ no. 171, 25: 577.

34. See Tianyin Yuanxiu's second reply to Hanyue and his comments in *Tianyin heshang yulu*, JXZ no. 171, 25: 577.

35. See Tianyin Yuanxiu's letter to Miyun, ibid., JXZ no. 171, 25: 577c.

36. Some Chan monks doubted the authenticity of these letters. See Hasebe, "Sanhō ichimon no ryūtai," II, p. 9.

37. Liu Daozhen hailed from Sichuan. He came to Suzhou in 1631 and was attracted by Hanyue's Chan teaching. He was later enlightened by Hanyue and received his dharma transmission. Refusing to surrender, he died as a martyr during the peasant rebel Zhang Xianzhong's rule in Sichuan. See his short biography in Xu Zi, *Xiao tian ji zhuan*, fasc. 51, p. 546; and Peng Shaosheng, *Jushi zhuan*, fasc. 51, Z no. 1646, 88: 280c–81a.

38. See Miyun's reply to Hanyue written in the summer of 1633 in his *Tiantong zhishuo*, fasc. 1, p. 3.

39. See Miyun's letter to Hanyue written in the spring of 1634 in his *Tiantong zhishuo*, fasc. 1, p. 5.

40. See Miyun's reply to Dingmu Hongche written in the summer of 1633, ibid., fasc. 1, pp. 3–4.

41. See Miyun's reply to Liu Daozhen written in the autumn of 1634, ibid., fasc. 1, pp. 6–32.

42. See Miyun's letter to Hanyue written in the winter of 1634, ibid., fasc. 1, pp. 32–36.

43. I have not yet located this letter.

44. Miyun Yuanwu, *Tiantong zhishuo*, 2: 23–30.

45. Although these letters are undated, Miyun's reply to Qi Junjia mentions the death of Hanyue, indicating that these letters must have been written after Fazang's death in 1635. See this letter in *Tiantong zhishuo*, 2: 37–38.

46. For his biography, see his recorded sayings *Rujiu Ruibai chanshi yulu*, JXZ no. 188, 26: 749–824.

47. These sources were incorporated in the first three fascicles of *Tiantong zhishuo*. These three essays are also known as the "three refutations" (*sanpi*).

48. See Dong Han, *Zhuanxiang zuibi*, fasc. 2, in *Zhongguo jindai xiaoshuo shiliao huibian*, vol. 20, p. 10. For reference to this essay, see *Sanfeng Qingliang chansi zhi* (1838 edition), ZFS 39: 126. See also *Sanfeng Qingliang chansi zhi* (1892 edition), fasc. 18, ZFS 41: 606.

49. Hanyue's acquaintance Xue Cai mentioned Tanji's eloquence in his journal. See Xue Cai, *Xue Xiemeng xiansheng biji*, fasc. 2, p. 22a. I thank Lynn Struve for sharing with me relevant pages of Xue Cai's journal.

50. As the compiler of this important work, Zhenqi should be important in Miyun's lineage. However, there is little information about him. According to Hasebe, he appeared to be a monk from Sichuan. He returned to Sichuan in 1640 and died a year later. See Hasebe, "Sanhō ichimon no ryūtai," II, p. 17.

51. This phrase refers to the three encounters between Huangbo and Linji, in which Linji was struck three times.

52. See Miyun's preface to the *Pi wangjiu lüeshuo* written on June 22, 1638, in XZJ 114: 219.

53. See Miyun Yuanwu, *Tiantong zhishuo*, fasc. 2, p. 28.

54. Jiyin, *Zongtong biannian*, fasc. 31, Z no. 1600, 86: 299b.

55. Miyun's chronological biography mentions this letter. See the record for the year 1634, JXZ no. 158, 10: 83c. According to Feiyin Tongrong, Miyun also wrote an essay to refute Chaozong Tongren. Several of Miyun's extant letters confirm that he wrote this work, which is no longer extant. See Miyun Yuanwu, *Miyun chanshi yulu*, JXZ 10: 45a and 47b.

56. See Feiyin Tongrong, *Feiyin chanshi bieji*, fasc. 3.

57. See Nukariya, *Zengaku shisōshi*, pp. 773–74.

58. See Feiyin Tongrong, *Feiyin chanshi bieji*, fascs. 4, 5, and 6. Feiyin was referred to as Master Jinsu because he resided in Jinsu monastery at that time.

59. See ibid., fasc. 7.

60. For Qian's biography, see ECCP, pp. 149–50. See also Lian, "Qian Qianyi de Fojiao shengya yu linian."

61. Qian edited Hanshan Deqing's collection himself and wrote a preface in 1657. For his commentary on the *Śuraṃgama Sūtra*, see *Shoulengyanjing shujie Mengchao*, XZJ, vol. 21.

62. See Yoshikawa, "Koji to shite no Sen Bokusai."

63. The other two "evils" were Christianity and the Jingling school of poems founded by Tan Yuanchun (1585–1637) and Zhong Xing (1574–1624). See Qian Qianyi, *Liechao shiji xiaozhuan*, vol. 4, fasc. 12, entry of Tan Yuanchun. See also Sterk, "Chan Grove Remarks on Poetry by Wang Shizhen," pp. 117–19; Lian, "Qian Qianyi de Fojiao shengya," pp. 331–34.

64. His relationship with Muchen Daomin deteriorated after the so-called second controversy over Miyun Yuanwu's plaque in Mount Jinshu. See Lian, "Qian Qianyi de Fojiao shengya," pp. 334–38.

65. Although Qian was among the first group of Ming officials who voluntarily surrendered to the Manchu regime, new evidence shows that he continued to involve himself in various loyalist activities. Because of his covert anti-Manchu activities, he was implicated in the case of his friend Huang Yuqi and jailed in Beijing for a year. See Wang Zhonghan, "Liu Rushi yu Qian Qianyi Xiang Qing wenti," p. 412. See also Chen Yinke, *Liu Rushi biezhuan*; Wakeman, *The Great Enterprise*, vol. 1, pp. 595–98.

66. See Chen Yuan, *Qingchu sengzheng ji*, pp. 34–42. See also Yamaguchi, "Kō Sōgi 'Sanhō zenji tōmei' kō." Huang was very critical of Buddhism in general and intended to purge the Buddhist influence from Confucianism. However, he maintained a friendly relationship with Buddhist monks. For example, he wrote a short essay attempting to solve the mystery of the two Daowus in the Tang, which I will analyze in appendix 3. For his biography, see ECCP, pp. 351–54.

67. See Chen Yuan, *Qingchu sengzheng ji*, pp. 48–55.

68. The "Jinsu fanzheng lu" is not extant, but its preface can be found in Muchen Daomin, *Bushuitai ji*, fasc. 6, JXZ, no. 181, 26: 334b. For his "Duni shuo," see *Bushuitai ji*, fasc. 24, JXZ no. 181, 26: 403a–b. He also wrote a letter to Jiqi Hongchu to express his view. For this letter, see *Bushuitai ji*, JXZ no. 181, 26: 418c–19c. See also Chen Yuan, *Qingchu sengzheng ji*, pp. 42–48.

69. The inflammatory titles suggest their polemical nature: "Panshi" (Rebelling against the master), "Chouzu" (Hating ancestors), "E'jiao" (Evil and cunning), "Minyu" (Pitying stupidity), and "Shemo" (Subduing demons). According to Chen Yuan, these essays, collectively referred to as *Wulun*, are preserved in Muyun Tongwen's *Lanzhai houji*, fasc. 6. I have not yet located these essays, and my account here is based on Chen Yuan's study. See Chen Yuan, *Qingchu sengzheng ji*, pp. 56–62.

70. His teacher was Ruo'an Tongwen, who brought dharma transmission to Li'an monastery in Hangzhou. This monastery was revived by Ruo'an Tongwen's ordination master Fayu Zhongguang (a.k.a. Rusong, *hao*. Foshi, 1569–1636). Tianli Xingzheng, as abbot of Jiashan monastery, received an audience with the Kangxi emperor when the emperor toured the south. He had been abbot of Li'an monastery for four times. His dharma heirs in Li'an such as Jialing Xingyin (1671–1726) became prominent in Bailin monastery in Beijing and was patronized by the Yongzheng and Qianlong emperors. For his short biography, see *Li'an si zhi*, ZFS 77: 232–239.

71. Yushan Shangsi's teacher was Jubo Jiheng (1605–1666), who was Jude Hongli's heir. He also received an audience with Kangxi when the emperor toured the south. For his short biography, see ZFR, p. 36.

72. For their dispute, see Hasebe, "Sanhō ichimon no ryūtai," III, pp. 137–38.

73. See this essay in *Yunlin si xuzhi*, fasc. 5, ZFS 62: 279–83. For a short biography of Qian, see ZFR, p. 1057.

CHAPTER 5

1. Linji Yixuan was a disciple of Huangbo Xiyun. After he left Huangbo Xiyun, Linji disseminated Chan teaching in Zhenzhou prefecture in Hebei. For Linji's biography, see Yanagida, "The Life of Lin-chi I-hsüan."

2. Baroni, *Obaku Zen*, p. 86. Baroni notices that Yinyuan lectured on the *Linji lu* frequently.

3. The earliest edition was published in 1120. For a study of various editions of the *Linji lu*, see Zhang, "Huanrao *Linjilu* zhuben de ruogan wenti." See also Welter, "The Textual History of the *Linji lu*." For a general review of the *yulu* genre in general, see Yanagida, "The 'Recorded Sayings' Texts of Chinese Ch'an Buddhism."

4. See *Linji lu*, T 47: 497a. Burton Watson translates this sentence as follows: "One phrase must be supplied with three dark gates. One dark gate must be supplied with three vital seals." See his *The Zen Teachings of Master Lin-chi*, p. 19.

5. See Huihong, *Linji zongzhi*, Z no. 1234, 63: 167–69; Fenyang Shanzhao, *Fenyang Wude chanshi yulu*, T no. 1992, 47: 594–628, especially 597–98, 603. For a translation of the *Linji zongzhi*, see Keyworth, "Transmitting the Lamp," pp. 169–88.

6. Fenyang Shanzhao, *Fenyang Wude chanshi yulu*, T no. 1992, 47: 597b. The translation is adopted from Keyworth, "Transmitting the Lamp," pp. 172–73.

7. Huihong was particularly critical of a Yunmen master named Jianfu Chenggu (970–1045). See Wu Limin et al., *Chanzong zongpai yuanliu*, pp. 293–95. See also Yang, "Fenyang Shanzhao jiqi chanfa."

8. Hanyue Fazang wrote an eulogy of the Linji school ("Jizong songyu"), which is collected in his *Wuzong yuan*, Z 65: 108.

9. Hanyue Fazang, *Wuzong yuan*, Z 65: 106c.

10. Ibid., Z 65: 107c.

11. See Foulk, "Controversies concerning the 'Separate Transmission,'" pp. 253–58.

12. Zongbao (ed.), *Liuzu fabao tanjing*, T no. 2008, 48: 349a–b. Translation is adopted from McRae (trans.), *The Platform Sutra of the Sixth Patriarch*, p. 35.

13. This passage appeared only in the Deyi and Zongbao editions. See *Enō kenkyū*, p.287. For the role of the robe, see Admek, "Robes Purple and Gold."

14. See Hanyue Fazang, *Wuzong yuan*, XZJ 114: 211. This phrase appeared as early as the second patriarch Huike's biography in the *Baolin Record(Baolin zhuan)*. For an alternative translation of this sentence, see Foulk, "Controversies concerning the 'Separate Transmission,'" p. 232.

15. The words for "transmission certificate" varied from time to time. In the Song, it was called *sishu*. In the late Ming, it was called *yuanliu* (origin and stream), and in modern times, according to Holmes Welch, it is called *fajuan* (dharma scroll). For details, see my article "Building a Dharma Transmission Monastery."

16. See Tanji Hongren, *Wuzong jiu*, p. 683.

17. This letter directed Miyun Yuanwu's attention to Hanyue Fazang's *Wuzong yuan*. In the subsequent exchange of polemical letters triggered by this letter, Miyun

Yuanwu totally rejected Hanyue's interpretation of the principles. See Miyun Yuanwu, *Tiantong zhishuo*, fasc. 1, p. 2.

18. Jiyin, *Zongtong biannian*, fasc. 14, Z 86: 171a.

19. Yuanwu Keqin, *Biyan lu*, T 48: 154c

20. See *Shinpan Zengaku daijiten*, p. 40. Miyun, however, misunderstood this term as *yijue* 一鑊. See Miyun's letter to Hanyue written in the spring of 1634, in his *Tiantong zhishuo*, fasc. 1, p. 29.

21. Miyun Yuanwu, *Tiantong zhishuo*, fasc. 3, p. 10.

22. Linji Yixuan, *Linji lu*, T 47: 504a. The context of this phrase is as follows: "At times my shout is like the precious sword of the Diamond King. At times, my shout is like a golden-haired lion crouching on the ground. At times, my shout is like the search pole and the shadow grass. At times my shout doesn't work like a shout at all." See Watson, *The Zen Teachings of Master Lin-chi*, p. 98.

23. As Yün-hua Jan records, in Chan history, there was a controversy about the role of Zongmi between Siming Zhili and Chan master Zining. At least in the Song, Zongmi had been regarded by orthodox Chan masters as *zhijie zongtu*. See Jan, *Zongmi*, pp. 228–29. See also Ziporyn, "Anti-Chan Polemics in Post Tang Tiantai."

24. For a detailed study, see Gregory, "Tsung-mi and the Single Word Awareness (*Chih*)."

25. Zongbao (ed.), *Liuzu dashi fabao tanjing*, T 48: 359b–c. Obviously, this insertion was the result of the demise of the Heze school. This derogatory attitude can be found in Qisong's edition as well, but not in Fahai's and Huixin's earlier versions. See Guo, *Tanjing duikan*, pp. 120–23; and "Gohon taishō Rokuso Dankyō" in *Enō kenkyū*, p. 366. For an introduction to various editions of the *Platform Sūtra*, see Schlütter, "A Study in the Genealogy of the *Platform Sūtra*."

26. See Poceski, *Original Mind as the Way*.

27. See *Linji lu*, T 47: 504c; and the translation in Watson, *The Zen Teachings of Master Lin-chi*, pp. 104–6.

28. See Yiru, *Da Ming sanzang fashu*.

29. According to the biography written by Tanji Hongren, Hanyue's teaching was influenced by Confucian classics. See Hanyue's biography written by Hongren in *Dengweishan Sheng'ensi zhi*, ZFS 44: 113–30.

30. T no. 12, 374: 376c. See Bernard Faure's explanation in his *The Rhetoric of Immediacy*, p. 197n44.

31. Tanji Hongren even attempted to reconstruct the ninety-seven kinds of the perfect circle used by Yangshan Huiji. See Tanji Hongren, *Wuzong jiu*, fasc. 9, pp. 703–4.

32. See Miyun's letter to Hanyue written in the spring of 1634 in his *Tiantong zhishuo*, fasc. 1, p. 5.

33. See Zongmi, *Zhonghua chuanxindi chanmen shizi chengxitu*, Z 63: 31a–36a.

34. See Tianyin Yuanxiu's second reply to Hanyue in his recorded sayings, JXZ 25: 577b.

35. See Charles Orzech's translation of the text, "Saving the Burning-Mouth Hungry Ghost."

36. Recent scholarship has seriously questioned the existence of such an esoteric school during the Tang. For a critical assessment of the esoteric school, see Sharf, "On Esoteric Buddhism in China," in his *Coming to Terms with Chinese Buddhism*, appendix 1. Charles Orzech, however, argues that the transmission of esoteric Buddhism indeed took place during the Tang dynasty. See his "Further Notes on Tantra, Metaphor Theory, Ritual and Sweet Dew."

37. See McRae, *The Northern School and the Formation of Early Ch'an Buddhism*, p. 344.

38. The Chinese scholar Hou Chong believes that a local esoteric tradition called *Azhali jiao*, which has been long regarded as either a form of Indian tantrism or a unique local ethnic religion, was actually the remainder of the institutionalized *jiao* division of Chinese Buddhism formulated by Zhu Yuanzhang. See Hou, "Yunnan Azhali jiao jingdian jiqi zai Zhongguo Fojiao yanjiu zhong de jiazhi."

39. Because during the Ming, Chinese people generally referred to Buddhists from Tibet, Tangut, India, and other Western Regions as "Tibetans," the so-called Tibetan influence on Chinese Buddhism needs to be further examined. For example, I hypothesized that the formation of the Mengshan Rite for Feeding the Hungry Ghosts (*Mengshan shishi yi*) might have originated from the Tangut state (1038–1227). This version of esoteric ritual was attributed to the Indian monk Budong (Sanskrit: Akṣobhya), who had served as national preceptor in the Xixia (Tangut) state. He might have had connections with the Tangut diasporic communities along the ancient Sino-Tibetan border in Sichuan. See my unpublished paper "The Rule of Marginality."

40. See Toh, "Tibetan Buddhism in Ming China," pp. 175–228. In addition to several accounts of contacts between Tibetan monks and the literati in the south, Jonathan Chaves notes that in 1599 Yuan Hongdao visited a hostel for foreign monks in a monastery in Beijing and recorded his seeing of a tantric statue (most likely a visual presentation of Yamāntaka according to Chaves). For the translation of Yuan's essay and discussion of its implication in Sino-Tibetan relationship, see Chaves, *Pilgrim of the Clouds*, pp. 105–6 and 135–7.

41. For esoteric Buddhism in late imperial China, see Yan, "Ming Qing shidai de Hanchuan Mijiao," in his *Hanchuan Mijiao*, pp. 52–64. See also Lü, *Zhongguo Mijiao shi*, pp. 514–64, especially pp. 547–54; Stevenson, "Text, Image, and Transformation in the History of the *Shuilu fahui*."

42. For the spread of the Cunti cult, see Gimello, "Icon and Incantation." See also Lü, *Zhongguo Mijiao shi*, pp. 547–554.

43. See Orzech, "Esoteric Buddhism and the *Shishi* in China," p. 65. Lü Jianfu believed that the popular form of the *Shishi* ritual was influenced by the Tibetan practice. See his *Zhongguo Mijiao shi*, pp. 554–60.

44. For the most comprehensive study of this rite in China, see Lye, "Feeding Ghosts: A Study of the *Yuqie Yankou* Rite."

45. I suspect that the character *shen* 滲 is a misprint for *can* 參. For a brief introduction to this work in Japanese, see Hasebe, "Sanhō ichimon no ryūtai," IV, pp. 30–36. Hasebe considers this text part of another Hanyue work, an esoteric text entitled *Yuqie jiyao shishi yi*, which is printed immediately after this text in the supplementary canon.

46. See Hanyue Fazang, *Yumi shen shishi zhigai*, Z no. 1082, 59: 302c.

47. See Amoghavajra, *Jin'gangding yuqie zhong fa a ru duo luo san miao san puti xin lun*, T no. 1665, 32: 573c.

48. For a brief history of the use of Lantsa scripts in China after the Song dynasty, see Takubo, *Bonji shittan*, pp. 100–110.

49. See Payne, "Ajikan."

50. For details about Mount Meru, see Mabbett, "The Symbolism of Mount Meru."

51. Linji Yixuan, *Linji lu*, T 47: 500b.

52. Hanyue Fazang, *Yumi shen shishi zhigai*, Z 59: 302. Obviously, Hanyue Fazang's account contains some historical errors because not all masters are from Central Asia.

53. See Orzech, *Politics and Transcendent Wisdom*.

54. Tanji Hongren, *Wuzong jiu*, 8: 696.

55. The exclamatory *yi* was widely used by Chan masters. Its first meaningful use appeared in Yunmen Wenyan's recorded sayings, in which he responded to students' questions with this word. See his *Yunmen Kuangzhen chanshi guanglu*, T no. 1988, 47: 553c.

56. See Miyun's reply to Liu Daozhen in his *Tiantong zhishuo*, fasc. 3, p. 21.

57. Tanji Hongren, *Wuzong jiu*, 8: 698.

58. See Zhanran Yuancheng, *Kaigu lu*, Z no. 1285, 65: 371c. See also Jiang Canteng's discussion of the decline of Buddhism in the late Ming, "Wanming Fojiao conglin shuaiwei yuanyin xiji," in his *Mingqing Minguo Fojiao sixiang shilun*, pp. 48–56.

59. Yongzheng, *Jianmo bianyi lu*, Z no. 1281, 65: 230c.

60. Qian Qianyi wrote a record for the rebuilding of a Buddhist cloister in Hangzhou ("Wulin chongxiu Baoguoyuan ji"), which is collected in his *Jianzhu Qian Muzhai quanji*, fasc. 42, pp. 5–6.

61. See Welch, *The Practice of Chinese Buddhism*.

CHAPTER 6

1. In addition to his refutation of Hanyue, Yongzheng's involvement in Buddhist affairs has been documented in his imperial decrees about Buddhism. See Yongzheng, "Qing shizong guanyu Foxue zhi yuzhi." See also Noguchi, "Yōseitei no Bukkyō shiryō ni tsuite."

2. Records of Kangxi's tour of these monasteries can be found in Jiyin, *Zongtong biannian*, XZJ 147: 506–11; and Gao Jin, *Nanxun shengdian*. See also Zhou, *Qingdai Fojiao shiliao jigao*, pp. 3–8.

3. For studies of their political use of religious symbolism, see Hung Wu, "Emperor's Masquerade"; and Berger, *Empire of Emptiness*.

4. For Yongzheng's Buddhist connections, see Feng, "Qing Shizong de chongfo he yongfo"; Tsukamoto, "Yōseitei no Bukkyō kyōdan hihhan" and "Yōseitei no Ju-Butsu-Dō sankyō ittaikan"; and Zhang Wenliang, *Yongzheng yu Chanzong*.

5. For the Chinese biography of the second ICang-skay master, see Yu Qian, *Xinxu gaoseng zhuan si ji*, fasc. 2. For a study of the third ICang-skya master, see

Wang, "Tibetan Buddhism at the Court of Qing;" and "the Qing Court's Tibet Connection." The lCang-skya lineage, belonging to the Gelukpa, originated from Youning monastery in Qinghai (Amdo). Both the second and third lCang-skya masters served the Manchu court as national preceptors.

6. See *Li'an si zhi*, ZFS 77: 97–104.

7. See *Baohua shan zhi*, ZFS 53: 1–2.

8. See Zhou Shujia, *Qingdai Fojiao shiliao jigao*, p. 175.

9. For the tax reform, see Zelin, "The Yung-cheng Reign," in *The Cambridge History of China*, vol. 9, pt. 1, pp. 183–229.

10. As Holmes Welch observes, monks in the late Qing and early Republican eras did have ordination certificates bearing government seals. However, these certificates were largely printed by the ordination centers themselves. As far as I know, the Qing dynasty never had its own official ordination platforms.

11. Farquhar, "Emperor as Bodhisattva in the Governance of the Ch'ing Empire, " p. 32. David Farquhar cites this passage from Lessing, *Yung-ho-kung*, p. 10.

12. Farquhar, "Emperor as Bodhisattva in the Governance of the Ch'ing Empire," p. 32.

13. Pei Huang, *Autocracy at Work*, p. 30.

14. Although he was praised by Yongzheng and given high status in the court, he was later denounced by the emperor. See Yongzheng, "Qing Shizong guanyu Fojiao zhi yuzhi," no. 1.

15. See Yongzheng's postscript in *Yuxuan yulu*, fasc. 18, Z no. 1319, 68: 696b.

16. Ibid.

17. Yongzheng discussed the meaning of this term in his *Yuanming jushi yulu*, Z 68: 696a and XZJ 119: 422a–b. According to him, it refers to the continuous effort of cultivation after the ultimate enlightenment.

18. Silas Wu, *Passage to Power*, p. 167.

19. Pei Huang, *Autocracy at Work*, p. 34.

20. For example, the Song master Huanglong Huinan (1002–1069) was famous for his use of "three passes," which were three questions he used in his encounters with students.

21. See Yongzheng's general preface in *Yuxuan yulu*, Z 68: 523–24.

22. Ibid.

23. For short biographies of the monks mentioned above, see ZFR, pp. 66, 370, 700, 701, 702. Some correspondences between Yongzheng and the monk Ruchuan Chaosheng are extant. See Zhang Wenliang, *Yongzheng yu Chanzong*, pp. 119–74.

24. For his biography, see Qing, *Zhongguo Daojiao*, vol. 1, p. 395.

25. ECCP, pp. 54–56. For a study of Zhang Tingyu, see Guy, "Zhang Tingyu and Reconciliation."

26. ECCP, pp. 601–3.

27. Ibid., p. 234.

28. Ibid., pp. 825–26.

29. Ibid., pp. 369–73.

30. Ibid., pp. 24–25.

31. Yongzheng invented the system of secret memorials, which were submitted directly to him by his trusted officials. However, in his communication with Fupeng, he devoted several pieces to spiritual issues occurring in their Chan practice. See Zhang, *Yongzheng yu Chanzong*, pp. 27–53.

32. Pei Huang, *Autocracy at Work*, p. 45. One of the Chan monks, Wenjue, became Yongzheng's political advisor and participated in many plots against Yongzheng's enemies. See Feng, *Yongzheng zhuan*, pp. 446, 507–52; and Yang Qiqiao, *Yongzheng di jiqi mizhe zhidu yanjiu*, pp. 20–26.

33. *Dangjin fahui* was incorporated into Yongzheng's *Yuxuan yulu*, fasc. 19, Z 68: 722–49.

34. I translate this passage from Zhang Wenliang's *Yongzheng yu Chanzong*, p. 181. These questions and answers resemble the kōan stories of early Chan patriarchs and the practice of capping phrases in Japanese Rinzai Zen. For a study on the Rinzai Zen practice of capping phrases, see Hori, *Zen Sand*.

35. Yongzheng, *Yuxuan yulu*, fasc. 14, XZJ 119: 508. Yongzheng publicly denounced the use of beating and shouting as seen in the teachings of Deshan Xuanjian and Danxia Tianran. For details, see Shengkong's and Liu Yuanchun's works listed in the bibliography.

36. Yongzheng, *Yuxuan yulu*, fasc. 14, XZJ 119: 537.

37. See Yongzheng's imperial edict issued in 1733, Z no. 1281-A, 68: 194a.

38. *Yongzheng yuzhi Fojiao dadian*, vol. 1, pp. 3–4.

39. See Yongzheng, "Qing Shizong guanyu Foxue zhi yuzhi."

40. Spence, *Treason by the Book*, p. 160.

41. Yongzheng, *Jianmo bianyi lu*, Z 65: 191.

42. Ibid.

43. Yangshan Huiji, *Yuanzhou Yanshan Huiji chanshi yulu*, T no. 1990, 47: 582a.

44. Guishan Lingyou, *Tanzhou Guishan Lingyou chanshi yulu*, T no. 1989, 47: 579c.

45. See Yongzheng, *Jianmo bianyi lu*, XZJ 114: 381.

46. The *Śūraṃgama Sūtra* starts with Ānanda's fall to sexual seduction and the Buddha's saving of him. For details, see my article "Knowledge for What?"

47. Given the fact that the emperor was also exposed to Tibetan Buddhism, Yongzheng could have appreciated Hanyue's association of Chan Buddhism with esoteric Buddhism. However, under this circumstance, Yongzheng intended to use this case to assert his spiritual authority and orthodox understanding of Chan Buddhism. It is unlikely that the emperor would have considered Hanyue's esotericism favorably even if he fully understood it.

48. This preface may be the one Hanyue wrote for the *Wujia yulu* compiled by Xuejiao Yuanxin and Guo Ningzhi. For my short discussion of this work, see chapter 4.

49. For my detailed explanation of Hanyue Fazang's analogical use of the image of a timber *stūpa*, see chapter 4.

50. Yongzheng, *Jianmo bianyi lu*, Z 65: 254b.

51. Yongzheng, *Jianmo bianyi lu*, XZJ 114: 382b. Hanyue did indicate his resentment about the line in Huineng's famous verse, "Originally not a single thing

existed." However, Noguchi suggests that the real target of Hanyue's criticism was Hanshan Deqing. For details, see Noguchi, "Honrai mu ichi butsu wa gedō no ho."

52. See Yongzheng's imperial edict in *Jianmo bianyi lu*, Z 65: 191a–b. See also Hasebe Yukei, "Sanhō ichimon no ryūtai," III, pp. 144–46.

53. See Yongzheng's imperial edict in *Jianmo bianyi lu*, Z 65: 193.

54. For this legend, see Nan Huaijin's preface to the *Yuxuan yulu* and *Xindeng lu*, reprinted in Zhang, *Yongzheng yu Chanzong*, pp. 346–47.

CHAPTER 7

1. To avoid using the first Song emperor's father's name, the character *xuan* 玄 was changed to *yuan* 元. In the Qing dynasty, this avoidance continued because the Kangxi emperor's name also contains the character *xuan*. See Chen Yuan, *Shihui juli*, pp. 153 and 169.

2. See Ying-shih Yü, "Some Preliminary Reflections on the Rise of Ch'ing Intellectualism."

3. See Elman, *From Philosophy to Philology*.

4. According to Weizhi Zhikai, Weizhong Jingfu commissioned his disciples, including Weizhi Zhikai, to conduct field surveys in sites of ancient monasteries in order to find new epigraphic evidence. See Weizhi Zhikai, *Zhengming lu*, fasc. 6, p. 73.

5. See the table of contents of the *Wudeng yantong*, Z 86: 547–48.

6. See Welter, "A Buddhist Response to the Confucian Revival."

7. Zanning, *Song gaoseng zhuan*, T no. 2061, 50: 769–70.

8. According to Kai-wing Chow's account, Feng Fang (*jinshi* 1523) fabricated a stele version of the *Great Learning* from the Wei dynasty (220–265). See Chow, "Between Canonicity and Heterodoxy," pp. 154–57. See also Rusk, "The Rogue Classicist."

9. See Saeki, *The Nestorian Documents and Relics in China*.

10. Qu Ruji was a Confucian scholar with an interest in Chan Buddhism. However, he was later converted by the Jesuit Matteo Ricci and became a Christian. For his relation with Christianity, see Fang, *Zhongguo Tianzhujiaoshi renwu zhuan*, vol. 1, pp. 274–83. See note 36 in chapter 2.

11. See Qu Ruji, *Zhiyue lu*, fasc. 9, pp. 55–57. This section, however, was altered in the Japanese *Zokuzōkyō* edition. For a comparison, see Z 83: 509a-c.

12. Qu's work may have been written around 1606 because Yuan Hongdao composed a similar essay for Tianhuang monastery in that year.

13. Huang Zongxi (comp.), *Ming wen hai*, fasc. 140, pp. 15–16, in *Siku quanshu*, 1454: 491–92.

14. See Guo Limei, *Jiaowai biechuan*, fasc. 7, XZJ 144: 139–40.

15. For Miyun Yuanwu's and Hanyue Fazang's prefaces, see Z nos. 1580-A and 1580-C, 84: 158.

16. Xuejiao Yuanxin and Guo Ningzhi (eds.), *Wujia yulu*, XZJ 119: 849–50 and Z 69: 21c–22b.

17. See Zhu Shi'en, *Fozu gangmu*, Z no. 1594, 85: 556b.

18. According to Muchen Daomin, Wu Tong also wrote "Diagram of the Patriarchs" (*Zushi tu*), which followed the two-Daowu theory. See Muchen Daomin, *Chandeng shipu*, Z 86: 319.

19. Muchen Daomin, *Chandeng shipu*, Z 86: 340.

20. Ibid., 457, 472.

21. Muchen Daomin, *Chandeng shipu*, Z 86: 318.

22. *Hufa zhengdeng lu*, pp. 1–3. In the text, the title was listed as "Huang sili Yuangong fa Xuedou gaoshi."

23. *Hufa zhengdeng lu*, p. 1

24. The account of this event is also preserved in Miyun Yuanwu's *Tiantong zhishuo*, fasc. 7.

25. This preface, written in 965, clearly states that Shenyan was a dharma heir of Xuefeng Yicun and five generations after Shitou. See *Gu zunsu yulu*, Z no. 1315, 68: 245c.

26. This letter has been reprinted in *Xuefeng Yicun chanshi yulu*. See XZJ 119: 943; *Hufa zhengdeng lu*, pp. 4–6; and Nukariya, *Zengaku shisōshi*, pp. 503–5.

27. See Wang Gu's essay in *Wudeng yantong xu*, Z no. 1567, 80: 546c–47b.

28. Wang Gu's observation is certainly correct. According to Albert Welter's study, Xuefeng Yicun and his followers showed a clear tendency to imitate Deshan Xuanjian's Chan teaching and thus their Chan style was close to Mazu's. See Welter, "Lineage and Context in the *Patriarch's Hall Collection*."

29. See Miyun Yuanwu's remark in his *Tiantong zhishuo*, fasc. 7, pp. 1–9.

CHAPTER 8

1. For this work, see Z no. 1566, 80: 443–540.

2. For the influence of this book in Japan, see my discussion in chapter 9.

3. Xu Changzhi was Feiyin's most loyal lay disciple. He hailed from Haiyan county in Jiangsu and studied with both Miyun and Feiyin. He supervised several publication projects initiated by his teachers, including the popular anti-Christian anthology *Shengchao poxie ji*. For his connection with the anti-Christian movement, see my dissertation, "Orthodoxy, Controversy, and the Transformation of Chan Buddhism," chapter 4.

4. The following list is based on Chen Shiqiang's summary. See his *Fodian jingjie*, pp. 669–70.

5. Feiyin Tongrong, *Wudeng yantong jiehuo pian*, Z no. 1569, 81: 318c–20a.

6. For a detailed analysis of this category in Chan historiography, see Hasebe, *Min Shin Bukkyō kyōdanshi kenkyū*, pp. 408–26.

7. Feiyin Tongrong, *Wudeng yantong jiehuo pian*, Z 81: 318b.

8. For my account of this debate, see appendix 2.C.

9. See Feiyin's letter to Xu Zhiyuan (Xinwei) in *Feiyin chanshi yulu*, JXZ no. 178, 26: 163c–64a.

10. Feiyin Tongrong, "Fuyan Feiyin Rong chanshi jinian lu," in *Feyin chanshi yulu*, JXZ 26: 187b. For a detailed account of this dispute, see Feiyin Tongrong's two

rebuttal essays against Muchen Daomin in his *Feiyin chanshi bieji*, fasc. 15, p. 8 and pp. 11–16.

11. Feiyin Tongrong, *Wudeng yantong*, Z 80: 531b.

12. Feiyin Tongrong, "Fuyan Feiyin Rong chanshi jinian lu," in *Feyin chanshi yulu*, JXZ 26: 189a–b.

13. The prefaces of the three essays are preserved in the *Hufa zhengdeng lu*.

14. See Qi Xiongjia's preface to "*Mingzong zhengwei*" in *Hufa zhengdeng lu*, p. 6.

15. See Wang Wei's preface to "Zhaiqi shuo" in ibid., p. 8.

16. See Z 81: 318c–20a.

17. Feiyin Tongrong, *Wudeng yantong jiehuo pian*, Z no. 1569, 81: 317b.

18. Ibid., 317a–18a.

19. Ibid.

20. Muchen Daomin, *Bushuitai ji*, fasc. 23, JXZ no. 181, 26: 400a.

21. See Lin Zhifan's preface in *Hufa zhengdeng lu*, p. 1.

22. See the petition from the literati in four counties in Zhejiang in *Hufa zhengdeng lu*, pp. 22–23.

23. See the petition from the literati in Fujian, which was appended to the end of the *Hufa zhengdeng lu* and renumbered as pp, 1–4.

24. For another account of this event, see Jiyin, *Zongtong biannian*, fasc. 32, Z 86: 306a.

25. Pan Lei also recorded this event. See Pan Lei's letter to Shilian Dashan in *Jiukuang bianyu*, pp. 26–27. See also Zhou Zheng's notes on the presiding officials in this trial in his "Feiyin chanshi shouza kaoshi," p. 145. Zhou argues convincingly that the character "Lü" was a misprint for "Li," and he identifies the only possible official of that name as Li Rifang, who served in Zhejiang around 1654.

26. *Hufa zhengdeng lu*, p. 24. See a slightly different version of this verdict in Pan Lei's letter to Shilian Dashan in his *Jiukuang bianyu*, pp. 26–27.

27. Chiyan was actually Jiqi Hongchu's disciple.

28. *Hufa zhengdeng lu*, p. 19.

29. This number was provided by Xu Changzhi. See his record of the year 1661 in *Wuyi daoren lu*, JXZ no. 127, 23: 335–56.

30. See Feiyin Tongrong, "Fuyan Feiyin Rong chanshi jinian lu," in *Feiyin chanshi yulu*, JXZ 26: 190b.

31. For this event, see Xu Changzhi's record of the year 1661 in his *Wuyi daoren lu*, JXZ 23: 344b.

CHAPTER 9

1. Liu Xianting, *Guangyang zaji*, p. 191.

2. See Shuijian Huihai's inscription written for rebuilding Tianwang monastery in his *Tianwang Shuijian Hai heshang liuhuilu*, JXZ no. 230, 29: 283b.

3. See Shuijian Huihai's inscription of the ancient iron lump discovered in Tianwang monastery in ibid., JXZ 29: 245–84.

4. For the content of this inscription, see Shuijian Huihai, *Tianwang Shuijian Hai heshang liuhuilu*, fasc. 10, JXZ 29: 284a–b. See also Huishan Jiexian's reply to the

monk Jiansou Kongzheng in *Famen chugui*, appendix, XZJ 147: 46b. For an account of this dispute, see Chen Yuan's discussion in *Qingchu sengzheng ji*, pp. 16–24. See also Liu Xianting, *Guangyang zaji*, p. 191.

5. Weizhong Jingfu, *Famen chugui*, Z 86: 486–95.

6. Ibid., 488a–89b.

7. Ibid., 486b–88a. Weizhong Jingfu repeated similar arguments in his *Zudeng bian'e*, pp. 93–94.

8. This essay can be found in Zhizhao, *Rentian yanmu*, fasc. 6, T no. 2006, 48: 333c–34b; and Z no. 1267-C, 64: 763a–c. Also in Yongjue Yuanxian, *Yongjue Yuanxian chanshi guanglu*, fasc. 16, Z no. 1437, 72: 480b. It is reprinted in its entirety in Nukariya, *Zengaku shisōshi*, pp. 506–8.

9. See Dangui Jinshi, *Bianxingtang ji*, fasc. 3, in *Chanmen yishu xubian*, 4: 103–5.

10. Weizhi Zhikai, *Zhengming lu*, pp. 13, 44–46.

11. Following his teacher Juelang Daosheng's instruction, Wuke Dazhi (Fang Yizhi) compiled this book. However, he did not have a chance to print this book before he died in 1671. Finally, Shilian Dashan helped to complete the work. After Shilian returned from Vietnam in 1696, he was accused of conducting illegal trade with the Vietnamese. Later, he died in exile. His involvement in the controversy about dharma transmission may have been one of the charges against him. See Jiang Boqin, *Shilian Dashan yu Aomen chanshi*, pp. 173–74.

12. For an account of this dispute, see Chen Yuan, *Qingchu sengzheng ji*, pp. 24–33.

13. The following list is based on Chen Shiqiang's summary. See his *Fodian jingjie*, pp. 699–700.

14. See Jilun Chaoyong, *Wudeng quanshu*, fasc. 13, Z 82: 515a.

15. Shilian Dashan's *Zhengwei lu* is not extant. Pan Lei's essay on Tianwang Daowu and his letter to Shilian Dashan preserved some of its contents. See Pan Lei, *Jiukuang bianyu*, pp. 26–32 and 65–70; Chen Yuan, *Qingchu sengzheng ji*, pp. 31–33; and Jiang Boqin, *Shilian Dashan yu Aomen chanshi*, pp. 166–73.

16. This rare book was only incorporated into the Puhui Buddhist canon published in Shanghai in 1945. See Hasebe, *Min Shin Bukkyō kenkyū shiryō*, pp. 82–88. See also his "Chikai san *Shōmei roku* ni tsuite," p. 329.

17. Weizhi Zhikai presented the most comprehensive list of evidence, most of which I discuss in appendix 3.

18. For a detailed summary of this dispute, see my discussion in appendix 2.B.

19. See Weizhi Zhikai, *Zhengming lu*, fasc. 14, pp. 209–27.

20. For his involvement in the dispute over the *Wudeng quanshu*, see Chen Yuan, *Qingchu sengzheng ji*, pp. 24–33.

21. Weizhi Zhikai, *Zhengming lu*, pp. 13, 44–46.

22. See Huang Zongxi's letter to Wang Weimei ("Da Wang Weimei wen Ji Dong liangzong zhengduan shu") in his *Nanlei Wenyue*, in *Lizhou yizhu huikan*, p. 43.

23. For his biography, see ECCP, pp. 521–22.

24. I have not located these sources. See Liu Xianting, *Guangyang zaji*, pp. 238–39.

25. According to Jiang Boqin, after Shilian Dashan returned from Vietnam with considerable wealth from trade and from the king's donation, Pan Lei solicited

monies from him but only received a little. See Jiang Boqin, *Shilian Dashan yu Aomen chanshi*, pp. 91–101.

26. For Pan Lei's short biography in English, see ECCP, pp. 606–7.

27. Shilian Dashan was eventually put in jail and died in exile. Pan Lei's *Jiukuang bianyu* was also listed as a forbidden book by the imperial court in 1780. Weilin Daopei wrote a letter to Dashan Tongqiu to discuss Shilian Dashan, which was preserved in Pan Lei's *Jiukuang bianyu*, p. 87.

28. See my account of these records in appendix 3.

29. See Pan Lei's investigation of Tianwang Daowu's inscription ("Tianwang bei kao") in his *Jiukuang bianyu*, pp. 26–32.

30. Keirin Sūshin was a monk from the Myōshinji line. In his book *Zenrin shūhei shū*, he was suspicious of the motives for Yinyuan's emigration to Japan. See Baroni, *Obaku Zen*, p. 39.

31. See Yinyuan Longqi's postscript and eulogy for the reprinted edition of the *Wudeng yantong*, Z 86: 315c.

32. *Riben Huangboshan Wanfusi cang lü Ri gaoseng Yinyuan Zhongtu laiwang shuxin ji*, letter no. 005, p. 65.

33. See Feiyin's biography written by Shuijian Huihai in *Tianwang Shuijian Hai heshang liuhuilu*, fasc. 2, JXZ 29: 277a–79a.

34. Here, Feiyin assumed that Yiyuan was invited by the Japanese emperor. But Yinyuan was actually invited by local Chinese patrons in Nagasaki. See my article "Leaving for the Rising Sun," pp. 97–100.

35. Yanagida, "Ingen no tōto to Nihon Ōbakuzen," p. 285.

36. For brief studies of Kokan Shiren, see Pollack, "Kokan Shiren and Musō Soseki"; Bielefeldt, "Kokan Shiren and the Sectarian Use of History." See Kokan Shiren's *Goke ben* in *Gozan bungaku zenshū*, vol. 1, pp. 196–98.

37. For his short biography, see *Nihon Bukke jinmei jisho*, p. 14.

38. See Yaoshan Weiyan's epitaph written by Tang Shen in *Quan Tang wen*, fasc. 536, pp. 2410–11. See also Xu Wenming, "Caodong zong guizong Qingyuan yixi de yuanyin chuxi."

39. Two essays, "Goke benshō" and "Goha itteki zu," are added as appendixes in the *Famen chugui*. See Z 86: 490a–94c.

40. See Zuxiu, *Longxing biannian tonglun*, XZJ 130: 660a.

41. Benjue, *Shishi tongjian*, XZJ 131: 954b.

42. Kokan's position has been sharply criticized by Sōtō historians such as Nukariya Kaiten and Ui Hakuju. In modern Japan, some Rinzai monks have voiced resentment against these Sōtō historians. See Torigoe, *Hiin zenji to sono cho*. I have not found his book, but his essay of the same title can be accessed in *Ōbaku bunka* 88 (June 1987): 3–6; and 89 (Sept. 1987): 3–5.

CHAPTER 10

1. My use of the term "mentality" is obviously influenced by historians of the Annales school. For introductions to the Annales school, see Stoianavitch, *French Historical Method*; and Burke, *The French Historical Revolution*.

2. This phrase is borrowed from Connery, *The Empire of the Text*.

3. See Lewis, *Writing and Authority in Early China*.

4. See Schopen, "Archaeology and Protestant Presuppositions in the Study of Indian Buddhism," p. 3.

5. Stock, *Listening for the Text*, p. 37. Recently, some Buddhist scholars have paid attention to the role of textual practice in the Buddhist tradition. For example, Anne Blackburn borrowed Brian Stock's term "textual communities" to explain the rise of Buddhism in eighteenth-century Sri Lanka. See her book *Buddhist Learning and Textual Practice*.

6. For a detailed discussion of this contrast, see Faure, *The Rhetoric of Immediacy*.

7. See Hanyue Fazang, *Yumi shen shishi zhigai*, Z no. 1082, 59: 302c.

8. See Faure, *Chan Insights and Oversights*, p. 233.

9. To some extent, their understanding is strikingly similar to that of earlier scholars of Indian Buddhism who held "Protestant presuppositions." Gregory Schopen's description of these assumptions fits well here to illuminate this literal hermeneutic strategy: "They all axiomatically assumed that the textual ideal either was or had been actually in operation, that if it said so in a text it must have been so in reality." See Schopen, "Archaeology and Protestant Presuppositions in the Study of Indian Buddhism," p. 3.

10. Halperin, *Out of the Cloister*, pp. 9–11.

11. Ibid., p. 110.

12. Welter, *Monks, Rulers, and Literati*, p. 207.

13. See Stock, *The Implications of Literacy*. See also Blackburn, *Buddhist Learning and Textual Practice*, pp. 10–11. For a further elaboration of these ideas, see Stock's "Textual Communities: Judaism, Christianity, and the Definitional Problem," in his *Listening for the Text*, pp. 140–58.

14. See Darnton, "What is the History of Books?" p. 65.

15. Although European studies on the role of printing, reading, and writing in religion are abundant, there are no substantial studies in China scholarship. For some discussion about this issue, see Bell, "A Precious Raft to Save the World," "Printing and Religion in China," and "Ritualization of Texts and Textualization of Ritual."

16. I analyzed the performance of Chan kōans in an unpublished paper, "Problems with Enlightenment."

17. Orzech, *Politics and Transcendent Wisdom*, p. 115.

18. Farquhar, "Emperor as Bodhisattva," pp. 5–34.

19. Elman, *From Philosophy to Philology*, p. 15.

20. See *Li'an si zhi*, ZFS 77: 23–24. Although he was praised by Yongzheng and given a high status, he was also denounced by the emperor. See Yongzheng, "Qing Shizong guanyu Fojiao zhi yuzhi," no. 1.

21. For some reflections on Chan institutions, see McRae, *Seeing through Zen*, pp. 115–16.

22. See my article "Building a Dharma Transmission Monastery."

23. Hasebe, *Min Shin Bukkyō kyōdanshi kenkyū*, p. 343.

24. The 1667 census gives the number of 140,193 clerics in total, including Buddhists and Taoists. The 1736–1739 census reports 340,112 clerics in total.

Among them, about 13–15 percent were Taoist clergy. See Goossaert, "Counting the Monks."

25. See Feiyin's critical comments in his *Feiyin chanshi bieji*, fasc. 15, pp. 12–16. For a brief account of this dispute, see appendix 2.C. I found that Yinyuan Longqi's seals in the Manpukuji collection were also effaced, suggesting Yinyuan's disciples had the same concern as Feiyin did. See Addiss, *Obaku, Zen Painting and Calligraphy*.

26. This event in Japan was called the "indirect transmission incident," or more precisely, "incident of transmission by proxy" (*daifu jiken*, or *daifu ronsō* in Japanese). Resulting in a famous scandal in the Japanese Ōbaku school, it reflected the struggle between conservatives, who wanted to enforce the principle of dharma transmission, and those who were willing to compromise based on circumstances. Helen Baroni has made a detailed study of this incident and, according to her, the incident involved the dharma transmission of the Japanese emperor Gomizunoo (1596–1680) who was converted to Ōbaku Buddhism. The incident began with Ryōkei Shōsen, who was converted from the Myōshinjiha and contributed greatly to the success of Ōbaku in Japan. But in 1670, he died tragically in a flood tide in Osaka. His death created a problem of dharma transmission because he left no dharma heirs except the Gomizunoo emperor, who unfortunately was unable to take students due to his political role as emperor. However, when the emperor was dying in 1680, Gaoquan Xingdun was entrusted to select official dharma heirs, acting on the emperor's proxy. This practice created a difficult situation because, as Baroni points out correctly, the Ōbaku practice of dharma transmission still followed Feiyin Tongrong's principle of strictness and denounced "transmission by proxy." The fourth abbot of Manpukuji, Duzhan Xingying (1628–1706), represented this conservative view. Despite criticisms, however, in 1685, five years after the emperor's death, Gaoquan conferred Gomizunnoo's transmission on the Japanese monk Kaiō Hōkō (1635–1712). The controversy ended with the *bakufu* judgment of Gaoquan's victory and led to Gaoquan's ascendancy to Manpukuji in 1692. See Baroni, *Obaku Zen*, pp. 176–80.

27. There are some discussions among social historians about the interactions between various kinds of vertical and horizontal associations in late imperial China. For example, in his study of local societies such as Songjiang prefecture (nowadays Shanghai), Kishimoto Mio describes vertical associations centering around local gentry and government (such as lineage organization) in the late sixteenth and seventeenth centuries as being organized by a relaionship of dependency. Contrary to "vertical," he uses the term "horizontal" to describe associations among the literati and the lower social class as being organized according to contractual relationships. These associations include various kinds of literary associations among the literati, secret societies, peasant associations, etc. In my opinion, when Buddhist monasteries were locally based, they represented a horizontal type of association. However, when these local monasteries were organized by the hierarchal relationship of dharma transmission, they became dharma transmission monasteries with a vertical structure. See Kishimoto, *Min Shin kōtai to Kōnan shakai*, pp. 3–10.

28. Brook, *Praying for Power*, p. 29.

29. See Xu Changzhi's account of his receiving dharma transmission from Miyun Yuanwu and Feiyin Tongrong in his *Wuyi daoren lu*, fasc. 1, ZH 90: 37532 and JXZ no. 127, 23: 336a.

CHAPTER 11

1. See Welch, *The Practice of Chinese Buddhism*.

2. Welch, "Dharma Scrolls and the Succession of Abbots in Chinese Monasteries," p. 144.

3. Both quotes are cited from ibid., p. 146.

4. Hanyue Fazang's *Hongjie fayi* was the first work that outlined the procedure of the Triple Platform Ordination Ceremony. For a detailed study of this work and other similar works on the invention of the ordination ceremony in the Ming and Qing dynasties, see Hasebe, *Min Shin Bukkyō kyōdanshi kenkyū*, pp. 157–68.

5. Yinyuan Longqi's work was reprinted in *Zengaku taikei*, vol. 7, pp. 1–68. For a textual analysis of these two works, see Hasebe's explanation in his *Min Shin Bukkyō kenkyū shiryō*, pp. 95–100.

6. Dangui Jinshi wrote an essay to oppose ordination ceremonies administered by Chan monks ("Zongmen bubi kaijie shuo"). According to him, Chan masters in his time believed that through offering the ordination ceremony traditionally administered by Vinaya masters, Chan Buddhism could be greatly strengthened. Jinshi lamented this confusion and complained that, instead of reviving Chan Buddhism, the solemnity of ordination was damaged when three platforms were offered together in just eight days. See Dangui Jinshi, *Bianxingtang ji*, in *Chanmen yishu xubian*, 4: 85–87. He also revealed that when Miyun Yuanwu first offered ordination in Mount Tiantong, even the requirement of "three masters and seven witnesses" could not be met. Only after listening to Vinaya master Sanmei Jiguang's admonishment did Miyun Yuanwu start to follow proper procedures.

7. See Barrett, "Buddhist Precepts in a Lawless World," especially pp. 114–7; Groner, "The Ordination Ritual in the *Platform Sūtra*."

8. For details, see my account of esoteric practices in the seventeenth century in chapter 5.

9. For a study of the liturgical tradition in Chinese Buddhism, see Pei-yan Chen, "Morning and Evening Service" and "Sound and Emptiness," pp. 24–25. See also Müller, "Buddhistische Morgen-und Abendliturgie Auf Taiwan."

10. Chen Jidong, "Zenmon nichiju no shohon ni tsuite."

11. See Hanshan Deqing, *Hanshan dashi mengyou ji*, fasc. 52, XZJ 127: 941–46.

12. Miyun Yuanwu's rules, entitled "Conglin shixun tiaogui dayue," has been preserved as part of the *Ōbaku shingi*. In this document, Miyun stressed the strict observance of precepts to regulate a large monastic community. For instance, monks were not allowed to disobey the master's will, to engage in business, to embezzle monastic property, to mingle with unlawful persons, etc. See Yinyuan Longqi, *Ōbaku shingi*, T no. 2607, 82: 777b–c. Feiyin Tongrong compiled *Conglin liangxu xuzhi*, which specifies the roles of each monastic officer. This text can be found in XZJ 112:

150–68. For an introduction to the compilation of monastic regulations in the late Ming, see Hasebe, *Min Shin Bukkyō kyōdanshi kenkyū*, p. 342.

13. According to Helen Baroni, although this work was published in 1673 and attributed to Yinyuan Longqi, the fifth abbot of Manpukuji, Gaoquan Xingdun, was responsible for the actual compilation. See Baroni, *Obaku Zen*, p. 88. Because it was composed in Japan, its contents must have been adapted to the Japanese monastic reality, as Yinyuan himself admitted. However, the essential ritual practices elaborated in these monastic codes were all derived from China.

14. For a study on the syncretism of Chan and Pure Land, see Sharf, "On Pure Land Buddhism and Ch'an/Pure Land Syncretism in Medieval China."

15. See Zürcher, "Buddhisme et Christianisme," p. 19.

16. See Foulk, "Myth, Ritual, and Monastic Practice in Sung Ch'an Buddhism." Yifa expresses a similar view in her analysis of *Pure Rules of Chan Monasteries*. See Yifa, "From the Chinese Vinaya Tradition to Chan Regulations."

17. Some scholars have noticed the importance of Chan Buddhism as part of the local tradition. Bernard Faure, for example, spells out two "incommensurable, yet coexisting visions of the world: the unlocalized (or 'utopian') conceptions of Buddhism as universal doctrine and the localized (and 'locative') beliefs of local religion as ritual practice." See Faure, *Chan Insights and Oversights*, p. 156. Welch also noticed strong local and regional ties within the monastic world in his *The Practice of Chinese Buddhism*.

18. To some degree, my proposal of the two models in the Buddhist world resonates with Robert Hymes's discussion of two similar models in Chinese religion. Based on his study of the rise of a Taoist sect in the Song, he proposes two different models of the relationship between humans and gods. The bureaucratic model, which was articulated clearly in the sect's liturgical manuals and divine laws, organized the pantheon of Taoist gods (deified extraordinary historical figures, or in Hymes's own words, "the elaborate intellectual construct of a tiny elite of practitioners and enthusiasts") into a hierarchy of celestial officials who delegated authority from superiors to subordinates and connected to humans through Taoist priests as intermediaries. However, there is another prevailing personal model, as Hymes terms it, which was manifested in local miracle stories, where gods as bureaucrats were seldom resorted to. Rather, the worshipers tended to build personal relationships with the gods through rituals unmediated by Taoist professionals and to appeal to their "inherent" supernatural qualities. The Taoist sect based on the bureaucratic model was a translocal and expansive phenomenon and did not attach to one particular place. On the contrary, in local eyes, the gods in the sect have strong ties with one locality, or in Hymes's words, the gods

> are "pre-adapted" to embody authority that is locally based: authority that resides in the locality, maintains close touch with the communities it serves, draws force from one place, is committed to remain there, and acts in direct and personal rather than bureaucratic or judicial terms, from a foundation of personally transmitted knowledge, textual learning, self-cultivation, virtue, and descent, rather than official standing. This was power that came from within, not from without. (Hymes, *Way and Byway*, p. 130)

For a better understanding of this book, I benefited from a graduate seminar that Hymes offered at Harvard in the spring of 2001. In this seminar, we read and discussed his manuscript.

19. See Welch, *The Buddhist Revival in China*, p. 264.

20. Ibid.

21. See Biechuan's biography written by Qu Ruji in his *Qu Jiongqing ji*, fasc. 11, *Siku quanshu cunmu congshu*, 187: 261b-263a.

22. See Chün-fang Yü, "Ming Buddhism," p. 921.

23. See Makita, *Sakugen nyūminki no kenkyū*, pp. 178–99. About fifty years before Sakugen's trip to China, the Korean official Ch'oe Pu (1454–1504) drifted to the China shore after a shipwreck and extensively traveled in China on his way back to Korea. He left a travelogue titled *R'yohae-rok*. However, because he harbored a neo-Confucian bias toward Buddhism, he showed no interest in Buddhist institutions in Ming China. This text was reprinted in Makita Tairyō's *Sakugen nyūminki no kenkyū*, pp. 237–345. See also John Meskill's English translation, *Ch'oe Pu's Diary*.

24. See Naquin, *Peking: Temples and City Life*; and Li and Naquin, "The Baoming Temple."

25. Some temples indeed maintained a few subtemples or branch temples. But most of these were located close to their home institution. See Welch, *The Practice of Chinese Buddhism*, pp. 134–38.

26. As Albert Welter shows, the intention of Buddhist clergy such as Zanning was not to create a Chan interpretation of Buddhism. Instead, they merely wanted to attract some literati who cherished the value of free spirits by creating a Chan style of *wen*. See Welter, *Monks, Rulers, and Literati*, p. 172. However, even this mild intellectual repositioning might be seen by some conservative Confucians as aggressive and thus intolerable.

27. See Gimello, "Marga and Culture"; Welter, "A Buddhist Response to the Confucian Revival."

28. Gimello, "Echoes of the *Platform Scripture* in Northern Sung Ch'an," p. 144.

29. Welch, *The Buddhist Revival*, p. 259.

30. Ibid., p. 9. For a study of Yang Wenhui, see Goldfuss, *Vers un bouddhisme du XXe siècle*.

31. Bol, "The 'Localist Turn' and "Local Identity,'" p. 4.

32. For a study of contemporary Buddhism in mainland China, see Birnbaum, "Buddhist China at the Century's Turn."

APPENDIX I

1. Issued on the thirteenth day of the fifth month of the tenth year of the Chongzhen reign (July 4, 1637). Translated from *Hufa zhengdeng lu*, pp. 1–3.

2. In the following verse, Miyun commented on Qingyuan Xingsi's encounter with Huineng, who was impressed by Qingyuan Xingsi's reply of "no holy truth and not falling down from the stage." Here, however, Miyun criticized Qingyuan Xingsi for indulging in the realm of "emptiness" without reaching the ultimate stage. See the original passage in Daoyuan (ed.), *Jingde chuandeng lu*, T no. 2076, 51: 240a.

3. In the following verse, Miyun commented on the kōan that Qingyuan Xingsi did not know the price of rice in the local market. See the original account of Qingyuan Xingsi's remark in Daoyuan (ed.), *Jingde chuandeng lu*, T no. 2076, 51: 240c.

4. I have not identified this source. I suspect that it may refer to Miyun's *Tiantong zhishuo*.

5. The identities of these two monks are unknown.

6. Traditionally, Chinese documents were written from right to left.

7. Translated from *Hufa zhengdeng lu*, pp. 24–25.

8. This verdict can be also found in Pan Lei, "Yu Changshou Shilian shu," in his *Jiukuang bianyu*, pp. 26–27. The wordings of these two records are slightly different.

9. Translated from *Hufa zhengdeng lu*, pp. 25–26.

10. Dong Hu was a famous official historian in the Jin kingdom during the Spring and Autumn periods (770–476 B.C.).

APPENDIX 2

1. Zijue's record appeared in *Zudeng datong*, fasc. 53. Weizhong Jingfu noted that this Zijue was also Lumen Zijue, but he did not highlight the significance of his change in the *Zudeng datong*. Instead, he explained in detail about his change in his *Zudeng bian'e*, fasc. 2, pp. 100–102.

2. The earliest reference to Lumen Zijue is a funerary inscription dated 1165 for Xingtong (1097–1165). This inscription is reproduced in Ishii, *Sōdai Zenshūshi no kenkyū*, pp. 536–37.

3. See Schlütter, "Chan Buddhism in Song-Dynasty China (960–1279)," pp. 156–61. See also Nukariya, *Zengaku shisōshi*, pp. 426–27; and Hasebe, "Tōmon no dōkō to sono keifu."

4. See Weizhong Jingfu, *Zudeng bian'e*, fasc. 2, pp. 100–101.

5. Weizhong Jingfu's claim was charged with containing serious historical errors. Weilin Daopei wrote two essays to criticize him. Both of them were entitled "Bianmiu" (discerning the errors) and were preserved in Pan Lei's *Jiukuang bianyu*, pp. 79–103. See also Weilin Daopei's reply to Dashan Tongqiu in ibid., p. 87.

6. To save space, in the following summary, I will not provide detailed documentation of all evidence. For details, consult Weizhi Zhikai, *Zhengming lu*, fascs. 5–7, pp. 52–101.

7. Weizhi Zhikai, *Zhengming lu*, p. 73.

8. For the sake of saving space, I will not provide documentation for each piece of evidence. Weizhi Zhikai excerpted most of them from the original work and commented on each one in his *Zhengming lu*, fascs. 8–14, pp. 102–227. Readers can also consult Hasebe Yūkei's relevant works listed in the bibliography.

9. See Shanci Tongji (comp.), *Dongming yilu*. In Weizhi Zhikai's *Zhengming lu*, this work was referred to as the *Tongming zudeng lu*. I came across this rare source in the Shanghai Library.

10. See McRae's four rules of Chan studies in his *Seeing through Zen*, pp. xix–xx.

11. For a catalog of and a brief introduction to the essays contained in this work, see Noguchi, "Minmatsu Shinsho sōsō kenkyū shiryō ni tsuite," p. 790.

12. Huanyou Zhengchuan's essays are collected in *Longchi Huanyou chanshi yulu*, fascs. 11 and 12, JXZ 25: 439–50. For a brief study, see Jiang Canteng's analysis of this debate in his *Wan Ming Fojiao conglin gaige yu Foxue zhengbian zhi yanjiu*, pp. 271–75.

13. For a brief study of his work, see ibid., pp. 265–71.

14. See Gaofeng Yuanmiao, *Gaofeng chanshi yulu*, XZJ 122: 678b–80a.

15. See *Tiantong zhishuo*, fasc. 7, pp. 7–32. See also Noguchi, "Minmatsu ni okeru shūjinko ronsō," p. 164.

16. This essay has been reprinted in *Zhongguo Fojiao sixiang ziliao xuanbian*, ser. 3, vol. 3, pp. 5–13.

17. For a brief study of Zhuhong's response, see Chün-fang Yü, *The Renewal of Buddhism in China*, pp. 87–90. For a brief study of Ouyi Zhixu's response, see Shengyan, *Minmatsu Chūgoku Bukkyō no kenkyū*, p. 144. For a German translation of Buddhist responses to Christianity in the seventeenth century, see Kern, *Buddhistische Kritik am Christentum im China*.

18. For Miyun's involvement in the anti-Christian campaign, see my dissertation, "Orthodoxy, Controversy, and the Transformation of Chan Buddhism in Seventeenth-century China," chapter 4, especially pp. 197–204.

19. See Feiyin's essays in fasc. 15 of the *Feiyin chanshi bieji*.

20. See Feiyin's essay in *Feiyin chanshi bieji*, fascs. 11–14. For a brief study of this debate, see Noguchi Yoshitaka, "Hiin Tsūyō no Rinzai-zen to sono zasetsu," pp. 70–74.

21. Feiyin Tongrong's four essays were collected in the following anthologies: *Feiyin chanshi bieji*, fasc. 16; *Honkoku byakujashū*, fasc. 2, reprinted in 1860 by the Fukuenji in Japan; and *Shengchao poxie ji*, reprinted in Japan in 1855. These editions differ from each other and from the early editions. For a brief study of Feiyin's essays, see my dissertation, "Orthodoxy, Controversy, and the Transformation of Chan Buddhism," chapter 4, especially pp. 204–18; see also my article "Buddhist Logic and Apologetics in Seventeenth-century China."

22. For Feiyin Tongrong's essays, see *Feiyin chanshi bieji*, fascs. 8–11.

23. See Huang Duanbo's preface to Wuming Huijing's recorded sayings, in Wuming Huijing, *Shouchang Wuming heshang yulu*, JXZ 25: 667c.

24. Chen Yuan, *Qingchu sengzheng ji*, pp. 63–70. According to Chen Yuan, Muchen Daomin's letter was written in 1667 and can be found in his *Baicheng ji*, fasc. 6. This rare book is preserved in the National Library in Beijing.

25. According to Chen Yuan, this essay is preserved in Muchen Daomin's *Baicheng ji*, fasc. 20. I have not seen this source. My account is based on Chen Yuan's study. See his *Qingchu sengzheng ji*, pp. 70–79.

26. See Hansong Zhicao, *Hansong Cao chanshi yulu*, fasc. 11, JXZ no. 392, 37: 601b–3c, especially 603b–c. In this edition, the title is written as *Pushuo*, and the work is dated the twelfth day of the eleventh month of 1673.

27. See Chen Yuan, *Qingchu sengzheng ji*, pp. 79–86. Because of Yulin Tongxiu's influence, the head of the Chen lineage was sentenced to death at the end of this dispute.

APPENDIX 3

1. *Baolin zhuan*, T 51: 217a.

2. In the earliest Chan anthology, *Zutang ji*, this verse was interpreted differently. For example, the character *yang* 陽 in the first line was taken as "Luoyang"; the phrase *rixia* from the third line was interpreted as the capital; the "pair of elephant and horse" (*shuangxiangma*), also from the third line, was understood as referring to Baozhi and Layman Fu. The "two tender branches" in the fourth line was rendered as "Shaolin temple" because "tender" means "young" (*shao* 少) and "two woods" means "forest" (*lin* 林). See Jing and Jun, *Zutang ji*, fasc. 2, p. 32b.

3. This passage was completely absent from the early edition. Even some versions of the Zongbao edition do not have this passage. See *Enō kenkyū*, p. 359.

4. Feiyin Tongrong, *Wudeng yantong jiehuo pian*, Z no. 1569, 86: 324c–25a.

5. Zongbao (ed.), *Liuzu dashi fabao tanjing*, T 48: 357b. Obviously, this episode was interpolated by others.

6. Z 63: 31a–36a. A new version containing about 200 more characters was discovered in Japan. For details, see Gregory, *Tsung-mi and the Sinification of Buddhism*, p. 318; and Ishii, "Shinpuku-ji bunko shozō no Hai Shū shūi mon no honkoku." In the Song dynasty, Juefan Huihong referred to this text as *Da Pei xiangguo zongqu zhuang*.

7. For an account of Faqin's life, see McRae, "The Ox-head School of Chinese Ch'an Buddhism," pp. 191–95.

8. He served as the minister of works. For his biography, see *Jiu Tang shu*, 12, fasc. 149, p. 4019.

9. See Zanning, *Song gaoseng zhuan*, T 50: 761a12.

10. For a short account of Quan's biography, see Poceski, *Ordinary Mind as the Way*, pp. 91–92.

11. For this inscription, see *Quan Tang wen*, p. 2262a. For an English translation of this text, see Poceski, "The Hongzhou School," pp. 512–15.

12. See Ouyang Xiu's postscripts in his *Jigu lu*, fasc. 8, in *Shike shiliao xinbian*, 24: 17903.

13. Chen Si, *Baoke congbian*, fasc. 19, in *Shike shiliao xinbian*, 24: 18353.

14. For a brief discussion of Daguan Tanying and his work, see Schlütter, "Chan Buddhism in Song-Dynasty China," pp. 38–40.

15. Juefan Huihong, *Linjian lu*, in *Siku quanshu*, 1052: 799a–b and Z no. 1624, 87: 248b–c. See also Ishii's Japanese translation in his *Chūgoku Zenshū shiwa*, pp. 448–49.

16. The meaning of this name (Juemengtang) cannot be determined at this moment. It could refer to a person's name. Chen Shiqiang thought this was Juefan Huihong's name but Wu Limin rejected this hypothesis. See Chen Shiqiang, *Fodian jingjie*, p. 660; and Wu Limin et al., *Chanzong zongpai yuanliu*, p. 288. Ui Hakuju suspects that this name may refer to a Yuan monk, Mengtang Tan'e (1285–1373). However, I have not yet found any evidence other than the similarity between the two names. See Ui, *Daini Zenshūshi kenkyū*, p. 458.

17. Lü was an influential official during the reign of the Yingzong emperor (1064–1067).

18. This preface has been preserved in Zhizhao (ed.), *Rentian yanmu*, fasc. 5. See Z 64: 758.

19. The current Taishō edition lists Xuedou Chongxian in the tenth generation after the sixth patriarch. See T no. 2007, 51: 475a. The confusion about Xuedou Chongxian's affiliation may derive from the fact that although he was an heir of Qingyuan's line, he (or his disciples) consciously claimed that he was the representative of Mazu's teaching. According to Albert Welter, such claims can be found in the *Zutang ji*. See Welter, "Lineage and Context in the *Patriarch's Hall Collection*." See also a revised version of this article in his book *Monks, Rulers, and Literati*, pp. 59–114.

20. For a short biography of Gongchen and his work, see *Jingzhong jianguo xu denglu*, T 51: 521c. The *Wudeng huiyuan* also contains a reference to the *Zuyuan tongyao*. Later polemicists may have adopted this reference without actually seeing the book. See Dachuan (ed.), *Wudeng huiyuan*, Z no. 1565, 80: 141b.

21. See Xuedou Chongxian, *Mingjue chanshi yulu*, T no. 1996, 47: 712a.

22. Dachuan (ed.), *Wudeng huiyuan*, fasc. 7, Z 80: 141–42.

23. *Fozu lidai tongzai*, fas. 15, T no. 2036, 49: 615.

24. I have consulted Koichi Shinohara's translation of these two biographies in his "Passages and Transmission in Tianhuang Daowu's Biographies," pp. 134–35. The authenticity of the two inscriptions was not Shinohara's primary concern. For the examination of the two sources, Shinohara largely based his study on Nukariya Kaiten's research on the subject in his Chan history. Nukariya's study drew on the sources used in the seventeenth-century debates in China.

25. *Fozu lidai tongzai*, fas. 15, T no. 2036, 49: 615a. In a later version of *Fozu lidai tongzai*, these two inscriptions appear in Z no. 1518, 76: 404b–405b.

26. Benjue, *Shishi tongjian*, XZJ 131: 954c.

27. See Jiyin, *Zongtong biannian*, Z 86: 257c. According to his source, the *Xindeng lu* did not circulate widely because of its audacious alteration of Chan lineage affiliations. This book might still have existed in the late Ming because its title appears in the catalog of a private library, *Qianqingtang*. See Huang Yuji, *Qianqing tang shumu*, p. 1208.

28. For this preface, see Z no. 1564, 80: 1. For Tingjun's biography, see Weizhong Jingfu, *Zudeng datong*, fasc. 82, vol. 4, pp. 141–2.

29. See Chen Shiqiang, *Fodian jingjie*, pp. 237–44.

30. See Jue'an, *Shishi jigu lue*, fasc. 3, T no. 2037, 49: 831c.

31. See ibid., 836b.

32. For a detailed study of the categories of the biographies of eminent monks, see Kieschnick, *The Eminent Monk*. He suggests that these categories may have reflected the "monastic imagination" rather than the actual situation in the monastic world.

33. For example, Juefan Huihong pointed out that the inclusion of Bodhidharma in the category "meditation practitioner" was totally unacceptable because Bodhidharma's practice of gazing toward a wall was not a way of meditating. He revealed an

important distinction between Chan as understood by Chan Buddhists themselves and *dhyāna* as a meditative technique. See Ishii, *Sōdai Zenshūshi no kenkyū*, p. 12.

34. His tomb was discovered in the 1950s in Shashi. See Cheng Xinren, "Shashi shijiao faxian Tangdai muta."

35. See T no. 2061, 50: 769.

36. Later Chan historiographies listed three disciples. However, Huang Zongxi pointed out that a phrase in Zanning's biography had been misread as a person's name. See my account of Huang's argument below.

37. Timothy Barrett believes that their relationship was impossible and the conversations between them, which were preserved in Daoyuan's *Jingde chuandeng lu*, must have been produced in the second half of the tenth century. See Barrett, *Li Ao*, p. 49.

38. The *Zutang ji* is the earliest existing anthology. However, it was lost in China, and Chan masters in the seventeenth century could not use it.

39. The current Taishō version of the *Jingde chuandeng lu* is a Ming edition that includes an appendix immediately after Tianhuang Daowu's biography. As the compilers of the Taishō note, this addition amounts to 1,028 Chinese characters and was appended to the Ming edition. See T no. 2067, 51: 309c–10b. In the earlier editions, however, there was no such appendix. See Yanagida (ed.), *Sōhan Kōraihon Keitoku dentōroku*.

40. The entry "Tianhuang Daowu" in the current Taishō edition of the *Jingde chuandeng lu* includes a note about the issue of Tianwang Daowu that quotes Juefan Huihong's and Juemengtang's accounts. See the *Jingde chuandeng lu*, T 51: 309–10.

41. Weizhi Zhikai, *Zhengming lu*, p. 11. The author of the polemical work *Zhengming lu* argued that the now-lost Chan genealogy *Xindeng lu*, composed by the monk Yunhe Rui, appeared too late to be considered seriously. Weizhong Jingfu indicated that Yehai Ziqing added this note in 1284. Yehai Ziqing received Huiji Yuanxi's (1238–1319) dharma transmission and was abbot in Tianyi monastery in Yuezhou. See his biography in Wenxiu, *Zengji xu chuandeng lu*, fasc. 14, in XZJ 142: 818b–19a.

42. Weizhong Jingfu, *Famen chugui*, Z 86: 486–95. For studies on Zhang Shangying, see Gimello, "Chang Shang-ying on Wu-t'ai Shan," pp. 91–97; Schmidt-Glintzer, "Zhang Shang-ying (1043–1122)."

43. Weizhi Zhikai, *Zhengming lu*, p. 13.

44. See Shichao Daning's preface to the *Famen chugui*, Z 86: 489a. Shichao Daning (?–1720) was Juelang Daosheng's dharma heir.

45. Daoyuan (ed.), *Jingde chuandeng lu*, T 51: 276a–b.

46. Weizhi Zhikai, *Zhengming lu*, p. 12.

47. Ibid., pp. 12–13.

48. Zanning, *Song gaoseng zhuan*, fasc. 10, T 50: 770.

49. See Huang Zongxi's letter to Wang Weimei ("Da Wang Weimei wen Ji Dong liangzong zhengduan shu") in his *Nanlei Wenyue*, in *Lizhou yizhu huikan*, p. 43. Wang Weimei was a Buddhist hermit. For a short biography, see ZFR, p. 315.

50. See Weizhi Zhikai, *Zhengming lu*, pp. 17–18.

51. See ibid., p. 17.

52. Xuefeng Yicun, *Xuefeng Yicun chanshi yulu* (or *Zhenjue chanshi yulu*), Z no. 1333, 69: 79b.

53. See Weizhi Zhikai, *Zhengming lu*, pp. 17–21.

54. Recently, some Chan scholars in the English world have discussed this issue as well. They tend to believe that Tianwang Daowu was a faked figure. See Welter, *Monks, Rulers, and Literati*, pp. 86–88; and Jia, *The Hongzhou School of Chan Buddhism*, pp. 22–26.

55. See Nukariya Kaiten's discussion about the debate in his *Zengaku shisōshi*, pp. 497–526.

56. The following works mention this issue briefly: Abe, *Zōtei Chūgoku Zenshūshi no kenkyū*, p. 38n1; Suzuki, *To Gōdai Zenshū shi*, pp. 430–31; Ishii, *Sōdai Zenshūshi no kenkyū*, p. 49.

57. Ui, *Daini Zenshūshi kenkyū*, pp. 458–60.

58. Ishii, *Chūgoku Zenshū shiwa*, pp. 447–52.

59. Chen Yuan, *Shishi yinian lu*, p. 123. See also Hou Yanqing's preface to Juefan Huihong's *Chanlin sengbao zhuan*, Z 78: 490c–91a. Chinese scholars such as Tang Yongton, Zhou Shujia, and Lü Cheng largely follow his argument. For some recent discussions, see Wu et al., *Chanzong zongpai yuanliu*, pp. 286–88; Ma, *Zhongguo Chanzong sixiang fazhan shi*, pp. 151–56. However, Ge Zhaoguang insists that the evidence against the inscription of Tianwang Daowu is not conclusive and calls for a reevaluation of the case. See his *Zhongguo Chan sixiang shi*, pp. 295–302.

60. See Yu Xianhao, *Tang cishi kao*, vol. 5, p. 2403.

61. Ibid., p. 2354.

62. See Cheng Xinren, "Shashi shijiao faxian Tangdai muta."

63. Jing and Jun, *Zutangji*, p. 78b.

64. Ibid., pp. 95–96. Albert Welter has also noticed the brevity of Tianhuang's biography in the *Zutang ji* regardless of his importance in Chan history. See Welter, *Monks, Rulers, and Literati*, pp. 86–88.

Bibliography

Anonymous works, monastic gazetteers, edited dictionaries, and major collections of primary sources are listed by titles.

Abe Chōichi 阿部肇一. "Hoku Sō no Chō Shōei to Bukkyō" 北宋の張商英と佛教. *Shūkyōgaku ronshū* 宗教學論集 14 (March 1988): 97–117.

———. *Zōtei Chūgoku Zenshūshi no kenkyū: Seiji shakaishiteki kōsatsu* 増訂中国禅宗史の研究: 政治社会史的考察. Tokyo: Kenbun Shuppan, 1986.

Addiss, Stephen. *Obaku, Zen Painting and Calligraphy*. Lawrence, Kans.: Helen Foresman Spencer Museum of Arts, 1978.

Admek, Wendi. "Robes Purple and Gold: Transmission of the Robe in the *Lidai fabao ji* (Record of the Dharma-Jewel through the Ages)." *History of Religions* 40.1 (Aug. 2000): 59–81.

Adshead, S. A. M. "The Seventeenth Century General Crisis." *Asian Profile* 1. 2 (Oct. 1973): 271–80.

Amoghavajra 不空, trans. *Fo shuo jiuba yankou egui tuoluoni jing* 佛說救拔焰口餓鬼陀羅尼經. T no. 1313, vol. 21.

———. *Jin'gangding yuqie zhong fa a ru duo luo san miao san puti xin lun* 金剛頂瑜伽中發阿褥多羅三藐三菩提心論. T no. 1665, vol. 32.

Ando Tomonobu 安藤智信. "Chō Shōei no *Gohōron* to sono haikei" 張商英の護法論とその背景. *Ōtani gakuhō* 大谷學報 42.3 (1963): 29–40.

———. "Sō no Chō Shōei ni tsuite: Bukkyō kankei no jiseki o chūshin to shite" 宋の張商英について: 佛教關係の事跡を中心として. *Tōhōgaku* 東方學 22 (July 1961): 57–63.

Araki Kengo 荒木見悟. *Bukkyō to Jukyō: Chūgoku shisō o keisei suru mono* 佛教と儒教: 中国思想を形するもの. Kyoto: Heirakuji Shoten, 1963.

———. *Bukkyō to Yōmeigaku* 仏教と陽明学. Tokyo: Daisan Bunmeisha, 1979.

———. *Chūgoku shingaku to kodō no Bukkyō* 中國心學と鼓動の仏教. Fukuoka: Chūgoku shoten, 1995. Tranlated into Chinese by Liao Zhaoheng as *Mingmo Qingchu de sixiang yu Fojiao* 明末清初的思想與佛教. Taibei: Lianjing chuban, 2006.

———. "Confucianism and Buddhism in the Late Ming." In *The Unfolding of Neo-Confucianism*, ed. William Theodore de Bary, pp. 39–66. New York: Columbia University Press, 1975.

———. "Kin Shōki to Yō Gyozan" 金正希と熊魚山. In his *Min Shin shisō ronkō* 明清思想論考, pp. 129–186. Tokyo: Kenbun Shuppan, 1992.

———. "Mindai ni okeru Ryogonkyō no ryūkō" 明代における楞嚴經の流行. In his *Yōmeigaku no kaiten to Bukkyō* 陽明學の開展と佛教, pp. 245–274. Tokyo: Kenbun shuppan, 1984.

———. *Mindai shisō kenkyū: Mindai ni okeru Jukyō to Bukkyō no kōryū* 明代思想研究: 明代における儒教と佛教の交流. Tokyo: Sōbunsha, 1972.

———. "Minmatsu ni okeru Enmei Enjū no eizō" 明末における永明延壽の影像. *Tōyō kotengaku kenkyū* 東洋古典學研究 19 (2005): 39–54.

———. "Minmatsu no Zensō Munen Shinyō ni tsuite" 明末の禪僧無念深有について. In *Zengaku ronkō: Yamada Mumon Rōshi kiju kinen* 禅学論攷: 山田無文老師喜壽記念, ed. Zen Bunka Kenkyūjo, pp. 273–96. Kyoto: Shibunkaku Shuppan, 1977.

———. *Minmatsu shūkyō shisō kenkyū: Kan Tōmei no shōgai to sono shisō* 明末宗教思想研究: 管東溟の生涯とその思想. Tokyo: Sōbunsha, 1979.

———. *Min Shin shisō ronkō* 明清思想論考. Tokyo: Kenbun Shuppan, 1992.

———. "*Shigetsu roku* no seritsu: Ku Ganritsu no Shōgai to sono shūhen" 指月錄の成立: 瞿元立の生涯とその周邊. *Kyūshū Chūgoku gakkai hō* 九州中國學會報 26 (May, 1987): 1–17.

———. "Shū Kaimon no shisō" 周海門の思想. In his *Mindai shisō kenkyū* 明代思想研究, pp. 227–64. Tokyo: Sōbunsha, 1972.

———. *Unsei Shukō no kenkyū* 雲棲袾宏の研究. Tokyo: Daizo shuppan, 1985. Translated into Chinese by Zhou Xianbo 周賢博 as *Jinshi Zhongguo Fojiao de shuguang: Yunqi Zhuhong zhi yanjiu* 近世中國佛教的曙光: 雲棲袾宏之研究. Taibei: Huiming wenhua, 2001.

———. *Yōmeigaku no kaiten to Bukkyō* 陽明学の開展と仏教. Tokyo: Kenbun Shuppan, 1984.

———. *Yōmeigaku to Zengaku: Toku ni tongo no mondai ni tsuite* 陽明學と禪學: 特に頓悟の問題について. Tokyo: Shibunkai, 1958.

———. *Yūkoku rekka Zen: Zensō Kakurō Dōsei no tatakai* 憂國烈火禪: 禪僧覚浪道盛 のたたかい. Tokyo: Kenbun Shuppan, 2000.

———. "Zensō Munen Shinyō to Ri Takugo" 禪僧無念深有と李卓吾. In his *Yōmeigaku no kaiten to Bukkyō*, pp. 174–196. Tokyo: Kenbun Shuppan, 1984.

———. "Zensō Gyōkushi Hōju to Yomei gakuha" 禪僧玉芝法聚と陽明學派. In his *Mindai shisō kenkyū* 明代思想研究, pp. 81–99. Tokyo: Sōbunsha, 1972.

Atwell, Williams S. "From Education to Politics: The Fushe." In *The Unfolding of Neo-Confucianism*, ed. W. T. de Bary, pp. 333–67. New York: Columbia University Press, 1975.

———. "Some Observations on the 'Seventeenth-Century Crisis' in China and Japan." *Journal of Asian Studies* 45.2 (Feb. 1986): 223–44.

Ayuwang shan zhi 阿育王山志. ZFS vols. 89 and 90.

Ayuwang si xinzhi 阿育王寺新志, ed. Sang Wenci 桑文磁, et al. 2 fascs. Ningbo: Ayuwang monastery, 1989.

Baohua shan zhi 寶華山志. ZFS vol. 53.

Baolin zhuan 寶林傳. In *Sōzō ichin: Hōrinden, Dentō gyokuei shū* 宋藏遺珍: 寶林傳, 傳燈玉英集, ed. Yanagida Seizan 柳田聖山. Kyoto: Chūbun, 1975.

Barnhart, Richard, and Fang-yu Wang. *Master of the Lotus Garden: The Life and Art of Bada shanren, 1626–1705.* New Haven and London: Yale University Press, 1990.

Baroni, Helen Josephine. "Bottled Anger: Episodes in Obaku Conflict in the Tokugawa Period." *Japanese Journal of Religious Studies* (Tokyo) 21.2–3 (June 1994): 191–210.

———. *Obaku Zen: The Emergence of the Third Sect of Zen in Tokugawa Japan.* Honolulu: University of Hawaii Press, 2000.

Barrett, Timothy H. *Li Ao: Buddhist, Taoist, or Neo-Confucian?* Oxford: Oxford University Press, 1992.

———. "Buddhist Precepts in a Lawless World: Some Comments on the Linhuai Ordination Schandal." In *Going Forth: Visions of Buddhist Vinaya*, ed. William M. Bodiford, pp. 101–23. Honolulu: University of Hawai'i Press, 2005.

Bell, Catherine. "'A Precious Raft to Save the World': The Interpretation of Scripture Traditions and Printing in a Chinese Morality." *Late Imperial China* 17.1 (June 1996): 158–200.

———. "Printing and Religion in China: Some Evidence from the *Taishang Ganying Pian*." *Journal of Chinese Religions* 20 (Fall 1992): 173–86.

———. "Ritualization of Texts and Textualization of Ritual in the Codification of Taoist Liturgy." *History of Religions* 27.4 (1988): 366–92.

Benjue 本覺. *Shishi tongjian* 釋氏通鑒. 12 fascs. 1270, reprinted in 1626. Z no. 1516, vol. 76; XZJ vol. 131.

Benn, James A. "Another Look at the Pseudo-*Śūraṃgama Sūtra*." In *Harvard Journal of Asiatic Studies* 68.1 (June 2008): 57–89.

Berger, Patricia. *Empire of Emptiness: Buddhist Art and Political Authority in Qing China.* Honolulu: University of Hawaii Press, 2003.

Berling, Judith. "Bringing the Buddha Down to Earth: Notes on the Emergence of Yülu as a Buddhist Genre." *History of Religions* 27 (1987): 56–88.

———. *The Syncretic Religion of Lin Chao-en.* New York: Columbia University Press, 1981.

Bie'an Xingtong 別庵性統. *Xudeng zhengtong* 續燈正統. 42 fascs. Z. no. 1582, vol. 84.

Bielefeldt, Carl. "Kokan Shiren and the Sectarian Use of History." In *The Origins of Japan's Medieval World*, ed. Jeffrey P. Mass, pp. 295–317. Stanford, Calif.: Stanford University Press, 1997.

Birnbaum, Raoul. "Buddhist China at the Century's Turn." In *Religion in China Today*, ed. Daniel Overmyer, pp. 122–44. Cambridge: Cambridge University Press, 2003.

Blackburn, Anne. *Buddhist Learning and Textual Practice in Eighteenth-century Lankan Monastic Culture.* Princeton, N.J.: Princeton University Press, 2001.

Bodiford, William M. "Dharma Transmission in Sōtō Zen: Manzan Dōhaku's Reform Movement." *Monumenta Nipponica* 46 (1991): 423–51.

——. *Sōtō Zen in Medieval Japan.* Honolulu: University of Hawaii Press, 1993.

Bodiford, William M., ed. *Going Forth: Visions of Buddhist Vinaya.* Honolulu: University of Hawai'i Press, 2005.

Bol, Peter K. "The 'Localist Turn' and 'Local Identity' in Late Imperial China." *Late Imperial China* 24.2 (Dec. 2003): 1–50.

——. "The Sung Examination System and the Shih." *Asia Major* (Princeton, N.J.), 3rd ser., 3.2 (1990): 149–71.

——. *"This Culture of Ours": Intellectual Transitions in T'ang and Sung China.* Stanford, Calif.: Stanford University Press, 1992.

Brokaw, Cynthia J. and Kai-wing Chow, ed. *Printing and Book Culture in Late Imperial China.* Berkeley: University of California Press, 2005.

Brook, Timothy. "At the Margin of Public Authority: The Ming State and Buddhism." In *Culture and State in Chinese History: Conventions, Accommodations, and Critiques,* ed. Theodore Huters, R. Bin Wong, and Pauline Yu, pp. 161–81. Stanford, Calif.: Stanford University Press, 1997.

——. *The Confusions of Pleasure: Commerce and Culture in Ming China.* Berkeley, Los Angeles, and London: University of California Press, 1998.

——. "Funerary Ritual and the Building of Lineages in Late Imperial China." *Harvard Journal of Asiatic Studies* 49.2 (Dec. 1989): 465–99.

——. *Geographical Sources of Ming-Qing History.* Ann Arbor: Center for Chinese Studies, University of Michigan, 1988.

——. "Institution." In *Critical Terms for the Study of Buddhism,* ed. Donald S. Lopez Jr. pp. 143–161. Chicago: The University of Chicago Press, 2005.

——. *Praying for Power: Buddhism and the Formation of Gentry Society in Late-Ming China.* Cambridge, Mass.: Harvard University Press, 1993.

——. "Rethinking Syncretism: The Unity of the Three Teachings and Their Joint Worship in Late-Imperial China." *Journal of Chinese Religions* 21 (1993): 13–44.

Broughton, Jeffrey L. "Kuei-feng Tsung-mi: The Convergence of Ch'an and the Teachings." Ph.D. diss., Columbia University, 1975.

——. "Tsung-mi's Zen Prolegomenon: Introduction to an Exemplary Zen Canon." In *The Zen Canon: Understanding the Classic Texts,* ed. Steven Heine and Dale S. Wright, pp. 11–52. New York: Oxford University Press, 2004.

Burke, Peter. *The French Historical Revolution: The Annales School.* Oxford: Oxford University Press, 1991.

Buswell, Robert E., Jr. *The Formation of Ch'an Ideology in China and Korea: The Vajrasamādhi-Sūtra, a Buddhist Apocryphon.* Princeton, N.J.: Princeton University Press, 1989.

——. "The 'Short-cut' Approach of K'an-hua Meditation: The Evolution of a Practical Subitism in Chinese Ch'an Buddhism." In *Sudden and Gradual: Approaches to Enlightenment in Chinese Thought,* ed. Peter N. Gregory, pp. 321–77. Honolulu: University of Hawaii Press, 1987.

——. *The Zen Monastic Experience.* Princeton, N.J.: Princeton University Press, 1992.

Cahill, James. "Tung Ch'i ch'ang's 'Southern and Northern Schools' in the History and Theory of Painting: A Reconsideration." In *Sudden and Gradual: Approaches to Enlightenment in Chinese Thought*, ed. Peter N. Gregory, pp. 429–46. Honolulu: University of Hawaii Press, 1987.

Cai Hongsheng 蔡鴻生. "Qu Dajun de taochan guiru yu pifo" 屈大均的逃禪歸儒和辟佛. In his *Qingchu Lingnan Fomen shilüe* 清初嶺南佛門事略, pp. 73–97. Guangzhou: Guangdong gaodeng jiaoyu chuban she, 1997.

Chan, Hok-lam. *Li Chih (1527–1602) in Contemporary Chinese Historiography: New Light on his Life and Works*. New York: M.E. Sharpe, 1980.

Chan, Wing-tsit. "How Buddhist Is Wang Yang-ming?" *Philosophy East and West* 12.3 (1962): 203–16.

Chang Qing 常青. *Zhongguo guta de yishu licheng* 中國古塔的藝術歷程. Xi'an: Shanxi renmin meishu chubanshe, 1998.

Chanlin kesong 禪林課誦 (Japanese: *Zenrin kaju*). 1662. Rare book in Komazawa University Library.

Chanmen risong 禪門日誦. Woodblock print. The Tianning monastery edition. Reprint. Guoqing monastery, Tiantai mountain, dates unknown.

Chanmen yishu chubian 禪門逸書初編, ed. Mingfu 明復. 10 vols. Taibei: Hansheng chubanshe, 1980.

Chanmen yishu xubian 禪門逸書續編, ed. Mingfu 明復. 10 vols. Taibei: Hansheng chubanshe, 1987.

Chanzong quanshu 禪宗全書, ed. Lan Jifu 藍吉富. 101 vols. Taibei: Wenshu wenhua youxian gongsi, 1990.

Chao Jiong 晁迥. *Daoyuan jiyao* 道院集要, 3 fascs. In *Siku quanshu*, 3rd series (*zibu*), vol. 1052.

———. *Fazang suijin lu* 法藏碎金錄, 10 fascs. In *Siku quanshu*, 3rd series (*zibu*), vol. 1052.

———. *Zhaode xinbian* 昭德新編, 2 fascs. In *Siku quanshu*, 3rd series (*zibu*), vol. 894.

Chaves, Jonathan, trans. *Pilgrim of the Clouds: Poems and Essays by Yüan Hung-tao and His Brothers*. New York, Weatherhill, 1978.

Chen Jidong 陳繼東. "Zenmon nichiju no shohon ni tsuite" 禅門日誦の諸本について. *Indogaku Bukkyōgaku kenkyū* 51.1 (Dec. 2002): 212–17.

Chen Jinghe 陳荊和, ed. *Shiqi shiji guangnan zhi xin shiliao* 十七世紀廣南之新史料. Taibei: Zhonghua congshu weiyuanhui, 1960.

Ch'en, Kenneth S. "The Role of Buddhist Monasteries in T'ang Society." *History of Religions* 15.3 (1976): 209–30.

Chen Lai 陳來. "Guanyu 'Yiyan lu,' 'Jishan chengyu' yu Wang Yangming yulu yiwen: Ji 'Yangming xiansheng yiyanlu,' 'Jishan chengyu'" 關於"遺言錄", "稽山承語"與王陽明語錄佚文: 記"陽明先生遺言錄", "稽山承語." *Qinghua hanxue yanjiu* 清華漢學研究 1 (1994): 176–193.

———. *You Wu zhi jing: Wang Yangming zhexue de jingshen* 有無之境: 王陽明哲學的精神. Beijing: Renmin chubanshe, 1991.

Chen Naiqian 陳乃乾. *Cangxue dashi xingji kaolue* 蒼雪大師行季考略. 1930. Reprinted in *Fojiao mingren nianpu (xia)* 佛教名人年譜(下), pp. 1–48. Beijing: Beijing Tushuguan, 2003.

Chen, Pi-yan. "Morning and Evening Service: The Ritual, Music, and Doctrine in the Chinese Buddhist Monastic Community." Ph.D. diss., University of Chicago, 1999.

———. "Sound and Emptiness: Music, Philosophy, and the Monastic Practice of Buddhist Doctrine." *History of Religions* 41.1 (2001): 24–25.

Chen Shiqian 陳士強. *Fodian jingjie* 佛典精解. Shanghai: Shanghai guji chubanshe, 1992.

———. "*Wudeng yantong* bing 'Wudeng yantong jiehuo pian' zhuizhi" "五燈嚴統"並 "五燈嚴統解惑篇"錐指. *Chanxue yanjiu* 禪學研究 1 (1992): 168–72.

Chen Si 陳思. *Baoke congbian* 寶刻叢編. In *Shike shiliao xinbian*, vol. 24.

Chen Yinke 陳寅恪. *Liu Rushi biezhuan* 柳如是別傳. Shanghai: Shanghai guji chubanshe, 1980.

Chen Yuan 陳垣. *Chen Yuan shixue lunzhu xuan* 陳垣史學論著選. Shanghai: Shanghai renmin chubanshe, 1981.

———. *Mingji Dian Qian Fojiao kao* 明季滇黔佛教攷. Beijing: Zhonghua shuju, 1959.

———. *Qingchu sengzheng ji* 清初僧諍記. Beijing: Zhonghua shuju, 1962.

———. *Shihui juli* 史諱舉例. Beijing: Zhonghua shuju, 1958.

———. *Shishi yinian lu* 釋氏疑年錄. Beijing: Zhonghua shuju, 1964.

———. "Tang Ruowang yu Muchen Min" 湯若望與木陳忞. *Furen xuezhi* 輔仁學志 7.1–2 (1938). Reprinted in *Chen Yuan ji* 陳垣集, ed. Huang Xianian 黃夏年, pp. 83–108. Beijing: Zhongguo shehui kexue chubanshe, 1995.

———. "Yulu yu Shunzhi gongting" 語錄與順治宮廷. *Furen xuezhi* 輔仁學志 8.1 (June 1939). Reprinted in *Chen Yuan ji* 陳垣集, ed. Huang Xianian 黃夏年, pp. 109–20. Beijing: Zhongguo shehui kexue chubanshe, 1995.

———. *Zhongguo Fojiao shiji gailun* 中國佛教史籍概論. Beijing: Zhonghua shuju, 1962.

Chen Zhichao 陳智超, ed. *Lü Ri gao seng Donggao Xinyue shi wen ji* 旅日高僧東皋心越詩文集. Beijing: Zhongguo she hui ke xue chu ban she, 1994.

Cheng, Chung-ying. "On Zen (Ch'an) Language and Zen Paradoxes." *Journal of Chinese Philosophy* 1 (1973): 77–102.

———. "Rejoinder to Michael Levin's Comments on the Paradoxicality of the Koans." *Journal of Chinese Philosophy* 3.3 (June 1976): 291–97.

Cheng, François. *Chu Ta, 1626–1705: Le génie du trait*. Paris: Phébus, 1999.

Cheng Xinren 程欣人. "Shashi shijiao faxian Tangdai muta" 沙市市郊發現唐代墓塔. *Wenwu* 文物 2 (1959): 75.

Chen-hua. *In Search of the Dharma: Memoirs of a Modern Chinese Buddhist Pilgrim*, ed. Chün-fang Yü, trans. Denis C. Mair. Albany: State University of New York Press, 1992.

Cherniack, Susan. "Book Culture and Textual Transmission in Sung China." *Harvard Journal of Asiastic Studies* 54.1 (June 1994): 5–126.

Chia, Lucille. *Printing for Profit: The Commercial Publishers of Jianyang, Fujian (11th–17th Centuries)*. Cambridge, Mass.: Harvard University Press, 2002.

Ch'ien, Edward. *Chiao Hung and the Restructuring of Neo-Confucianism in the Late Ming*. New York: Columbia University Press, 1986.

———. "The Conception of Language and the Use of Paradox in Buddhism and Taoism." *Journal of Chinese Philosophy* 9. 3 (Sept. 1982): 307–28.

Chikusa Masaaki 竺沙雅章. *Chūgoku Bukkyō shakaishi kenkyū* 中國佛教社會史研究. Kyoto: Dōhosha, 1982.

———. "Enkin Daito no Kegonshū: Hōshūji to Sūkokujiso tachi" 燕京大都の華嚴宗: 寶集寺と崇国寺僧たち. *Ōtani daigaku shigaku ronkyū* 大谷大學史學論究 6 (2000): 1–26.

———. "Mindai jiden no fueki ni tsuite" 明代寺田の賦役について. In *Minshin jidai no seiji to shakai* 明清時代の政治と社會, ed. Ono Kazuko 小野和子, pp. 487–512. Kyoto: Kyōtō Daigaku Jinbun Kagaku Kenkyūjo, 1983.

———. "Sōdai Fukken no shakai to jiin" 宋代福建の社會と寺院. In his *Chūgoku Bukkyō shakaishi kenkyū*, pp. 181–87. Kyoto: Dohōsha, 1982.

Chow, Kai-wing. "Between Canonicity and Heterodoxy: Hermeneutical Moments of the Great Learning (Ta-hsueh)." In *Imagining Boundaries: Changing Confucian Doctrines, Texts, and Hermeneutics*, ed. Kai-wing Chow, On-cho Ng, and John B. Henderson, pp. 147–63. Albany: State University of New York Press, 1999.

———. *Publishing, Culture, and Power in Early Modern China*. Stanford, Calif.: Stanford University Press, 2004.

Chuiwan Guangzhen 吹萬廣真. *Chuiwan chanshi yulu* 吹萬禪師語錄. JXZ no. 239, vol. 29.

Ciyuan 辭源, rev. ed. Beijing: Shangwu yinshuguan, 1988.

Cleary, J. C. *Zibo: The Last Great Zen Master of China*. Berkeley, Calif.: AHP Paperbacks, 1989.

Cleary, Thomas, and J. C. Cleary. *The Blue Cliff Record*. 3 vols. Boulder, Colo., and London: Shambhala, 1977.

Clunas, Craig. "Books and Things: Ming Literary Culture and Material Culture." In *Chinese Studies*, ed. Frances Wood, pp. 136–43. London, British Library, 1988.

———. *Superfluous Things: Material Culture and Social Status in Early Modern China*. Cambridge: Polity, 1991.

Collcutt, Martin. "Buddhism: The Threat of Eradication." In *Japan in Transition: From Tokugawa to Meiji*, ed. Marius B. Jansen and Gilbert Rozman, pp. 143–67. Princeton, N.J.: Princeton University Press, 1986.

———. "The Early Ch'an Monastic Rule: Ch'ing Kuei and the Shaping of Ch'an Community Life." In *Early Ch'an in China and Tibet*, ed. Whalen Lai and Lewis R. Lancaster, pp. 165–84. Berkeley, Calif.: Asian Humanities Press, 1983.

———. *Five Mountains: The Rinzai Zen Monastic Institution in Medieval Japan*. Cambridge, Mass.: Harvard University Press, 1981.

———. "The Zen Monastery in Kamakura Society." In *Court and Bakufu in Japan: Essays in Kamakura History*, ed. Jeffrey P. Mass, pp. 191–220. New Haven, Conn.: Yale University Press, 1982.

Connery, Christopher Leigh. *The Empire of the Text: Writing and Authority in Early Imperial China*. New York: Rowman and Littlefield, 1998.

Da Zhaoqing lüsi zhi 大昭慶律寺志. 1882. ZFS vol. 71.

Dachuan 大川, ed. *Wudeng huiyuan* 五燈會元. Z no. 1565, vol. 80

Dangui Jinshi 澹歸今釋 (Jin Bao 金堡). *Bianxingtang ji* 遍行堂集. In *Chanmen yishu xubian*, vol. 4.

Daoyuan 道元, ed. *Jingde chuandeng lu* 景德傳燈錄. T no. 2076, vol. 51.

Darnton, Robert. "What is the History of Books?" *Daedalus* 111.3 (Summer 1982): 65–83.

Dazangjing bubian 大藏經補編, ed. Lan Jifu 藍吉富. 37 vols. Taibei: Huayu chubanshe, 1984–1986.

de Bary, William T. "Buddhism and the Chinese Tradition." *Diogenes* 47 (1964): 102–24.

———. "Individualism and Humanitarianism in Late Ming Thought." In his *Self and Society in Ming Thought*, pp. 145–248. New York: Columbia University Press, 1970.

———. *Learning for One's Self: Essays on the Individual in Neo-Confucian Thought*. New York: Columbia University Press, 1991.

———. *The Liberal Tradition in China*. New York: Columbia University Press, 1983.

Demiéville, Paul, trans. *Entretiens de Lin-tsi*. Paris: Fayard, 1972.

———. "The Mirror of the Mind." In *Sudden and Gradual: Approaches to Enlightenment in Chinese Thought*, ed. Peter N. Gregory, pp. 13–40. Honolulu: University of Hawaii Press, 1987.

Demiéville, Paul, et al., eds. *Hōbōgirin: Dictionanaire encyclopédique du bouddhisme d'aprè les sources chinoises et japonaises*, vols. 1–6. Paris: Adrien Maisonneuve, 1929–1983.

Deng Huoqu 鄧豁渠. *Nanxun lu* 南詢錄. 1599. Rare book in Naikaku bunko 內閣文庫. Reprinted in *Zhongguo zhexue* 中國哲學, vol. 19, puctruated and edited by Huang Xuanmin 黃宣民, pp. 377–414. Changsha: Yuelu shushe, 1998,

Dengweishan Sheng'en si zhi 鄧蔚山聖恩寺志. ZFS vols. 44 and 45.

Dictionary of Ming Biography, 1368–1644, ed. L. Carrington Goodrich. New York and London: Columbia University Press, 1976.

Dimberg, Ronald G. *The Sage and Society: The Life and Thought of Ho Hsin-yin*. Honolulu: University of Hawaii Press, 1974.

Dongchu 釋東初. *Zhongri fojiao jiaotongshi* 中日佛教交通史. In *Tongchu laoren quanji* 東初老人全集, vol. 7. Taibei: Dongchu chubanshe, 1985.

Dong Han 董含. *Zhuanxiang zuibi* 篔鄉贅筆. Reprinted in *Zhongguo jindai xiaoshuo shiliao huibian* 中國近代小說史料彙編, vol. 20. Taibei: Guangwen shuju, 1980.

Dong Qun 董群. *Zushi chan* 祖師禪. Hangzhou: Zhejiang renmin chubanshe, 1997.

Eberhard, Wolfram. "Temple-Building Activities in Medieval and Modern China." *Monumenta Serica* 23 (1964): 264–318.

Eichman, Jennifer Lynn. "Spiritual Seekers in a Fluid Landscape: A Chinese Buddhist Network in the Wanli Period (1573–1620)." Ph.D. diss., Princeton University, 2005.

Elman, Benjamin. *A Cultural History of Civil Service Exam in Late Imperial China*. Berkeley: University of California Press, 2000.

———. *From Philosophy to Philology: Intellectual and Social Aspects of Change in Late Imperial China*. Cambridge, Mass.: Harvard University Press, 1984.

Eminent Chinese of the Ch'ing Period (1644–1912), ed. Arthur W. Hummel. Taipei: Literature House, 1964.

Enō kenkyū: Enō no denki to shiryō ni kansuru kisoteki kenkyū 慧能研究: 慧能の伝記と資料に関する基礎的研究, ed. Komazawa Daigaku Zenshūshi Kenkyūkai. Tokyo: Taishūkan Shoten, 1978.

Fang Hao 方豪. *Zhongguo Tianzhujiaoshi renwu zhuan* 中國天主教史人物傳. 3 vols. Beijing: Zhonghua shuju, 1988.

Farmer, Edward Lewis, Romeyn Taylor, and Ann Waltner. *Ming History: An Introductory Guide to Research.* Minneapolis: University of Minnesota, 1994.

Farquhar, David M. "Emperor as Bodhisattva in the Governance of the Ch'ing Empire." *Harvard Journal of Asiatic Studies* 38.1 (June 1978): 5–34.

Faure, Bernard. *Chan Insights and Oversights: An Epistemological Critique of the Chan Tradition.* Princeton, N.J.: Princeton University Press, 1993.

———. *The Rhetoric of Immediacy: A Cultural Critique of Chan/Zen Buddhism.* Princeton, N.J.: Princeton University Press, 1991.

Feiyin Tongrong 費隱通容. *Bore Xinjing zhuolun jie* 般若心經斲輪解. 1 fasc. Z no. 548, vol. 26.

———. *Conglin liangxu xuzhi* 叢林兩序須知. 1 fasc. Z no. 1251, vol. 63; XZJ vol. 112.

———. *Feiyin chanshi bieji* 費隱禪師別集. Manuscript. Preface dated 1648. 18 fascs. Originally in Keizuiji 慶瑞寺 in Osaka, now in Komazawa University Library.

———. *Feiyin chanshi yulu* 費隱禪師語錄. 14 fascs. JXZ no. 178, vol. 26.

———. "Fuyan Feiyin Rong chanshi jinian lu" 福嚴費隱容禪師紀年錄. In *Feiyin chanshi yulu.* JXZ no. 178, vol. 26

———. "Miyun chanshi nianpu" 密雲禪師年譜. In *Miyun chanshi yulu*, JXZ no. 158, vol. 10.

———. *Wudeng yantong* 五燈嚴統. 25 fascs. 1653. Z no. 1568, vols. 80 and 81.

———. *Wudeng yantong jiehuo pian* 五燈嚴通解惑篇. 1 fasc. Z no. 1569, vol. 81.

———. *Yuandao pixie shuo* 原道闢邪説. 1 fasc. In *Feiyin chanshi bieji*, fasc. 16; also in *Honkoku byakujashū* 翻刻闢邪集, fasc 2. Reprinted in *Fukuenji* 福圓寺, Japan, 1860; also in *Shengchao poxie ji* 聖朝破邪集, ed. Xu Changzhi, fasc. 8. 1639. Reprint. Japan, 1855.

———. *Zuting qianchui lu* 祖庭鉗鎚錄. Z no. 1286, vol. 65.

Feng Er'kang 馮爾康. "Qing Shizong de chongfo he yongfo" 清世宗的崇佛和用佛. In *Fojiao yu Zhongguo wenhua* 佛教與中國文化, pp. 304–13. Beijing: Zhonghua shuju, 1988.

———. *Qingshi shiliao xue chugao* 清史史料學初稿. Tianjin: Nankai daxue chubanshe, 1986.

———. *Yongzheng zhuan* 雍正傳. Beijing: Renmin chubanshe, 1985.

Fenyang Shanzhao 汾陽善昭. *Fenyang Wude chanshi yulu* 汾陽無德禪師語錄. T no. 1992, vol. 47.

Fojiao dazangjing 佛教大藏經. ed. Lan Jifu 藍吉富. 84 vols. Taibei: Fojiao chuban she, 1977–1983.

Fojiao mingren nianpu 佛教名人年譜. 3 vols. Beijing: Beijing Tushuguan, 2003.

Foulk, T. Griffith. "The 'Ch'an School' and Its Place in the Buddhist Monastic Tradition." Ph.D. diss., University of Michigan, 1987.

———. "Controversies concerning the 'Separate Transmission.'" In *Buddhism in the Sung*, ed. Peter N. Gregory and Dan Getz, pp. 253–58. Honolulu: University of Hawaii Press, 1999.

———. "Myth, Ritual, and Monastic Practice in Sung Ch'an Buddhism." In *Religion and Society in T'ang and Sung China*, ed. Patricia Ebrey and Peter Gregory, pp. 147–208. Honolulu: University of Hawaii Press, 1993.

Foulk, T. Griffith, and Robert H. Sharf. "On the Ritual Use of Ch'an Portraiture in Medieval China." *Cahiers d'Extrême-Asie* 7 (1993–1994): 149–219.

Franke, Wolfgang. "Li Zhi's Tomb." In his *Sino-Malaysiana: Selected Papers on Ming & Qing History and on the Overseas Chinese in Southeast Asia 1942–1988*, pp. 191–205. Singapore: South Seas Society, 1989.

Fuju 福聚, comp. *Nanshan zongtong* 南山宗統. 1744. Reprint. 1936. Rare source in the Shanghai Library.

Fukushima Shunō 福島俊翁. *Kokan* 虎關. Tokyo: Yūzankaku, 1944. Reprinted in *Fukushima Shunō chosakushū* 福島俊翁著作集, vol. 2. Tokyo: Mokujisha, 1974.

Gao Jin 高晉. *Nanxun shengdian* 南巡盛典. Reprint. Taibei: Wenhai chubanshe, 1970.

Gaofeng Yuanmiao 高峰原妙. *Gaofeng chanshi yulu* 高峰禪師語錄. XZJ vol. 122.

Gaoming si zhi 高明寺志, ed. Zhu Feng'ao 朱封鰲 and Wei Yanduo 韋彥鐸. Beijing: Dangdai zhongguo chubanshe, 1995.

Gardner, Daniel, K. "Modes of Thinking and Modes of Discourse in the Sung: Some Thoughts on the Yülu (Recorded Conversations) Texts." *Journal of Asian Studies* 50.3 (1991): 574–603.

Ge Zhaoguang 葛兆光. *Chanzong yu Zhongguo wenhua* 禪宗與中國文化. Shanghai: Shanghai renmin chubanshe, 1986.

———. *Zhongguo Chan sixiang shi, liu shiji dao jiu shiji* 中国禅思想史: 6世纪到 9世纪. Beijing: Beijing daxue chubanshe, 1995.

Gernet, Jacques. *Buddhism in Chinese Society: An Economic History from the Fifth to the Tenth Centuries*, trans. Franciscus Verellen. New York: Columbia University Press, 1995.

———. *China and the Christian Impact: A Conflict of Cultures*. Cambridge and New York: Cambridge University Press, 1985.

Gimello, Robert M. "Apophatic and Kataphatic Discourse in Mahāyāna: A Chinese View." *Philosophy East and West* 26.2 (1976): 116–36.

———. "The Buddhism of a 'Confucian' Scholar: Some Remarks Preliminary to a Study of Ch'ao Yueh-chih 晁說之 (1059–1129) and His Relationship to T'ien-t'ai 天台." In *Fojiao yu Zhongguo wenhua guoji xueshu huiyi lunwenji* 佛教與中國文化國際學術會議論文集, pp. 863–900. Taibei: Zhonghua wenhua fuxing yundong zonghui Zongjiao yanjiu weiyuanhui, 1995.

———. "Chang Shang-ying on Wu-t'ai Shan." In *Pilgrims and Sacred Sites in China*, ed. Chün-fang Yü and Susan Naquin, pp. 89–149. Berkeley: University of California Press, 1992.

———. "Echoes of *The Platform Scripture* in Northern Sung Ch'an." In *Fo Kuang Shan Report of International Conference on Ch'an Buddhism*, pp. 142–160. Gaoxiong: Foguangshan press, 1990.

———. "Icon and Incantation: The Goddess Zhunti and the Role of Images in the Occult Buddhism of China." In *Images in Asian Religions: Texts and Contexts*, ed. Phyllis Granoff and Koichi Shinohara, pp. 225–56. Vancouver: UBC Press, 2004.

———. "Imperial Patronage of Buddhism during the Northern Sung." In *Proceedings of the First International Symposium on Church and State in China*, pp. 71–85. Taipei: Tamkang Univeristy Press, 1987.

———. "Li T'ung-hsüan and the Practical Dimensions of Hua-yen." In *Studies in Ch'an and Hua-yen*, ed. Robert M. Gimello and Peter Gregory, pp. 321–390. Honolulu: University of Hawaii Press, 1983.

———. "Marga and Culture: Learning, Letters, and Liberation in Northern Sung Ch'an." In *Paths to Liberation: The Marga and Its Transformations in Buddhist Thought*, ed. Robert M. Gimello and Robert E. Buswell, Jr., pp. 371–437. Honolulu: University of Hawaii Press, 1992.

———. "Poetry and the *Kung-an* in Ch'an Practice." *Ten Directions* 7 (Spring/Summer 1986): 9–10.

———. "The Sudden/Gradual Polarity: A Recurrent Theme in Chinese Thought." *Journal of Chinese Philosophy* 9 (1982): 471–86.

Goldfuss, Gabriele. *Vers un bouddhisme du XXe siècle: Yang Wenhui (1837–1911), réformateur laïque et imprimeur.* Paris: Collège de France, Institut des Hautes Etudes Chinoises, 2001.

Goossaert, Vincent. "Counting the Monks: The 1736–1739 Census of the Chinese Clergy." *Late Imperial China* 21.2 (2000): 40–85.

Gozan bungaku zenshū 五山文學全集, ed. Kamimura Kankō 上村觀光. 5 vols. Tokyo: Gozan bungaku zenshū Kankōkai, 1936.

Granoff, Phyllis, and Koichi Shinohara, eds. *Monks and Magicians: Religious Biographies in Asia.* Oakville, N.Y., and London: Mosaic, 1988.

Grant, Beata. "Female Holder of the Lineage: Linji Chan Master Zhiyuan Xinggang (1597–1654)." *Late Imperial China* 17.2 (Dec. 1996): 51–76.

———. *Mount Lu Revisited: Buddhism in the Life and Writings of Su Shi.* Honolulu: University of Hawaii Press, 1994.

———. "The Red Cord United: Buddhist Nuns in Eighteenth-Century China." In *Buddhist Women across Culture: Realizations*, ed. Karma Lekshe Tsomo, pp. 91–104. Albany: State University of New York Press, 1999.

———. "Through the Empty Gate: The Poetry of Buddhist Nuns in Late Imperial China." In *Cultural Intersections in Late Chinese Buddhism*, ed. Marsha Weidner, pp. 87–113. Honolulu: University of Hawaii Press, 2001.

———. "Who Is This I? Who Is That Other? The Poetry of an Eighteenth Century Buddhist Lay Woman." *Late Imperial China* 15 (1994): 47–86.

———. "Writing Nuns." In *The Red Brush: Writing Women of Imperial China*, ed. Wilt Idema and Beata Grant, pp. 455–70. Cambridge, Mass.: Harvard University Press, 2004.

Gregory, Peter N. "The Buddhism of the Cultured Elite." In *Religions of China in Practice*, ed. Donald Lopez, Jr., pp. 381–89. Princeton, N.J.: Princeton University Press, 1996.

———. "Tsung-mi and the Single Word Awareness (*Chih*)." *Philosophy East and West* 18 (1985): 249–69.

———. *Tsung-mi and the Sinification of Buddhism*. Princeton, N.J.: Princeton University Press, 1991.

Gregory, Peter N., and Dan Getz, eds. *Buddhism in the Sung*. Honolulu: University of Hawaii Press, 1999.

Griffiths, Paul J. *Religious Reading: The Place of Reading in the Practice of Religion*. New York: Oxford University Press, 1999.

Groner, Paul. "The *Fan-wang ching* and Monastic Discipline in Japanese Tendai: A Study of Annen's *Futsū jubosatsutai kōshaku*." In *Chinese Buddhist Apocrypha*, ed. Robert Buswell, pp. 251–90. Honolulu: University of Hawaii Press, 1989.

———. "The Ordination Ritual in the *Platform Sūtra*: Within the Context of the East Asian Buddhist Vinaya Tradtion." In *Fo Kuang Shan Report of International Conference on Ch'an Buddhism*, pp. 220–50. Gaoxiong: Foguangshan press, 1990.

Guishan Lingyou 溈山靈祐. *Tanzhou Guishan Lingyou chanshi yulu* 潭州溈山靈祐禪師語錄. T no. 1989, vol. 47.

Guo Limei 郭黎眉, comp. *Jiaowai biechuan* 教外別傳. 16 fascs. Z no. 1580, vol. 84; XZJ vol. 144.

Guo Peng 郭朋. *Ming Qing Fojiao* 明清佛教. Fuzhou: Fujian renmin chuban she, 1982.

———. *Tanjing duikan* 壇經對勘. Jinan: Qilu shushe, 1981.

Guoxiang 果祥. *Zibo dashi yanjiu* 紫柏大師研究. Taibei: Dongchu chubanshe, 1987.

Gushan zhi 鼓山志. 1761. ZFS vol. 97.

Guy, Kent. "Zhang Tingyu and Reconciliation: the Scholar and the State in the Early Qianlong Reign." *Late Imperial China* 7.1 (June 1986): 50–62.

Haichao yin 海潮音. 1920–1949. Reprint, 41 vols. Shanghai: Shanghai guji chubanshe, 2003.

Halperin, Mark. *Out of the Cloister: Literati Perspectives on Buddhism in Sung China 960–1279*. Cambridge, Mass.: Harvard University Press, 2006.

Hanshan Deqing 憨山德清. *Hanshan dashi mengyou ji* 憨山大師夢游集. 52 fascs. Z no. 1456, vol. 73; JXZ nos. 115, 116, 117, vol. 22.

Hansong Zhicao 寒松智操. *Hansong Cao chanshi yulu* 寒松操禪師語錄. JXZ no. 392, vol. 37.

Hanyue Fazang 漢月法藏. *Hongjie fayi* 弘戒法儀 or *Chuanshou santan Hongjie fayi* 傳授三壇弘戒法儀. ZH, vol. 116 and JXZ no. 397, vol. 37.

———. "Sanfeng Fazang chanshi nianpu" 三峰法藏禪師年譜. In *Sanfeng Zang heshang yulu*. JXZ no. 299, vol. 34.

———. *Sanfeng Zang heshang yulu* 三峰藏和尚語錄. 16 fascs. JXZ no. 299, vol. 34.

———. *Wuzong yuan* 五宗原. 1 fasc. Z no. 1279, vol. 65; XZJ vol. 114.

———. *Yumi shen shishi zhigai* 於密滲施食旨概. ca. 1626. Z no. 1082, vol. 59.

Hasebe Kōichi 長谷部好一. "Tōmon no dōkō to sono keifu: Fuyōkai ka ni tsuite" 洞門の動向とその系譜: 芙蓉楷下について. *Indogaku Bukkyōgaku kenkyū* 18.1 (1969): 91–96.

Hasebe Yūkei 長谷部幽蹊. "Hakuzan no monryū" 博山の門流. *Indogaku Bukkyōgaku kenkyū* 印度學佛教學研究 49 (1976): 251–54.

———. "Chikai san *Shōmei roku* ni tsuite" 智楷撰《正名錄》について. *Indogaku Bukkyōgaku kenkyū* 印度學佛教學研究 30.1 (1982): 329–34.

———. "Chūgoku kindai ni okeru gukai hogi" 中國近代における具戒法儀. *Aichi daigaku zenkenkyūjo kiyō* 愛知學院禪研究所紀要 28 (2000): 1–22.

———. "Fukeizō shoshū no zenseki ippon ni tsuite" 普慧藏所收の禪籍一本について. *Aichi daigaku zenkenkyūjo kiyō* 愛知學院禪研究所紀要 9 (1970): 47–76.

———. "Kosoha no sho ritsuso gyōgō kiryaku" 古祖派の諸律祖行業記略. *Aichi daigaku zenkenkyūjo kiyō* 愛知學院禪研究所紀要 I, 24 (1996): 81–102; II, 25 (1996): 129–207; III, 26 (1996): 51–78.

———. *Min Shin Bukkyō kenkyū shiryō* 明清佛教研究資料. Nagoya: self-published, 1987.

———. *Min Shin Bukkyō kyōdanshi kenkyū* 明清佛教教團史研究. Tokyo: Dōhōha, 1993.

———. "Min Shin Bukkyō no seikaku o kangaeru" 明清佛教の性格を考える. *Aichi daigaku zenkenkyūjo kiyō* 愛知學院禪研究所紀要 18–19 (1990–1991): 87–109.

———. *Min Shin Bukkyōshi kenkyū josetsu* 明清佛教史研究序說. Taibei: Xinwenfeng chuban gongsi, 1979.

———. "Min Shin jidai kyūkai no tembō" 明清時代教界の展望. *Aichi gakuin zenkenkyūjo kiyō* 愛知學院禪研究所紀要 6–7 (1976–1977): 189–225.

———. "Min Shin jidai ni okeru Zen Ritsu ryōshū kōka no dōkō" 明清時代における禅律両宗弘化の動向. *Aichi gakuin zenkenkyūjo kiyō* 愛知學院禪研究所紀要 20 (Mar. 1992): 183–203.

———. "Sanhō ichimon no ryūtai" 三峰一門の隆替. *Aichi gakuin daigaku ronsō ippan kyōiku kenkyū* 愛知學院大學論叢一般教育研究 I, 31.4 (1984): 29–69; II, 32.1 (1985): 3–35; III, 32.2 (1985): 133–50; IV, 33.3 (1986): 29–47; V, 33.4 (1986): 59–80.

———. "Zokutō shōtō to Shūōn Tsuiman homon" 續燈正統と聚雲吹萬法門 *Aichi gakuin zenkenkyūjo kiyō* 愛知學院禪研究所紀要 31 (2003): 31–52.

———. "Sotō benka' kōshaku" 祖灯辨訛考釈. *Aichi gakuin zenkenkyūjo kiyō* 愛知學院禪研究所紀要 I, 13(1984): 31–85; II, 14 (1985): 41–111.

Hay, Jonathan. *Shitao: Painting and Modernity in Early Qing China.* Cambridge: Cambridge University Press, 2001.

Hayada Yoshio 林田芳雄. "Mindai ni okeru Fukken to Bukkyō" 明代にわける福建と佛教. *Kyoto Joshi gaku'en Bukkyō bunka kenkyūjo kenkyū kiyō* 京都女子學園佛教文化研究所研究紀要 17 (1987): 111–45.

He Bingsong 何炳松. *Zhedong xuepai suyuan* 浙東學派溯源. Shanghai: Shangwu yinshuguan, 1933.

He Mianshan 何綿山. "Qiantan Fujian Fojiao de tedian" 淺談福建佛教的特點. *Zongjiaoxue yanjiu* 宗教學研究 2 (Apr. 1996): 67–71.

He Lingxiu 何齡修. "Huang Yuqi de fu Ming huodong ji Huang Yuqi an" 黃毓祺的復明活動及黃毓祺案. In his *Wukuzhai Qingshi conggao* 五庫斋清史叢稿, pp. 324–39 Beijing: Xueyuan chubanshe, 2004.

He Xiaorong 何孝榮. *Mingdai Nanjing siyuan yanjiu* 明代南京寺院研究. Beijing: Zhongguo shehui kexue chubanshe, 2000.

Henderson, John B. *The Construction of Orthodoxy and Heresy: Neo-Confucian, Islamic, Jewish, and Early Christian Patterns.* Albany: State University of New York Press, 1998.

Hirakubo Akira 平久保章. *Ingen* 隱元. Kyoto: Yoshikawa kobunkan, 1974.

———. *Shinsan Kōtei Ingen zenshū* 新纂校訂隱元全集. Kyoto: Kaimei shoin, 1979.

Hobsbawm, Eric and Terence Ranger, ed. *The Invention of* Tradition. Cambridge and New York: Cambridge University Press, 1983.

Hong Xiuping 洪修平 and Sun Yiping 孫亦平. *Rulai Chan* 如來禪. Hangzhou: Zhejiang renmin chubanshe, 1997.

Hori, Victor Sōgen. *Zen Sand: The Book of Capping Phrases for Kōan Practice.* Honolulu: University of Hawaii Press, 2003.

Hou Chong 侯沖. "Yunnan Azhali jiao jingdian jiqi zai Zhongguo Fojiao yanjiu zhong de jiazhi" 雲南阿吒力教經典及其在中國佛教研究中的價值. In *Zangwai Fojiao wenxian* 藏外佛教文獻, no. 6, ed. Fang Guangchang 方廣錩. Beijing: Zongjiao wenhua chubanshe, 1998. Reprinted in Hou Chong, *Yunnan yu Bashu Fojiao yanjiu lungao* 雲南與巴蜀佛教研究論稿, pp. 196–209. Beijing: Zongjiao wenhua chubanshe, 2006.

———. "Yunnan Jizushan de jueqi jiqi zhuyao Chanxi" 雲南雞足山的崛起及其主要禪係. Reprinted in Hou Chong, *Yunnan yu Bashu Fojiao yanjiu lungao* 雲南與巴蜀佛教研究論稿, pp. 425–454. Beijing: Zongjiao wenhua chubanshe, 2006.

Hou Wailu 侯外廬. *Zhongguo sixiang tongshi* 中國思想通史. 5 vols. Beijing, Renmin chubanshe, 1957–1960.

Hsieh, Ding-hwa Evelyn. "A Study of the Evolution of K'an-hua Ch'an in Sung China: Yuan-wu K'o-ch'in (1063–1135) and the Function of Kung-an in Ch'an Pedagogy and Praxis." Ph. D diss., University of California, Los Angeles, 1993.

———. "Yuan-wu K'o-ch'in's (1063–1135) Teaching of Ch'an Kung-an Practice: A Transition from Literary Study of Ch'an Kung-an to the Practical K'an-hua Ch'an." *Journal of the International Association of Buddhist Studies* 17 (1994): 66–95.

Hsu, Sung-peng. *A Buddhist Leader in Ming China.* University Park: Pennsylvania State University Press, 1979.

Hu Shih. "Ch'an (Zen) Buddhism in China: Its History and Method." *Philosophy East and West* 3.1 (1953): 3–24.

———. "The Development of Zen Buddhism in China." *Chinese Social and Political Science Review* 15.4 (1932): 475–505.

Huang Chi-chiang 黃啟江. "Zhang Shangying hufa de lishi yiyi" 張商英護法的歷史意義. *Zhonghua Foxue bao* 中華佛學學報 9 (July 1996): 123–66.

Huang Duanbo 黃端伯. *Yaoguang ge waiji* 瑤光閣外集. 2 fasc. In *Siku quanshu cunmu congshu*, vol. 193.

Huang, Pei. *Autocracy at Work: A Study of the Yung-cheng Period, 1723–1735.* Bloomington: Indiana University Press, 1974.

———. "Five Major Sources for the Yung-cheng Period, 1723–1735." *Journal of Asian Studies* 27 (1968): 847–57.

Huang Yuji 黃虞稷. *Qianqing tang shu mu* 千頃堂書目. Reprint. Taibei: Guangwen shuju, 1967.

Huang Zongxi 黃宗羲. *Lizhou yizhu huikan* 梨洲遺著彙刊. 57 fascs. Shanghai: Shizhong shuju, 1910.

———. *Mingru xue'an* 明儒學案. 2 vols. Reprint. Beijing: Zhonghua shuju, 1985.

———. *Nanlei wending qianji houji sanji* 南雷文定前集後集三集. Shanghai: Shangwu yinshuguan, 1937.

———. *The Records of Ming Scholars*, trans. and ed. Julia Ching. Honolulu: University of Hawaii Press, 1987.

Huang Zongxi 黃宗羲, comp. *Ming wen hai* 明文海. In *Siku quanshu*, vol. 1454.

Huanlun 幻輪, comp. *Shishi jigu lue xuji* 釋氏稽古略續集. 3 fascs. T no. 2038, vol. 49.

Huanyou Zhengchuan 幻有正傳. *Longchi Huanyou chanshi yulu* 龍池幻有禪師語錄. 12 fascs. JXZ no. 169, vol. 25.

Hucker, Charles O. *A Dictionary of Official Titles in Imperial China*. Stanford, Calif.: Stanford University Press, 1985.

———. "An Index of Terms and Titles in 'Governmental Organization of Ming Dynasty.'" *Harvard Journal of Asiatic Studies* 23 (1960–1961): 127–51.

Hucker, Charles O, ed. *Chinese Government in Ming Times: Seven Studies*. New York: Columbia University Press, 1969.

Hufa zhengdeng lu 護法正燈錄. 1 fasc. Rare book in the Shanghai Library.

Huihong 慧洪. *Chanlin sengbao zhuan* 禪林僧寶傳. 30 fascs. Z no. 1560, 79: 490–556.

———. *Linji zongzhi* 臨濟宗旨. 1 fasc. Z no. 1234, vol. 63.

———. *Linjian lu* 林間錄. 2 fascs. Z no. 1624, vol. 87.

Huiyan 釋慧嚴. "Mingmo Qingchu Mintai Fojiao de hudong" 明末清初閩台佛教的互動. *Zhonghua Foxue bao* 中華佛學報 9 (1996): 209–42.

Hurvitz, Leon. "Chu-hung's One Mind of Pure Land and Ch'an Buddhism." In *Self and Society in Ming Thought*, ed. William Theodore de Bary, pp. 451–76. New York: Columbia University Press, 1970.

Hymes, Robert. "Not Quite Gentlemen? Doctors in Sung and Yuan." *Chinese Science* (Philadelphia) 8 (1987): 9–76.

———. *Way and Byway: Taoism, Local Religion, and Models of Divinity in Sung and Modern China*. Berkeley: University of California Press, 2002.

Ishan Ining 一山一寧. *Issan kokushi goroku* 一山國師語錄. T no. 2553, vol. 80.

Ishii Shūdō 石井修道. *Chūgoku Zenshū shiwa* 中國禪宗史話. Kyoto: Zen Bunka Kenkyūjo, 1988.

———. "Minmatsu Shinsho no Tendōzan to Mitsuun Engo" 明末清初の天童山と密雲圓悟. *Komazawa daigaku bukkyō gakubu ronshū* 6 (1975): 78–96.

———. "Shinpuku-ji bunko shozō no Hai Shū shūi mon no honkoku" 真福寺文庫所藏の "裴修拾遺問" の翻刻. *Zengaku kenkyū* 60 (1981): 71–104.

———. *Sōdai Zenshūshi no kenkyū* 宋代禪宗史の研究. Tokyo: Daitō Shuppan, 1987.

Jaffe, Richard. "Ingen and the Threat to the Myōshinjiha." *Komazawa daigaku zen kenkyūsho nenpō* 2 (1991): 1–35.

Jan, Yün-hua. "Chinese Buddhism in Ta-tu: The New Situation and New Problems." In *Yuan Thought: Chinese Thought and Religion under the Mongols*, ed. Hok-lam Chan and William Theodore de Bary, pp. 375–417. New York: Columbia University Press, 1982.

———. "Li Ping-shan and His Refutation of Neo-Confucian Criticism of Buddhism." In *Developments in Buddhist Thought: Canadian Contributions to Buddhist Studies*, ed. Roy C. Amore, pp. 162–93. Waterloo, Ont.: Wilfrid Laurier University Press, 1979.

———. *Zongmi* 宗密. Taibei: Dongda tushu, 1988.

Jilun Chaoyong 霽崙超永. *Wudeng quanshu* 五燈全書. 120 fascs, 1693. Z no. 1571, vols. 81 and 82.

Ji Wenfu 嵇文甫. *Zuopai Wang xue* 左派王學. Reprint. Taibei: Guowen tiandi zazhi she, 1990.

Jia, Jinhua. *The Hongzhou School of Chan Buddhism in Eighth-through Tenth-Century China*. Albany: State University of New York Press, 2006.

Jiang Boqin 姜伯勤. *Shilian Dashan yu Aomen chanshi: Qingchu Lingnan chanxue shi yanjiu* 石濂大汕與澳門禪史: 清初嶺南禪學史研究. Shanghai: Xuelin chubanshe, 1999.

Jiang Canteng 江燦騰. *Mingqing Minguo Fojiao sixiang shilun* 明清民國佛教思想史論. Beijing: Zhongguo shehui kexue chuban she, 1996.

———. *Wan Ming Fojiao conglin gaige yu Foxue zhengbian zhi yanjiu* 晚明佛教叢林改革與佛學爭辯之研究. Taibei: Xinwenfeng, 1990.

Jiangling xianzhi 江陵縣志. 1794. Reprinted in *Huibei fangzhi* 湖北方志, no. 12. Taibei: Taiwan Shuju, 1970.

Jianyi 見一. "Hanyue fazang zhi chanfa yanjiu" 漢月法藏之禪法研究. *Zhonghua Foxue bao* 中華佛學報 11 (1998): 181–225.

Jiao Hong 焦竑, ed. *Guochao xianzheng lu* 国朝獻征錄. Reprinted in *Mingdai zhuanji congkan* 明代傳記叢刊, no. 114. Taibei: Mingwen Shuju, 1991.

Jing 靜 and Jun 筠. *Sodō shū* 祖堂集, ed. Yanagida Seizan. Reprint. Kyoto: Chūbun shuppansha, 1972.

Jiu Tang shu 舊唐書. Reprint. Beijing: Zhonghua shuju, 1976.

Jiyin 紀蔭. *Zongtong biannian* 宗統編年. 1689. Z no. 1600, vol. 86; XZJ vol. 147.

Johnson, David, ed. *Popular Culture in Late Imperial China*. Berkeley: University of California Press, 1985.

Jones, Charles B. "Apologetic Strategies in Late Imperial Chinese Pure Land Buddhism." *Journal of Chinese Religions* 29 (2001): 69–90.

———. "Mentally Constructing What Already Exists: the Pure Land Thought of Chan Master Jixing Chewu (1741–1810)." *Journal of the International Association of Buddhist Studies* 23.1 (Summer 2000): 43–70.

———. "Toward a Typology of Nien-fo: a Study in Methods of Buddha-Invocation in Chinese Pure Land Buddhism." *Pacific World: Journal of the Institute of Buddhist Studies* 3rd series, 3 (Fall 2001): 219–239.

Jorgensen, John. "The 'Imperial' Lineage of Ch'an Buddhism: The Role of Confucian Ritual and Ancestor Worship in Ch'an's Search for Legitimization in the Mid-T'ang Dynasty." *Papers in Far Eastern History* 35 (1987): 89–133.

Juding 居頂, comp. *Xu Chuandeng lu* 續傳燈錄. T no. 2077, vol. 51.

Jue'an 覺岸. *Shishi jigu lue* 釋氏稽古略. T no. 2037, vol. 49.

Juelang Daosheng 覺浪道盛. *Tianjie Juelang Sheng chanshi quanlu* 天界覺浪盛禪師全錄. JXZ no. 311, vol. 34.

Kern, Iso. *Buddhistische Kritik am Christentum im China des 17 Jahrhunderts. Texte von Yu Shunxi (?–1621), Zhuhong (1535–1615), Yuanwu (1566–1642), Tongrong (1539–1679), Xingyuan (1611–1662), Zhixu (1599–1655)*. Bern: Peter Lang, 1992.

———. "Matteo Riccis Verhaltnis zum Buddhismus." *Monumenta Serica* 36 (1984–1985): 65–126.

Keyworth, George Albert, III. "Transmitting the Lamp of Learning in Classical Chan Buddhism: Juefan Huihong (1071–1128) and Literary Chan." Ph.D. diss., University of California, Los Angeles, 2001.

Kieschnick, John. *The Eminent Monk: Buddhist Ideals in Medieval Chinese Hagiography.* Honolulu: University of Hawaii Press, 1997.

———. *The Impact of Buddhism on Chinese Material Culture.* Princeton, N.J.: Princeton University Press, 2003.

Kishimoto Mio 岸本美緒. *Min Shin kōtai to Kōnan shakai: 17-seiki Chūgoku no chitsujo mondai* 明清交替と江南社会: 17世紀中国の秩序問題. Tokyo: Tōkyō daigaku shuppankai, 1999.

Kokan Shiren 虎關師錬. *Saihokushū* 濟北集. In *Gozan bungaku zenshū* 五山文學全集, vol. 1, ed. Kamimura Kankō 上村觀光. Tokyo, Gozan bungaku zenshū Kankōkai, 1936.

Kuo, Jason C. *Austere Landscape: The Paintings of Hungjen.* Taipei and New York: SMC, 1990.

Kusumoto Bunyū 久須本文雄. *Ō Yōmei no Zen teki shisō kenkyū* 王陽明の禪的思想研究. Nagoya: Nisshindō Shoten, 1958.

Lai, Whalen. "The Buddhist-Christian Dialogue in China." In *Religious Issues and Interreligious Dialogues: An Analysis and Sourcebook of Developments since 1945,* ed. Charles Wei-hsun Fu and Gerhard Spiegler, pp. 613–31. New York and London: Greenwood, 1989.

———. "Ma-tsu tao-i and the Unfolding of Southern Zen." *Journal of Japanese Religions* 12 (1985): 173–92.

———. "The Transmission Verses of the Ch'an Patriarchs." *Han Hsüeh yen-chiu* 1.2 (1983): 593–624.

Lan Jifu 藍吉富. "Jiaxing dazangjing de tese jiqi shiliao jiazhi" 嘉興大藏經的特色及其史料價值. In *Fojiao de sixiang yu wenhua: Yinshun daoshi bazhi jinliu shouqing lunwenji* 佛教的思想與文化-印順導師八秩晉六壽慶論文集, pp. 255–66. Taibei: Faguang chubanshe, 1991.

Langlois, John, and K'o K'uan Sun. "Three Teachings Syncretism and the Thought of Ming T'ai Tsu." *Harvard Journal of Asiatic Studies* 43.1 (June 1983): 97–139.

Lee, Thomas H. C. "Books and Bookworms in Song China: Book Collection and the Appreciation of Books." *Journal of Sung-Yuan Studies* 25 (1995): 193–218.

———. *Education in Traditional China: A History.* Leiden: Brill, 2000.

Lessing, Ferdinand Diederich. *Yung-ho-kung: An Iconography of the Lamaist Cathedral in Peking, with Notes on Lamaist Mythology and Cult, Sino-Swedish Expedition (1927–1935).* Stockholm: Goteborg, Elanders boktryckeri aktiebolag, 1942.

Levering, Miriam. "Ch'an Enlightenment for Laymen: Ta-hui and the New Religious Culture of the Sung." Ph.D. diss., Harvard University, 1978.

———. "Dahui Zonggao and Zhang Shangying: The Importance of a Scholar in the Education of a Song Chan Master." *Journal of Sung-Yuan Studies* 30 (2000): 115–40.

————. "The Dragon Girl and the Abbess of Miao-shan: Gender and Status in the Ch'an Buddhist Tradition." *Journal of the International Association of Buddhist Studies* 5.1 (1982): 19–35.

————. "Ta-hui and Lay Buddhists: Ch'an Sermons on Death." In *Buddhist and Taoist Practice in Medieval Chinese Society*, ed. David W. Chappell, pp. 181–214. Honolulu: University of Hawaii Press, 1987.

Lewis, Mark Edward. *Writing and Authority in Early China*. Albany: State University of New York Press, 1999.

Lidai fabao ji 歷代法寶記. Reprinted in *Shoki no Zenshi* 初期の禪史, ed. Yanagida Seizan. Tokyo: Chikuma shobō, 1976. A reprinted version can be also found in T 51: 179a–196a.

Li Li'an 李利安. "Mingmo Qingchu Zhongguo Hanchuan Fojiao ge zongpai de jiben tedian" 明末清初中國漢傳佛教各宗派的基本特點. *Xibei daxue xuebao* 西北大學學報(哲學社會科學版) 1 (1998): 83–86.

Li, Thomas Shiyu, and Susan Naquin. "The Baoming Temple: Religion and the Throne in Ming and Qing China." *Harvard Journal of Asiatic Studies* 48.1 (June 1988): 131–88.

Li, Wai-yee. "The Rhetoric of Spontaneity in Late-Ming Literature." *Ming Studies* 35 (Aug. 1995): 32–52.

Li Zhi 李贄. *Li Zhi wenji* 李贄文集. 7 vols. Beijing: Shehui kexue wenxian chubanshe, 2000.

Li'an si zhi 理安寺志. 1877. ZFS, vol. 77.

Lian Ruizhi 連瑞枝. "Hanyue Fazang yu wan Ming Sanfengzongpai de jianli" 漢月法藏 (1573–1635) 與晚明三峰宗派的建立. *Zhonghua Foxue bao* 中華佛學報 9 (1996): 167–208.

————. "Qian Qianyi de Fojiao shengya yu linian" 錢謙益的佛教生涯与理念. *Zhonghua Foxue xuebao* 中華佛學報 7 (1994): 317–70.

Liao Zhaoheng 廖肇亨. "Diyideng toulan shamen: Xuejiao Yuanxin yu Mingmo Qingchu de Chanzong" 第一等偷懶沙門: 雪嶠圓信與明末清初的禪宗. *Donghua hanxue* 東華漢學 1 (Feb. 2003): 229–59.

————. "Jin Bao de jieyi guan yu lishi pingjia tanxi" 金堡的節義觀與歷史評價探析. *Zhongyang yanjiuyuan wenzhesuo tongxun* 中央研究院文哲所通訊 9.4 (Dec. 1999): 95–116.

————. "Kin Hō *Hengyōdō shū* ni yoru Minmatsu Shinsho Kōnan bunjin no seishin yōshiki no saikentō" 金堡《遍行堂集》による明末清初江南文人の精神樣式の再檢討. *Nihon Chūgoku gakukaiho* 日本中國學會報 51 (Oct. 1999): 152–65.

————. "Mingmo Qingchu yimin tao Chan zhi feng yanjiu" 明末清初遺民逃禪之風研究. Master's thesis, National Taiwan University, 1994.

————. "Wanming sengren shanju shi lunxi: Yi Hanyue Fazang wei zhongxin" 晚明僧人山居詩論析: 以漢月法藏為中心. In *Disijie tongsu wenxue yu yazheng wenxue quanguo xueshu yantao hui huiyi lunwen ji* 第四屆通俗文學與雅正文學全國學術研討會會議論文集, pp. 49–74. Taibei: Xinwenfeng chuban she, 2003.

————. "Xuelang Hong'en chutan: Jianti Dongjing Neige wenku suocang 'Guxiang lu'" 雪浪洪恩初探: 兼題東京內閣文庫所藏"谷響錄". *Hanxue yanjiu* 漢學研究 14.2 (Dec. 1996): 35–57.

Lin Haiquan 林海權. *Li Zhi nianpu kaolue* 李贄年譜考略. Fuzhou: Fujian renmin chubanshe, 1992.

Lin Yuanbai 林元白. "Huishan heshang de shengping jiqi *Chanmen duanlian shuo*" 晦山和尚的生平及其禪門鍛煉說. *Xiandai Foxue* 現代佛學 6 (1960): 17–22.

Lin Ziqing 林子清. "Yuanxian chanshi de 'Gushan chan' jiqi shengping" 元賢禪師的 '鼓山禪' 及其生平. *Xiandai Foxue* 現代佛學 8 (1958): 19–22.

Linji Yixuan 臨濟義玄. *Linji lu* 臨濟錄, or *Zhenzhou Linji Huizhao chanshi yulu* 鎮州臨濟慧照禪師語錄. T no. 1985, vol. 47.

Liu Xianting 劉獻庭. *Guangyang zaji* 廣陽雜記. Reprint. Beijing: Zhonghua shuju, 1957.

Liu Yuanchun 劉元春. "Mingmo Chanmen sengzheng yu Qing Yongzheng di *Jianmo bianyi* pingxi" 明末禪門僧諍與清雍正帝揀魔辯異評析. In *Juequn xueshu lunwen ji* 覺群學術論文集, ed. Juexing 覺醒, pp. 49–74. Beijing: Shangwu yinshu guan, 2001.

Long, Darui 龍達瑞. "A Note on the Hongwu Nanzang, a Rare Edition of the Buddhist Canon." *East Asian Library Journal* 9.2 (Fall 2000): 112–47.

Lu K'uan Yü (Charles Luk). *The Secrets of Chinese Meditation*. York Beach: Samuel Weiser, 1969.

Lü Cheng 呂澂. "Lengyan baiwei" 楞嚴百偽. *Zhongguo zhexue* 中國哲學 2 (1980): 185–97. Reprinted in *Lü Cheng Foxue lunzhu xuanji* 呂澂佛學論著選集, vol. 1, pp. 370–95. Jinan: Qilu shushe, 1991.

Lü Jianfu 呂建福. *Zhongguo Mijiao shi* 中国密教史. Beijing: Zhongguo shehui kexue chubanshe, 1995.

Lümen zuting huizhi 律門祖庭匯誌. Nanjing, 1904.

Lye, Hun Yeow. "Feeding Ghosts: A Study of the *Yuqie Yankou* Rite." Ph.D. diss., University of Virginia, 2003.

Ma Tianxiang 麻天祥. *Zhongguo Chanzong sixiang fazhan shi* 中國禪宗思想發展史. Wuhan: Hunan jiaoyu chubanshe, 1997.

Mabbett, Ian W. "The Symbolism of Mount Meru." *History of Religions* 23 (August 1983): 64–83.

Makita Tairyō 牧田諦亮. *Chūgoku kinsei Bukkyōshi kenkyū* 中國近世佛教史研究. Kyoto, Heirakuji Shoten, 1957.

———. *Sakugen nyūminki no kenkyū* 策彥入明記の研究. Kyoto: Hōzōkan, 1959.

Mano Senryū 間野潛龍. "Mindai no Bukkyō to Minchō" 明代の佛教と明朝. In his *Mindai bunka shi kenkyū* 明代文化史研究, pp. 243–334. Kyoto: Dōhōsha, 1979.

Mano Shōjun 真野正順. *Bukkyō ni okeru shūkannen no seiritsu* 佛教にねける宗觀念の成立. Tokyo: Risōha, 1964.

Maraldo, John C. "Is There Historical Consciousness with Ch'an?" *Japanese Journal of Religious Studies* 12.2–3 (June–Sept. 1985): 141–72.

McDermott, Joseph P. *A Social History of the Chinese Book: Books and Literati Culture in Late Imerpial China*. Hong Kong: Hong Kong University Press, 2006.

McRae, John R. "The Antecedents of Encounter Dialogue in Chinese Ch'an Buddhism." In *The Kōan: Texts and Contexts in Zen Buddhism*, ed. Steven Heine and Dale S. Wright, pp. 46–74. New York: Oxford University Press, 2000.

————. "Encounter Dialogue and the Transformation of the Spiritual Path in Chinese Ch'an." In *Paths to Liberation: The Marga and its Transformations in Buddhist Thought*, ed. Robert M. Gimello, pp. 339–69. Honolulu: University of Hawaii Press, 1992.

————. "Daoxuan's Vision of Jetavana: The Ordination Platform Movement in Medieval Chinese Buddhism." In *Going Forth: Visions of Buddhist Vinaya*, ed. William M. Bodiford, pp. 68–100. Honolulu: University of Hawaii Press, 2005.

————. *The Northern School and the Formation of Early Ch'an Buddhism*. Honolulu: University of Hawaii Press, 1986.

————. "The Ox-head School of Chinese Ch'an Buddhism: From Early Ch'an to the Golden Age." In *Studies in Ch'an and Hua-yen*, ed. Robert Gimello and Peter Gregory, pp. 169–253. Honolulu: University of Hawaii Press, 1983.

————. *Seeing through Zen: Encounter, Transformation, and Genealogy in Chinese Chan Buddhism*. Berkeley: University of California Press, 2003.

McRae, John R, trans. *The Platform Sutra of the Sixth Patriarch: Translated from the Chinese of Tsung-pao*. Berkeley: Numata Center for Buddhist Translation and Research, 2000.

Meng Sen 孟森. "Shizu chujia shi kaoshi" 世祖出家事考實. In *Qingchu sanda yi'an kaoshi* 清初三大疑案考實. Reprinted in *Jindai Zhongguo shiliao congkan* 近代中國史料叢刊, ed. Shen Yunlong 沈云龍, ser. 36, pp. 23–68. Taibei: Wenhai chubanshe, 1966.

Meskill, John, trans. *Ch'oe Pu's Diary: A Record of Drifting across the Sea*. Tucson: University of Arizona Press, 1965.

Ming shilu 明實錄. Reprint. Taibei: Zhongyang yanjiuyuan lishi yuyan yanjiusuo, 1962–1968.

Ming shilu leizuan 明實錄類纂 (*Wenjiao keji juan* 文教科技卷), ed. Wu Bosen et al. Wuhan: Wuhan chubanshe, 1992.

Mingban Jiaxing dazang jing 明版嘉興大藏經. 40 vols. Reprint of *Zhonghua dazang jing di er ji*. Taibei: Xinwenfeng, 1987.

Mingji liechen zhuang 明季烈臣傳. In *Xijian Mingshi shiji jicun*, vols. 23–29.

Miyazaki Ichisada 宮崎市定. *Yōseitei: Chūgoku no dokusai kunshu* 雍正帝: 中國の獨裁君主. Tokyo: Iwanami shoten, 1950.

Miyun Yuanwu 密雲圓悟. *Miyun chanshi yulu* 密雲禪師語錄. 12 fascs. JXZ no. 158, vol. 10.

————. *Pi wangjiu lueshuo* 闢妄救略說. 10 fascs. 1638. Z no. 1280, vol. 65.

————. *Tiantong zhishuo* 天童直說, or *Miyun Yuanwu chanshi Tiantong zhishuo* 密雲圓悟禪師天童直說. 9 fascs., comp. Muchen Daomin, ca. 1642–1643. Rare book in Tōhō Bunka Gakuen Tōkyō Kenkyūshō 東方文化學院東京研究所.

Mohr, Michel. "Zen Buddhism during the Tokugawa Period: The Challenge to Go beyond Sectarian Consciousness." *Japanese Journal of Religious Studies* 21.4 (1994): 341–72.

Mote, Frederik, and Howard L. Goodman. *A Research Manual for Ming History*. Princeton, N.J.: Princeton University Press, 1984.

Mou Zongsan 牟宗三. "Rulai chan yu Zushi chan" 如來禪与祖師禪. In *Chanzong sixiang yu lishi* 禪宗思想与歷史, *Xiandai Fojiao xueshu congkan* 現代佛教學術叢刊,

no. 52, ed. Zhang Mantao 張曼濤, pp. 77–112. Taibei: Dacheng wenhua chubanshe, 1978.

Mu Konghui 穆孔暉. *Daxue qianlü* 大學千慮. 1 fasc. In *Siku quanshu cunmu congshu*, 156: 626–55.

———. *Mu Wenjian gong huangao* 穆文簡公宦稿. 2 fascs. Rare book in National Library, Taiwan.

Muchen Daomin 木陳道忞. *Beiyou ji* 北遊集 or *Tiantong Hongjue Min chanshi Beiyou ji* 天童弘覺忞禪師北游集. JXZ no. 180, vol. 26.

———. *Bushuitai ji* 布水臺集. JXZ no. 181, vol. 26.

———. *Chandeng shipu* 禪燈世譜. 1632. Z no. 1601, vol. 86.

———. *Shanweng Min chanshi suinian zipu* 山翁忞禪師隨年自譜. 1 fasc. *Dongfang xuebao* 東方學報 (Singapore) 1.1 (1957): 289–304.

———. *Tiantong Hongjue Min chanshi yulu* 天童弘覺忞禪師語錄. 20 fascs. JXZ no. 179, vol. 26.

Muchen Daomin 木陳道忞, comp. "Tiantong Miyun chanshi nianpu" 天童密雲禪師年譜. 1 fasc. In *Beijing tushuguan cang zhenben nianpu congkan* 北京圖書館藏珍本年譜叢刊, vol. 55. Beijing: Beijing tushuguan chubanshe, 1999.

Müller, Wilhelm 彌維禮. "Buddhistische Morgen-und Abendliturgie Auf Taiwan." In *Guoji hanxue* 國際漢學, no. 2, ed. Ren Jiyu, 322–63. Zhengzhou: Daxiang chubanshe, 1998.

Nagai Masashi 永井政之. "Sōtōshū Jushōha to sono seisui" 曹洞宗壽昌派とその盛衰. In *Dōgen shisō no ayumi* 道元思想のあゆみ, ed. Sōtō shūgaku kenkyūjo, pp. 120–54. Tokyo: Yoshikawa Kōbunkan. 1993.

———. "Tōkō Shin'etsu kenkyū josetsu" 東皋心越研究序說. In *Zenshū no shomondai* 禪宗の諸問題, ed. Imaeda Aishin 今枝愛真, pp. 365–85. Tokyo:Yūzankaku, 1979.

Nakajima Ryūzo 中嶋隆藏. "Shinbunhō shuppan kōsi inkō Minpan 'Jiaxing' daizokyō nitsuite" 新文豐出版公司印行《明版嘉興大藏經》について. *Shūkan Tōyōgaku* 集刊 東洋學 87 (May 2002): 71–82.

Nakamura Hajime 中村元. *Bukkyōgo daijiten* 佛教語大辭典. 3 vols. Tokyo: Tōkyō shoseki, 1975.

Naquin, Susan. *Peking: Temples and City Life: 1400–1900.* Berkeley: University of California Press, 2000.

Nattier, Jan. *A Few Good Men: The Bodhisattva Path according to the Inquiry of Ugra (Ugraparipcchā).* Honolulu: University of Hawaii Press, 2003.

———. *Once upon a Future Time: Studies in a Buddhist Prophecy of Decline.* Berkeley: Asian Humanities Press, 1991.

Nianchang 念常, comp. *Fozu lidai tongzai* 佛祖歷代通載. 22 fascs. T no. 2036, vol. 49.

Nihon Bukke jinmei jisho 日本佛家人名辭書, ed. Washio Junkei 鷲尾順敬. Tokyo: 1911. Reprint. Tokyo: Tokyo Bijutsu, 1982.

Noguchi Yoshitaka 野口善敬. "Hiin Tsūyō no Rinzai-zen to sono zasetsu: Mokuchin Dōbin tono tairitsu o megutte" 費隱通容の臨濟禪とその挫折: 木陳道忞との對立を巡って. *Zengaku kenkyū* 禪學研究 64 (1985): 57–81.

———. "Honrai mu ichi butsu wa gedō no hō" 本来無一物は外道の法. *Aichi gakuin zenkenkyūjo kiyo* 愛知學院禪研究所紀要 18 (1992): 1–50.

————. "Iminsō Kaizan Kaiken ni tsuite" 遺民僧晦山戒顯について. *Aichi gakuin Zenkenkyūjo kiyō* 愛知學院禪研究所紀要 16 (1990): 251–74.

————. "Kaizan Kaiken nenpu kō" 晦山戒顯年譜稿. In *Disijie Zhongguo yuwai hanji guoji xueshu huiyi lunwenji* 第四屆中國域外漢籍國際學術會議論文集, pp. 307–32. Taibei: Lianhebao wenhua jijinhui guoxue wenxian guan, 1991.

————. "Kangetsu Hōzō to shitaifu tachi: Yōseitei kara mazō to yobareta sōryo" 漢月法蔵と士大夫たち―雍正帝から魔蔵と呼ばれた僧侶. *Tōyō kotengaku kenkyū* 東洋古典学研究 2 (1996): 33–35.

————. "Minmatsu Kokyūha no genryū: Shōgan Tokuhō to Genyū Shōden 明末虎丘派の源流―笑巌徳宝と幻有正伝." *Tetsugaku Nenpō* 哲學年報 42 (January 1983): 121–140,

————. "Minmatsu ni okeru shūjinko ronsō: Mitsuun Engo no Rinzaizen no seikaku o megutte" 明末にゐける主人公論爭: 密雲圓悟の臨濟禪の性格を巡って. *Tetsugaku Nenpō* 45 (Feb. 1986): 149–82.

————. "Minmatsu no Bukkyō koji Ō Tanhaku o megutte" 明末の仏教居士黄端伯を巡って. *Tetsugaku Nenpō* 哲學年報 43 (Feb. 1984): 113–38.

————. "Minmatsu Shinsho sōsō kenkyū shiryō ni tsuite" 明末清初僧浄研究資料 について. In *Diyijie Zhongguo yuwai hanji guoji xueshu huiyi lunwen ji* 第一屆中國域外漢籍國際學術會議論文集, pp. 753–90. Taibei: Lianjing chuban shiye gongsi, 1987.

————. "Yōseitei no Bukkyō shiryō ni tsuite" 雍正帝の佛教資料について. *Tōyō kotengaku kenkyū* 東洋古典學研究 9 (May 2000): 42–65.

Noguchi Yoshitaka 野口善敬, trans. *Yakuchū Shisho sōsōki: Chūgoku Bukkyō no kunō to shitaifu tachi* 譯注清初僧浄記: 中國佛教の苦惱と士大夫たち. Kyoto: Chūgaku shoten, 1989.

Nōnin Kōdō 能仁晃道, comp. *Ingen Zenji Nenpu* 隠元禅師年譜. Kyoto: 1999.

Nozawa Yoshimi 野澤佳美. *Daizōkyō kankei kenkyū bunken mokuroku* 大藏經關係研究文獻目錄. Tokyo: Risshō University, 1993.

————. *Mindai Daizōkyō shi no kenkyū: Nanzō no rekishigaku teki kiso kenkyū* 明代大蔵経史の研究: 南蔵の歴史学的基礎研究. Tokyo: Kyūko Shoin, 1998.

Nukariya Kaiten 忽滑谷快天. *Zengaku shisōshi* 禪學思想史. Tokyo: Genkōsha, 1979.

Ōbaku bunka 黄檗文化, ed. Hayashi Yukimitsu 林雪光. Uji: Manupukuji, 1972.

Ōbaku bunka jinmei jiten 黄檗文化人名字典, ed. Hayashi Yukimitsu 林雪光. Kyoto: Shibunkaku, 1988.

Ōbaku Ingen: Ingen Zenji goseitan yonhyakunen kinen 黄檗隠元: 隠元禪師御生誕四百年記念. Uji: Manpukuji, 1992.

Oishi Morio 大石守雄. "Ōbaku shingi no kenkyū" 黄檗清規の研究. *Zengaku kenkyū* 禪學研究 49 (1959): 142–49.

Ono Kazuko 小野和子. "Dōran no jidai o ukita Ingen zenji" 動亂の時代を生きた隠元禪師. *Zenbunka* 禪文化 124 (1987): 83–92.

————. *Kō Sōgi* 黄宗義. Tokyo: Jimbutsu ōraisha, 1967.

————. "Shinsho no kōkeihai ni tsuite" 清初の講經會について. *Tōhō gakuhō* 東方學報 36 (1964): 633–61.

Ono Gemmyō 小野玄妙. *Bussho kaisetsu daijiten* 佛書解説大辭典. 12 vols. Tokyo: Daitō shuppan sha, 1932–1936.

Orzech, Charles D. "Esoteric Buddhism and the *Shishi* in China." In *The Esoteric Buddhist Tradition: Selected Papers from the 1989 SBS Conference*, ed. Henrik H. Sørensen, pp. 51–72. Copenhagen and Arhus: Seminar for Buddhist Studies, 1994.

——. "Further Notes on Tantra, Metaphor Theory, Ritual and Sweet Dew." Unpublished paper presented at the seminar Tantra and Daoism: A Multidisciplinary Conference on the Globalization of Religion and Its Experience, Boston University, April 19–21, 2002.

——. *Politics and Transcendent Wisdom: The Scripture for Humane Kings in the Creation of Chinese Buddhism*. University Park: Pennsylvania State University Press, 1998.

——. "Seeing Chen-Yen Buddhism: Traditional Scholarship and the Vajrayana in China." *History of Religions* 29.2 (Nov. 1989): 87–114.

Orzech, Charles D., trans. "Saving the Burning-Mouth Hungry Ghost." In *Religions of China in Practice*, ed. Donald S. Lopez, Jr., pp. 278–83. Princeton, N.J.: Princeton University Press, 1996.

Ouyang Xiu 歐陽修. *Jigu lu* 集古錄. 8 fascs. In *Shike shiliao xinbian*, vol. 24.

Overmyer, Daniel. *Folk Buddhist Religion: Dissenting Sects in Late Traditional China*. Cambridge, Mass.: Harvard University Press, 1976.

Pan Guiming 潘桂明. *Zhongguo Chanzong sixiang licheng* 中國禪宗思想歷程. Beijing: Jinri zhongguo chubanshe, 1992.

——. *Zhongguo jushi Fojiao shi* 中國居士佛教史. Beijing: Zhongguo shehui kexue chubanshe, 2000.

Pan Guiming 潘桂明 and Wu Zhongwei 吳忠偉. *Zhongguo Tiantaizong tongshi* 中國天台宗通史. Nanjing: Jiangsu guji chubanshe, 2001.

Pan Lei 潘耒. *Jiukuang bianyu* 救狂砭語. Reprint. Shanghai: Shanghai guji chubanshe, 1983.

Payne, Richard K. "Ajikan: Ritual and Meditation in the Shingon Tradition." In *Re-visioning "Kamakura" Buddhism*, ed. Richard K. Payne, pp. 219–48. Honolulu: University of Hawaii Press, 1998.

Peng Guodong 彭國棟. "Qing Shizu taochan kao" 清世祖逃禪考. In *Mingqing Fojiao shi pian* 明清佛教史篇, ed. Zhang Mantao 張曼濤, pp. 275–302. Taibei: Dacheng wenhua chuban she, 1977–1979.

Peng Shaosheng 彭紹升. *Jushi zhuan* 居士傳. 51 fascs. Z no. 1646, vol. 88.

Peterson, Willard J. *Bitter Gourd: Fang I Chih and the Impetus for Intellectual Change*. New Haven, Conn.: Yale University Press, 1979.

——. "Fang I-chih: Western Learning and the 'Investigation of Things.'" In *The Unfolding of Neo-Confucianism*, ed. William T. de Bary, pp. 369–401. New York: Columbia University Press, 1975.

——. "From Interest to Indifference: Fang I-chih and Western Learning." *Ching-shih wen-t'i* 3.5 (Nov. 1976): 60–80.

——. "The Life of Ku Yen-wu (1613–1682)." *Harvard Journal of Asiatic Studies* I, 28 (1968): 114–56; II, 29 (1969): 201–47.

Pittman, Don A. *Towards a Modern Chinese Buddhism*. Honolulu: University of Hawaii Press, 2001.

Poceski, Mario. "The Hongzhou School of Chan Buddhism during the Mid-Tang Period." Ph.D. diss., University of California, Los Angeles, 2000.

———. *Ordinary Mind as the Way: The Hongzhou School and the Growth of Chan Buddhism*. New York: Oxford Univesity Press, 2006.

Pollack, David. "Kokan Shiren and Musō Soseki: 'Chinese' vs. 'Japaneseness' in Thirteenth and Fourteenth Century Japan." *Journal of the International Association of Buddhist Studies* 7.2 (1984): 143–68.

Power, John. *The Concise Encyclopedia of Buddhism*. Oxford: Oneworld Publications, 2000.

Qi Biaojia 祁彪佳. *Qi Biaojia ji* 祁彪佳集. Reprint. Shanghai: Zhonghua shuju, 1960.

———. *Qi Zhongmin gong riji*. 祁忠敏公日記. Reprint. Hangzhou: Hangzhou gujiu shudian, 1982.

Qian Bocheng 錢伯城. *Yuan Hongdao ji jianjiao* 袁宏道集箋校. Shanghai: Guji chubanshe, 1981.

Qian Qianyi 錢謙益. *Jianzhu Qian Muzhai quanji* 箋注錢牧齋全集. 163 fascs. Wujiang: Suihan zhai, 1910.

———. *Lengyan jing shujie mengchao* 楞嚴經疏解蒙鈔. 28 fascs. Z no. 287, vol. 13.

Qian Qianyi 錢謙益, comp. *Liechao shiji xiaozhuan* 列朝詩集小傳. Reprint. Shanghai: Zhonghua shuju, 1961.

Qianlong dazang jing 乾隆大藏經. 1735–1738. Reprint. 169 vols. Taibei: Chuanzheng youxian gongsi, 2002.

Qing Xitai 卿希泰. *Zhongguo Daojiao* 中國道教, vol. 1. Shanghai: Dongfang chuban zhongxin, 1996.

Qingliang shan zhi 清涼山志. 8 fascs. 1933. ZFS vol. 9.

Qingyuan zhilüe 青原志略. Kangxi edition. ZFS vol. 18.

Qiu Gaoxing 邱高興. "Qingdai Fojiao yanjiu xianzhuang" 清代佛教研究現狀. *Pumen xuebao* 普門學報 16 (July 2003): 311–22.

———. *Yizhi duxiu: Qingdai Chanzong longxing* 一枝獨秀: 清代禪宗隆興. Shenyang: Liaoning renmin chubanshe, 1997.

Qiu Minjie 邱敏捷. *Canchan yu nianfo: Wanming Yuan hongdao de Fojiao sixiang* 參禪與念佛: 晚明袁宏道的佛教思想. Taibei: Shangding wenhua faxing, 1993.

Qu Ruji 瞿汝稷. *Qu Jiongqing ji* 瞿冏卿集. 14 fascs. 1611. *Siku quanshu cunmu congshu*, series 4 (*jibu*), 187: 62–331.

———. *Zhiyue lu* 指月錄. Reprint. 4 vols. Taibei: Zhenshanmei chubanshe, 1968. Also in Z no. 1578, vol. 83.

Quan Tang wen 全唐文, ed. Dong Gao 董誥 et al. 1,000 fascs. 1814. Reprint. Shanghai, 1990.

Rao Zongyi 饒宗頤. "Qingchu seng Daomin jiqi *Bushuitai ji*" 清初僧道忞及其布水台集. In *Kanda Kiichirō hakushi tsuitō Chūgokugaku ronshū* 神田喜一郎博士追悼中國學論集, pp. 644–52. Tokyo: Nigensha, 1986.

Rawski, Evelyn. *The Last Emperors: A Social History of Qing Imperial Institutions*. Berkeley: University of California Press, 1998.

Ren Daobin 任道斌. *Fang Yizhi nianpu* 方以智年譜. Hefei: Anhui jiaoyu chuban she, 1983.

Ren Fangqiu 任訪秋. *Yuan Zhonglang yanjiu* 袁中郎研究. Shanghai: Shanghai guji chubanshe, 1983.

Ren Jiyu 任繼愈. "A Brief Discussion of the Philosophical Thought of Chan Buddhism." *Chinese Studies in Philosophy* 15.4 (1984): 3–69.

———. "Buddhism and Chinese Culture." In *Freedom, Progress, and Society: Essays in Honour of Professor K. SatchidanandaMurty*, ed. R. Balasubramanian and Sibajiban Bhattacharyya, pp. 118–24. Delhi: Motilal Banarsidass, 1986.

———. "On Hu Shih's Mistakes in His Study of the History of the Chan Sect." *Chinese Studies in Philosophy* 15.4 (1984): 70–98.

Riben Huangboshan Wanfusi cang lü Ri gaoseng Yinyuan Zhongtu laiwang shuxin ji 日本黃檗山萬福寺藏旅日高僧隱元中土來往書信集, ed. Chen Zhichao 陳智超, Wei Zuhui 韋祖輝, and He Lingxiu 何齡修. Beijing: Quanguo tushuguan wenxian suowei fuzhi zhongxin, 1995.

Ruibai Mingxue 瑞白明雪. *Rujiu Ruibai chanshi yulu* 入就瑞白禪師語錄. JXZ no. 188, vol. 26.

Rujin 如巹, comp. *Chanzong zhengmai* 禪宗正脈. Z no. 1593, vol. 85.

Rusk, Bruce. "The Rogue Classicist: Feng Fang (1493–1566) and His Forgeries." Ph. D. diss., University of California, Berkeley, 2004.

Sanfeng Qingliang chansi zhi 三峰清涼禪寺志. 2 fascs. 1838. ZFS vol. 39.

Sanfeng Qingliang chansi zhi 三峰清涼禪寺志. 18 fascs. 1892. ZFS vols. 40 and 41.

Saeki, Yoshirō. *The Nestorian Documents and Relics in China*. Tokyo: Toho Bunka Gakuin, 1951.

Sasaki, Ruth Fuller, and Yoshitaka Iriya. *The Recorded Sayings of Ch'an Master Lin-chi Hui-chao of Chen Prefecture*. Kyoto: Institute for Zen Studies, Hanazono College, 1975.

Schlütter, Morten. "Chan Buddhism in Song-Dynasty China (960–1279): The Rise of the Caodong Tradition and the Formation of the Chan School." Ph.D. diss., Yale University, 1999.

———. "The *Record of Hongzhi* and the Recorded Sayings Literature of Song-Dynasty Chan." In *The Zen Canon: Understanding the Classic Texts*, ed. Steven Heine and Dale S. Wright, pp. 181–206. New York: Oxford University Press, 2004.

———. "A Study in the Genealogy of the *Platform Sūtra*." *Studies in Central and East Asian Religions* 2 (1989): 53–114.

———. "Vinaya Monasteries, Public Abbacies, and State Control of Buddhism under the Song (960–1279)." In *Going Forth: Visions of Buddhist Vinaya*, ed. William M. Bodiford, pp. 136–61. Honolulu: University of Hawaii Press, 2005.

Schmidt-Glintzer, Helwig. "Zhang Shang-ying (1043–1122): An Embarrassing Policy Adviser under the Northern Sung." In *Studies in Sung History: A Festschrift for Dr. James T. C. Liu*, ed. Kinugawa Tsuyoshi 衣川強, pp. 521–30. Kyoto: Dōbōsa, 1989.

Schopen, Gregory. "Archaeology and Protestant Presuppositions in the Study of Indian Buddhism." *History of Religions* 31 (1991): 1–23. Reprinted in his *Bones, Stones, and Buddhist Monks*, pp. 1–22. Honolulu: University of Hawaii Press, 1997.

Shahar, Meir. "Ming-period Evidence of Shaolin Martial Practice." *Harvard Journal of Asiatic Studies* 61.2 (Dec. 2001): 359–413.

Shanci Tongji 山茨通際, comp. *Dongming yilu* 東明遺錄, or *Tongming zudeng lu* 東明祖燈錄. 3 fascs. 1635. Rare book in the Shanghai Library.

Shanmi 善璨. *Zhengzong xinyin houxu lianfang* 正宗心印後續聯芳. Z no. 1617, vol. 87.

Shaolin si zhi 少林寺志. Qianlong edition. ZFS vol. 6.

Sharf, Elizabeth Horton. "Chinzo and Obaku Portraiture." In *Contacts between Cultures: Eastern Asia: Literature and Humanities*, vol. 3, ed. Bernard Hung-Kay Luk, pp. 422–27. Lewiston, N.Y.: Mellen, 1992.

———. "Obaku Zen Portrait Painting: A Revisionist Analysis." Ph.D. diss., University of Michigan, 1994.

———. "Ōbaku Zen Portrait Painting and Its Sino-Japanese Heritage." In *Images in Asian Religions: Texts and Contexts*, ed. Phyllis Granoff and Koichi Shinohara, pp. 290–345. Vancouver: UBC Press, 2004.

Sharf, Robert. *Coming to Terms with Chinese Buddhism: A Reading with the Treasure Store Treatise*. Honolulu: University of Hawaii Press, 2001.

———. "The Idolization of Enlightenment: On the Mummification of Ch'an Masters in Medieval China." *History of Religions* 32.1 (1992): 1–31.

———. "On Pure Land Buddhism and Ch'an/Pure Land Syncretism in Medieval China." *T'oung Pao* 88.4–5 (2002): 282–332.

———. "The Zen of Japanese Nationalism." *History of Religions* 33.1 (1993): 1–43. Reprinted in *Curators of the Buddha: The Study of Buddhism under Colonialism*, ed. Donald S. Lopez, Jr., pp. 107–60. Chicago: University of Chicago Press, 1995.

She Changji 佘常吉. "Yongqing dawen" 永慶答問. In *Li Wening waiji* 李溫陵外集, ed. Pan Zenghong 潘曾纮, fasc. 1, pp. 43–58. Reprint. Taibei: Weiwen tushu, 1977.

Shen Defu 沈德符. *Wanli yehuo pian* 萬厲野獲篇. Reprint. Beijing: Zhonghua shuju, 1959.

Shengkong 聖空. "Shixi Yongzheng zai *Jianmo bianyi lu* zhong dui Hanyue Fazang de pipan" 試析雍正在揀魔辨異錄中對漢月法藏的批判. *Zhonghua Foxue yanjiu* 中華佛學研究 5 (Mar. 2001): 411–39.

Shengyan 聖嚴. *Minmatsu Chūgoku Bukkyō no kenkyū* 明末中國佛教の研究. Tokyo: Sankibō bunsshorin, 1975.

———. *Mingmo Fojiao yanjiu* 明末佛教研究. Taibei: Tongchu chubanshe, 1987.

Shi Dun 史惇. *Tong yu zaji* 慟餘雜記. 1 fasc. *Siku jinhuishu congkan*, series 2 (*shibu*), 72: 107–124.

Shiina Kōyū 椎名宏雄. *Sō Gen ban zenseki no kenkyū* 宋元版禪籍の研究. Tokyo: Daitō shuppansha, 1993.

———. "Sūzan ni okeru Hokushū Zen no tenkai" 嵩山における北宗禪の展開. *Shūgaku kenkyū* 宗學研究 10 (1968): 173–85.

Shike shiliao xinbian 石刻史料新編. Taibei: Xinwenfeng, 1982.

Shilian Dashan 石濂大汕. *Haiwai jishi* 海外紀事. Reprint. Beijing: Zhonghua shuju, 1958.

Shinohara, Koichi. "Passages and Transmission in Tianhuang Daowu's Biographies." In *Other Selves: Autobiography and Biography in Cross-cultural Perspective*, ed. Phyllis Granoff and Koichi Shinohara, pp. 132–49. Oakville, Ontario: Mosaic, 1994.

Shinpan Zengaku daijiten 新版禪學大辭典. Tokyo: Taishūkan, 1985.

Shinsan dai Nihon Zokuzōkyō 新纂大日本續藏經. 90 vols. Tokyo: Kokusho Kankōkai, 1975–1989. Originally published as *Dainihon zokuzōkyō* 大日本續藏經. 750 vols. Kyoto: Zōkyō Shoin, 1905–1912.

Shinsan kōtei Ingen zenshū 新纂校訂隱元全集, ed. Hirakubo Akira 平久保章. 12 vols. Kyoto: Kaimei shoin, 1979.

Shuijian Huihai 水鑑會海. *Tianwang Shuijian Hai heshang liuhuilu* 天王水鑑海和尚六會錄. 10 fascs. JXZ no. 230, vol. 29.

Siku jinhuishu congkan 四庫禁毀書叢刊. 311 vols. Beijing: Beijing chubanshe, 1997–1999.

Siku quanshu 四庫全書. The Wenyuange 文淵閣 edition. 1500 vols. Taibei: Shangwu yinshuguan, 1983–96.

Siku quanshu cunmu congsu 四庫全書存目叢書. 426 vols. Jinan: Qilu shushe, 1997.

Smith, Joanna F. Handlin. "Gardens in Ch'i Piao-chia's Social World: Wealth and Values in Late-Ming Kiangnan." *Journal of Asian Studies* 51.1 (1992): 55–81.

———. "Liberating Animals in Ming-Qing China: Buddhist Inspiration and Elite Imagination." *Journal of Asian Studies* 58.1 (Feb. 1999): 51–84.

Spence, Jonathan D. *The Memory Palace of Matteo Ricci.* New York: Viking Penguin, 1984.

———. *Return to Dragon Mountain: Memories of a Late Ming Man.* New York: Viking, 2007.

———. *Treason by the Book.* New York: Viking, 2001.

Spence, Jonathan, and John E. Wills, Jr., eds. *From Ming to Ch'ing: Conquest, Regions and Continuity in Seventeenth-century China.* New Haven, Conn., and London: Yale University Press, 1979.

Steinhardt, Nancy, ed. *Chinese Traditional Architecture.* New York: China Institute in America, 1984.

Sterk, Darryl Cameron. "Chan Grove Remarks on Poetry by Wang Shizhen: A Discussion and Translation." M.A. Thesis, University of Toronto, 2002.

Stevenson, Daniel B. "Protocols of Power: Tz'u-yun Tsun-shih (964–1032) and T'ien-t'ai lay Buddhist Ritual in the Sung." In *Buddhism in the Sung*, ed. Peter N. Gregory and Daniel A. Getz, Jr., pp. 340–408. Honolulu: University of Hawaii Press, 1999.

———. "Text, Image, and Transformation in the History of the *Shuilu fahui*, the Buddhist Rite for Deliverance of Creatures of Water and Land." In *Cultural Intersections in Later Chinese Buddhism*, ed. Marsha Weidner, pp. 30–70. Honolulu: University of Hawaii Press, 2001.

Stock, Brian. *The Implications of Literacy.* Princeton, N.J.: Princeton University Press, 1983.

———. *Listening for the Text: On the Uses of the Past.* Philadelphia: University of Pennsylvania Press, 1996.

Stoianavitch, Traian. *French Historical Method: The Annales Paradigm.* Ithaca, N.Y., and London: Cornell University Press, 1976.

Struve, Lynn. "Ancestor *Édité* in Republican China: The Shuffled Journal of Xue Cai (1595–1665)." *East Asian Library Journal* (Princeton). 13.1 (2007), forthcoming.

———. "Dreaming and Self-search during the Ming Collapse: *The Xue Xiemeng biji*, 1642–1646." *Toung P'ao*, 93.1 (March 2007). 159–192.

———. *Ming-Qing Conflict: A Historiography and Source Guide*. Ann Arbor, Mich.: Association for Asian Studies, 1998.

———. *The Southern Ming 1644–1662*. New Haven, Conn.: Yale University Press, 1984.

Sun Changwu 孫昌武. "Shiseng Cangxue" 詩僧蒼雪. *Pumen xuebao* 普門學報 20 (Mar. 2004): 351–68.

Sun Zongzeng 孫中曾. "Mingmo Chanzong zai Zhedong xingsheng zhi yuanyou tantao" 明末禪宗在浙東興盛之緣由探討. *Guoji Foxue yanjiu* 國際佛學研究 12 (1992): 141–76.

Suzuki Tetsuo 鈴木哲雄. *To Gōdai Zenshū shi* 唐五代禅宗史. Tokyo: Sankibō Busshorin, 1985.

Taishō shinshū daizōkyō 大正新修大藏經, ed. Takakusu Junjirō 高楠順次郎 et al. 100 vols. Tokyo: Daizōkyōkai shuppan, 1922–1933.

Takubo Shūyo 田久保周譽. *Bonji shittan* 梵字悉曇. Tokyo: Hirakawa shuppansha, 1981.

Tan Zhaowen 覃召文. *Lingnan Chan wenhua* 嶺南禪文化. Guangzhou: Guangdong renmin chubanshe, 1996.

Tanji Hongren 潭吉弘忍. *Wuzong jiu* 五宗救. 10 fascs. In *Zhongguo Fojiao congshu: Chanzong bian* 中國佛教叢書: 禪宗編, ed. Re Jiyu 任繼愈, vol. 6. Nanjing: Jiansu guji, 1993; also in *Chanzong quanshu* 禪宗全書, ed. Lan Jifu, vol. 33. Taibei: Wenshu wenhua youxian gongsi, 1990; also in *Fojiao dazangjing* 佛教大藏經, ed. Lan Jifu, vol. 110. Taibei: Fojiao chuban she, 1977–1983.

Tatsuike Kiyoshi 龍池清. "Mindai no okeru baichō" 明代における賣牒. *Tōhō gakuhō* 東方學報 11.2 (1940): 279–90.

———. "Mindai no sōkan" 明代の僧官. *Shina Bukkyō shigaku* 支那佛教史學 4.3 (1940): 35–46.

———. "Mindai no Yūga kyōsō" 明代の瑜伽教僧. *Tōhō gakuhō* 東方學報 11.1 (1940): 405–13.

———. "Mindai Pekin ni okeru Rama kyōdan" 明代北京における喇嘛教團. *Bukkyō kenkyū* 佛教研究 4.6 (1941): 65–76.

———. "Minsho no jiin" 明初の寺院. *Shina Bukkyō shigaku* 支那佛教史學 2.4 (Dec. 1938): 9–29.

Thich Thien-An. *Buddhism and Zen in Vietnam: In Relation to the Development of Buddhism in Asia*, ed. Carol Smith. Los Angeles: College of Oriental School 1975.

Tiantai shan fangwai zhi 天台山方外志. 1603. 30 fascs. ZFS vol. 81.

Tiantong si zhi 天童寺志. ZFS vols. 84 and 85.

Tianyin Yuanxiu 天隱圓修. *Tianyin heshang yulu* 天隱和尚語錄. 15 fascs. JXZ no. 171, vol. 25.

T'ien Ju-k'ang. "The Decadence of Buddhist Temples in Fukien in Late Ming and Early Ch'ing." In *Development and Decline of Fukien Province in the 17th and 18th Ccenturies*, ed. E. B. Vermeer, pp. 83–101. Leiden: Brill, 1990.

Toh, Hoong Teik. "Tibetan Buddhism in Ming China." Ph.D. diss., Harvard University, 2004.

Tokiwa Daijō 常盤大定. "Ōbaku to Rinzai" 黄檗と臨濟. *Zenshū* 禪宗 413 (1929): 21–26.

———. *Shina Bukkyō shiseki chōsa* 支那佛教史蹟調查. Tokyo: Ryūginsha, 1938.

Torigoe Bunpō 島越文邦. *Hiin zenji to sono cho: Gotō entō*. 費隱禪師と其の著: 五燈嚴統. Omuta: Daijizan enichi zenji 大慈山慧日禪寺, 1986.

Tsukamoto Shunkō 塚本俊孝. "Kenryūtei no kyōdan shukusei seisaku to Yōseitei" 乾隆帝の教團肅正政策と雍正帝. *Bukkyō bunka kenkyū* 佛教文化研究 11 (1962): 63.

———. "Yōsei Kenryū nitei no Butsugaku" 雍正乾隆二帝の佛學. *Indogaku Bukkyōgaku kenkyū* 印度學佛教學研究 22(11.2) (1963): 178–79.

———. "Yōseitei no Bukkyō kyōdan e no kunkai" 雍正帝の仏教教団への訓誨. *Indogaku Bukkyōgaku kenkyū* 印度學佛教學研究 17(9.1) (1961): 323–26.

———. "Yōseitei no Bukkyō kyōdan hihhan" 雍正帝の佛教教團批判. *Indogaku Bukkyōgaku kenkyū* 印度學佛教學研究 7.1 (1958): 158–59.

———. "Yōseitei no Ju-Butsu-Dō sankyō ittaikan" 雍正帝の儒佛道三教一體觀. *Tōyōshi kenkyū* 東洋史研究 18.3 (1959): 44–60.

———. "Yōseitei no nenbutsuzen" 雍正帝の念佛禪. *Indogaku Bukkyōgaku kenkyū* 印度學佛教學研究 15(8.1) (1960): 168–69.

Tsukamoto Zenryū 塚本善隆. *Chūgoku kinsei Bukkyōshi no shomondai* 中國近世佛教史の諸問題. Tokyo: Daitō shuppansha, 1975.

Tu Long 屠隆. *Suoluo guan qingyan* 娑羅館清言. In *Congshu jicheng* 叢書集成, series 1, no. 2986. Shanghai: Shangwu yinshu guan, 1936.

Tu, Weiming 杜維明. *Neo-Confucian Thought in Action: Wang Yang-ming's Youth (1472–1509)*. Berkeley: University of California Press, 1976.

Ui Hakuju 宇井伯壽. *Daini Zenshūshi kenkyū* 第二禪宗史研究. Tokyo: Iwanami shoten, 1942.

Van Gulik, Robert Hans 高羅佩. *Mingmo yiseng Donggao chanshi jikan* 明末義僧東皋禪師集刊. Chongqing: Shang wu yin shu guan, 1944.

Veblen, Thorstein. *The Theory of the Leisure Class: An Economic Study of Institutions.* 1899. Reprint. New York: New American Library, 1953.

Wakeman, Frederic, Jr. "China and the Seventeenth-century Crisis." *Late Imperial China* 7.1 (June 1986): 1–26.

———. *The Great Enterprise: The Manchu Reconstruction of Imperial Order in Seventeenth-century China.* 2 vols. Berkeley: University of California Press, 1985.

———. "Localism and Loyalism during the Ch'ing Conquest of Kiangnan." In *Conflict and Control in Late Imperial China*, ed. Frederic Wakeman and C. Grant, pp. 43–85. Berkeley: University of California Press, 1975.

———. "Romantics, Stoics, and Martyrs in Seventeenth-century China." *Journal of Asian Studies* 43.4 (Aug. 1984): 631–66.

Wan zi xu zang jing 卐字續藏經. 150 vols. Reprint of *Dai-Nihon zokuzōkyō* 大日本續藏經, originally published in 1912. Taibei, 1976.

Wang, Chen-main. *The Life and Career of Hung Ch'eng-ch'ou (1593–1665): Public Service in a Time of Dynastic Change.* Ann Arbor, Mich.: Association for Asian Studies, 1999.

Wang Fansen 王汎森. "Classics Discussion Societies in Early Qing." *Bulletin of the Institute of History and Philology of Academia Sinica* 68.3 (1997): 503–87.

Wang Guichen 王貴忱. "Ji Ming Wanli keben *Liuzu tanjing*" 記明萬厲刻本六祖壇經. In *Liuzu Huneng sixiang yanjiu* 六祖慧能思想研究, vol. 2, ed. Lin Youneng 林有能 and Huo Qichang 霍啓昌, pp. 290–2. Hong Kong: Xianggang chubanshe, 2003.

Wang Gu 王谷. *Zongmen zhengming lu* 宗門正名錄. Z no. 1567, vol. 80.

Wang Luping 王路平. *Guizhou Fojiao shi* 贵州佛教史. Guiyang: Guizhou renmin chubanshe, 2001.

Wang, Xiangyun. "The Qing Court's Tibet Connection: lCang skya Rol pa'i rdo rje and the Qianlong Emperor." *Harvard Journal of Asiatic Studies* 60 (2001): 125–63.

———. "Tibetan Buddhism at the Court of Qing: The Life and Work of lCang-skya Rol-pa'i-rdo-rje, 1717–86." Ph.D. diss., Harvard University, 1995.

Wang Yangming quanji 王陽明全集. 2 vols., ed. Wu Guang 吳光, et. al. Shanghai: Shanghai guji chubanshe, 1992.

Wang Zhonghan 王鍾翰. "Liu Rushi yu Qian Qianyi xiang Qing wenti" 柳如是与錢謙益降清問題. In his *Wang Zhonghan xueshu lunzhu zixuan ji* 王鍾翰學術論著自選集, pp. 404–24. Beijing: Zhongyang minzu daxue chubanshe, 1999.

Wang Zongyan 汪宗衍. *Mingji Shengren heshang nianpu* 明季剩人和尚年譜. Taibei: Shangwu yinshuguan, 1986.

———. *Tianran chanshi nianpu* 天然禪師年譜. 1943. Reprinted in *Fojiao mingren nianpu (xia)*, pp. 51–124. Beijing: Beijing Tushuguan, 2003.

Watson, Burton. *The Zen Teachings of Master Lin-chi: A Translation of the Lin-chi Lu*. New York: Columbia University Press, 1999.

Wei Daoru 魏道儒. *Zhongguo Huayan zong tongshi* 中國華嚴宗通史. Nanjing: Jiangsu guji chubanshe, 1998.

Weibai 惟白, comp. *Jingzhong jianguo xu denglu* 靖中建國續燈錄. T no. 2007, vol. 51.

Weidner, Marsha, ed. *Cultural Intersections in Later Chinese Buddhism*. Honolulu: University of Hawaii Press, 2001.

———. *Latter Days of the Law: Images of Chinese Buddhism: 850–1850*. Lawrence, Kans.: Spencer Museum of Art, 1994.

Weinstein, Stanley. *Buddhism under the T'ang*. Cambridge and New York: Cambridge University Press, 1987.

———. "The Schools of Chinese Buddhism." In *Buddhism and Asian History*, ed. Joseph M. Kitagawa and Mark D. Cummings, pp. 257–65. New York: Macmillan, 1989.

Weizhi Zhikai 惟直智楷. *Zhengming lu* 正名錄. 1694. Reprinted in the Puhui 普慧 canon, 1945. Rare book in the Shanghai Library. Also reprinted in *Dazangjing bubian*, vol. 24.

Weizhong Jingfu 位中淨符. *Famen chugui* 法門鋤宄. 1 fasc. Z no. 1604, vol. 86.

———. *Zongmen niangu huiji* 宗門拈古彙集. 45 fascs. Z no. 1296, vol. 66.

———. *Zudeng bian'e* 祖燈辨訛. 2 fascs. 1672. Reprinted in *Zudeng datong*, vol. 1, pp.83–108. Hong Kong: Xianggang Foxue shuju, 1994. The 1672 edition is preserved in the Shanghai Library.

———. *Zudeng datong* 祖燈大統. 98 fascs. 1672. Reprint the *Puhui dazang jing* 普慧大藏經 edition in 1944, 4 vols.; Hong Kong: Xianggang Foxue shuju, 1994. Also in

Fojiao dazangjing, no. 2291, vols. 109–10. The 1672 edition is preserved in the Shanghai Library.

Welch, Holmes. *The Buddhist Revival in China*. Cambridge, Mass.: Harvard University Press, 1968.

———. "Dharma Scrolls and the Succession of Abbots in Chinese Monasteries." *T'oung Pao* 50 (1963): 93–149.

———. *The Practice of Chinese Buddhism, 1900–1950*. Cambridge, Mass.: Harvard University Press, 1967.

Welter, Albert. "A Buddhist Response to the Confucian Revival: Tsan-ning and the Debate over *Wen* in the Early Sung." In *Buddhism in the Sung*, ed. Peter N. Gregory and Daniel A. Getz, Jr., pp. 21–61. Honolulu: University of Hawaii Press, 1999.

———. "Lineage and Context in the *Patriarch's Hall Collection* and the *Transmission of the Lamp*." In *The Zen Canon: Understanding the Classic Texts*, ed. Steven Heine and Dale S. Wright, pp. 137–80. New York: Oxford University Press, 2004.

———. *Monks, Rulers, and Literati: The Political Ascendancy of Chan Buddhism*. New York: Oxford University Press, 2006.

———. "The Textual History of the *Linji lu* (Record of Linji): The Earliest Recorded Fragments." Paper presented at the American Association of Religion annual meeting, Toronto, November 2002.

Wen Bing 文秉. *Jiayi shi'an* 甲乙事案. 2 fascs. *Siku jinhuishu congkan*, series 2 (*shibu*), 72: 43–106.

———. *Shanxi xunfu Cai Yunyi xiansheng xunnan shimo zhuan* 山西巡撫蔡雲怡先生殉難始末傳. In *Xijian Mingshi shiji jicun*, 17: 1–11.

Wen Ruilin 溫睿臨. *Nanjiang yishi* 南疆逸史. Reprinted in *Han Min shiryō sōsho* 晚明史料叢書. Tokyo: Dai'an, 1967.

Wenxiu 文琇, comp. *Zengji xu chuandeng lu* 增集續傳燈錄. Z no. 1574, vol. 83.

Williams, Paul. *Mahayana Buddhism: The Doctrinal Foundations*. London: Routledge, 1989.

Wilson, Thomas A. *Genealogy of the Way: The Construction and Uses of the Confucian Tradition in Late Imperial China*. Stanford, Calif.: Stanford University Press, 1995.

Wright, Dale S. *Philosophical Meditations on Zen Buddhism*. New York: Cambridge University Press, 1998.

Wu, Hung. "Emperor's Masquerade: Costume Portraits of Yongzheng and Qinglong." *Orientations* 26.7 (July–Aug. 1995): 25–41.

Wu, Jiang. "Buddhist Logic and Apologetics in Seventeenth-century China: an Analysis of the Use of Buddhist Syllogisms in an Anti-Christian Polemic." *Dao: A Journal of Comparative Philosophy* II.2 (June 2003): 273–289.

———. "Building a Dharma Transmission Monastery in Seventeenth-century China." *Journal of East Asian History* 31 (June 2006): 29–52.

———. "The Commentarial Tradition of the *Śūraṃgama Sūtra*." Paper presented at the annual meeting of the American Association of Religion, November 18–21, 2006, Washington, D.C.

————. "Knowledge for What? The Buddhist Concept of Learning in the *Śuragama Sūtra*." *Journal of Chinese Philosophy* 33.4 (Dec. 2006): 491–503.

————. "Leaving for the Rising Sun: The Historical Background of Yinyuan Longqi's Migration to Japan in 1654." *Asia Major*, 3rd ser., 17.2 (2004): 89–120.

————. "Orthodoxy, Controversy, and the Transformation of Chan Buddhism in Seventeenth-century China." Ph.D. diss., Harvard University, 2002.

————. "Problems with Enlightenment: The Performance of Encounter Dialogue in Seventeenth-century Chinese Chan Buddhism." Paper presented at Zen Seminar at the annual meeting of the American Association of Religion, November 20, 2005, Philadelphia.

————. "The Rule of Marginality: Hypothesizing the Transmission of the Mengshan Rite for Feeding the Hungry Ghosts in Late Imperial China." Paper presented at Conference on Tantra: Constructions and Deployments of Power, October 11–13, 2002, Flagstaff, Arizona.

Wu Limin 吳立民, Xu Sunming 徐孫銘, et al. *Chanzong zongpai yuanliu* 禪宗宗派源流. Beijing: Zhongguo shehui kexue chubanshe, 1998.

Wu, Silas H. L. *Passage to Power: K'ang-hsi and His Heir Apparent, 1661–1722.* Cambridge, Mass.: Harvard University Press, 1979.

Wu Tianren 吳天任. *Dangui chanshi nianpu* 澹歸禪師年譜. Hong Kong: Zhilian jingshe, 1991.

Wujia yulu 五家語錄, compiled by Xuejiao Yuanxin 雪嶠圓信 and Guo Ningzhi 郭凝之. In Z no. 1326, vol. 69 and XZJ vol. 119.

Wuke Dazhi 無可大智 (Fang Yizhi 方以智). *Qingyuan Yuzhe Zhi chanshi yulu* 青原愚者智禪師語錄. 4 fascs. JXZ no. 331, vol. 34.

Wuming Huijing 無明慧經. *Shouchang Wuming heshang yulu* 壽昌無明和尚語錄. 2 fascs. JXZ no. 173, vol. 25.

Wunian Shenyou 無念深有. *Huangbo Wunian chanshi fuwen* 黃檗無念禪師復問. JXZ no. 98, vol. 20; ZH vol. 79.

Xie Guozhen 謝國楨. "Qingchu Dongbei liuren kao" 清初東北流人考. 1948. Reprinted in his *Mingmo Qingchu de xuefeng* 明末清初的學風, pp. 1–52. Beijing: Renmin chubanshe, 1982.

Xijian Mingshi shiji jicun 稀見明史史籍輯存, ed. Su Xiaojun 蘇曉君 and Yu Bing 俞冰. 30 vols. Beijing: Xianzhuang shuju, 2003.

Xinxiu Tiantong shan sizhi 新修天童山寺志. Beijing: Zhongjiao wenhua chubanshe, 1997.

Xinxu Gaoseng zhuan siji 新修高僧傳四集, ed. Yu Qian 喻謙. Reprint. Taibei: Guangwen shuju, 1977.

Xiuxi Yuqie jiyao shishi yi 修習瑜伽集要施食儀. 1 fasc. Z no. 1081, vol. 59.

Xuxiu siku quanshu 續修四庫全書. 1,800 vols. Shanghai: Shanghai guji chubanshe, 1994–2002.

Xu Changzhi 徐昌治, comp. *Shengchao poxie ji* 聖朝破邪集. 8 fascs. 1639. Reprint. Japan, 1865.

————. *Wuyi daoren lu* 無依道人錄. 2 fascs. JXZ no. 127, vol. 23.

Xu Wenming 徐文明. "Caodong zong guizong Qingyuan yixi de yuanyin chuxi" 曹洞宗歸宗青原一系的原因初析. *Pumen xuebao* 普門學報 2 (2001): 126–36.

Xu Zi 徐鼒. *Xiao tian ji zhuan* 小腆紀傳. Reprint. Beijing: Zhonghua shuju, 1958.

Xue Cai 薛寀. *Xue Xiemeng xiansheng biji* 薛諧孟(先生)筆記. 2 fascs. Reprint. Changzhou, 1939.

Xue Feng 薛锋 and Xue Xiang 薛翔. *Kuncan* 髡残. Changchun: Jilin meishu chuban-she, 1996.

Xuedou Chongxian 雪竇重顯. *Mingjue chanshi yulu* 明覺禪師語錄. 6 fascs. T no. 1996, vol. 47.

Xuefeng Yicun 雪峰義存. *Xuefeng Yicun chanshi yulu* 雪峰義存禪師語錄, or *Zhenjue chanshi yulu* 真覺禪師語錄. 1 fasc. Z no. 1333, vol. 69.

Xuelang Hong'en 雪浪洪恩. *Xuelang ji* 雪浪集. Reprinted in *Chanmen yishu xubian*, no. 217, vol. 2.

———. *Xuelang xuji* 雪浪續集. Reprinted in *Chanmen yishu xubian*, no. 218, vol. 2.

Yamaguchi Hisakazu 山口久和. "Kō Sōgi 'Sanhō zenji tōmei' kō" 黄宗羲三峰禅师塔铭考. *Osaka Shiritsu Daigaku Jimbun Kenkyū* 大阪市立大学人文研究 I, 32.2 (1981): 84–94; II, 33.1 (1982): 687–703.

Yan Jun 顏鈞. *Yan Jun ji* 顏鈞集, ed. Huang Xuanmin 黃宣民. Beijing: Zhongguo shehui kexue chubanshe, 1996.

Yan Yaozhong 嚴耀中. "Ming Qing shidai de Hanchuan Mijiao" 明清時代的漢傳密教. In his *Hanchuan Mijiao* 漢傳密教, pp. 52–64. Shanghai: Xuelin chubanshe, 1999.

Yanagida Seizan 柳田聖山. "Ingen no tōto to Nihon Ōbakuzen" 隱元の東渡と日本黃檗禪. In *Shūkyō* 宗教, *Nitchū bunka koryūshi sūsho* 日中文化交流史叢書 4, ed. Minamoto Ryōen 源了圓 and Yang Zengwen 楊曾文, pp. 276–95. Tokyo: Taishūkan Shoten, 1996.

———. "The Life of Lin-chi I-hsüan," trans. by Ruth Sasaki. *The East Buddhist* 5. 2 (October 1972): 70–94.

———. "The 'Recorded Sayings' Texts of Chinese Ch'an Buddhism," trans. John R. McRae. In *Early Ch'an in China and Tibet*, ed. Whalen Lai and Lewis R. Lancaster, pp. 185–206. Berkeley, Calif.: Berkeley Buddhist Studies Series, 1983.

———. *Shoki Zenshū shisho no kenkyū* 初期禪宗史書の研究. Kyoto: Hōzōkan, 1967.

Yanagida Seizan 柳田聖山, ed. *Sōhan Kōraihon Keitoku dentōroku* 宋版高麗本景德傳燈錄. Kyōto: Chūbun Shuppansha, 1984.

Yang Haiying 楊海英. *Hong Chengchou yu Ming Qing yidai yanjiu* 洪承疇與明清易代研究. Beijing: Shangwu yinshuguan, 2006.

Yang Qiqiao 楊啓樵. *Yongzheng di jiqi mizhe zhidu yanjiu* 雍正帝及其密摺制度研究. Hong Kong: Sanlian shudian, 1981.

Yang Zengwen 楊曾文. "Fenyang Shanzhao jiqi chanfa" 汾陽善昭及其禪法. *Zhonghua Foxue bao* 15 (2002): 219–53.

Yangshan Huiji 仰山慧濟. *Yuanzhou Yanshan Huiji chanshi yulu* 袁州仰山慧寂禪師語錄. T no. 1990, vol. 47.

Yifa. *The Origins of Buddhist Monastic Codes in China: An Annotated Translation and Study of the Chanyuan qinggui*. Honolulu: University of Hawaii Press, 2002.

———. "From the Chinese Vinaya Tradition to Chan Regulations: Continuity and Adaptation." In *Going Forth: Visions of Buddhist Vinaya*, ed. William M. Bodiford, pp. 124–35. Honolulu: University of Hawai'i Press, 2005.

Yim, Chi-hung. "The Poetics of Historical Memory in the Ming-Qing Transition: A Study of Qian Qianyi's (1582–1664) Later Poetry." Ph.D. diss., Yale University, 1998.

———. "Political Exile, Chan Buddhist Master, Poetry Club Founder: A Cantonese Monk in Manchuria during the Ming-Qing Transition." Paper presented at the annual meeting of the Society for Ming Studies, March 23, 2001, Chicago.

Yinyuan Longqi 隱元隆琦. *Fushō gokushi goroku* 普照國師語錄. T no. 2605, vol 82.

———. *Fushō gokushi hōgo* 普照國師法語. T no. 2606, vol. 82.

———. *Hongjie fayi* 弘戒法儀 (adapted from Hanyue's work with the same title). In *Zengaku taikei* 禪學大系, ed. *Zengaku taikei* hensankyoku, vol. 7, pp. 1–68. Tokyo: Kokusho kankōkai, 1913.

———. *Huangboshan si zhi* 黃檗山寺志. 8 fascs. In *Xuxiu Siku quanshu*, vol. 719.

———. *Ōbaku shingi* 黃檗清規. T no. 2607, vol. 82.

———. *Yinyuan chanshi yulu* 隱元禪師語錄. 16 fascs. 1655. JXZ no. 193, vol. 27.

Yiru 一如. *Da Ming sanzang fashu* 大明三藏法數. Reprint. Taipei: Xinwenfeng chuban gongsi, 1978.

Yongjue Yuanxian 永覺元賢. *Yongjue Yuanxian chanshi guanglu* 永覺元賢禪師廣錄. Z no. 1437, vol. 72.

Yongzheng 雍正. *Jianmo bianyi lu* 揀魔辨異錄. 8 fascs. Z no. 1281, vol. 65.

———. "Qing Shizong guanyu Foxue zhi yuzhi" 清世宗關於佛學之諭旨. Reprinted in *Wenxian congbian* 文獻叢編, ser. 3 and 4. Beijing: Guoli Beiping Gugong bowuyuan wenxianguan, 1932.

———. *Yuanming jushi yulu* 圓明居士語錄. In *Yuxuan yulu*, Z 68: 553–77.

———. *Yulu jinghai yidi* 御錄經海一滴. Reprinted in *Yongzheng yuzhi Fojiao dadian*, vol. 3.

———. *Yulu Zongjing dagang* 御錄宗鏡大綱. Reprinted in *Yongzheng yuzhi Fojiao dadian*, vol. 4.

———. *Yuxuan yulu* 御選語錄. Z no. 1319, vol. 68; XZJ vol. 119.

Yongzheng 雍正, comp. *Yuexin ji* 悅心集. Reprint. Taibei: Laogu wenhua, 1998.

Yongzheng yuzhi Fojiao dadian 雍正御制佛教大典, ed. Shi Yuanpeng 史原朋. 4 vols. Beijing: Zhongguo shehui kexue chubanshe, 2003.

Yoshikawa Kōjirō 吉川幸次郎. "Koji to shite no Sen Bokusai: Sen Bokusai to Bukkyō" 居士としての錢牧齋: 錢牧齋と佛教. In *Fukui hakushi shōju kinen: Tōyō shisō ronshū* 福井博士頌壽記念. 東洋思想論集, pp. 738–58. Tokyo: Fukui Hakushi Shōju Kinen Ronbunshū Kankōkai.

Youxi biezhi 幽谿別志. 16 fascs. Chongzhen edition. ZFS supplement, vol. 9.

Yü, Chün-fang (Kristin Yu Greenblat). "Chu-hung and Lay Buddhism in the Late Ming." In *The Unfolding of Neo-Confucianism*, ed. William Theodore de Bary, pp. 93–140. New York: Columbia University Press, 1975.

———. "Chung-feng Ming-pen and Ch'an Buddhism in the Yüan." In *Yüan Thought: Chinese Thought and Religion under the Mongols*, ed. Hok-lam Chan and William Theodore de Bary, pp. 419–77. New York: Columbia University Press, 1982.

———. "Ming Buddhism." In *Cambridge History of China*, ed. F. W. Mote and D. Twitchett, vol. 8, Part II, pp. 893–952. Cambridge: Cambridge University Press, 1990.

————. "P'u-t'o Shan: Pilgrimage and the Creation of the Chinese Potalaka." In *Pilgrims and Sacred Sites in China*, ed. Susan Naquin and Chün-fang Yü, pp. 190–245. Berkeley: University of California Press, 1992.

————. *The Renewal of Buddhism in China: Chu-hung and the Late Ming Synthesis*. New York: Columbia University Press, 1981.

Yu, Li. "A History of Reading in Late Imperial China, 1000–1800." Ph.D. diss., Ohio State University, 2003.

Yu Xianhao 郁賢皓. *Tang cishi kao* 唐刺史攷. Hong Kong and Nanjing: Zhonghua shuju and Jiangsu guji chubanshe, 1987.

Yü, Ying-shih 余英時. *Fang Yizhi wanjie kao* 方以智晚節考. Hong Kong: Xinya yanjiusuo, 1972.

————. "Some Preliminary Reflections on the Rise of Ch'ing Intellectualism." *Tsing Hua Journal of Chinese Studies* 11 (1975): 105–43.

Yuan Hongdao 袁宏道. *Jinxie bian* 金屑編. 1 fasc. Rare book preserved in the Naikaku bunko Archive in Japan. The same edition preserved in the Beijing Library was reprinted in *Xuxiu siku quanshu*, series 3(*zibu*), vol. 1131.

————. *Shanhu lin* 珊瑚林, 2 fascs. Rare book preserved in the Naikaku bunko Archive in Japan. Reprinted in *Sango rin: Chūgoku bunjin no Zen mondōshū* 珊瑚林: 中国文人の禪問答集, edited and translated by Araki Kengo, et al. Tokyo: Perikansha, 2001. The same edition preserved in the Beijing Library was reprinted in *Xuxiu siku quanshu*, series 3(*zibu*), vol. 1131.

Yuan Zhongdao 袁中道, comp. "Zuolin ji tan" 柞林紀譚. In *Li Wenling waiji* 李溫陵外紀. pp. 59–102. Taibei: Weiwen tushu chubanshe, 1978.

Yuanliang 源諒, comp. *Lüzong dengpu* 律宗燈譜. Qianlong edition. Reprinted in the Republican era. Rare source in the Shanghai Library; also in *Dazangjing bubian*, no. 118, vol. 22.

Yuanmen Jingzhu 遠門淨柱. *Wudeng huiyuan xulue* 五燈會元續略. Z no. 1566, vol. 80.

Yuanwu Keqin 圓悟克勤. *Yuanwu Keqin Foguo chanshi yulu* 圓悟佛果禪師語錄. 20 fascs. T no. 1997, vol. 47.

Yuanwu Keqin 圓悟克勤, comp. *Biyan lu* 碧巌錄. 10 fascs. T no. 2003, vol. 48.

Yunlin si xuzhi 雲林寺續志. ZFS vol. 62.

Yunmen Wenyan 雲門文偃. *Yunmen Kuangzhen chanshi guanglu* 雲門匡真禪師廣錄. T no. 1988, vol. 47.

Yunmen Xiansheng si zhi 雲門顯聖寺志. Yongzheng edition. ZFS vol. 4.

Yunqi Zhuhong 雲棲袾宏. *Huang Ming gaoseng jilüe* 皇明高僧輯略. Z no. 1581, vol. 84.

————. *Yunqi fahui* 雲棲法匯. JXZ no. 277, vol. 33.

————. *Yuqie jiyao shishi yigui* 瑜伽集要施食儀軌. 1606. Z no. 1080, vol. 59.

————. *Zhuchuan suibi* 竹窗隨筆. In *Yunqi fahui*, JXZ no. 277, vol. 33; also in *Dazangjing bubian*, no. 123, vol. 23.

Yuqie jiyao yankou shishi yi 瑜伽集要燄口施食儀. 1 fasc. T no. 1320, vol. 21.

Yuquan zhi 玉泉志. ZFS vol. 14.

Zanning 贊寧. *Song gaoseng zhuan* 宋高僧傳. T no. 2061, vol. 50.

Zengaku taikei 禪學大系. 8 vols. Tokyo: Kokusho kankōkai, 1910–1915.

Zengo jiten 禅語辞典, ed. Iriya Yoshitaka 入矢義高 and Koga Hidehiko 古賀英彦. Kyōto: Shibunkaku Shuppan, 1991.

Zelin, Madeleine. "The Yung-cheng Reign." In *The Cambridge History of China*, vol. 9, pt. 1: *The Ch'ing Empire to 1800*, ed. Willard J. Peterson, pp. 183–229. Cambridge: Cambridge University Press, 2002.

Zezang 賾藏, ed. *Gu zunsu yulu* 古尊宿語錄. 48 fascs. Z no. 1315, vol. 68.

Zha Jizhuo 查繼佐. *Guo shou lu* 国壽錄. Reprinted in *Han Min shiryō sōsho* 晚明史料叢書. Tokyo: Dai'an, 1967.

Zhang Bowei 張伯偉. "Huanrao Linjilu zhuben de ruogan wenti" 環繞臨濟錄諸本的若干問題. In *Zhongguo dianji yu wenhua luncong* 中國典籍與文化論叢, ser. 2, pp. 388–401. Beijing: Zhonghua shuju, 1995.

Zhang Dai 張岱. *Tao'an mengyi* 陶庵夢憶. Reprint. Shanghai: Shanghai yuandong chubanshe, 1996.

Zhang Mantao 張曼濤, ed. *Dacheng qixin lun yu Lengyanjing kaobian* 大乘起信論與楞嚴經考辨. Taibei: Dacheng wenhua chubanshe, 1978.

Zhang Wenliang 張文良. "Hanyue Fazang lun Rulai Chan yu Zushi Chan" 漢月法藏論如來禪与祖師禪. *Fayin* 法音 3 (1995): 29–35.

———. *Yongzheng yu Chanzong* 雍正與禪宗. Taibei: Laogu wenhua shiye gufen youxian gongsi, 1997.

Zhang Zhiqiang 張志強. "Weishi sixiang yu wanming weishixue yanjiu" 唯識思想与晚明唯識學研究. Ph.D. diss., Beijing University, 1997. Reprinted in *Zhongguo Fojiao xueshu lundian* 中國佛教學術論典, vol. 7, pp. 291–439. Gaoxiong: Foguang chubanshe, 2000.

Zhanran Yuancheng 湛然圓澄. *Kaigu lu* 慨古錄. Z no. 1285, vol. 65.

———. *Kuaiji Yunmen Zhanran Cheng chanshi yulu* 會稽云門湛然澄禪師語錄. JXZ no. 172, vol. 25.

Zhao, Jie. "Chou Ju-teng (1547–1629) at Nanking: Reassessing a Confucian Scholar in the Late Ming Intellectual World." Ph.D. diss., Princeton University, 1995.

———. "Reassessing the Place of Chou Ju-teng (1547–1629) in late Ming Thought." *Ming Studies* 33 (August 1994): 1–11.

Zhao Mengfu 趙孟頫. *Zhao Mengfu ji* 趙孟頫集, ed. Ren Daobin 任道斌. Hangzhou: Zhejiang guji chubanshe, 1986.

Zhao Yuan 趙園. *Ming Qing zhiji shidafu yanjiu* 明清之際士大夫研究. Beijing: Beijing daxue chubanshe, 1999.

Zhaoqing si zhi 昭慶寺志. 1882. ZFS vol. 71.

Zhizhao 智昭, ed. *Rentian yanmu* 人天眼目. T no. 2006, vol. 48; Z no. 1267, vol. 64.

Zhongguo Fojiao congshu Chanzong bian 中國佛教叢書禪宗編, ed. Ren Jiyu 任繼愈. 12 vols. Nanjing: Jiangsu guji chubanshe, 1993.

Zhongguo Fojiao renming dacidian 中國佛教人名大辭典, posthumuous work by Zhenhua 震華, ed. Zhenchan 真禪 and Wang Xin 王新. 1999. Reprint. Shanghai: Shanghai cishu chubanshe, 2002.

Zhongguo Fojiao sixiang ziliao xuan bian 中國佛教思想資料選編, ed. Lou Yulie 樓宇烈. 5 series. Beijing: Zhonghua shuju, since 1981.

Zhongguo Fosi shi zhi hui kan 中國佛寺史志彙刊, ed. Du Jiexiang 杜潔祥. 1st ser., 35 vols.; 2nd ser., 21 vols.; 3rd ser., 30 vols. Taibei: Ming wen shu ju, 1980.

Zhongguo Fosi zhi congkan 中国佛寺志叢刊, ed. Bai Huawen 白化文, Liu Yongming 刘永明, and Zhang Zhi 张智. 120 vols. Yangzhou: Jiangsu guangling guji keyin she, 1996.

Zhongguo Fosi zhi congkan xubian 中國佛寺志叢刊續編, ed. Bai Huawen 白化文, Liu Yongming 刘永明, and Zhang Zhi 张智. 10 vols. Yangzhou: Jiangsu guji chubanshe, 2001.

Zhongguo lidai chanshi zhuanji huibian zongmu 中國歷代禪師傳記資料彙編總目, ed. Xu Ziqiang 徐自強. 3 vols. Beijing: Quanguo tushuguan wenxian suowei fuzhi zhongxin, 1994.

Zhonghua dazang jing di er ji 中華大藏經第二輯. Reprint of *Jiaxing zhengzang* 嘉興正藏, *Jiaxing xuzang* 嘉興續藏, and *Jiaxing you xuzang* 嘉興又續藏. Taibei: Xiuding Zhonghua dazang jing hui 修訂中華大藏經會, 1962.

Zhou Er'fang 周馹方. "Pa Tiantong Miyun chanshi *Biantianshuo*" 跋天童密雲禪師辨天說. *Wenwu* 文物 4 (1999): 285–87.

Zhou Qi 周齊. *Mingdai Fojiao yu zhengzhi wenhua* 明代佛教與政治文化. Beijing: Renmin chubanshe, 2005.

Zhou Rudeng 周汝登. *Fofa zhenglun* 佛法正輪, or *Zhixin bian* 直心編. 2 fascs. 1603. In *Meiguo Hafo daxue Hafo Yanjing tushuguan cang zhongwen shanben huikan* 美國哈佛大學哈佛燕京圖書館藏中文善本彙刊, vol. 33, pp. 105–34. Guilin: Guangxi shifan daxue chubanshe, 2003.

———. *Zhou Haimen xiansheng wenlu* 周海門先生文錄. Wanli edition. Reprinted in *Siku quanshu cunmu congshu*, vol. 165.

Zhou Shujia 周叔迦. *Qingdai Fojiao shiliao jigao* 清代佛教史料輯稿, ed. Jiang Canteng 江燦騰. Taibei: Xinwenfeng, 2000.

Zhou Zheng 周錚. "Feiyin chanshi shouza kaoshi" 費隱禪師手札考釋. *Shijie zongjiao yanjiu* 世界宗教研究 4 (1985). 143–47.

Zhu Shi'en 朱時恩. *Fozu gangmu* 佛祖綱目. 1634. Z no. 1594, vol. 85.

Ziporyn, Brook. "Anti-Chan Polemics in Post Tang Tiantai." *Journal of the International Association of Buddhist Studies* 17.1 (Summer 1994): 26–65.

Zongbao 宗寶, ed. *Liuzu dashi fabao tanjing*. T no. 2008, vol. 48.

Zongmi 宗密. *Chanyuan zhu quanji duxu* 禪源諸詮集都序. 2 fascs. T no. 2015, vol. 48.

———. *Zhonghua chuanxindi chanmen shizi chengxitu* 中華傳心地禪門師資承襲圖. 1 fasc. Z no. 1225, vol. 63.

Zürcher, Erik. "Buddhisme et Christianisme." In his *Bouddhisme, Christianisme et Societe Chinoise*, pp. 11–42. Paris: Julliard, 1990.

———. *The Buddhist Conquest of China: The Spread and Adaptation of Buddhism in Early Medieval China*. Leiden: Brill, 1972.

Zuxiu 祖琇. *Longxing biannian tonglun* 隆興編年通論. 29 fascs. Z no. 1512, vol. 75.

Index

Amitābha Sūtra, 66

antinomianism, 9, 12, 13, 39, 44–45, 52–53, 76, 82, 92, 107, 136, 154, 174–76, 250, 273, 275
   Huang Duanbo and, 80

Araki Kengo, 61, 68, 81–82

asceticism, 33, 40–41, 50

associations, vertical and horizontal, 261, 393n27

authority, 12, 26, 132, 140, 143, 183, 204–5, 241–42, 250, 287, 288, 296, 395n18
   patriarchal, 6, 241–42
   political, 177, 203, 207, 215, 222, 241, 257
   spiritual, 71, 108, 134, 155, 169, 251, 252, 253, 258, 386n47
   textual, 48, 65, 67, 102, 108, 196, 241, 242, 246, 252

autonomy, monastic, 30, 166

Avataṃsaka (Huayan) Sūtra, 25, 63, 325
   Li Tongxuan and, 26–27
   literati and, 66, 26–27

awareness (*zhi*), 141

Ayuwang monastery, 23, 27, 49, 73, 77–78, 278, 374n50

Azhali jiao, as reminiscence of esoteric institutions in the early Ming dynasty, 383n38

Bada Shanren, 103

Baichi Xingyuan, 196, 221, 222, 296

Bailin monastery, 164, 165, 167, 257, 380n70

Baima Tanzhao, biography of, 327–28

Baisong Xingfeng, 310

Baiting Xufa, 26

Baizhang Huaihai, 95, 96, 152, 153, 189c, 240c, 267, 378n38

Bankei Yōtaku, 99

Bao'en monastery, 25, 26, 65

Baofeng monastery, 95

Baofeng Xuan (Mingxuan or Zhixuan), 38, 39c, 301–2, 304–5

Baolin monastery, 76

Baroni, Helen, 393n26, 395n13

de Bary, William Theodore, 50

beating and shouting practice, 12, 13, 14, 45, 53, 97, 106, 109, 122, 131, 135, 136, 152, 153, 154, 155, 157, 158, 160, 248, 250, 273, 308. *See also* encounter dialogue
   disappearance of, 160, 246, 256, 265, 267, 272
   Feiyin Tongrong on, 309
   Hanyue Fazang on, 117, 120, 157
   imitation of, 265
   Miyun Yuanwu and, 7, 77, 87, 118, 126
   as public performance, 9
   Qian Qianyi criticizing, 159
   superficiality of, 140
   as a way of Chan training, 9, 11
   Yongzheng criticizing, 159, 178, 386n35

Bianrong Zhenyuan, 24

Biyan lu, 136, 141

Blackburn, Anne, 392n5

Bodhidharma, 139, 218, 324, 312, 400n33

Bol, Peter, 284

The Book of Changes, 96, 142

Brook, Timothy, 13, 22, 23, 24, 33, 47, 48, 49, 53, 84, 87, 101, 107, 261–62, 273, 274, 275, 357n22, 373n40

Buddhism, 84. *See also* Chan Buddhism; Chinese Buddhism
  anti-, 22, 24
  boundaries of, 279–80, 285
  Chan Buddhism reintegrating all of, 270
  Chan masters' role in, 14
  Confucianism and, 14, 47, 60, 74, 279, 369n94
  Confucianism/Taoism integrated with, 50
  decline of, 23–24
  esoteric, 145–51, 256, 277, 273, 275
  historical cycles of, 277, 279, 280
  Indian, 392n9
  Japanese Shingon, 148
  models of, lineage and local, 275, 276, 395n18,
  modern Chinese, 14, 160–61, 245, 260, 266, 267, 269, 270, 271, 273, 283, 381n15
  Ōbaku, 87, 93, 99, 238, 239, 253, 261, 270, 272, 393n26
  patterns/stages of revival of, 280–85
  persecution of, 3
  revival and outside influence, 283, 289
  revival of, 22, 24–25, 31, 32, 277, 282
  revival of, documentation, 22
  separation of, from society, 23, 258
  Shunzhi emperor and, 85, 90, 91, 97, 101, 373n37
  sinification of, 3, 288
  Tibetan, 22, 24, 146, 148, 163, 383n39, 386n47
  transformation and, 3, 4
  in twentieth century, 266–67, 269
  vitality of, 113
  Wanli emperor stimulating recovery of, 24–25
  Yongzheng emperor supporting, 164, 165
  Zen, 99, 239
Buddhist Abhidharma tradition, 142
Buddhist ordination. *See* ordination
The Buddhist Revival in China (by Welch), 276–77. *See also* Holmes Welch
Buddhist scholasticism, 13, 14, 25–26, 39, 47, 273, 282. *See also* Tiantai school, Huayan school, and Yogācāra school
Buddhist syllogisms, 27
Budong, 271, 383n39

Cai Maode, 79, 368n89
calligraphy, 58, 102, 108, 164, 168, 253
  Feiyin Tongrong, 255*f*
  Miyun Yuanwu, 254*f*
  Shunzhi emperor, 91*f*
  Yongzheng emperor, 182*f*
Cangxue Duche, 26, 358n26
Caodong masters/monks, 93, 189, 225, 226, 305, 313, 314, 326, 328, 329
  Daowu debate and, 190–94, 227–35, 324–30
  Feiyin Tongrong and, 7, 8, 92, 212, 214, 220, 221, 222–23

Linji monks compared with, 94
  Qi family and, 78–79
  in Shaolin monastery, 94
Caodong school, 6, 7, 14, 32, 39, 51,77, 78, 84, 92, 106, 187, 192, 201–2, 208, 209, 210–11, 229, 234, 245, 293–94, 295
  dharma transmission, 36, 72, 201–2, 234, 267
  further spread of, 98–99
  inadequate study of, 288
  inconsistent genealogy of, 36, 297–301
  principle of, 123, 308
  revival of, 93–96
Caoxi monastery, 34, 272, 361n60
Cao Yinru, 66
Central Buddhist Registration (*Seng lu si*), 28
ceremony of ascending the hall (*shangtang*), 9, 72, 95, 96, 153, 158
Chan anthologies, 173, 174
  literati's, 59, 60, 61, 107, 188
Chan Buddhism, 163. *See also* Patriarch Chan (*Zushi Chan*); Tathāgata Chan (*Rulai Chan*)
  Buddhism reintegrated through, 270
  Chan literature and rise of, 245–46
  Chinese Buddhism and, 273–76
  controversies in, 7–8, 15, 113–14, 120, 121, 122, 201, 222, 223, 245, 287, 288, 297
  decline of, 5, 12, 33, 93, 106, 245, 255, 275, 262–63, 268, 277
  disruption of, 12–13, 14
  dormancy of, in the mid-Ming, 32–34
  in eighteenth century, 267–68
  Hanyue Fazang's interpretation of, 114, 115, 117, 121, 135, 137–40, 151, 157
  Hanyue Fazang systematizing/theorizing, 142, 144
  intellectualism and, 275
  legacies of, 266, 268
  literati and rise of, 13, 14, 21, 27, 45, 47–48, 49, 50, 72–73, 100, 249–50, 289
  lost cultural identity and, during the Ming-Qing transition, 4, 269
  Miyun Yuanwu's interpretation of, 43, 120, 126, 135, 136, 140, 142, 151
  monastic/secular world linked by, 273
  Northern School of, 35, 38, 39, 145, 205, 283, 361n64
  outside influences and, 13, 283, 289
  objectivity and subjectivity in, 143–44
  paradox of, 44, 143
  politics and, 250, 256
  power structure of, 8, 183, 223, 258, 274, 276
  practices of, 7, 9, 11, 12, 13, 14, 21, 33, 40, 41
  practices of, becoming shallow, 42
  reading normative texts in, 16, 357n22
  as reinvented tradition, 11–14
  rise of, 3–8, 13, 15, 17, 21, 31, 35–36, 44, 74, 83–85, 208, 262–63, 277, 287
  ritualistic nature of, 247
  Shaolin monastery and, 36

society and, 84, 105–9, 284, 288
spreading of, 96–99, 288
stages of revival of, 105–7
Taizhou school and, 51–53
textual communities and, 254–55
textual practice *vs.* reality in, 246–49, 253
transformation of, 8–11, 12–14
two aspects of transmission in, 137–38, 140
as unifying force, 274–75
Wang Yangming and, 48–49, 68
Yongzheng emperor teaching, 169–73, 175, 178
Yunqi Zhuhong's understanding of, 66
Chandeng shipu (by Muchen Daomin), 200, 201, 202, 218, 220, 291, 303, 309
debate over, 200–5
Huang Duanbo and, 200, 201–3
Chan genealogy(ies), 4, 6, 11, 35, 60, 199, 200, 245, 256, 282. *See also* lineage(s); *Wudeng huiyuan; Wudeng quanshu; Wudeng yantong, Chandeng shipu*
disrupted, 215
gap in, 32
Muchen Daomin and, 201
new editions of, in the seventeenth century, 208
Yuanmen Jingzhu and, 208, 209
by Yunhe Rui, 322
Chanlin kesong, 271, 272f
Chanlin sengbao zhuan (by Juefan Huihong), 326, 331
Chan literature, 12, 16, 106, 200, 205. *See also* recorded sayings; textual practice
Confucian literati and, 48, 53–54, 55–56, 57, 73, 246
Confucian literati composing, 59–64, 82
Confucian literati editing, 61
controversies through interpretation of, 249
as culturally binding force, 250–51
increase of, as index to religious and social changes, 106
lamp transmissions in, 247
offensive language in, 61
production/proliferation of, 254
reinterpretation of, to reinvent the past, 247
rise of Chan Buddhism and, 245–46
scarcity of, in the early and mid-Ming, 21, 33
two types of, 5–6
Chan masters/monks, 4, 5, 9, 10, 12, 13, 16, 21, 39, 109. *See also* Caodong masters and Linji masters
Buddhism and role of, 14, 41
Confucian literati and, 47, 48, 253
doctrinal studies of, as young monk, 31, 44, 372n25
as entrepreneurs, 273
Feiyin Tongrong criticizing, 308–9
laymen and, 68–71
literary skills of, 64, 65, 253

literati acting as, 68–71
literati influencing, 64–67, 250, 256, 257, 278, 281
literati patronizing, 47, 48, 49, 71, 72, 73, 77, 108
ordination ceremonies performed by, 31, 270–71
patriarchal authority of, 241
textual communities and, 249–56
Chan monastery, 11, 12. *See also* dharma transmission monasteries
Chan Pure Regulation (*qinggui*), 4, 12, 145
Chan rhetoric, 273, 275, 281, 288
Changshou monastery, 98
Chan, Wing-tsit, 68
Chanzong zhengmai (by Rujin), 32
Chao Jiong, as example of literati's religious reading, 56
Chaozong Tongren
Feiyin Tongrong and, 130–31
Miyun Yuanwu and, 130–31
Chow, Kai-wing, 107, 387n8
Chaves, Jonathan, 383n40
Chenghua emperor, 35
Chengzong emperor of the Yuan dynasty, 356n15
Chen Yuan, 43, 219, 371n97
on Chan Buddhism in Yunnan and Guizhou, 97, 104
on controversies, 113, 131, 132, 133, 207, 306, 310, 311, 331
Chen Zhichao, 17
Ch'ien, Edward, 363n9
childlike mind (*tongxin*), 51
Chinese Buddhism, 266, 267, 269, 270, 271
Chan Buddhism and, 273–76
Future revival of, 283–85
homogeneity in, 274
jiao division of, in the Ming dynasty, 22, 23, 146, 383n38
Lineage model of, 275–76
local model of, 266–67, 276
as mixture of doctrinal studies, esotericism, meditation, and Pure Land practice, 273, 275
modern and contemporary, 14, 160–61, 245, 260, 266, 267, 269, 270, 271, 273, 283, 381n15
pattern of revival of, 280–83
power structure lacking in, 266–67, 273, 276
Chiyan, 222, 296
Ch'oe Pu, 396n23
Chongzhen emperor, 113, 202
Christianity, 90, 197, 262, 273, 274, 282, 307, 309, 365n36, 369n91, 372n25, 380n63, 387n10, 388n3, 398n17
Chuanfa zhengzong ji (by Qisong), 216–18
Chuiwan Guangzhen, 37, 362n69
Chün-fang Yü, 22, 33, 40, 42, 43
Chushi Fanqi, 43

Cisheng, Dowager Empress (Madame Li), 22
  Buddhism recovery stimulated by, 24–25
Cizhou Fangnian, 6, 71–72
Clunas, Craig, 55
Confucianism, 13, 21, 35, 56, 73, 88, 96, 163,
    194–95, 216, 255
  Buddhism and, 14, 47, 60, 74, 279, 369n94
  Chan monks and, 253
  codes of behavior of, 49
  eremitism in, 84
  neo-, 49, 195
  self-cultivation in, 50
  Taoism/Buddhism integrated with, 50
Controversies/disputes
  in Chan Buddhism, 7–8, 15, 113–14, 120, 121,
    122, 201, 222, 223, 245, 287, 288, 297
  Chan text interpretations creating, 249
  Chen Yuan on, 113, 131, 132, 133, 207, 306, 310,
    311, 331
  as index to religious and social changes, 8,
    287
  over property at Shanquan monastery, 310
  purpose of, 8
  for social networking, 15
  textual nature of, 245–46, 248
cult of patriarchs, 12

Daguan Tanying, 315, 330
Dahui Zonggao, 85, 116, 229, 250, 258,
    356n15
  popularity of, 5
  influence in the late Ming, 5, 36–37, 40, 43,
    130
  literati and, 54, 63, 74
  Yongzheng's exclusion of, 174, 258
Dangui Jinshi, 229, 270
  Daowu debate and, 229
Danxia Tianran, Yongzheng emperor criticizing,
    174, 386n35
Daowu debate, 7–8, 15, 187, 188, 189–90, 191,
    210, 231, 291–94. See also Feiyin Tongrong;
    lineage(s); Tianhuang Daowu; Tianwang
    Daowu
  Caodong monks and, 227–35
  comparing inscriptions in, 319
  Dangui Jinshi and, 229
  evidence against two Daowus in, 324–30
  Japan and, 238–41
  Juefan Huihong and, 315–16
  literati and, 197–98, 235–38
  modern scholarship on, 330–32
  Muchen Daomin and, 200–201
  Shichao Daning and, 227
  support for two Daowus in, 311–23
  Weizhi Zhikai and, 232–35
  Weizhong Jingfu and, 227–28
  Yongjue Yuanxian and, 228
  Yongzheng and, 174
  Zhang Shangying and, 316–18

Daoyuan, dharma transmission diagram
    according to, 189f
Daozhe Chaoyuan, 99, 374n43
Darnton, Robert, 253
Datian Tongli, 26
Da Xinglong monastery, 26, 278
Da Xingshan monastery, 236
Deng Huoqu, 100–101
Deqing monastery, 88
Deshan Xuanjian, 189, 194, 198, 202, 204, 240,
    292, 317, 318, 326, 388n28
  inscription of, 329
  Yongzheng emperor criticizing, 74, 386n35
devotional practices, 40, 57, 277
  textual spirituality vs., 54, 58, 64, 82
dharma robe, 138–39
Dharma-spreading Spring (Hongfa quan), 266f
dharma transmission, 4, 5, 17, 32, 33, 37–40, 43,
    94, 106, 109, 187, 281. See also Daowu
    debate; lineage(s)
  Caodong, 36, 72, 201–2, 234, 267
  Certificate (yuanliu), 139f, 381n15
  Chan principles and, 135, 137–40
  confusion of, 8, 34–40
  consistency of teaching and practice and, 38,
    114
  debates about, 7, 194, 195–205, 207
  diagram of, according to Daoyuan, 189f
  diagram of, according to Feiyin Tongrong, 190f
  diagram of, according to Kokan Shiren, 240f
  disputed Linji, 39f
  evidence of, 36, 233
  Feiyin Tongrong's, 92
  Feiyin Tongrong's definition of, 210, 211, 212,
    213, 393n26
  Hanshan Deqing questioning value of, 41
  Hanyue Fazang's, 119, 120, 151
  history of, 6
  institutional implication of, 258–62
  integrating function of, 274, 275, 276
  Linji, 36–38, 39f, 85, 128, 234, 267, 301, 302,
    305, 306, 309
  literati accepting, 84
  literati promoting, 71–73
  Miyun Yuanwu's, 6, 301–6
  monasteries, 208, 216, 259, 261, 262, 276,
    296, 393n27
  as one of two aspects of Chan transmission,
    137–38, 140
  through personal acquaintance, 211
  by proxy (daifu), 10, 34, 210, 212, 258, 259,
    260, 393n26
  by remote succession (yaosi), 10, 34, 35, 210,
    212, 258, 259, 260
  of Shaolin monastery, 36
  standard/authenticity of, 10, 12
  strength of, 270
  strict definition of, 6, 45, 210, 211, 212, 213,
    233, 258, 259, 273

Tianhuang Daowu/Tianwang Daowu, lines, 191, 193–94, 199–201, 202, 203, 207
value of, questioned, 41
Dinghu monastery, 98, 373n40
doctrinal instruction, 14, 22, 26, 27, 39, 40, 44, 92, 106, 143, 247, 275, 277, 352n25, 395n17. *See also* Buddhist scholasticism
Dōgen, 298
Donggao Xinyue. See Xinyue Xingchou
Dongming monastery, 17, 303
Dongming yilu (by Shanci Tongji), 17, 38*f*, 303. *See also* Shanci Tongji
Dongming zudeng lu. See *Dongming yilu*
Dong Qichang, 200
Dongshan Liangjia, 5
Dumen monastery, 35
Duoduo (Prince Yu), 80
Duzhan Xingying, 393n26
dynasty
    early Ming, 5, 12, 16, 17, 22, 28, 32, 198
    early Qing, 15, 21, 114, 132, 219, 256
    late Ming, 9, 13, 14, 15, 16, 21, 22, 24, 29, 31, 32, 47, 49, 53, 59, 62, 63, 64, 71, 73, 94, 114, 118, 188, 197, 235, 255
    late Tang, 116, 141, 190
    Liao, 359n38
    mid-Ming, 12, 21, 32, 277
    Ming, 3, 5, 6, 13, 17, 22, 25, 57, 77, 84, 103, 142, 146, 208, 216, 299
    Qing, 5, 6, 17, 28, 84, 104, 109, 163–64, 165, 197, 235, 257, 282
    Song, 3, 4, 6, 7, 11, 12, 16, 22, 25, 36, 57, 62, 85, 169, 196, 249, 250, 282, 284, 314–15
    Southern Ming, 78, 79, 80, 97, 102, 103, 104, 108, 365n36, 369n92, 370n96, 375n62
    Southern Song, 5, 85, 217, 300, 301, 319, 322, 323
    Tang, 4, 6, 7, 10, 11, 12, 16, 85, 140, 145, 187, 188, 197, 225, 277, 311, 313
    Yuan, 3, 5, 12, 22, 36, 319

Eastern Zhejiang, 48, 76, 78, 79, 82, 83, 84, 86, 102, 207
    Chan revival and, 55–63
    literati in, 51, 72–73, 77, 252
Eberhard, Wolfram, 23
economic growth and Buddhist revival in the late Ming, 48–49
E'ertai, 171, 172, 173
elite culture, 54, 282
    love of reading/writing in, 55, 56, 281
    conspicuous consumption in, 54
Elman, Benjamin, 194, 255, 257
emperor(s). *See also specific emperors*
    Qing, 163–64
    religiousness of, 163–64
    setting boundaries for religion, 256–58
emptiness, 81, 148, 169, 393n2

encounter dialogues (*jiyuan wenda*), 9, 35–36, 52, 57, 60, 70, 94, 123, 176, 249, 255, 277
    criticism of, 158–60
    enlightenment and, 135, 136, 157
    Hanyue Fazang's, with Miyun Yuanwu, 152–56
    Miyun Yuanwu interpreting, with Hanyue Fazang, 156–57
    as public performance, 9
    as spontaneous practice, 9, 36
    theatrical aspect of, 158–60, 161
    of Wuming Huijing, 96
enlightenment, 47, 101, 109, 229
    arrogance created by, 134
    encounter dialogue and, 135, 136, 157
    evaluating, 135, 136, 143
    Feiyin Tongrong and lineage *vs.*, 213
    of Hanyue Fazang, 119, 377n18
    literati and, 55, 68
    of Miyun Yuanwu, 86
    objectification of, 136, 140, 143
    obstacles for, 80
    personal, of mind as one of two aspects of Chan trasnmission, 137–38, 140
    politics and, 182, 183
    publishing, experiences, 143
    seal of the recognition (*yinke*) of, 118
    through self-cultivation, 40–41, 59
    subjective, 144
    sudden, 4, 9, 12, 41, 49, 107, 122, 135, 141
    taken for granted, 137
    of Wunian Shenyou, 69–70
    of Yongzheng emperor, 166–68, 169, 257
esotericism, 145–51, 256, 273, 275, 386n47
    of perfect circle, 151, 271
    Hanyue Fazang's, 147–51
evidential scholarship, 195–96, 197
    forgery detection in, 195, 197
    literati and, 196, 198–99
    monks using, 194–96
Famen chugui (by Weizhong Jingfu), 227
Fang Yizhi, 104, 105. *See also* Wuke Dazhi.
Farquhar, David, 166
Faure, Bernard, 248
Fayan school, 8, 32, 123, 188, 189, 209, 230, 231, 291, 294, 295
Feiyin Tongrong, 5, 7, 15, 40, 86, 131, 195, 196, 210, 239, 241, 253, 258, 259, 301, 306, 313. See also *Wudeng yantong*
    accusations against, 214–15, 221, 222, 294, 295
    anti-Christian essays by, 398n21
    biography of, 92–93, 372n26
    calligraphy, 255*f*
    Caodong monks and, 212, 214, 220, 221, 222–23
    Chan lineage changed by, 187, 211, 212–18, 222, 225
    Chan masters criticized by, 308–9

Feiyin Tongrong, (continued)
   Chaozong Tongren and, 130–31
   defending Wudeng yantong, 215–18
   definition of dharma transmission and, 210,
      211, 212, 213, 393n26
   dharma heirs of, 93, 97, 99, 119, 226
   dharma transmission diagram according to,
      190f
   dharma transmission of, 92
   Jesuits and, 309
   lawsuit against, 8, 15, 17, 187, 207, 214, 218,
      219, 221–22
   letters from, to Yinyuan Longqi, 17
   lineage vs. enlightenment and, 213
   literati and, 215, 217, 218, 219, 221
   longevity pagoda of, 268f
   Miyun Yuanwu and, 92, 187, 213, 262,
      265–66
   Muchen Daomin and, 212, 213, 260–61, 308
   Memorial Pavilion (Feiyin ting) built by
      Japanese pilgrims, 269f
   polemical essays by, 208
   police chief Wang's public notice against,
      295–96
   portrait of, 93f
   prophecy interpreted by, 311–12
   Ruibai Mingxue and, 308
   warrant for, 222
Feiyin chanshi bieji (by Feiyin Tongrong), 17,
   209f, 306
Feng Fang, 387n8
Fenyang Shanzhao, 137
fire, 96, 148, 149
The Five Superfluous Generations in the
   Caodong School, 37f, 297–301
Fofa zhenglun (by Zhou Rudeng), 74
Foulk, Griffith, 275
Fozu gangmu (by Zhu Shi'en), 200
Fu, Prince, 80
function (yong), 170
Furong Daokai, 36, 37c, 93, 234, 298, 299, 300

Gaofeng Yuanmiao, 5, 114–15, 118, 154
Gaoming ("Youxi") monastery, 27
Gaoquan Xingdun, 393n26, 395n13
Gaoyuan Mingyu, 26
Geng Dingli, 252
Geng Dingxiang, 52, 66, 252
gentry, monasteries and, 47–48, 49, 108,
   261–62, 361n63
Genxin Xingmi, 374n41
Gimello, Robert, 56, 146, 282, 358n28
gods, humans and, 395n18
Gomizunoo, Japanese emperor, 393n26
Gongchen, 318
government, 241, 281
   control in the Ming dynasty, 28
   policies in the Ming dynasty, 23, 24
Grant, Beata, 372n14

Great Learning, 50, 63, 197
Griffiths, Paul, on religious reading, 55, 59
Guangxiao monastery, 98
Guan Zhidao, 50, 252
Guishan Lingyou, 5, 116, 178
Guo Limei (Guo Ningzhi), 117, 199, 355n4,
   366n48
Gushan monastery, 96
Gu Xiancheng, 88
Guxin Ruxin, as reformer of ordination
   ceremonies, 30–31
Gu Yanwu, 105

Haichao yin, 356n20
Haiyin monastery, 23
Haizhou Ci, 17, 27
   debate, 301–6
   inscription and, debate, 304
Haizhou Puci, 37, 302, 303, 305
Haizhou Yongci, 304, 305
Halperin, Mark, 57, 249, 250
Hanpu Xingcong, 97, 98, 164
Hanshan Deqing, 4, 7, 13, 23, 24, 26, 27, 34, 65,
   76, 83, 84, 105, 272
   dharma transmission value questioned by, 41
   new Linji lineage criticized by, 42–43
   practices of, 40
   views on meditation, 40–41
Hanyue Fazang, 5, 7, 17, 26, 29, 31, 199, 247,
   270, 271, 372n15, 386n47. See also Wuzong
   yuan
   antagonism between lineages of Miyun and,
      129–30
   on beating and shouting practice, 157
   biography of, 88, 90, 114–15, 360n46, 377n18
   Chan Buddhism interpretation of, 114, 115,
      117, 121, 135, 137–40, 151, 157
   Chan Buddhism systematized/theorized by,
      142, 144
   cognitive understanding used by, 141, 178
   dharma heirs of, 90, 129, 371n12
   dharma transmission of, 119, 120, 151
   female disciples of, 90
   Juefan Huihong and, 137
   letters between, and Miyun Yuanwu, 125–26
   letters between, and Tianyin Yuanxiu, 123–25,
      140
   Miyun Yuanwu interpreting encounter
      dialogue with, 156–57
   Miyun Yuanwu's dispute with, 7, 15, 113–14,
      120, 121–22, 123, 124, 128–29, 135, 136,
      140–42, 257, 302
   Miyun Yuanwu's encounter dialogue with,
      152–56
   Miyun Yuanwu's relationship with, 118,
      119–20
   need for master rejected by, 138
   numerology and, 142
   Patriarch Chan represented by, 117

principle and, 135, 137, 138, 141, 161
Rite for Releasing the Hungry Ghosts (shishi)
    and, 145, 147–51, 179
three mysteries/three essentials and, 141, 144,
    179
on yijue yingchan, 140–41
Yongzheng emperor and Miyun Yuanwu's
    dispute with, 163, 176–77, 181, 183, 184
Yongzheng emperor on, 179–81, 257
Hasebe Yūkei, 6, 22, 219
Heart Sūtra, 25
He Xinyin, 52, 53
Histories of Lamp Transmissions (dengshi), 5.
    See also Chan genealogies
historiography, Buddhist, 8, 17, 34, 194, 195, 197,
    205, 210, 215–17, 227, 230, 240
Hobsbawn, Eric, 11
Hong Chengchou, 373n38
Hongjie fayi (by Hanyue Fazang), 31
Hongren, the fifth patriarch, 138
Hongzhi emperor, 363n8
Hongzhi Zhengjue, 250
Hou Chong
    on Azhali in Yunnan, 373n36
    on Jizu mountain in Yunnan, 383n38
Houses, Chan monasteries divided by, 33, 361n57
Huangbo monastery, 77, 92, 261, 266, 268, 269
Huangbo qinggui (by Yinyuan Longqi), 272
Huangbo Wunian chanshi fuwen (by Wunian
    Shenyou), 367n60
Huangbo Xiyun, 127, 142, 153, 189f, 190f, 240f,
    356n15, 381n1
Huang Duanbo, 118, 188, 200, 220, 309
    antinomianism and, 80
    martyr death of, 79, 80, 81, 369n94
    Miyun Yuanwu and, 77–78, 201–4, 291–94
    Muchen Daomin and, 102, 201
    nonduality and, 79, 80
    patronage of, 77
    translation of public notice by, 291–94
    Yu Dacheng and, 203–4
Huang, Pei, 166–67, 168, 325, 332
Huang Yuqi, 79, 369n90, 380n65
Huang Zongxi, 43, 52, 75, 79, 83, 105, 236, 314,
    328–29
    on Chan Buddhism, 31, 32, 41,
    on Chan Buddhism and loyalism, 369–70n94
    on Chan and Confucianism, 75–76
    on Daowu debate, 193, 235, 236, 314, 328–29,
    Qian Qianyi and, 130, 132
    on Taizhou scholars, 52–53, 74
Huanyou Zhengchuan, 6, 27, 40, 85, 234, 301,
    305, 310, 371n5
    dharma heir of, 361n62
    as Miyun Yuanwu's master, 86–87
Huayan helun (by Li Tongxuan), 26. See also Li
    Tongxuan
Huayan school, 3, 13, 21, 25, 26
Huayan Sūtra, 66

Hufa zhengdeng lu, 15, 17, 207
    table of contents of, 219–20, 221f
Huineng, 34, 67, 115, 124, 138, 141, 180, 188,
    189f, 190f, 210, 240f, 271, 293, 312, 329,
    366n41. See also Platform Sūtra
    verses of, altered, 378n30
Huishan Jiexian, 103
    Tianwang monastery inscription by, 226–27,
    228
Huqiu Shaolong, 85, 301
Hymes, Robert, 395n18

ICang-skya masters, 164, 167
    Yongzheng and the second, 164 167, 168
    Yongzheng and the third, 164
India, 151
intellectualism, 194, 197, 256, 288
    Chan Buddhism and, 275
    transition towards, in the eighteenth century,
    246
"invented tradition," 11–12
Ishii Shūdō, 87, 331
isolation, policy of, 23, 258

Japan, 15, 17, 93, 99, 121, 136, 148, 261, 270, 271,
    288
    Daowu debate in, 238–41
    Feiyin Tongrong's memorial pavilion built by
    pilgrims from, 269f
    Feiyin Tongrong requesting copies of Wudeng
    yantong sent from, 239
    Wudeng yantong reprinted in, 238
    Xinyue Xingchou emigrating to, 99, 374n45
    Yanagida Seizan on Wudeng yantong in, 239
    Yinyuan Longqi emigrating to, 99, 238,
    391n34
Jesuit missionaries, 16, 307, 309
Jiajing emperor, 22, 24, 113, 359n41
    prohibiting ordination, 29–30
Jialing Xingyin, Yongzheng and, 164–65, 167,
    168, 257
Jianmo bianyi lu (by Yongzheng emperor), 7, 106.
    See also Yongzheng emperor
    Comparison between, and Dayi juemi lu, 177
    Content of, 177–82
Jianyue Duti, 30, 31
Jiaowai biechuan (by Guo Limei), 199. See also
    Guo Limei
Jiashan monastery, 380n70
Jiaxing Buddhist canon, 16, 25, 251
Jin Bao. See Dangui Jinshi
Jingde chuandeng lu (by Daoyuan), 5, 7, 8, 32,
    216–18, 188, 202, 215, 222, 291, 315, 318,
    319, 323, 331
    Tianhuang Daowu and, 326
Jingde emperor, 5
Jingling school of poems, 380n63
Jingshan canon. See Jiaxing Buddhist canon
Jingyin monastery, 298

Jingyin Zijue, 298–300. *See also* The Five Superfluous Generations in the Caodong school
Jingzhong jianguo xu denglu (by Weibai), 318
Jinling fancha zhi (by Ge Yinliang), 24
Jin Sheng, 79, 375n53
  biography of, 369n91
  converted to Christianity, 369n91
Jinsu monastery, 93, 132, 151, 153
  as subtemple of Tiantong monastery, 262
Jinxie bian (by Yuan Hongdao), 60, 61
Jiqi Hongchu, 90, 129, 222, 371n12, 375n53, 380n68, 389n27
  Muchen Daomin's dispute with, 132–33
  Disputes settled by, 129, 130
Jones, Charles, 366n42
Jude Hongli, 103, 309, 310, 375n53, 380n71
Juefan Huihong, 114–15, 118, 137, 154, 192, 232, 313, 331
  Daowu debate and, 315–16
  Hanyue Fazang and, 137
Juelang Daosheng, 83, 105, 119, 131, 209, 229, 231, 299, 373n34, 377n17, 390n11
  criticizing literati, 58, 65
  disciples of, 98, 99, 103, 104, 375n65, 391n44
  philosophy of, 96
Jushō tradition (Japan), 99. *See also* Xinyue Xingchou

Kaiō Hōkō, 373n26
kaitang shuofa, 9. *See also* ceremony of ascending the hall
Kaixian monastery, 354n50
Kangxi emperor, 6, 164, 168, 229, 354n41, 360n70
Keirin Sūshin, 238, 371n30
Kishimoto Mio, 373n27
kōans, 9, 12, 40, 41, 54, 57, 92, 94, 137, 250
  reenactment of, 41, 106, 160
Kokan Shiren, 331
  Diagram of Chan Dharma Transmission according to, 240*f*
  radical change of Chan genealogy by, 240
  Yinyuan Longqi discovering works by, 239
Komazawa University, 331
Kongyin Zhencheng, 27, 306
Kuangyuan Benkao, 98
Kusumoto Bunyū, 68

Laṅkāvatāra Sūtra, 25
Lantsa scripts, 149, 149*f*
lectures, public, 73, 76, 101
lecture meetings (*jianghui*), 49, 73, 74, 86, 101
legal codes about religion in the Ming dynasty, 219
leisure class, canon of tastes of, 54–55
  Thorstein Veblen on, 54
Lengyan huijie (by Tianru Weize), 358n20
Lengyan monastery, 25
Lewis, Mark, 246

Li'an monastery, 164, 380n70
  Jialing Xingyin and, 165
  Yongzheng patronizing, 165
Lian Ruizhi, 119
Li Ao, 326, 401n37
Liao dynasty, 359n38
lineage(s), 10, 215, 230–31, 235, 281
  antagonism between Hanyue Fazang's and Miyun Yuanwu's, 129–30
  Caodong, 201–3, 208, 209, 210–11, 229, 234, 293–94, 295, 297–301
  continuity by remote succession, 10, 34, 35, 210, 212, 258, 259, 260
  continuity by transmission by proxy, 10, 34, 210, 212, 258, 259, 260, 393n26
  Feiyin Tongrong and enlightenment *vs.*, 213
  Feiyin Tongrong changing Chan, 187, 211, 212–18, 222, 225
  Hanshan Deqing criticizing Linji, 42–43
  Linji, 201–3, 208, 209, 210–11, 229, 234, 267, 293–94, 295, 301, 302, 305, 306, 309
  Longtan Chongxin's, 329–30
  Miyun Yuanwu's, 97, 302–6
  Nanyue Huairang's, 311, 312
  Tianyin Yuanxiu's, 85, 98, 371n6
  unknown (*sifa weixiang*), 7, 43, 187, 201, 212, 214, 218, 301
  Wuming Huijing's, 6, 95–96
  Xuejiao Yuanxin's, 6, 35, 85, 218, 309, 355n6
  Zhanran Yuancheng's, 6, 36, 94–95
  Zongbao Daodu's, 98
Linggu monastery, 30
Linjian lu (by Huihong), 191, 192, 228, 237, 328, 331
  Tianwang Daowu's biography in, 315–16
Linji lu (by Linji Yixuan), 136, 142, 148
Linji masters/monks, 43, 77, 85, 193, 194, 222, 229, 259, 288, 297, 301, 302, 306
Linji school, 6, 12, 14, 32, 34, 39, 51, 77, 84, 94, 98, 106, 118, 119, 123, 143, 208, 209, 210–11, 229, 234, 267, 293–94, 295, 301, 302, 305, 306, 309
  dharma transmission of, 36–38, 39*f*, 85, 128, 234, 267, 301, 302, 305, 306, 309
  Hanshan Deqing criticizing, 42–43
  principle of, 135–37, 140, 153, 154, 308
Linji Yixuan, 7, 9, 43, 78, 115, 128, 136, 137, 142, 148, 153, 306, 356n15
Linji zhengzong ji (by Yuanwu Keqin), 356n15
Linji zongzhi (by Juefan Huihong), 115, 137
  translation of, 381n5
Li Rifang, 294
literati, Confucian, 25, 26, 45, 195, 225, 265, 279
  authority in textual practice, 48, 102, 246
  becoming Chan masters, 68–71
  becoming monks, 100–101, 102–4
  Chan Buddhism's rise and, 13, 14, 21, 27, 45, 47–48, 49, 50, 72–73, 100, 249–50, 289
  Chan literature and, 48, 53–54, 55–56, 57, 73, 246

Chan literature edited by, 61
Chan literature composed by, 59–64, 82
Chan masters patronized by, 47, 48, 49, 71, 72, 73, 77, 108
Chan monks influenced by, 64–67, 250, 256, 257, 278, 281
Daowu debate and, 197–98, 235–38
dharma transmission accepted by, 84
dharma transmission promoted by, 71–73
enlightenment and, 55, 68
evidential scholarship and, 196, 198–99
Feiyin Tongrong and, 215, 217, 218, 219, 221
knowledge/action issue and, 60
leisure class of, 54–55
monasteries supported by, 72
patronage of, 77, 108
reading practices of, 55–56, 57–58, 59, 82, 281
textual communities and, 249–56
textual spirituality of, 35–46
Śuraṃgama Sūtra and, 50, 57, 59, 131
Li Tongxuan, 26
liturgical tradition, 271
Liu Daozhen, 378n37
Liu Xianting, 236–37
Liu Zongzhou, 74, 78, 81
Li Zhi, 63, 101, 252
   biography of, 50–51
   as Chan teacher, 68, 69–71
   intellectual community forming around, 50, 252
   literati gathering with, in Yongqing monastery, 70–71
   shaving head, 71, 101
   thought of, 51
   Wunian Shenyou and, 68–69, 70
   Yuan Hongdao and, 52, 63
Li Zicheng, 78, 369n89
localist turn, 284–85
Longqing emperor, 73, 113
Longtan Chongxin, 188, 198, 199, 291, 292, 311, 322
   biography of, 324–26, 332
   lineage of, 329–30
   significance of, 8, 189
Lotus Sūtra, 50
Lou Jinyuan, 171
Lumen monastery, 298. *See also* the Five Superfluous Generations in the Caodong school
Luo Rufang, 50, 52, 70, 74
Lu, Regent, 79
Lü Liuliang, 177, 180
Lü Xiaqing, 191, 292, 317, 318
Lü Zuqian, 216

Ma'anshan monastery, 359n41, 371n97
"mad Chan" (*kuangchan*), 52
   Taizhou school and, 50–53
   Huang Zongxi's comment on, 52–53

Madhyamaka theory, 27
Mahāparinirvanāna Sūtra, 142
Mahāyāna tradition, 30, 31, 59, 138
Manchu rule, 3, 4, 91, 97, 99, 103, 106, 109, 164, 181, 257, 310, 360
   surrender to, 79, 80, 84
Mañjusrī, bodhisattva, 30
Manpukuji monastery (Japan), 9, 17, 88, 89f, 93f, 100f, 139f, 209f, 238, 255f, 261, 357n26, 393n26, 395n13
mantra, 145, 147, 149
Maoxi Xingsen, 101, 171, 174
martyr death, of Huang Duanbo and Qi Biaojiao, 79, 80, 81, 349n94
Ma Shiqi, 79, 348n89
Ma Shiying, 80
master-disciple relationship, 5, 9, 114, 143
Mazu Daoyi, 8, 154, 199, 237, 239, 240, 241, 291, 292, 324, 388n28
   dharma heirs of, 188, 189, 201, 313, 318, 322
   epitaph of, 313
   prophecy about, 311–12
meditation, 12, 13, 21, 50, 92, 116, 273, 275
   cells (*chanku*), 40
   on critical phrases (*huatou*), 14, 40, 63, 106
   Hanshan Deqing's views on, 40–41
   silent, 250
   stages/passes of, articulated by Yongzheng, 169–70
Mengtang Tan'e, 399n16
Mengshan Rite for Feeding the Hungry Ghosts (*Mengshan shishi yi*), 271, 383n39
Miaofeng Zhenjue, 27
migration, overseas, 98–99, 108–9
   Chan Buddhism and, 98–99
mind and principle, in enlightenment experience, 138–39
mind-to-mind transmission, 34
Ming dynasty, 3, 5, 6, 13, 17, 22, 25, 57, 77, 84, 103, 142, 146, 208, 216, 299
   early, 5, 12, 16, 17, 22, 28, 32, 198
   late, 9, 13, 14, 15, 16, 21, 22, 24, 29, 31, 32, 47, 49, 53, 59, 62, 63, 64, 71, 73, 94, 114, 118, 188, 197, 235, 255
   mid, 12, 21, 32, 277
   Southern, 78, 79, 80, 97, 102, 103, 104, 108, 365n36, 369n92, 370n96, 375n62
Ming History (Mingshi), 257
Ming loyalists, 77, 84, 91, 98, 103, 201
   Chan Buddhism and, 79–81, 369–70n94
Ministry of Rites, 304
   disrobing of Buddhist monks/nuns by, 24
Miyun Yuanwu, 5, 6, 9, 10, 13, 14, 17, 31, 40, 49, 73, 75–76, 83, 102, 123, 199, 200, 234, 253, 258, 301, 303, 330, 356n20
   antagonism between lineages of Hanyue Fazang and, 129–30
   biography of, 86–87
   calligraphy, 89f, 254f

Miyun Yuanwu, (*continued*)
    Chaozong Tongren and, 130–31
    criticizing Qingyuan Xingsi, 396n2, 397n3
    Daowu debate and, 200, 201
    debate between Jesuits and, 307
    debate between Ruibai Mingxue and, 307
    debate over the epitaph of, 131–32
    dharma heirs of, 85–86, 88, 90, 97, 98, 119,
        136, 208, 259, 260–61, 308, 377n17
    encounter dialogue with Hanyue interpreted
        by, 156–57
    Feiyin Tongrong and, 92, 187, 213, 262,
        265–66
    Hanyue Fazang's dispute with, 7, 15, 113–14,
        120, 121–22, 123, 124, 128–29, 135, 136,
        140–42, 257, 302
    Hanyue Fazang's encounter dialogue with,
        152–56
    Hanyue Fazang's relationship with, 118,
        119–20
    Huang Duanbo and, 77–78, 201–4, 291–94
    Huanyou Zhengchuan as master of, 86–87
    interpreting Chan Buddhism, 43, 120, 126,
        135, 136, 140, 142, 151
    influence in Southwest China, 97
    lack of education of, 118–19, 125, 377n16
    letters between, and Hanyue Fazang, 125–26
    lineage of, 97, 302–6
    Muchen Daomin and, 201
    Muchen Daomin editing works of, 374n5,
        377n22
    polemical essays of, 120–21, 122, 126–27,
        306–7
    portrait of, 89*f*
    principle and, 141, 142, 144,
    Qi Family and, 78
    talents of, 87
    Tao Wangling and, 86–87
    Tathāgata Chan represented by, 117
    Tiantong monastery and, 77, 87–88
    Yongzheng emperor and Hanyue Fazang's
        dispute with, 163, 176–77, 181, 183, 184
    Yongzheng emperor as reincarnation of, 182
    Yongzheng emperor praising, 182*f*
    Zhou Rudeng and, 86
Miyun Yuanwu chanshi Tiantong zhishuo, 17. See
    also *Tiantong zhishuo.*
monastery(ies)
    Ayuwang, 23, 27, 49, 73, 77
    Bailin, 164, 165, 167, 257, 380n70
    Bao'en, 25, 26, 65
    Baofeng, 95
    Baolin, 76
    Caoxi, 34, 272, 361n60
    Chan, 11, 12
    Changshou, 98
    consolidation of, in the early Ming dynasty,
        340n57
    Da Xinglong, 26, 278

    Da Xingshan, 236
    Deqing, 88
    destruction of, 24
    devided into houses, 33
    dharma transmission, 36, 259, 276
    Dinghu, 98, 373n40
    Dongming, 17, 303
    Dumen, 35
    Gaoming ("Youxi"), 27
    gentry and, 261–62
    Guangxiao, 98
    Gushan, 96
    Haiyin, 23
    Huangbo, 77, 92, 261, 266, 268*f*, 269*f*
    institutional framework of, 261, 273, 275, 288,
        363n2
    Jiashan, 380n70
    Jingyin, 298
    Jinsu, 93, 132
    Kaixian, 374n50
    Lengyan, 25
    Li'an, 164, 380n70
    Linggu, 30
    literati supporting, 72
    Lumen, 298
    Ma'anshan, 359n41, 371n97
    Manpukuji, 9, 17, 88, 89*f*, 93*f*, 100*f*, 139*f*, 209*f*,
        238, 255*f*, 261, 357n26, 393n26, 395n13
    Nanjing, 24
    network of, 11, 269, 270
    Nianhua, 171
    Xishan jietai si, 28, 359n38
    Pingyang, 310
    property of, 266–67
    Puyang, 35
    Qingyuan, 104
    rebuilding, 268
    reviving Buddhist, 49
    routine in, 272, 275
    rules, monastic, 271–72, 275, 366n51, 393n12
    Sakugen Shūryō observing Chinese, 278,
        279
    Shanquan, dispute over property at, 310
    Shaolin, 6, 36, 94
    Sheng'en, 122
    Shouchang, 95
    taxation of, in the early Ming, 23
    Tanzhe monastery, 359n37
    Tianhuang, 188, 198, 293, 321
    Tianjie, 40, 65
    Tianning (T'ien-ning), 29
    Tiantong, 14, 33, 49, 73, 77, 87–88, 89*f*, 182,
        266*f*, 267*f*, 356n20
    Tianwang, 193, 225–27, 321, 327
    White Horse, 327
    Xuedou, 202, 291
    Yishan, 304
    Yongqing, 71
    Yunmen, 73, 78, 95

Yunqi, 73
Yuquan, 35, 361n63
Zhaoqing, 24, 33, 359n41
Zhulin, 324
monastic discipline, decline in, 33, 363n2
Monks, Rulers, and Literati (by Welter), 250
moon-disc, 147, 148
morality, 67
  debasement of, 113
  good/evil and, 74–75
  perfection of, 51
  unconventional behavior and, 51–52
Muchen Daomin, 5, 101, 127, 131, 202, 218, 220,
    259, 309–10, 361n62. See also *Chandeng
    shipu.*
  autobiography of, 374n50
  biography of, 90–92, 102
  as Buddhist sinner, 91
  Chan genealogies and, 201
  Daowu debate and, 200–201
  Feiyin Tongrong and, 212, 213, 260–61, 308
  Jiqi Hongchu's dispute with, 132–33
  as literary monk, 102
  Miyun Yuanwu and, 201
  Miyun Yuanwu's works edited by, 374n51,
    377n22
  Shunzhi emperor and, 90, 91, 98, 101
  Yongzheng emperor denouncing, 176
mudrā, 145, 147, 149
Mu Konghui, 363n8
Muyun Tongmen, polemical essays
    of, 132–33

Nanjio Bunyū, 283
Nanxun lu (by Deng Huoqu), 101
Nanyang Huizhong, 144, 151
Nanyue Huairang, 8, 188, 204, 217, 233, 237,
    292, 301
  inscription of, 313
  lineage of, 311, 312
Naquin, Susan, 26, 279
Nattier, Jan, 357n22
National Buddhist Association, 270
nature inclusion (*xingju*), 27
networking, 11, 15, 269, 270
Nguyên Phúc Chu, the Vietnamese king, 99
Nianhua monastery, 171
Noguchi Yoshitaka, 118
nonduality, 49, 74–75, 369n94
  Huang Duanbo and, 79, 80
Northern School, during the Ming, 35, 38, 39,
    361n64
Nukariya Kaiten, 330
numerology, Hanyue Fazang and, 142

Ōbaku school (Japan), 87, 93, 99, 238, 239, 253,
    261, 270, 272, 393n26
Oboi, 171
On Friendship (by Matteo Ricci), 365n36

ordination, 165, 359n38, 359n41
  ban on, 28
  bodhisattva, 31
  ceremonies, 28, 44, 247, 394n6
  ceremonies reformed by Guxin Ruxin, 30–31
  certificate, 385n10
  Chan monks performing, ceremonies, 270–71
  men/women intermingling during, 29
  prohibition of, platforms, 29–30
  Qing government giving up control of, 165–66
  Triple Platform, 30–31, 99, 166, 247, 267, 270,
    394n4
  Wanshou, platform, 30
Orzech, Charles, 146, 256, 383n36
Ouyi Zhixu, 131, 307, 366n38, 398n17

Pan Lei, 237–38
  Shilian Dashan and, 237
Panshan (or Qingshan) transmission of Tianyin
    Yuanxiu, 85
Patriarch Chan (*Zushi Chan*), 53, 118
  Hanyue Fazang representing, 117
  difference between, and Tathāgata Chan, 115,
    116
perfect circle (*yuanxiang*), 122–23, 124, 126, 129,
    142, 150, 178, 179
  Ajikan and, 148
  esotericism of, 151, 271
  meaning of, 135, 144
  use of, in Chan history, 144
  visualization and, 147–48
Peterson, Willard, 105
Pingyang monastery, 310
pirate invasions, Japanese, 24
Pi wangjiu lueshuo (by Miyun Yuanwu), 114, 122,
    128–29, 303
Platform Sūtra, 5, 67, 86, 124, 138, 141, 271, 312.
    See also Huineng
  Miyun Yuanwu and, 86
  Yuan Hongdao's edition of, 61, 62f
polemical essays, 17, 157, 161, 288, 374n51
  decline in production of, 235
  features of, 133–34
  Feiyin Tongrong's, 208
  Miyun Yuanwu's, 120–21, 122, 126–27, 306–7
  Muyun Tongmen's, 132–33
  quality of, 194
  by Shilian Dashan, 231–32
  textual communities and, 253
Poshan Haiming, 97, 259
power
  redistribution of, 205
  structure lacking in Chinese Buddhism,
    266–67, 273, 276
  structure of Chan Buddhism, 258
Prajñātāra, 312
principle (*zongzhi*), 7, 9
  of Caodong school, 123, 308
  Chan, 135, 137–40, 138, 139

principle (*zongzhi*), (*continued*)
   dharma transmission and, 135, 137–40
   Hanyue Fazang and, 135, 137, 138, 141, 161
   of Linji school, 135–37, 140, 153, 154, 308
   mind and, as two aspects of Chan
     transmission, 138–39
   Miyun Yuanwu's understanding of, 144
print culture, 251, 281
   Chan Buddhism and, 107
Pure Land practice, 9, 13, 21, 33, 40, 64, 84, 106,
   118, 273, 275
   belittled by literati, 66
   Yuan Hongdao and, 75, 346n42
   Yunqi Zhuhong on, 66
Puyang monastery, 35

Qian Bangqi (Dacuo), 104, 360n65
Qianlong emperor, 166, 360n70
Qian Luchan, 133
Qian Qianyi, 131, 159, 160, 338n20
Qian Sule, 79, 349n92
Qi Bansun, 350n97
Qi Biaojia, 73, 126, 350n96, 350n97
   biography of, 78
   Caodong monks and, 78
   inviting Miyun Yuanwu, 77, 78
   Jonathan Spence on, 79
   martyr death of, 79, 81
Qi Chenghan, 78, 126, 348n82
Qi Family, 95
   library of, 348n82
   Minyun Yuanwu and, 78
   patronage of, 78–79, 81
   Zhanran Yuancheng and, 78
Qi Junjia, 73, 78, 126, 129, 359n45
Qing dynasty, 5, 6, 17, 28, 84, 104, 109, 165, 197,
   235, 257, 282
   emperors of, 163–64
Qing dynasty, early, 15, 21, 114, 132, 219, 256
Qingyuan monastery, 104
Qingyuan Xingsi, 188, 201, 203, 233, 237, 291,
   293, 311, 330
   Miyun Yuanwu criticizing, 376n2,
     377n3
Qingzhou Yibian, 299
Qisong, 203, 204, 215, 216, 227, 326,
   362n25
Qiu Yuansu, 201, 229, 292
   doubt of existence of, 327
   identity of, 193, 331–32
   poem by, 314
Qi Xiongjia, 79, 214, 220
Qi Zhijia, 79
Quan Deyu, 313
Qu Ruji, 32, 60, 200, 278. See also
   Zhiyue lu
   Tianwang Daowu discovered by, 198
   converted by Matteo Ricci, 345n36
   observing Vinaya decline, 28

Qu Shigu, 365n36
Qu Shisi, 365n36

reading practices, 107, 392n15
   Chao Jiong's, 56
   literati's, 55–56, 57–58, 59, 82, 281
   Juelang Dasheng's view on, 58
   religious, 53, 54, 55, 56, 59, 62, 82
   Yuan Hongdao's, 62–64
recorded sayings, 4, 9, 13, 16, 21, 32, 57, 62, 85,
   136, 199, 245, 247, 256, 267
religious suppression, in early Ming, 23
remote succession (*yaosi*), 10, 34, 210, 212, 258,
   259, 260
   dharma transmission by, 10, 34, 35, 210, 212,
     258, 259, 260
   of Xuejiao Yuanxin, 35
renaissance patriarchs, 96
Republican era, 277, 282, 284, 285, 356n20
Ricci, Matteo, 365n36
Rite for Releasing the Hungry Ghosts (*shishi* or
   fang yankou), 144, 218, 248, 271. *See also*
   Mengshan Rite for Feeding the Hungry
   Ghosts
   Hanyue Fazang and, 145, 147–51, 179
   Holmes Welch on, 267
   meaning of, 145
   in the Ming dynasty, 146
   performance of, 146
   use of Siddham or Lantsa scripts in, 148, 149*f*
ritual(s), 12, 143, 148, 149, 395n17. *See also*
   esotericism
   Chan Buddhism and, 247
   esoteric, performance (*jiao*), 22, 35, 247, 248
   performance for the dead, 146
   of Rite for Releasing the Hungry Ghosts,
     144–51, 179, 218, 267, 271
   systematizing/codifying of, 270, 271, 272, 288
romantic perspective, 82, 247, 249, 265, 289
Ruibai Mingxue
   Feiyin Tongrong and, 308
   Miyun Yuanwu's debate with, 307
Ruo'an Tongwen, 85, 380n70

Sakugen Shūryō, traveling in Ming China, 278
Śākyamuni Buddha, 5, 12, 137, 138, 318
Sanmei Jiguang, 31, 394n6
Sanshan Denglai, 362n69
Sanyi Mingyu, 113
   essays by, 214, 215
   lawsuit against Feiyin Tongrong by, 8, 15, 17, 187
Schall von Bell, Adam, Shunzhi emperor and,
   90
scholarship, modern, Daowu debate, 330–32
school(s)
   Caodong, 6, 7, 14, 32, 36, 39, 51, 72, 77, 78, 84,
     92, 93–94, 98, 99, 106, 123, 187, 192,
     201–3, 208, 209, 210–11, 212–18, 234, 267,
     293–94, 295, 297–301, 308

Chan Buddhism's five, 122, 123, 136
Chinese philosophical, 3
Donglin, 88
Fayan, 8, 32, 123, 188, 189, 209, 230, 231, 291, 294, 295
Gong'an, 75
Guiyang, 8, 32, 123, 144, 209
Hongzhou, 141, 190, 284
Huayan, 3, 13, 21, 25, 26
Japanese Sōtō, 99
Linji, 6, 12, 14, 32, 34, 35, 36–38, 39, 42–43, 51, 77, 84, 94, 98, 106, 118, 119, 123, 128, 143, 153, 154, 201–3, 208, 209, 210–11, 229, 234, 267, 293–94, 295, 301, 302, 305, 306, 308, 309
Northern, 35, 38, 283, 361n64
Ōbaku, 87, 93, 99, 238, 239, 253, 261, 270, 272, 393n26
Sanfeng, 181
Southern, 39
Taizhou, 47, 52–53, 73, 74, 101
Tiantai, 3, 13, 21, 25, 27
Vinaya, 21, 24, 28, 30, 98, 165, 247
of Wang Yangming, 82
Yogācāra, 13, 14, 21, 25, 67
Yunmen, 8, 32, 35, 85, 123, 188, 189, 230, 231, 291, 293, 295
Schopen, Gregory, 247, 392n9
self-cultivation, 59
Confucian, 50
enlightenment through, 40–41, 59
as wisdom without teachers (wushizhi), 41
shamanism, 163
Shanci Tongji, 17, 303
Shanghai Library, 17, 38f, 219, 221f, 232, 233f, 375n51, 397n9
Shanhu lin (by Yuan Hongdao), 62, 63, 64
Shanquan monastery, 310
Shaolin lianfang bei, 36
Shaolin monastery, 6, 36, 94
Sheng'en monastery, 122
Shenhui, 115, 141
Shichao Daning, Daowu debate and, 227
Shilian Dashan, 237–38, 390n11
as Juelang Daosheng's dharma heir, 98
Pan Lei and, 237
polemical essays by, 231–32
trip to Vietnam, 99
Shiqi shi xiangjie (by Lü Zuqian), 216
Shishi jigu lue (by Jue'an), 323
Shishi tongjian (by Benjue) (Compendium of Buddhist history), 322
Shitao Yuanji, 103
Shitou Xiqian, 8, 291, 320, 321, 324
Shiyu Mingfang, 78, 95, 208, 227
Shouchang monastery, 95
Shouzun Yuanzhao, Vietnamese Thiên Buddhism and, 98–99

Shuijian Huihai, Tianwang monastery rebuilt by, 226, 228
Shunzhi emperor, 6, 85, 90, 91, 97, 101, 164, 165, 176, 309
Buddhism and, 373n37
calligraphy by, 91f
favoring Xuejiao Yuanxin, 309
Muchen Daomin and, 90, 91, 98, 101
religious belief of, 90
Shuquan ji (by Jiqi Hongchu), 132
Siku quanshu, 257
Sima Guang, 216
Siming Zhili, 27
society, 3
Chan Buddhism and, 84, 105–9, 284, 288
separation from, 23, 258
solitary confinement (biguan), 40, 115
Song dynasty, 3, 4, 6, 7, 11, 12, 16, 22, 25, 36, 57, 62, 85, 169, 196, 249, 250, 282, 284, 314–15
Song gaoseng zhuan (by Zanning), 192, 197, 203, 228, 331
Tianhuang Daowu's biography in, 324–26
Southern Song dynasty, 5
Spence, Jonathan
on Qi Biaojia's death, 79
on Yongzheng's Dayi juemi lu, 177
spontaneity, 9, 36, 47, 52, 75, 107, 154, 158, 160, 255, 275, 281, 283, 289
Stock, Brian, 15, 247, 251, 392n5
Struve, Lynn, 371n12
substance (ti), 170
Supplementary Biographies of Eminent Monks (by Yu Qian), 277
Śuraṃgama Sūtra (Shoulengyan jing), 25, 50, 57, 59, 358n20
literati and, 50, 57, 59, 131
syncretism, 44

Taiping Rebellion, 282
Taixu, 277, 283, 356n20
Taizhou school, 47, 52–53, 73, 74, 101
Chan Buddhism and, 51
Chan-like teachings of, 51–53
Huang Zongxi's comment on, 52–53, 74
"Mad Chan" and, 50–53
members of, 50
Tang dynasty, 4, 6, 7, 10, 11, 12, 16, 85, 140, 145, 187, 188, 197, 225, 277, 311, 313
late, 116, 141, 190
Tanji Hongren, 114, 139–40, 142, 152, 159, 177, 179, 180, 303, 360n46. See also Wuzong jiu
biography of, 127
Yongzheng emperor destroying work of, 376n13
Tanjing jielu (by Yuan Hongdao), 62, 62f
Tang Tai (Dandang Puhe), 104, 375n63
tantrism, 145–46, 150, 271, 383n40
Chan Buddhism and, 150
Tan Yuanchun, 380n63

Tanzhe monastery, 359n37
Taoism, 22, 24, 56, 74, 163
    Confucianism/Buddhism integrated with, 50
Tao Shiling, 73, 75
Tao Wangling, 51, 61,71, 75, 76, 94, 252
    Miyun Yuanwu and, 86–87
    Zhanran Yuancheng and, 71–73, 94
    Zhou Rudeng and, 73–76
Tathāgata Chan (*Rulai Chan*), 115, 116, 118
    Miyun Yuanwu representing, 117
    difference between, and Patriarch Chan, 115, 116
Tatsuike Kiyoshi, 22
taxation, of monasteries, 23
temple, increase in, building, 49
textual authority, 48, 102, 241, 242
textual communities, 281, 285, 392n5
    Anne Blackburn on, 392n5
    Brian Stock on, 247, 251
    Chan Buddhism and, 254–55
    formation of, 252
    literati/monks and, 249–56
    polemical essays and, 253
textual practice
    China and, 246, 253
    literati, Confucian's authority in, 48, 102, 246
    reality *vs.*, in Chan Buddhism, 246–49, 253
    textual double created by, 246
textual spirituality, 57, 67, 248
    devotion-based spirituality *vs.*, 54, 58, 64, 82
    literati and, 35–46
Things Do Not Shift (*Wubu qian*) (by Sengzhao), 27, 306–7
three mysteries and three essentials, 115, 120, 122, 123, 124, 129, 136–37, 356n15
    Hanyue Fazang and, 141, 144, 179
three teachings, 56, 63
Tiangsheng guangdeng lu, 138
Tianhuang Daowu, 7–8, 15, 187, 188, 189–90, 197–98, 210, 291, 292, 317–18, 332. *See also* Daowu debate
    biography of, 324–26
    dharma transmission lines regarding, and Tianwang Daowu, 191, 193–94, 199–201, 202, 203, 207
    inscription of, 192–93, 203, 215, 236
    in *Jingde chuandeng lu*, 326
    newly discoverly pagoda of, 332
    in *Song gaoseng zhuan*, 324–26
    translation of inscription of, 319–20, 328–29
    in *Zutang ji*, 332
Tianhuang monastery, 188, 198, 293, 321
Tianjie monastery, 40, 65
Tianjuan reign, 298
Tianning (T'ien-ning) monastery, 29
Tianran Hanshi, 98, 103, 104, 131
Tianru Weize, 358n20
Tiantai masters, 27
Tiantai school, 3, 13, 21, 25, 27

Tiantong monastery, 14, 33, 49, 73, 77, 182, 356n20
    dharma-spreading spring (*Hongfa quan*) in, 266f, 267f
    entrance hall of, 89f
    Miyun Yuanwu and, 77, 87–88
Tiantong quanlu (by Miyun Yuanwu), 294
Tiantong Rujing, 299
Tiantong zhishuo (by Miyun Yuanwu), 17, 121f, 306
Tianwang Daowu, 7–8, 15, 187, 188, 189–90, 197–98, 210, 225, 311, 312, 313, 318, 332. *See also* Daowu debate
    dharma transmission lines regarding, and Tianhuang Daowu, 191, 193–94, 199–201, 202, 203, 207
    identity of, 322, 323
    inscription of, 192–93, 197, 203, 215, 217, 232, 236, 292, 314, 316, 327–28, 330, 331
    Qu Ruji discovering, 198
    translation of inscription of, 320–21
Tianwang monastery, 193, 321
    doubt about existence of, 327
    Huishan Jiexian's inscription at, 226–27, 228
    Shuijian Huihai rebuilding, 225–28
Tianyin Yuanxiu, 6, 85, 121, 144
    letters between, and Hanyue Fazang, 123–25, 140
    lineage of, 85, 98, 371n6
Tianxi Shoudeng, 27
Tianzhu Manxiu, 35, 38
Tibetan Buddhism, 22, 24, 146, 163, 164. *See also* Buddhism
    ambiguous reference to, 383n39
    in Beijing, 146, 383n40
    literati and, 146
    in the Ming dynasty, 146, 357n14
Touzi Datong, 204
transformation
    Buddhism and, 3, 4
    of Chan Buddhism, 8–11, 12–14
    intellectual/social, 13, 49, 197, 280
    spiritual, 4, 287
Triple Platform Ordination Ceremony, 30–31, 99, 166, 247, 267, 270, 394n4
    Chan monks performing, 31, 270–71
    Shilian Dashan offering, in Vietnam, 99
    Guxin Ruxin reforming, 30
Tu Long, 57
Tu Weiming, 68

Ui Hakuju, 330–31

Vajrabodhi, 145, 151
Veblen, Thorstein, on leisure class, 54
Vietnam, 98–99, 288
    Shilian Dashan's trip to, 99
    Shouzun Yuanzhao's trip to, 98
Vinaya master(s)/monk(s), 28, 29, 31

Chan masters as, 270–71
Hanyue Fazang as, 31
Zhihuan Daofu as, 28, 29
Vinaya school, 21, 24, 98, 165, 247
Chan Buddhism and, 31, 270–71
revival of, 28, 30
Zhihuan Daofu and, 28, 29
visualization, 145
perfect circle and, 147–48
of syllables, 148, 149

Wakeman, Frederic, on Huang Duanbo's death, 80
Wanfeng Shiwei, 37, 38, 302, 303
Wang An'shi, 192
Wang Gen, 51, 52, 53
Wang Gu, 204
Wang Guocai, 372n19
Wang Ji, 74, 75
Wang, police chief, Feiyin Tongrong and, 295–96
Wang Yangming, 13, 21, 45, 60, 62, 66, 74, 75, 76, 101, 255, 369n94
Chan Buddhism and, 48–49, 68
declining influence of, 195
intellectual movement of, 47, 49, 82, 100
"learning of the mind" (xinxue) and, 49, 50, 73, 78, 82, 107, 194, 246
school of, 82
teaching of innate knowledge of goodness by, 49, 52
Yuzhi Faju and, 68
Wanli emperor, 5, 22, 23, 24, 25, 29, 30, 31, 32, 44, 73, 75, 83, 85, 105
Buddhist recovery stimulated by, 24–25
bestowing the Buddhist canon, 25
Wansong Xingxiu, 37c, 93, 300
Weilin Daopei, 96, 237, 299, 391n27, 397n5
Weiyin Buddha, 151
Weizhi Zhikai, 17, 299–301, 305, 326, 328–29.
See also Zhengming lu
Daowu debate and, 232–35
on Linji transmissions in the early Ming, 304
Weizhong Jingfu, 234, 298–99, 330, 397n5
Daowu debate and, 227–28
Welch, Holmes, 269, 280
on Buddhism in modern China, 266–67,
on Buddhist revival, 276–77,
on outside influence on modern Chinese Buddhism, 282–83
Welter, Albert, 57, 197, 250, 396n26, 388n28
Wenhai Fuju, 165
Wenxue, 329–30
White Horse monastery, 327
"Wok for a Thousand Monks," 88f
Wubuqian zhengliang lun (by Kongyin Zhencheng), 27
Wudeng huiyuan, 5, 199, 202, 203, 209, 212, 217, 231, 319, 323, 326

Wudeng huiyuan xulüe (by Yuanmen Jingzhu), 208, 213
Wudeng quanshu, 15, 95, 225, 229, 233–34
content of, 230–31
dispute about, 229–35
Wudeng yantong (by Feiyin Tongrong), 7, 15, 17, 40, 94, 99, 113, 187, 196, 207, 213, 220, 221, 225, 231, 241, 258, 301, 303, 306
banning of, 222, 294–95
content of, 210–11
debate over, 207–23
publication of, 208, 214
Yinyuan Longqi reprinting, in Japan, 238–39
Wudeng yantong jiehuo pian (by Feiyin Tongrong), 215
content of, 215–18
Wu emperor, 312
Wujia yulu, 85, 117, 199
Hanyue Fazang's preface to, 199
Miyun Yuanwu's preface to, 199
Wujia zongpai (by Daguan Tanying), and Daowu debate, 315
Wuji Mingxin, 26, 39
Wujin Chuandeng, 27
Wuji Zhenghui, 35, 38, 39
Wuke Dazhi, 229, 370n11. See also Fang Yizhi.
Wulou Chuanping, 27
Wuming Huijing, 7, 83, 92, 201, 209, 231
biography of, 95–96
dharma heirs of, 96, 214
encounter dialogues of, 96
lineage unknown regarding, 212
Wunian Shenyou, 68, 69, 71, 252, 362n69
biography of, 68
enlightenment of, 69–70
as messenger for Li Zhi, 70
in literati gathering with Li Zhi, 70–71
Yuan Hongdao and, 62–64, 367n60
Wuyi Yuanlai, 92, 209
dharma heirs of, 98
Wuzong jiu (by Tanji Hongren), 114, 122, 142, 159, 177, 303
content of, 127–28
Wuzong pi (by Muchen Daomin), 127
Wuzong yuan (by Hanyue Fazang), 113, 120–21, 126, 127, 138
content of, 122–23

Xiangzong bayao (by Xuelang Hong'en), 26
Xiaofeng Daran, 104, 229, 235, 327
Xiaoyan Debao, 40, 85, 201, 305
dharma heir of, 37n5
Xiangya Xingting, 97
Xifang helun (by Yuan Hongdao), 63
Xindeng lu (by Yunhe Rui), 326
Xinghua Cunjiang, 174, 305
Xinglang Daoxiong, 101, 374n47
Xinyue Xingchou (Donggao Xinyue), 99, 374n45

Xiong Kaiyuan (Bo'an Zhengzhi), 103, 108, 132, 133, 369n91
Xishan Jietai monastery, 359n38
Xixiebian yin (by Chen Danzhong), 82
Xuande emperor, 23
Xu Changzhi, 388n3
Xu chuandeng lu (by Juding), 32
Xue Cai, journal of, 371n12
Xuedou Chongxian, 318, 400n19
Xuedou monastery, 202, 291
Xuefeng guanglu, 292
Xuefeng Yicun, 203–4, 330
Xuejiao Yuanxin, 6, 85, 361n62
    debate over memorial pagoda of, 309
    remote succession of, 35
Xuelang Hong'en, 26, 131, 358n25
Xueting Fuyu, 36, 37c, 94
    reviving Shaolin monastery, 36
Xu Guangqi, 369n91

Yanagida Seizan, 9, 239
    on *Wudeng yantong* in Japan, 239
Yang Qiyuan, 70
Yangshan Huiji, 5, 116, 144, 151, 178
Yang Wenhui, 283
Yang Yi, 365n28
Yan Jun, 52, 53
Yinyuan Longqi, 15, 17, 99, 253, 270, 271, 272
    burying Qian Sule at Mount Huangbo, 79
    dharma heirs of, 119
    emigration to Japan by, 99, 238
    portrait of, 100f
    transmission certificate of, 139f
    Wudeng yantong reprinted by, 238–39
Yiran Xingrong, 238
Yishan monastery, 304
Yogācāra school, 13, 14, 21, 25, 67
    dreams interpreted by, 67
Yongjue Yuanxian, 234
    Daowu debate and, 228
    Gushan monastery and, 96
Yongle emperor, 23, 25
Yongming Yanshou, 61. See also *Zongjing lu*
Yongqing monastery, 71
Yongzheng emperor, 7, 15, 91, 106, 109, 123, 151, 159, 279, 380n70, 386n47
    ascendancy to throne of, 168–69
    Buddhism supported by, 164, 165
    calligraphy, 182f
    Chan community around, 170–73
    Chan historiography of, 173–75
    Chan taught by, 169–73, 175, 178
    enlightenment of, 166–68, 169, 257
    Dayi juemi lu and, 177
    on Hanyue Fazang, 179–81, 257
    Jialing Xingyin and, 164–65, 167, 168, 257
    Jonathan Spence on, 177
    Miyun/Hanyue dispute and, 163, 176–77, 181, 183, 184

Miyun Yuanwu praised by, 182f
    Muchen Daomin denounced by, 176
    patronizing Li'an monastery, 165
    political intentions of, 181–82, 183
    ordination reform and, 166
    as reincarnation of Miyun Yuanwu, 182
    scriptural studies of, 175–76
    secret memorials of, 386n31
    Tanji Hongren's work destroyed by, 376n13
    tax reform of, 166
Yuan dynasty, 3, 5, 12, 22, 36, 319
Yuan Hongdao, 60, 61, 62–63, 64, 75, 198, 346n51, 347n60, 363n40
    editing the *Platform Sūtra*, 61, 62f
    editing the *Zongjing lu*, 61
    Pure Land beliefs of, 75, 366n42
    Li Zhi and, 52, 63,
    Shanhu lin by, 62, 63
    Wunian Shenyou and, 62–64, 367n60
Yuanmen Jingzhu, 234
    Chan genealogy by, 208, 209
    essays by, 214, 215
Yuanwu Keqin, 141, 356n15
Yuan Zhongdao, 62, 69, 366n40, 366n51
Yu Dacheng (Yu Jisheng),
    Huang Duanbo and, 203–4
    Daowu debate and, 203
Yueting Mingde, 27
Yuexin ji (by Yongzheng emperor), 167
Yulin Tongxiu, 85, 101, 109, 171, 174, 176, 310
    Muchen Daomin criticizing, 310
    Shunzhi emperor and, 85, 164
Yungu Fahui, 40, 43
Yunhe Rui, 326. See also *Xindeng lu*
    Chan genealogy by, 322
Yunmen monastery, 73, 78, 95
    Qi family and, 78
Yunmen school, 8, 32, 35, 85, 123, 188, 189, 230, 231, 291, 294, 295
    Xuejiao Yuanxin's self-identification with, 35
Yunmen Wenyan, 141, 188, 309
Yunqi Zhuhong, 4, 7, 13, 27, 33, 65, 75, 83, 84, 101, 105, 131, 156, 161, 212, 271, 307, 360n46, 366n49, 366n51, 367n71, 371n5
    Cao Yinru arguing with, 66
    Criticizing Chan Buddhism, 41, 42, 43, 58–59, 66
    Criticizing literati, 66
    On Pure Land practice, 40, 66
    Miyun Yuanwu's negative view of, 376n15
    offering novice ordination, 30
    Yongzheng and, 174
    Yuan Hongdao and, 63
    Zhanran Yuancheng and, 94
Yunqi monastery, 73

Yuxuan yulu (by Yongzheng emperor), 169, 176
    Content of, 173–75
Yuzhi Faju, Wang Yangming and, 68

Zaisan Hongzan, 98
Zanning, 324–26, 331, 393n26
Zen Buddhism. *See* Buddhism
Zeng Jing, 177, 180
Zhang Boduan, Yongzheng emperor praising, 174
Zhang Dai, 81, 87
Zhang Juzheng, 29–30
Zhang Shangying, 77, 192, 326–27
    Daowu debate and, 316–18
Zhang Tingyu, 171, 172
Zhang Xianzhong, 97, 378n37
Zhangxue Tongzui, 97
Zhang Ying, 171
Zhanran Yuancheng, 6, 7, 36, 66–67, 74, 75–76, 83, 92, 158, 209, 297, 367n68, 372n21
    biography of, 94–95
    Cizhou Fangnian and, 71–73
    dharma heirs of, 95, 214
    as head of Yunmen monastery, 78
    Qi Family and, 78
    Tao Wangling and, 71–73, 94
Zhao Mengfu, 356n15
Zhaoqing monastery, 24, 33, 359n41
Zhao Zhenji, 50, 278
Zhaozhou Congshen, 164, 173
Zheng Chenggong, 374n44
Zhenghe reign, 298
Zhengming lu (by Weizhi Zhikai), 17, 107, 204, 229, 232, 233*f*, 305, 330
    on Daowu debate, 232–35
    Deshan Xuanjian's epitaph in, 329–30
    on the five superfluous generation in the Caodong school, 234–35, 299–301
    on Linji transmission in the early Ming, 234, 302–5
Zhengtong emperor, 23, 28
Zhenqi, 379n50
Zhenyuan reign, 313, 314

Zhihuan Daofu, 28, 29
Zhiyue lu (by Qu Ruji), 60, 328, 366n38
    Daowu debate and, 198
    becoming new Chan classic, 61
Zhizheng zhuan (by Juefang Huihong), 142
    Hanyue Fazang's use of, 115
Zhongfeng Mingben, 85, 124, 301
Zhonghua chuanxindi Chanmen shizi chengxi tu (by Zongmi), 313
Zhongtian Zhengyuan, 362n65
Zhong Xing, 380n63
Zhong Yuchang, 65
Zhou Rudeng, 66–67, 73–76, 79, 94
    Miyun Yuanwu and, 86
Zhulin monastery, 324
Zhuo'an Zhipu, 235
Zhunti (Cunti) cult, 146
Zhu Xi, 49, 50, 216, 255
Zhu Yuanzhang, 32, 258, 277, 357n2, 383n38
    restricting Buddhism, 22–23
Zibo Zhenke, 4, 7, 13, 27, 32, 43, 76, 83, 84, 95, 105, 131, 132
    on Chan practice, 24, 42
    initiating the Jiaxing canon, 25
    visiting Shaolin monastery, 42
    writing new Chan genealogy, 32
Zijue debate, 298–300. *See also* The Five Superfluous Generations in the Caodong School.
Zongbao Daodu, lineage of, 98
Zongjing lu (by Yongming Yanshou), 61
    Tao Wangling's edition of, 61
    Yongzheng emperor's edition of, 175, 176
    Yuan Hongdao's edition of, 61
Zongmi, 115–16, 141, 144, 313
Zudeng datong (by Weizhong Jingfu), 227, 234, 298
Zürcher, Eric, on the spread of Buddhism and Christianity in China, 274, 275
Zutang ji, 332
Zuxin Hanke, 98, 373n38
Zuyuan tongyao (by Gongchen), 318